PHYSICS OF ELECTRONIC CONDUCTION IN SOLIDS

Physics of Electronic Conduction in Solids

Frank J. Blatt
Professor of Physics
Michigan State University

McGraw-Hill Book Company
New York   St. Louis
San Francisco
Toronto   London
Sydney

Physics of Electronic Conduction in Solids

Preface

In discussions over the years with graduate students in physics and engineering, I was often surprised to find that they viewed conduction in metals and semiconductors as distinct and almost unrelated phenomena. All too often physicists interested in transport phenomena concentrate their attention on metallic conduction, relegating semiconductors to their more applied brethren, whereas students of semiconductor physics are perhaps fascinated by the multitude of device potentialities before they have gained a proper perspective of electronic conduction in solids. This attitude, which I consider unfortunate, is further strengthened by the fact that many books treating electronic conduction in solids strongly emphasize metals and dispose all too quickly of semiconductors, creating the impression that the latter group of materials poses relatively few interesting fundamental problems and deserves the attention only of device engineers. There exist, of course, many fine books on semiconductor physics, but they, in turn, devote little space or attention to metals.

The aim of this book, then, is to provide the reader with a self-contained treatment of the physical process of conduction and of related electronic phenomena in solids. If there is one principal thread that runs through the fabric of this text, it is the viewpoint that electronic conduction in both metals and semiconductors is fundamentally one and the same phenomenon, described in terms of the same transport equation, limited by the same kind of relaxation process, and which may be employed as a useful and flexible tool in the study of the same parameters, such as effective masses and shapes of constant-energy surfaces in wave-vector space. Once the student recognizes that there is no substantial difference between the mechanisms of charge transport in metals and in semiconductors, he can, I believe, appreciate better the reasons for the differences in the properties and behavior of these materials.

The text is divided into three principal sections. The first establishes the necessary background in solid-state physics and encompasses Chaps. 1 through 4. The second presents the general treatment of electronic transport and contains Chap. 5 (Boltzmann Equation) and Chap. 6 (Relaxation Mechanisms), which serve as a springboard for the third part, consisting of Chaps. 7 through 11. Chapters 7 and 8 are devoted to conductivity and low-field galvanomagnetic effects in homogeneous metals and semiconductors, respectively. Chapter 9 presents a brief qualitative discussion of rectifying junctions and transistors, and Chap. 10 is devoted to photoelectric properties of semiconductors. The final chapter, 11, summarizes developments in the study of electronic properties at high magnetic fields in metals and semiconductors, including cyclotron resonance, magnetooptical effects, the de Haas-van Alphen effect, magnetoacoustic resonance, etc., which have all played a very major role in elucidating the band structure and Fermi surfaces of crystals.

Although rectifying junctions, transistors, infrared detectors, and photodiodes are discussed in the text, emphasis is not on application, selection of suitable materials for particular device purposes, or analysis of device performance, but on the method by which experimental results using such devices may shed light on the band structure, effective masses, lifetimes, and other interesting physical parameters.

The book was written with the expectation that it could be read profitably by seniors or beginning graduate students in physics, graduate students in material science, electrical engineering, and physical metallurgy, and research scientists working in these fields. Familiarity with only the rudiments of quantum mechanics is assumed and the principal results of elementary quantum mechanics are summarized in an appendix.

This is a book, not a review article, and I have exercised to the limit the author's prerogative to select the bibliography. At the end of each chapter

I have appended a list of relevant books and review articles which the reader may wish to consult for further details or an alternative viewpoint. Undoubtedly, I have failed to mention some material that perhaps should have been included in these bibliographies. If these are the only errors I have committed I shall be delighted.

It is a distinct pleasure to take this opportunity to thank Professor G. Busch and Professor W. Känzig of the Eidgenössische Technische Hochschule, Zürich, for their kind hospitality during the academic year 1963–64, when a major portion of the text was written. The friendly, stimulating atmosphere at the E.T.H. contributed greatly to the progress of my work. I also wish to express my appreciation to the Physics Division of the Aspen Institute for Humanistic Studies for their hospitality during the summer of 1966, when the manuscript was revised for the last time. Last, but by no means least, I am deeply grateful to my friend and colleague, Professor P. A. Schroeder, who read the manuscript with painstaking care, made many valuable suggestions and caught a number of errors; those that remain are, of course, my sole responsibility.

Frank J. Blatt

Contents

PHYSICS OF ELECTRONIC CONDUCTION IN SOLIDS

1
Classification of Solids

1.1 INTRODUCTION

In this text we shall be concerned primarily with electron transport phenomena, i.e., phenomena which depend on the motion of electrons within the substance. Before we can discuss these properties, however, we must have available a certain amount of knowledge of a rather general nature. The first few chapters will be concerned with the presentation of this introductory material.

This first chapter is divided into two parts, both of which are concerned with the classification of solids. In the first part, we base our classification upon the physical properties of the solids, and in particular show that it is convenient to classify these materials according to the forces which are principally responsible for the cohesive energy of the material. As we shall see, most of the important physical properties of solids can be understood, at least qualitatively, in the light of the binding forces.

The second part is concerned with the purely geometrical aspects of crystals, their symmetry properties. Although crystalline symmetry can be described entirely within formal mathematical terms (group theory), the symmetry properties also reflect themselves in the physical behavior of a crystal. For example, the electrical conductivity, which is a tensor property since it relates two vectors (the electric current density and the electric field intensity), must be a multiple of the unit tensor if the crystal is cubic. Also, as another example, we may cite the fact that a crystal displaying optical activity cannot have a center of inversion.

1.2 PHYSICAL PROPERTIES OF SOLIDS

In a general way, one may define a solid as any substance which deforms elastically under small shear stresses. This definition evidently excludes gases and liquids; they exhibit only viscous resistance to shear. Viscosity opposes shear deformation but does not give rise to restoring forces.

We shall, moreover, restrict our attention to crystalline solids. A *crystal* is a substance which may be constructed by the regular repetition in three dimensions of identical units which themselves contain one or more atoms. Most frequently, a crystalline solid consists of an agglomeration of a large number of small crystalline grains, oriented relative to each other in a more or less random fashion and joined at interfaces known as *grain boundaries*. The substance is said to be *polycrystalline*.

Single crystals of most materials can be prepared using a variety of techniques, such as growing from a saturated solution or pulling from the melt. It will become clear as we proceed that measurements made on single crystals yield a maximum amount of information about the basic properties of the material. In recent years, the techniques of crystal growing have been perfected to a high degree. An introduction to this technology may be found in a number of texts, listed at the end of this chapter, and particular details dealing with recent advances abound in the periodical literature.

Numerous solids, however, do not fall into the category of crystalline substances, among them glasses and plastics. These substances do display some regularity in the arrangement of the constituent atoms over short distances of the order of several interatomic spacings. However, over distances of perhaps a few hundred interatomic spacings (an interatomic spacing is roughly 3 Å, that is, 3×10^{-8} cm in most solids) no correlation between the positions of the atoms remains. We shall not concern ourselves with such substances in this book.

Even among crystalline solids there is such a profusion, both natural and synthetic, that we shall restrict our attention to relatively few. Although the study of solids (henceforth the adjective "crystalline" will be understood) has occupied physicists, chemists, and metallurgists for many years and has progressed at an accelerated pace in the past few decades, only the simplest structures have been analyzed in great detail. Our understanding of crystals such as barium chlorate, which might seem to fall into the group of "simple" structures, is very inadequate. The difficulty lies not in our lack of basic knowledge, but in the formidable complexity of the problem posed by the interaction of a large number of particles.

It is, of course, quite impossible to describe in minutest detail the internal dynamics of a material containing 10^{22} to 10^{23} atoms per cubic centimeter and, thus, 10^{23} to 10^{25} particles per cubic centimeter (nuclei and electrons). Even if this feat could be accomplished, such work would be of questionable value. One, therefore, turns to statistical mechanics, which concerns itself with the macroscopic response of a system composed of a large number of particles. We shall not, in this text, derive the results of statistical mechanics but only use them.

If, then, we must discard at the outset all hope of obtaining an exact solution, our best recourse is to look for appropriate approximation methods based on a simplified construction, i.e., a *model* which reproduces with reasonable faithfulness the dominant features of the real crystal. Although a physical model is not essential and our approximations can be discussed in a purely formal way, it does help, whenever possible, to create a visual image, provided one is careful not to take such models too literally.

A model may conceivably obscure a salient feature of the true crystal, and no calculation based on it, no matter how exactingly carried to its solution, will ever reveal physical properties fundamentally at variance with the initial assumptions. For example, the classical theory of elasticity predicts certain relationships—the Cauchy relations—among the elastic constants. However, most crystals do not obey these. Since a crystal is not an elastic continuum, one might attempt to explain these deviations as originating in the atomic nature of the solid and compute the elastic energy assuming a spherically symmetric interaction potential $V(r_{ab})$ between atoms at positions a and b. The simplest approximation, of course, is to neglect all but nearest-neighbor interactions; then again, one obtains the Cauchy relations. An obvious refinement is to extend the calculation so as to include next-nearest-neighbor and even longer-range interactions. Still, no deviation from the Cauchy relations will ever result from such calculations. The Cauchy relations are a direct consequence of the assumed spherical symmetry of $V(r_{ab})$; only when that aspect of the model is discarded can the theory yield results at variance with the Cauchy relations.

The widely divergent characteristics of solids, e.g., the existence of very good conductors and very good insulators, suggest that it may be difficult to construct a universal model, one which, for example, will be equally useful as a framework for calculations of the properties of metals and of ionic crystals, such as sodium chloride. In fact, our model is generally constructed so as to reflect the dominant physical properties of the substance. Here a classification of solids based on the forces which hold the constituent atoms together proves to be a particularly valuable guide.

It is common practice to classify solids into four types according to the binding forces. The types and their predominant characteristics are listed in Table 1.1 in order of diminishing cohesive energy. Cohesive energy is that energy which must be expended in order to separate the constituents of the crystal into neutral units (atoms or molecules) at rest and infinitely far removed from each other. In other words, the cohesive energy is the energy which would be released if the atoms, or molecules, originally in the gaseous state at very low temperature were permitted to condense into the solid phase. To a close approximation this energy is equal to the sublimation energy.

A. Ionic Crystals

Ionic crystals generally form from a combination of strongly electropositive metals and strongly electronegative atoms, such as the halides. In sodium chloride, for example, the sodium atom is ionized and the valence electron of the neutral sodium atom attaches itself to a chlorine atom, forming a Cl^- ion. The resulting ions then have the closed-shell electronic configuration characteristic of inert gases. This closed-shell configuration of the individual ions is one of the outstanding features of ionic crystals. Since in the free atom the electronic-charge distribution associated with a closed shell is spherically symmetric, a model in which one imagines the ions as spheres carrying equal charges of opposite sign is a reasonable one. The radii of these spheres are not equal, however. In fact, the radius of the Cl^- ion in NaCl is approximately twice that of the Na^+ ion; thus, the Cl^- ions occupy roughly 85 percent of the volume of the crystal (Fig. 1.1).

The binding energy of ionic crystals is largely the result of the mutual coulomb attraction between these charged spheres. The equilibrium separation between the ions in the crystal represents a compromise between these attractive forces and the strong, but short-range, repulsive forces which come into play whenever the ions approach each other sufficiently to cause appreciable overlap of the charge distributions of the closed shells.

Energetically, the most favorable arrangement of the ions is evidently one in which every positive ion finds only negative ions as its nearest neighbors, and vice versa. Among several possible structures

Table 1.1

Solid type	Cohesive energy, kcal/mole	Electronic conduction	Magnetic property	Optical	Crystal structure
Ionic crystals	150–400	No electronic conduction. Conductivity due to ionic motion, very low	Diamagnetic	Strong infrared and uv absorption; photoconduction in visible range of spectrum	Fcc, bcc determined by coulomb forces
LiF	216				
NaCl	153				
CaF_2	401				
Na_2Se	172				
MgO	242				
Covalent crystals	80–300	Semiconductors, σ dependent on impurity content	Diamagnetic	Infrared absorption; photoconduction in infrared	Determined by valence
Diamond	170				
Ge	85				
SiC	283				
Metals	20–200	High conductivity	Paramagnetic or diamagnetic	Reflection of visible radiation	Various
K	19.8				
Na	25.9				
Cu	81.2				
Zn	27.4				
Be	75				
La	90				
Ga	52				
Fe	94				
W	210				
Pt	127				
Mo	160				
Molecular crystals	1–20	Very good insulators	Generally diamagnetic	Characterized by properties of the molecules	Various
A	1.77				
H_2	2.44				
I_2	18.9				
CH_4	2.40				

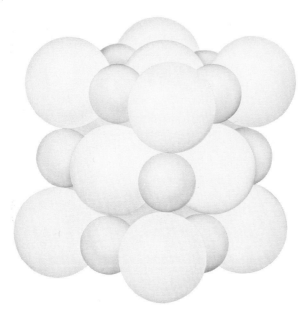

Fig. 1.1   The NaCl lattice showing the ions with their respective ionic radii.   The smaller Na^+ ions occupy the octahedral holes of the face-centered cubic structure.

fulfilling this requirement, that of sodium chloride, consisting of two interpenetrating face-centered cubic lattices, is by far the most common of the monovalent metal halides.

Not only the monovalent metals and halogens form ionic crystals; compounds of the II-VI, I_2-VI, II-VII$_2$, and I_3-V types also generally display ionic characteristics.† However, when we come to the III-V compounds, such as indium antimonide or gallium arsenide (both semiconductors with very useful and interesting properties), it is difficult to specify precisely the nature of the binding forces.   Here we encounter a situation not at all uncommon, namely, that of solids which fall into borderline cases, neither clearly ionic nor clearly covalent.

One can give a fairly satisfactory account of the physical properties of ionic crystals in terms of the model we have outlined above.   We note that the valence electrons are tightly bound to the respective ions.   It is, therefore, impossible for electrons to contribute to charge transport, and we anticipate that ionic crystals are insulators.   However, at high temperatures the constituent atoms can diffuse through the solid, and

† The roman numerals are used to designate the column in the periodic table of elements that is occupied by the constituent atoms, and the subscripts conform to standard chemical convention.

in an ionic crystal it is the ions which participate in the diffusion process. At elevated temperatures, therefore, an ionic crystal does conduct electricity by diffusion of positively or negatively charged ions. This ionic conductivity is many orders of magnitude smaller than the electronic conductivity of metals, in part because the mass of the ions is about 10^4 times the mass of electrons and, hence, the ions are less mobile. Since the diffusion constant of a solid increases exponentially with increasing temperature, the conductivity of an ionic crystal should exhibit approximately the same behavior; such is, indeed, the case. One can readily show with the aid of reasonable simplifying assumptions that the ionic conductivity σ and the diffusion constant D of the mobile ions are related to each other in the following manner:

$$\sigma = \frac{ne^2D}{kT} \tag{1.1}$$

Here n is the number of mobile ions per unit volume, e is the electronic charge, k is Boltzmann's constant, and T is the absolute temperature. Equation (1.1) is known as the *Einstein relation*.

We previously remarked that in the alkali halides the alkali ions are very much smaller than the halogen ions. In these crystals, only the alkali ions are relatively mobile, and they make the dominant contribution to ionic charge transport. Typical curves of the diffusion constant are shown in Fig. 1.2.

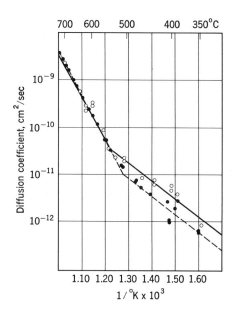

Fig. 1.2 Temperature dependence of the diffusion coefficient of sodium in sodium chloride. ○ measured directly; ● calculated from measured conductivity. [*From D. Mapother, H. N. Crooks, and R. Maurer, J. Chem. Phys.*, **18**: 1234 (1950).]

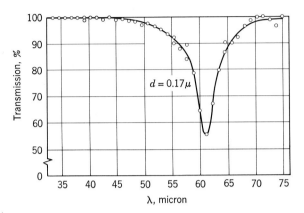

Fig. 1.3 Transmission of infrared radiation through a thin (0.17μ) NaCl film. [*From R. B. Barnes and M. Czerny, Z. Physik,* **72**: 451 (1931).]

The curves of Fig. 1.2 show markedly different behavior at high and low temperatures. It is found experimentally that in the low-temperature region the diffusion constant is closely related to the purity and stoichiometry of the crystal, whereas in the high-temperature region the conductivity and diffusivity are almost independent of purity. Since diffusion in the high-temperature region is characteristic of the particular material and is insensitive to contamination by impurities, it is said to be *intrinsic*. The low-temperature region is by contrast called the *extrinsic* range—sensitive to external influences, namely, concentration and type of solute. The transition from the extrinsic to the intrinsic region will, of course, vary from specimen to specimen, appearing at lower temperatures the purer the material. The reader will find detailed discussions of diffusion and conduction in ionic crystals in the references listed at the end of this chapter.

We can also understand why, with the exception of crystals containing transition-metal ions, ionic crystals are diamagnetic. The electronic configuration is that of closed shells, leaving no unpaired electron spins which, by virtue of the associated intrinsic magnetic moment, might make a paramagnetic contribution to the susceptibility.

The strong infrared absorption of ionic crystals is associated with forced vibrations of the ions induced by the oscillating electric field of the electromagnetic radiation. When the frequencies of the incident radiation and of the normal modes of oscillation of the ions are equal, one would expect a resonant absorption peak. A typical transmission curve of an ionic crystal is shown in Fig. 1.3; the shape of the curve is clearly of the form generally associated with a resonance phenomenon.

B.   Covalent (Homopolar) Crystals

We saw that in ionic crystals the electrostatic binding forces were the
result of the transfer of electrons from the metallic to the halogen atoms,
leaving one positively and the other negatively charged.   In a covalent
crystal the source of the electrostatic binding forces may be visualized as
follows.   The valence electrons of each atom, which in the free state
might be distributed with spherical symmetry about the nucleus, preferentially occupy the regions between neighboring atoms in the crystal.
The spaces occupied by the atomic cores are, thus, in effect positively
charged, whereas the regions between atomic cores carry an excess negative charge located predominantly along lines joining the lattice points.
This situation is in sharp contrast to that in ionic crystals, in which
alternate lattice points carry charges of opposite sign.   The charge
distribution in a covalent crystal is shown schematically in Fig. 1.4.

In a homopolar crystal each atom contributes one electron to the
charge distribution associated with each bond, known to chemists as the
electron-pair bond.   As we shall see more clearly later, the Pauli principle
applied to electrons in solids gives rise to a correlation in their motion
which keeps electrons of parallel spin away from each other.   The two
electrons which form the homopolar bond occupy the same small region
of space and, therefore, must have antiparallel spin orientations.

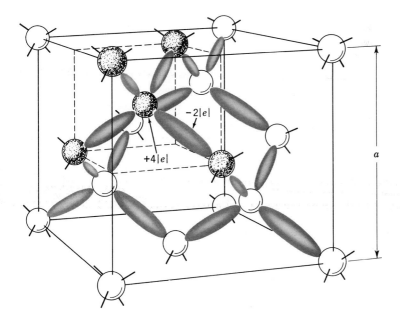

Fig. 1.4   Charge distribution of a covalent crystal (germanium).

As in the case of ionic crystals, the crystal structure of covalent crystals is largely dictated by the nature of the bond itself. Carbon (diamond), germanium, and silicon, all covalently bonded, have four valence electrons which can participate in bonding. Each atom is capable of contributing to four bonds; the structure of the crystals is one in which each atom is at the center of a tetrahedron, symmetrically surrounded by four neighbors located at the vertices of the tetrahedron.

Covalent crystals should be insulators because each valence electron is an integral part of a bond and, therefore, not free to move through the crystal. Indeed, covalent crystals of high purity are insulators at low temperatures. Yet many, e.g., germanium, silicon, and silicon carbide, display semiconducting properties. They show electronic conduction at any temperature by virtue of small concentrations of various kinds of impurities. Even crystals of the highest purity become electronic conductors at elevated temperatures. We shall have occasion to consider these and related properties of Ge, Si, and other semiconductors in great detail in subsequent chapters. For the moment, we shall give only a cursory account of this behavior.

Suppose, for example, that in a crystal of germanium one atom is replaced by a pentavalent atom, arsenic or phosphorous. It is reasonable to expect that four of the five valence electrons of the impurity atom will participate in the formation of the covalent bonds which were broken when the germanium atom was removed. The remaining electron, however, is then comparatively free to move through the crystal. In this fashion, impurities may transform an insulating homopolar crystal into an electronic conductor.

Even in a pure crystal the forces holding the valence electrons in their bonding orbits are not nearly as strong as those which confine electrons to closed shells in ionic crystals. At sufficiently high temperatures, the thermal energy of vibration of the crystal is then adequate to break an occasional bond and, thereby, release an electron. This electron is now able to move more or less undisturbed through the solid. Moreover, the unsaturated bond which is left behind may shift about; that is, the "hole" thus formed is also relatively mobile. Since it carries an effective positive charge due to the absence of an electron which would provide local electrical neutrality, motion of holes also contributes to an electric current.

As in the case of ionic conductivity, one distinguishes between the two physical mechanisms which give rise to charge transport in a semiconductor. If the conductivity is due to the presence of impurities it is said to be *extrinsic*. *Intrinsic* conductivity is the result of thermal excitation of valence electrons. It is obviously incorrect usage to apply this terminology to a particular sample without specifying the temperature range.   At very low temperatures, conductivity in any semiconductor is the result of the presence of impurity atoms.   If the temperature is raised sufficiently, any extrinsic, or impurity, semiconductor will become intrinsic as the number of thermally excited electrons, increasing exponentially with increasing temperature, exceeds the number of impurity atoms.

Pure covalent crystals are diamagnetic because there is complete pairing of electron magnetic moments within each bond.   However, covalent crystals into which impurities have been introduced (which have been "doped," to use semiconductor parlance) show evidence of paramagnetism due to either an excess or a deficiency of bonding electrons.   In fact, the study of the magnetic susceptibility of semiconductors has received much attention in recent years because of the light which it sheds on the fundamental properties of these materials.

C. Metallic Crystals

Energy is released when free metallic atoms condense into the solid phase, largely as the result of a compromise between the kinetic and potential energies of the valence electrons.   In the free atom the valence electron of a monovalent metal occupies a region of space which exceeds the atomic volume in the solid.†   According to the Heisenberg uncertainty principle, the electron's more severe limitation in space implies a greater uncertainty in its momentum.   Consequently, $\langle p^2 \rangle_{avg}$ is enhanced, and the kinetic energy of the valence electrons in the solid will, on the average, be greater than in the free atom.   This effect inhibits condensation. On the other hand, each valence electron in the solid spends more time near the attractive potential of the ion core than it does in the gaseous phase.   Using somewhat different terminology, the probability density of the valence electron in the region near the ion cores is enhanced when the atoms condense into a solid.   Hence, the average potential energy of the valence electrons is reduced on condensation.   The net effect, increase in kinetic energy and decrease in potential energy, is such as to favor the solid phase energetically.

As this model suggests, the distribution of valence electrons in metals is fairly uniform.   Also, the binding energies of metals are considerably smaller than those of ionic or covalent crystals, though transition metals do have fairly high binding energies, attributed by some workers to a covalent bond which may be formed by the d electrons of the unfilled shells.

The outstanding characteristic of metals is their high electrical conductivity.   One can appreciate this behavior in the light of the model

† The atomic volume is the volume associated with each atom in the crystal; if there are N atoms per cubic centimeter in a solid, the atomic volume is $(1/N)$ cm³.

presented above; the binding forces involve only the average behavior of the valence electrons, and there is no tendency for these electrons to be localized within any given portion of the structure. Thus, there are some 10^{23} electrons per cubic centimeter which can contribute to charge transport in metals. Because of their participation in the conduction of electric currents, valence electrons in metals are referred to as *conduction* electrons.

In the absence of a magnetic field, the spins and magnetic moments of the conduction electrons are evenly paired, except in ferromagnetic metals. However, this balance of magnetic moments is readily upset by the application of an external magnetic field. Metals are frequently paramagnetic, although the conduction electrons as well as the ions make a diamagnetic contribution to the susceptibility which may mask the paramagnetism due to the alignment of the intrinsic magnetic moments of the conduction electrons with the applied magnetic field. It is impossible to predict the magnetic behavior of metals without performing long and difficult calculations, and even then the results do not always agree too well with experiment. It is, of course, possible to carry through some elementary calculations based on a much simplified model, the so-called free-electron model; one then finds that the magnetic susceptibility is given by

$$\chi = \frac{n_0 \mu_B^2}{\eta} \tag{1.2}$$

where μ_B is the Bohr magneton, i.e., the magnetic moment of a free electron, and η is the Fermi energy (see Chap. 3), an energy characteristic of the electrons in the metal and closely related to n_0, the number of conduction electrons per unit volume. The susceptibility of the conduction electrons is actually the sum of two terms: the paramagnetic contribution due to the alignment of the spin magnetic moments under the action of the magnetic field, and the diamagnetic susceptibility due to the orbital motion of the electrons. The latter effect is strictly a quantum-mechanical phenomenon and does not lend itself to a satisfactory classical explanation. We shall consider the susceptibility of metals in more detail in Chap. 3.

D. Molecular Crystals

We shall not have occasion to discuss the properties of molecular crystals in this text and shall say only a few words here. These substances generally have very small binding energies and, consequently, low melting and boiling points. The forces (so-called van der Waals forces) which hold the saturated molecules together in the solid phase arise in the following way.

Although the molecules in the solid carry neither net electric charge nor permanent electric dipole moments, there may be fluctuations of the electronic charge distributions, resulting in instantaneous dipole moments. The instantaneous dipole moment on one molecule will then give rise to an electric field which induces dipole moments on neighboring molecules.   The interaction between these time-varying electric dipoles is, on the average, an attractive one, and it is this interaction which is primarily responsible for the cohesive energy of molecular crystals and the rare-gas solids.   One may think of the dipole moment of each molecule as fluctuating rapidly in time in a random manner, with fluctuations of neighboring dipoles correlated through weak short-range electric interactions.

Since the individual molecules of molecular crystals are electrically neutral and interact only weakly with one another, it is not surprising that molecular crystals are good insulators, showing neither electronic nor ionic conductivity.

The magnetic behavior of these crystals is determined by the magnetic properties of the individual molecules.   If these are paramagnetic the crystal also exhibits paramagnetism.   Generally, however, molecular crystals are diamagnetic, as are nearly all saturated molecules.   The notable exception to this rule is oxygen.

1.3 CRYSTAL SYMMETRY

A crystalline solid is distinguished from all other aggregates of atoms by the three-dimensional periodicity of the atomic arrangement.   Thus, choosing a suitable small polyhedron as our basic building block, we can construct the crystal by repeatedly displacing this building block along three noncoplanar directions by certain amounts.   Suitable geometric shapes for such building blocks are, for example, the cube, the regular dodecahedron, the truncated octahedron, or any arbitrary parallelepiped.

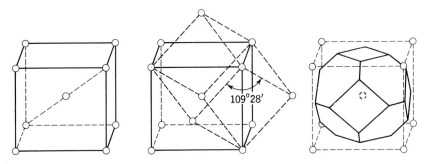

Fig. 1.5   Three possible unit cells of a body-centered cubic lattice.   (*a*) Unit cube; (*b*) primitive cell; (*c*) polyhedral cell.

The basic building block is called the *unit cell* of the crystal.   The unit cell of a given crystal is not unique (see Fig. 1.5).   It is possible to choose a variety of unit cells for a particular structure, although generally there will be one which is most convenient and descriptive of the crystal.

If the shape of the unit cell is specified, and if we also know the arrangement of all the atoms within the unit cell, we have a complete geometric description of the crystal.   This follows because there is then only one way in which the unit cells can be stacked together to fill all space.

Let us first consider the various possible arrangements of unit cells. The description is most readily achieved by means of the space lattice, a concept introduced by Bravais.   A *space lattice*, a purely mathematical construct, is an arrangement of points in space such that the placement of points about any given point is the same for all points of the lattice.

Space lattices are constructed with the aid of three primitive, non-coplanar translation vectors **a**, **b**, and **c**.   The act of translating a point by a vector **T** is known as a *translation operation*.   The space lattices are then generated by applying all translation operations of the form $\mathbf{T} = n_1\mathbf{a} + n_2\mathbf{b} + n_3\mathbf{c}$ (where n_i are integers) to a given point, for example, the origin.   Two arbitrary points of the resulting Bravais lattice, whose coordinates are given by the position vectors **r** and **r'**, will satisfy the relation

$$\mathbf{r} - \mathbf{r}' = n_a\mathbf{a} + n_b\mathbf{b} + n_c\mathbf{c} \tag{1.3}$$

where n_a, n_b, and n_c are integers.   The number of possible arrangements of points satisfying Eq. (1.3) is limited; in fact, there are only 14 unique Bravais lattices.   These 14 lattices are divided into seven crystal systems according to the orientation and relative lengths of the primitive translation vectors.   The seven crystal systems and the 14 Bravais lattices are listed in Table 1.2 and shown in Fig. 1.6.

The parallelepiped formed from the three translation vectors **a**, **b**, **c** is called the *primitive cell*.   It has the property that points of the space lattice occur at and only at the corners of the primitive cell.   The volume of the primitive cell of a particular Bravais lattice is unique, in distinction to that of the unit cell.

The primitive cells of the face-centered cubic (fcc) lattice and the body-centered cubic (bcc) lattice are shown in Fig. 1.7.   From their shape, the cubic symmetry of the lattices is not immediately apparent. For this reason, the primitive cell is not always the most convenient building block, since it is generally desirable to select a unit cell which most forcefully exhibits the full symmetry of the lattice.   As we have mentioned before, there is an infinite number of shapes and sizes of primitive as well as unit cells.   These can, however, be classified accord-

Table 1.2   The Seven Crystal Systems, 14 Bravais Lattices, and 32 Crystal Classes

System†	*Bravais lattices*	*Crystal classes*‡§
Triclinic $a \leq b \leq c$ $\alpha \neq 90°,\ \beta \neq 90°,\ \gamma \neq 90°$	Simple	$C_1,\ S_2$
Monoclinic $a \geq c,\ b$ arbitrary $\alpha = \gamma = 90°,\ \beta \neq 90°$	Simple; base-centered	$C_2,\ C_s,\ C_{2h}$
Orthorhombic $a < b < c$ $\alpha = \beta = \gamma = 90°$	Simple; base-centered; body-centered; face- centered	$D_2,\ C_{2v},\ D_{2h}$
Tetragonal $a = b \neq c$ $\alpha = \beta = \gamma = 90°$	Simple; body-centered	$C_4,\ C_{4h},\ S_4,\ D_{2d},\ D_4,$ $D_{4h},\ C_{4v}$
Cubic $a = b = c$ $\alpha = \beta = \gamma = 90°$	Simple; body-centered; face-centered	$T,\ T_h,\ T_d,\ O,\ O_h$
Trigonal $a = b = c$ $\alpha = \beta = \gamma \neq 90°$	Simple	$C_3,\ C_{3v},\ S_6,\ D_3,\ D_{3d}$
Hexagonal $a = b,\ c$ arbitrary $\alpha = \beta = 90°,\ \gamma = 120°$	Simple	$C_6,\ C_{6h},\ C_{6v},\ C_{3h},\ D_6,$ $D_{6h},\ D_{3h}$

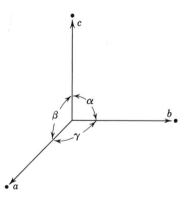

† a,b,c denote the crystal axes and α,β,γ the angles between these axes, as indicated in the figure.

‡ The crystal classes are listed according to the Schoenflies notation, as explained below. The crystal systems are easily identified by the first rotational element listed in the third column of Table 1.2.

C_n denotes a symmetry group with one n-fold rotation axis.

D_n denotes a symmetry group with one n-fold rotation axis and n twofold axes normal to the n-fold axis.

S_n denotes a symmetry group with one n-fold rotation-reflection axis.

T denotes a symmetry group with four threefold rotation axes corresponding to the axes of a regular tetrahedron (Tetrahedral group).

O denotes a symmetry group with three mutually perpendicular fourfold rotation axes.

§ Subscripts:

s denotes the presence of a mirror plane

v denotes the presence of a mirror plane containing the symmetry axis.

h denotes the presence of a mirror plane normal to the symmetry axis.

d denotes the presence of a mirror plane bisecting the angle between two twofold axes.

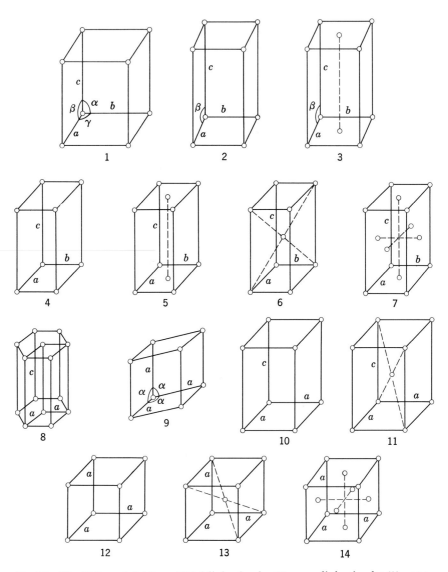

Fig. 1.6 The 14 Bravais lattices: (1) triclinic, simple; (2) monoclinic, simple; (3) monoclinic, base-centered; (4) orthorhombic, simple; (5) orthorhombic, base-centered; (6) orthorhombic, body-centered; (7) orthorhombic, face-centered; (8) hexagonal; (9) rhombohedral; (10) tetragonal, simple; (11) tetragonal, body-centered; (12) cubic, simple; (13) body-centered cubic; (14) face-centered cubic.

ing to their symmetry properties.   Symmetry is an extremely important consideration in crystalline solids because the symmetry displayed by the physical properties of the substance, such as its elastic, magnetic, electric, and thermal behavior, reflects and is determined by the symmetry of the lattice.   Consequently, the unit cube is often selected as the unit cell of the fcc and bcc lattices.   These unit cells, however, contain more than one lattice point per cell.   For example, the central point of the bcc unit cube belongs solely to that unit cube.   Each corner point is also a corner point of seven other unit cubes, and, thus, only one-eighth of each corner point belongs to the particular unit cube under consideration.   There are eight such points.   Hence, the unit cube of the bcc lattice contains one corner point and one body-center point, or a total of two points.   Similar arguments may be used to show that there are four lattice points per unit cube of the fcc lattice. Although there is nothing wrong in principle in selecting a unit cell which includes more than one lattice point, it is generally desirable to work with a cell which contains only one lattice point of the Bravais lattice.   We can, indeed, construct a unit cell which not only clearly displays the full symmetry of the cubic lattice but also contains only one point.   This, the smallest unit cell, is the one most frequently used in calculations.   It is obtained by means of the following geometrical construction.   Draw lines from a given point of the lattice to all other points, to the nearest neighbors, next-nearest neighbors, and so on.   The planes which bisect these lines normally will form a polyhedron about the central point, and this polyhedron is the desired unit cell, known as the *Wigner-Seitz cell*.   The Wigner-Seitz cells for the bcc and fcc lattices are shown in Fig. 1.8.

In general, a real crystal is not a perfect replica of a Bravais lattice with identical atoms at every point of the Bravais lattice.   A crystal is, instead, an arrangement of atoms such that with any given crystal one

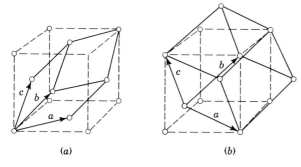

(a)   (b)

Fig. 1.7   Primitive cell of the fcc (a) and bcc (b) lattices.

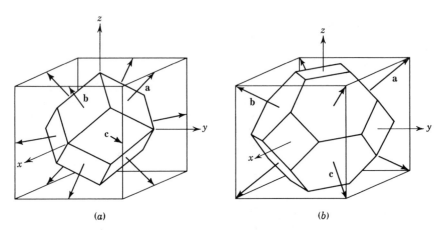

Fig. 1.8 Polyhedral unit cells of fcc (*a*) and bcc (*b*) lattices. (*After J. C. Slater, "Quantum Theory of Molecules and Solids," vol. 2, McGraw-Hill Book Company, New York, 1963.*)

may *associate* a particular Bravais lattice. In the real crystal, however, there is generally a set of atoms, whose internal symmetry is restricted only by the requirement of translational periodicity, which must be associated with each point of the corresponding Bravais lattice. This set of atoms is known as the *basis*. If we now translate this basis using all the allowed translation vectors **T** for a given Bravais lattice, we will generate the actual crystal.

We have, so far, limited our attention to only one type of symmetry operation, namely, the translation operation. A brief glance at the Bravais lattices of Fig. 1.6 shows other obvious symmetry operations that may be applied to one or another lattice and leave the lattice invariant. These additional operations, applied about a point of the lattice, are elements of the point group. The point-group operations involve one or more of the following elements:

1. *Rotation.* If rotation about some axis through an angle of $2\pi/n$ radians leaves the lattice invariant, we say that the lattice contains an n-fold rotation axis. One can show that the requirement of translational symmetry restricts the possible values of n to 1, 2, 3, 4, and 6. Examples of rotation axes are the three cube axes of a cubic crystal, which are fourfold rotation axes; moreover, the body diagonals are threefold rotation axes.

2. *Reflection.* In many cases, a lattice will be invariant under reflection in a plane through the lattice. For example, the faces of the unit cube are reflection planes.

3. *Inversion.* Every Bravais lattice possesses inversion symmetry; that is to say, we obtain the exact same lattice if we replace every lattice point whose coordinate is **r** by the point at −**r**. Although all monatomic crystals do have a center of inversion, inversion symmetry is not a general property of all crystals. For example, the one-dimensional crystal shown in Fig. 1.9 is not invariant under inversion. If, however, the two "atoms" are identical, then, although the lattice still has a basis of two atoms, it is nevertheless centrosymmetric, the center of symmetry being midway between the two atoms (Fig. 1.9b).

4. *Improper rotations.* An improper rotation is a rotation followed by an inversion. If a lattice contains an *n*-fold rotation-inversion axis, we can bring it into self-coincidence by performing first the *n*-fold rotation followed by the inversion. For example, the linear chain of Fig. 1.9a has a twofold rotation-inversion axis, namely, an axis midway between the two points of the basis and perpendicular to the linear chain.

No inversion symmetry   Center of inversion at X

Fig. 1.9 One-dimensional lattice without and with inversion symmetry.

There are 32 distinct classes of point-group operations associated with the 14 Bravais lattices. These 32 classes are enumerated in Table 1.2. The notation is that introduced by Schoenflies and is explained in Table 1.2.

In addition to the operations of the point group, a lattice with a basis may contain *glide planes* or a *screw axis*. A glide plane refers to a symmetry operation consisting of a reflection in a plane followed by a translation along a direction within the plane. A screw axis is a rotation axis which brings the lattice into coincidence if, following the rotation about $2\pi/n$, the lattice is translated in the direction of the axis by a distance a/n, where a is the lattice parameter along the direction of the screw axis. A spiral staircase is a macroscopic screw axis.

The symmetry of a real crystal is determined by the symmetry of the basis and of the Bravais lattice to which the crystal belongs. The mathematical equivalent of a real crystal is a space group, an array of symmetry elements located on a Bravais lattice. There are 230 different space groups that are realizable in three dimensions.

Directions in a crystal are specified by a set of three integers u, v, w defining a vector $u\mathbf{a} + v\mathbf{b} + w\mathbf{c}$ which points along the chosen direction. For most directions of interest u, v, w are small. The integers are

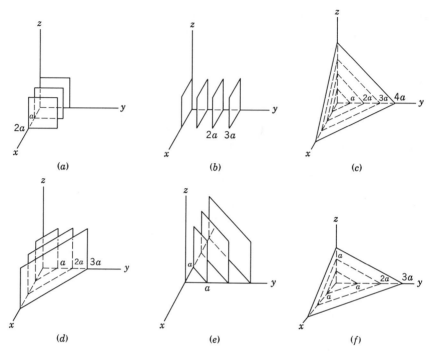

Fig. 1.10 Important cubic planes: (a) (100); (b) (010); (c) (111); (d) (110); (e) (1$\bar{1}$0); (f) (112). (*From C. A. Wert and R. W. Thomson, "Physics of Solids," McGraw-Hill Book Company, New York, 1964.*)

enclosed in square brackets [uvw] and have no common integral divisor. A negative integer is represented by placing a bar above the integer. A complete set of equivalent directions is denoted by the symbol $\langle uvw \rangle$. For example, in a cubic crystal there are 12 directions along the face diagonals, namely, [110], [$\bar{1}$10], [1$\bar{1}$0], [$\bar{1}\bar{1}$0], [101], [$\bar{1}$01], [10$\bar{1}$], etc. These twelve directions are collectively grouped into the symbol $\langle 110 \rangle$.

The symbol (hkl)—note the parenthesis—where h, k, l are small integers, denotes a crystal plane. The three integers are related to the orientation of the plane in the following manner (Fig. 1.10). If h', k', and l' are the intercepts of the particular plane on the three crystal axes in units of the lattice constants (units of $|\mathbf{a}|$, $|\mathbf{b}|$, and $|\mathbf{c}|$), then h, k, l are the smallest three integers satisfying the relation

$$hh' = kk' = ll'$$

h, k, and l are known as the *Miller indices*. If one of the intercepts, say, k', is infinity, the corresponding Miller index k is zero; for example, the

(100) planes of a cubic crystal. A set of equivalent planes is denoted collectively by enclosing the Miller indices in curly brackets, for example, {100}.

PROBLEMS

1.1. Gold has a density of 19.32 g/cm³, an atomic weight of 197.0, and an fcc structure.

    (a) Calculate the number of gold atoms per cubic centimeter.
    (b) Calculate the length of the edge of a unit cube.
    (c) Calculate the atomic radius of gold.

1.2. Show that the c/a ratio of an ideal hexagonal close-packed structure is $\sqrt{\frac{8}{3}}$. Compare this with the experimental values of six metals which possess this structure.

1.3. Show that the fraction of the volume filled by hard spheres in various arrangements is

    (a) Simple cubic $\dfrac{\pi}{6}$

    (b) Body-centered cubic $\dfrac{\pi}{8}\sqrt{3}$

    (c) Face-centered cubic $\dfrac{\pi}{6}\sqrt{2}$

    (d) Close-packed hexagonal $\dfrac{\pi}{6}\sqrt{2}$

1.4. Show that the distance between adjacent planes in a cubic crystal with Miller indices (hkl) is given by

$$d = \frac{a}{\sqrt{h^2 + k^2 + l^2}}$$

where a is the length of the cube edge.

1.5. Show that the base-centered tetragonal lattice is already contained among the Bravais lattices of Table 1.2.

1.6. Draw the $(3\bar{1}2)$ plane of a simple cubic lattice.

BIBLIOGRAPHY

General

Azaroff, L. V.: "Introduction to Solids," McGraw-Hill Book Company, New York, 1960.
Kittel, C.: "Introduction to Solid State Physics," 3d ed., John Wiley & Sons, Inc., New York, 1967.

Diffusion

Girifalco, L. A.: "Atomic Migration in Crystals," Blaisdell Publishing Co., Inc., New York, 1964.

Lazarus, D.: Diffusion in Metals, *Solid State Phys.*, **10** (1960).

Shewmon, P. G.: "Diffusion in Solids," McGraw-Hill Book Company, New York, 1963.

Crystal Growth

Brooks, M. S., and J. K. Kennedy: "Ultrapurification of Semiconductor Materials," The MacMillan Company, New York, 1963.

Buckley, H. E.: "Crystal Growth," 2d ed., John Wiley & Sons, Inc., New York, 1951.

Doremus, R. H., B. W. Roberts, and D. Turnbull: "Growth and Perfection of Crystals," John Wiley & Sons, Inc., New York, 1958.

Lawson, W. D., and S. Nielsen: "Preparation of Single Crystals," Butterworth & Co. (Publishers), Ltd., London, 1958.

Pfann, W. G.: Techniques of Zone Melting and Crystal Growing, *Solid State Phys.*, **4** (1957).

Crystal Structure and Symmetry

Flugge, S. (ed.): Crystal Physics I, in "Encyclopedia of Physics," vol. VII/1, Springer-Verlag OHG, Berlin, 1955.

Pearson, W. B.: "Lattice Spacings and Structures of Metals and Alloys," Pergamon Press, New York, 1958.

Slater, J. C.: "Quantum Theory of Molecules and Solids," vol. 2., McGraw-Hill Book Company, New York, 1965.

Tinkham, M.: "Group Theory and Quantum Mechanics," McGraw-Hill Book Company, New York, 1964.

Weinreich, G.: "Solids: Elementary Theory for Advanced Students," John Wiley & Sons, Inc., New York, 1965.

Wyckoff, R. W. G.: "Crystal Structures," 2d ed., Interscience Publishers, New York, 1963.

Crystallography

Buerger, M. J.: "Elementary Crystallography," John Wiley & Sons, Inc., New York, 1963.

Cullity, B. D.: "Elements of X-ray Diffraction," Addison-Wesley Publishing Company, Inc., Reading, Mass., 1956.

Phillips, F. C.: "An Introduction to Crystallography," Longmans, Green & Co., Ltd., London, 1946.

2
Lattice Vibrations and Lattice Specific Heat

2.1 INTRODUCTION

In this chapter we consider the thermal properties of crystalline lattices. This and the following two chapters, which are devoted to a presentation of important results of the electronic theory of perfect crystals, provide the necessary foundation for the development of the theory of electronic conduction in solids.

One of the most important processes which inhibits the motion of electrons in metals and semiconductors is scattering of the charge carriers by lattice vibrations. It is this interaction between the electrons and the lattice that is responsible for the temperature dependence of the resistivity of metals and determines the temperature dependence of the mobility of electrons and holes in semiconductors at elevated temperatures. Moreover, the electron-lattice interaction plays a crucial role in other solid-state phenomena, such as superconductivity, spin-lattice relaxation in nuclear and paramagnetic resonance, and in the thermoelectric effects in metals and semiconductors.

The various effects to which we have just referred arise because the ions in a crystal are not stationary, but are, in fact, vibrating about their equilibrium positions. At any finite temperature the thermal energy of a solid is in large measure contained in the vibrational energy of the ions. Even at the absolute zero of temperature the ions are not stationary, but participate in the so-called zero-point vibrations.

Following a careful classical treatment of the properties of monatomic and diatomic linear chains, we generalize the expressions to three dimensions. We then extend the discussion to the quantum-mechanical description and apply the results to derivations of the Einstein and Debye theories of the specific heat of solids. This procedure is satisfactory here because many of the important results of classical mechanics retain their validity in the quantum-mechanical treatment.

2.2   MONATOMIC LINEAR CHAIN

We begin our discussion by concentrating attention on the simplest model, a linear chain of identical masses connected to each other by identical massless springs assumed to obey Hooke's law. Though it may seem at first that this model is adequate for a "one-dimensional crystal" (by which we mean a linear array of atoms), we have, in fact, already made several approximations in selecting our model. First, the only forces which appear are nearest-neighbor forces; that is, the force on the mass m_0 of Fig. 2.1 depends only on the displacements of m_0 relative to m_{-1} and m_{+1} and not on the displacements of any other masses of the chain. If m_2 suffers a displacement from its equilibrium position, no force is experienced by m_0, provided m_1, m_0, and m_{-1} are held fixed. In a real lattice the displacement of next-nearest and even more distant neighbors induces forces on a particular ion, though weaker than those due to corresponding displacements of nearest neighbors.

Second, we are assuming at the outset that the forces between neighbors obey Hooke's law. There is abundant evidence to show that in a real crystal the force law deviates from this simple form, though, for

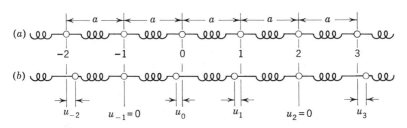

Fig. 2.1 The linear chain. (*a*) Masses in their equilibrium positions; (*b*) masses in displaced positions.

small displacements, the dominant term is always

$$F_i = -\beta\mu_i \tag{2.1}$$

where μ_i is the change in length of the ith spring and F_i is the force exerted by the ith spring. The difference between the true force law and Eq. (2.1) is responsible for such physical phenomena as thermal expansion, the difference between the specific heats at constant pressure and constant volume, and the dependence of the elastic constants on temperature.

Let us now consider the dynamics of an infinitely long chain, such as the one shown in Fig. 2.1. We denote the equilibrium distance between the masses by the symbol a, so that at equilibrium the nth mass is at position na along the chain, and the displacement of the nth mass from this position by the symbol u_n. Since the chain is assumed to be of infinite length, we have obviated end-effect difficulties and have assured that the equations of motion of all masses are identical. We can therefore restrict our attention to m_0, knowing that it is representative of all other masses.

If, then, m_0, m_1, and m_{-1} suffer displacements u_0, u_1, and u_{-1}, respectively, the force on m_0 is given by

$$F_0 = -\beta(u_0 - u_1) - \beta(u_0 - u_{-1}) \tag{2.2}$$

where all displacements and forces are measured along the positive x direction. Hence, the equation of motion for m_0 is

$$m_0\ddot{u}_0 = \beta(u_1 + u_{-1} - 2u_0)$$

and, in general,

$$m\ddot{u}_i = \beta(u_{i+1} + u_{i-1} - 2u_i) \tag{2.3}$$

Equation (2.3) is somewhat reminiscent of the equation of motion of a harmonic oscillator, suggesting the solution

$$u_i = A_i e^{-i\omega t} \tag{2.4}$$

Substitution of Eq. (2.4) into the equation of motion (2.3) gives

$$mA_i\omega^2 = \beta(2A_i - A_{i+1} - A_{i-1}) \tag{2.5}$$

showing that the assumed time dependence is indeed correct.

Since there is nothing to distinguish position i from position j in the chain, the solution for the displacement u_i can differ from the solution for u_j only by a constant (time-independent) factor; that is, we can set

$$u_{i+1} = \Gamma u_i \tag{2.6}$$

As a matter of convenience we let this factor $\Gamma = \exp{(iqa)}$, where q is as yet completely arbitrary and may take on real or complex values.

Equation (2.5) now reduces to

$$m\omega^2 = \beta(2 - e^{iqa} - e^{-iqa}) = 2\beta(1 - \cos qa) \qquad (2.7)$$

We have thus obtained the following result: The displacement of any mass is of the form

$$u_n = A e^{i(qna - \omega t)} \qquad (2.8)$$

characterized by a wave of amplitude A, a propagation number q, and an angular frequency ω. The dispersion relation for these waves, i.e., the relation between the frequency and the propagation, or wave number, q, is obtained by solving Eq. (2.7) for ω:

$$\omega(q) = \sqrt{\frac{4\beta}{m}} \left| \sin \frac{qa}{2} \right| \qquad \omega(q) = \omega(-q^*) \qquad (2.9)$$

For the solution, Eq. (2.8), to represent a steady state, both q and ω must be real. If, for example, q were complex, the displacements would grow exponentially in one direction along the chain. Correspondingly, if ω were complex, the vibrational waves would either grow or decay exponentially with time, a condition which cannot represent a steady state.

The allowed real values of the propagation number q, for which a real solution for ω exists, depend on the boundary conditions. Strictly speaking, we can impose no boundary conditions, since we assumed at the outset that the chain is of infinite length. We can, however, approximate the infinite chain by forming a large circle of a chain of finite length containing N masses, where $N \gg 1$. The boundary conditions which our solutions must then satisfy are of cyclic character; that is, since the $(N + n)$th mass is identical to the nth mass, we require that

$$u_{N+n}(t) = u_n(t) \qquad (2.10)$$

From Eq. (2.8) we see that the condition (2.10) requires

$$e^{iqNa} = 1 \qquad q = \frac{2\pi n}{Na} \qquad (2.11)$$

where n is an integer. Thus, the propagation number q can take on only certain discrete values given by Eq. (2.11).

There is yet one further limitation on the propagation number, not the result of boundary conditions, but intimately connected with the fact that the chain is not a continuous medium. To see how the finite spacing between the masses limits the choice of propagation number, let

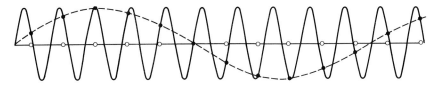

Fig. 2.2 Two waves of different wavelengths resulting in identical displacements of particles in a linear chain. (*From J. M. Ziman, "Electrons and Phonons," p. 15, Oxford University Press, London, 1960.*)

us add to a particular q number, say, q_j, a value K, where

$$K = \frac{2\pi}{a} n' \qquad n' \text{ is an integer} \tag{2.12}$$

We then find, substituting the new value of the propagation number into Eq. (2.7), that the angular frequency of this mode of vibration is given by

$$\omega^2(q_j + K) = \frac{2\beta}{m} [1 - \cos{(q_j a + 2\pi n')}] = \frac{2\beta}{m} [1 - \cos{(q_j a)}] = \omega^2(q_j)$$

Thus the frequencies of modes of propagation numbers q_j and $q_j + K$ are identical.   Also, the displacements u_i are identical for both modes.

This result is by no means fortuitous.   It reflects the fact that the only physically significant displacements are those of the masses m, so that waves of wavelengths shorter than $2a$ do not correspond to new modes of vibration.   The situation is illustrated in Fig. 2.2, which shows the displacements of particles of a linear chain for two modes of vibration, one whose wavelength λ is greater than $2a$, and the other whose wavelength λ' is less than $2a$, the two modes being related to each other through

$$q' = q + K \qquad \lambda = \frac{2\pi}{q} \qquad \lambda' = \frac{2\pi}{q'}$$

Since only the displacements of the masses are physically meaningful, both modes describe the identical behavior of the linear chain, and it is proper that the frequencies of these "two" modes be one and the same.

We conclude, therefore, that the allowed and physically meaningful normal modes are those whose wave numbers q satisfy the relation (2.11) and are contained in the region

$$-\frac{\pi}{a} < q \leq \frac{\pi}{a} \tag{2.13}$$

This range of q values is known as the *Brillouin zone* (BZ) of the one-dimensional chain.

The restriction on the possible q values given by Eq. (2.13) is also perfectly reasonable when approached from an entirely different point of view. Our circular "lattice" consists of N masses, each restricted to motion in one dimension. The number of degrees of freedom of the system is therefore equal to N, and hence the number of independent modes of vibration must also be N. If each q value describes a separate normal mode of vibration of the chain, the total number of different q values should be N, which, by (2.11), is just the total number contained in the interval (2.13).

The most general displacement of the nth mass in the linear chain is a linear combination of the solutions which we have obtained; that is, in general

$$u_n = \sum_q Q_q e^{iqna} \tag{2.14}$$

where the summation extends over the entire Brillouin zone. Here the Q_q's may be thought of as time-dependent coordinates. Substitution of Eq. (2.14) into Eq. (2.3) leads to the relation

$$\ddot{Q}_q + \omega^2(q)Q_q = 0 \tag{2.15}$$

which the reader will recognize as the equation of motion of the harmonic oscillator. Furthermore, since the differential equation for each coordinate Q_q involves only this one coordinate and not another, say $Q_{q'}$, it follows that these are indeed the proper normal coordinates of the problem.

There are N allowed and significant values of q; hence there are also N equations of the form (2.15), one for each value of q. Since Eq. (2.15) is a second-order differential equation, it must have two independent solutions, and it would seem, then, as though we are led to $2N$ independent solutions even though physically there are only N degrees of freedom. Put in another way, the solutions to Eq. (2.15) are complex, with independent real and imaginary parts. When considered in this light, the difficulty is more apparent and its resolution rather obvious. Although the Q_q's may be complex, the displacements u_n must be real, these being physically measurable quantities. The requirement that the displacements be real imposes the condition

$$Q_q = Q_{-q}^* \tag{2.16}$$

on the solutions, where the asterisk denotes complex conjugation. Application of Eq. (2.16) reduces the number of independent solutions to N.

Let us turn now to the dispersion relation, Eq. (2.7) or Eq. (2.9). A plot of Eq. (2.9) is shown in Fig. 2.3, where for comparison we also show

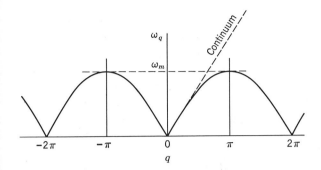

Fig. 2.3   The dispersion relation for a linear chain.   (*After J. M. Ziman, "Electrons and Phonons," p.* 14, *Oxford University Press, London,* 1960.)

the relationship between ω and q for a dispersionless medium.   In the limit of long wavelength, the linear chain behaves as a dispersionless medium in which the wave velocity and group velocity, defined by

$$v_p = \frac{\omega(q)}{q} \quad \text{and} \quad v_g = \frac{d\omega(q)}{dq} \tag{2.17}$$

are both equal to

$$a\sqrt{\frac{\beta}{m}}$$

provided

$$qa \ll 1$$

This similarity between the chain and a continuum is to be expected when $qa \ll 1$, for in this region the wavelength $\lambda = 2\pi/q$ is much longer than the characteristic length of the lattice, a.

As the wavelength becomes shorter and comparable to the lattice spacing, we expect the behavior of the chain to deviate markedly from that of a continuum, and, as shown in Fig. 2.3, such is indeed the case. In fact, the group velocity vanishes at $qa = \pm\pi$, indicating that these modes represent standing waves in the lattice.

It may be of interest to call to mind the orders of magnitude involved for an average solid.   Interatomic distances in solids are of the order of 3 Å; sound velocities are in the neighborhood of 10^5 cm/sec; and since on an atomic scale these correspond to long-wavelength vibrations even at ultrasonic frequencies, we see that

$$\sqrt{\frac{\beta}{m}} \simeq 3 \times 10^{12} \text{ sec}^{-1}$$

The vibrational mode of highest frequency which the lattice can support is $\omega_m = 2\sqrt{\beta/m} \simeq 6 \times 10^{12}\,\text{sec}^{-1}$. Frequencies of this order of magnitude belong in the infrared region of the spectrum.

One of our assumptions which may readily be removed in principle, though not in practice, is the limitation to nearest-neighbor forces. If this restriction is lifted, one finds that the solution to the equation of motion is unchanged in form, and, moreover, the conditions which determine and limit the allowed q values remain valid. The dispersion relation, however, is no longer given correctly by Eq. (2.9), but is of a more complicated form, involving more than one spring constant. Nevertheless, certain qualitative features persist, namely, the approach to the dispersionless continuum at long wavelengths and the vanishing group velocity for the mode $q = \pi/a$.

2.3 DIATOMIC LINEAR CHAIN

In the previous discussion we assumed that all masses were identical. Such a chain might serve as a model for a linear monatomic crystal, but it cannot reveal certain interesting features of diatomic crystals, such as NaCl. We now turn our attention to a one-dimensional analog of an alkali halide crystal. The model is shown in Fig. 2.4, where we assume that the chain contains two different masses in alternate positions.

The equations of motion now are

$$m\ddot{u}_{2n+1} = \beta(u_{2n+2} + u_{2n} - 2u_{2n+1})$$
$$M\ddot{u}_{2n} = \beta(u_{2n+1} + u_{2n-1} - 2u_{2n}) \tag{2.18}$$

We again look for wavelike solutions. However, because alternate lattice points are associated with different masses, the amplitudes and phases of the wave at these alternate points may differ. We therefore let

$$u_{2n} = A_e e^{i(2nqa-\omega t)}$$
$$u_{2n+1} = A_o e^{i[(2n+1)qa-\omega t]} \tag{2.19}$$

and find that the equations of motion take the form

$$2\beta A_e - M\omega^2 A_e - 2\beta A_o \cos(qa) = 0$$
$$-2\beta A_e \cos(qa) + 2\beta A_o - m\omega^2 A_o = 0 \tag{2.20}$$

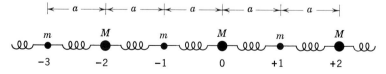

Fig. 2.4 The linear chain with a basis.

These two simultaneous linear equations have nontrivial solutions if and only if the determinant of the coefficients A_e and A_o vanishes. The frequencies ω must therefore satisfy the "secular" equation

$$\begin{vmatrix} 2\beta - M\omega^2 & -2\beta \cos{(qa)} \\ -2\beta \cos{(qa)} & 2\beta - m\omega^2 \end{vmatrix} = 0 \tag{2.21}$$

whose solution is

$$\omega^2 = \frac{\beta}{\bar{m}} \left\{ 1 \pm \left[1 - \frac{4\bar{m} \sin^2{(qa)}}{M + m} \right]^{\frac{1}{2}} \right\} \tag{2.22}$$

where $\bar{m}$ is the reduced mass

$$\bar{m} = \frac{mM}{m + M} \tag{2.23}$$

Using the same arguments as before, one finds that the allowed values of q are given by

$$q = \frac{\pi n}{Na} \tag{2.24}$$

where N is the number of masses of one kind in the chain (which is again assumed to be closed on itself) and n is an integer. Moreover, all physically significant solutions are again contained within a certain interval, namely,

$$-\frac{\pi}{2a} < q \le \frac{\pi}{2a} \tag{2.25}$$

This is just the Brillouin zone in wave-number space for a lattice whose lattice parameter is $2a$. (Although the distance between adjacent masses is a, the period of the lattice is $2a$, this being the distance after which the pattern repeats itself.)

The outstanding difference between the solution of the chain with a basis and the result for the monatomic chain is the presence of two different solutions for ω for each value of q. To appreciate the significance of these two solutions, we consider the solutions in the limit of long wavelength, i.e., in the limit $qa \to 0$. Using the positive sign in Eq. (2.22) and letting $qa \to 0$, one obtains

$$\omega = \sqrt{\frac{2\beta}{\bar{m}}} \qquad \frac{A_e}{A_o} = -\frac{m}{M} \tag{2.26}$$

If the negative sign is employed,

$$\omega = \left(\frac{2\beta}{M+m}\right)^{\frac{1}{2}} qa \qquad \frac{A_e}{A_o} = 1 \tag{2.27}$$

The solution (2.27) is identical to the one for the monatomic chain, provided one replaces the mass per atom by the average mass $(M+m)/2$. Moreover, we see that since A_e/A_o equals unity, the masses on odd and even lattice sites are moving in phase in the limit of infinite wavelength.

The other solution, Eq. (2.26), however, is quite unlike that for the monatomic lattice. The frequency is nonvanishing even in the limit $qa \rightarrow 0$, and in this limit is independent of the wavelength. Consequently, the group velocity for these waves vanishes at $q = 0$, and this mode of vibration must therefore be a standing wave. The ratio of the amplitude factors shows that in this mode of vibration alternate masses are exactly π radian out of phase, the amplitudes being inversely proportional to the masses.

The modes corresponding to the negative sign in Eq. (2.22) are known as *acoustical modes of vibration* because these are the modes that would be excited if a crystalline rod were connected to and driven by an acoustic transducer which generates pressure waves in the rod. The other set of solutions, corresponding to the positive choice of sign in Eq. (2.22), are known as *optical modes of vibration*. Such modes are excited in an alkali halide crystal subjected to electromagnetic radiation whose frequency is equal to $\sqrt{2\beta/\overline{m}}$. Since the two types of ions of an alkali halide are oppositely charged, they will experience forces in opposite direction under the influence of an electric field. Thus their motion will tend to be out of phase; and if the frequency at which the electric field alternates is equal to the frequency of the corresponding normal mode of the system, resonant absorption will take place, as evidenced by a typical transmission curve shown in Fig. 1.3.

As the wave number increases from zero to $\pi/2a$, the frequency of the acoustical modes increases from zero to $\sqrt{2\beta/M}$, whereas the frequency of the optical modes decreases from $\omega = \sqrt{2\beta/\overline{m}}$ to $\omega = \sqrt{2\beta/m}$. The dispersion relation for these two branches of the vibrational spectrum is shown in Fig. 2.5.

A noteworthy feature of the frequency spectrum is the appearance of a "forbidden gap" between $\omega = \sqrt{2\beta/M}$ and $\omega = \sqrt{2\beta/m}$. The forbidden region corresponds to frequencies which cannot propagate unattenuated through the linear chain. To see this we need only substitute a value of ω falling in the forbidden region into Eq. (2.20). We then find that the equations of motion can be satisfied only if the propagation number takes on a complex value, indicating that the wave is

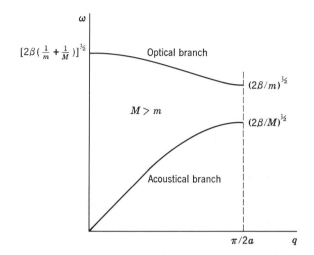

Fig. 2.5 Acoustic and optical branches of the frequency-versus-wave-number relation for a diatomic linear chain. *(From C. Kittel, "Introduction to Solid State Physics," 2d ed., John Wiley & Sons., Inc., New York, 1956.)*

attenuated.   We shall encounter similar forbidden regions in the energy spectrum of electrons propagating in a perfect crystal.

2.4   LATTICE VIBRATIONS IN THREE DIMENSIONS

Extension to three dimensions is simple enough.   Rather than belabor the obvious, we present below the results, calling attention to the analogy with the one-dimensional system.

We consider a crystal with N unit cells containing r atoms each, with masses M_j, $j = 1, 2, \ldots, r$.   Again we assume that the forces between the atoms obey Hooke's law.   The displacements $\mathbf{u}_{j,n}$ are then

$$\mathbf{u}_{j.n} = \sqrt{\frac{1}{NM_j}} \sum_{\mathbf{q},s} Q_{\mathbf{q},s} e^{i\mathbf{q} \cdot \mathbf{a}_n} \boldsymbol{\xi}_j(\mathbf{q},s)$$

$$= \sqrt{\frac{1}{NM_j}} {\sum_{\mathbf{q},s}}' [Q_{\mathbf{q},s} \boldsymbol{\xi}_j(\mathbf{q},s) e^{i\mathbf{q} \cdot \mathbf{a}_n} + Q_{\mathbf{q},s}^* \boldsymbol{\xi}_j(\mathbf{q},s) e^{-i\mathbf{q} \cdot \mathbf{a}_n}] \tag{2.28}$$

Here the symbols have the following meanings: $\mathbf{q}$ is the *wave vector* of the vibrational wave; $\boldsymbol{\xi}_j(\mathbf{q},s)$ is a unit vector which defines the *direction of polarization* of the wave and is characterized by the index s; the prime on the summation indicates that only one of the two possible choices, $+\mathbf{q}$ or $-\mathbf{q}$, shall be included in the sum; and the factor $(1/NM_j)^{\frac{1}{2}}$ is introduced as a matter of convenience and serves as a normalization factor.

The $Q_{q,s}$ are complex, time-dependent normal coordinates which obey the harmonic oscillator equation of motion

$$\ddot{Q}_{q,s} + \omega^2(q,s)Q_{q,s} = 0 \tag{2.29}$$

where, as before, these coordinates must satisfy the reality condition for the displacements $u_{j,n}$:

$$Q_{q,s} = Q^*_{-q,s}$$

If the crystal is of the Bravais type, that is, has only one atom per unit cell, there are three possible directions of polarization of the wave for each value of the propagation vector q. In the long-wavelength limit they appear as one longitudinal and two transverse polarizations. In the first case, the motion of the atoms is along the direction of q, whereas for transverse vibrations the motion of the atoms is in the plane perpendicular to the direction of propagation. These three polarization directions correspond, in effect, to the three degrees of freedom per atom. In general, i.e., when $q \cdot a \sim 1$, it is not possible to classify the waves as strictly transverse or longitudinal, although there are always three independent polarizations for each q vector.

If the crystal contains more than one atom per unit cell, the index s runs from 1 to $3r$. For example, if $r = 2$, then $s = 1, 2, 3$ could designate the three polarizations for the acoustical modes and $s = 4, 5, 6$, the three optical modes that the crystal can support.

The allowed propagation vectors q are again determined by applying appropriate boundary conditions. In the case of a three-dimensional system it is, of course, difficult to imagine a situation in which the system closes upon itself. Nevertheless, it has become accepted practice to use analogous boundary conditions, the periodic or Born-von Kármán boundary conditions. In applying these, one imagines a large crystal as being divided into smaller, but macroscopic, parallelepipeds. Since the boundaries between the parallelepipeds are purely fictitious, the solution to the equations of motion must be continuous across these boundaries.

Let a_1, a_2, and a_3 be the three noncoplanar primitive-lattice vectors, and let these three vectors define our coordinate system. We assume that the lengths of the sides of the parallelepiped are L_1, L_2, and L_3 in the directions defined by the primitive-lattice vectors. The periodic boundary conditions then require that

$$e^{iq_1L_1} = e^{iq_2L_2} = e^{iq_3L_3} = 1 \tag{2.30}$$

where q_1, q_2, and q_3 are the components of the propagation vector along the directions a_1, a_2, and a_3. It follows that the components q_1, q_2, and q_3

must be given by

$$q_1 = \frac{2\pi}{L_1} n_1 \qquad q_2 = \frac{2\pi}{L_2} n_2 \qquad q_3 = \frac{2\pi}{L_3} n_3 \tag{2.31}$$

where n_1, n_2, and n_3 are integers.

As in the one-dimensional case, one can show that two modes whose polarization vectors are identical and whose wave vectors $\mathbf{q}$ and $\mathbf{q}'$ are related by

$$(\mathbf{q}' - \mathbf{q}) \cdot \mathbf{a}_j = 2\pi m \tag{2.32}$$

where m is an integer, are in fact one and the same mode. Thus all physically significant and unique solutions are contained in the Brillouin zone, a finite region in $\mathbf{q}$ space, the space spanned by the propagation vectors. The limits on $\mathbf{q}$ corresponding to (2.13) are

$$-\frac{\pi}{a_1} < q_1 \le \frac{\pi}{a_1} \qquad -\frac{\pi}{a_2} < q_2 \le \frac{\pi}{a_2} \qquad -\frac{\pi}{a_3} < q_3 \le \frac{\pi}{a_3}$$

2.5 RECIPROCAL LATTICE

It is convenient to introduce new vectors $\mathbf{K}_m$ which satisfy the condition

$$e^{i\mathbf{K}_m \cdot \mathbf{a}_n} = 1 \qquad \text{for all } n \text{ and } m \tag{2.33}$$

These vectors define a lattice in $\mathbf{q}$ space just as the translation vectors $\mathbf{a}_n$ define the real lattice in coordinate space. For reasons which will soon be obvious they are called *reciprocal-lattice vectors*.

To prove that the $\mathbf{K}_m$ vectors do in fact define a lattice, consider first the three vectors $\mathbf{K}_1$, $\mathbf{K}_2$, and $\mathbf{K}_3$ which satisfy the conditions

$$\mathbf{K}_i \cdot \mathbf{a}_j = 2\pi \delta_{ij} \tag{2.34}$$

where the $\mathbf{a}_j$ are the primitive vectors of the real lattice, and

$$\delta_{ij} = \begin{cases} 0 & \text{if } i \ne j \\ 1 & \text{if } i = j \end{cases}$$

It is a simple matter to show that the vectors $\mathbf{K}_i$ are given by

$$\mathbf{K}_1 = 2\pi \frac{\mathbf{a}_2 \times \mathbf{a}_3}{\mathbf{a}_1 \cdot (\mathbf{a}_2 \times \mathbf{a}_3)} \qquad \mathbf{K}_2 = 2\pi \frac{\mathbf{a}_3 \times \mathbf{a}_1}{\mathbf{a}_2 \cdot (\mathbf{a}_3 \times \mathbf{a}_1)} \qquad \mathbf{K}_3 = 2\pi \frac{\mathbf{a}_1 \times \mathbf{a}_2}{\mathbf{a}_3 \cdot (\mathbf{a}_1 \times \mathbf{a}_2)} \tag{2.35}$$

These three vectors form the *primitive vectors of the reciprocal lattice*. From Eq. (2.34) it follows that

$$\mathbf{K}_m \cdot \mathbf{a}_n = 2\pi(m_1 n_1 + m_2 n_2 + m_3 n_3) \qquad m_j, n_j \text{ integers}$$

where $\mathbf{K}_m = m_1\mathbf{K}_1 + m_2\mathbf{K}_2 + m_3\mathbf{K}_3$ and $\mathbf{a}_n = n_1\mathbf{a}_1 + n_2\mathbf{a}_2 + n_3\mathbf{a}_3$; therefore, Eq. (2.33) is satisfied for all $\mathbf{K}_m$ and $\mathbf{a}_n$.

The Brillouin zone may now be obtained most conveniently from the reciprocal lattice. Since the Brillouin zone is that region in $\mathbf{q}$ space within which two points differ by no more than one of the reciprocal-lattice vectors, this region is just the unit cell of the reciprocal lattice. Thus, we obtain the Brillouin zone, as we did the unit cell of the real lattice, by constructing planes which normally bisect the reciprocal-lattice vectors emanating from the origin in $\mathbf{q}$ space. The smallest polyhedron formed from these planes is the Brillouin zone. Any wave vector $\mathbf{q}$ which falls outside this polyhedron may be mapped into the polyhedron by translation through a reciprocal-lattice vector.

Just as the unit cell and primitive cell of a Bravais lattice are of equal volume, namely, $\Omega = \mathbf{a}_1 \cdot (\mathbf{a}_2 \times \mathbf{a}_3)$, so the volume of the Brillouin zone is equal to the volume of the primitive cell of the reciprocal lattice, namely,

$$\Omega_B = \mathbf{K}_1 \cdot (\mathbf{K}_2 \times \mathbf{K}_3) = \frac{8\pi^3}{\Omega} \tag{2.36}$$

Let us now determine the number of wave vectors contained within the Brillouin zone. As a matter of convenience, we assume that the principal vectors $\mathbf{a}_j$ are mutually orthogonal. From Eq. (2.31) we see that the number of $\mathbf{q}$ vectors which terminate within the volume element $d\mathbf{q}_1\, d\mathbf{q}_2\, d\mathbf{q}_3$ is equal to

$$\left(\frac{L_1}{2\pi}\, d\mathbf{q}_1\right)\left(\frac{L_2}{2\pi}\, d\mathbf{q}_2\right)\left(\frac{L_3}{2\pi}\, d\mathbf{q}_3\right) = \frac{\mathsf{V}}{8\pi^3}\, d\mathbf{q}_1\, d\mathbf{q}_2\, d\mathbf{q}_3$$

where V is the volume $L_1 L_2 L_3$.

Since the density of vectors in $\mathbf{q}$ space is uniform, i.e., the number of $\mathbf{q}$ vectors terminating in a given volume element in $\mathbf{q}$ space is independent of the location of that volume element, the total number of $\mathbf{q}$ vectors contained in the Brillouin zone is just equal to the density of $\mathbf{q}$ vectors times the volume of the Brillouin zone. Thus, the total number of $\mathbf{q}$ vectors within the Brillouin zone is

$$\frac{\mathsf{V}}{8\pi^3}\, \Omega_B = \frac{\mathsf{V}}{\Omega} = N$$

where N is the number of unit cells in the volume V.

This result is, of course, to be expected. Since the entire crystal contains $r\mathsf{V}/\Omega$ atoms, the number of degrees of freedom is $3r\mathsf{V}/\Omega$. Now we have seen previously that the index s, which determines the branch and polarization of a vibrational mode, can take on any one of $3r$ values for each choice of **q**.   Thus, the total number of independent modes of vibration that can be excited in the crystal is $3rV/\Omega$, equal to the number of degrees of freedom.

A three-dimensional Bravais lattice will support only acoustic modes of vibration; but in contrast to the one-dimensional case, we now find three acoustic branches, one for each direction of polarization.   In general, the three branches are nondegenerate, that is, there will be three different frequencies associated with each value of **q**.   However, in Bravais lattices displaying a high degree of symmetry, such as the cubic lattices, and in all lattices at long wavelengths, the two transverse modes of vibration are degenerate.   Generally, these two degenerate modes will split as **q** increases.   Dispersion curves for a three-dimensional crystal are shown in Fig. 2.6.   As indicated in Fig. 2.6, the transverse modes

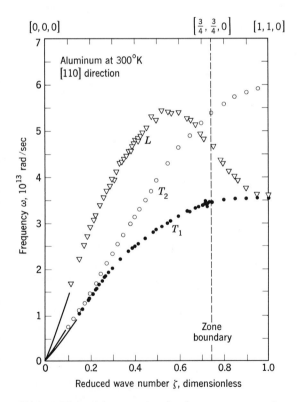

Fig. 2.6 Dispersion curves for elastic waves propagating along the [110] axis in aluminum. [*From R. F. Wallis (ed.), "Lattice Dynamics," p. 60, Pergamon Press, New York,* **1965.**]

normally have lower frequencies than the longitudinal mode of equal wavelength.

2.6 TRANSITION TO QUANTUM MECHANICS

The results which we have obtained were based entirely on the application of classical mechanics to the problem of the motion of atoms in a crystalline solid. For many purposes this classical description is entirely adequate. However, we shall consider later the interaction between electrons and moving lattice ions; since the description of electrons requires the use of quantum mechanics, the system with which these electrons interact must, then, be formulated within the same framework.

The transition to quantum mechanics is quite simple. We have seen that in the present instance the apparently formidable problem of describing the motion of a large number of interacting particles reduces to that of the behavior of a collection of harmonic oscillators. This simplification is possible only within the limitation imposed on the interaction potential between ions, namely, that the potential is proportional to the square of the displacement from the equilibrium position.

The reduction to normal coordinates is valid also in the quantum-mechanical treatment. It is only the description of the oscillators themselves which must now be carried through according to quantum theory. This is done in Sec. A.3 of the Appendix and we quote here the pertinent results.

1. The energy ϵ of an oscillator is quantized:

$$\epsilon = \epsilon_n = (\mathfrak{n} + \tfrac{1}{2})\hbar\omega \tag{2.37}$$

where $\mathfrak{n}$ is a positive integer or zero, and ω is the angular frequency of vibration of the oscillator.

For the case considered here, where each mode of vibration corresponds to a propagating wave,

$$\epsilon_n(\mathbf{q},s) = (\mathfrak{n}_{\mathbf{q},s} + \tfrac{1}{2})\hbar\omega(\mathbf{q},s) \tag{2.38}$$

where $\mathbf{q}$ and s again denote the wave vector and the polarization of the wave, respectively.

2. The quantities $\mathfrak{n}_{\mathbf{q},s}$ in (2.38) are called *occupation numbers:* they specify the degree of excitation of each mode, $\mathbf{q},s$. If $\mathfrak{n}_{\mathbf{q},s}$ is large, the vibrational mode of wave vector $\mathbf{q}$ and of polarization s is highly excited. Classically, we would say that this mode is vibrating with large amplitude.

3. The normal coordinates $Q_{q,s}$ are to be thought of as operators in the quantum-mechanical sense. The only nonvanishing matrix elements of the operators $\mathbf{Q}$ and $\mathbf{Q}^*$ are given by

$$(\mathfrak{n}_{q,s} - 1|\mathbf{Q}_{q,s}|\mathfrak{n}_{q,s}) = \left[\frac{\hbar}{2\omega(q,s)} \right]^{\frac{1}{2}} (\mathfrak{n}_{q,s})^{\frac{1}{2}}$$

$$(\mathfrak{n}_{q,s} + 1|\mathbf{Q}_{q,s}^*|\mathfrak{n}_{q,s}) = \left[\frac{\hbar}{2\omega(q,s)} \right]^{\frac{1}{2}} (\mathfrak{n}_{q,s} + 1)^{\frac{1}{2}}$$

$$(2.39)$$

In the language of quantum mechanics, Eq. (2.39) states that the operator $\mathbf{Q}_{q,s}$ connects the state of occupation number $\mathfrak{n}_{q,s}$ to one of occupation number $(\mathfrak{n}_{q,s} - 1)$. $\mathbf{Q}_{q,s}^*$ connects the same state to one of higher occupation number $(\mathfrak{n}_{q,s} + 1)$. For this reason the operators $\mathbf{Q}$ and $\mathbf{Q}^*$ are referred to as *annihilation* and *creation operators*, respectively, since acting on a state of specified occupation number they destroy and create one quantum of energy of that polarization and wave vector. Note that these operators connect only states with the same wave vector and polarization.

4. The reader acquainted with the quantum theory of electromagnetic radiation will see the close resemblance between it and the preceding description of a collection of harmonic oscillators. It is because of this close similarity (which is by no means accidental) that a quantum of lattice vibration has been given the name *phonon* in analogy to the *photon*, a quantum of electromagnetic radiation. We shall henceforth use this terminology throughout the text.

2.7 SPECIFIC HEAT OF SOLIDS

It has been known for over a century that at room temperature the molar specific heat at constant pressure, C_p, is almost the same for nearly all solids, namely, slightly more than 6 cal/deg-mole. From thermodynamic considerations one can show that C_p and C_v, the specific heat at constant volume, are related by

$$C_p - C_v = \beta^2 K \mathbf{v} T \tag{2.40}$$

where β is the volume coefficient of thermal expansion at constant pressure, K is the isothermal bulk modulus, and $\mathbf{v}$ is the molar volume. One now finds that, generally, C_v is almost independent of temperature as T is increased above room temperature, and is nearly the same for all solids. The magnitude of C_v is also very close to 6 cal/deg-mole, or $3R$, where R is the universal gas constant. Since R is just the product of Boltzmann's constant k and Avogadro's number N_0, these experimental results imply that the specific heat per atom is $3k$, regardless of the substance.

A specific heat of $3k$ per atom is consistent with a model of a solid in which each atom is a three-dimensional harmonic oscillator whose average kinetic energy per degree of freedom is $\frac{1}{2}kT$, giving an average kinetic energy of $\frac{3}{2}kT$ per atom. According to the virial theorem, a particle moving in a parabolic potential well has an average total energy twice its kinetic energy, in this case $3kT$. Hence the specific heat per atom should be $3k$, and per mole, $3R$. The observation that indeed $C_v \simeq 3R$ is known as the *law of Dulong and Petit*, in honor of the scientists who first formulated this empirical relation.

Curiously enough, though it initially lent strong support to classical statistical mechanics, and in particular to Maxwell's equipartition law, subsequent experiments on the specific heats of solids provided one of the first indications that the description of atomic systems required a drastic revision of classical mechanics. Whereas classical mechanics predicted that the specific heat of a solid should remain constant down to the lowest temperature, all data clearly indicated that C_v decreases as the temperature is lowered.

The first successful microscopic theory of the specific heat of solids was given by Einstein.[†] This theory, which we shall now present, is based firmly upon Planck's quantization rule, and, following closely upon Einstein's explanation of the photoelectric effect, its success provided yet another justification for the revolutionary proposals of Planck and Born. Einstein's theory, although in good qualitative agreement with the experiments, predicted that C_v should diminish with decreasing temperature more rapidly than observed. An improvement in that theory, which had already been suggested by Einstein himself, was published by Debye in 1912.

A. Einstein's Theory

Einstein combined classical concepts and the new hypothesis of Planck in an eminently successful manner. He visualized a solid as a collection of atoms, vibrating harmonically and independently of each other, all with one identical frequency of vibration ν. He then departed from classical theory and adopted Planck's rule that the energy of any one oscillator must take on the value

$$\epsilon_i = n_i h \nu = n_i \hbar \omega \tag{2.41}$$

[†] At about the time that these observations were reported, and shortly before Einstein's theory of the specific heat of solids was published, Nernst was able to predict from thermodynamic arguments that the specific heat of all matter should approach zero as the temperature approaches the absolute zero.

The probability that a particular atom oscillates with such ampli-
tude that its energy is ϵ_i is given by the Boltzmann factor exp $(-\epsilon_i/kT)$.
The relative probability that the oscillator is in the quantum state
specified by the quantum number n_i is therefore

$$p_i = \frac{e^{-n_i\hbar\omega/kT}}{\sum_{n_i=0}^{\infty} e^{-n_i\hbar\omega/kT}} \tag{2.42}$$

The average energy of an oscillator is then†

$$\bar{\epsilon} = \frac{\Sigma n\hbar\omega e^{-n\hbar\omega/kT}}{\Sigma e^{-n\hbar\omega/kT}} \tag{2.43}$$

Here we have dropped the subscript i, since in Einstein's theory all
oscillators are assumed identical.

Since each atom has three degrees of freedom, we associate with
each atom three independent oscillators. Einstein, therefore, assumed
that there are $3N_0$ oscillators per mole of a monatomic crystal. The
average total energy of such a solid is then $\bar{E} = 3N_0\bar{\epsilon}$. An analytic
expression for $\bar{\epsilon}$ may be obtained as follows.

We introduce the variable

$$x = \epsilon^{-\hbar\omega/kT} \tag{2.44}$$

Equation (2.43) now becomes

$$\bar{\epsilon} = \hbar\omega x \frac{\Sigma n x^{n-1}}{\Sigma x^n}$$

$$= \hbar\omega \left[\frac{d}{dx} \left(\ln \sum_0^{\infty} x^n \right) \right]$$

$$= \hbar\omega x \left[\frac{d}{dx} \ln \left(\frac{1}{1-x} \right) \right]$$

$$= \hbar\omega \frac{x}{1-x} \tag{2.45}$$

† As is shown in Sec. A.3 of the Appendix, the energy levels of an oscillator
are given by $\epsilon_n = (n + \frac{1}{2})\hbar\omega$ rather than by Eq. (2.41). The energy $\hbar\omega/2$, known
as the *zero-point energy* of the oscillator, arises because of the restrictions imposed by
the uncertainty principle. In calculating the specific heat of a solid, this zero-point
energy can be taken into account, carrying the term $\hbar\omega/2$ through the calculations.
However, since the total zero-point energy is temperature-independent, it does not
contribute to the specific heat, and the final result is identical to that which we shall
find.

Consequently, the average energy per mole is

$$\bar{E} = 3N_0\hbar\omega \frac{e^{-\hbar\omega/kT}}{1 - e^{-\hbar\omega/kT}} = \frac{3N_0\hbar\omega}{e^{\hbar\omega/kT} - 1} \tag{2.46}$$

To obtain an expression for the specific heat, we differentiate Eq. (2.46) with respect to T:

$$C_v = 3N_0 k \left(\frac{\hbar\omega}{kT}\right)^2 \frac{e^{\hbar\omega/kT}}{(e^{\hbar\omega/kT} - 1)^2} \tag{2.47}$$

Equation (2.47) is most conveniently written in terms of the new parameter $\Theta_E = \hbar\omega/k$, the characteristic *Einstein temperature:*

$$C_v = 3R \left(\frac{\Theta_E}{T}\right)^2 \frac{e^{\Theta_E/T}}{(e^{\Theta_E/T} - 1)^2} \tag{2.48}$$

For most solids the Einstein temperature, i.e., the value of Θ_E for which Eq. (2.48) most closely approximates the experimental results, is in the neighborhood of room temperature, about 300°K. The corresponding characteristic frequency ν is about 5×10^{12} cps. This is roughly the same frequency as the maximum frequency which we obtained for the linear chain in which we assumed a sound velocity equal to that for an average solid. Hence the adjustable parameter which appears in the Einstein results has, physically, the right order of magnitude.

The behavior of the specific heat at high and low temperatures is readily determined from Eq. (2.48) by going to the limits $T \gg \Theta_E$ and $T \ll \Theta_E$. In the first instance, when $T \gg \Theta_E$

$$e^{\Theta_E/T} \simeq 1 + \frac{\Theta_E}{T} + \cdots$$

and

$$C_v \simeq 3R \left(\frac{\Theta_E}{T}\right)^2 \frac{1}{(1 + \Theta_E/T - 1)^2} = 3R \qquad T \gg \Theta_E \tag{2.49}$$

At high temperatures Einstein's expression reduces to the classical result.

At low temperatures $e^{\Theta_E/T} \gg 1$, and Eq. (2.48) now simplifies to

$$C_v \simeq 3R \left(\frac{\Theta_E}{T}\right)^2 e^{-\Theta_E/T} \qquad T \ll \Theta_E \tag{2.50}$$

We see that the specific heat does approach zero as T approaches zero. Moreover, when $T \ll \Theta_E$, the dominant factor in Eq. (2.50) is the exponential, and it determines the behavior of C_v. Accordingly, C_v diminishes very quickly when T falls below $0.2\Theta_E$ (see Fig. 2.7). It is particularly

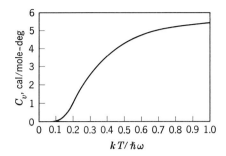

Fig. 2.7 The Einstein atomic heat. [*From J. DeLaunay, Solid State Phys.*, **2**: 223 (1951).]

in this temperature range that the Einstein theory and measured specific heats disagree, the latter approaching zero much more slowly. It is this disagreement which was removed by the refinement suggested by Einstein and carried through by Debye.

B. Debye's Theory

We have seen already that a linear chain, and also a crystal, can support vibrational modes whose frequencies extend from zero to a maximum value which is of order $k\Theta_E/h$. In Einstein's model it is assumed that only one mode, that for which the frequency is exactly $k\Theta_E/h$, can be excited. Since the quanta for this vibrational mode are of fairly high energy, it is not surprising that the internal energy of the system falls rapidly as the temperature is lowered to the point where a phonon of energy $\hbar\omega_E$ is unlikely to be excited thermally.

Debye relaxed the restriction on the frequencies of oscillation and assumed that all modes with ω within the range $\omega_{min} \leq \omega \leq \omega_{max}$ could be excited. The formal evaluation of the average energy of the system of oscillators follows the previous section very closely. However, the calculation requires one new piece of information, namely, the distribution of vibrational modes among the range of possible frequencies. This information is necessary because the average total energy of the system is now given by

$$\bar{E} = \int_{\omega_{min}}^{\omega_{max}} g(\omega)\bar{\epsilon}(\omega) \, d\omega \tag{2.51}$$

where $g(\omega)$ is the spectral density; that is, $g(\omega) \, d\omega$ is the number of modes within the frequency interval ω and $\omega + d\omega$. The first step in the evaluation of the internal energy, therefore, requires the determination of the function $g(\omega)$.

We have seen already that the number of $\mathbf{q}$ vectors which terminate in the volume element $d\mathbf{q}$ is $(V/8\pi^3) \, d\mathbf{q}$. Since there are three directions of polarization per wave vector, the number of modes in the volume element $d\mathbf{q}$ is

$$N(\mathbf{q})\, d\mathbf{q} = \frac{3V}{8\pi^3}\, d\mathbf{q} \tag{2.52}$$

and in the interval $d\omega$

$$g(\omega)\, d\omega = N(\mathbf{q}) \left(\frac{d\omega}{dq}\right)^{-1} d\omega \tag{2.53}$$

From Eq. (2.53) we see that the density function $g(\omega)$ can be evaluated only if the dispersion relation $\omega(\mathbf{q})$ is known.

Debye assumed that the crystalline solid is an isotropic dispersionless homogeneous continuum; hence

$$\omega = v_p q = v_g q \tag{2.54}$$

where v_p and v_g are the phase and group velocities.

The assumption of isotropy means that v_p is independent of the direction of $\mathbf{q}$; it is then convenient to consider a spherical shell in $\mathbf{q}$ space. The number of modes within such a spherical shell is, according to Eq. (2.52),

$$N'(q)\, d\mathbf{q} = \frac{3V}{8\pi^3}\, 4\pi q^2\, dq = \frac{3V}{2\pi^2}\, q^2\, dq$$

The density function $g(\omega)$ now becomes

$$g(\omega) = \frac{3Vq^2}{2\pi^2 v} = \frac{3V}{2\pi^2}\frac{\omega^2}{v^3} \tag{2.55}$$

In Eq. (2.55) we have omitted the subscript on v, since the group and phase velocities are assumed equal. However, we see from Eq. (2.53) that it is the group velocity which appears in the denominator of the first expression in Eq. (2.55). Thus, generally, we can write

$$g(\omega) = \frac{3V}{2\pi^2}\frac{\omega^2}{v_g v_p^2}$$

provided the material, though dispersive, is still isotropic. If it is not isotropic, $g(\omega)$ will be a function of the direction of propagation of the vibrational waves.

We have assumed that the velocities of transverse and longitudinally polarized waves are the same.   This assumption is not justified, even in the case of an elastically isotropic continuum.   Equation (2.55) is easily generalized to cover the situation in which the velocity depends on polarization, but remains, for each polarization, independent of q, namely,

$$g(\omega) = \frac{V}{2\pi^2} \omega^2 \left[\frac{1}{v_l^3} + \frac{2}{v_t^3} \right] \tag{2.56}$$

We shall assume hereafter that the velocity which appears in the denominator of Eq. (2.55) is an appropriate average of transverse and longitudinal velocities and use Eq. (2.55) rather than Eq. (2.56) in the remainder of the chapter.

We are now in a position to evaluate Eq. (2.51), find the internal energy of the solid, and then, differentiating the resulting expression, determine the specific heat.   Before we can do that, however, we must still decide what limits should be placed on the integral in Eq. (2.51).

The lower limit ω_{min} should be the frequency corresponding to the longest wavelength mode that can propagate through the crystal.   For crystals of reasonable dimensions the frequency ω_{min} is so small that $\hbar\omega_{min}$, the energy of one quantum, is negligible compared to kT, even at a temperature as low as 0.01°K.   We shall, therefore, set $\omega_{min} = 0$, confident that this approximation will not introduce a significant error in the calculation.   However, if the dimensions of a crystal are so small that the longest possible wavelength for which the boundary conditions can be satisfied corresponds to a frequency such that $\hbar\omega_{min} = kT'$, then for temperatures lower than T', deviations of the experimental results from the Debye theory may be expected.   Such deviations have, in fact, been observed in measurements of the specific heats of finely divided powders.

The upper limit on the integral in (2.51) is determined as follows: We know that the total number of modes must equal the number of degrees of freedom.   Formally, we can express this condition by

$$\int_0^{\omega_{max}} g(\omega)\, d\omega = 3N \tag{2.57}$$

We now substitute Eq. (2.55) into Eq. (2.57), evaluate the integral, and solve for ω_{max}:

$$\omega_{max} = \left[\frac{6\pi^2 N}{V} \right]^{\frac{1}{3}} v = [6\pi^2 n]^{\frac{1}{3}} v \tag{2.58}$$

where n is the number of atoms per unit volume.

Neglecting, as before, the zero-point energy of the system, we now have

$$\bar{E} = \int_0^{\omega_{max}} g(\omega)\bar{\epsilon}(\omega)\, d\omega$$

$$= \int_0^{\omega_{max}} \left(\frac{3}{2\pi^2}\right)\left(\frac{\hbar\omega^3}{v^3}\right)(e^{\hbar\omega/kT} - 1)^{-1}\, d\omega$$

$$= \frac{3k^4 T^4}{2\pi^2\hbar^3 v^3}\int_0^{y_{max}} \frac{y^3\, dy}{e^y - 1} \tag{2.59}$$

where $y = \hbar\omega/kT$ and $y_{max} = \hbar\omega_{max}/kT = \Theta_D/T$. $\qquad$ (2.60)

The parameter Θ_D is the *Debye temperature*. It is that temperature at which the thermal energy $k\Theta_D$ is just equal to the maximum energy of one quantum of vibrational energy.

The specific heat per unit volume is obtained by differentiating (2.59) with respect to T. The result is

$$C_v = 9nk\left(\frac{T}{\Theta_D}\right)^3 \int_0^{y_{max}} \frac{e^y y^4\, dy}{(e^y - 1)^2}$$

The internal energy and specific heat per mole are given by

$$\bar{E} = 9R\Theta_D\left(\frac{T}{\Theta_D}\right)^4 \int_0^{\Theta_D/T} \frac{y^3\, dy}{e^y - 1} \qquad \text{cal/mole} \tag{2.61}$$

$$C_v = 9R\left(\frac{T}{\Theta_D}\right)^3 \int_0^{\Theta_D/T} \frac{e^y y^4\, dy}{(e^y - 1)^2} \qquad \text{cal/deg-mole} \tag{2.62}$$

The integrals which appear in the above formulas cannot be evaluated in closed form. These and related thermodynamic functions have been evaluated numerically and tabulated as functions of T/Θ_D.

We can, however, find analytic expressions for the specific heat in the limits $T \gg \Theta_D$ and $T \ll \Theta_D$. At high temperatures the variable y is always much smaller than one, and an adequate approximation may be obtained by expanding the exponential in ascending powers of y. Equation (2.62) then simplifies to

$$C_v = 3R \qquad T \gg \Theta_D \tag{2.63}$$

the classical result.

At low temperatures, the upper limit Θ_D/T approaches infinity. We may then approximate the finite integral in (2.62) by an integral whose limits are zero and infinity. This definite integral is

$$\int_0^\infty \frac{y^3 \, dy}{e^y - 1} = 6\zeta(4) = \frac{\pi^4}{15}$$

Hence, in this limit

$$\bar{E} = \frac{3R\pi^4 T^4}{5\Theta_D{}^3} \tag{2.64}$$

and

$$C_v = \frac{12\pi^4}{5} R \left(\frac{T}{\Theta_D}\right)^3 \qquad T \ll \Theta_D \tag{2.65}$$

We see that in contrast to the exponential behavior of the Einstein model, Debye's theory predicts a T^3 dependence for the specific heat at low temperatures. This more gradual dependence of C_v on T arises from the inclusion of low frequency modes which can be excited at low temperatures. In other words, the Debye theory takes into account modes that can be excited and can contribute to the specific heat of the system at a temperature so low that the single Einstein mode would be excited only very feebly.

The reader may have noted the close resemblance between the form of Eq. (2.64) and the expression for the energy density of a blackbody. The latter also depends on the fourth power of the absolute temperature. The difference between the blackbody and the Debye dispersionless elastic continuum is only that, in the former, all frequencies for which the boundary conditions are satisfied may be excited, whereas, in the latter, there is an artificial cutoff imposed on the highest frequency, determined by the number of degrees of freedom. At low temperatures, however, the higher-frequency modes, those near the cutoff frequency, are not significantly excited in any event; and it is for this reason that we were justified in extending our range of integration from Θ_D/T to infinity. Once that is done, the difference between the dispersionless elastic continuum and the blackbody is obviated, and the results are formally identical.

The parameter Θ_D can be determined experimentally by a variety of independent measurements. One of these is, of course, a calorimetric experiment in which one measures the specific heat as a function of temperature and then fits the Debye curve to the experimental curve. Another method, applicable to metals only, involves the measurement of the resistivity as a function of temperature. As we shall show in a later chapter, the temperature dependence of the resistivity of a pure metal is also a universal function of T/Θ_D.

Table 2-1   Debye Temperature of the Elements, °K

Atomic number	Element	Θ_D					
		1†	2	3	4	5	6–9
3	Li	400	430	370	363		
4	Be	1000	980	1160	1160		
5	B	1250					
6	C (diamond)	1860	1940	2230			
6	C (graphite)			420			
10	Ne	63					
11	Na	150	160	158	160		
12	Mg	318	330	400	330		
13	Al	394	380	428	419		
14	Si	625		640			
18	A	85					
19	K	100	99	90	100		
20	Ca	230	230	230	219		
22	Ti	380		420	278	280	
23	V	390		360	300	326	
24	Cr	460	405	630	403	418	
25	Mn	400		450	410	410	
26	Fe	420		467	462	464	
27	Co	385		445	445	443	
28	Ni	375		450	413	413	
29	Cu	315	310	343	335		
30	Zn	234	240	310	190		
31	Ga	240		320	125		
32	Ge	360		370			
33	As	285					
34	Se			90			
37	Rb			52	68		
38	Sr			147	148		
39	Y						214 [6]
40	Zr	250		310	270	265	
41	Nb			230	250	254	
42	Mo	380	375	450	425	445	
44	Ru			600	426	426	
45	Rh			480	370	370	
46	Pd	275		300	275	275	
47	Ag	215	220	226	210		
48	Cd	120	165	188	300		
49	In	129		108	109		
50	Sn (gray)	260		210			
50	Sn (white)	170		178	160		

Table 2.1   Debye Temperature of the Elements, °K *(Continued)*

Atomic number	Element	Θ_D 1†	2	3	4	5	6–9
51	Sb	200		207	201		
52	Te			153			
55	Cs				54		
56	Ba			110	133		
57	La	132		142	132		131 [6]
59	Pr	74					
64	Gd	152					152 [7]
65	Tb						158 [8]
66	Dy			140			158 [9]
71	Lu						166 [6]
72	Hf			260	254	213	
73	Ta	225		240	247	264	
74	W	310	315	400	380		
75	Re			430	310	262	
76	Os			500		256	
77	Ir			420	316	285	
78	Pt	230	225	240	233	233	
79	Au	170	185	164	165		
80	Hg	100	90	80	69		
81	Tl	96		87	89		
82	Pb	88	86	110	90		
83	Bi	120		119	120		
90	Th	100		170			
92	U			200			

† The numbers 1 to 9 correspond to the following references:

1. J. deLaunay, *Solid State Phys.*, **2**: 219 (1956).
2. M. Blackman, "Encyclopedia of Physics," vol. VII/1, p. 325, Springer-Verlag OHG, Berlin, 1955.
3. "American Institute of Physics Handbook," McGraw-Hill Book Company, New York, 1963.
4. A. N. Gerritsen, "Encyclopedia of Physics," vol. XIX, p. 137, Springer-Verlag OHG, Berlin, 1956.
5. J. Horowitz and J. G. Daunt, *Phys. Rev.*, **91**: 1099 (1953).
6. L. D. Jennings, R. E. Miller, and F. H. Spedding, *J. Chem. Phys.*, **33**: 1849 (1960).
7. M. Griffel, R. E. Stockdopole, and F. H. Spedding, *Phys. Rev.*, **93**: 657 (1954).
8. L. D. Jennings, R. M. Staunton, and F. H. Spedding, *J. Chem. Phys.*, **27**: 909 (1957).
9. M. Griffel, R. E. Stockdopole, and F. M. Spedding, *J. Chem. Phys.*, **25**: 75 (1956).

Table 2-2 The Specific Heat as a Function of T/Θ_D

For $T/\Theta_D < 0.06$, $C_v/R = 233.8\ (T/\Theta_D)^3$

T/Θ_D	C_v/R	T/Θ_D	C_v/R	T/Θ_D	C_v/R	T/Θ_D	C_v/R	T/Θ_D	C_v/R
0.060	0.0505	0.098	0.2150	0.145	0.592	0.240	1.436	0.50	2.477
0.062	0.0557	0.100	0.2276	0.150	0.639	0.245	1.473	0.55	2.557
0.064	0.0612	0.102	0.2406	0.155	0.686	0.250	1.509	0.60	2.621
0.066	0.0671	0.104	0.2539	0.160	0.734	0.26	1.579	0.65	2.673
0.068	0.0734	0.106	0.2675	0.165	0.782	0.27	1.646	0.70	2.714
0.070	0.0801	0.108	0.2814	0.170	0.830	0.28	1.709	0.75	2.748
0.072	0.0871	0.110	0.2956	0.175	0.877	0.29	1.767	0.80	2.777
0.074	0.0946	0.112	0.3103	0.180	0.925	0.30	1.823	0.90	2.822
0.076	0.1024	0.114	0.3253	0.185	0.971	0.31	1.876	1.0	2.855
0.078	0.1107	0.116	0.3408	0.190	1.017	0.32	1.925	1.2	2.898
0.080	0.1194	0.118	0.3567	0.195	1.063	0.33	1.973	1.4	2.924
0.082	0.1284	0.120	0.3730	0.200	1.107	0.34	2.017	1.6	2.942
0.084	0.1378	0.122	0.3894	0.205	1.152	0.35	2.060	1.8	2.954
0.086	0.1476	0.124	0.4060	0.210	1.196	0.36	2.100	2.0	2.963
0.088	0.1578	0.126	0.4229	0.215	1.238	0.37	2.137	2.5	2.976
0.090	0.1686	0.128	0.4399	0.220	1.280	0.38	2.172	4.0	2.990
0.092	0.1796	0.130	0.4571	0.225	1.320	0.39	2.206	5.0	2.994
0.094	0.1911	0.135	0.501	0.230	1.359	0.40	2.238	10.0	2.998
0.096	0.2029	0.140	0.546	0.235	1.398	0.45	2.373		

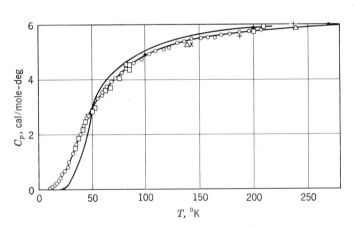

Fig. 2.8 The specific heat of silver and the corresponding Debye curve; also shown is the Einstein specific heat curve. (*From C. Kittel, "Introduction to Solid State Physics," 2d ed., John Wiley & Sons, Inc., New York, 1956.*)

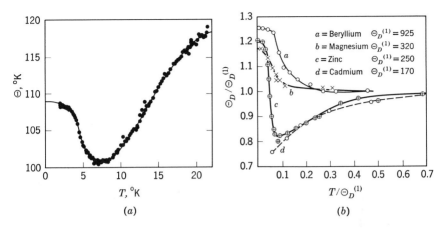

Fig. 2.9 (*a*) The temperature variation of the Debye temperature of indium [*From J. DeLaunay, Solid State Phys.*, **2**: 223 (1951).]; (*b*) the reduced Debye temperature as a function of reduced temperature for several hexagonal metals. $\Theta_D^{(1)}$ is the Debye temperature at $T \sim \Theta_D$. (*From M. Blackman, The Specific Heat of Solids, in "Encyclopedia of Physics,"* vol. VII/1, p. 362, *Springer-Verlag OHG, Berlin,* 1955.)

In Fig. 2.8 are shown the experimental specific heat curve of silver and the Debye curve which gives the best fit. We have also shown there the corresponding "best" Einstein curve. It is apparent that the Debye theory does reproduce the experimental data very closely, and is far superior to the Einstein result at low temperatures.

At this point one may well ask to what extent the Debye theory is correct. In most cases the Debye result and the experimental data are in very good agreement, although it is generally not possible to obtain a perfect fit by means of a single choice for Θ_D that is valid at all temperatures. It has now become accepted practice to consider the Debye temperature as a temperature-dependent parameter. A few typical curves of Θ_D versus T are shown in Fig. 2.9.

The fact that the Debye temperature is not a fixed parameter for a given material, but must be permitted to vary with temperature to obtain a close fit to the experimental data, implies that one or more of the approximations made in the derivation of Eq. (2.62) are not valid. We briefly review these approximations now and consider to what extent a real crystal might deviate from the ideal behavior, and how such a deviation might influence the thermal properties. The following approximations were made.

1. The solid was assumed to be a continuous medium.
2. The medium was assumed to be elastically isotropic.

3. The medium was assumed to be dispersionless.
4. The elastic properties were assumed to be independent of temperature.

The first of these assumptions is the cornerstone of the Debye theory. The atomic nature of the crystal is taken into account only by limiting the possible modes of vibration.

Elastic isotropy is certainly not a good assumption for many crystals. Anisotropy of the elastic constants results in a dependence of the velocity of sound on direction in the crystal. Consequently, the cutoff frequency generally is a function of the direction of propagation of the vibrational wave. Moreover, the function $g(\omega)$ is modified if v depends on direction.

We have seen that even under the simplest possible assumptions a model which takes the atomic character of the crystal into account inevitably leads to dispersion. Hence, the group velocity and wave velocity are not the same, and both are functions of the frequency. The spectral density $g(\omega)$, which depends on group and wave velocities, is in the real crystal a much more complicated function than Eq. (2.55). A typical frequency spectrum is shown in Fig. 2.10. Although in its gross aspects the frequency spectrum resembles the quadratic relation, Eq. (2.55), there are several prominent peaks and valleys in Fig. 2.10. The assumption leading to Eq. (2.55), namely, assumption 3, is clearly not justified, and leads to the most pronounced differences in the behavior of a real solid from that predicted by the Debye theory.

Elastic constants do, in general, depend on temperature. Such temperature variations could be taken into account in the theory by treating the sound velocity as a temperature dependent function. The variation of sound velocity with temperature would reflect itself in a temperature dependence of the Debye temperature. These variations, however, are not very pronounced and are usually neglected.

In retrospect, in view of the many assumptions which go into the Debye theory, it is surprising that it is as satisfactory as it appears to be.

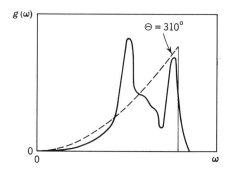

Fig. 2.10 The frequency spectrum of tungsten. The corresponding Debye spectrum is also indicated. [*From J. DeLaunay, Solid State Phys.*, **2**: 223 (1951).]

PROBLEMS

2.1. Give a thermodynamic derivation of Eq. (2.40). Estimate $C_p - C_v$ for copper at 300°K and 600°K.

2.2. Consider a linear chain (Fig. 2.1) and derive an expression for the specific heat at low temperatures using the Debye approach.

2.3. Repeat Prob. 2.2 for a two-dimensional square array.

2.4. Table 2.1 shows that the Debye temperature of solids, whose chemical and structural properties are similar, diminishes with increasing atomic mass. Thus, e.g.,

Element	Li	Na	K	Rb	Cs	C	Si	Ge	Sn	Cu	Ag	Au
Approx. Θ_D	400	160	100	65	55	1900	630	360	260	320	220	170

Discuss this pattern and show that it is consistent with the Debye theory. Use the Debye theory to estimate Θ_D of Li, K, Rb, and Cs from that of Na and compare your values with the experimental results.

2.5. In deriving the law of DuLong and Petit, one uses the result that the total energy of a harmonic oscillator is twice its average kinetic energy. Prove this statement.

2.6. The harmonic potential is only a first approximation. Show that the approximate heat capacity of a classical one-dimensional oscillator having the potential $V(x) = ax^2 + bx^3$, $b < a$, is

$$C \approx k\left[1 + \frac{15b^2}{8a^3} kT\right]$$

2.7. Solve the equations of motion for a linear chain of identical masses but connected to each other by springs with spring constants β_1 and β_2 in alternating positions.

2.8. The elastic energy per unit cell in a cubic crystal is $\frac{1}{2}ce^2a^3$, where c is an average elastic constant, e the elastic strain. Estimate the average thermal strain in a cubic crystal at 300°K and 1000°K.

BIBLIOGRAPHY

Bak, T. A. (ed.): "Phonons and Phonon Interactions," W. A. Benjamin, Inc., New York, 1964.

Blackman, M.: Specific Heat of Solids, "Encyclopedia of Physics," vol. VII/1, pp. 325–382, Springer-Verlag OHG, Berlin, 1955.

Born, M., and K. Huang: "Dynamical Theory of Crystal Lattices," Oxford University Press, London, 1956.

DeLaunay, J.: Theory of Specific Heats and Lattice Vibrations, *Solid State Phys.*, **2** (1956).

Maradudin, A. A., E. W. Montroll, and G. H. Weiss: "Theory of Lattice Dynamics in the Harmonic Approximation," Academic Press Inc., New York, 1963.

Peierls, R. E.: "Quantum Theory of Solids," Oxford University Press, London, 1955.

Ziman, J. M.: "Electrons and Phonons," Oxford University Press, London, 1960.

3
Equilibrium Properties of a
Free-electron Gas

3.1 INTRODUCTION

Electrons in solids—metals, semiconductors, and insulators—move in
and are strongly influenced by the periodic electrostatic potential of the
crystal lattice.   In large measure, it is this potential which determines
to which of the three categories a material belongs.   Nevertheless, even
today, despite the development of ever more sophisticated and reliable
theoretical methods for treating a difficult many-body problem,† the
free-electron theory remains the most convenient for many purposes.
To be sure, one cannot apply it blindly, and almost without exception
some adjustable parameter has to be introduced (e.g., an "effective mass"
which differs from the free-electron mass).   Yet, most electronic phenomena can be described and understood, at least semiquantitatively,
within its very simple framework.

One reason for its apparent success is that the free-electron theory
embodies one of the most fundamental and far-reaching results of quan-

† A brief qualitative discussion of the many-body aspect of solid-state physics
is presented in Sec. 4.2.

tum theory, the Pauli exclusion principle.   Application of the exclusion principle leads to a statistical description of a free-electron gas that is in sharp contrast to the classical.† In this chapter we shall be principally concerned with the profound changes wrought by Fermi-Dirac statistics as applied to an equilibrium distribution of free electrons.

We first give a brief quantum description of the free-electron gas and derive the relation between an important parameter, the "Fermi energy," and the electron density.   Since the mathematics simplifies considerably in two extremes, those of high and low electron density, which correspond, physically, to conduction electrons in metals and most semiconductors, respectively, we quickly turn our attention to these cases—the "degenerate" and "classical" limits.   The results are then applied to discussions of two important equilibrium properties, specific heat and magnetic susceptibility.

3.2 FREE ELECTRON GAS

The Schroedinger equation for a free electron is‡

$$-\frac{\hbar^2}{2m}\nabla^2\psi_k = \epsilon_k\psi_k \tag{3.1}$$

which has solutions of the form

$$\psi_k = \frac{1}{V^{\frac{1}{2}}} e^{i\mathbf{k}\cdot\mathbf{r}} \tag{3.2}$$

where V is the volume within which the electron is confined.

Substitution of Eq. (3.2) into Eq. (3.1) leads to the relationship between the wave vector $\mathbf{k}$ and the energy ϵ_k

$$\epsilon_k = \frac{\hbar^2}{2m} k^2 \tag{3.3}$$

It now remains to determine what conditions, if any, should be imposed on the wave vector itself.   As with lattice waves, the limitations on $\mathbf{k}$ are provided by the boundary conditions.   In the preceding chapter the concept of periodic boundary conditions was introduced in the discussion of traveling vibrational waves in a crystal lattice; the same periodic boundary conditions prove to be convenient also in dealing with electron waves.   Consider the electron to be confined in a cube of

† See, for example, F. Reif, "Statistical and Thermal Physics," McGraw-Hill Book Company, 1965.

‡ The reader who is not familiar with the elements of quantum mechanics is advised to consult Appendix A at this point.

lengths L, and impose the periodic boundary conditions on the wave function ψ_k, that is,

$$\psi_k(x + L,y,z) = \psi_k(x,y,z) \qquad \text{similarly for } y \text{ and } z \qquad (3.4)$$

Equation (3.4) will be satisfied if

$$\mathbf{k} = (k_x,k_y,k_z) = \left(\frac{2\pi}{L}\, n_x,\ \frac{2\pi}{L}\, n_y,\ \frac{2\pi}{L}\, n_z\right) \qquad (3.5)$$

where n_x,n_y,n_z are integers. Either these integers or, more simply, the components of the wave vector can serve as a set of three quantum numbers that characterizes the eigenstate of a free electron.

Indeed, these quantum numbers would completely specify the state of the free electron, were it not for the additional degree of freedom provided by its intrinsic spin of $\frac{1}{2}\hbar$. The spin quantum number m_s tells us whether the electron's spin is parallel or antiparallel to a particular spatial direction, according as $m_s = +\frac{1}{2}$ or $= -\frac{1}{2}$. The quantum state of a free electron is, then, fully specified by the wave vector $\mathbf{k}$ and the value of m_s.

The lowest energy level of the system is evidently the state $\mathbf{k} = 0$. According to classical statistical mechanics, we should find that at $T = 0°\text{K}$ all electrons within the volume V have condensed to this lowest state. As we shall see shortly, the application of classical statistical mechanics to the free-electron gas led to the most difficult paradox of the classical free-electron theory proposed by Drude and Lorentz.

The dilemma was resolved by the Pauli exclusion principle, which states that in any system of particles of half-integral spin (spin of $\frac{1}{2}$, $\frac{3}{2}$, etc.) a given quantum state can accommodate only one particle. Consequently, only two electrons can go into the $\mathbf{k} = 0$ level, one electron whose $m_s = +\frac{1}{2}$, the other whose $m_s = -\frac{1}{2}$. The remaining electrons, assuming there are more than two in the volume V, must occupy higher energy levels. At $T = 0°\text{K}$, electrons will occupy not merely the lowest two levels ($\mathbf{k} = 0$), but as many levels as there are electrons, until all levels below a certain energy η_0 are filled and none above that energy are occupied. The energy η_0 which marks the boundary between the filled and empty states is called the *Fermi energy* at absolute zero.

To determine η_0 we must first compute the number of available states of a given spin orientation between the energy ϵ and $\epsilon + d\epsilon$. That is, we wish to find the *density of states* $\mathcal{N}(\epsilon)$ such that

$$\mathcal{N}(\epsilon)\, d\epsilon = \text{number of states of given spin orientation per unit volume}$$
$$\text{between } \epsilon \text{ and } \epsilon + d\epsilon \qquad (3.6)$$

Consider the density of states in the space spanned by the wave vectors $\mathbf{k}$.

Since n_x, n_y, n_z are integers the number of available states in the volume element of $\mathbf{k}$ space,

$$\Delta \mathbf{k} = \Delta k_x \, \Delta k_y \, \Delta k_z = \frac{8\pi^3}{V} \, \Delta n_x \, \Delta n_y \, \Delta n_z$$

is equal to the product $\Delta n_x \, \Delta n_y \, \Delta n_z$. Now $n(k)$, the number of states contained within a sphere of radius $|\mathbf{k}|$ in $\mathbf{k}$ space, is equal to the volume of that sphere times the number of states per unit volume of $\mathbf{k}$ space. Thus,

$$n(k) = \tfrac{4}{3}\pi k^3 \, \frac{V}{8\pi^3}$$

We now write, in analogy to Eq. (2.53),

$$\mathscr{N}(\epsilon) = \frac{1}{V} \frac{dn(k)/dk}{d\epsilon/dk} \tag{3.7}$$

and obtain

$$\mathscr{N}(\epsilon) = \frac{(2m)^{\frac{3}{2}}}{4\pi^2 \hbar^3} \epsilon^{\frac{1}{2}} \tag{3.8}$$

This important relationship is valid whenever the energy is proportional to the square of the magnitude of the wave vector. We shall find in the next chapter that in crystals, too, the relationship between ϵ and $\mathbf{k}$ is often of the form $\epsilon_\mathbf{k} = (\hbar^2/2m^*)k^2$, where m^* is a parameter whose dimension is that of a mass, though its magnitude may differ from that of the free-electron mass. The density of states is then given correctly by Eq. (3.8), provided m is replaced by m^*.

We now proceed with the calculation of η_0, the energy of the highest occupied level at $T = 0°K$. [Compare this with the calculation of ω_{max}, Eq. (2.57).] We denote by n_0 the density of the electron gas, i.e., the number of electrons per unit volume. It follows that

$$n_0 = 2 \int_0^{\eta_0} \mathscr{N}(\epsilon) \, d\epsilon = \frac{(2m)^{\frac{3}{2}}}{2\pi^2 \hbar^3} \int_0^{\eta_0} \epsilon^{\frac{1}{2}} \, d\epsilon = \frac{(2m)^{\frac{3}{2}}}{3\pi^2 \hbar^3} \eta_0^{\frac{3}{2}} \tag{3.9}$$

where the factor 2 takes account of the two possible spin states allowed for each $\mathbf{k}$ state. According to Eq. (3.9), the Fermi energy at $T = 0°K$ is

$$\eta_0 = \frac{\pi^2 \hbar^2}{2m} \left(\frac{3n_0}{\pi} \right)^{\frac{2}{3}} \tag{3.10}$$

We note that η_0 increases monotonically as n_0 increases. This is expected, since electrons added to a system containing n electrons which are already occupying the lowest possible energy states must necessarily go into higher energy states, thereby increasing the energy η_0 which divides the occupied from the unoccupied regions. The increase of η_0 with n_0 is less than linear, because the density of states $\mathcal{N}(\epsilon)$ increases with increasing energy. Consequently, as one proceeds to higher energies it is possible to accommodate a larger number of electrons within a given energy interval.

At $T > 0°K$, thermal agitation will promote some electrons to higher energy states, leaving some states below η_0 unoccupied. The equilibrium distribution of free electrons at any temperature T is given by the *Fermi-Dirac distribution function*

$$f_0(\epsilon) = \frac{1}{1 + e^{(\epsilon - \eta)/kT}} \tag{3.11}$$

Here $f_0(\epsilon)$ is the probability that a quantum state of energy ϵ is occupied by an electron. η is the electrochemical potential, a parameter specified by the electron density and the temperature. η is generally designated "the Fermi energy"; it is that energy at which $f_0(\epsilon) = \frac{1}{2}$. The function $f_0(\epsilon)$ is shown for a number of values of kT in Fig. 3.1. We see that as $T \to 0$, Eq. (3.11) takes on the form which we specified in the previous section; namely, unit probability of occupancy for $\epsilon < \eta = \eta_0$, and zero probability of occupancy for $\epsilon > \eta = \eta_0$. With the aid of the Fermi-Dirac distribution we can now extend the discussion to finite temperatures. This generalization is achieved by replacing Eq. (3.9) by

$$n_0 = 2 \int_0^\infty \mathcal{N}(\epsilon) f_0(\epsilon)\, d\epsilon \tag{3.12}$$

which evidently reduces to Eq. (3.9) in the limit $T \to 0$.

Substitution of Eqs. (3.8) and (3.11) into Eq. (3.12) gives

$$n_0 = \frac{(2m)^{\frac{3}{2}}}{2\pi^2\hbar^3} \int_0^\infty \epsilon^{\frac{1}{2}} f_0(\epsilon)\, d\epsilon \tag{3.13}$$

$$n_0 = \frac{(2mkT)^{\frac{3}{2}}}{2\pi^2\hbar^3} \mathfrak{F}_{\frac{1}{2}}(w) \tag{3.13a}$$

where $w = \eta/kT$ and $\mathfrak{F}_{\frac{1}{2}}(w)$ is the Fermi-Dirac function of order $\frac{1}{2}$. The

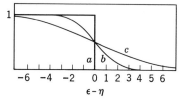

Fig. 3.1 The Fermi distribution, shown as a function of $\epsilon - \eta$, for several values of kT. (*After J. C. Slater, "Quantum Theory of Matter," p. 351, McGraw-Hill Book Company, New York, 1951.*)

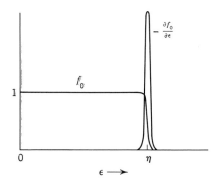

Fig. 3.2 The Fermi distribution in the degenerate limit at finite temperatures. Also shown is the derivative $-\partial f_0/\partial \epsilon$. (*After F. Seitz, "The Modern Theory of Solids," p.* 148, *McGraw-Hill Book Company, New York,* 1951.)

Fermi-Dirac functions of order n, defined by

$$\mathfrak{F}_n(w) = \int_0^\infty \frac{x^n}{1 + e^{x-w}}\, dx \tag{3.14}$$

occur quite frequently in calculations of the properties of an electron gas or of other assemblies of fermions. Tables of Fermi-Dirac functions for the half-integral values $n = -\frac{1}{2}, \frac{1}{2}, \frac{3}{2}, \ldots, \frac{11}{2}$ have been compiled by McDougall and Stoner and by Beer and coworkers [1,2]†. $\mathfrak{F}_n(w)$ for $n = 1, 2, 3,$ and 4 have been computed and tabulated by Rhodes [3].

From Eq. (3.13a) and the tabulated values of $\mathfrak{F}_{\frac{1}{2}}(w)$, the Fermi energy for arbitrary electron density and temperature is readily determined. Fortunately, it is rarely necessary to refer to tables of $\mathfrak{F}_{\frac{1}{2}}(w)$ since the electron distribution in most situations of physical interest is either highly degenerate (metals), or closely resembles the classical Boltzmann distribution (semiconductors and photoconductors). These two limiting cases can be dealt with most effectively by the following approximation methods, which lead to simple analytic solutions.

3.3 LIMIT OF EXTREME DEGENERACY

The degenerate limit is usually encountered in metals where the conduction electron density n_0 is so high (10^{22} cm^{-3} or more) that it forces the Fermi energy to values considerably in excess of kT. The distribution function then has the shape shown schematically in Fig. 3.2.

In every instance the integrals which we shall encounter are of the form $\int_0^\infty F(\epsilon) f_0(\epsilon)\, d\epsilon$, where $F(\epsilon)$ is a well-behaved function of the electron energy. Let us replace $F(\epsilon)$ by $dg(\epsilon)/d\epsilon$ and consider

$$I = \int_0^\infty \frac{dg}{d\epsilon} f_0(\epsilon)\, d\epsilon \tag{3.15}$$

† Numbers in brackets refer to References at the end of the chapter.

Integration by parts gives

$$I = -g(0) - \int_0^\infty g(\epsilon) \frac{\partial f_0(\epsilon)}{\partial \epsilon} \, d\epsilon \tag{3.16}$$

In the degenerate limit, $-\partial f_0/\partial \epsilon$ is a sharply peaked function, as shown in Fig. 3.2. This function is virtually zero everywhere except in the immediate neighborhood of $\epsilon = \eta$. Consequently, a Taylor's expansion of the integrand in Eq. (3.16) about $\epsilon = \eta$ leads to a rapidly converging series, namely,

$$-\int_0^\infty g(\epsilon) \frac{\partial f_0}{\partial \epsilon} \, d\epsilon = \int_{-\eta/kT}^\infty \sum_{\nu=0}^\infty \left[\frac{y^\nu}{\nu!} \left(\frac{d^\nu g}{dy^\nu} \right)_{y=0} \right] \frac{dy}{(1 + e^y)(1 + e^{-y})} \tag{3.17}$$

where $y = (\epsilon - \eta)/kT$. Since the expansion converges rapidly only if $\eta/kT \gg 1$, we may replace the lower limit of the integral on the right-hand side of (3.17) by $-\infty$. The result is then

$$-\int_0^\infty g(\epsilon) \frac{\partial f_0}{\partial \epsilon} \, d\epsilon = g(\eta) + 2 \sum_{\nu=1}^\infty C_{2\nu}(kT)^{2\nu} \left(\frac{d^{2\nu}g}{d\epsilon^{2\nu}} \right)_{\epsilon=\eta} \tag{3.18}$$

$$C_{2\nu} = \sum \frac{(-1)^{n+1}}{n^{2\nu}} = (1 - 2^{1-2\nu})\varsigma(2\nu)$$

where $\varsigma(x)$ is the Riemann zeta function. The first two coefficients of the series are

$$C_2 = \frac{\pi^2}{12} \qquad C_4 = \frac{7\pi^4}{720}$$

We shall never have occasion to use terms beyond $\nu = 1$. The higher terms are generally of order $(kT/\eta)^2$, as compared to the last term retained in the expansion. We then have as our final approximate result

$$I = \int_0^\infty \frac{dg(\epsilon)}{d\epsilon} f_0(\epsilon) \, d\epsilon \approx g(\eta) - g(0) + \frac{\pi^2}{6} (kT)^2 \left(\frac{d^2g}{d\epsilon^2} \right)_{\epsilon=\eta} \tag{3.19}$$

As an example of the application of Eq. (3.19) we now evaluate Eq. (3.13) in the degenerate limit. Here $F(\epsilon) = \epsilon^{\frac{1}{2}}$, and thus $g(\epsilon) = \frac{2}{3}\epsilon^{\frac{3}{2}}$. We obtain

$$\int_0^\infty \epsilon^{\frac{1}{2}} f_0(\epsilon) \, d\epsilon = g(\eta) - g(0) + \frac{\pi^2}{6} (kT)^2 \left[\frac{d^2g}{d\epsilon^2} \right]_{\epsilon=\eta}$$

$$= \frac{2}{3}\eta^{\frac{3}{2}} \left[1 + \frac{\pi^2}{8} \left(\frac{kT}{\eta} \right)^2 \right]$$

and find that

$$n_0 = \frac{(2m)^{\frac{3}{2}}}{3\pi^2 \hbar^3} \eta^{\frac{3}{2}} \left[1 + \frac{\pi^2}{8} \left(\frac{kT}{\eta} \right)^2 \right] \tag{3.20}$$

This expression evidently reduces to Eq. (3.9) as $T \to 0$.

We obtain the Fermi energy at any temperature (provided $kT \ll \eta$) by solving Eq. (3.20) for η. This gives

$$\eta = \eta_0 \left[1 - \frac{\pi^2}{12} \left(\frac{kT}{\eta_0} \right)^2 \right] \tag{3.21}$$

where

$$\eta_0 = \frac{\pi^2 \hbar^2}{2m} \left(\frac{3n_0}{\pi} \right)^{\frac{2}{3}} \tag{3.10}$$

is the Fermi energy at $T = 0°K$.

The temperature dependence of the Fermi energy as given by Eq. (3.21) assumes that the electron density n_0 is independent of temperature. In actual fact, thermal expansion decreases n_0, and η_0 changes accordingly (see Prob. 3.3).

The Fermi energy of the monovalent metals is in the neighborhood of 5 ev. At room temperature, $kT = 0.025$ ev; the second term in Eq. (3.21) therefore represents a correction of only a fraction of a percent, even at the melting point of these metals.

3.4 CLASSICAL LIMIT

When the electron density is sufficiently small and/or the temperature sufficiently high, the effect of the exclusion principle on the electronic distribution function becomes unimportant. This "classical limit" is attained when $e^{\eta/kT} \ll 1$, i.e., when $\eta/kT \ll -1$. In that case the allowed energy states which constitute the spectrum for $\epsilon \geq 0$ fall into the high-energy tail of the Fermi distribution, as shown schematically in Fig. 3.3. For positive energy states the Fermi-Dirac distribution is then given by the approximation

$$f_0(\epsilon) = \frac{1}{1 + e^{(\epsilon - \eta)/kT}} \approx e^{\eta/kT} e^{-\epsilon/kT} \tag{3.22}$$

Using this approximate expression for $f_0(\epsilon)$, Eq. (3.13) is quickly integrated and gives

$$n_0 = \frac{(2m\pi kT)^{\frac{3}{2}}}{4\pi^3 \hbar^3} e^{\eta/kT} \tag{3.23}$$

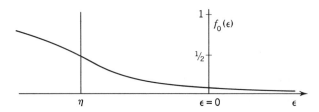

Fig. 3.3 The Fermi distribution in the "classical limit."

The Fermi energy

$$\eta = kT \ln \left[\frac{4\pi^3\hbar^3 n_0}{(2m\pi kT)^{\frac{3}{2}}} \right] \tag{3.24}$$

is now a sensitive function of the temperature. The validity criterion for the application of the classical limit is

$$e^{\eta/kT} = \frac{4\pi^3\hbar^3 n_0}{(2m\pi kT)^{\frac{3}{2}}} \ll 1 \tag{3.25}$$

At room temperature the free-electron gas satisfies the above inequality if $n_0 \leq 10^{19}$. If the temperature is lowered and the electron density maintained constant, the electron gas ultimately approaches the degenerate limit. In that case there will be some temperature region within which the electron gas cannot be approximated properly by either the classical or the degenerate limits. It will then be necessary to take recourse to the tables of Fermi functions. One also enters this domain, of course, if the temperature is maintained fixed and the electron density is increased in some manner. Although the latter eventuality may seem unlikely now, we shall see that in some semiconductors one can attain just such electron concentrations.

In a metal, that is, in a dense electron gas at normal temperatures, the electronic energy levels from $\epsilon = 0$ upward have virtually unit probability for occupancy to an energy $\epsilon \approx \eta$. Again, for $\epsilon \gg \eta$ the probability of occupancy of an energy level is effectively zero. It is only within a relatively narrow energy range of order kT in width and centered about $\epsilon = \eta$ that the probability for occupancy of an energy state is sensitive to the temperature of the electron gas. Thus, the major fraction of the electrons are "unaware," so to speak, of temperature changes. As we shall see shortly, this property of the degenerate gas reflects itself most forcefully in the specific heat and magnetic susceptibility of the gas.

In the classical limit the Pauli principle still holds. However, the probability of occupancy of any level whose energy is equal to or greater than zero is very small.   Consequently, if the only allowed states of the system have positive energies, the chance that *two* electrons might occupy the same level (identical spin and wave vector) is negligibly small, and, consequently, the Pauli principle does not significantly alter the distribution function.

The expressions which have been given in the preceding sections were based on the "independent-particle model" as applied to a gas of free electrons.   This independent-particle model assumes, as its name implies, that the motion of any given electron is independent of the coordinates and momenta of all the other electrons of the gas.   Only by virtue of this assumption could we write Eq. (3.1).

But can one neglect the mutual coulomb interaction between the negatively charged electrons?   The answer is clearly "no," because these interactions correlate the motion of the electrons.   Moreover, there is another correlation effect, which has its origin in the Pauli principle. This so-called exchange correlation also tends to keep electrons out of each other's way, but operates only on electrons of the same spin orientation (same m_s quantum number).

A treatment of the free-electron gas that includes exchange and coulomb correlations has been developed by Bohm and Pines.   An account of this work is well beyond the scope of this book; the interested reader is referred to review articles by Pines.

3.5 ELECTRONIC SPECIFIC HEAT

The earliest theory of metallic conduction was formulated by Drude and Lorentz and assumed that the valence electrons of a metal are free to move about the interior of the substance and can, by virtue of their mobility, contribute to charge transport.   For the monovalent metals the number of these free electrons per unit volume agreed reasonably well with the electron density deduced from measurements of the Hall effect (see Chap. 7).   Perhaps the most notable achievement of the Drude-Lorentz theory was the prediction of the Wiedemann-Franz law, which all metals obey rather well at room temperature (see Chaps. 5 and 7).

The Drude-Lorentz theory was not, however, an unqualified success. For example, it proved difficult to account for the temperature dependence of the conductivity.   The most serious problem, however, arose in connection with the measured specific heats of metals and insulators. Experiments clearly showed that both types of substance obeyed the law of Dulong and Petit (see Chap. 2).   This result could not be reconciled with the classical free-electron theory of metals.   In an insulator, classical arguments lead to a molar specific heat of $3R$ at high temperatures. The ions of a metal should likewise contribute a specific heat of $3R$ per mole, but in addition there should be a specific heat of $\frac{3}{2}RZ$ (Z = number of valence electrons per atom) attributable to the free electrons. Hence, one would expect the specific heat of insulators to be $3R$ per mole, but that of monovalent metals to be $\frac{9}{2}R$ per mole. The experimental results, however, seemed to show that the electron gas, if it exists, has a vanishingly small specific heat.

This dilemma was resolved with the advent of quantum statistics. Before we proceed to the detailed quantitative calculation of the specific heat of a degenerate electron gas, we shall consider qualitatively how the use of a Fermi-Dirac distribution law profoundly alters the situation. In the preceding section we pointed out that in the degenerate case, only electrons within an energy range of about kT of the Fermi energy are responsive to temperature changes. It is these electrons which, when excited thermally by energy increments of the order kT, can in fact change their energy. Electrons deep down in the "Fermi sea" cannot be excited thermally to states of higher energy, because these states are already occupied by electrons, and the Pauli principle excludes the possibility of simultaneous occupancy of a given state by two electrons. Thus, roughly only a fraction kT/η_0 of the total number of electrons can absorb thermal energy from the surroundings, and these will, on the average, increase their energy by an increment kT. Consequently, the energy change per mole of the gas is

$$\Delta E \approx kT \times \text{number of electrons affected}$$

$$\approx kT \, \frac{NkT}{\eta_0}$$

where N is the number of electrons per mole $= ZN_0$. The specific heat thus is approximately

$$C_v \sim ZR \, \frac{kT}{\eta_0}$$

This argument, crude as it may appear, leads to essentially the right result. The electronic specific heat *is* proportional to the temperature, and its value *is* reduced below that of a classical gas by a factor whose magnitude is kT/η_0. We have remarked above that η_0 for most metals is about 5 ev. Consequently, at room temperature kT/η_0 is about 0.005. It is then not surprising that the contribution of the electron gas to the specific heat of metals had not been observed.

We now turn to the detailed calculation of the electronic specific heat. The energy of a degenerate gas containing n_0 electrons per unit volume is

$$E = 2 \int_0^\infty \epsilon \mathcal{N}(\epsilon) f_0(\epsilon) \, d\epsilon$$

$$= \frac{(2m)^{\frac{3}{2}}}{2\pi^2\hbar^3} \int_0^\infty \epsilon^{\frac{3}{2}} f_0(\epsilon) \, d\epsilon \tag{3.26}$$

The integral appearing in Eq. (3.26) is of the form (3.15) with $g(\epsilon) = \frac{2}{5}\epsilon^{\frac{5}{2}}$. Applying (3.19) to (3.26) we obtain

$$E = \frac{(2m)^{\frac{3}{2}}}{2\pi^2\hbar^3} \left[\frac{2}{5} \eta^{\frac{5}{2}} + \frac{\pi^2}{4} (kT)^2 \eta^{\frac{1}{2}} \right] \tag{3.27}$$

We now differentiate (3.27) with respect to T, bearing in mind that η is itself a function of T, and obtain

$$C_v = \frac{\partial E}{\partial T} = \frac{(2m)^{\frac{3}{2}}}{2\pi^2\hbar^3} \eta_0^{\frac{1}{2}} \frac{\pi^2}{3} k^2 T = k n_0 \frac{\pi^2}{3} \frac{kT}{\eta_0} = ZR \frac{\pi^2}{3} \frac{kT}{\eta_0} \tag{3.28}$$

where Z is the number of valence electrons per atom.

Except for the numerical factor $\pi^2/3$, (3.28) is identical with the previous estimate.

It is left as a problem (Prob. 3.4) to show that in the case where the density of states differs from Eq. (3.8), the specific heat is given by the more general relation

$$C_v = \frac{2}{3}\pi^2 k^2 T \mathcal{N}(\eta_0) \tag{3.29}$$

At room temperature the electronic specific heat of metals is negligible compared to $3R$, the contribution due to the lattice vibrations. Since the vibrational specific heat is, according to Eq. (2.63), independent of temperature at high temperatures, one might hope to discern the electronic contribution experimentally by performing measurements at high temperatures. In most cases this approach is doomed to failure for a variety of reasons. First, even near the melting point of most metals, kT/η_0 is small compared to unity, and the electronic specific heat therefore represents still a small fraction of the total heat capacity. Second, and more important, the harmonic-oscillator approximation, the foundation on which the Debye theory of specific heat is constructed, becomes less reliable as the amplitude of lattice vibrations increases. If one considers the influence of anharmonicity on the lattice specific heat, one obtains additional terms, of which the most significant are linear in the temperature (see Prob. 2.6). Third, near the melting point of solids, vacancies and interstitial atoms are generated thermally. These defects also contribute to the specific heat, and their contribution increases approximately exponentially with temperature. For these reasons it is

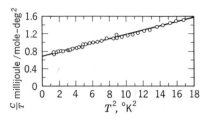

Fig. 3.4 The atomic heat of copper (at low temperatures) as a function of T^2. From the intercept, one obtains $\gamma = (0.668 \pm 0.004) \times 10^{-3}$ joule-mole^{-1}-deg^{-2} and from the slope $\Theta_D = 343.2 \pm 1.3°K$. [*After W. S. Corak et. al., Phys. Rev.,* **98,** 1699 (1955).]

usually a hopeless task to attempt to sort out the electronic specific heat from among the various effects which enhance the total specific heat above the Dulong and Petit value of $3R$.

The electronic specific heat can, however, be measured by going to the opposite extreme in temperature. The lattice specific heat is proportional to T^3 at low temperatures, thus decreasing much more rapidly than the electronic specific heat as the temperature is lowered. Indeed, at sufficiently low temperatures (generally below 4°K) the electronic specific heat is dominant.

The procedure by which the electronic specific heat is determined is, then, as follows. The total specific heat of the metal is measured over a fairly wide temperature range, say, between the lowest temperature that is attainable in the laboratory (perhaps about 4°K) and about 10°K. Since, presumably,

$$C_v = C_v^L + C_v^e = AT^3 + \gamma T$$

where the superscripts L and e denote lattice and electronic contributions, respectively, a plot of C_v/T versus T^2 should be a straight line whose slope

Table 3.1 γ **Values of Metals, millijoules-mole^{-1}-deg^{-2}**

Li	1.8	Ga	0.60	Lu	9.5
Be	0.23	Rb	2.6	Hf	2.6
Na	1.4	Y	8.5	Ta	5.9
Mg	1.3	Sr	3.6	W	1.3
Al	1.35	Zr	3.0	Re	2.3
K	2.2	Nb	7.6	Os	2.4
Ca	2.9	Mo	2.0	Ir	3.1
Ti	3.5	Ru	3.3	Pt	6.8
V	9.3	Rh	4.9	Au	0.75
Cr	1.40	Pd	9.9	Hg	2.1
Mn	18	Ag	0.611	Tl	2.6
Fe	5.0	Cd	0.63	Pb	3.3
Co	4.7	In	1.6	Bi	0.021
Ni	7.1	Sb	0.24	Th	4.7
Cu	0.688	Ba	2.7	U	11
Zn	0.65	La	10		

is A and whose intercept, when extrapolated to $T = 0°K$, equals γ.   A typical plot of C_v/T versus T^2 is shown in Fig. 3.4 and values of γ for various metals are listed in Table 3.1.

3.6 ELECTRONIC SPIN PARAMAGNETISM

It follows from the existence of an intrinsic electronic magnetic moment that an assembly of free electrons should show a net magnetization under the influence of an applied magnetic field.   The individual magnetic moments will tend to align themselves parallel to the field, perfect alignment of all moments being prevented at any finite temperature by thermal agitation.   Before we consider the paramagnetism of a degenerate electron gas, we shall treat first the situation which prevails when classical statistics are applicable.   This is by no means a fictitious situation. On the contrary, the susceptibility of paramagnetic salts and also the nuclear susceptibility, measurable at extremely low temperatures, are given correctly by the expression which we now derive.

The energy of a magnetic moment in a field $\mathbf{H}$ is given by

$$W = -\mathbf{\mu} \cdot \mathbf{H}$$

The intrinsic magnetic moment of a particle is generally written $g\mu_B s$, where g is a numerical factor ($g = 2$ for a free electron), μ_B is the Bohr magneton ($\mu_B = e\hbar/2mc$), and s is the spin quantum number (the maximum value of the z component of the spin angular momentum).   Since the electronic charge is negative, the direction of the magnetic moment is opposite to the direction of the spin.   The energy-level diagram of a free electron in a magnetic field H is therefore as shown in Fig. 3.5, where we have taken the z axis to point in the direction of the magnetic field.[†]

We denote the number of electrons with $m_s = +\frac{1}{2}$ by N_+ and those

[†] We are neglecting here the kinetic energy of the electron.   This simplification is not really permissible, for a magnetic field not only acts on the intrinsic magnetic moments, tending to align these, but also influences the orbital motion through the Lorentz force $(e\mathbf{H}/c) \times \mathbf{v}$.   This latter interaction poses a slightly more difficult problem for free electrons (and an extremely difficult one for electrons in real solids) than does that of the spin paramagnetism.   We treat the problem of orbital quantization due to a magnetic field in Appendix A.

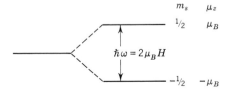

	m_s	μ_z
	$\frac{1}{2}$	μ_B
$\hbar\omega = 2\mu_B H$		
	$-\frac{1}{2}$	$-\mu_B$

Fig. 3.5 Energy levels of an electron in a magnetic field; the energy separation is $2\mu_B H$.

with $m_s = -\frac{1}{2}$ by N_-. In thermal equilibrium the probability that a given state of energy ϵ is occupied is proportional to the Boltzmann factor $\exp(-\epsilon/kT)$; thus

$$\frac{N_+}{N} = \frac{e^{-\mu H/kT}}{e^{\mu H/kT} + e^{-\mu H/kT}}$$

$$\frac{N_-}{N} = \frac{e^{\mu H/kT}}{e^{\mu H/kT} + e^{-\mu H/kT}}$$

(3.30)

where $N = N_+ + N_-$, and we have written μ for $g\mu_B s$.

The net magnetization $\mathbf{M}$ is

$$\mathbf{M} = (N_+ - N_-)\mu = N\mu \frac{e^x - e^{-x}}{e^x + e^{-x}} = N\mu \tanh(x) \qquad x = \frac{\mu H}{kT} \qquad (3.31)$$

The magnetic moment of an electron is about 10^{-20} erg/gauss. Consequently, even in a field of 10^4 gauss, μH is only about 10^{-16} erg, corresponding to a thermal energy near 1°K, so that at temperatures above that of liquid helium the parameter x is much less than unity. We can, therefore, expand the hyperbolic tangent for small argument and write, neglecting higher-order terms,

$$\mathbf{M} = \frac{N\mu^2 \mathbf{H}}{kT}$$

(3.32)

For the susceptibility we now have

$$\chi = \frac{\partial M}{\partial H} = \frac{N\mu^2}{kT}$$

(3.33)

In general, the orbital motion of electrons will also contribute to the magnetic moment, so that Eq. (3.32) does not give the total magnetic moment of the electron assembly.

If the electrons are bound to atoms, their magnetic moments are given by

$$\mu = g\mu_B J$$

where J is the total angular-momentum quantum number, and the Landé g factor is

$$g = 1 + \frac{J(J + 1) + S(S + 1) - L(L + 1)}{2J(J + 1)}$$

(3.34)

Here S and L are the total spin and orbital angular-momentum quantum numbers. If, now, the total angular momentum J exceeds $\frac{1}{2}$, the atomic levels will be $(2J + 1)$-fold degenerate in the absence of a magnetic field, not just doubly degenerate ($m_s = \pm\frac{1}{2}$).   This degeneracy is lifted by the application of a magnetic field leading to a set of $2J + 1$ levels, separated in energy by $g\mu_B H$, and specified by the magnetic quantum number m_J ($m_J = J, J - 1, \ldots, -J$).   The susceptibility, in the limit $x' = gJ\mu_B H/kT \ll 1$, is given by an expression similar to Eq. (3.33):

$$\chi = NJ(J + 1)\frac{g^2\mu_B{}^2}{3kT} \tag{3.35}$$

The above expression reduces, of course, to Eq. (3.33) when $J = S = \frac{1}{2}$.

To summarize, the paramagnetic susceptibility of a *classical* gas of free electrons is given by Eq. (3.33); for electrons bound to atoms, the susceptibility depends on the orbital as well as the spin angular momentum and is given by Eq. (3.35).   Here g is the Landé g factor, whose magnitude is determined from Eq. (3.34).   In any case a characteristic feature of the magnetic susceptibility is its linear increase with $1/T$.   A typical curve of χ versus $1/T$ is shown in Fig. 3.6.

If, now, conduction electrons in metals behaved as free particles obeying Boltzmann statistics, we would expect a susceptibility propor-

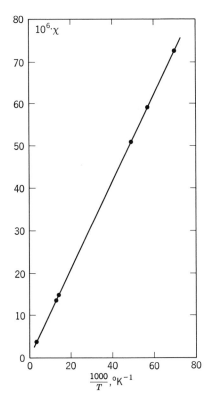

Fig. 3.6 The susceptibility of $CuSO_4 \cdot K_2SO_4 \cdot 6H_2O$ as a function of $1/T$ between room temperature and 14°K.   (*From C. Kittel, "Introduction to Solid State Physics," 2d ed., p. 217, John Wiley & Sons, Inc., New York, 1956.*)

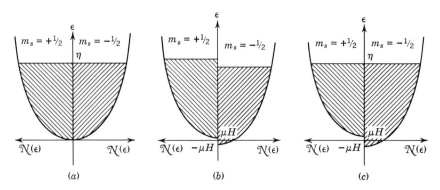

Fig. 3.7 The occupied states for the two spin orientations in a degenerate electron gas (a) For $H = 0$; (b) in a field H before reorientation of the spins; and (c) after equilibrium is established.

tional to $1/T$. If we set $N \approx 10^{23}$ cm^{-3} we find a room temperature susceptibility of about 10^{-4} cgs units (and a correspondingly larger one at lower temperatures). The measured paramagnetic susceptibility of conduction electrons is some two orders of magnitude smaller at room temperature and is, moreover, temperature-independent.

These discrepancies are again resolved by application of Fermi statistics. It is convenient to consider separately the $m_s = +\frac{1}{2}$ and $m_s = -\frac{1}{2}$ groups of electrons and to plot for each of these groups the density of states as a function of total electron energy, as shown in Fig. 3.7. The available states will all be filled (at $T = 0°$K) up to the Fermi energy, which will, however, be slightly different from its value when $H = 0$. Summing over the two spin states and applying (3.31) we have

$$M = \mu\!\int[\mathcal{N}(\epsilon + \mu H) - \mathcal{N}(\epsilon - \mu H)]f(\epsilon)\,d\epsilon \qquad (3.36)$$

Clearly only those electrons near the Fermi energy can actually reverse their spin orientation and can, thereby, contribute to the total magnetization. To see that this is so we need only imagine the two curves of Fig. 3.7a shifted by $\pm\mu H$, keeping the number of occupied states the same as in Fig. 3.7a. We then have the situation shown schematically in Fig. 3.7b. Electrons whose kinetic energy is less than $\eta_0 - \mu H$ cannot reverse their spins, because the state of opposite spin is already occupied. As in the case of the specific heat, the operation of the Pauli principle limits the number of "active" electrons to a small fraction of the total.

Even with the highest magnetic fields currently attainable $(H \sim 10^7$ gauss), $\mu H \ll \eta$. Consequently, an expansion of $\mathcal{N}(\epsilon + \mu H)$ in a power series in μH about $\epsilon = \eta$ will converge rapidly. Retaining only the lowest term, Eq. (3.36) reduces to

$$M = 2\mu^2 H \int f(\epsilon) \frac{d\mathscr{N}(\epsilon)}{d\epsilon} d\epsilon = 2\mu^2 H \mathscr{N}(\eta) \left\{ 1 + \frac{\pi^2}{6} (kT)^2 \left[\frac{d^2 \mathscr{N}(\epsilon)}{d\epsilon^2} \right]_{\eta_0} \right\}$$

(3.37)

where Eq. (3.19) has been employed in the evaluation of the integral. Neglecting the small term proportional to T^2,

$$\chi_p = 2\mu_B^2 \mathscr{N}(\eta) \approx 2\mu_B^2 \mathscr{N}(\eta_0)$$

(3.38)

where we have set $\mu = \mu_B$, the free-electron spin magnetic moment. For free electrons $\mathscr{N}(\eta_0) = 3n_0/4\eta_0$. Thus,

$$\chi_p = \frac{3n_0 \mu_B^2}{2\eta_0}$$

(3.39)

This is the Pauli result. The susceptibility is independent of temperature and is reduced below the classical value by a factor of about kT/η_0.

We have so far neglected to consider the influence of a magnetic field on the orbital motion of free electrons. It was first demonstrated by Landau [4] that free-electron wave functions and energy levels are modified by a uniform magnetic field in such a manner as to give rise to a diamagnetic susceptibility whose magnitude is one-third of the Pauli paramagnetic susceptibility. Consequently, the total magnetic susceptibility of a degenerate free-electron gas is

$$\chi_T = \tfrac{2}{3}\chi_p = \frac{n_0 \mu_B^2}{\eta_0}$$

(3.40)

Direct comparison of these results with experiment is difficult for several reasons. First, the ions in a metallic crystal also make a contribution to the diamagnetic susceptibility which cannot be measured directly and can only be estimated. Fortunately, this correction is relatively small, and small errors in estimating it will therefore be of little importance in the final result. Second and more serious than the above uncertainty, is the fact that electrons in metals are not truly "free." Several calculations of the diamagnetism of metallic electrons have appeared in recent years, and it is evident from these that not only do the results differ from the Landau value, but that they are rather sensitive to the assumptions made in the course of the calculations.

In a few cases, however, χ_p has been determined directly by an ingenious technique developed by Slichter [5]. The results show that

χ_p is larger than the Pauli susceptibility, especially in Li. This discrepancy appears to be related on the one hand to the neglect, in the Pauli treatment, of exchange and coulomb correlations, and on the other hand to the use of a density-of-states curve which does not take account of the "effective mass" of conduction electrons. Susceptibilities calculated by Pines taking account of these effects are in good agreement with the experimental data.

Finally, we call attention to the fact that the paramagnetic susceptibility is, in general, not a measure of the electron density. It is evident from Eq. (3.38) that the magnetization is a measure of the density of states at the Fermi energy, and that Eqs. (3.39) and (3.40) are valid only if the density of states is proportional to $\epsilon^{\frac{1}{2}}$ over the entire occupied region of the energy band. (See Prob. 3.6.)

PROBLEMS

3.1. Calculate the Fermi energy at $T = 0°K$ for sodium and potassium, taking $m^* = m$.

3.2. Calculate the change in the Fermi energy of sodium between $0°$ and $300°K$ using Eq. (3.21).

3.3. Repeat Prob. 3.2 taking into account the thermal expansion of sodium. The average coefficient of linear expansion of sodium between $0°$ and $300°K$ is 50×10^{-6} °K^{-1}. How important is the correction due to thermal expansion?

3.4. Derive Eq. (3.29) for the electronic specific heat.

3.5. As the temperature increases, the Fermi function $f_0(\epsilon)$ broadens symmetrically about the Fermi energy η. Nevertheless, $\eta(T)$ diminishes with increasing temperature. Give a physical explanation for this behavior.

3.6. Assume that the dispersion relation for free electrons is $\epsilon = \beta k^4$, where β is a constant.
(a) Calculate the density of states $\mathcal{N}(\epsilon)$.
(b) Calculate the Fermi energy at $T = 0°K$, η_0.
(c) Calculate the relative change in Fermi energy with temperature.
(d) Calculate the electronic specific heat to lowest order.
    Compare these results with those for the usual dispersion relation $\epsilon = \alpha k^2$.

3.7. For an electron gas of density n_0, calculate the mean energy $\bar{\epsilon}$ of an electron at $T = 0°K$. Express your result in terms of η_0.

3.8. (a) Using the relation $p = -(\partial \bar{E}/\partial V)_T$, where $\bar{E}$ is the total mean energy in the volume V, derive an expression for the pressure of a degenerate electron gas at $T = 0°K$. Show that the result is $p = \frac{2}{3}\bar{E}n_0$.
(b) Use your result to compute the pressure exerted by conduction electrons in sodium. Express your result in atmospheres.

3.9. Show that the compressibility $K_e = -(1/V)(dV/dp)$ of a degenerate electron gas is given by $K_e = 3/2n_0\eta_0$. Compare the value calculated from the above relation with the compressibility of sodium $K(\text{Na}) \approx 15 \times 10^{-11}$ m²/newton.

3.10. Calculate the ratio of the electronic to lattice specific heat for copper at $T = 300°$, $77°$, $4.2°$, $1°$, and $0.3°K$. Cooling from $1°$ to $0.3°K$ can be achieved by placing the substance in thermal contact with liquid He³ at $0.3°K$. If 1 joule of heat evaporates 1.25 cm³ of liquid He³, determine the amount of liquid He³ required to cool 50 g of copper from $1°$ to $0.3°K$.

3.11. Calculate the magnetic susceptibility of sodium and compare your result to the experimental value $\chi_{exp} = 0.63 \times 10^{-6}$ (cgs units).

3.12. A long uniform bar AB of a metal is suspended from a balance in a magnet as shown in the figure. The magnetic field at the center of the pole faces is homogeneous and the fringing field at A is negligible.

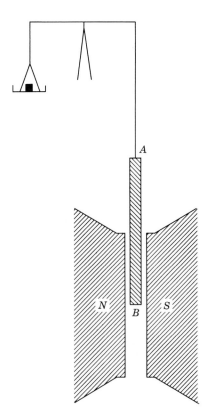

(*a*) Derive an expression relating the force exerted by the action of the magnetic field H on the bar to the susceptibility of the bar.

(*b*) If this were a 100-g, 20-cm-long bar of sodium, calculate the weight that would have to be added to the left-hand pan of the balance if the magnetic field is increased from 0 to 20,000 gauss (2 weber/m²).

REFERENCES

1. McDougall, J., and E. C. Stoner: *Phil. Trans. Roy. Soc. London*, **A237**: 350 (1938).
2. Beer, A. C., M. N. Chase, and P. F. Choquard: *Helv. Phys. Acta*, **28**: 529 (1955).
3. Rhodes, P.: *Proc. Roy. Soc. London*, **A204**: 396 (1950).
4. Landau, L.: *Z. Physik*, **64**: 629 (1930). (English translation appears in "Collected Papers of L. Landau," p. 31, Pergamon Press, London, 1965.)
5. Schumacher, R. T., and C. P. Slichter: *Phys. Rev.*, **101**: 58 (1956).

BIBLIOGRAPHY

Blakemore, J. S.: "Semiconductor Statistics," Pergamon Press, New York, 1962.
Kittel, C.: "Elementary Statistical Mechanics," John Wiley & Sons, Inc., New York, 1958.
Pines, D.: Electron Interaction in Metals, *Solid State Phys.*, **1**: 368 (1955).
———: "The Many-Body Problem," W. A. Benjamin, Inc., New York, 1961.
Reif, F.: "Fundamentals of Statistical and Thermal Physics," McGraw-Hill Book Company, New York, 1965.
Smith, R. A.: "Wave Mechanics of Crystalline Solids," Chapman & Hall, Ltd., London, 1961.
Spenke, E.: "Electronic Semiconductors," McGraw-Hill Book Company, New York, 1958.
Wilson, A. H.: "The Theory of Metals," Cambridge University Press, London, 1954.

4
Electrons in a Periodic Lattice

4.1 INTRODUCTION

In this chapter we shall be concerned with the solution of the Schroedinger equation for electrons in crystals. Before we can consider the behavior of electrons in metals and semiconductors under the influence of applied electric and magnetic fields, we must first have a satisfactory quantum-mechanical description of electrons in a crystal in the absence of external fields.

The results which we shall obtain will resemble in many respects those of Chaps. 2 and 3. The eigenfunctions for electrons are propagating waves whose (complex) amplitudes are periodic functions in the lattice; a particular solution of the wave equation can be specified by means of a quantum number n and a wave vector $\mathbf{k}$. The quantum number n serves much the same purpose as the parameter r in the description of lattice waves; that is, n specifies the "branch" of the energy spectrum in $\mathbf{k}$ space to which the electron is assigned. To make the analogy even more complete, all the physically significant and unique solutions belonging to a given branch of the spectrum are contained within the same limited volume in $\mathbf{k}$ space, the Brillouin zone.

We begin our discussion by considering first the difficulties inherent in a many-body problem. We shall find that the complexity of the problem forces us to adopt certain approximation procedures, even though their application is sometimes questionable. We shall resurrect the one-dimensional crystal, simplify the detailed features as much as we can, and solve the resulting wave equation. The solution, although physically inapplicable, does display certain qualitative features common to any periodic structure. We then consider a three-dimensional crystal and shall solve the Schroedinger equation in two limiting cases, known as the approximation of nearly free electrons and the tight-binding approximation. Finally, we shall consider the acceleration and velocity of electrons in a crystal and shall show that, to good approximation, these electrons behave very much as do free electrons.

4.2 MANY-BODY PROBLEM

It is well known that the equations of motion of celestial objects have never been solved exactly. Even the apparently simple problem of the motion of three interacting objects has not yielded to an analytic solution. The difficulties which one encounters arise because the force acting on a given object is not only a function of its position but depends on the disposition of all other objects as well.

In celestial mechanics this obstacle is overcome, though not circumvented, with the recognition that, since the mass of the sun is much greater than that of any planet, the most important gravitational force on a given planet is that between it and the sun. The forces between planets may then be treated as small perturbations, which give rise to small deviations of the true motion from that calculated under the assumption that the only objects in the heavens are the sun and that particular planet.

Despite the commonly quoted analogy between the solar system and the atomic system of nucleus and electrons, it fails deplorably in detail. In particular, the influence of one "planetary" electron on other electrons is so great that a perturbation method cannot be justified here.

Let us consider first the simplest atomic many-body system, namely, the helium atom, consisting of a nucleus and two electrons. The hamiltonian of the system, neglecting the kinetic energy of the nucleus and magnetic interactions, is given by

$$\mathcal{H} = \sum_{i=1}^{2} \left(-\frac{\hbar^2}{2m_i} \nabla_i^2 \right) + V_1(\mathbf{r}_1) + V_2(\mathbf{r}_2) + V_{12}(\mathbf{r}_{12}) \tag{4.1}$$

$$\mathbf{r}_{12} = \mathbf{r}_1 - \mathbf{r}_2$$

Here the first term is the sum of the kinetic energies of the electrons; the next two terms are the potential energies of the two electrons, arbitrarily designated by the subscripts 1 and 2, in the field of the nucleus. The last term represents the potential energy due to the interaction between the two electrons. Now r_{12} is of the same order of magnitude as r_1 or r_2, and, furthermore, the nuclear and electronic charges are of the same order of magnitude. Hence V_{12} and V_1 are roughly the same, and to neglect the interaction potential in this problem would be a crude oversimplification.

The eigenfunctions ψ, i.e., the solutions of Schroedinger's equation

$$\mathcal{K}\psi(r_1, r_2) = \epsilon\psi(r_1, r_2) \tag{4.2}$$

are functions of the electron coordinates r_1 and r_2. If the last term in (4.1) were negligible the wave equation would be separable, and the wave functions would be of the form

$$\psi(r_1, r_2) = \psi_1(r_1)\psi_2(r_2) \tag{4.3}$$

The energy eigenvalues are then

$$\epsilon = \epsilon_1 + \epsilon_2$$

the sum of the energies of two noninteracting electrons in the field of the nucleus.

The simplification of the wave function to the form (4.3) implies that the probability of finding electron 1 at the point r_1 depends only on r_1, that is, only on the coordinate of that one electron. Obviously, if there is an interaction between electron 1 and electron 2, the probability density for electron 1 will involve the coordinates of electron 2. Nevertheless, the "one-electron" approximation, on which until recent years nearly the sum and substance of the theory of solids was based, assumes that a product function of the type (4.3) is a good approximation to the true wave function.

In this approximation the interaction potential is, however, not entirely neglected, nor is it treated as a small perturbation. The procedure that is adopted is briefly as follows. First, one can derive, by a variational theorem, the equations which the functions $\psi_i(r_i)$ should satisfy. Once these equations have been obtained, the remainder of the problem is concerned with their solution. The energy eigenvalues calculated by this procedure are not the true eigenvalues of the many-electron system, even if the one-electron eigenfunctions are exact solutions of the differential equation derived from the variational principle. The reason is, of course, that we have started out with an assumed product wave function, which we know is incorrect. The effects which we have neglected are those resulting from correlations among the motions of the various electrons.

We shall not here derive the differential equation which the one-electron function $\psi_i(\mathbf{r}_i)$ must satisfy. If it is assumed that the wave function for the n electrons of the system is of the form

$$\psi = \psi_\alpha(\mathbf{r}_1)\psi_\beta(\mathbf{r}_2)\psi_\gamma(\mathbf{r}_3) \cdots \psi_\nu(\mathbf{r}_n) \tag{4.4}$$

one can show that the "best" functions satisfy the equation

$$\frac{-\hbar^2}{2m} \nabla_j^2\psi_\mu(\mathbf{r}_j) + V_j\psi_\mu(\mathbf{r}_j) + e^2 \sum_{\nu \neq \mu} \left[\frac{|\psi_\nu(\mathbf{r}_i)|^2}{\mathbf{r}_{ij}} d\tau_i \right] \psi_\mu(\mathbf{r}_j) = \epsilon_\mu\psi_\mu(\mathbf{r}_j) \tag{4.5}$$

Equation (4.5) is Hartree's "self-consistent" equation. The adjective refers to the fact that, since the equation for $\psi_\mu(\mathbf{r}_j)$ contains all other wave functions through the presence of the third term of Eq. (4.5), the solution for $\psi_\mu(\mathbf{r}_j)$ must be consistent with the solutions for the wave functions of the other electrons. This third term is evidently the average coulomb potential of the electron in the eigenstate described by $\psi_\mu(\mathbf{r}_j)$ due to all the remaining electrons. Thus the one-electron approximation does not neglect mutual coulomb interactions between electrons but replaces it by a reasonable average potential. Whereas the solution of Eq. (4.5) for a many-electron atom was once a formidable task, the advent of high-speed computing machines has greatly facilitated the numerical work. The mechanics of solving such a set of self-consistent equations has been outlined in a book by Hartree [1], and a summary of the available self-consistent solutions has been compiled by Knox [2].

A serious flaw of the Hartree equations is that they do not take account of the Pauli principle; i.e., there is no formal requirement within the framework of the Hartree approximation which corresponds to the Pauli exclusion principle. Now, one can show that the constraint that the wave function of a many-electron system be antisymmetric with respect to an interchange of the coordinates of any two electrons is completely equivalent to the exclusion principle. An antisymmetric linear combination may be formed from the product functions (4.4). Such a combination, known as a *Slater determinant,* is†

$$\Psi = \begin{vmatrix} \psi_\alpha(\mathbf{r}_1) & \psi_\alpha(\mathbf{r}_2) & \psi_\alpha(\mathbf{r}_3) & \cdots & \psi_\alpha(\mathbf{r}_n) \\ \psi_\beta(\mathbf{r}_1) & \psi_\beta(\mathbf{r}_2) & \psi_\beta(\mathbf{r}_3) & \cdots & \psi_\beta(\mathbf{r}_n) \\ \psi_\gamma(\mathbf{r}_1) & \psi_\gamma(\mathbf{r}_2) & \psi_\gamma(\mathbf{r}_3) & \cdots & \psi_\gamma(\mathbf{r}_n) \\ \cdot & & & & \\ \cdot & & & & \\ \cdot & & & & \\ \psi_\nu(\mathbf{r}_1) & \psi_\nu(\mathbf{r}_2) & \psi_\nu(\mathbf{r}_3) & \cdots & \psi_\nu(\mathbf{r}_n) \end{vmatrix} \tag{4.6}$$

† In the following the symbol $\mathbf{r}_j$ refers to *space and spin* coordinates of the jth electron.

It is a simple matter to prove that the wave function (4.6) is indeed antisymmetric with respect to the interchange of the coordinates of any two electrons.   Use of wave functions of the form (4.6) also leads to a set of self-consistent equations for the $\psi_\nu(\mathbf{r}_n)$.   These equations, the Hartree-Fock equations, differ from the simpler Hartree equations in that they contain an additional term, the so-called exchange term, which reflects the correlation in the motion of electrons of identical spin quantum number imposed by the exclusion principle.   In addition to this "exchange" correlation, the electrons are correlated due to the coulomb interaction between them.   This correlation, absent in the Hartree-Fock as in the Hartree equations, has been the focus of much theoretical research during the past decade.   Although methods for taking account of coulomb correlations have now been developed, their discussion is beyond the scope of this book.

In the solution of the atomic problem, the zero-order one-electron wave functions would naturally be atomic orbitals.   In the application of the one-electron method to crystals, the translational symmetry of the crystal imposes restrictions on the form of the wave function.   Suitable wave functions must obey the Bloch-Floquet theorem, which follows.

4.3   BLOCH THEOREM

The theorem due to Bloch states that the most general solution of the one-electron Schroedinger equation for an electron in a crystal is of the form

$$\psi_\mathbf{k}(\mathbf{r}) = e^{i\mathbf{k}\cdot\mathbf{r}}u_\mathbf{k}(\mathbf{r}) \tag{4.7}$$

where $u_\mathbf{k}(\mathbf{r})$ is a function with the same spatial periodicity as the crystal lattice.

The Schroedinger equation of which $\psi_\mathbf{k}(\mathbf{r})$ is a solution is

$$-\frac{\hbar^2}{2m}\nabla^2\psi_\mathbf{k}(\mathbf{r}) + V(\mathbf{r})\psi_\mathbf{k}(\mathbf{r}) = \epsilon_\mathbf{k}\psi_\mathbf{k}(\mathbf{r}) \tag{4.8}$$

Here $V(\mathbf{r})$ is the potential in which the electron is moving.   It is obvious that this potential, which arises from the presence of ions at regularly spaced points in the lattice, has the same periodicity in space as does the lattice itself.   Consequently, if $\mathbf{R}_j$ is a translation vector of the lattice, then

$$V(\mathbf{r} + \mathbf{R}_j) = V(\mathbf{r}) \tag{4.9}$$

Let us now consider the operator $\mathbf{T}_j$, defined by

$$\mathbf{T}_j F(\mathbf{r}) \equiv F(\mathbf{r} + \mathbf{R}_j) \tag{4.10}$$

We note the following properties. First, the operators $\mathbf{T}_j$ and $\mathbf{T}_i$ commute. This property follows from the fact that the order of translation is immaterial. Moreover, since the hamiltonian of Eq. (4.8) has the periodicity of the lattice, it follows that

$$\mathbf{T}_j \mathfrak{K}\psi = \mathfrak{K}\mathbf{T}_j\psi$$

That is, the translation operators commute with the hamiltonian. Consequently, it must be possible to find eigenfunctions of the hamiltonian which are also eigenfunctions of the translation operators. Let these eigenfunctions be denoted by $\psi_k(\mathbf{r})$. We now prove that these functions are indeed of the form of Eq. (4.7).

Since $\psi_k(\mathbf{r})$ is an eigenfunction of $\mathbf{T}_j$,

$$\mathbf{T}_j\psi_k(\mathbf{r}) = \psi_k(\mathbf{r} + \mathbf{R}_j) = \mathbf{\mu}_j\psi_k(\mathbf{r}) \tag{4.11}$$

where $\mathbf{\mu}_j$ is a number, the eigenvalue of the operator $\mathbf{T}_j$. We let

$$\mathbf{\mu}_j = e^{i\mathbf{k}\cdot\mathbf{R}_j} \tag{4.11a}$$

where $\mathbf{k}$ is a complex vector. Writing the eigenvalue $\mathbf{\mu}_j$ in this form leaves it completely general. We now consider the successive operations $\mathbf{T}_j\mathbf{T}_i$. From (4.11) we have

$$\mathbf{T}_j\mathbf{T}_i\psi_k(\mathbf{r}) = \mathbf{T}_j\mathbf{\mu}_i\psi_k(\mathbf{r}) = \mathbf{\mu}_j\mathbf{\mu}_i\psi_k(\mathbf{r}) = e^{i\mathbf{k}\cdot(\mathbf{R}_i+\mathbf{R}_j)}\psi_k(\mathbf{r}) \tag{4.12}$$

Since successive operations by $\mathbf{T}$ operators correspond to translation by a vector equal to the sum of the individual translation vectors, the reason for choosing $\mathbf{\mu}_j$ to be of the form of Eq. (4.11a) is apparent from (4.12). We also see that we must restrict $\mathbf{k}$ to the real domain. Otherwise, the wave function will grow exponentially in some directions. In a crystal of infinite extent such a solution is clearly inadmissible.†

We now define a function $u_k(\mathbf{r})$ as follows:

$$u_k(\mathbf{r}) = e^{-i\mathbf{k}\cdot\mathbf{r}}\psi_k(\mathbf{r}) \tag{4.13}$$

With the aid of Eq. (4.10) and Eqs. (4.11) and (4.11a), we find

$$\begin{aligned}
\mathbf{T}_j u_k(\mathbf{r}) = u_k(\mathbf{r} + \mathbf{R}_j) &= \mathbf{T}_j[e^{-i\mathbf{k}\cdot\mathbf{r}}\psi_k(\mathbf{r})] \\
&= e^{-i\mathbf{k}\cdot(\mathbf{r}+\mathbf{R}_j)}\mathbf{T}_j\psi_k(\mathbf{r}) \\
&= e^{-i\mathbf{k}\cdot(r+\mathbf{R}_j)}e^{i\mathbf{k}\cdot\mathbf{R}_j}\psi_k(\mathbf{r}) \\
&= e^{-i\mathbf{k}\cdot\mathbf{r}}\psi_k(\mathbf{r}) = u_k(\mathbf{r}) \tag{4.14}
\end{aligned}$$

† Near an external or internal boundary, however, solutions with complex wave vectors cannot be discarded a priori; the resulting electronic surface states, known as *Tamm states*, have been studied in some detail.

We see, then, from Eq. (4.14) that the function $u_k(\mathbf{r})$ is periodic in the lattice; that is, $u_k(\mathbf{r} + \mathbf{R}_j) = u_k(\mathbf{r})$. Consequently, the eigenfunctions $\psi_k(\mathbf{r})$ can be written as products,

$$\psi_k(\mathbf{r}) = e^{i\mathbf{k}\cdot\mathbf{r}}u_k(\mathbf{r}) \tag{4.7}$$

by multiplying both sides of Eq. (4.13) by $\exp(i\mathbf{k}\cdot\mathbf{r})$. This completes the proof of Bloch's theorem.

The detailed shape of the function $u_k(\mathbf{r})$ depends on the energy eigenvalue ϵ_k and on the crystal potential $V(\mathbf{r})$ of Eq. (4.8). We shall see later just what these functions look like in certain cases. For the moment all we do know is that once we have solved $u_k(\mathbf{r})$ within the confines of one unit cell of the crystal, we have completed our problem, for according to the Bloch theorem, $u_k(\mathbf{r})$ does not change as one goes from a given unit cell within the crystal to any other unit cell.

4.4 ONE-DIMENSIONAL CRYSTAL

We now attempt to solve the Schroedinger equation for an electron moving in a one-dimensional periodic potential. The one-dimensional crystal potential which a valence electron of a monatomic crystal might see is shown schematically in Fig. 4.1.

For such a potential we cannot find analytic solutions to Schroedinger's equation, and we therefore replace it by a potential which, in certain respects, resembles the crystal potential, but for which the Schroedinger equation yields a very simple analytic solution. In this model, shown in Fig. 4.2, and first employed by Kronig and Penney [3], the periodic potential is assumed to consist of an infinite number of potential barriers of width b spaced at intervals $a + b$, leaving regions of zero potential of width a between the barriers. The height of each barrier is taken to be V_0.

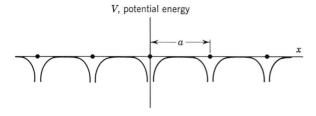

Fig. 4.1 The crystal potential of a monatomic, one-dimensional lattice. (*From C. Kittel, "Introduction to Solid State Physics," 2d ed., p. 273, John Wiley & Sons, Inc., New York, 1956.*)

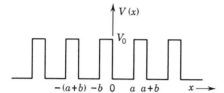

Fig. 4.2   The Kronig-Penney potential. *(From C. Kittel, "Introduction to Solid State Physics," 2d ed., p. 280, John Wiley & Sons, Inc., New York, 1956.)*

The Schroedinger equation for a particle moving in the above one-dimensional periodic potential is solved as follows. Solutions to the differential equation in the region $0 \le x \le a$ and in the adjoining region $a \le x \le a + b$ are obtained. In order for these to be acceptable solutions over the entire period $0 \le x \le a + b$, they and their first derivatives must be continuous everywhere, in particular at a, the boundary between the two regions. Finally, we impose the periodicity condition, which, as we know already, leads to the requirement that the solutions be of the Bloch form (4.7).

In the case of a one-dimensional crystal, Eqs. (4.7) and (4.14) become

$$\psi(x) = e^{ikx}u(x) \qquad u(x) = u(x + a + b)$$

$$\psi(x + a + b) = e^{ik(a+b)}e^{ikx}u(x) \quad (4.15)$$

In region I, $0 \le x \le a$, the general solution to the one-dimensional Schroedinger equation $-(\hbar^2/2m)(d^2\psi/dx^2) + V(x)\psi = \epsilon\psi$ is

$$\psi_{\mathrm{I}} = A\cos\beta x + B\sin\beta x \qquad \beta = \left(\frac{2m\epsilon}{\hbar^2}\right)^{\frac{1}{2}} \tag{4.16}$$

In region II, $a \le x \le a + b$, the solution takes the form

$$\psi_{\mathrm{II}} = C\cosh\gamma x + D\sinh\gamma x \qquad \gamma = \left[\frac{2m(V_0 - \epsilon)}{\hbar^2}\right]^{\frac{1}{2}} \tag{4.17}$$

The two constants C and D appearing in Eq. (4.17) may be eliminated by applying the continuity conditions on the wave function and its derivative. One then obtains the following expression for $\psi_{\mathrm{II}}(x)$:

$$\psi_{\mathrm{II}}(x) = A\cos\beta a\cosh\gamma(x - a) - A\left(\frac{\beta}{\gamma}\right)\sin\beta a\sinh\gamma(x - a)$$

$$+ B\sin\beta a\cosh\gamma(x - a) + B\left(\frac{\beta}{\gamma}\right)\cos\beta a\sinh\gamma(x - a) \tag{4.18}$$

Next we impose the periodicity condition on the wave function, namely, Eq. (4.15), and the corresponding condition obtained by taking the derivative of both sides of (4.15). At the point $x = 0$ these equations are

$$\psi_{\text{II}}(a + b) = \psi_{\text{I}}(0)e^{ik(a+b)}$$
$$\psi'_{\text{II}}(a + b) = \psi'_{\text{I}}(0)e^{ik(a+b)} \tag{4.19}$$

If we now substitute Eqs. (4.16) and (4.18) into the above two relations, we obtain the two simultaneous equations for the coefficients A and B:

$$A \cos \beta a \cosh \gamma b - A \left(\frac{\beta}{\gamma}\right) \sin \beta a \sinh \gamma b + B \sin \beta a \cosh \gamma b$$

$$+ B \left(\frac{\beta}{\gamma}\right) \cos \beta a \sinh \gamma b - A e^{ik(a+b)} = 0$$

$$\gamma A \cos \beta a \sinh \gamma b - A \sin \beta a \cosh \gamma b + \gamma B \sin \beta a \sinh \gamma b$$

$$+ B \cos \beta a \cosh \gamma b - B e^{ik(a+b)} = 0$$

which have nontrivial solutions only if the determinant of the coefficients of A and B vanishes. The solution of the secular equation is

$$\cos k(a + b) = \cos \beta a \cosh \gamma b + \frac{\gamma^2 - \beta^2}{2\gamma\beta} \sin \beta a \sinh \gamma b \tag{4.20}$$

In principle, Eq. (4.20) gives the energy for any value of k, or, alternatively, the value of k associated with a particular energy ϵ. Although the transcendental equation is still too complicated to permit one to deduce the functional relationship between ϵ and k in a simple manner, it is already apparent from Eq. (4.20) that the energy will be a *multi-valued* function of the wave number k. To clarify the problem we simplify still further by going to the limit $b \to 0$, $V_0 \to \infty$, such that the product bV_0 remains constant. One then finds that Eq. (4.20) reduces to

$$\cos ka = \cos \beta a + \frac{P}{\beta a} \sin \beta a \qquad P = \frac{V_0 mab}{\hbar^2} \tag{4.21}$$

In Fig. 4.3 we have plotted the right-hand side of Eq. (4.21) as a function of βa. Since for k real, $-1 \le \cos ka \le +1$, the requirement that the wave numbers be real limits βa to certain well-defined regions. In other words, there will be only certain allowed energy bands, shown shaded in Fig. 4.3, for which the wave equation leads to a solution in the form of an unattenuated wave.

It is interesting to note that the widths of the allowed energy bands increase with increasing values of βa, i.e., with increasing energy. Also, for any particular band, the width decreases with increasing P. The physical reason for this behavior is easily found. The parameter P is characteristic of the strength of the potential barriers which separate

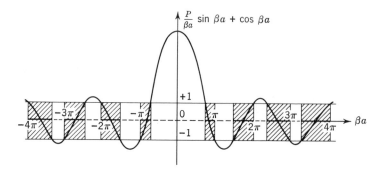

Fig. 4.3   The quantity $\cos \beta a + (P/\beta a) \sin \beta a$ as a function of βa. For real $k, -1 \le \cos ka \le +1$.   This restricts the acceptable range of βa to the shaded regions.   *(From C. Kittel, "Introduction to Solid State Physics," 2d ed., p. 280, John Wiley & Sons, Inc., New York, 1956.)*

regions of zero potential.   As the energy of the electron increases, and P is kept constant, the electron can more readily surmount, or penetrate, the potential barriers, and the presence of the potential barriers becomes less and less important as far as the behavior of the electron is concerned; ultimately, as β approaches infinity, the electron behaves as though free.

Going toward the other extreme, the width of any energy band decreases as P increases.   In the limit as P approaches infinity, the only allowed solutions are those for which βa is a multiple of π.   These are just the solutions for the energy levels of a particle in one-dimensional motion confined to a "box" of width a.   In other words, as the potential barriers between the regions of vanishing potential become impenetrable, a particle is unaware of the existence of other regions of zero potential which lie beyond the barriers.   Consequently, the behavior of the particle is the same as if these other regions did not exist at all.

These two limiting conditions, namely, one in which the barriers are relatively unimportant and the wave function of the electron resembles that of a free electron, and the other in which the barriers are very great, have their analogs in real crystals.   The two cases are known as the approximation of *nearly free electrons* and the *tight-binding approximation*, respectively.

The energy spectrum corresponding to Fig. 4.3 is shown in Fig. 4.4. The allowed energy bands occupy regions of equal extent in wave-number space—the intervals $ka = 0$ to $ka = \pi$, $ka = \pi$ to $ka = 2\pi$, etc.   (Of course the corresponding negative values of ka also correspond to the same energies since $\cos ka$ is an even function of ka.)   The lowest energy bands are comparatively narrow, the bandwidth increasing with increasing energy.   Also, the forbidden energy regions between the bands, at first relatively wide, decrease as the energy increases.   In the limit of infinite energy, the solutions of the Kronig-Penney model approach the free-electron result (dashed curve).

The appearance of energy bands is, of course, very reminiscent of the allowed energy bands in the solution of the vibrational motion of a crystal lattice.   Moreover, the solutions to the Schroedinger equation can be restricted without loss of generality to the first Brillouin zone of the one-dimensional lattice.   To each particular value of the wave number k there corresponds a solution $\psi_k(x)$ of the wave equation.   We know already from the Bloch theorem that the function $\psi_k(x)$ will be of the form

$$\psi_k(x) = e^{ikx}u_k(x)$$

where $u_k(x)$ is periodic in the lattice.   For a second wave number k', related to k by $k' = k + 2\pi n/a$, the wave function will be

$$\psi_{k'}(x) = e^{ikx}e^{2\pi inx/a}u_{k'}(x)$$

The factor $e^{2\pi inx/a}$ is, of course, also periodic in the lattice and may be absorbed into the function $u_{k'}(x)$; thus

$$\psi_{k'}(x) = e^{ikx}u_{k,n}(x) = \psi_{k,n}(x)$$

We see that the assignments of particular k values to the solutions of the wave equation are not unique.   We may, and we shall, henceforth, consider the energy and the wave function as multivalued functions of the wave number k, where now k is constrained to lie within the first Brillouin

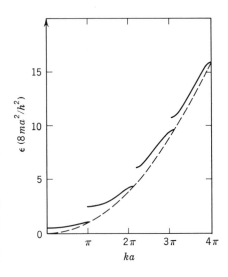

Fig. 4.4   The energy spectrum for the periodic potential of Fig. 4.3.   (*From C. Kittel, "Introduction to Solid State Physics," 2d ed., p. 280, John Wiley & Sons, Inc., 1956.*)

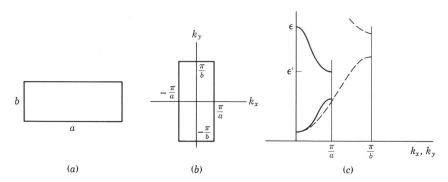

Fig. 4.5 The energy spectrum of a hypothetical rectangular lattice. (a) The unit cell of the lattice; (b) the first Brillouin zone of the lattice; (c) the energy spectrum in the reduced-zone scheme. The solid line is for **k** along the x, the dashed line for **k** along the y direction. Overlap commences when $\epsilon > \epsilon'$.

zone of the lattice. This method of classification of electron wave functions in a crystal is known as the *reduced-zone scheme*.

The extension of the periodic-potential problem to three dimensions leads to wave functions that are of the Bloch form, and may again be considered multivalued functions of a wave vector **k**, where **k** is constrained to lie within the first Brillouin zone of the lattice. Since the Brillouin zone is a property of the lattice, related to its translational periodicity, the geometry of the Brillouin zone for electron waves is exactly the same as that for lattice vibrational waves. We refer the reader to Chap. 2 for a discussion of the Brillouin zone.

There is, however, one important qualitative difference between the one-dimensional case and the two- and three-dimensional cases. In the former, we found that there was of necessity a discontinuity in the energy at the edge of the zone. Hence, the energy spectrum was divided into bands of allowed energy separated by forbidden energy regions. In the two- and three-dimensional cases there will again appear forbidden energy gaps at the zone boundaries. However, the forbidden gaps may occur at *different energies* for *different directions* of the wave vector **k**. This situation is illustrated in Fig. 4.5, where we show a hypothetical energy spectrum for a rectangular plane lattice whose lattice parameters are a and b. The boundaries of the Brillouin zone occur, then, at $k_x = \pi/a$ and $k_y = \pi/b$. It is now quite conceivable that the forbidden gaps for the x and y directions occur at different energies. In that case, there will be no energy regions which are truly forbidden. This crude model shows, therefore, that the existence of zone boundaries does not, by itself, require the existence of forbidden energy regions. In the case illustrated here we speak of *zone overlap*. That is, as the energy levels in the first zone are gradually filled, the second zone begins to accommo-date electrons even before the first zone is completely occupied. Hence, given enough electrons, the occupied electron states will overlap, or spill over, into the next zone. Whether, in any particular case, a forbidden gap does appear depends not only on the geometry of the crystal but also on the details of the crystal potential in which the electrons move.

4.5 APPROXIMATION OF NEARLY FREE ELECTRONS

We have seen already that as the parameter P in the Kronig-Penney model becomes small compared to the electronic kinetic energy, the behavior of the electron in this periodic potential approaches that of a free electron. We now consider the properties of electrons in a more realistic three-dimensional lattice potential, but shall introduce this periodic potential as a perturbation, assumed small compared to the electron energy.

The Schroedinger equation which we wish to solve is

$$-\frac{\hbar^2}{2m}\nabla^2\psi_{\mathbf{k}} + V\psi_{\mathbf{k}} = \epsilon_{\mathbf{k}}\psi_{\mathbf{k}} \tag{4.22}$$

where $V = V(\mathbf{r})$ is a potential which has the periodicity of the lattice. The wave equation for the unperturbed case is simply

$$-\frac{\hbar^2}{2m}\nabla^2\psi_{\mathbf{k}}^0 = \epsilon_{\mathbf{k}}^0\psi_{\mathbf{k}}^0 \tag{4.23}$$

whose solutions are

$$\psi_{\mathbf{k}}^0 = \left(\frac{1}{\mathsf{V}}\right)^{\frac{1}{2}} e^{i\mathbf{k}\cdot\mathbf{r}} \quad \text{and} \quad \epsilon_{\mathbf{k}}^0 = \frac{\hbar^2 k^2}{2m} \tag{4.24}$$

where V is the volume of the crystal. We now write the perturbation $V(\mathbf{r})$ as a three-dimensional Fourier series

$$V(\mathbf{r}) = \sum_{\mathbf{K}_j} v(\mathbf{K}_j)e^{-\mathbf{K}_j\cdot\mathbf{r}} \tag{4.25}$$

and calculate the matrix elements of V between the unperturbed states specified by wave vectors $\mathbf{k}$ and $\mathbf{k}'$. Once these matrix elements are known, we can then make use of the results of Sec. A.5 of Appendix A and determine the perturbed wave functions and the new energy levels.†

† In Sec. A.5 the unperturbed wave functions are designated by φ_{n0}. In the present calculation the wave vectors $\mathbf{k}$ and $\mathbf{k}'$ constitute the quantum numbers of the unperturbed, plain wave functions and correspond to the indices n and m of Sec. A.5.

Thus we require

$$(\mathbf{k'}|V|\mathbf{k}) = \frac{1}{V} \int e^{-i\mathbf{k'}\cdot\mathbf{r}} \sum_{\mathbf{K}_j} v(\mathbf{K}_j) e^{-i\mathbf{K}_j\cdot\mathbf{r}} e^{i\mathbf{k}\cdot\mathbf{r}} \, d\tau \tag{4.26}$$

The integral in (4.26) may be evaluated term by term; it is apparent, then, that all terms will vanish except that for which $\mathbf{k'} = \mathbf{k} - \mathbf{K}_j$. The matrix element for this term is just

$$v(\mathbf{K}_j) = \frac{1}{\Omega} \int V e^{i\mathbf{K}_j\cdot\mathbf{r}} \, d\tau_0$$

where $d\tau_0$ denotes integration over one unit cell.

Let us assume that the average value of $V(\mathbf{r})$ vanishes; then $v(0) = 0$. Since the Fourier expansion of the lattice potential contains only the reciprocal-lattice vectors $\mathbf{K}_j$, we find

$$(\mathbf{k'}|V|\mathbf{k}) = \frac{1}{V} \int V(\mathbf{r}) e^{i\mathbf{K}_j\cdot\mathbf{r}} \, d\tau = v(\mathbf{K}_j) \qquad \mathbf{k'} = \mathbf{k} - \mathbf{K}_j \tag{4.27}$$

We can now make use of the results of Sec. A.5 of Appendix A to find the perturbed wave functions to lowest order in the perturbation. Substituting Eq. (4.27) into (A.51) we obtain

$$\psi_{\mathbf{k}} = \frac{1}{V^{\frac{1}{2}}} e^{i\mathbf{k}\cdot\mathbf{r}} \left[1 + \sum_{\mathbf{K}_j} \frac{v(\mathbf{K}_j)}{\epsilon_{\mathbf{k}}^0 - \epsilon_{\mathbf{k'}}^0} e^{-i\mathbf{K}_j\cdot\mathbf{r}} \right] \qquad \mathbf{k'} = \mathbf{k} - \mathbf{K}_j \tag{4.28}$$

From (A.52) we find that

$$\epsilon_{\mathbf{k}} = \epsilon_{\mathbf{k}}^0 + \sum_{\mathbf{K}_j} \frac{|v(\mathbf{K}_j)|^2}{\epsilon_{\mathbf{k}}^0 - \epsilon_{\mathbf{k'}}^0} \qquad \mathbf{k'} = \mathbf{k} - \mathbf{K}_j \tag{4.29}$$

We see immediately that the wave function $\psi_{\mathbf{k}}$ is indeed of the Bloch form. The summation in Eq. (4.28) is over the reciprocal-lattice vectors $\mathbf{K}_j$. It follows from the definition of these vectors that the factor within the brackets will remain unchanged if we replace $\mathbf{r}$ by $\mathbf{r} + \mathbf{R}_j$, where $\mathbf{R}_j$ is a lattice translation vector.

Equations (4.28) and (4.29) are valid provided the denominators $\epsilon_{\mathbf{k}}^0 - \epsilon_{\mathbf{k'}}^0$ do not vanish. However,

$$\epsilon_{\mathbf{k}}^0 - \epsilon_{\mathbf{k'}}^0 = \frac{\hbar^2}{2m} (k^2 - |\mathbf{k} - \mathbf{K}_j|^2)$$

will vanish if

$$\mathbf{k} \cdot \mathbf{K}_j - \frac{K_j^2}{2} = 0 \qquad \text{i.e.} \qquad \mathbf{k} \cdot \mathbf{K}_j = \frac{K_j^2}{2} \tag{4.30}$$

The conditions for which the energy denominator vanishes are just the conditions which define the boundaries of the Brillouin zone. In other words, whenever the unperturbed wave functions have wave vectors which terminate on a zone boundary, the perturbation procedure which we have used will fail. In that case there will be one term in the summation in (4.28) of unusual magnitude, and we can circumvent the divergence difficulty of the perturbation procedure by selecting at the outset a different unperturbed wave function in the calculation of the perturbed energy. Let

$$\psi_{\mathbf{k}}^0 = A_0 e^{i\mathbf{k}\cdot\mathbf{r}} + A_n e^{i\mathbf{k}_n\cdot\mathbf{r}} \qquad \mathbf{k}_n = \mathbf{k} - \mathbf{K}_n \tag{4.31}$$

We substitute this trial function into the wave equation (4.22) and obtain

$$-\frac{\hbar^2}{2m} \nabla^2 (A_0 e^{i\mathbf{k}\cdot\mathbf{r}} + A_n e^{i\mathbf{k}_n\cdot\mathbf{r}}) + (V - \epsilon_{\mathbf{k}})(A_0 e^{i\mathbf{k}\cdot\mathbf{r}} + A_n e^{i\mathbf{k}_n\cdot\mathbf{r}})$$

$$= \left[\frac{\hbar^2 k^2}{2m} + (V - \epsilon_{\mathbf{k}})\right] A_0 e^{i\mathbf{k}\cdot\mathbf{r}} + \left[\frac{\hbar^2 k_n^2}{2m} + (V - \epsilon_{\mathbf{k}})\right] A_n e^{i\mathbf{k}_n\cdot\mathbf{r}} = 0 \tag{4.32}$$

We now multiply Eq. (4.32) first by $\exp(-i\mathbf{k}\cdot\mathbf{r})$ and integrate over all space; next we multiply Eq. (4.32) by $\exp(-i\mathbf{k}_n\cdot\mathbf{r})$ and again integrate over all space. The resulting equations are

$$\begin{aligned}
A_0(\epsilon_{\mathbf{k}}^0 - \epsilon_{\mathbf{k}}) - A_n v_n^* &= 0 \qquad v_n^* = v^*(\mathbf{K}_n) \\
A_0 v_n - A_n(\epsilon_{\mathbf{k}} - \epsilon_{\mathbf{k}_n}^0) &= 0 \qquad v_n = v(\mathbf{K}_n)
\end{aligned} \tag{4.33}$$

These two simultaneous linear equations for A_0 and A_n have nonvanishing solutions only if the secular determinant vanishes. The solution of the determinantal equation gives

$$\epsilon_{\mathbf{k}} = \tfrac{1}{2}[\epsilon_{\mathbf{k}}^0 + \epsilon_{\mathbf{k}_n}^0 \pm \sqrt{(\epsilon_{\mathbf{k}}^0 - \epsilon_{\mathbf{k}_n}^0)^2 + 4v_n v_n^*}] \tag{4.34}$$

We see from (4.34) that at a zone boundary there is a discontinuity in the energy equal to $2|v_n|$. A typical energy spectrum is shown schematically in Fig. 4.6. The approximation of nearly free electrons, therefore, agrees in all respects with the conclusions which we had drawn from the Kronig-Penney model: (1) The wave functions are of the Bloch form. (2) Except near a zone boundary, the energy spectrum resembles closely that of free electrons. (3) The energy spectrum shows a discontinuity at a zone boundary. However, whereas in the Kronig-Penney model an energy discontinuity necessarily occurred at every zone boundary, we see that for a more realistic potential function this requirement is appar-

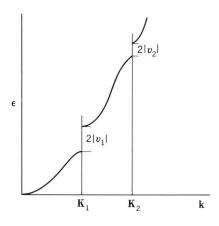

Fig. 4.6 The energy spectrum of electrons showing the discontinuities at the first and second zone boundaries in the extended-zone scheme.

ently relaxed. If the Fourier coefficient of the potential corresponding to the reciprocal-lattice vector $\mathbf{K}_n$ vanishes, then, to lowest order, the energy will be continuous across the zone boundary corresponding to the lattice vector $\mathbf{K}_n$. The reason no such exceptions could be found in the Kronig-Penney case is obvious: The potential assumed there, a delta function, is one which contains nonvanishing Fourier components for all multiples of the principal reciprocal-lattice vectors.

The vanishing of the Fourier component $v(\mathbf{K}_n)$ of the crystal potential $V(\mathbf{r})$ is not, however, a sufficient condition for the absence of an energy discontinuity across the corresponding zone boundary. It must be remembered that the foregoing was a perturbation calculation carried only to second order. In a higher order of the perturbation expansion there appear terms that describe the interaction of unperturbed states $\mathbf{k}$ and $\mathbf{k}' = \mathbf{k} + \mathbf{K}_n$ through intermediate states $\mathbf{k}_p = \mathbf{k} + \mathbf{K}_p$ and $\mathbf{k}'_p = \mathbf{k}' + \mathbf{K}'_p$ such that $\mathbf{K}_p + \mathbf{K}'_p = \mathbf{K}_n$. Since, in general, $v(\mathbf{K}_p)$ and $v(\mathbf{K}'_p)$ are nonvanishing, a finite energy gap will appear even though $v(\mathbf{K}_n) = 0$.

4.6 TIGHT–BINDING APPROXIMATION

We shall now consider the opposite extreme to the approximation of nearly free electrons. The tight-binding approximation, or LCAO method (linear combination of atomic orbitals), is appropriate whenever the electrons are fairly well localized about their attractive ion cores and the overlap of the electron wave function centered at one lattice point into adjacent unit cells is relatively small. For example, the core electron wave functions of sodium would satisfy this condition, whereas the valence electrons are better treated by the free-electron approximation.

As the name implies, we start by constructing our wave function from a combination of atomic orbitals, each orbital being centered at a different lattice site.

$$\psi_{\mathbf{k}}^{(n)} = \frac{1}{\sqrt{N}} \sum_j C_j(\mathbf{k}) \phi_n(\mathbf{r} - \mathbf{R}_j) \tag{4.35}$$

where N is the number of atoms per unit volume.

The function $\phi_n(\mathbf{r})$ is an atomic wave function; the index n denotes the appropriate quantum numbers of the atomic energy level, assumed nondegenerate, which the electron occupies in the free atom. The normalization, $N^{-\frac{1}{2}}$, is correct only if overlap of atomic orbitals centered on different atoms is negligible; thus, we further assume

$$\int \phi_n^*(\mathbf{r} - \mathbf{R}_i) \phi_n(\mathbf{r} - \mathbf{R}_j) \, d\tau = \delta_{ij} \tag{4.36}$$

Since the functions $\psi_{\mathbf{k}}^{(n)}$ are solutions of the Schroedinger equation in the crystal, they are of the Bloch form; hence, the coefficients of the sum must be

$$C_j(\mathbf{k}) = e^{i\mathbf{k}\cdot\mathbf{R}_j} \tag{4.37}$$

for, if we substitute (4.37) into (4.35), we see that indeed

$$\psi_{\mathbf{k}}^{(n)}(\mathbf{r}) = e^{i\mathbf{k}\cdot\mathbf{r}} N^{-\frac{1}{2}} \sum_j e^{-i\mathbf{k}\cdot(\mathbf{r}-\mathbf{R}_j)} \phi_n(\mathbf{r} - \mathbf{R}_j) = e^{i\mathbf{k}\cdot\mathbf{r}} u_{\mathbf{k},n}(\mathbf{r})$$

where $u_{\mathbf{k},n}(\mathbf{r})$ is periodic in the lattice.

We now wish to find the energy levels and their dependence on the wave vector $\mathbf{k}$.

Since the functions $\phi_n(\mathbf{r})$ are atomic orbitals they satisfy the free-atom Schroedinger equation

$$\left[-\frac{\hbar^2}{2m} \nabla^2 + V_n^0(\mathbf{r} - \mathbf{R}_j) \right] \phi_n(\mathbf{r} - \mathbf{R}_j) = \epsilon_n \phi_n(\mathbf{r} - \mathbf{R}_j) \tag{4.38}$$

The function $\psi_{\mathbf{k}}^{(n)}(\mathbf{r})$, on the other hand, is a solution of

$$\mathfrak{K}\psi_{\mathbf{k}}^{(n)}(\mathbf{r}) = \left[-\frac{\hbar^2}{2m} \nabla^2 + V(\mathbf{r}) \right] \psi_{\mathbf{k}}^{(n)}(\mathbf{r}) = \epsilon_{\mathbf{k}}^{(n)} \psi_{\mathbf{k}}^{(n)}(\mathbf{r}) \tag{4.39}$$

where $V(\mathbf{r})$ is the periodic crystal potential.

The energy $\epsilon_{\mathbf{k}}^{(n)}$ is given by

$$\epsilon_{\mathbf{k}}^{(n)} = \int \psi_{\mathbf{k}}^{(n)*}(\mathbf{r}) \mathfrak{K}\psi_{\mathbf{k}}^{(n)}(\mathbf{r}) \, d\tau$$

$$= \frac{1}{N} \int \sum_{ij} e^{-i\mathbf{k}\cdot\mathbf{R}_i} e^{i\mathbf{k}\cdot\mathbf{R}_j} \phi_n^*(\mathbf{r} - \mathbf{R}_i) \left[-\frac{\hbar^2}{2m} \nabla^2 + V(\mathbf{r}) \right] \phi_n(\mathbf{r} - \mathbf{R}_j) \, d\tau \tag{4.40}$$

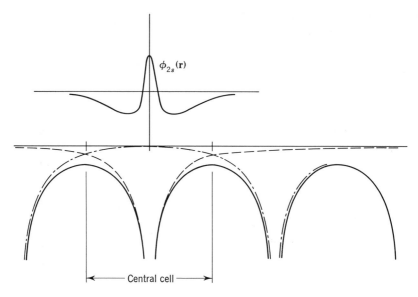

Fig. 4.7 Potentials in the tight-binding approximation. ——— crystal potential; – – – – atomic potential, $V_n^0(\mathbf{r})$; — · — · - perturbation potential, $V'(\mathbf{r})$. Also shown, schematically, a 2s-type wave function centered at the origin.

We now write $V(\mathbf{r} - \mathbf{R}_j) = V_n^0(\mathbf{r} - \mathbf{R}_j) + V'(\mathbf{r} - \mathbf{R}_j)$, i.e., as a sum of two potentials, one the atomic potential† centered at $\mathbf{R}_j$ and the other a correction term which will be small inside the cell centered at $\mathbf{R}_j$ and large outside that cell (see Fig. 4.7). We then obtain

$$\epsilon_{\mathbf{k}}^{(n)} = \frac{1}{N} \left\{ \int \sum_{ij} e^{i\mathbf{k}\cdot(\mathbf{R}_j - \mathbf{R}_i)} \phi_n^*(\mathbf{r} - \mathbf{R}_i) \left[-\frac{\hbar^2}{2m} \nabla^2 + V_n^0(\mathbf{r} - \mathbf{R}_j) \right] \right.$$

$$\left. \phi_n(\mathbf{r} - \mathbf{R}_j)\, d\tau + \int \sum_{ij} e^{i\mathbf{k}\cdot(\mathbf{R}_j - \mathbf{R}_i)} \phi_n^*(\mathbf{r} - \mathbf{R}_i) V'(\mathbf{r} - \mathbf{R}_j) \phi_n(\mathbf{r} - \mathbf{R}_j)\, d\tau \right\}$$

$$(4.40a)$$

In (4.40a) the first integral just gives us the atomic energy level according to (4.38). In the first summation, terms for which $\mathbf{R}_i \neq \mathbf{R}_j$ vanish by assumption (4.36). The second sum in (4.40a) is then conveniently separated into two terms, one corresponding to $\mathbf{R}_i = \mathbf{R}_j$, the

† The atomic potential $V_n^0(\mathbf{r})$ depends on the energy level ϵ_n due to shielding effects of the other atomic electrons. Thus, the 1s electrons "see" a potential which is approximately that of the nucleus shielded by one electron, namely, the other 1s electron. Electrons in higher energy states, and thus farther from the nucleus move in a potential which is weakened through shielding of the nuclear charge by the innermost electrons.

other to $\mathbf{R}_i \neq \mathbf{R}_j$.   We obtain the result given below by shifting our coordinate origin to $\mathbf{R}_j$.   Thus

$$\epsilon_{\mathbf{k}}^{(n)} = \epsilon_n - \alpha_n - \sum_{\mathbf{R}_i \neq 0} \beta_n(\mathbf{R}_i) e^{i\mathbf{k}\cdot\mathbf{R}_i} \tag{4.41}$$

where

$$\alpha_n = -\int \phi_n^*(\mathbf{r}) V'(\mathbf{r}) \phi_n(\mathbf{r}) \, d\tau \tag{4.42a}$$

$$\beta_n(\mathbf{R}_i) = -\int \phi_n^*(\mathbf{r} - \mathbf{R}_i) V'(\mathbf{r}) \phi_n(\mathbf{r}) \, d\tau \tag{4.42b}$$

In those cases in which the LCAO method is most applicable, both α_n and β_n are small perturbation terms. α_n is small because the perturbation potential V' is small in that region of space where $\phi_n(\mathbf{r})$ is large; V' does attain significance outside the region of the central unit cell, where, however, $\phi_n(\mathbf{r})$ is already decreasing exponentially.   This fact is illustrated in Fig. 4.7, where we have drawn, schematically, the lattice potential, the potential V_n^0, the correction (perturbation) potential $V'(\mathbf{r})$, and the wave function of a $2s$ electron centered about the origin.   It is apparent that there is no region in which $V'(\mathbf{r})$ and $\phi_{2s}(\mathbf{r})$ are simultaneously of significant magnitude.

As regards $\beta_n(\mathbf{R}_i)$ we note the following.   First, since $V'(\mathbf{r})$ has the point symmetry of the lattice, $\beta_n(\mathbf{R}_m) = \beta_n(\mathbf{R}_q)$ if $\mathbf{R}_m$ and $\mathbf{R}_q$ specify equivalent lattice sites.   For such a set of equivalent lattice vectors $\beta_n(\mathbf{R}_i)$ may be taken outside the summation in (4.41).   Also, since we have assumed at the outset that the atomic functions $\phi_n(\mathbf{r})$ overlap very little, it will then suffice to consider only those terms $\beta_n(\mathbf{R}_i)$ for which $\mathbf{R}_i$ is a vector to a nearest neighbor site.

To illustrate the LCAO method we consider atomic s functions in a simple cubic lattice of lattice parameter a.   There are six nearest-neighbor sites at equivalent positions, each site at a distance a from the origin. The integral $\beta_n(a)$ is, therefore, the same for all six sites.   Since $V'(\mathbf{r})$ is negative and the atomic s functions are of the same sign in the region of overlap, both α_n and $\beta_n(a)$ are positive parameters.   The energy is then given by

$$\epsilon_{\mathbf{k}}^{(n)} = \epsilon_n - \alpha_n - 2\beta_n(a)(\cos k_x a + \cos k_y a + \cos k_z a) \tag{4.43}$$

This energy band is shown in Fig. 4.8 for the [100] and the [111] directions in the crystal.   From the form of the expansion coefficients, Eq. (4.37), $C_j(\mathbf{k}) = C_j(\mathbf{k} + \mathbf{K}_i)$; hence, we must again restrict the allowed values of the wave vector $\mathbf{k}$ to the first Brillouin zone.

Next, we draw attention to the following qualitative features. The bandwidth, $12\beta_n(a)$, is determined to large measure by the amount of wave-function overlap.   In the limit of infinite separation of atoms, that is, zero overlap of the wave functions, $\beta_n(a)$ and α_n vanish and the "band"

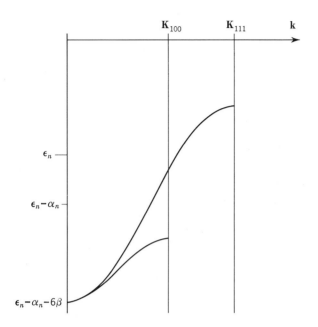

Fig. 4.8 Energy bands for a cubic crystal in the tight-binding approximation along the [100] and [111] directions.

reduces to one N-fold degenerate level of energy ϵ_n.   As a decreases, the
overlap of wave functions is enhanced and, also, $V'(\mathbf{r})$ becomes more
important even within the central cell.   Consequently, the bandwidth
will increase and the difference between the mean energy of the band and
the atomic-energy level ϵ_n will also increase.

From Eq. (4.42) it would seem that the shape of the energy band
in $\mathbf{k}$ space, as distinguished from its width, is completely determined by
the crystal symmetry and the symmetry of the atomic wave functions.
This result is correct for the case considered, where only nearest-neighbor
overlap integrals have been used.   If, however, the additional contributions arising from overlap with next-nearest-neighbor functions are also
considered, one finds that the band shape depends not only on crystal
symmetry, but also on the relative magnitudes of these various overlap
integrals.

This section is intended to serve merely as an introduction to the
tight-binding method.   The treatment has been extended and refined
by many workers, but a discussion of these formulations is beyond the
scope and intent of this book.   The reader is encouraged to consult the
Bibliography, particularly the review article by Reitz.

Let us now summarize the pertinent results of band theory.   Before the atoms condense into a crystal, the electrons within each atom occupy well defined energy levels. These atomic levels, known from spectroscopic data, are the same for all the atoms which form a monatomic crystal such as copper. Electrons closest to the nuclei, the core electrons, are most tightly bound to the nuclei, i.e., their energy levels are quite low, and the wave functions of these electrons do not extend very far. The energy levels of the outermost valence electrons are relatively high, though still negative, and the valence-electron wave functions extend relatively far.

As the atoms are brought close to each other, the well defined N-fold degenerate energy levels of the N atoms gradually broaden into energy bands. As the tight-binding approximation demonstrates, broadening into energy bands takes place as electron wave functions on neighboring atoms begin to overlap. Since the wave functions of greatest extent in the free atom are those of the valence electrons, the band of greatest width will be the valence band (neglecting for the moment bands associated with excited atomic states). In the solid, even the energy levels of the core electrons will, in principle, be spread into bands, but the bandwidth is negligibly small compared to the energy separation between neighboring energy bands.

We have seen, using only general arguments, that the wave function of an electron in a crystal must be of the form

$$\psi_{k,n}(\mathbf{r}) = u_{k,n}(\mathbf{r})e^{i\mathbf{k}\cdot\mathbf{r}}$$

In the tight-binding approximation, where the Bloch function is constructed from a linear combination of atomic orbitals (LCAO), the similarity between the modulating function $u_{k,n}(\mathbf{r})$ and the atomic function $\phi_n(\mathbf{r})$ is assured by the choice of the method itself. However, even in cases where the tight-binding method is not suitable, as, for example, for the conduction bands of metals, the form of the modulating function is still similar to the wave function of the atomic state whose energy is approximately the same as that of the energy band in question. It is, therefore, common practice to speak of "the 3d band of iron," by which one means that energy band whose modulating function has the character of a 3d atomic function; this is also the band which, in the LCAO method, arises from the overlap of the 3d atomic wave functions on neighboring atoms. While the modulating factor $u_{k,n}(\mathbf{r})$ represents a link between electronic wave functions in the crystal and in the isolated atom, the plane-wave factor $\exp(i\mathbf{k}\cdot\mathbf{r})$ suggests that in some respects, at least, electrons in crystals resemble free electrons. We expect a close similarity to free electrons, of course, if energy bands are derived from the approximation of nearly free electrons. There we used free-electron wave functions as descriptive of the unperturbed state and assumed that the crystal potential is sufficiently weak to permit a perturbation treatment. Indeed, the dependence of energy on wave vector is then very similar to that of a free electron.   To see this more clearly, let us consider a simplification of Eq. (4.29).

We restrict ourselves to a one-dimensional lattice once more, and assume, moreover, that the only nonvanishing Fourier coefficients of the crystal potential are $v(\pi/a)$ and $v(-\pi/a)$.   We know already (see page 28) that the reality of $V(\mathbf{r})$ requires that $v(\pi/a) = v^*(-\pi/a)$.   Equation (4.29) now reduces to

$$\epsilon_k = \epsilon_k^0 + \frac{|v(\pi/a)|^2}{\epsilon_k^0 - \epsilon_{k-\pi/a}^0} + \frac{|v(\pi/a)|^2}{\epsilon_k^0 - \epsilon_{k+\pi/a}^0} \tag{4.44}$$

If we focus our attention on the region of small wave number, that is, the region near the band edge at $k = 0$, we can expand (4.44) in powers of $2ka/\pi$ and obtain

$$\epsilon_k = -\frac{4m|v(\pi/a)|^2 a^2}{\hbar^2\pi^2} + \frac{\hbar^2 k^2}{2m}\left[1 - \frac{32m^2 a^4 |v(\pi/a)|^2}{\hbar^4\pi^4}\right] \tag{4.45}$$

We see that the dependence of energy on wave number k is functionally the same as for free electrons, that is

$$\epsilon_k = \text{const} + \frac{\hbar^2}{2m^*}\, k^2$$

Now, however, an electron appears to have an *effective mass*

$$m^* = \frac{m}{1 - (32m^2 a^4/\hbar^4\pi^4)|v(\pi/a)|^2} \tag{4.46}$$

which differs from the free-electron mass m by an amount determined by the magnitude of the Fourier coefficient $v(\pi/a)$.   At this point the effective mass appears merely as a proportionality constant relating the energy to the square of the wave vector.   We shall see later that the effective-mass concept is extremely useful in conductivity theory as well as in other branches of solid-state physics.   First, however, we show that in the tight-binding approximation the energy near a band edge is again a quadratic function of k, and that, therefore, an effective mass also emerges from this treatment.

We restrict our attention to crystals which have a center of symmetry.   In these cases the summation in Eq. (4.42) must necessarily lead to expressions which are polynomials of products of cosine functions of argument $pk_i a_i$, where p is a numerical factor and a_i is the primitive translation vector in the ith direction ($i = 1, 2, 3$).   If we then expand these trigonometric functions about $k_i a_i = 0$, the lowest term in k_i, aside from a term independent of k_i, will be of the form bk_i^2. Hence, at the band edge, we can always write

$$\epsilon_{\mathbf{k}} = \text{const} + \frac{\hbar^2}{2m^*} k^2$$

To illustrate, consider the case of a simple cubic lattice in the most elementary treatment of the tight-binding method. Here $\epsilon_{\mathbf{k}}^{(n)}$ is given by Eq. (4.43). We now expand the cosine functions for small $k_x a$, $k_y a$, $k_z a$ and obtain

$$\epsilon_{\mathbf{k}}^{(n)} = \text{const} + \beta_n(a)a^2 k^2 = \text{const} + \frac{\hbar^2}{2m^*} k^2$$

where the effective mass is given by

$$m^* = \frac{\hbar^2}{2\beta_n(a)a^2} \tag{4.47a}$$

It is also of interest to consider the region near the top of the band, expanding $\epsilon_{\mathbf{k}}^{(n)}$ about $k_x = k_y = k_z = \pi/a$. Once more we obtain the result

$$\epsilon_{\mathbf{k}}^{(n)} = \text{const} + \frac{\hbar^2}{2m^*} k^2$$

where, however, now

$$m^* = -\frac{\hbar^2}{2\beta_n(a)a^2} \tag{4.47b}$$

The effective mass is now negative.

The effective mass, as we have introduced it here, is merely characteristic of the shape of the band near the band edge. It is a parameter which defines the curvature of the ϵ versus $\mathbf{k}$ curve. If m^* is positive, the band curves upward, and the reverse is true if m^* is negative. Moreover, the smaller the effective mass, the faster does the energy increase, or decrease, as k increases.

Finally, we call attention here to the fact that m^* may, and in general does, depend on the direction of the wave vector in the crystal. Consequently, one generally speaks of an effective-mass *tensor* **m**. The anisotropy of the effective-mass tensor emerges most clearly if we consider the tight-binding approach applied to a tetragonal crystal. In that case Eq. (4.43) becomes

$$\epsilon_{\mathbf{k}}^{(n)} = \text{const} - 2\beta_n(a) \cos k_1 a - 2\beta_n(a) \cos k_2 a - 2\beta_n(b) \cos k_3 b$$

It is now apparent that an expansion about $k_1 = k_2 = k_3 = 0$ will, in general, lead to different effective masses along $\mathbf{k}_1$ or $\mathbf{k}_2$ and $\mathbf{k}_3$.

4.7 CELLULAR (WIGNER SEITZ) METHOD

We now turn to the method of calculating energy levels and wave functions first proposed by Wigner and Seitz [4]. Consider a body-centered cubic crystal, for example, sodium. The unit cell, with one atom at its center, is the truncated octahedron shown in Fig. 4.9. From the inversion symmetry of the crystal and the periodicity conditions, it follows that over the entire boundary of the unit cell the wave function for $\mathbf{k} = 0$, $\psi_0(\mathbf{r}) = u_0(\mathbf{r})$, must satisfy the requirement

$$\frac{\partial u_0}{\partial \mathbf{n}} = 0 \tag{4.48}$$

where $\mathbf{n}$ is the unit vector normal to the cell surface.

In the Wigner-Seitz approximation, the polyhedral cell is replaced by a sphere of equal volume, the Wigner-Seitz or s sphere, whose radius is

$$r_s = \left(\frac{3}{4\pi N}\right)^{\frac{1}{3}} \tag{4.49}$$

and the true boundary condition is replaced by

$$\left(\frac{\partial u}{\partial r}\right)_{r_s} = 0 \tag{4.50}$$

In the alkali metals, the ionic radius is considerably less than half the nearest-neighbor distance—or, for that matter, r_s. For example, the ionic radius of Na^+ is about $0.95\,\text{Å}$, whereas $r_s = 2.2\,\text{Å}$. Thus, over most

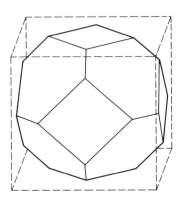

Fig. 4.9 The Wigner-Seitz polyhedral cell for a body-centered cubic structure. (*From C. Kittel, "Quantum Theory of Solids," p. 251, John Wiley & Sons, Inc., New York, 1963.*)

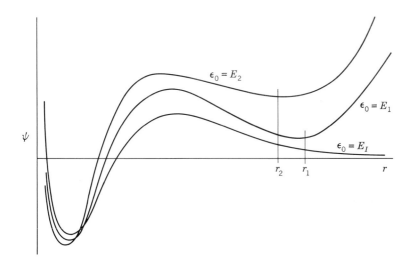

Fig. 4.10 $3s$-like radial wave functions (schematic) for three choices of energy, $E_2 < E_1 < E_I$. For $\epsilon_0 = E_I$, the wave function vanishes at infinity. For $\epsilon_0 = E_1$ and E_2, ψ diverges as r increases; however, $\partial\psi/\partial r = 0$ at r_1 and r_2, respectively.

of the atomic volume, the valence electron moves in the coulomb potential of only a single positive charge located at the center of the cell. Since each unit cell is electrically neutral, the potential beyond $r = r_s$ vanishes to lowest order.

Within the ionic radius the potential is strong and rapidly varying. Here the wave function, that of a $3s$ electron, also oscillates fairly rapidly.

For the $\mathbf{k} = 0$, $3s$-like state, the solution of the Schroedinger equation in the crystal reduces to the solution of the radial wave equation

$$\left[-\frac{\hbar^2}{2mr^2} \frac{\partial}{\partial r} \left(r^2 \frac{\partial}{\partial r} \right) + V(r) \right] u_0(r) = \epsilon_0 u_0(r) \tag{4.51}$$

subject to the boundary condition (4.50). $V(r)$ is the Hartree—or Hartree-Fock—self-consistent potential for Na^+.

In practice the procedure for solving Eqs. (4.51) and (4.50) is as follows. One starts with a reasonable value for ϵ_0 and integrates (4.51) numerically. For $\epsilon_0 = E_I$, where E_I is the ionization potential of the free atom, $u_0(r)$ approaches zero exponentially as $r \to \infty$. Solutions for $\epsilon_0 < E_I$ are sketched in Fig. 4.10, where we have also shown the position where $\partial u/\partial r = 0$. The desired solution is that for which $\partial u/\partial r = 0$ at $r = r_s$; a few choices of ϵ_0 usually suffice to fix the energy quite accurately. The $\mathbf{k} = 0$, $3s$-like wave function in sodium is shown in Fig. 4.11. Evidently $u_0(r)$ is nearly constant over 90 percent of the cellular volume.

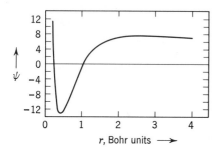

Fig. 4.11 The $\mathbf{k} = 0$ wave function of the conduction band of sodium. (*From C. Kittel, "Quantum Theory of Solids," p. 252, John Wiley & Sons, Inc., New York, 1963.*)

In writing Eq. (4.51) we neglected all higher angular-momentum states. This is, in fact, an excellent approximation for the following reason. The only angular-momentum states that could be admixed through the presence of the crystal potential are those with full cubic symmetry. The $l = 0$ state is one such, and the next-higher angular-momentum state is one with $l = 4$, a g state. In Na the $5g$ state is about 5 ev above the $3s$ state, and its admixture should, therefore, be quite small.

For the states $\mathbf{k} \neq 0$ the $l = 0$ radial wave equation leads to the following differential equation for the Bloch function $u_{\mathbf{k}}(r)$:

$$\left[-\frac{\hbar^2}{2m} \nabla^2 - \frac{i\hbar^2}{m} \nabla \cdot \mathbf{k} + V(r) \right] u_{\mathbf{k}}(r) = \left(\epsilon_{\mathbf{k}} - \frac{\hbar^2 k^2}{2m} \right) u_{\mathbf{k}}(r) \qquad (4.52)$$

If we could neglect the $\nabla \cdot \mathbf{k}$ term on the left-hand side of (4.52), the solution would be

$$\epsilon_{\mathbf{k}} = \epsilon_0 + \frac{\hbar^2 k^2}{2m} \qquad u_{\mathbf{k}}(r) = u_0(r)$$

that is, the energy would be exactly the same as that of a free electron of wave vector $\mathbf{k}$. For small values of $\mathbf{k}$ we may treat the $\nabla \cdot \mathbf{k}$ term as a small perturbation; the procedure outlined in Sec. A.5 of Appendix A then gives

$$\epsilon_{\mathbf{k}} = \epsilon_0 + \frac{\hbar^2 k^2}{2m} \left(1 + \frac{2}{m} \sum_n \frac{\langle 0|\mathbf{p}_j|n \rangle \langle n|\mathbf{p}_j|0 \rangle}{\epsilon_0 - \epsilon_n} \right) \qquad (4.53)$$

where $\mathbf{p}_j = i\hbar \nabla_j$ is the jth component (x, y, or z) of the momentum operator, n is a band index with 0 denoting the band under consideration. Thus, we are once again led to the effective-mass concept, where now

$$\frac{1}{m^*} = \frac{1}{m} \left(1 + \frac{2}{m} \sum_n \frac{\langle 0|\mathbf{p}_j|n \rangle \langle n|\mathbf{p}_j|0 \rangle}{\epsilon_0 - \epsilon_n} \right) \qquad (4.54)$$

We have given here only the bare outlines of the theory of energy bands in solids. The theories have been greatly extended and refined in recent years, and the advent of modern high-speed computing machines has made detailed calculations practicable. An excellent account of this work is contained in the book by Callaway, where reference to the earlier literature may be found.

4.8 VELOCITY AND ACCELERATION OF ELECTRONS IN SOLIDS

We have seen that the eigenfunctions of electrons in crystals are Bloch waves, $\psi_k(\mathbf{r}) = \exp(i\mathbf{k} \cdot \mathbf{r})u_k(\mathbf{r})$. These functions are not localized, but extend over the entire crystal. To describe the motion of an electron, as a *particle*, we must, therefore, construct a *wave packet* centered about a given $\mathbf{k}$ and investigate its behavior under the influence of applied electric and magnetic fields. Such a wave packet travels with a group velocity

$$\mathbf{v}_g = \frac{d\omega}{d\mathbf{k}} = \frac{1}{\hbar}\frac{\partial\epsilon(\mathbf{k})}{\partial\mathbf{k}} = \frac{1}{\hbar}\nabla_k\epsilon(\mathbf{k}) = \mathbf{v}(\mathbf{k}) \tag{4.55}$$

where we have set $\hbar\omega = \epsilon$.

This result, which can be derived in a more rigorous manner, is of fundamental importance. According to (4.55), the velocity of an electron in the state $\mathbf{k}$ is not equal to $\hbar\mathbf{k}/m^*$. The velocity *is* always normal to the constant-energy surface at every point in $\mathbf{k}$ space, but depends on the derivative of the energy with respect to $\mathbf{k}$, and only indirectly on $\mathbf{k}$ itself. Only if $\epsilon(\mathbf{k}) = \hbar^2k^2/2m^*$ is $\mathbf{v}(\mathbf{k}) = \hbar\mathbf{k}/m^*$. If, for example, the constant-energy contours are spheroidal rather than spherical, $\mathbf{v}(\mathbf{k})$ and $\mathbf{k}$ will not, in general, be colinear (see Fig. 4.12).

Let us now assume that an external force $\mathbf{F}$ acts on the electron. In a small time interval δt the energy gained by the electron from the force field is

$\delta\epsilon = \mathbf{F} \cdot \mathbf{v}\delta t$

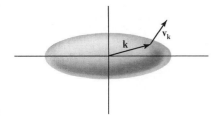

Fig. 4.12 Velocity and wave vector of an electron on a spheroidal energy surface. $\mathbf{v}_k$ is normal to the surface; $\mathbf{k}$ will, in general, not be colinear with $\mathbf{v}_k$.

If we now write $\delta\epsilon = (\nabla_k\epsilon) \cdot \delta k$ and make use of (4.55), we obtain

$$\hbar\delta k = F\delta t$$

Thus, under the influence of an external force field, the wave vector of the electron changes with time according to the relation

$$\hbar\dot{k} = F \tag{4.56}$$

The simple argument leading to (4.56) constitutes, of course, no adequate derivation of that relation. Clearly, at best, we can only conclude that $\hbar$ times the component of $\dot{k}$ in the direction v equals the corresponding component of F. In particular, we can say nothing whatever concerning the influence of a magnetic field on the motion of electrons in a crystal. A more elaborate and, also, more difficult derivation can, however, be given with the result that (4.56) is, indeed, correct in the general case, at least as a first approximation. It is important to note here that Eq. (4.56) is *not* equivalent to Newton's law $F = \dot{p}$. It is the rate of change of the *wave vector* that is proportional to the force F; only in rather special circumstances may one associate $\hbar k$ with the momentum mv_k of the electron.

The two fundamental relations, Eqs. (4.55) and (4.56), can also be deduced from the correspondence principle and from the classical hamiltonian equations of motion

$$\dot{r} = \frac{\partial \mathcal{H}}{\partial p} \qquad \dot{p} = -\frac{\partial \mathcal{H}}{\partial r}$$

If we identify p with $\hbar k$, (4.55) and (4.56) follow immediately. Because of this close association and, also, the identity $p = \hbar k$ *for free electrons*, the quantity $\hbar k$ is frequently spoken of as the *crystal momentum* of electrons in solids. It is certainly not, however, the true momentum, as one can see immediately from the fact that though k is a good quantum number the Bloch functions are not eigenfunctions of the momentum operator.

Finally, we can now obtain an expression for m that is suitable to kinematic problems. From (4.55) the acceleration of an electron is

$$a_k = \dot{v}_k = \frac{1}{\hbar}\frac{d}{dt}(\nabla_k\epsilon) = \frac{1}{\hbar}\frac{\partial^2\epsilon}{\partial k\,\partial k}\cdot\dot{k} = \frac{1}{\hbar^2}\frac{\partial^2\epsilon}{\partial k\,\partial k}\cdot F \tag{4.57}$$

Comparison of (4.57) with Newton's law, $F = ma$, leads to

$$\dot{v}_k = (m)^{-1}F$$

where $(m)^{-1}$ is the *reciprocal-mass tensor* whose components are

$$(m)_{ij}^{-1} = \frac{1}{\hbar^2}\frac{\partial^2\epsilon}{\partial k_i\,\partial k_j} \tag{4.58}$$

4.9 RELATIONSHIP BETWEEN VARIOUS PHYSICAL PROPERTIES AND THE EFFECTIVE MASS

When the electron energy in the conduction band is given by

$$\epsilon_k = \frac{\hbar^2 k^2}{2m^*} \tag{4.59}$$

we can adapt the results of Chap. 3 merely by replacing m with m^* in all of the expressions appearing there. Thus, we find, for example, that the density of states is proportional to $(m^*)^{\frac{3}{2}}$ and the Fermi energy η_0 is inversely proportional to m^*.

It then follows that measurements of specific heat, Fermi energy, and paramagnetic susceptibility may be used to deduce average effective masses of electrons in metals.

It is well to remember that, in general, the electron energy is not given correctly by Eq. (4.59). If ϵ is a function of $|\mathbf{k}|$ but the shape of the band is not of "standard form" (i.e., a plot of ϵ versus $|\mathbf{k}|^2$ is not a straight line), measurements of C_v^e and χ_p provide information only on the density of states at the Fermi energy. In other words, such measurements may be used to deduce a value for $(\partial \epsilon / \partial k)_\eta$. In this more general situation it is not possible to deduce m^* from such measurements, since the relationship between $m^* = [(1/\hbar^2)(\partial^2 \epsilon / \partial k^2)]^{-1}$ and $\partial \epsilon / \partial k$ is unknown. In such cases independent measurements of m^* and of η_0 could provide valuable information on the deviation of the band shape from standard form.

Direct determination of m in metals is a difficult and exacting task. In some instances it has been possible to measure the effective mass by the cyclotron-resonance technique, using an experimental modification suggested by Azbel' and Kaner [5]. In many materials, oscillations of the susceptibility with magnetic field at low temperatures (de Haas-van Alphen effect) have shed light on the conduction-band structure and provided information on m. The theory of these effects will be considered later. For the moment, let it suffice to say that there are techniques now available which, in favorable instances, yield results from which m can be deduced with considerable accuracy.

The Fermi energy may be measured in an independent manner by a study of the soft x-ray emission bands of metals. Figure 4.13 shows schematically the energy levels in a metal such as sodium. Electron, or hard x-ray, bombardment serves to excite electrons from the low-lying, very narrow energy band associated with the core electrons. Following the excitation, soft x-ray emission takes place as electrons from the conduction band make transitions to these low-lying, vacant energy

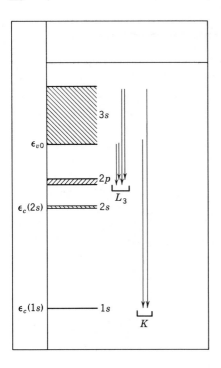

Fig. 4.13 Energy levels in metallic sodium (schematic). The K and L x-ray transitions are indicated.

levels.   The frequency of the emitted radiation is given by

$$h\nu = \Delta\epsilon = \epsilon_v - \epsilon_c$$

where $\Delta\epsilon$ is the energy difference between the initial state ϵ_v in the valence band and the final state ϵ_c in the core "band."

Any electron in the valence band can contribute to the emission of x-rays, and the intensity of the emitted radiation in a given frequency interval is determined largely by the corresponding density of occupied states in the valence band.   The long-wavelength limit (smallest x-ray energy) corresponds to the energy difference between the valence-band edge ϵ_{v_0} and the core-state energy ϵ_c.   The short-wavelength limit is determined by the energy difference between the highest *occupied* state in the valence band and ϵ_c.   At low temperatures the highest occupied state in the valence band is the state whose energy equals the Fermi energy.   Consequently, the width of the x-ray emission band provides a direct measure of the Fermi energy relative to the bottom of the valence band.   Characteristic soft x-ray emission bands are shown in Fig. 4.14.

Although the long-wavelength edge of the band is not clearly discernible from the measurements, one can, nevertheless, determine this edge with some accuracy.   We know that in this region of the valence band, ϵ_v must be proportional to k^2 (higher-order terms being negligible for small k). It follows that the density of states is proportional to $\epsilon^{\frac{1}{2}}$ near ϵ_{v_0}, and the change in x-ray intensity with energy may be fitted to a theoretical expression which assumes that energy dependence for $\mathcal{N}(\epsilon)$.

The density of states at the Fermi energy is most conveniently obtained from data on the electronic specific heat. The method by which C_v^e is measured has already been discussed. The valence-electron density n_0 is given by the valency of the atom and the density of the solid. (This statement really holds only for the few monovalent metals; in all others, band overlap occurs, and the total number of valence electrons is shared among several bands.)

In favorable cases one can obtain the following parameters by independent means: n_0, $\mathcal{N}(\eta)$, η_0, and $\partial^2\epsilon/\partial k_i\,\partial k_j$, as well as the cross-sectional area of the Fermi surface in $\mathbf{k}$ space and the diameter ("caliper dimension") of the Fermi surface along various crystallographic directions (see Chap. 11). If one now expresses $\epsilon_\mathbf{k}$ as a series in ascending powers of $\mathbf{k}$,

$$\epsilon_\mathbf{k} = a_{\alpha\beta}k_\alpha k_\beta + a_{\alpha\beta\gamma}k_\alpha k_\beta k_\gamma + a_{\alpha\beta\gamma\delta}k_\alpha k_\beta k_\gamma k_\delta + \cdots \qquad \alpha,\beta,\gamma,\delta = 1,2,3$$

it is then possible to deduce the values of some of the coefficients a_n (see Prob. 4.8).

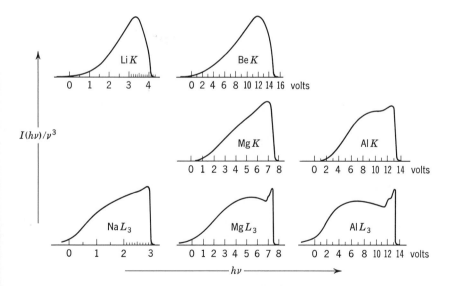

Fig. 4.14 The soft x-ray-emission spectra of various solids. K and L_3 designate the x-ray band in the usual notation. The intensity divided by (frequency)[3] is plotted because this function should be proportional to the density of occupied energy levels. [*From H. W. B. Skinner, Rept. Progr. Phys.*, **5**: 271 (1938).]

Some of the methods frequently employed for determining m in metals are not suitable in semiconductors. For example, specific-heat measurements shed little light on m because in these materials the number of conduction electrons is itself a sensitive function of temperature, and the energy required to generate conduction electrons makes a significant contribution to the specific heat. On the other hand, cyclotron resonance (see Chap. 11) is a very effective technique here. Moreover, much can be learned about the band structure of semiconductors from transport measurements and from careful studies of optical properties.

PROBLEMS

4.1. Show that the reciprocal lattice of the face-centered cubic lattice is the body-centered cubic lattice.

4.2. Use arguments based on symmetry considerations to show that the reciprocal lattice of a Bravais lattice belongs to the same crystal system as the real space lattice.

4.3. Use the free-electron approximation to calculate the electron density at which the Fermi sphere just touches the nearest Brillouin-zone boundary for

(a) the simple cubic lattice
(b) the bcc lattice
(c) the fcc lattice

4.4. Using the tight-binding approximation, derive $\epsilon(\mathbf{k})$ for the bcc and fcc lattices. Limit overlap integrals to nearest neighbors only.

4.5. Discuss, qualitatively, the form of energy bands in a layered structure, such as graphite.

4.6. Use the data of Table 3.1 to obtain values of m^*/m for Li, Na, Cu, and Au.

4.7. Assume that the probability for the transition of a conduction electron into an unoccupied core state is independent of the initial $\mathbf{k}$ vector. Calculate the frequency dependence of the soft x-ray emission spectrum near the long-wavelength cutoff and relate the result to the conduction-band effective mass.

4.8. Assuming that, in a Wigner-Seitz cellular calculation, the ionic potential in the unit cell may be replaced by the coulomb potential $V = Ze/r$, calculate the fractional change between $V(r)$ at the centers of the (111) and (100) cell boundaries in a bcc lattice. Compare $V(r)_{111}$ and $V(r)_{100}$ with $V(r_s)$.

4.9. In some materials (for example, Ge, InSb) the effective mass m^* of electrons in the conduction band is significantly smaller than the free-electron mass. Give a qualitative explanation of this observation in terms of the nearly free-electron approximation using the reduced-zone scheme.

4.10. Assume the following $\epsilon(k)$ relation:

$$\epsilon(k) = \alpha k^2 + \beta |k|^3 + \delta k^4$$

Calculate $\mathscr{N}(\epsilon)$, $\partial\epsilon/\partial k$, and $\partial^2\epsilon/\partial k^2$. Using these results, sketch curves showing how the Fermi energy η_0, the effective mass m^*, and the electronic specific-heat coefficient γ would vary with the electron concentration n_0.

4.11. In the free-electron approximation calculate the energy $\epsilon(k_{100})$ in a simple cubic crystal of cube edge $= 2 \times 10^{-8}$ cm, where k_{100} is the wave vector from the center of the Brillouin zone to the (100) zone face. How large, in units of $\epsilon(k_{100})$, must the energy gap at the (100) zone boundary be to prevent overlap of energy states of the first and second Brillouin zones?

REFERENCES

1. Hartree, D. R.: "Calculation of Atomic Structures," John Wiley & Sons, Inc., New York, 1957.
2. Knox, R. S.: Bibliography of Atomic Wave Functions, *Solid State Phys.*, **4**: 413 (1957).
3. Kronig, R. deL., and W. G. Penney: *Proc. Roy. Soc. London*, **130**: 499 (1931).
4. Wigner, E., and F. Seitz: *Phys. Rev.*, **43**, 804 (1933); **46**, 509 (1934).
5. Azbel', M. Ya., and E. A. Kaner: *Soviet Phys. JETP*, **3**: 773 (1956); **5**: 730 (1957).

BIBLIOGRAPHY

General

Kittel, C.: "Introduction to Solid State Physics," 3d ed., John Wiley & Sons, Inc., New York, 1967.
Raimes, S.: "Wave Mechanics of Electrons in Metals," North Holland Publishing Company, Amsterdam, 1961.
Smith, R. A.: "Wave Mechanics of Crystalline Solids," Chapman & Hall, Ltd., London, 1961.
Weinreich, G.: "Solids, Elementary Theory for Advanced Students," John Wiley & Sons, Inc., New York, 1965.
Ziman, J. M.: "Principles of the Theory of Solids," Cambridge University Press, London, 1964.

Many-body Effects; Hartree Calculations

Anderson, P. W.: "Concepts in Solids," W. A. Benjamin, Inc., New York, 1963.
Hartree, D. R.: "The Calculation of Atomic Structures," John Wiley & Sons, Inc., New York, 1957.
Knox, R. S.: Bibliography of Atomic Wave Functions, *Solid State Phys.*, **4**: 413 (1957).
Pines, D.: Electron Interactions in Metals, *Solid State Phys.*, **1**: 368 (1955).
———: "The Many-Body Problem," W. A. Benjamin, Inc., New York, 1961.

Band Theory

Callaway, J.: "Energy Band Theory," Academic Press Inc., New York, 1964.
Jones, H.: "The Theory of Brillouin Zones and Electronic States in Crystals," North Holland Publishing Company, Amsterdam, 1960.
Reitz, J. R.: Methods of the One-Electron Theory of Solids, *Solid State Phys.*, **1**: 1 (1955).
Slater, J. C.: "Quantum Theory of Molecules and Solids," vol. 2, McGraw-Hill Book Company, New York, 1965.

5
Transport Equation

5.1 INTRODUCTION

In preceding chapters we developed the background which allows us to treat electronic conduction in solids in a reasonably concise and systematic manner.   It is well, however, to emphasize at the very beginning of this second section of the book that, though we rely on the quantum theory of solids and use its results, we shall not present a correct quantum theory of transport.   In essence what we shall do is resort to a classical treatment which we hope to make plausible and palatable by reference to the quantum theory of solids.

In recent years considerable theoretical effort has been devoted to the formulation of a valid quantum theory of transport.   Almost invariably it is found that the semiclassical theory constitutes an excellent and reliable approximation, and has, moreover, the great virtue of lending itself to vivid physical interpretations.   References to the newer quantum transport theory are listed at the end of the chapter.

In this chapter we first derive the Boltzmann transport equation and present its solution subject to the simplifying approximation that all collision processes can be described in terms of a unique relaxation time. We next consider the justification for this approximation and obtain the relevant validity criteria.   We then discuss thermal and electrical conductivity, i.e., the Wiedemann-Franz ratio, in metallic conductors.   The chapter concludes with a discussion of the variational solution of the Boltzmann equation.

In Chap. 4 we showed that electrons in some solids behave similarly to free electrons.   The quasi-free-electron approach not only allowed us to determine many equilibrium properties of valence electrons, but we also found that, even under the influence of external force fields, electrons in solids behave much like free electrons.   We showed that the velocity of an electron in a crystal is given by

$$\mathbf{v_k} = \frac{1}{\hbar}\, \nabla_k \epsilon(\mathbf{k}) \tag{5.1}$$

and that the wave vector $\mathbf{k}$ of an electronic state changes with time according to

$$\hbar \dot{\mathbf{k}} = \mathbf{F} \tag{5.2}$$

where $\mathbf{F}$ is the force acting on the electron.

We shall describe the *assembly* of conducting electrons by means of a *distribution function*.   We have already made use of such a distribution function in our treatment of the specific heat and magnetic susceptibility of an electron gas.   In that case, the occupation probability of a given quantum state at a specified temperature depended only on the energy of that state relative to a suitably chosen zero energy.   When the electron gas is subjected to electric fields, the probability of occupancy of a given quantum state $\mathbf{k}$ depends not only on the energy of that state, $\epsilon(\mathbf{k})$, but also on the wave vector $\mathbf{k}$ itself.   This follows from Eq. (5.2), which shows that under the influence of a force field $\mathbf{F}$ an electron in a state $\mathbf{k}$ at a given time will suffer a change $\delta \mathbf{k}$ during a subsequent time interval δt.   Moreover, since the equilibrium probability depends on $(\epsilon - \eta)/kT$ rather than on ϵ, we expect that the new probability will be a function of position should there exist temperature gradients in the specimen.   We, therefore, choose to describe our electronic system by means of a distribution function $f(\mathbf{k},\mathbf{r},t)$, defined such that the number of electrons in the six-dimensional volume element $d\mathbf{k}\, d\tau$ at time t is given by

$$\frac{1}{4\pi^3}\, f(\mathbf{k},\mathbf{r},t)\, d\mathbf{k}\, d\tau$$

At equilibrium, $f(\mathbf{k},\mathbf{r},t)$ depends only on ϵ and reduces to the Fermi distribution $f_0(\epsilon)$, Eq. (3.11).   As defined above, $f(\mathbf{k},\mathbf{r},t)$ is normalized to unit volume.

In principle, the electronic properties of a conductor are completely specified once $f(\mathbf{k},\mathbf{r},t)$ is known. For example, the current contributed by an electron in the state $\mathbf{k}$ is the electronic charge e times the velocity $\mathbf{v_k}$ of that electron. Consequently, the current density at position $\mathbf{r}$ and at time t is obtained simply by summing the individual current contributions of all the electrons. This summation is achieved by integrating the velocity over all values of $\mathbf{k}$ and weighing each velocity by the probability distribution $f(\mathbf{k},\mathbf{r},t)$. Thus, we have

$$\mathbf{J}(\mathbf{r},t) = \frac{e}{4\pi^3} \int \mathbf{v_k} f(\mathbf{k},\mathbf{r},t) \, d\mathbf{k} \tag{5.3}$$

Formally, then, the central problem is one of finding the correct distribution function under certain specified boundary conditions. This task is accomplished in two steps. The first step is that of deriving the equation which $f(\mathbf{k},\mathbf{r},t)$ must satisfy. The second step is the solution of that equation subject to appropriate boundary conditions. The first step is relatively simple in the semiclassical treatment, although it presents the most interesting problem in the formulation of a quantum theory of transport. The second step, that of solving the equation for $f(\mathbf{k},\mathbf{r},t)$, presents formal though not conceptual difficulties even in the semiclassical treatment under all but the most idealized conditions.

5.2 BOLTZMANN EQUATION

Electrons, which at time t are within the volume element $d\mathbf{k}\,d\tau$, may leave it as a result of the following processes:

1. They may leave the element $d\tau$ centered about $\mathbf{r}$ by virtue of their velocities, which carry them out of that volume element in coordinate space.
2. They may leave the element $d\mathbf{k}$ centered about $\mathbf{k}$ by virtue of their crystal acceleration $\hbar\dot{\mathbf{k}}$, caused by an externally applied force field.
3. They may be scattered out of the element $d\mathbf{k}$.

According to Liouville's theorem, electrons which at time t are in $d\tau\,d\mathbf{k}$ centered about $\mathbf{r},\mathbf{k}$ will at time $t + dt$ be located in an equal volume centered about $\mathbf{r} + \dot{\mathbf{r}}\,dt$, $\mathbf{k} + \dot{\mathbf{k}}\,dt$. Scattering must then account for the difference between $f(\mathbf{k} + \dot{\mathbf{k}}\,dt,\, \mathbf{r} + \dot{\mathbf{r}}\,dt,\, t + dt)$ and $f(\mathbf{k},\mathbf{r},t)$. Thus, we find

$$\frac{df}{dt} = -\dot{\mathbf{k}}\cdot\nabla_{\mathbf{k}}f - \mathbf{v}\cdot\nabla_{\mathbf{r}}f + \frac{\partial f}{\partial t} + \left(\frac{\partial f}{\partial t}\right)_c \tag{5.4}$$

where $(\partial f/\partial t)_c$ denotes the rate of accretion of electrons in $d\tau \, d\mathbf{k}$ due to scattering events. Equation (5.4) is the Boltzmann transport equation.

We shall, hereafter, restrict our attention to steady-state conditions under the influence of time-independent forces; we shall, therefore, be primarily concerned with solutions of Eq. (5.4) when $\partial f/\partial t = 0$. Thus, the Boltzmann equation to which we shall address ourselves is

$$\dot{\mathbf{k}} \cdot \nabla_{\mathbf{k}} f + \mathbf{v} \cdot \nabla_{\mathbf{r}} f = \left(\frac{\partial f}{\partial t}\right)_c \tag{5.5}$$

Some of the difficulties encountered in the solution of the apparently simple differential equation (5.5) become apparent as soon as the collision term $(\partial f/\partial t)_c$ is written in a slightly more explicit form. We introduce the quantity $\mathfrak{S}(\mathbf{k},\mathbf{k}')$, which is the probability per unit time that an electron in the state $\mathbf{k}$ will be scattered into the state $\mathbf{k}'$. The problem of calculating $\mathfrak{S}(\mathbf{k},\mathbf{k}')$ will be considered in some detail in a later chapter. For the moment, we shall assume that such a calculation can be carried through and that an explicit expression for $\mathfrak{S}(\mathbf{k},\mathbf{k}')$ can be derived. In terms of $\mathfrak{S}(\mathbf{k},\mathbf{k}')$, we can then write the collision term as follows:

$$\left(\frac{\partial f}{\partial t}\right)_c = \int \{\mathfrak{S}(\mathbf{k}',\mathbf{k})f(\mathbf{k}')[1 - f(\mathbf{k})] - \mathfrak{S}(\mathbf{k},\mathbf{k}')f(\mathbf{k})[1 - f(\mathbf{k}')]\} \, d\mathbf{k}' \tag{5.6}$$

In Eq. (5.6) the first term in the integrand equals the number of electrons scattered from the element $d\mathbf{k}'$ into the volume element $d\mathbf{k}$ per unit time. The factor $\mathfrak{S}(\mathbf{k}',\mathbf{k})$ gives the a priori probability of the scattering event, and $f(\mathbf{k}')$ and $[1 - f(\mathbf{k})]$ give the probabilities that (1) an electron initially did occupy the state $\mathbf{k}'$, and (2) the state $\mathbf{k}$ into which this electron is to be scattered is initially unoccupied and can, therefore, accept an electron. Correspondingly, the second term in the integrand equals the number of electrons scattered out of the element $d\mathbf{k}$ into the element $d\mathbf{k}'$ per unit time.

At equilibrium, when $f(\mathbf{k},\mathbf{r},t) = f_0(\epsilon)$, detailed balance requires that

$$\mathfrak{S}(\mathbf{k}',\mathbf{k})f_0(\epsilon')[1 - f_0(\epsilon)] = \mathfrak{S}(\mathbf{k},\mathbf{k}')f_0(\epsilon)[1 - f_0(\epsilon')] \tag{5.6a}$$

It is reasonable to assume that the scattering probability $\mathfrak{S}(\mathbf{k},\mathbf{k}')$ will not depend on applied electric or magnetic fields.[†] One can then make use of the detailed balance relationship and rewrite Eq. (5.6) as follows:

$$\left(\frac{\partial f}{\partial t}\right)_c = \int \mathfrak{S}(\mathbf{k},\mathbf{k}')f_0(\epsilon)[1 - f_0(\epsilon')] \left\{\frac{f(\mathbf{k}')[1 - f(\mathbf{k})]}{f_0(\epsilon')[1 - f_0(\epsilon)]} - \frac{f(\mathbf{k})[1 - f(\mathbf{k}')]}{f_0(\epsilon)[1 - f_0(\epsilon')]}\right\} \, d\mathbf{k}' \tag{5.7}$$

[†] See, however, p. 120.

We now write the distribution function as the sum of two terms: the first is the equilibrium Fermi distribution, and the second represents the deviation of the true distribution from equilibrium. That is, we take

$$f(\mathbf{k},\mathbf{r}) = f_0(\epsilon) + f_1(\mathbf{k},\mathbf{r}) \tag{5.8}$$

and shall find it convenient to write

$$f_1 = -\phi(\mathbf{k},\mathbf{r})\frac{\partial f_0}{\partial \epsilon} \tag{5.9}$$

which leaves the generality of f_1 unimpaired since ϕ is unrestricted.

Although the effect of external fields in generating electric and thermal currents may be quite startling, it is, nevertheless, true that in nearly all cases the deviation of the steady-state distribution from the equilibrium distribution is rather small. The linear relationship between cause and effect, i.e., Ohm's law, is a manifestation of this small deviation, since this linear relationship shows that in the solution of Boltzmann's equation only terms linear in f_1 need be retained. Only in semiconductors subjected to rather strong electric fields does one observe deviations from Ohm's law.

Substitution of Eqs. (5.8) and (5.9) into Eq. (5.7) gives, to first order in f_1,

$$\left(\frac{\partial f}{\partial t}\right)_c = \frac{1}{kT}\int \mathfrak{S}(\mathbf{k},\mathbf{k}')f_0(\epsilon)[1 - f_0(\epsilon')][\phi(\mathbf{k}') - \phi(\mathbf{k})]\,d\mathbf{k}' \tag{5.10}$$

where we have made use of the identity

$$f_0(\epsilon)[1 - f_0(\epsilon)] = -kT\frac{\partial f_0}{\partial \epsilon} \tag{5.11}$$

We will refer to the integral in (5.10) as the *collision integral*.

The transport equation now reads†

$$\mathfrak{e}\left[\mathbf{E} + \frac{1}{c\hbar}\nabla_{\mathbf{k}}\epsilon \times \mathbf{H}\right] \cdot \frac{1}{\hbar}\nabla_{\mathbf{k}}f(\mathbf{k},\mathbf{r}) + \frac{1}{\hbar}\nabla_{\mathbf{k}}\epsilon \cdot \nabla f(\mathbf{k},\mathbf{r})$$

$$= \frac{1}{kT}\int \mathfrak{S}(\mathbf{k},\mathbf{k}')f_0(\epsilon)[1 - f_0(\epsilon')][\phi(\mathbf{k}') - \phi(\mathbf{k})]\,d\mathbf{k}' \tag{5.12}$$

where $\mathfrak{e}[\mathbf{E} + (1/c\hbar)\nabla_{\mathbf{k}}\epsilon \times \mathbf{H}]$ is the force acting on an electron as a result of an electric field $\mathbf{E}$ and a magnetic field $\mathbf{H}$.

Thus, we see that Boltzmann's equation when linearized leads to an integral equation, known as the *Bloch equation*. In general, a solution

---

† We omit the subscript $\mathbf{r}$ on the gradient symbol ∇. Hereafter it is understood that ∇ refers to the gradient in coordinate space.

to this equation cannot be obtained in closed form.   The most powerful and elegant method of solution involves the use of a variational principle first advanced by Kohler [1].   The application of this procedure requires first the selection of a suitable trial function containing parameters which are then adjusted in accordance with the variational principle.   The trial function which has been used most commonly is a power series in the energy, and the coefficients of the terms in that series constitute the adjustable parameters.

In the variational method the transport coefficients (electrical conductivity, thermal conductivity, and thermoelectric power) appear as ratios of determinants of infinite dimensionality.   Although these determinants may not be convergent, their ratios do converge rapidly, and excellent approximations are obtained by retaining only the first nonvanishing terms of the desired expansion.

The other, and most direct, avenue leading to solution of the Bloch equation, relies on the use of a *relaxation time* τ defined by

$$\left(\frac{\partial f}{\partial t}\right)_c = -\frac{f - f_0}{\tau} = -\frac{f_1}{\tau} \tag{5.13}$$

The significance of τ is that of a time constant in the exponential approach of a disturbed distribution $f = f_0 + f_1$ to the equilibrium distribution f_0. We shall show that the relaxation time is always a useful concept when applied to: (1) scattering of electrons by acoustical phonons or impurities in semiconductors; (2) rather impure metals; and (3) pure metals at temperatures higher than their Debye temperature.

In pure metals at temperatures below about $\Theta_D/2$, the relaxation-time approximation fails and another approach must be employed.   We shall, then, use the more elegant variational method.   The solution of the Bloch equation by the variational technique requires explicit expressions for the transition probabilities $\mathfrak{S}(\mathbf{k},\mathbf{k}')$, as these enter directly in the variational integrals.   Since we shall determine $\mathfrak{S}(\mathbf{k},\mathbf{k}')$ due to electron-phonon interactions in the next chapter, we defer to a later portion of the text the detailed discussion of the variational solution of the Bloch equation.

Instead of the variational method, an iterative procedure may be employed at low temperatures.   One then assumes that in a slightly impure metal, scattering by phonons is unimportant compared to elastic scattering of electrons by stationary imperfections.   As we shall see presently, the latter process can be described by a relaxation time.   The Bloch equation is now solved, in the relaxation-time approximation, with complete neglect of phonon scattering.   This zero-order solution is then used to evaluate that portion of the collision integral—the right-hand side of Eq. (5.12)—where $\mathfrak{S}(\mathbf{k},\mathbf{k}')$ is the transition probability due to electron-phonon scattering. Finally, it is assumed that the ideal resistivity, i.e., the resistivity of the ideally pure metal, is given by Matthiessen's rule

$$\rho_T = \rho_i + \rho_r$$

where ρ_T, ρ_i, and ρ_r are the total, ideal, and residual (impurity) resistivities, respectively. Since ρ_i is calculated using in the collision integral a perturbed distribution characteristic of elastic scattering only, the iterative method is no more accurate than the variational method, which presumes a certain form for the perturbed distribution. Moreover, the iterative procedure is at least as cumbersome as the variational, and we shall, therefore, not refer to it again hereafter.

5.3 SOLUTION OF BLOCH EQUATION. RELAXATION-TIME APPROXIMATION

We have stated above, without proof, that under many conditions the collision integral, Eq. (5.10), can be replaced by Eq. (5.13). We shall first develop the solution of the Bloch equation assuming the validity of Eq. (5.13) and shall then consider the conditions under which this approximation to the collision integral is justified.

We start by rewriting the left-hand side of Eq. (5.12) keeping only the lowest nonvanishing terms and equating it to the right-hand side of Eq. (5.13). With the aid of the relation

$$\nabla f \approx \nabla f_0 = \frac{\partial f_0}{\partial T} \nabla T = -\frac{\partial f_0}{\partial \epsilon} [\nabla \eta + (\epsilon - \eta) \nabla \ln T]$$

and recalling that in steady state the Fermi energy is constant throughout the material, one obtains

$$\mathbf{P} \cdot \mathbf{v} \frac{\partial f_0}{\partial \epsilon} + \frac{e}{c\hbar} (\mathbf{v} \times \mathbf{H}) \cdot \nabla_\mathbf{k} f = \frac{\phi}{\tau} \frac{\partial f_0}{\partial \epsilon} \tag{5.14}$$

where

$$\mathbf{P} = e\mathbf{E} - (\epsilon - \eta) \nabla \ln T \tag{5.15}$$

The second term on the left-hand side of (5.14) is

$$\frac{e}{c\hbar} (\mathbf{v} \times \mathbf{H}) \cdot \nabla_\mathbf{k} f = \frac{e}{c} (\mathbf{v} \times \mathbf{H}) \cdot \mathbf{v} \frac{\partial f_0}{\partial \epsilon} + \frac{e}{c\hbar} (\mathbf{v} \times \mathbf{H}) \cdot \nabla_\mathbf{k} f_1$$

The term in $\partial f_0/\partial \epsilon$ evidently vanishes as $\mathbf{v} \times \mathbf{H}$ is normal to $\mathbf{v}$. The second term may be rewritten as follows:

$$\frac{e}{c\hbar} (\mathbf{v} \times \mathbf{H}) \cdot \nabla_\mathbf{k} f_1 = \frac{e}{c\hbar} \mathbf{H} \cdot (\nabla_\mathbf{k} f_1 \times \mathbf{v}) = -\frac{e}{c\hbar^2} [\mathbf{H} \cdot \Omega(f_1)]$$

where Ω is the operator

$$\Omega = \nabla_{\mathbf{k}}\epsilon \times \nabla_{\mathbf{k}} \tag{5.16}$$

Making use of the identity

$$\Omega g(\epsilon) = 0$$

where $g(\epsilon)$ is a function only of energy, we now obtain the Lorentz force term of the Bloch equation in the form which we shall find most useful:

$$\frac{e}{c\hbar}\,(\mathbf{v} \times \mathbf{H}) \cdot \nabla_{\mathbf{k}} f = \frac{e}{c\hbar^2}\,\mathbf{H} \cdot (\Omega\phi)\,\frac{\partial f_0}{\partial \epsilon}$$

By means of Eq. (5.13) the Bloch *integral* equation has been reduced to the following simple *differential* equation:

$$\phi = \tau\mathbf{P} \cdot \mathbf{v} + \frac{e\tau}{c\hbar^2}\,(\mathbf{H} \cdot \Omega\phi) \tag{5.17}$$

Equation (5.17) is the basic equation in those cases where a meaningful relaxation time can be defined.   We shall consider various physical phenomena, such as electrical and thermal conductivities, Hall effect, and the thermoelectric and thermomagnetic effects in detail in Chaps. 7 and 8.   In the following discussion we shall only be concerned with the solutions of Eq. (5.17) subject to various boundary conditions and with the physical interpretations which attach to these solutions.

Although a formal solution of Eq. (5.17) can be written in closed form, it is so cumbersome that it has rarely been employed for computations.   Instead, when conditions are such as to make simple elementary solutions invalid, expansions in powers of $\mathbf{H}$ have been sought.   We consider three separate situations: (1) $H = 0$; (2) $H \neq 0$, $\epsilon = \hbar^2 k^2/2m^*$; and (3) $H \neq 0$, ϵ an arbitrary, well-behaved function of $\mathbf{k}$.

Case 1: $H = 0$. This is by far the simplest case, and for this reason allows a better insight into the character of the steady-state distribution function.   The solution of Eq. (5.17) is evidently

$$\phi = \tau\mathbf{P} \cdot \mathbf{v} \tag{5.18}$$

It is instructive to consider two special conditions, one in which $\mathbf{E} \neq 0$ and $\nabla T = 0$, the other corresponding to $\mathbf{E} = 0$ and $\nabla T \neq 0$.   In the first instance $\mathbf{P} = e\mathbf{E}$.   Insight into the form of the steady-state distribution under this situation is best gained by reference to Eqs. (5.1), (5.8), and (5.9).   If cartesian coordinates are chosen such that the electric field lies along the x axis, we have

$$f = f_0 - \frac{e\tau E}{\hbar}\,\frac{\partial f_0}{\partial k_x}$$

The steady-state distribution f is, therefore, very simply related to the equilibrium distribution, namely,

$$f(k_x,k_y,k_z) = f_0\left(k_x - \frac{eE\tau}{\hbar}, k_y,k_z\right)$$
(5.19)

Equation (5.19) shows that the distribution f is identical to the equilibrium distribution f_0, except that the origin of f in $\mathbf{k}$ space has been shifted from the point $\mathbf{k} = (0,0,0)$ to the point $(eE\tau/\hbar,0,0)$. The equilibrium and steady-state distributions are shown schematically in Fig. 5.1, where, for convenience, we have made the further simplifying assumptions that the surfaces of constant energy in $\mathbf{k}$ space are spheres and that

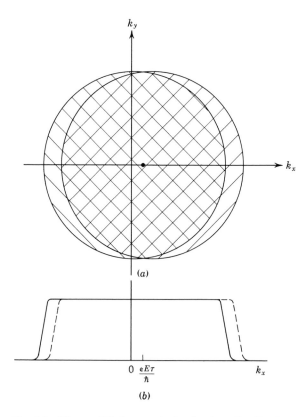

(a)

(b)

Fig. 5.1 The equilibrium and steady-state distribution functions for charge flow. (a) Two Fermi spheres in $\mathbf{k}$ space, one centered at $k_x = 0$, the other at $k_x = eE\tau/\hbar$; (b) the probability distribution in k_x space for the equilibrium (solid) and displaced (dashed) distributions.

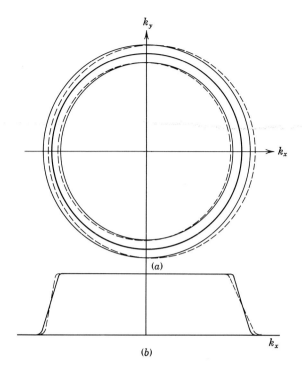

Fig. 5.2 The equilibrium and steady-state distributions for heat flow. (*a*) Two Fermi spheres in **k** space with the fine and dashed circles indicating the "width" of the distribution; (*b*) the distribution in k_x space, the solid line representing the equilibrium, the dashed the steady-state distribution.

the relaxation time is a function only of energy, i.e., is independent of direction.

That an electric field should simply shift the distribution in **k** space is understandable in view of the effect of the field on each quantum state **k**. According to Eq. (5.2), the rate of change of **k** is the same for all electrons. Consequently, if there exists no relaxation mechanism which tends to restore the distribution function to equilibrium, a force field ϵE causes the distribution to drift, unaltered in shape, through **k** space at constant velocity $\dot{\mathbf{k}} = \epsilon E/\hbar$. Relaxation mechanisms, tending to restore the equilibrium distribution, limit this drift to a displacement $\Delta \mathbf{k} = \epsilon E \tau/\hbar$.

Consider next the perturbation to the distribution function occasioned by a temperature gradient. According to Eqs. (5.1), (5.9), (5.15), and (5.17), we now have

$$f_1 = -\phi \frac{\partial f_0}{\partial \epsilon} = \tau(\epsilon - \eta) \frac{1}{T} \frac{\partial T}{\partial x} \frac{1}{\hbar} \frac{\partial f_0}{\partial \epsilon} \frac{\partial \epsilon}{\partial k_x}$$

where we have chosen our x axis to coincide with the temperature gradient. We may simplify the above expression by performing a Taylor expansion of $(\epsilon - \eta)$ about the Fermi energy $\eta = \hbar^2 k_0^2 / 2m^*$. Provided $|\epsilon - \eta| \ll \eta$, we can replace $(\epsilon - \eta)$ by $\dfrac{\hbar^2 k_0}{m^*} (k - k_0)$ and obtain

$$f_1 = \frac{\tau \hbar k_0}{m^* T} (k - k_0) \frac{\partial T}{\partial x} \frac{\partial f_0}{\partial k_x} = f - f_0$$

It follows from the above that the steady-state distribution is given by

$$f(k_x, k_y, k_z) = f_0(k_x + \delta, k_y, k_z) \qquad \delta = \frac{\tau \hbar k_0}{m^* T} (k - k_0) \frac{\partial T}{\partial x} \qquad (5.20)$$

Equation (5.20) bears a close similarity to Eq. (5.19); as in the latter instance, surfaces of constant energy in **k** space again have their centers shifted by the perturbation. However, whereas in the case of an electric field *all* surfaces of constant energy suffered the *same* displacement in **k** space, in the present instance the displacement of the center of a given energy surface *depends on the energy* of that surface relative to the Fermi energy. In particular, the distribution of states on the Fermi surface, $k = k_0$, is not influenced by the temperature gradient; that is, $\delta(k_0) = 0$. Surfaces corresponding to energies in excess of the Fermi energy have their centers shifted in **k** space opposite to the direction of the temperature gradient, whereas surfaces of lower energy have their centers shifted in the direction of the temperature gradient. The resulting steady-state distribution function is shown in Fig. 5.2. It is again possible to understand the shape of this perturbed distribution with the aid of simple physical arguments.

The influence of temperature on the equilibrium distribution has been discussed previously. We recall here that as T increases, the energy range in which $f_0(\epsilon)$ differs significantly from the limiting values of 1 and 0 becomes increasingly wide. This "width" of the Fermi distribution is roughly equal to $2kT$. Now an electron at the point **r** in the crystal and moving in the direction of increasing temperature (the direction of the temperature gradient) must have suffered its last previous collision at a point where the temperature was less than $T(\mathbf{r})$. It then follows that the width of the distribution will be relatively small for electrons moving up the temperature gradient. Similarly, at point **r**, electrons moving opposite to the temperature gradient must have suffered their last collision at a higher temperature.   Hence, the width of the distribution for electrons moving down the temperature gradient must be greater than average.   Thus, the steady-state distribution is wide in the $-\nabla T$ direction and narrow in the ∇T direction.

It is now evident from Figs. 5.1 and 5.2 that the shape of the perturbed distribution function depends sensitively on the character of the perturbation.   Consequently, the efficacy of a given relaxation mechanism in restoring these two distributions to equilibrium may also differ markedly.   In that case, it would be difficult indeed to define a suitable relaxation time of universal applicability.

Case 2: $H \neq 0$, $\epsilon = \hbar^2 k^2/2m^*$.   In this case we can still obtain an exact solution of Eq. (5.17) which is sufficiently simple to allow its use in calculations of the transport coefficients.   The simplification arises from the fact that now $\mathbf{v} = \hbar\mathbf{k}/m^*$.   Equation (5.17) then reads

$$\phi = \frac{\tau \mathbf{P} \cdot \hbar \mathbf{k}}{m^*} + \frac{e\tau}{c\hbar^2} \mathbf{H} \cdot \frac{\hbar^2 \mathbf{k}}{m^*} \times \nabla_{\mathbf{k}}\phi \tag{5.21}$$

The solution of Eq. (5.21) is of the form

$$\phi = \mathbf{k} \cdot \boldsymbol{\psi} \tag{5.22}$$

where $\boldsymbol{\psi}$ is independent of the direction of $\mathbf{k}$ but may be a function of ϵ as well as of the electric and magnetic fields and of the thermal gradient. That (5.22) is the correct form is readily seen by substitution into Eq. (5.21).   The resulting equation for $\boldsymbol{\psi}$ is

$$\boldsymbol{\psi} + \frac{e\tau}{m^*c} \mathbf{H} \times \boldsymbol{\psi} = \frac{\hbar\tau}{m^*} \mathbf{P} \tag{5.23}$$

Equation (5.23) has the solution

$$\boldsymbol{\psi} = \frac{\tau[\mathbf{P} - \alpha\tau\mathbf{H} \times \mathbf{P} + (\alpha\tau)^2\mathbf{H}(\mathbf{H} \cdot \mathbf{P})]}{1 + (\alpha\tau H)^2} \qquad \alpha = \frac{e}{m^*c} \tag{5.24}$$

We shall later have occasion to use Eq. (5.24) in the calculation of galvano- and thermomagnetic coefficients.   For the moment, we call attention only to one physical implication which is immediately apparent.

If $\mathbf{H}$ and $\mathbf{P}$ are colinear, Eq. (5.24) reduces upon multiplication by $\mathbf{k}$ to Eq. (5.18).   It follows that under these conditions the magnetic field has no influence whatever on the transport properties of the electron gas. In other words, a quasi-free-electron gas† cannot display longitudinal magnetoresistance or any other longitudinal magnetic effects.   If a given substance does show a longitudinal magnetoresistance, it is almost certain

---

† We use this nomenclature to indicate that $\epsilon(\mathbf{k}) = \hbar^2 k^2/2m^*$, where m^*, though different from m (the free-electron mass) is, nevertheless, a scalar (see Chap. 4).

that the conduction band in that material is not of standard parabolic form. The qualification "almost" relates to the assumption, implicit in Eq. (5.17) and all subsequent relations, that τ is independent of H. In weak magnetic fields, weak being defined here by the condition

$$\alpha \tau H \ll 1 \qquad (5.25)$$

the relaxation time is independent of H to very good approximation. However, strong fields $(\alpha \tau H > 1)$ can so modify the electronic energy levels and wave functions that τ may depend rather sensitively on the magnetic field. Of course, when $\alpha \tau H > 1$, the use of the Boltzmann equation is also questionable. In this limit, quantum effects become of paramount importance and cannot be ignored.

Absence of longitudinal effects at low magnetic fields in the case of spherical energy surfaces can be understood on physical grounds as follows. The effect of a force field $\mathbf{P}$ is to displace each surface of constant energy in momentum space parallel to $\mathbf{P}$. Depending on $\mathbf{P}$, the displacement may result in a distribution function of the form indicated in Fig. 5.1 or in Fig. 5.2. The displacement of each energy surface is characterized by the vector function $\psi_0 = (\hbar \tau / m^*)\mathbf{P}$, where the subscript $_0$ is used to indicate that we are taking $\mathbf{H} = 0$. A magnetic field, through the Lorentz force, tends to rotate the distribution about an axis parallel to $\mathbf{H}$ and passing through the origin of $\mathbf{k}$ space. If $\mathbf{H}$ is parallel to $\mathbf{P}$, and, consequently, also to ψ_0, this rotation does not influence the distribution function, which now rotates about its symmetry axis—provided, of course, that the magnetic field is sufficiently weak that quantum effects can be neglected and the assumption of an isotropic relaxation time is valid. Since the distribution function is unaffected by the longitudinal field, the presence of the field cannot give rise to measurable effects.

Case 3: $H \neq 0$, arbitrary energy surfaces. In this case the only solution of Eq. (5.17) is one which does not lend itself to computation. The procedure which has been applied with greatest success is based on an iterative expansion of ϕ in ascending powers of the magnetic field. The expansion converges well in the low-field limit, $\alpha \tau H \ll 1$.

Let us assume that the term in $\mathbf{H}$ in Eq. (5.17) is small compared to the term $\tau \mathbf{P} \cdot \mathbf{v}$. We then may take as our lowest approximation to the true function ϕ the solution

$$\phi^0 = \tau \mathbf{P} \cdot \mathbf{v}$$

If this solution is now substituted into the right-hand side of Eq. (5.17), one obtains, as the next-higher approximation,

$$\phi' = \tau \mathbf{P} \cdot \mathbf{v} + \frac{e\tau}{c\hbar^2} \mathbf{H} \cdot \Omega(\tau \mathbf{P} \cdot \mathbf{v})$$

Further iteration yields

$$\phi = \tau \mathbf{P} \cdot \mathbf{v} + \frac{e\tau}{c\hbar^2} \mathbf{H} \cdot \Omega \left[\tau \mathbf{P} \cdot \mathbf{v} + \frac{e\tau}{c\hbar^2} \mathbf{H} \cdot \Omega(\tau \mathbf{P} \cdot \mathbf{v}) \right] + \cdots$$

$$= \tau \left\{ \mathbf{P} \cdot \mathbf{v} + \frac{e}{c\hbar^2} \mathbf{H} \cdot \Omega(\tau \mathbf{P} \cdot \mathbf{v}) + \left(\frac{e}{c\hbar^2}\right)^2 \mathbf{H} \cdot \Omega[\tau \mathbf{H} \cdot \Omega(\tau \mathbf{P} \cdot \mathbf{v})] + \cdots \right\}$$

$$(5.26)$$

with obvious extension to higher-order terms.

It is left as a problem to show that in Eq. (5.26) all terms in $\mathbf{H}$ vanish if $\mathbf{H}$ and $\mathbf{P}$ are parallel and if $\epsilon = \hbar^2 k^2 / 2m^*$ and τ is isotropic. If $\epsilon(\mathbf{k})$ and/or $\tau(\mathbf{k})$ are anisotropic, these terms do not vanish in the longitudinal case. Thus, in general, a longitudinal magnetic field can affect the distribution and can, therefore, also give rise to magnetoresistance.

5.4 JUSTIFICATION OF A RELAXATION TIME IN THE BLOCH EQUATION

In the preceding section we presented solutions of the Bloch equation predicated on the replacement of the collision integral by the expression $-(f - f_0)/\tau$. We now consider the validity of this approximation so that we may know when the simplification which it allows is, in fact, justified.

It is, of course, possible to define a relaxation time in any circumstance. Having in some way solved the Bloch integral equation and obtained an expression for $\phi(\mathbf{k})$, one may now define τ by

$$\tau(\mathbf{k}) = \phi(\mathbf{k}) \frac{\partial f_0 / \partial \epsilon}{(\partial f / \partial t)_c}$$

According to Eqs. (5.10) and (5.11), we can write this in a more detailed form:

$$\frac{1}{\tau(\mathbf{k})} = \int \mathfrak{S}(\mathbf{k},\mathbf{k'}) \left[\frac{1 - f_0(\epsilon')}{1 - f_0(\epsilon)} \right] \left[1 - \frac{\phi(\mathbf{k'})}{\phi(\mathbf{k})} \right] d\mathbf{k'} \qquad (5.27)$$

Equation (5.27) provides us with a useful and physically meaningful parameter only if it is characteristic of the specimen and independent of the type and strength of the perturbation which caused the departure of the distribution function from equilibrium.

Apart from a possible dependence of τ on the strength of the perturbation—a situation with which the *linearized* Bloch equation cannot cope—the relaxation time will be a meaningful parameter only if it is independent of the *type* of perturbation. In other words, the approach to equilibrium should be exponential, governed by the same time constant whether f is of the form shown in Fig. 5.1 or in Fig. 5.2.

Let us consider first perfectly elastic scattering processes. With this restriction $\mathfrak{S}(\mathbf{k},\mathbf{k}')$ vanishes whenever $\epsilon(\mathbf{k}) \neq \epsilon(\mathbf{k}')$. Therefore, we may set $f_0(\epsilon') = f_0(\epsilon)$ in the integrand of Eq. (5.27) and obtain

$$\frac{1}{\tau(\mathbf{k})} = \int \mathfrak{S}(\mathbf{k},\mathbf{k}') \left[1 - \frac{\phi(\mathbf{k}')}{\phi(\mathbf{k})} \right] d\mathbf{k}' \tag{5.28}$$

We have assumed at the very outset that $\mathfrak{S}(\mathbf{k},\mathbf{k}')$ is the same in the steady state as it is in equilibrium, and it now remains to see if the ratio $\phi(\mathbf{k}')/\phi(\mathbf{k})$ is independent of the perturbation.

According to Eq. (5.18), $\phi(\mathbf{k}) = \tau(\mathbf{k})\mathbf{P} \cdot \mathbf{v}(\mathbf{k})$. If only an electric field $\mathbf{E} = (E,0,0)$ is acting, we have

$$\frac{\phi(\mathbf{k}')}{\phi(\mathbf{k})} = \frac{\tau(\mathbf{k}')e\mathbf{E} \cdot \mathbf{v}(\mathbf{k}')}{\tau(\mathbf{k})e\mathbf{E} \cdot \mathbf{v}(\mathbf{k})} = \frac{\tau(\mathbf{k}')v_x(\mathbf{k}')}{\tau(\mathbf{k})v_x(\mathbf{k})} \tag{5.29}$$

where $v_x(\mathbf{k})$ denotes the x component of the velocity of an electron in the quantum state $\mathbf{k}$.

If $\mathbf{E} = 0$ and only a temperature gradient $\nabla T = (\partial T/\partial x,0,0)$ perturbs the equilibrium, the ratio is given by

$$\frac{\phi(\mathbf{k}')}{\phi(\mathbf{k})} = \frac{\tau(\mathbf{k}')\{[\epsilon(\mathbf{k}') - \eta]\nabla \ln T\} \cdot \mathbf{v}(\mathbf{k}')}{\tau(\mathbf{k})\{[\epsilon(\mathbf{k}) - \eta]\nabla \ln T\} \cdot \mathbf{v}(\mathbf{k})}$$

$$= \frac{\tau(\mathbf{k}')v_x(\mathbf{k}')}{\tau(\mathbf{k})v_x(\mathbf{k})} \cdot \left[\frac{\epsilon(\mathbf{k}') - \eta}{\epsilon(\mathbf{k}) - \eta} \right] \tag{5.30}$$

Expressions (5.29) and (5.30) are, as expected, independent of $\mathbf{E}$ and ∇T. We note, however, that these two expressions are identical only in the case which we are presently considering, namely, elastic scattering for which $\epsilon(\mathbf{k}') = \epsilon(\mathbf{k})$. We conclude that in the limit of elastic scattering a meaningful relaxation time can always be defined.

If, on the other hand, the scattering events are inelastic, the relaxation time as defined by Eq. (5.27) will depend on the relative magnitudes of $e\mathbf{E}$ and $(\epsilon - \eta)\nabla \ln T$, and a single relaxation time descriptive of electrical as well as thermal resistivity cannot be defined.

We expect, however, that the transition between the two extreme cases will be gradual rather than sudden. Presumably, even if the collisions are inelastic, τ will still be a useful parameter, provided $\Delta\epsilon$, the energy change suffered by an electron per collision, is sufficiently small. Thus, we anticipate an energy criterion of the form

$$\begin{aligned}
\left(\frac{\partial f}{\partial t}\right)_c &= -\frac{f_1}{\tau} \qquad \text{if } \Delta\epsilon < \delta \\
\left(\frac{\partial f}{\partial t}\right)_c &\neq -\frac{f_1}{\tau} \qquad \text{if } \Delta\epsilon > \delta
\end{aligned} \tag{5.31}$$

There is only one reasonable characteristic energy† in this problem, namely,

$$\delta = kT \tag{5.31a}$$

Equation (5.31) is, in fact, the correct validity criterion for the application of a relaxation time to the solution of the Bloch equation. From Eq. (5.10) we see that the integrand will be of significant magnitude only in the energy region $\epsilon < \eta + kT$, $\epsilon' > \eta - kT$, for otherwise the factor $f_0(\epsilon)[1 - f_0(\epsilon')]$ is vanishingly small. If $|\epsilon(\mathbf{k}') - \epsilon(\mathbf{k})| < kT$, the ratio $[\epsilon(\mathbf{k}') - \eta]/[\epsilon(\mathbf{k}) - \eta]$ which appears in Eq. (5.30) will, when averaged over $\mathbf{k}'$, be close to unity. On the other hand, if $|\epsilon(\mathbf{k}') - \epsilon(\mathbf{k})| > kT$, the averages of Eq. (5.29) and of (5.30) will differ considerably. Thus, we may summarize with the statement that

a meaningful relaxation time $\tau(\mathbf{k})$ can be defined whenever the energy change of an electron per collision is small compared to kT.

Let us now investigate under what physical conditions a meaningful τ can be defined in the case of conduction in metals and in semiconductors.

When an electron of wave vector $\mathbf{k}$ is scattered by a phonon into the state $\mathbf{k}'$, the electron either absorbs or emits a phonon of wave vector $\mathbf{q}$, where

$$\mathbf{k}' = \mathbf{k} \pm \mathbf{q} \tag{5.32}$$

In this process the electron either gains or loses a quantum of energy $\hbar\omega_q$. Conservation of energy for the system as a whole imposes the additional requirement‡

$$\epsilon' = \epsilon \pm \hbar\omega_q \tag{5.33}$$

Phonon wave vectors can take on magnitudes ranging from $q = 0$ to $q_0 = k\Theta_D/\hbar u = (6\pi^2/\Omega)^{\frac{1}{3}}$. Here Ω is the volume of a unit cell, u is the velocity of sound in the solid, and we have used the Debye approximation in which the unit cell in wave-vector space is replaced by a sphere of equal volume. The wave vector q_0 is, in fact, the radius of a sphere in $\mathbf{k}$ space whose volume is equal to that of the first Brillouin zone.

† The only other characteristic energy parameter is η, which is of the order of a few electron volts in metals and roughly of equal magnitude, but negative, for conduction electrons in nondegenerate semiconductors. An energy loss or gain of this magnitude by collision is evidently unrealistic.

‡ Although the energy-conservation condition, Eq. (5.33), is correct as stated, the condition on the conservation of crystal momentum, Eq. (5.32), is "the truth," but not "the whole truth." We have omitted here "Umklapp" processes, to avoid beclouding the central issue. This germanic behavior of electrons will be dealt with in some detail in the following chapter.

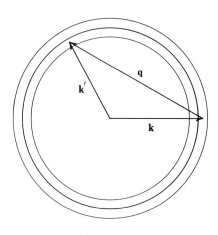

Fig. 5.3 Large-angle scattering of electrons by phonons. The process here is quasi-elastic; the energy change of the electrons is small compared to kT, the width of the distribution.

In metals, k_0, the wave vector at the Fermi surface, is of the same order of magnitude as q_0. In a solid crystallizing in a monatomic Bravais lattice, the first Brillouin zone can accommodate two electrons per atom; in that case, the Brillouin zone should be half full, and, assuming spherical energy surfaces, we have $k_0 = (\frac{1}{2})^{\frac{1}{3}} q_0 = 0.79 q_0$.

The Fermi energy in metals is of the order of 5 ev, whereas the maximum phonon energy $k\Theta_D$ is of the order of $\frac{1}{40}$ ev for most metals (see Table 2.1 for values of Θ_D). Thus, absorption or emission of phonons can cause a significant change in the direction of the electron's crystal momentum ($|\mathbf{k}' - \mathbf{k}|$ can be, and often is, the same magnitude as k_0), but can change its energy by no more than $k\Theta_D$, an energy increment very small compared to the Fermi energy η. Even so, we have just shown that a scattering event can be considered quasi-elastic only if the energy change per collision is small compared to kT, irrespective of the value of the Fermi energy. Applying this criterion to the present situation of electron-phonon scattering, we conclude that this relaxation mechanism is quasi-elastic only at high temperatures, when $kT > k\Theta_D$.

At temperatures below Θ_D the phonon energy is comparable to kT, and, consequently, electron-phonon scattering is inelastic. Furthermore, at low temperatures, $T \ll \Theta_D$, phonons of energy $\hbar\omega_q \approx kT \ll k\Theta_D$ and with wave vector $q \ll q_0$ will dominate the vibrational spectrum. Consequently, at low temperatures $k_0 \gg q$, and electrons are scattered through small angles only.

The dominant scattering events in metals in the two extreme temperature limits are indicated schematically in Figs. 5.3 and 5.4. To summarize:

in metals at high temperatures $(T > \Theta_D)$ electron-phonon interaction leads to quasi-elastic scattering through large angles; at low temperatures $(T < \Theta_D)$ the same interaction results in inelastic small-angle scattering.

Let us now investigate the physical reasons for the breakdown of the relaxation-time approximation in metallic conduction at low temperatures. We have already remarked that the only sense in which the relaxation time may fail as a useful and meaningful parameter is that it may depend on the type of perturbation. Linearization of the Boltzmann equation, leading to the Bloch equation, automatically assures that all calculated currents will be linear functions of the respective driving forces.

The steady-state distribution function resulting from the application of a uniform electric field is shown in Fig. 5.1. The important relaxation processes in this case are those which scatter electrons on the Fermi surface moving in the direction $e\mathbf{E}$ into other states, also on the Fermi surface, whose velocity vectors make large angles with $e\mathbf{E}$. Thus, *large-angle* elastic (or quasi-elastic) scattering is extremely effective in relaxing the steady-state distribution of Fig. 5.1 toward one which is spherically symmetric in $\mathbf{k}$ space and which, consequently, cannot admit of charge or mass transport. Hence, the effective conductivity relaxation rate $1/\tau_\sigma$ is an average over all collisions in which large-angle scattering events are weighted preferentially; that is,

$$\frac{1}{\tau_\sigma} = \left\langle \frac{1}{\tau(\theta)} (1 - \cos\theta) \right\rangle \qquad (5.34)$$

where $\tau(\theta)$ is the collision time for scattering through an angle θ.

If the steady-state distribution is of the form shown in Fig. 5.2, it is convenient to distinguish between two different kinds of relaxation

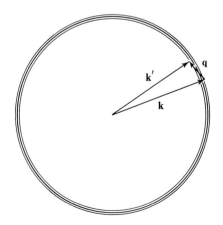

Fig. 5.4 Electron-phonon scattering at low temperature. Here, although the momentum and energy changes are small, the process is, nonetheless, inelastic in the sense that the change in energy is comparable to kT, the width of the Fermi distribution.

processes: First, large-angle elastic scattering, the process described in the preceding paragraph; second, processes which scatter electrons predominantly through small angles but do change their energy by a significant amount. Of course, the division of relaxation mechanisms into two such distinct categories is somewhat artificial. It is, nevertheless, a physically important distinction and, as we have already seen, correctly describes the characteristic features of electron-phonon scattering at high and low temperatures, respectively. Both processes serve to restore the distribution of Fig. 5.2 to equilibrium. At high temperature, when large-angle elastic scattering is characteristic of electron-phonon scattering, the relaxation times for the decay to equilibrium of Figs. 5.1 and 5.2 are one and the same. At low temperatures, however, when $T \ll \theta$, electron-phonon scattering is inelastic and the angle through which an electron is scattered is of order $q/k_0 \approx q/q_0 = T/\Theta_D$. The relaxation rate for energy change, $1/\tau_\kappa$, is of order $1/\tau$. It follows from Eq. (5.34), and the expansion of $\cos \theta$ for small θ, that the relaxation rate for momentum change (the electrical-conductivity relaxation rate) is approximately

$$\frac{1}{\tau_\sigma} = \frac{1}{\tau}\left(\frac{T}{\Theta_D}\right)^2 \tag{5.35}$$

It is immediately apparent that the two relaxation times τ_κ and τ_σ differ greatly at low temperatures. As the subscript suggests, the first of these relaxation times is associated with thermal conduction, a process arising from an *energy* unbalance of the distribution function. We have here the situation of which we spoke earlier: The relaxation time depends sensitively on the type of perturbation.

Having carried the qualitative analysis of electrical and thermal conduction to this juncture, we can now predict the temperature dependences of the electrical and thermal conductivities of metals with some degree of certainty. To do this we anticipate here two results derived in Chap. 7, namely,

$$\sigma = \frac{n_0 e^2 \tau_\sigma}{m^*} \tag{5.36}$$

$$\kappa = \frac{n_0 \pi^2 k^2 T \tau_\kappa}{3m^*} \tag{5.37}$$

where σ and κ are the electrical and thermal conductivities, respectively.

In collision processes, the transition probability for scattering is generally proportional to the number of scattering centers. In the case of electron-phonon scattering, the number of scattering centers is the number of phonons which exist in the lattice at thermal equilibrium. At high temperatures the number of phonons is proportional to the absolute temperature.   Consequently, in that temperature range, $\tau \propto 1/T$, and the electrical conductivity will be inversely proportional to T, whereas the thermal conductivity will be independent of T.   These predictions are substantiated by experimental results on the conductivities of metals.

At low temperatures the total energy due to lattice vibrations is proportional to T^4 [see Eq. (2.64)].   Since the average energy of a phonon in that temperature region is kT, we conclude that the number of phonons and, therefore, $1/\tau$ as well, is proportional to T^3.   From Eqs. (5.35), (5.36), and (5.37) it follows that at low temperatures the thermal conductivity will be proportional to T^{-2}, whereas the electrical conductivity will go as T^{-5}.

These temperature dependences are observed in pure metals at low temperatures.   At extremely low temperature, even in the purest specimen, the relaxation mechanism which arises from elastic scattering of electrons by impurities ultimately takes preeminence over the ever diminishing electron-phonon scattering.   Thus, at sufficiently low temperatures elastic scattering again takes hold and the collision integral can again be characterized by a meaningful relaxation time.

Finally, we consider the manner in which the Wiedemann-Franz ratio $L = \kappa/\sigma T$ depends on temperature.   First, we must remark that electrons, though making a very large contribution to the heat flow in metals and a significant one in semiconductors, are not solely responsible for thermal conduction.   Heat transport by lattice vibrations takes place in metals and semiconductors as in insulators.   While lattice conductivity is the only important mechanism of heat transport in insulators, it decreases in relative magnitude as the number of conduction electrons increases.   In pure metals, lattice thermal conductivity is generally responsible for only a few percent of the total heat flow.   Nevertheless, before comparing experimental and theoretical values of the Wiedemann-Franz ratio, it is essential that the lattice contribution to thermal conduction be subtracted from the total heat flow.   In the following, it will be assumed that this correction has been made, and hereafter we shall mean *electronic contribution to the thermal conductivity* whenever we write simply *thermal conductivity*.

If τ_σ and τ_κ are equal, as is the case at high temperatures, the Wiedemann-Franz ratio

$$\frac{\kappa}{\sigma T} = L \tag{5.38}$$

is given by the Lorenz number $L_0 = (\pi^2/3)(k/e)^2$.†   The Wiedemann-

---

† If the electron gas approximates a classical Boltzmann gas, the numerical factor $\pi^2/3$, which appears in Eqs. (5.37) and (5.38), must be replaced by the factor

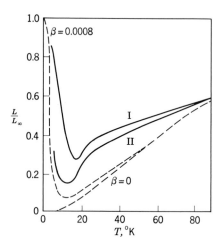

Fig. 5.5 The Wiedemann-Franz ratio of two sodium specimens as a function of temperature. The residual resistances of the two specimens are indicated by the parameter $\beta = \rho_r/\rho_i (T = 4\Theta)$, the ratio of the residual to the ideal resistivity at $T = 4\Theta$. The dashed curves are theoretical. *(From A. H. Wilson, "Theory of Metals," p. 291, Cambridge University Press, London, 1958.)*

Franz Law, which states that L is independent of temperature, is obeyed provided one and the same relaxation time governs the approach of the steady-state distribution function to equilibrium, irrespective of the perturbing fields which cause the deviation from equilibrium.

At high, and again at extremely low temperatures, the existence of a meaningful relaxation time assures that the Wiedemann-Franz ratio will take on the value L_0. At intermediate temperatures the electrical conductivity decreases with T much more rapidly than κ/T. From the predicted temperature dependence of the two conductivities, $\sigma \propto T^{-5}$ and $\kappa \propto T^{-2}$, we see that at sufficiently low temperatures

$$L = \frac{\kappa}{\sigma T} \propto T^2$$

Typical experimental and theoretical curves of the Wiedemann-Franz ratio of metals are shown in Fig. 5.5. The residual resistivity ρ_r is used there as an index of the degree of purity of the metal samples.

We now turn our attention to electron-phonon scattering in semiconductors. We shall restrict ourselves here to scattering by phonons of the acoustical branches of the vibration spectrum.†

$p + \frac{5}{2}$ if the relaxation time shows an energy dependence expressible by $\tau(\epsilon) = \epsilon^p$. Though the Lorentz number in semiconductors differs slightly from its value in metals, this is a rather unimportant detail.

† The crystal structure of all known semiconductors is such that the unit cell contains at least two atoms. Therefore, the vibrational spectrum boasts at least three optical branches. Consequently, conclusions based on acoustical-mode scattering only may require modification later. Still, the relatively high energy of excitation of optical phonons precludes their active participation in electron-phonon scattering at low temperatures. Hence, qualitative conclusions which refer to that temperature range should be, and are, correct.

In most semiconductors the electron gas is of such low density that the classical approximation (see Chap. 3) is applicable. Hence, the average kinetic energy of an electron is $\frac{3}{2}kT$. For purposes of rough qualitative discussions, it will suffice to consider all conduction electrons in a semiconductor as confined to the surface of a sphere in **k** space of radius k_s where

$$\frac{\hbar^2 k_s{}^2}{2m^*} = \frac{3kT}{2} \qquad k_s = \frac{(3m^*kT)^{\frac{1}{2}}}{\hbar} \tag{5.39}$$

Assuming, as before, the validity of the standard-band approximation, one obtains the following conditions from Eqs. (5.32) and (5.33):

Phonon absorption:
$$\frac{\hbar q}{2m^*} = u - \frac{\hbar k_s \cos \vartheta}{m^*} \tag{5.40a}$$

Phonon emission:
$$\frac{\hbar q}{2m^*} = \frac{\hbar k_s \cos \vartheta}{m^*} - u \tag{5.40b}$$

Here ϑ is the angle between the initial direction of k_s and q (see Fig. 5.6); u denotes the velocity of sound, ω_q/q.

In Eq. (5.40) one may neglect u as compared to $\hbar k_s/m^*$, except at extremely low temperatures. To see that this is a valid approximation, note that $\hbar k/m^*$ is the velocity of an electron of wave vector k. Thus, $\hbar k/m^*$ will equal u when the velocity of the electron equals that of sound. The latter in most solids is about 3×10^5 cm/sec. An electron with such velocity has a kinetic energy of 0.5×10^{-16} erg, equivalent to the thermal energy corresponding to a temperature less than 1°K. At such very low temperatures, scattering of electrons is accomplished largely by stationary imperfections, such as impurities and dislocations, and lattice scattering makes a negligible contribution to the relaxation rate.

It follows from Eqs. (5.40a) and (5.40b), with $u \approx 0$, that in nondegenerate semiconductors, only those acoustical phonons whose wave vectors are less than or equal to $2k$ can interact with an electron of wave vector k. Moreover, we have just observed that for electrons of thermal

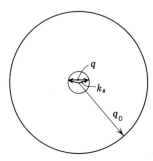

Fig. 5.6 Electron-phonon scattering in semiconductors, showing the Debye sphere, of radius q_0, and the region in **k** space, bounded by the sphere of radius k_s, occupied by electrons.

energy, $\hbar k_s/m^* \gg u$ at all interesting temperatures. If we multiply this inequality by $\hbar k_s/2 = \hbar q$, we have

$$\tfrac{3}{2}kT = \frac{\hbar^2 k_s^2}{2m^*} \gg \hbar q u = \hbar \omega_q = \Delta\epsilon \tag{5.41}$$

Equation (5.41) is, of course, just the requirement for quasi-elastic scattering of electrons by phonons. We conclude that

> scattering of electrons by acoustical phonons in nondegenerate semiconductors is a quasi-elastic process at all relevant temperatures. For these processes a meaningful relaxation time does exist.

We have devoted considerable space to the formal solution of the Boltzmann equation in the relaxation time approximation because of the many virtues of that method. It is devoid of mathematical difficulties and, therefore, allows one to draw a clear picture of the important physical features of the conduction process on a slate unspoiled by mathematical formalities. Also, the relaxation time itself is a most useful and attractive construct, and one with which the reader is probably already familiar from previous readings. Finally, we shall adhere to the accepted manner and present our discussion of the transport properties of metals and semiconductors almost exclusively within the framework of the solutions presented in the preceding section. We shall be talking quite often of the relaxation time, its energy and temperature dependence and its anisotropy, and shall no longer concern ourselves with justifying the concept. Obviously, we must then omit from our discussion that temperature range in metals in which a meaningful relaxation time cannot be defined; nor should we include in these discussions scattering of electrons in semiconductors by optical phonons.

5.5 VARIATIONAL SOLUTION OF THE TRANSPORT EQUATION

Attractive as the relaxation-time approximation may be, there are many situations in which it is clearly inapplicable and leads to incorrect results if it is employed blindly. The best, and also, fortunately, the easiest method of solving the Bloch equation in these situations is also the most elegant and general method now known. The procedure is referred to as the *variational method*, since it rests on a variational principle which, once formulated *ad hoc*, is relatively easy to prove. Our primary aim in this section, however, is not the formal presentation and proof of a variational theorem; instead, we shall attempt to show the physical basis of the principle and, thereby, hope to remove it from the realm of abstract formalism and make its application less of a mystic ritual.

The variation principle as first formulated was restricted to problems involving no magnetic fields and it was only some two decades later that the method was extended to include magnetic effects. The variation principle in the presence of a magnetic field is rather weaker than it is for the case $H = 0$. Partly for this reason, and also to retain the desirable compactness and simplicity of the original theorem, we restrict ourselves here to the case of a vanishing magnetic field.

The reader is undoubtedly familiar with one variational principle of physics, a fundamental theorem of statistical mechanics, based on Boltzmann's famous H-theorem. The H-theorem shows that the entropy of an assembly of particles can never decrease; and from this it follows that the equilibrium distribution of an assembly of particles with given boundary conditions (number of particles, total energy, volume) is that distribution which maximizes the entropy.

At equilibrium, the entropy of a Fermi gas is given by

$$S = k\int\{f(\mathbf{k})\ln f(\mathbf{k}) + [1 - f(\mathbf{k})]\ln[1 - f(\mathbf{k})]\}\,d\mathbf{k} \qquad (5.42)$$

We shall assume that the above is correct, even if $f(\mathbf{k})$ is not the equilibrium distribution, but differs from it slightly.

The Boltzmann equation (5.5) is fundamentally just an equation of continuity which we may conveniently write as

$$[\dot{f}(\mathbf{k})]_c + [\dot{f}(\mathbf{k})]_{\text{drift}} = 0$$

$$[\dot{f}(\mathbf{k})]_{\text{drift}} = -\dot{\mathbf{k}}\cdot\nabla_{\mathbf{k}}f - \mathbf{v}\cdot\nabla f \qquad (5.43)$$

displaying the approach to steady state by the simultaneous operation of two opposing processes—drift and collisions.

In steady state, $\dot{f}(\mathbf{k}) = 0$, and thus S according to Eq. (5.42), though not a maximum, must also be constant in time. By analogy to Eq. (5.43) it is, therefore, reasonable to write

$$\dot{S} = 0 = \dot{S}_c + \dot{S}_{\text{drift}} \qquad (5.44)$$

in the expectation that some physical meaning may attach to these two terms. To deduce this physical significance, we write $\dot{S}$ explicitly in terms of the function $\phi(\mathbf{k},\mathbf{r})$. From Eqs. (5.8), (5.9), (5.11), and, presumably, (5.42) we obtain, to lowest order†

$$\dot{S} = -\frac{1}{T}\int\phi(\mathbf{k})\dot{f}(\mathbf{k})\,d\mathbf{k} \qquad (5.45)$$

† A second term, $(1/T)\int\epsilon(\mathbf{k})\dot{f}(\mathbf{k})\,d\mathbf{k}$, is of higher order than the one appearing in Eq. (5.45). This second term is the rate of entropy increase associated with an increase in the average energy of the assembly. In the linearized Boltzmann equation, the change in the distribution is such as to leave the total energy invariant. Failure of this approximation is well-known in semiconductors and leads to nonohmic behavior at high electric fields.

The next obvious step in the association of Eq. (5.44) with Eq. (5.43) is to replace $\dot{f}(\mathbf{k})$ in the integrand of Eq. (5.45) by the expression on the right-hand side of Eq. (5.10) to obtain the first term of Eq. (5.44); from Eq. (5.14) with $H = 0$, we have

$$\dot{f}(\mathbf{k})_{\text{drift}} = -\mathbf{P} \cdot \mathbf{v}\frac{\partial f_0}{\partial \epsilon}$$

and it is this expression which should be substituted into Eq. (5.45) to yield $\dot{S}_{\text{drift}}$. Thus,

$$\dot{S}_c = -\frac{1}{kT^2} \iint \phi(\mathbf{k}) \mathfrak{S}(\mathbf{k},\mathbf{k}')f_0(\epsilon)[1 - f_0(\epsilon')][\phi(\mathbf{k}') - \phi(\mathbf{k})]\,d\mathbf{k}\,d\mathbf{k}' \quad (5.46)$$

$$\dot{S}_{\text{drift}} = \frac{1}{T} \int \left(\mathbf{P} \cdot \mathbf{v}\frac{\partial f_0}{\partial \epsilon}\right) \phi(\mathbf{k})\,d\mathbf{k} = -\frac{1}{T} \int \mathbf{P} \cdot \mathbf{v}f(\mathbf{k})\,d\mathbf{k}$$

and from Eq. (5.15)

$$\dot{S}_{\text{drift}} = -\frac{1}{T}\mathbf{E} \cdot \mathbf{J} - \frac{\nabla T}{T^2} \int (\epsilon - \eta)\mathbf{v}f(\mathbf{k})\,d\mathbf{k} \quad (5.47)$$

Directing attention first to the drift term, the reader will recognize the product $\mathbf{E} \cdot \mathbf{J}$ as the Joule heat developed per unit volume. We now assert that

> the second term in Eq. (5.47) is the negative of the rate of entropy production associated with a uniform heat flow in a temperature gradient, ∇T. $\quad (5.47a)$

This assertion may be justified as follows. The heat flux due to a flux of particles is given by the energy flux minus the flux of free energy. The latter is the particle flux times the electrochemical potential of the particles. Thus, the heat flux $\mathbf{U}$ is given by

$$\mathbf{U} = \int \epsilon \mathbf{v}f(\mathbf{k})\,d\mathbf{k} - \int \eta \mathbf{v}f(\mathbf{k})\,d\mathbf{k} = \int (\epsilon - \eta)\mathbf{v}f(\mathbf{k})\,d\mathbf{k} \quad (5.48)$$

One now associates an entropy flux $\mathbf{U}/T$ with this uniform heat flux. From the continuity equation,

$$\dot{S} = \nabla \cdot \frac{\mathbf{U}}{T} = \mathbf{U} \cdot \nabla \frac{1}{T}$$

and from Eq. (5.48), the assertion (5.47a) follows directly.

It is noteworthy that $\dot{S}_{\text{drift}}$ is negative, leading to an entropy *decrease* with time. Indeed, an entropy decrease due to the force field $\mathbf{P}$ is to be expected, for the displacement of the Fermi distribution in

k space which it evokes implies a distribution with a higher degree of order than the equilibrium distribution.

Consider next $\dot{S}_c$. From the symmetry relation (5.6a), it follows that

$$\iint \phi(\mathbf{k})\mathfrak{S}(\mathbf{k},\mathbf{k}')f_0(\epsilon)[1 - f_0(\epsilon')][\phi(\mathbf{k}') - \phi(\mathbf{k})]\, d\mathbf{k}\, d\mathbf{k}'$$
$$= \iint \phi(\mathbf{k}')\mathfrak{S}(\mathbf{k},\mathbf{k}')f_0(\epsilon)[1 - f_0(\epsilon')][\phi(\mathbf{k}) - \phi(\mathbf{k}')]\, d\mathbf{k}\, d\mathbf{k}' \quad (5.49)$$

Equation (5.46) may, thus, be written in the following symmetric form:

$$\dot{S}_c = \frac{1}{2kT^2} \iint \mathfrak{S}(\mathbf{k},\mathbf{k}')f_0(\epsilon)[1 - f_0(\epsilon')][\phi(\mathbf{k}) - \phi(\mathbf{k}')]^2\, d\mathbf{k}\, d\mathbf{k}' \quad (5.50)$$

The integrand of Eq. (5.50) is positive definite since $\mathfrak{S}(\mathbf{k},\mathbf{k}')$, f_0, and $1 - f_0$ are probabilities, and, hence, positive. Equation (5.50) states that the entropy change due to random collisions is positive; indeed, Eq. (5.50) is the famous H-theorem of Boltzmann as it applies to a Fermi gas.

The variational principle now asserts that of all distribution functions satisfying the equation

$$\dot{S}_{\text{drift}} + \dot{S}_c = 0$$

the function $f(\mathbf{k})$, which is a solution of the Bloch equation, will maximize $\dot{S}_c$. The physical significance of the variational principle is manifest: Under given perturbing forces **P**, the steady-state distribution which is achieved is such that, were the perturbation removed suddenly, the return to equilibrium would be the most rapid for a given relaxation mechanism.

We now turn to the formal statement of the variation principle. It proves convenient here to introduce the following shorthand notation.

1. The collision operator **C** is defined as follows:

$$\mathbf{C}\phi(\mathbf{k}) \equiv \frac{1}{kT} \int \mathfrak{S}(\mathbf{k},\mathbf{k}')f_0(\epsilon)[1 - f_0(\epsilon')][\phi(\mathbf{k}') - \phi(\mathbf{k})]\, d\mathbf{k}' \quad (5.51)$$

2. The drift term in the Bloch equation for zero magnetic field is a known function which we represent by $-F(\mathbf{k})$; thus,

$$F(\mathbf{k}) = \mathbf{P} \cdot \mathbf{v} \frac{\partial f_0}{\partial \epsilon} \quad (5.52)$$

The Bloch integral equation then takes on the formally simple appearance

$$F(\mathbf{k}) = \mathbf{C}\phi(\mathbf{k}) \quad (5.53)$$

The two rates of entropy production are expressed very simply in terms of $F(\mathbf{k})$ and the collision operator **C**. We have

$$\dot{S}_{\text{drift}} = -\frac{1}{T}(\phi, F) \tag{5.54}$$

$$\dot{S}_c = \frac{1}{T}(\phi, \mathbf{C}\phi) \tag{5.55}$$

Here the symbol (a,b) denotes the "inner product" of the two functions $a(\mathbf{k})$ and $b(\mathbf{k})$:

$$(a,b) \equiv \int a(\mathbf{k})b(\mathbf{k})\, d\mathbf{k} \tag{5.56}$$

When $\phi(\mathbf{k})$ satisfies the Bloch equation (5.53), we have

$$(\phi, F) = (\phi, \mathbf{C}\phi) \tag{5.57}$$

Equation (5.57) is, however, a weaker condition on the function ϕ than is (5.53). It is quite possible that there may be functions which satisfy Eq. (5.57) but which are not solutions to Eq. (5.53). The variational theorem maintains:

> of all the functions which satisfy (5.57), that function which is also a solution of Eq. (5.53) will maximize the inner product $(\phi, \mathbf{C}\phi)$. (5.58)

An equivalent statement of the theorem which is more convenient for many purposes is

$$\frac{(\phi, \mathbf{C}\phi)}{[(\phi, F)]^2} \quad \text{is a minimum when } \phi \text{ is a solution of Eq. (5.53).} \tag{5.59}$$

We shall at no point in this text apply the variation principle to detailed calculations. We shall, however, not turn our back on this elegant method altogether, but shall employ what may be called thermodynamic or variational expressions for various transport coefficients. These expressions can be deduced from entropy arguments, that is, from Eq. (5.59) and the rates of entropy production, Eqs. (5.54) and (5.55). As an example of this procedure, we now derive an expression for the resistivity.

The resistivity is defined by the relation

$$\mathbf{E} = \rho \mathbf{J} \tag{5.60}$$

From Eq. (5.47) it follows that

$$\dot{S}_{\text{drift}} = -\frac{1}{T}\,\rho J^2 \tag{5.61}$$

According to Eq. (5.44), $\dot{S}_{\text{drift}} = \dot{S}_c$ when steady state has been reached. Turning, then, to Eq. (5.55) one obtains, using (5.3),

$$\rho = \frac{(\phi, \mathbf{C}\phi)}{J^2} = \frac{\dfrac{8\pi^6}{kT}\displaystyle\iint \mathfrak{S}(\mathbf{k},\mathbf{k}')f_0(\epsilon)[1 - f_0(\epsilon')][\phi(\mathbf{k}) - \phi(\mathbf{k}')]^2 \, d\mathbf{k}\, d\mathbf{k}'}{e^2 \left[\displaystyle\int v\phi(\mathbf{k})\frac{\partial f_0}{\partial \epsilon}\, d\mathbf{k}\right]^2} \tag{5.62}$$

By a parallel route one arrives at the relation for the thermal resistivity

$$W = \frac{1}{\kappa} = \frac{T(\phi, \mathbf{C}\phi)}{U^2}$$

$$= \frac{\dfrac{8\pi^6}{k}\displaystyle\iint \mathfrak{S}(\mathbf{k},\mathbf{k}')f_0(\epsilon)[1 - f_0(\epsilon')][\phi(\mathbf{k}) - \phi(\mathbf{k}')]^2 \, d\mathbf{k}\, d\mathbf{k}'}{\left[\displaystyle\int v(\epsilon - \eta)\phi(\mathbf{k})\frac{\partial f_0}{\partial \epsilon}\, d\mathbf{k}\right]^2} \tag{5.63}$$

Proper application of the variational method would require the selection of a suitable trial function for $\phi(\mathbf{k})$. This trial function should contain certain parameters which would, then, be determined by recourse to the variational theorem. The formidable expressions, involving the ratios of bordered determinants found in some of the literature, are the results of that procedure.

We shall later apply Eqs. (5.62) and (5.63) to compute the resistivities in that temperature region in which the relaxation time approximation is invalid. However, we shall be rather cavalier about the use of a "variational trial function"; in truth, we shall allow for no variation of parameters at all, but shall, in the selection of a trial function of reasonable form, be guided by the solution of the Bloch equation in the relaxation-time approximation.

PROBLEMS

5.1 Use arguments based on elementary kinetic theory to show that $\kappa/\sigma T$ is a constant.

5.2 Derive the expression for $(\partial f/\partial t)_c$, equivalent to Eq. (5.6), appropriate to particles obeying classical statistics. Show that in the limit of elastic scattering the relaxation time again reduces to Eq. (5.28). Explain the equivalence of the two results.

5.3 Show, using Eq. (5.26), that longitudinal magnetic effects vanish if the Fermi surface is spherical.

5.4 Starting from Eq. (5.28) show, with the use of Eq. (5.18), that in the limit of elastic scattering and spherical energy surfaces the relaxation rate is given by Eq. (5.34).

REFERENCE

1. Kohler, M.: *Ann. Physik*, **40**: 601 (1942).

BIBLIOGRAPHY

General

Blatt, F. J.: Theory of Mobility of Electrons in Solids, *Solid State Phys.*, **4**: 199–366 (1957).
Wilson, A. H.: *"The Theory of Metals,"* Cambridge University Press, London, 1954.
Ziman, J. M.: *"Electrons and Phonons,"* Oxford University Press, London, 1960.

Quantum Theory of Transport

Ambegaokar, V.: Green's Functions in Many-Body Problems, *"Astrophysics and the Many-Body Problem,"* W. A. Benjamin, Inc., New York, 1963.
Dresden, M.: Recent Developments in the Quantum Theory of Transport and Galvanomagnetic Phenomena, *Rev. Mod. Phys.*, **33**: 265 (1961).
Kadanoff, L. P., and G. Baym: *"Quantum Statistical Mechanics,"* W. A. Benjamin, Inc., New York, 1962.

6
Relaxation Mechanisms

6.1 INTRODUCTION

The arguments of the preceding chapter clearly identify the collision term as the most interesting and significant in the transport equation. In this chapter we consider the various relaxation mechanisms and shall compute the corresponding relaxation rates. We shall treat metals (degenerate electron gas), semiconductors (nondegenerate electron gas and nonpolar crystals), and photoconducting ionic crystals (nondegenerate electron gas and polar crystals) in that order.

It was demonstrated in Chap. 4 that in a perfect crystal the expectation value of the velocity of an electron in the state $\mathbf{k}$ is nonvanishing and equal to $(1/\hbar)\nabla_{\mathbf{k}}\epsilon_{\mathbf{k}}$. Since the Bloch functions $\psi_{\mathbf{k}} = \exp(i\mathbf{k} \cdot \mathbf{r})u_{\mathbf{k}}(\mathbf{r})$ are eigenfunctions in the perfect crystal, it follows that a net electron flux in a *perfect* crystal, once established by any means whatever, cannot decay. Relaxation to an equilibrium distribution (vanishing particle and energy flux) must, therefore, be associated with the failure of a real crystal to achieve the ideal perfection demanded for the validity of Bloch's theorem.

6.2 STATIONARY CRYSTAL IMPERFECTIONS: CLASSIFICATION AND DESCRIPTION

No real solid is a perfect periodic structure. In addition to phonons, which constitute time-dependent imperfections, every crystal contains some stationary imperfections. The latter may be point imperfections, such as vacancies, interstitials and impurity atoms, linear imperfections—dislocations, and two-dimensional, planar imperfections—external and internal crystal boundaries.

A. Planar Imperfections

Every crystal is of finite extent; the boundaries themselves constitute imperfections which often play a most decisive role. Moreover, most solids are not single crystals but are polycrystalline; the *grain boundaries* separating the individual crystalline grains represent internal surfaces of disregister—that is, of crystal imperfection. Besides grain boundaries, many crystals exhibit yet another type of planar imperfection, called a *stacking fault*. These we shall describe in greater detail later in this chapter.

B. Linear Imperfections

It is a safe assertion that all solids, except a very few prepared under the most exacting conditions, contain *dislocations*, imperfections of linear extent. There are several types of dislocations of which the easiest to visualize is the edge dislocation, also known as a Taylor-Orowan dislocation.

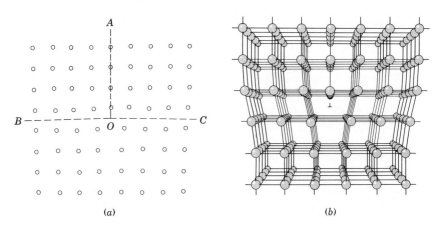

Fig. 6.1 Atomic arrangement in the neighborhood of an edge dislocation of unit Burgers vector in a simple cubic crystal. (*a*) Cross-sectional view (*From A. H. Cottrell, "Dislocations and Plastic Flow in Crystals," p. 23, Oxford University Press, 1953.*); (*b*) perspective view. (*From C. A. Wert and R. W. Thomson, "Physics of Solids," McGraw-Hill Book Company, New York, 1964.*)

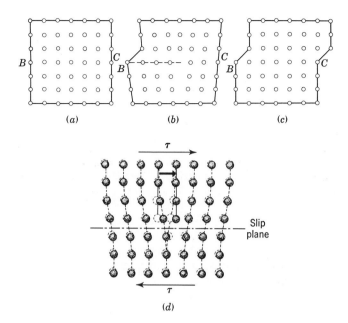

Fig. 6.2 (a), (b), (c) Motion of a positive edge dislocation of unit Burgers vector in the direction BC through a cubic lattice. Passage of the dislocation produces a slip of one lattice parameter of the upper portion of the crystal relative to the lower (*From C. Kittel, "Introduction to Solid State Physics," 2d ed., John Wiley & Sons, Inc., New York, 1956.*); (d) rearrangement of atoms as the edge dislocation moves one lattice parameter under the influence of shear stress τ. (*From H. W. Hayden, W. G. Moffatt, and J. Wulff, "The Structure and Properties of Materials," vol. III, John Wiley & Sons, Inc., New York, 1965.*)

An *edge dislocation* may best be visualized by imagining a perfect crystal which is cut open along the line AO, the plane of the cut being perpendicular to that of the page (see Fig. 6.1). An extra monolayer crystal plane of depth AO is then inserted in the cut and the crystal is "repaired" as best it can be, leaving a line perpendicular to the plane of the paper and passing through the point O, around which the crystal structure is seriously distorted.

A dislocation is defined by its *Burgers vector*. Figure 6.2a shows the lattice prior to the formation of the dislocation. After the dislocation has been introduced we have the atomic arrangement shown in Fig. 6.2b, where we have followed the displacements of the individual atoms of Fig. 6.2a. We now see that some distance away from the core of the dislocation the effect of the dislocation appears as a uniform displacement

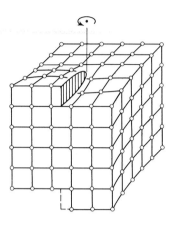

Fig. 6.3 Atomic arrangement in the neighborhood of a screw dislocation of unit Burgers vector in a simple cubic lattice. (*From H. W. Hayden, W. G. Moffatt, and J. Wulff, "The Structure and Properties of Materials," vol. III, John Wiley & Sons, Inc., New York, 1965.*)

of the upper half of the crystal to the right by one lattice distance. The Burgers vector is the vector whose length and direction specify the distance and direction of motion of that portion of the crystal which lies above the glide plane *BOC* and to one side of the plane *AO*. Finally one speaks of positive and negative dislocations, according as the extra half plane is inserted above or below the glide plane, respectively.

Another type of dislocation, the *screw dislocation*, is shown in Fig. 6.3. Here, the relative displacements of the two halves of the crystal are in the direction of the dislocation line rather than normal to it. Again, the Burgers vector is used to specify the amount of displacement that has occurred.

The energy associated with the presence of a dislocation in a crystal is of elastic origin. Referring to Fig. 6.1, it is evident that in the region above the glide plane the crystal is essentially in compression, whereas below, it is in tension. One can show that the elastic energy associated with an edge dislocation is given by

$$E = \frac{\mu b^2}{4\pi(1 - \nu)} \ln \frac{R}{r_0} \tag{6.1}$$

where b is the Burgers vector, μ is the shear modulus, and ν is Poisson's ratio. Here r_0 is the radius of the core of the dislocation, roughly 10^{-7} cm, and R is the distance between dislocations, i.e., roughly 10^{-3} cm. Hence, the logarithmic term is of order 10. The above expression assumes that the crystal can be approximated by an isotropic elastic continuum. An important feature of Eq. (6.1) is the dependence of the elastic energy on the square of the Burgers vector. This tells us immediately that dislocations whose Burgers vectors are multiples of a lattice parameter will never occur in a crystal, for such a dislocation would spontaneously break up into several unit dislocations, thereby releasing elastic energy. Indeed, we may anticipate that a unit dislocation might separate into two or more partial dislocations if such a process can occur without seriously disrupting the crystal register in the region between the partial dislocations.

Dislocations were originally postulated to account for the relative ease of plastic deformation of crystals. Figure 6.4 is a photograph of a single crystal of cadmium which has been deformed under tension. It is clear that the deformation has occurred through the slipping of complete segments of the crystal over parallel crystal planes which make an angle of roughly 45° with the tensile stress. Elementary calculation shows that the stress required to force half of a crystal to slip relative to the other half in such a way that all the atoms move in unison is orders of magnitude greater than the observed critical shear stress at which plastic deformation commences. Taylor [1], and independently Orowan [2], suggested that deformation could occur by the motion of an edge dislocation from one end of the crystal to the other. Each time a positive dislocation moves from left to right over the entire glide plane, the upper half of the crystal of Fig. 6.2 is displaced relative to the lower half by one lattice parameter. Motion of successive dislocations could produce any desired amount of slip. The calculated shear stress required to initiate and sustain motion of a dislocation line is relatively small and in order-of-magnitude agreement with the observed critical shear stress of single crystals.

Fig. 6.4 Slip bands on a deformed single crystal. (*From C. A. Wert and R. W. Thomson, "Physics of Solids," McGraw-Hill Book Company, New York, 1964.*)

Since dislocations were first postulated, their properties have been the subject of much theoretical and experimental investigation that provided ample evidence of their existence in solids. Moreover, many properties of solids, such as work-hardening, polygonization, and crystal growth, have been successfully interpreted in terms of dislocation theory.

C. Point Imperfections

Consider a perfect crystal and imagine removing an atom from its interior and placing it on the surface. Although this creation of a *vacancy* requires an expense of energy, since the atom on the surface is less tightly bound than one in the interior of the crystal, the entropy of the crystal containing a vacancy is greater than that of the perfect crystal. Consequently, at any finite temperature the presence of a few vacancies will lower the free energy, and the imperfect crystal, therefore, represents the thermodynamically stable configuration. At high temperatures, vacancies migrate readily, and it is through this mechanism that diffusion takes place in many solids. Vacancy mobility, just as vacancy formation, is thermally activated; and, as the temperature is lowered, such vacancies as remain in the solid are effectively immobilized. Continued reduction of the temperature cannot diminish the vacancy concentration further because these defects are now "quenched" into the crystal lattice. Since crystal growth, especially growth of good single crystals, proceeds at elevated temperatures, every crystal, though cooled to very low temperatures, nevertheless contains a small but finite number of vacancies. In the same category as vacancies we also place *interstitial atoms*—atoms not located on normal lattice sites, but in the "interstices" between these.

Interstitial atoms and vacancies obviously do not constitute the only point defects. While many substances can now be obtained commercially 99.999 percent pure, no crystal is ever ideally free of chemical contamination. Frequently, the impurities dissolve in the solid; that is to say, the impurity atoms appear substitutionally at random lattice points. Sometimes, as the impurity concentration is increased, impurity atoms tend to segregate and form small clusters. Moreover, impurities may also induce phase changes in the crystal.

D. Disorder

Lastly, we come to a rather different type of stationary imperfection which we may denote as *disorder*. Here we make a further division into alloy disorder and magnetic disorder.

Many alloys when prepared in appropriate stoichiometric proportions tend to form an ordered structure. One example of such an alloy is a 50-50 copper-zinc alloy, beta brass. Beta brass forms a body-centered cubic structure, and at temperatures above 360°C copper and zinc atoms appear to be placed on the lattice sites in a random manner. Below this critical transition temperature the lattice orders in such a way that it now resembles the CsCl structure, with copper atoms on corner sites, say, and zinc at the body-center positions. The degree of order is generally described by means of a long-range-order parameter s, whose value ranges between 0 and 1. Let us denote the body-center sites as A sites, the corner sites as B sites, and designate the zinc and copper atoms by A and B, respectively. Let N_{AA} and N_{AB} be the number of A atoms on A sites and the number of A atoms on B sites, respectively. The order parameter s is then defined by

$$s = \frac{N_{AA} - N_{AB}}{N_A} \tag{6.2}$$

where N_A is the number of A atoms present.

Even when $s = 0$ some local order persists. That is, even though over a large region A- and B-type atoms occupy lattice sites without preference, there will still be a higher probability of finding a B atom next to an A atom than of finding another A atom at the neighboring site. Whereas long-range order, a cooperative phenomenon whose effects extend over the entire crystal, falls precipitously to zero as the critical temperature is approached, short-range order decreases with temperature somewhat more gradually. The theoretical variations of long- and short-range order for an AB-type alloy are shown in Fig. 6.5.

A 50-50 composition is not the only one which allows an ordered structure. For example, the copper-gold system forms two ordered phases, CuAu and Cu₃Au.

It is to be expected that an ordered alloy behaves very much like a pure metal. However, the unit cell now contains two or more atoms, and the Brillouin zone is correspondingly reduced in size. Thus, the band structure of the ordered AB alloy is surely different from that of pure A or pure B. Moreover, one would not consider each B atom as an imperfection in the lattice of A atoms when A and B atoms array themselves in an ordered fashion. Indeed, the resistivities of highly ordered

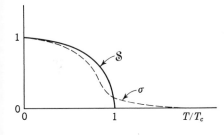

Fig. 6.5 Long-range- and short-range-order parameters s and σ as functions of T/T_c for an AB alloy according to the Bethe-Peierls theory.

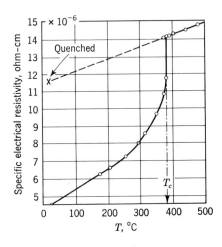

Fig. 6.6 Electrical resistivity of $AuCu_3$ as a function of temperature. [*From F. C. Nix and W. Shockley, Rev. Mod. Phys.*, **10**: 5 (1938).]

alloys are often roughly the same as those of the separate pure metals which formed the alloy.

Suppose we start with a perfectly ordered AB alloy and introduce some disorder by interchanging a pair of AB atoms. We have now introduced a disturbance in an otherwise perfect lattice, and expect that this disturbance will give rise to scattering of electrons, thereby increasing the resistivity. As the temperature is increased and order is progressively destroyed, one does find an anomalous increase in resistivity with temperature which is most pronounced just below the critical temperature; that is, in that temperature range where S drops cataclysmically. A typical curve of resistivity versus temperature of an order-disorder alloy is shown in Fig. 6.6.

A very similar type of disorder scattering appears to occur in ferromagnetic and antiferromagnetic metals and alloys. Here one may associate a magnetic moment with each ion. In the ferromagnetic case all magnetic moments are aligned parallel at $T = 0°K$; in the antiferromagnetic case they are aligned antiparallel throughout a magnetic domain. In either case we have to do with a perfect magnetic lattice. As the Curie temperature is approached, the ordered arrangement is destroyed with ever increasing rapidity, the curve of spontaneous magnetization of a ferromagnet versus temperature resembling rather closely the curve of S versus T of Fig. 6.5. In these metals disorder in the spin (magnetic-moment) lattice can give rise to scattering of conduction electrons, the interaction arising through the quantum-mechanical exchange force between the "magnetic" d-shell electrons and the conduction electrons. One again finds nearly discontinuous behavior of the transport properties of these metals near the Curie temperature. Figures

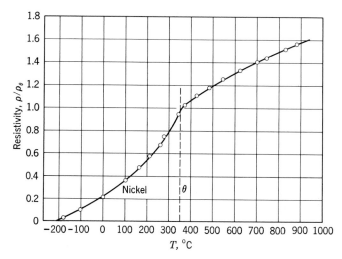

Fig. 6.7 The resistivity of nickel as a function of temperature. (*After R. M. Bozorth, "Ferromagnetism," D. Van Nostrand Company, Inc., Princeton, N.J., 1951.*)

6.7 and 6.8 show typical curves of resistivity and of thermoelectric power versus temperature.

6.3 LATTICE VIBRATIONS

In addition to the various stationary imperfections, lattice vibrations also destroy perfect lattice periodicity.   Though the time average of each

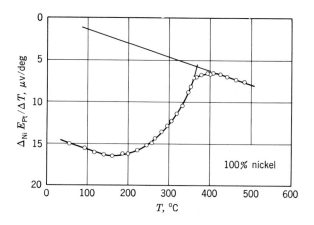

Fig. 6.8 The thermoelectric power of a nickel-platinum thermocouple near the Curie temperature of nickel. [*From K. E. Grew, Phys. Rev.,* **41**: 356 (1932).]

ion's position is that of its respective lattice point, a "snapshot" of the ions would reveal a somewhat distorted crystal, the degree of distortion depending on temperature. Lattice vibrations, which themselves are conveniently categorized into acoustic, optical, longitudinal, and transverse modes, constitute time-dependent imperfections.

6.4 SCATTERING OF ELECTRONS BY IMPERFECTIONS

In the remaining pages of this chapter we shall calculate the probability for transition of an electron from a state $\mathbf{k}$ to another eigenstate $\mathbf{k'}$, when the interaction which gives rise to the transition is due to one of the imperfections listed above.

The electronic energy levels and eigenfunctions of a perfect lattice formed the topic of Chap. 4. It is apparent now that this perfect lattice is a fiction—albeit a lovely one—which leads to the conclusion that all perfect metals should exhibit infinite conductivity.†

We must, then, extend the horizons of the electronic theory of solids to encompass the imperfect as well as the perfect lattice. One obvious approach is through perturbation theory. Unfortunately, the validity of this procedure is difficult to establish and, consequently, considerable effort has been devoted in recent years to the development of more powerful and reliable theoretical methods. A discussion of this work is well outside the scope of this book. Happily, its major conclusions agree with those of the more pedestrian perturbation treatment that we shall follow.

We consider the ideally perfect lattice and the associated assembly of conduction electrons as the unperturbed system. All imperfections are then treated as perturbations which induce transitions between the stationary states of the unperturbed crystal. This procedure is intuitively reasonable when the perturbation is an occasional impurity atom in an otherwise perfect crystal. Here one can readily visualize the process of scattering of an electron from one stationary state to another in essentially classical terms. Whether, in any given instance, perturbation theory is appropriate for the description of such scattering events depends on the strength of the perturbing potential.

The justification of perturbation theory in electron-phonon scattering (scattering of electrons by lattice vibrations) deserves further scrutiny. It rests, initially, on the adiabatic approximation, also

---

† Superconductivity, a topic which will be omitted from discussion, is not the external manifestation of crystal perfection. Even before an acceptable theory of superconductivity was proposed, the demonstration of the isotope effect by Maxwell [3] showed that the *motion* of the ions played a crucial role in the phenomenon.

known as the Born-Oppenheimer approximation. Consider the conduction electrons and the ions of the crystal as the quantum-mechanical system. The total hamiltonian is then a sum of terms

$$\mathcal{H}_T = T_e + T_i + V_{ee} + V_{ii} + V_{ei} \tag{6.3}$$

representing the electronic kinetic energy, the kinetic energy of the ions, and the electron-electron, ion-ion, and electron-ion interactions in that order. Here V_{ei} is *not* the perturbation which we wish to consider. Our stationary electronic states refer to an unperturbed hamiltonian which already contains the time-*independent* part of V_{ei}—the potential of the ions fixed at regularly spaced lattice points. It is only the *time-dependent* part of V_{ei} which induces transitions between the stationary states ψ_k and $\psi_{k'}$. The perturbation potential U is, accordingly, the difference between the crystal potential at time t and the crystal potential of the perfect lattice; that is,

$$U = U(\mathbf{r},t) = V_{\text{crystal}}(\mathbf{r},t) - V_{\substack{\text{perfect}\\ \text{crystal}}}(\mathbf{r}) \tag{6.4}$$

In the Born-Oppenheimer approximation it is assumed that the motion of the ions is so sluggish compared to that of the electrons that the electrons are able to adjust to this motion adiabatically. In that case, the electronic wave functions contain the ionic coordinates only as parameters. The complete unperturbed wave function can then be written as a product of an electronic and a lattice function

$$\varphi(\mathbf{r},\mathbf{R}) = \psi_k(\mathbf{r})\Phi_L(\mathbf{R}) \tag{6.5}$$

The eigenstates of the system are specified by the quantum numbers n and $\mathbf{k}$ (electronic quantum numbers) and n_q and s (phonon quantum numbers; the subscript L on the lattice wave function contains all lattice quantum numbers). The perturbing potential $U(\mathbf{r},t)$ induces transitions between the eigenstates of the system at a rate which we now calculate.

6.5   PHONON–INDUCED TRANSITIONS: METALS†

In Appendix A we have sketched the derivation of an important result of quantum mechanics relating to the probability for transitions between stationary states. According to Eq. (A.59) the transition probability

---

† This section is rather more difficult than the norm of the text. In subsequent chapters only the final result, Eq. (6.22), will reappear, and the reader may skip most of this section without loss of continuity. However, the discussion relating to Normal (N) and Umklapp (U) processes should be read before proceeding.

$\mathfrak{S}(\mathbf{k},\mathbf{k}')$ is given by†

$$\mathfrak{S}(\mathbf{k},\mathbf{k}') = \frac{2\pi}{\hbar}\,|(\mathbf{k}'|U|\mathbf{k})|^2\delta[E(\mathbf{k}) - E(\mathbf{k}')] \tag{6.6}$$

where $(\mathbf{k}'|U|\mathbf{k})$ is the matrix element of the perturbation U, and $\delta(g)$ is the Dirac delta function. This last factor is a formal way of expressing the requirement of energy conservation. The energy E here denotes the energy of the entire system, electronic and phonon.

The perturbing potential $U(\mathbf{r},t)$ is derived by means of the "rigid-ion" model, introduced by Houston and Nordheim [4], which assumes that as each ion vibrates its potential moves with it rigidly. In the perfect lattice the crystal potential is the sum of the ionic potentials, that is,

$$V(\mathbf{r}) = \sum_n v(\mathbf{r} - \mathbf{a}_n) \tag{6.7}$$

In the perturbed lattice, in which the nth atom is displaced by $\mathbf{u}_n$ from its equilibrium position, the crystal potential is

$$V'(\mathbf{r}) = \sum_n v(\mathbf{r} - \mathbf{a}_n - \mathbf{u}_n) \tag{6.8}$$

According to Eq. (6.4) the perturbing potential is the difference between Eq. (6.8) and Eq. (6.7). Retaining only the lowest nonvanishing term of a Taylor expansion, we have

$$U(\mathbf{r}) = -\sum_n \mathbf{u}_n \cdot \nabla v(\mathbf{r} - \mathbf{a}_n) \tag{6.9}$$

The displacements $\mathbf{u}_n$ are given by Eq. (2.28). Since we are now embarking on a quantum-mechanical calculation involving the lattice vibrations, we shall treat the quantities $\mathbf{Q}_{q,s}$ and $\mathbf{Q}_{q,s}^*$ as annihilation and creation operators whose matrix elements are given by Eq. (2.39). The complete expression for the matrix element connecting an electronic state $\mathbf{k}$ with the state $\mathbf{k}'$ via the electron-phonon interaction will then contain two similar terms, one involving $\mathbf{Q}$ and the other $\mathbf{Q}^*$. The procedure of evaluating these two terms is essentially the same, and so we concentrate attention on only one, that involving $\mathbf{Q}^*$. Moreover, to simplify matters we restrict ourselves to scattering in a Bravais lattice where we have only one atom per unit cell.

---

† To be precise, we should write the function $\mathcal{O}\,[E(\mathbf{k}) - E(\mathbf{k}')]$ [see Eq. (A.59)] instead of the Dirac delta function in Eq. (6.6). Although for our present purposes the replacement of $\mathcal{O}\,(x)$ by $\delta(x)$ is permissible, there are occasional circumstances when some caution must be exercised [see M. Dresden, *Rev. Mod. Phys.*, **33**: 265 (1961)].

We now have—for the $\mathbf{Q}^*$ part of the matrix element—

$$(\mathbf{k'}|U|\mathbf{k}) = (NM)^{-\frac{1}{2}} \int \psi_{\mathbf{k'}}^* \Phi_{L'}^* \left[\sum_{q,s,n} \mathbf{Q}_{q,s}^* e^{-iq\cdot a_n} \xi(q,s) \cdot \nabla v(\mathbf{r} - \mathbf{a}_n) \right] \psi_{\mathbf{k}} \Phi_L \, d\tau$$

which can be factored into phonon and electron parts. The phonon part is readily evaluated with the aid of Eq. (2.39) and yields

$$(\mathbf{k'}|U|\mathbf{k}) = B \sum_n \int e^{-iq\cdot a_n} e^{-i\mathbf{k'}\cdot\mathbf{r}} u_{\mathbf{k'}}^*(\mathbf{r}) \xi \cdot \nabla v(\mathbf{r} - \mathbf{a}_n) e^{i\mathbf{k}\cdot\mathbf{r}} u_{\mathbf{k}}(\mathbf{r}) \, d\tau$$

$$B = (NM)^{-\frac{1}{2}} \left[\frac{\hbar}{2\omega(q,s)} \right]^{\frac{1}{2}} (\mathfrak{n}_{q,s} + 1)^{\frac{1}{2}}$$

(6.10)

In Eq. (6.10) we have expressed the electronic eigenfunctions in the Bloch form, $\exp(i\mathbf{k}\cdot\mathbf{r})u_{\mathbf{k}}(\mathbf{r})$.

Each term in the sum in Eq. (6.10) is an integral over the entire crystal. It is convenient to translate the center of coordinates of each of these terms by $\mathbf{a}_n$ so that the ion which is displaced is always at the origin. Since the functions $u_{\mathbf{k'}}^*(\mathbf{r})$ and $u_{\mathbf{k}}(\mathbf{r})$ are periodic in the lattice, this translation is accomplished by multiplication by $\exp[i(\mathbf{k} - \mathbf{k}') \cdot \mathbf{a}_n]$. We now have

$$(\mathbf{k'}|U|\mathbf{k}) = B \sum_n e^{i(\mathbf{k}-\mathbf{k'}-q)\cdot a_n} \mathfrak{M}_q(\mathbf{k'},\mathbf{k})$$

(6.11)

$$\mathfrak{M}_q(\mathbf{k'},\mathbf{k}) = \int \psi_{\mathbf{k'}}^* \xi \cdot \nabla v(\mathbf{r})\psi_{\mathbf{k}} \, d\tau_0$$

(6.12)

The subscript $_0$ on the volume integral $(d\tau_0)$ denotes that the integration is restricted to a unit cell. The matrix element of U is the product of an as yet unknown quantity $\mathfrak{M}_q(\mathbf{k'},\mathbf{k})$ times a sum of $\exp[i(\mathbf{k} - \mathbf{k} - q) \cdot \mathbf{a}_n]$ over all basis vectors $\mathbf{a}_n$. This sum is just N times the Kroneker delta, $\delta_{\mathbf{k}-\mathbf{k'}-q,\mathbf{K}}.$†

We have here one of the important selection rules for electron-phonon interaction: The matrix element vanishes unless

$$\mathbf{k} - \mathbf{k'} - q = \mathbf{K}$$

(6.13)

The physical significance of the above requirement is apparent when we recall that we have been considering here the term involving the creation operator $\mathbf{Q}^*$; i.e., an interaction in which a phonon of wave vector q and polarization s is created. It is convenient to discuss the two cases $\mathbf{K} = 0$ and $\mathbf{K} \neq 0$ separately.

If $\mathbf{K} = 0$, the final total wave vector is $\mathbf{k'} + q$ and must be equal to the wave vector $\mathbf{k}$ of the electron in its initial stationary state. That is,

---

† The factor N is most conveniently absorbed in the normalization of the electronic wave functions.

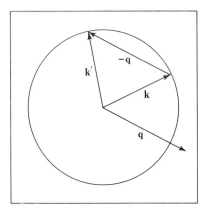

Fig. 6.9 Normal (N) scattering of an electron in a simple cubic crystal from the state **k** to the state **k′** through the emission of a phonon of wave vector **q**. The Fermi surface is assumed spherical and we have neglected the energy change of the electron due to the emission of the phonon (elastic approximation). The square represents the surfaces of the Brillouin zone.

the electron crystal momentum $\hbar\mathbf{k}$ has been diminished in the interaction by the momentum $\hbar\mathbf{q}$ of the phonon which was created in the process. Thus, Eq. (6.13) represents the conservation of momentum selection rule in the interaction of electrons and phonons in crystals. The events for which $\mathbf{K} = 0$ are known as *Normal* (N) *processes.*

Events in which $\mathbf{K} \neq 0$ have been designated *Umklapp* (U) *processes* by Peierls. Scattering by U processes may be viewed as the creation of a phonon of wave vector **q** with the simultaneous internal Bragg reflection of the electron. Such a U process is shown schematically in Fig. 6.10, with Fig. 6.9 showing the typical geometry of an N process. Figures 6.9 and 6.10 are drawn according to the reduced zone scheme. In Fig. 6.11 we show the same scattering event as in Fig. 6.10 but now in the periodically extended zone scheme.

The matrix element for the dual process in which a phonon is *absorbed* rather than created differs only in that the factor $(n_{\mathbf{q},s} + 1)^{\frac{1}{2}}$

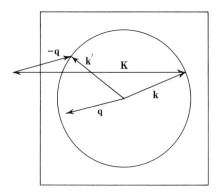

Fig. 6.10 Umklapp (U) scattering of an electron in a simple cubic crystal from the state **k** to the state **k′** through the emission of a phonon of wave vector **q**. The process is shown in the reduced zone scheme. The Fermi surface is assumed spherical and we have neglected the energy change of the electron due to the emission of the phonon (elastic approximation). The square represents the surfaces of the Brillouin zone.

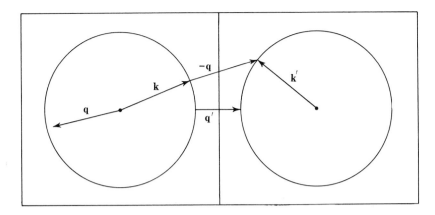

Fig. 6.11   The U process of Fig. 6.10 in the periodically extended zone scheme. q' is the wave vector of the least energetic phonon capable of participating in a U process.

in B is replaced by $(\mathfrak{n}_{q,s})^{\frac{1}{2}}$, and the momentum selection rule now reads

$$\mathbf{k} - \mathbf{k}' + \mathbf{q} = \mathbf{K} \tag{6.13a}$$

There remains the evaluation of $\mathfrak{M}_q(\mathbf{k}',\mathbf{k})$. If we continue to adhere strictly to the rigid-ion approximation, this poses no serious difficulties. The integral we need is

$$\int \psi_{\mathbf{k}'}^* \boldsymbol{\nabla} v(\mathbf{r}) \psi_{\mathbf{k}} \, d\tau_0 \tag{6.14}$$

We recall that in the Wigner-Seitz method it is assumed that the potential $v(\mathbf{r})$ is the ionic potential within the central cell, but vanishes outside the cell boundaries. As a further simplification, the polyhedral cell is replaced by a sphere of equal volume, i.e., of radius $r_s = [(3/4\pi)\Omega]^{\frac{1}{3}}$. Within the unit cell the wave function $\psi_{\mathbf{k}}(\mathbf{r})$ is a solution of the Schroedinger equation

$$\frac{\hbar^2}{2m} \nabla^2 \psi_{\mathbf{k}} + (\epsilon_{\mathbf{k}} - v)\psi_{\mathbf{k}} = 0 \tag{6.15}$$

Since the energy of the phonon which is either absorbed or emitted in the interaction is a very small fraction of the Fermi energy, only electrons near the Fermi energy can be scattered into unoccupied states. We shall, therefore, introduce no serious error if in the evaluation of $\mathfrak{M}_q(\mathbf{k}',\mathbf{k})$ we set $\epsilon_{\mathbf{k}'} = \epsilon_{\mathbf{k}}$.

We now differentiate Eq. (6.15), multiply by $\psi_{\mathbf{k}'}^*$, and make use of the relation

$$\nabla\psi_{\mathbf{k}} = i\mathbf{k}\psi_{\mathbf{k}} + e^{i\mathbf{k}\cdot\mathbf{r}}\,\nabla u_{\mathbf{k}}(\mathbf{r}) \tag{6.16}$$

to obtain

$$\psi_{\mathbf{k}'}^*\psi_{\mathbf{k}}\nabla v = i\mathbf{k}\psi_{\mathbf{k}'}^*\left[\frac{\hbar^2}{2m}\nabla^2 + (\epsilon_{\mathbf{k}} - v)\right]\psi_{\mathbf{k}} + \frac{\hbar^2}{2m}\{\psi_{\mathbf{k}'}^*\nabla^2[e^{i\mathbf{k}\cdot\mathbf{r}}\nabla u_{\mathbf{k}}(\mathbf{r})]$$
$$- e^{i\mathbf{k}\cdot\mathbf{r}}\,\nabla u_{\mathbf{k}}(\mathbf{r})(\nabla^2\psi_{\mathbf{k}'}^*)\} \tag{6.17}$$

The first term on the right-hand side of Eq. (6.17) vanishes because of Eq. (6.15). The volume integral of the second may be transformed into an integral over the surface of the Wigner-Seitz sphere. If we now make the further assumption that $u_{\mathbf{k}}(\mathbf{r}) = u_0(\mathbf{r})$, where $u_0(\mathbf{r})$ is spherically symmetric and has a vanishing derivative over the surface of the Wigner-Seitz sphere, we obtain

$$\int\psi_{\mathbf{k}'}^*\nabla v\psi_{\mathbf{k}}\,d\tau = \frac{\hbar^2}{2m}\oint\psi_{\mathbf{k}'}^*e^{i\mathbf{k}\cdot\mathbf{r}}\nabla^2 u_0(\mathbf{r})\,d\mathbf{S} \tag{6.18}$$

Once again we make use of the Schroedinger equation, replace $(\hbar^2/2m)[\nabla^2 u_0(\mathbf{r})]_{r=r_s}$ by $[v(r_s) - \epsilon_0]u_0(r_s)$, and are led to the simple expression

$$\int\psi_{\mathbf{k}'}^*\nabla v\psi_{\mathbf{k}}\,d\tau_0 = [v(r_s) - \epsilon_0]\oint\psi_{\mathbf{k}'}^*\psi_{\mathbf{k}}\,d\mathbf{S}$$
$$= [v(r_s) - \epsilon_0]\int\nabla(\psi_{\mathbf{k}'}^*\psi_{\mathbf{k}})\,d\tau_0 \tag{6.19}$$

Here $v(r_s)$ is the ionic potential at the surface of the Wigner-Seitz sphere and ϵ_0 is the energy of an electron at the bottom of the conduction band, i.e., in the state $\mathbf{k} = 0$. The further reduction of the matrix element makes use of the fact that $u_0(r)$ is nearly constant over most of the unit cell. For normalization in a unit cell this means that we may take $u_0(r) \simeq 1$ and arrive at the final result

$$\mathfrak{M}_q(\mathbf{k}',\mathbf{k}) = i\boldsymbol{\xi}\cdot(\mathbf{k} - \mathbf{k}')[v(r_s) - \epsilon_0]\int\psi_{\mathbf{k}'}^*\psi_{\mathbf{k}}\,d\tau_0 \tag{6.20}$$

In the free-electron approximation the interference integral $\int\psi_{\mathbf{k}'}^*\psi_{\mathbf{k}}\,d\tau_0$ can be evaluated and gives

$$\int\psi_{\mathbf{k}'}^*\psi_{\mathbf{k}}\,d\tau_0 = \mathfrak{F}(|\mathbf{k} - \mathbf{k}'|r_s) \qquad \mathfrak{F}(x) = \frac{3\,(x\cos x - \sin x)}{x^3} \tag{6.21}$$

Since the square of the matrix element of U enters in Eq. (6.6), it is the square of the function $\mathfrak{F}$ which largely determines the behavior of the transition probability as a function of the change of electron momentum.

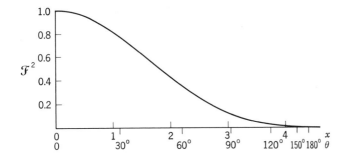

Fig. 6.12   The square of the interference function $\mathfrak{F}(x)$ as a function of x and the scattering angle θ for a monovalent free-electron metal. (*From J. M. Ziman, "Electrons and Phonons," Oxford University Press, London, 1960.*)

Since $|\mathbf{k}| \simeq |\mathbf{k'}|$, $|\mathbf{k} - \mathbf{k'}| = |\mathbf{k}| \sin (\theta/2)$ is a measure of the angle θ through which the electron is scattered. The dependence of $|\mathfrak{F}^2|$ on the scattering angle for a monovalent metal is shown in Fig. 6.12. Evidently, the probabilities for large-angle scattering are severely attenuated. Nevertheless, large-angle events are quite important in inhibiting conduction, because of the preferential weighting by the factor $1 - \cos \theta$ (see page 125).

The numerical value of the energy factor $[v(r_s) - \epsilon_0]$ may also be estimated from the free-electron approximation where it equals $2\eta/3$; we expect, therefore, that the energy factor is of the order of 1 ev.

Quite apart from the various other approximations we have made, the expression for $\mathfrak{M}_q(\mathbf{k'},\mathbf{k})$ which has been derived cannot be correct, since it rests on the somewhat unrealistic rigid-ion assumption. A better calculation has been carried out by Bardeen [5], who took account of screening of the rigid-ion potential by the conduction electrons in a self-consistent manner. The result which he obtained differs in certain details from Eq. (6.20) but is akin to it in its most important features. These are summarized below.

1. *The polarization factor* $\boldsymbol{\xi} \cdot (\mathbf{k} - \mathbf{k'})$ shows that in N processes, for which $(\mathbf{k} - \mathbf{k'}) = \pm \mathbf{q}$, only longitudinal phonons can participate. This restriction is, however, predicated on the assumption of a spherical Fermi surface, implicit in the reduction of $\mathfrak{M}_q(\mathbf{k'},\mathbf{k})$ indicated in the preceding pages. The Fermi surfaces of the noble metals are known to touch the (111) zone boundaries; and even the Fermi surfaces of the alkali metals , with the exception of Na and K, deviate somewhat from spherical form. Transverse and

longitudinal phonons can always contribute to U processes since in these events $(\mathbf{k} - \mathbf{k}')$ and $\mathbf{q}$ are not colinear (see Fig. 6.10).

2. The strength of the electron-phonon interaction, given by the *energy factor* $[v(r_s) - \epsilon_0]$ in the rigid-ion approximation, is of the order of magnitude of the Fermi energy.

3. The square of the matrix element, that is to say the transition probability, depends sensitively on the scattering angle. This dependence is expressed primarily through the function $\mathfrak{F}^2(|\mathbf{k} - \mathbf{k}'|r_s)$ of Eq. (6.21), and is shown graphically in Fig. 6.12 for the ideal electron gas of a monovalent metal.

Collecting our results, we can now write the following explicit expression for the transition probability in the case of lattice scattering:

$$\mathfrak{S}(\mathbf{k},\mathbf{k}') = \frac{4\pi}{9}\, \eta^2\mathfrak{F}^2(|\mathbf{k} - \mathbf{k}'|r_s)\, \frac{[\boldsymbol{\xi} \cdot (\mathbf{k} - \mathbf{k}')]^2}{NM} \left[\frac{\mathfrak{n}_q}{\omega_q}\, \delta(\epsilon_{\mathbf{k}'} - \epsilon_{\mathbf{k}} - \hbar\omega_q) \right.$$
$$\left. + \frac{\mathfrak{n}_{q'} + 1}{\omega_{q'}}\, \delta(\epsilon_{\mathbf{k}'} - \epsilon_{\mathbf{k}} + \hbar\omega_{q'}) \right] \quad (6.22)$$

Here the first term in the brackets corresponds to absorption of a phonon of wave vector $\mathbf{q} = \mathbf{k} - \mathbf{k}' + \mathbf{K}$ and the second, to emission of a phonon of wave vector $\mathbf{q}' = \mathbf{k} - \mathbf{k}' + \mathbf{K}$.

6.6 SCATTERING BY STATIONARY IMPERFECTIONS: METALS

A. Point Imperfections

Although the perturbing potential due to an impurity ion in a solid acquires the symmetry of the host lattice, we will, nevertheless, assume that it is spherically symmetric. This assumption is analogous to the replacement of the unit-cell polyhedron by an equivalent sphere in the Wigner-Seitz approximation.

Since scattering by stationary imperfections is of necessity elastic, we know that a meaningful relaxation time can be defined (see discussion on page 121ff). The calculation of this relaxation time is accomplished most conveniently with the aid of the "differential scattering cross section," $\sigma(\theta,\phi)$. This is a concept much in vogue in nuclear physics, and the calculation of $\sigma(\theta,\phi)$ for a spherically symmetric scattering potential is dealt with in all standard texts on quantum mechanics.

To understand the meaning of $\sigma(\theta,\phi)$, consider a flux of N electrons per unit time and unit area which is incident on a target whose scattering potential has spherical symmetry and vanishes at large distances from the center of the target. The geometry of the scattering process is shown

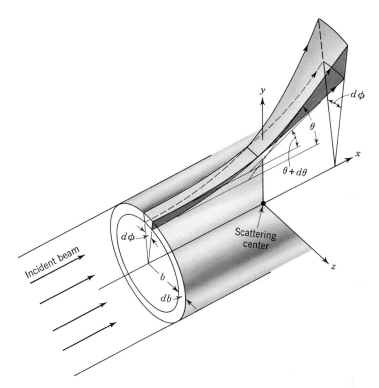

Fig. 6.13 Scattering by a point imperfection. Electrons passing through the area $2\pi b\,db$ are scattered through angles between θ_c and $\theta_c + d\theta_c$. (*From R. B. Leighton, "Principles of Modern Physics," McGraw-Hill Book Company, New York, 1959.*)

in Fig. 6.13. We now write the number of electrons which are scattered per unit time into the solid angle $d\omega$, centered about the polar and azimuthal angles θ and ϕ,

$$n(\theta,\phi)\,d\omega = N\sigma(\theta,\phi)\,d\omega \tag{6.23}$$

The quantity σ so defined has the dimension of an area and is, in fact, the differential scattering cross section. The physical significance of the differential scattering cross section, at least in the classical model, is also shown in Fig. 6.13. It is that small area of the infinite plane normal to the incident flux through which those particles that are to be scattered into the specified solid angle must pass.

There is a simple relationship between $\sigma(\theta,\phi)$ and $\mathfrak{S}(|\mathbf{k} - \mathbf{k}|) = \mathfrak{S}(\theta\ \phi)$, the corresponding transition probability. Note that, since the scattering event is elastic, $|\mathbf{k}| = |\mathbf{k}'|$, and the assumption of isotropy ensures that $\mathfrak{S}(\mathbf{k},\mathbf{k}')$ is independent of the initial direction of motion, i.e., of the direction of $\mathbf{k}$.   Provided the scattering centers are sufficiently dispersed they will scatter incoherently and $\mathfrak{S}(\theta,\phi)$ will be proportional to their density, N_I.   Normalized to a density of one electron per unit volume, the incident flux is just equal to v, the velocity of the electron. According to Eq. (6.23) the differential scattering cross section is then the scattering probability per unit flux per scattering center.   Thus, we have

$$\mathfrak{S}(\theta,\phi) = N_I\sigma(\theta,\phi)v \tag{6.24}$$

From Eqs. (5.28) and (5.29) we obtain

$$\frac{1}{\tau(k)} = \frac{1}{\tau(\epsilon)} = N_I v \int (1 - \cos\theta)\sigma(\theta,\phi)\,d\omega \tag{6.25}$$

where we have made use of the fact that $|\mathbf{k}| = |\mathbf{k}'|$ to reduce the volume integral in $\mathbf{k}$ space to a surface integral over the sphere of energy $\epsilon(k)$. Equation (6.25) exhibits very clearly the importance of large-angle scattering events in restoring the equilibrium distribution.   Instead of the total collision cross section

$$\sigma_T = \int \sigma(\theta,\phi)\,d\omega$$

the effective conductivity collision cross section is one which is suitably weighed in favor of large angle events through the factor $1 - \cos\theta$.

The differential scattering cross section appropriate to a given imperfection can be calculated once the perturbation potential has been ascertained.   Consider, for example, the effect of an impurity of valence Z in solid solution in a monovalent metal.   Presumably, the valence electrons of the impurity atom go into the conduction (valence) band of the solvent crystal, leaving the impurity ion with a positive charge Z. The ions of the host lattice are singly charged.   At first sight, a reasonable perturbing potential might be $V'(r) = (Z - 1)e/r$, the coulomb potential of a point charge $(Z - 1)e$.   This choice cannot be correct, however, for it completely ignores the fact that the mobile conduction electrons, attracted to this excess positive charge, will tend to screen it at large distances.   A more realistic potential is

$$V'(r) = \frac{(Z - 1)e}{r} e^{-r/r_0} \tag{6.26}$$

where the screening radius r_0, a function of the conduction-electron concentration, is, in metals, roughly one interatomic distance.

Once the scattering potential has been selected, the differential scattering cross section can be evaluated quite easily by perturbation theory, provided the potential is sufficiently weak.   The procedure is known as the *Born approximation* and yields the result

$$\sigma(\theta,\phi) = \left(\frac{m}{2\pi\hbar^2}\right)^2 \left| \int V'(r)e^{i(\mathbf{k} - \mathbf{k}')\cdot\mathbf{r}} \, d\tau \right|^2 \tag{6.27}$$

One immediate consequence of Eq. (6.27) and Eq. (6.26) is that σ, and consequently also $1/\tau(\epsilon)$, must be proportional to $(Z - 1)^2$, i.e., to the square of the valence difference between solute and solvent atom. We shall see later that this prediction is in accord with observation although application of Eq. (6.27) rather overestimates the scattering cross section and leads to incorrect magnitudes for the resistivities due to impurities in monovalent metals.

The difficulty with Eq. (6.27) is that $V'(r)$ is not, in fact, a "weak" potential in the sense of perturbation theory; the Born approximation cannot be justified here.   A rather more lengthy and tedious calculation, known as the *method of partial waves* and expounded in all standard quantum mechanics texts, must be employed.   The crucial parameters which determine $\sigma(\theta)$ are now the *phase shifts* δ_l, which characterize the extent to which an incident electron wave corresponding to an electron with angular momentum $\hbar l$ about the impurity center is modified by the scattering potential.

The phase-shift method, though more tedious to apply than Eq. (6.27), has two great advantages.   First, it is an exact method, not an approximation as is Eq. (6.27).   Second, Friedel [6] has derived an extremely useful sum rule which the phase shifts must satisfy, namely,

$$\frac{2}{\pi} \sum_l (2l + 1)\delta_l = \mathfrak{N} \tag{6.28}$$

where $\mathfrak{N}$ is the excess charge which must be screened by the conduction electrons.   The condition (6.28) arises from the requirement that at large distances the perturbing potential be completely screened by the mobile electrons which accommodate themselves to the disturbance.   The importance of Eq. (6.28) is that it prescribes one parameter of the scattering potential in a fully self-consistent manner.

The integral (6.25) can be expressed in terms of the phase shifts directly, so that there is no need to evaluate the differential scattering cross section as such.   The desired relation is

$$\int (1 - \cos\theta)\sigma(\theta) \, d\omega = \frac{4\pi}{k^2} \sum_{l=1}^{\infty} l \sin^2(\delta_{l-1} - \delta_l) \tag{6.29}$$

B. Scattering by Dislocations; the Deformation Potential

In calculations of the scattering of conduction electrons by dislocations, one must take account of two effects: first, the influence of the long-range elastic strain field of the dislocation, and second, the influence of the "core" of the dislocation line. Scattering by the strain field was calculated by Hunter and Nabarro [7], who applied the method of the deformation potential. The influence of the core was disregarded by Hunter and Nabarro. However, a rough calculation by Harrison [8] showed it to be of at least the same magnitude as that due to the long-range strain field.

The *method of the deformation potential*, which we shall outline here, was first developed by Bardeen and Shockley [9] for the purpose of calculating lattice scattering of electrons in semiconductors. It is applicable whenever the strain in the lattice varies inappreciably over a distance of a lattice parameter. Thus, for example, the method is useful in the treatment of scattering of electrons by *long-wavelength* phonons. We consider here the simplest situation in which the strain is a pure dilatation and contains no shear components.

It follows from the Wigner-Seitz method that ϵ_0, the energy at the bottom of the conduction band, is a function of r_s, the radius of the Wigner-Seitz sphere. Consider, then, an electron in the state $\mathbf{k}$ in the unstrained portion of the crystal which enters the strained region where the dilatation is $\Delta(\mathbf{r})$. When $\Delta(\mathbf{r})$ is a slowly varying function of $\mathbf{r}$ the energy of the electron is still given by

$$\epsilon(\mathbf{k}) = \epsilon_0(r_s) + \frac{\hbar^2}{2m^*} k^2 \tag{6.30}$$

Thus, as the electron enters the region of dilatation its energy in the state $\mathbf{k}$ changes just as though it had passed through a region in which there is a perturbation potential

$$V'(\mathbf{r}) = \tfrac{1}{3} r_s \frac{\partial \epsilon_0}{\partial r_s} \Delta(\mathbf{r}) \tag{6.31}$$

The derivative which determines the strength of the deformation potential may be estimated by recourse to the free-electron approximation. It follows from the constancy of the Fermi energy relative to a fixed reference potential external to the metal that η must be independent of the dilatation. In a monovalent metal the wave vector at the Fermi energy is related to the local free-electron density by

$$k_0 r_s = \left(\frac{9\pi}{4} \right)^{\frac{1}{3}}$$

From the relation

$$\eta = \epsilon_0(r_s) + \frac{\hbar^2}{2m^*} k_0^2$$

we now obtain

$$\frac{\partial \epsilon_0}{\partial r_s} = \frac{2\eta}{r_s}$$

Hence, in the free-electron limit the deformation potential corresponding to a pure compressional strain is

$$V'(\mathbf{r}) = \tfrac{2}{3}\eta\Delta(\mathbf{r}) \tag{6.32}$$

The method may be extended to include shear as well as compression and leads to the result

$$V'(\mathbf{r}) = \tfrac{2}{3}\eta\Delta(\mathbf{r}) + \mathcal{E}_s \sum_{\alpha,\beta} (Y_{\alpha\beta} - \tfrac{1}{3}\Delta\delta_{\alpha\beta}) \frac{k_\alpha k_\beta}{k^2} \tag{6.33}$$

Here $Y_{\alpha\beta}$ is the $\alpha\beta$ component of the strain tensor and $\mathcal{E}_s$ is the deformation-potential coefficient for shear deformation. In some instances, notably in semiconductors, $\mathcal{E}_s$ can be deduced from elastoresistance measurements. Unfortunately, there are no similar reliable methods for estimating $\mathcal{E}_s$ in metals.

To return now to the matter of scattering of electrons by dislocations, the procedure followed by Hunter and Nabarro involves the substitution of the dislocation strain field into Eq. (6.33). Hunter and Nabarro estimated that $\mathcal{E}_s \simeq \eta$ in Cu and $\mathcal{E}_s \simeq \eta/2$ in Na, but these values cannot be considered well established.

Once $V'(\mathbf{r})$ is fixed the calculation proceeds by standard perturbation theory, i.e., Born approximation, which, in this instance, is valid.

C.   Scattering by Planar Imperfections; Stacking Faults

A stacking fault, as its name implies, is an imperfection relating to the ordered arrangement of crystal planes. These faults are known to occur in cold-worked fcc metals, such as the noble metals and their alloys.

Consider the arrangement of atomic planes in a fcc lattice. The atoms labeled A in Fig. 6.14 are arranged in one of the close-packed (111) planes. The atoms in the next-higher plane may be positioned in a triangular pattern with their centers above either the B or C positions. Suppose we place them in the B positions. We then have the choice of placing the atoms of the third plane in either the C or A positions; that is, in the latter case, directly above the atoms of the first layer. If we choose the C positions, we have selected the stacking order of the

fcc lattice—$ABCABCABCABC$ . . . ; if, instead, we had selected the
pattern $ABABABABA$ . . . , the lattice would be hcp.

Suppose, now, that at some point we disturb this fcc order so that
the pattern becomes

. . . $CABCABABCABCA$ . . .
$\uparrow$

or

. . . $CABCACBCABCAB$ . . .
$\uparrow$

In the first instance a C plane has been removed where indicated;
in the other, such a plane has been added to the normal stacking order,
resulting in "stacking faults."

If the extra or missing plane of the fault is bounded within the
crystal, its circumference resembles a dislocation loop. The manner
in which a stacking fault is created through the separation of a full
dislocation into two partial dislocations is shown in Fig. 6.14. Note that,
though the magnitude of each partial Burgers vector is greater than half
a full Burgers vector, dissociation of the full dislocation into two partials
is still favored energetically according to Eq. (6.1).

One can show that two dislocations of equal sign with Burgers
vectors in the same direction repel one another. The Burgers vectors
$\mathbf{b}_2$ and $\mathbf{b}_3$ of the partial dislocations formed by the dissociation of the
dislocation $\mathbf{b}_1$ are essentially in the same direction. The strain field will,
therefore, force the separation of the two partial dislocations, creating,
thereby, a stacking fault in the intervening region. The extent of the
fault is determined by a compromise between the energy of the repulsive
interaction between the partial dislocations and the surface energy of
the stacking fault itself.

The principal physical characteristic of a stacking fault is the phase
change in the lattice. This phase change must reflect itself in the
electronic wave function, and, by analogy to scattering of electromagnetic
waves at an interface, one expects an incident electron wave to be partly
transmitted and partly reflected.

The matter is, however, not dealt with quite so simply. In the
extreme free-electron approximation, a stacking fault must be an unob-
servable disturbance, since the ionic and electronic charge densities are
unaltered by the stacking fault and there are no dilatations introduced
into the lattice.

The analogy to the electromagnetic problem suggests a wave-
matching procedure. Here, however, one must proceed with some caution, for the phase shift in the lattice bears no immediate relation to a
phase shift in the plane-wave portion, $\exp(i\mathbf{k} \cdot \mathbf{r})$, of the Bloch function.

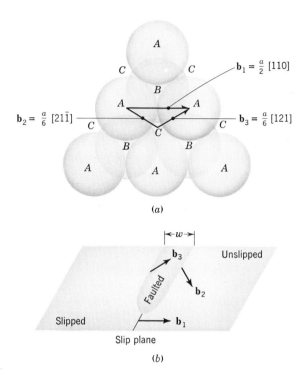

Fig. 6.14 ⟨110⟩ slip in fcc crystals. The unit slip vector of the complete dislocation b_1 is $a/2$ [110]; two partial slip vectors, the sum of which produces the same net motion as b_1, are b_2 and b_3. (*After H. W. Hayden, W. G. Moffatt, and J. Wulff, "Structure and Properties of Materials," vol. III, John Wiley & Sons, Inc., New York, 1965.*)

The crux of the matter is that the phase shift in the lattice must be reflected in a corresponding shift in phase of the periodic factor $u_k(\mathbf{r})$ of the Bloch function, for it is this factor which is intimately related to the crystal potential. The results of such calculations are not entirely conclusive but show that when the Fermi surface is badly distorted—especially when it touches some zone boundaries—the reflection coefficient may be quite large, approaching unity.

These wave-matching methods as well as certain other approaches suffer from one serious oversimplification [10]. While it is true that in the perfect lattice the periodic boundary conditions impose the Bloch form on the solutions of the Schroedinger equation, in the vicinity of an external or internal boundary the Born-von Kármán conditions cannot be applied. In these regions other solutions to the wave equation are admissible, though these solutions must decay exponentially with distance from the boundaries. A matching procedure which neglects the localized electronic surface states is at best a rough approximation. A calculation taking account of surface states has been carried through by Howie [11] and is probably the most reliable at present.

6.7 SCATTERING OF CHARGE CARRIERS IN SEMICONDUCTORS

Scattering of charge carriers in semiconductors and in metals is fundamentally the same process. The difference between the metal and semiconductor from the point of view of their electronic properties is largely a quantitative difference in the electron (or hole) concentration. This quantitative difference results, however, in essentially qualitative differences in the reaction of the electrons to external influences.

To illustrate, consider lattice scattering of electrons in an n-type semiconductor whose conduction band is of standard form. By this we mean that $\epsilon(\mathbf{k}) = (\hbar^2/2m^*)k^2$; that is, $\epsilon(k)$ has an extremum at $\mathbf{k} = 0$, is parabolic, and surfaces of constant energy are spherical in $\mathbf{k}$ space (see Fig. 6.15). As in metals, the scattering process is one in which a phonon is either absorbed or emitted, crystal momentum and total energy being conserved in the event. In Chap. 5 we showed that in a semiconductor only phonons of wave vector $q \lesssim 2k$ can scatter electrons of wave vector

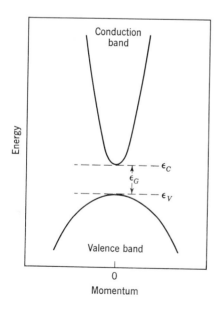

Fig. 6.15 The idealized band structure of a semiconductor. [*From E. Burstein and P. Egli, Advan. Electron. Electron. Phys.*, **7**: 10 (1954).]

k.   Since, for all electrons in this ideal semiconductor, $k \ll K$, it follows that:

1   Only long-wavelength phonons can be effective in scattering.
2   The energy change of an electron through collision with a phonon is much smaller than kT; i.e., scattering is essentially elastic.
3   Umklapp processes cannot occur.

The first two conclusions have been discussed already in some detail in Chap. 5.   The last follows from the first: All energetically allowed scattering events correspond to values of $|\mathbf{k} - \mathbf{k}'|$ that are small compared to a reciprocal-lattice vector.   Hence, all possible combinations of initial and final electronic states are connected through phonon emission or absorption in which q is small and is contained well within the Brillouin zone.   Consequently, there are no scattering events which require an Umklapp process.

These three conclusions apply, however, only to the idealized semiconductor with its standard band, and even then, only to scattering by acoustic modes.   Let us now consider in turn the various complications that arise in real crystals.

All known semiconductors crystallize in lattices which are not of the Bravais type.   Thus, there are two or more atoms per unit cell and, consequently, the phonon spectrum contains at least three optical branches (one longitudinal and two transverse).

From our analysis of Chap. 2 we recognize that the energy of optical phonons is relatively high, even though the wave vector may be small. It is, in fact, a rather good approximation to assume that the energy of optical phonons is independent of q altogether.   Some of the methods by which these energies may be deduced have been discussed previously; typical values for $\hbar\omega_0 = k\Theta_0$ lie at about $\Theta_0 \approx 400°K$.

It follows that an electron–optical-phonon collision is decidedly inelastic.   It is, therefore, not possible to reduce the collision integral to the form $(f - f_0)/\tau$; the variational method or one equivalent to it must be invoked.

Another qualitative difference between acoustic and optical-phonon scattering relates to the phonon distribution.   Both types of mode are, of course, properly described by Bose-Einstein statistics, which leads to the Planck distribution

$$\mathfrak{n}_q = (e^{\hbar\omega_q/kT} - 1)^{-1} \tag{6.34}$$

Since those acoustic phonons which interact with the charge carriers have energies $\hbar\omega_q \ll kT$ (except at very low temperatures where, however, scattering by stationary imperfections dominates), we may expand the

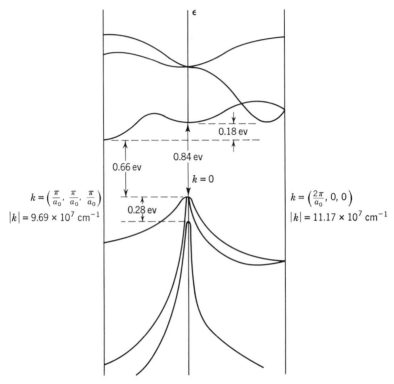

Fig. 6.16 The valence and conduction bands of germanium.   [*From F. J. Blatt, Solid State Phys.*, **4**: 278 (1953).]

exponential and write

$$\mathfrak{n}_q \simeq \frac{\hbar \omega_q}{kT} \quad \text{(acoustic phonons)} \tag{6.35}$$

For optical phonons, on the other hand, we have $\hbar \omega_q / k \approx \Theta_0 \approx 400°\text{K}$. Thus, at room temperature and below we may neglect unity compared to $\exp(\hbar \omega_q / kT)$ and obtain

$$\mathfrak{n}_q \simeq e^{-\hbar \omega_0 / kT} \quad \text{(optical phonons)} \tag{6.36}$$

Since the mobility† $\mu = \sigma / n e$ is roughly inversely proportional to the number of effective phonons, we see that the temperature variation of μ

† Transport properties of semiconductors are generally discussed in terms of the average mobility μ of the individual charge carriers.   The fairly drastic changes of conductivity σ with temperature and impurity concentration in semiconductors are largely due to order of magnitude variations of n. The mobility, its temperature and concentration dependence, a characteristic property of individual charge carriers, is usually the physically interesting and significant parameter.

will depend quite sensitively on the relative importance of acoustic- and optical-phonon scattering.   Specifically, if optical-mode scattering dominates at $T < \Theta_0$, the temperature dependence of μ should be decided principally by the exponential factor in Eq. (6.36), and μ should, therefore, increase steeply with decreasing temperature.

The other qualification for validity of the three conclusions of page 163 relates to the band structure.   The band structure of the idealized semiconductor is shown in Fig. 6.15.   In this case, the surfaces of constant energy in **k** space are spheres centered about the point **k** = 0. The structure of the valence and conduction bands of germanium and silicon are shown in Figs. 6.16 and 6.17.   The bands do have the full symmetry of the cube, for example, inversion symmetry through the point **k** = 0; the apparent lack of symmetry in Figs. 6.16 and 6.17 arises

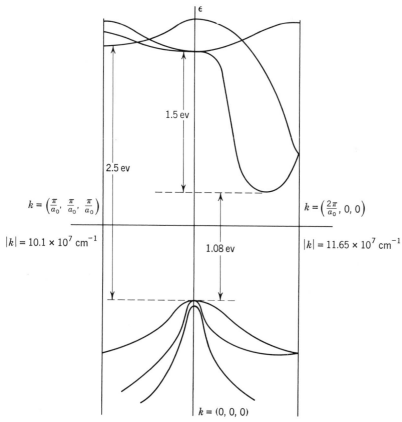

Fig. 6.17   The valence and conduction bands of silicon.   [*From F. J. Blatt, Solid State Phys.*, **4**: 278 (1953).]

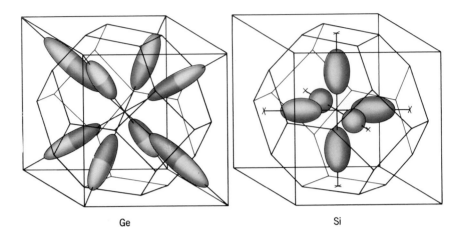

Ge   Si

Fig. 6.18   Constant-energy spheroids in the conduction bands of germanium and silicon. (*After J. M. Ziman, "Electrons and Phonons," Oxford University Press London,* 1960.)

because the electron energies are plotted along different crystallographic directions in the two halves of each figure.

   These bands display several noteworthy features.   First, the minima of the conduction bands of Ge and Si do not occur at $\mathbf{k} = 0$.   In Si, the minima appear to be about $\frac{2}{3}$ of the way to the zone boundary along the $\langle 100 \rangle$ directions.   The minima in Ge fall just at the zone boundaries along the $\langle 111 \rangle$ directions.   In both substances the surfaces of constant energy are prolate spheroids rather than spheres.   The major axes of the spheroids are the $\langle 100 \rangle$ axes in Si, the $\langle 111 \rangle$ axes in Ge.   Full cubic symmetry is preserved by the symmetric disposition of identical spheroids along the equivalent crystallographic directions.   The constant-energy spheroids for Si and Ge are shown in Fig. 6.18.   Since the energy contours show not one central depression but several equivalent ones, it is natural to speak here of a "many-valley model."

   The curvature of the band parallel and normal to the spheroidal axis is characterized by effective-mass parameters $m_{\parallel}$ and $m_{\perp}$, defined by

$$\epsilon_{\mathbf{k}}^{i} = \frac{\hbar^2}{2m_{\parallel}} (k_{\parallel}^{i})^2 + \frac{\hbar^2}{2m_{\perp}} (k_{\perp}^{i})^2 \tag{6.37}$$

Here $\epsilon_{\mathbf{k}}^{i}$ is the energy in the ith spheroid measured relative to the bottom of the spheroidal depression. $k_{\parallel}^{i}$ and $k_{\perp}^{i}$ are the wave-vector components in the ith spheroid, parallel and normal to the spheroidal axis, measured relative to the position of the ith energy minimum.

Before considering the qualitative modifications in the transport properties induced by the many-valley model, we focus our attention on the valence-band structure.   The valence bands are formed—in the tight-binding limit—from atomic p orbitals, resulting in four states of $p_{\frac{3}{2}}$ and two states of $p_{\frac{1}{2}}$ symmetry for every value of $\mathbf{k}$.   Thus, we may conveniently denote these bands as $p_{\frac{3}{2}}^{|\frac{3}{2}|}$, $p_{\frac{3}{2}}^{|\frac{1}{2}|}$, and $p_{\frac{1}{2}}^{|\frac{1}{2}|}$ bands, each band remaining doubly degenerate (spin degeneracy) in the absence of an external magnetic field.

These three bands would be degenerate at $\mathbf{k} = 0$, were it not for the spin-orbit interaction which depresses the energy of the $p_{\frac{1}{2}}^{|\frac{1}{2}|}$ band well below that of the $p_{\frac{3}{2}}$ bands.   The two $p_{\frac{3}{2}}$ bands are degenerate at $\mathbf{k} = 0$, where both have their energy maxima.   The degeneracy is removed when $\mathbf{k} \neq 0$, and the interaction between the bands leads to an energy-versus-$\mathbf{k}$ relation of the form

$$\epsilon_{\mathbf{k}} = Ak^2 \pm [B^2k^4 + C^2(k_x{}^2k_y{}^2 + k_y{}^2k_z{}^2 + k_z{}^2k_x{}^2)]^{\frac{1}{2}} \tag{6.38}$$

Were it not for the C^2 term, the constant-energy contours would be two concentric spheres; i.e., each band would be of standard parabolic form with effective masses given by

$$m^* = \frac{\hbar^2}{2(A \pm B)}$$

The C^2 term distorts the energy surfaces in a cubically symmetric manner. The resulting contours are "warped spheres," as shown in Fig. 6.19.

Even though the valence-band energy surfaces are warped, it is often sufficiently accurate to treat the valence bands as though of standard form and assign to each an appropriate average effective mass.   It is natural then to employ the nomenclature of "heavy" and "light" holes, according as the negative or positive sign is taken in Eq. (6.38).

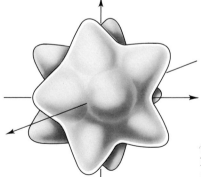

Fig. 6.19   The constant-energy surface of heavy holes in silicon.   (*From J. M. Ziman, "Electrons and Phonons," Oxford University Press, London,* 1960.)

Table 6.1   Band Parameters of Carriers in Si and Ge

	Top of valence band (units of $\hbar^2/2m$)			Holes (units of m)		Electrons (units of m)	
	A	$|B|$	$|C|$	m_1	m_2	$m_\parallel$	$m_\perp$
Si	-4.0	1.1	4.1	0.16	0.5	0.98	0.19
Ge	-13.1	8.3	12.5	0.04	0.3	1.64	0.082

The band parameters for Ge and Si are given in Table 6.1.

Let us now consider the qualitative changes in the scattering of electrons and holes which might follow in consequence of these drastic modifications from the standard band structure.

First, as regards the electrons, these are now found not in one but in several valleys positioned symmetrically in **k** space. Since the energy surface of any given valley is anisotropic, the relaxation time and the effective mass will reflect this anisotropy. For one valley we may introduce a relaxation-time tensor τ_{jk}^i which is diagonal in a coordinate system in which $\epsilon_\mathbf{k}$ is also diagonal and whose components are $\tau_\parallel^i$, $\tau_\perp^i$, $\tau_\perp^i$. The mobility tensor for electrons of the ith valley is then also diagonal and has components $\mu_\parallel^i$, $\mu_\perp^i$, $\mu_\perp^i$. The effective masses and relaxation times generally appear in the combinations $\tau_\parallel^i/m_\parallel^i$ and $\tau_\perp^i/m_\perp^i$. Since $m_\parallel^i > m_\perp^i$ and detailed calculations indicate that for phonon scattering the relaxation-time tensor is approximately a multiple of the unit tensor, one concludes that $\mu_\perp^i > \mu_\parallel^i$.

Though the mobilities of the individual valleys are strongly anisotropic, a result which has considerable bearing on the elastoresistance of these materials, isotropy is restored on averaging over all valleys in a cubically symmetric arrangement. The expression for the mobility reduces to

$$\mu = e\,\frac{\langle\tau\rangle}{m'} \tag{6.39}$$

where $\langle\tau\rangle$ is a suitable average of the relaxation time (see Chap. 8) and m' is defined by

$$\frac{1}{m'} = \frac{1}{3}\left[\frac{2}{m_\perp} + \frac{1}{m_\parallel}\right] \tag{6.40}$$

Except for these modifications the many-valley model does not, as yet, suggest significant departures from the standard band model. We have, however, glossed over one very important new feature, the possibility of *intervalley scattering*.

For *intra*valley scattering—scattering of an electron from the state
$\mathbf{k}$ to $\mathbf{k}'$, where both $\mathbf{k}$ and $\mathbf{k}'$ terminate on an energy surface belonging
to the same valley—the rules of page 163 again apply, for we have, in
effect, only changed our origin of coordinates in $\mathbf{k}$ space (and, of course,
introduced some anisotropy of the energy surfaces). The important
criterion for the validity of rules 1 to 3 is that $|\mathbf{k} - \mathbf{k}'|$ be small compared
to a reciprocal-lattice vector; and this condition is certainly satisfied in
intravalley scattering. Thus, taking proper account of anisotropy, we
shall be able to use the results of the standard band approximation when
discussing intravalley scattering.

In addition to this scattering mechanism, the many-valley model
also allows for *inter*valley scattering of electrons. Here the change in
electron wave vector is large, being essentially equal to the vector which
connects the minimum of the valley in which the electron originates
and that into which it is scattered. Consequently $\mathbf{q}$, the wave vector
of the phonon which must be absorbed or emitted, is correspondingly
large, of the order of the radius of the Debye sphere.† The process is
inelastic, involving an energy change of order $k\Theta_D$. Thus, intervalley
scattering by acoustical modes closely resembles scattering by optical
modes in the ideal semiconductor. In particular, intervalley scattering
will decrease approximately exponentially with decreasing temperature if
$T < \Theta_D$.

Scattering of holes in Ge and Si can proceed by *intra-* or *interband*
processes. That is, a light hole may be scattered into either another
state in the light-hole band or into a state in the heavy-hole band, and
vice versa. In contrast to intervalley scattering, interband scattering
of holes in Ge and Si is quasi-elastic, as both band extrema are centered
at $\mathbf{k} = 0$. Therefore, rules 1 to 3 apply here. However, since the
relaxation rate is proportional to the density of final states, scattering
into the heavy-hole band will largely determine the relaxation time for
light as well as heavy holes, leading to nearly equal relaxation times for
both types of carrier.

In the following section we consider the calculation of lattice scattering in semiconductors in some detail. The reader who is primarily
interested in the final expressions for relaxation times and mobilities may
pass over this portion without loss of continuity. The calculation of

---

† In Si, two narrow bands of acoustical phonons are effective in intervalley
scattering. The first band induces transitions from, say, the valley labeled 1 to the
four valleys 2, 3, 4, 5 which are in equivalent positions about valley 1. The second
band contributes to Umklapp scattering to valley 6. In Ge, the magnitude of $\mathbf{q}$ for
intervalley scattering is the same for all combinations of valleys. However, it should
be remembered that not only acoustical but also optical phonons may cause these
transitions.

scattering by stationary impurities is quite elementary and follows the section on lattice scattering.

6.8 CALCULATION OF LATTICE SCATTERING IN SEMICONDUCTORS

A. Acoustic Modes

We treat here only the simplest case, corresponding to the ideal semiconductor with spherical energy surfaces. Since only long-wavelength phonons can scatter carriers (there is only one valley of electrons), the method of the deformation potential is admirably suited. Moreover, in this simple case, only dilatation and not shear strains create a perturbation.

We write the perturbation potential as

$$U(\mathbf{r}) = \mathcal{E}_1 \Delta(\mathbf{r}) = \mathcal{E}_1 \nabla \cdot \mathbf{u}(\mathbf{r}) \tag{6.41}$$

where $\mathcal{E}_1$, the deformation potential constant, is the shift of the band edge per unit dilatation, $\Delta(\mathbf{r})$ is the dilatation, and $\mathbf{u}(\mathbf{r})$ is the elastic displacement of the lattice at the point $\mathbf{r}$. We now represent $\mathbf{u}(\mathbf{r})$ by the normal-mode expansion Eq. (2.28). The matrix element $(\mathbf{k}'|U|\mathbf{k})$ is then evidently of the same form as Eq. (6.10) except that $\nabla v(\mathbf{r} - \mathbf{a}_n)$ is replaced by $\mathcal{E}_1 \mathbf{q}$. We now recall that $|\mathbf{k} - \mathbf{k}'|r_s$ is small compared to unity, so that the interference integral (6.21) is unity. Thus, we are quickly led to the result, corresponding to Eq. (6.22),

$$\mathcal{S}(\mathbf{k},\mathbf{k}') = \frac{2\pi^2 \mathfrak{n}_q}{N M \omega_q} \mathcal{E}_1^2 q^2 \tag{6.42}$$

B.   Interaction of Electrons with Optical Modes; Polar Crystals

We limit our discussion to polar crystals because here the interaction between an electron and the optical phonons is very apparent and allows fairly precise numerical estimates for the mobility of the carrier. Normally, of course, polar crystals, of which NaCl and CsCl are prototypes, do not contain conduction electrons. Electrons may, however, be excited into the conduction band optically and their behavior studied in suitably devised experiments. There are also a large number of semiconducting crystals, the intermetallic compounds, such as InSb, GaAs, etc., which have at least partly polar character. Here, however, the strength of the interaction is difficult to determine a priori.

Polar crystals do, of course, support acoustical as well as optical vibrational modes. We need not concern ourselves with the former for two reasons. First, the treatment follows that already described above. Second, the electrostatic interaction between the charged carrier and the internal polarization field due to optical vibrations is much stronger than the deformation potential interaction.

This former interaction is simply

$$U = e\phi(\mathbf{r}) \tag{6.43}$$

where $\phi(\mathbf{r})$ is related to the polarization $\mathbf{P}(\mathbf{r})$ through

$$4\pi\mathbf{P}(\mathbf{r}) = \nabla\phi(\mathbf{r}) \tag{6.44}$$

The polarization is completely specified by the vibrations themselves, and is most conveniently expressed in the normal-mode formalism

$$\mathbf{P}(\mathbf{r}) = \left(\frac{\hbar\omega_0}{8\pi\mathbf{x}'}\right)^{\frac{1}{2}} \sum_{\mathbf{q}} [e^{i\mathbf{q}\cdot\mathbf{r}}\mathbf{Q}_{\mathbf{q}} + e^{-i\mathbf{q}\cdot\mathbf{r}}\mathbf{Q}_{\mathbf{q}}^*] \tag{6.45}$$

ω_0 is the frequency of the optical phonons, here assumed independent of the wave vector $\mathbf{q}$, and, consequently, taken outside the summation.

In Eq. (6.45), $\mathbf{x}'$ is an effective dielectric constant

$$\mathbf{x}' = \left(\frac{1}{\mathbf{x}_\infty} - \frac{1}{\mathbf{x}_0}\right)^{-1} \tag{6.46}$$

where $\mathbf{x}_\infty$ and $\mathbf{x}_0$ are the high-frequency and static dielectric constants, respectively. The polarization due to a static field arises from the simultaneous displacement of the ions and the distortion of the closed electron shells of the ions. At high frequencies (ultraviolet) the ionic motion is too sluggish to follow the excitation and only the electrons contribute to the polarization. In the present case we are concerned not with the polarization due to an externally applied electric field, but with the polarization caused by the thermally activated vibrations of the ions. In this case the electron shells will tend to screen the ionic polarization rather than add to it, and will therefore reduce the polarization below that which one would calculate under a "rigid-ion" assumption. Consideration of this shielding effect, whose efficacy is characterized by $1/\mathbf{x}_\infty$, leads to (6.46).

From Eqs. (6.43), (6.44), and (6.45) we now obtain the interaction hamiltonian

$$U = ie\left(\frac{2\pi\hbar\omega_0}{\mathbf{x}'}\right)^{\frac{1}{2}} \sum_{\mathbf{q}} \frac{\mathbf{q}\cdot\boldsymbol{\xi}}{q^2} [\mathbf{Q}^*e^{-i\mathbf{q}\cdot\mathbf{r}} - \mathbf{Q}e^{i\mathbf{q}\cdot\mathbf{r}}] \tag{6.47}$$

Calculation of the matrix elements proceeds in quite the same manner as before. There will, again, be two terms, one corresponding to emission, the other to absorption of an optical phonon. Since we shall be largely concerned with the mobility of electrons of thermal energy near room temperature or below, energy conservation precludes the emission process, except for those very few electrons (in the high-energy tail of the Boltzmann distribution) which have sufficient energy to permit the creation of a quantum of optical vibration. Thus, we need concern ourselves only with the absorption process, though the inclusion of emission is trivial. The interesting matrix element is then

$$(\mathbf{k}',\mathfrak{n} - 1|U|\mathbf{k},\mathfrak{n}) = -4\pi i e \left(\frac{2\pi\hbar\omega_0}{\varkappa'}\right)^{\frac{1}{2}} \cdot \frac{\mathfrak{n}_q^{\frac{1}{2}}}{q} \tag{6.48}$$

and the corresponding transition probability is

$$\mathfrak{S}(\mathbf{k},\mathbf{k}') = \frac{64\pi^3 e^2 \omega_0 \mathfrak{n}_q}{\varkappa' q^2} \delta(\epsilon_{\mathbf{k}'} - \epsilon_{\mathbf{k}} - \hbar\omega_0) \tag{6.49}$$

subject to the usual selection rule

$$\mathbf{k}' = \mathbf{k} + \mathbf{q}$$

The preceding calculation appears to be straightforward and at first glance might seem acceptable. In fact, this is not the case. The interaction of a free electron with the polarizable crystal is so strong that perturbation theory is of doubtful validity. The obstacle of strong coupling can be negotiated using techniques of field theory, but these procedures lie outside the scope of this book. They are discussed in review articles by Froehlich and Allcock [12]; the calculation of the mobility along these lines was first given by Low and Pines [13]. Here, we restrict ourselves to a purely qualitative consideration of these questions.

If a free charge (an electron, say) is placed at position $\mathbf{r}$ in a polar crystal, the electrostatic field of that charge polarizes the surrounding region. Suppose we now apply an external electric field. This field will exert a force on the charge and accelerate it. However, as the charge moves through the crystal, the cloud of local polarization will tend to move with it. Thus, we need to accelerate not only the free charge but also its polarization field, a complex christened the *polaron*. It is intuitively clear that the acceleration of the polaron per unit field will be less than that of the corresponding free charge. Another way of expressing the same thought is to say that the effective mass of the polaron, $m_\mathfrak{p}^*$, is greater than that of the free charge carrier. If the interaction with the polarization field is relatively weak, m^* may be evaluated by perturbation theory. The result is

$$m_\mathfrak{p}^* = m\left(1 + \frac{\alpha}{6}\right) \qquad \alpha < 1 \tag{6.50}$$

where

$$\alpha = e^2 \left(\frac{1}{\varkappa_\infty} - \frac{1}{\varkappa_0} \right) \left(\frac{m}{2\omega_0 \hbar^3} \right)^{\frac{1}{2}}$$

is a measure of the strength of the interaction.

If $\alpha \gg 1$, the effective polaron mass is given by

$$m_p^* = 0.02 m \alpha^4 \tag{6.51}$$

Unfortunately, there are no reliable calculations which cover the physically interesting region $\alpha \gtrsim 1$.   Presumably, the transition from Eq. (6.50) to (6.51) is a smooth one.

The calculation of $\mathfrak{S}(\mathbf{k},\mathbf{k}')$ should take account of the existence of the polaron.   We presented the derivation of $\mathfrak{S}(\mathbf{k},\mathbf{k}')$ appropriate to a nude electron, one not clothed in its polarization shield.   Though this procedure is not justified, it does, apparently, lead to quite acceptable numerical results.

6.9 IMPURITY SCATTERING IN SEMICONDUCTORS

A. Impurity Energy Levels

Consider a donor atom, for example As, in germanium.   Suppose that we remove one of the five valence electrons of the As atom, leaving the remaining four to form the homopolar bonds and the impurity with a single net positive charge.   The potential about this ion at large distances is given by

$$V(r) = \frac{e}{\varkappa r} \tag{6.52}$$

where $\varkappa$ is the dielectric constant of germanium.   This is the potential in which the extra electron will move if it is now permitted to approach the region about the impurity ion, provided it does not come into the immediate vicinity of the impurity where the approximation of a homogeneous dielectric medium cannot hold.   The electron in the field of the donor is described by the Schroedinger equation

$$\left(-\frac{\hbar^2}{2m^*} \nabla^2 - \frac{e^2}{\varkappa r} \right) \psi = \epsilon \psi \tag{6.53}$$

which differs from the hydrogen-atom equation only by the replacement of the free-electron mass by the effective mass m^* and by the reduction of the ionic charge by the factor $1/\varkappa$.   Consequently, there will be bound-state solutions of Eq. (6.53) with energy

$$\epsilon_n = -\frac{1}{n^2}\left[\frac{(e^2/\varkappa)^2}{2\hbar^2 m^*}\right] = -\left(\frac{1}{n^2}\right)\left(\frac{e^2}{2\hbar^2 m^*}\right)\left(\frac{m}{m^*\varkappa^2}\right) \qquad (6.54)$$

where ϵ_n is measured relative to the edge of the conduction band, which here corresponds to the continuum of the free hydrogen-atom case.

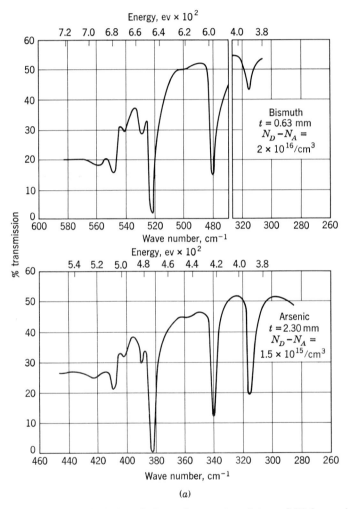

(a)

Fig. 6.20 (a) The infrared absorption spectra of As and Bi donors in silicon at 4.2°K [*After J. Phys. Chem. Solids*, **7**: 237 (1958)]; (b) the infrared absorption spectra of B, Al, and Ga acceptors in silicon. [*From W. Kohn, Solid State Phys.*, **5**: 264 (1954).]

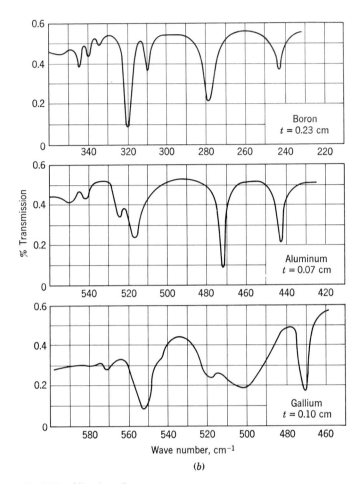

Fig. 6.20   (*Continued*)

The lowest bound state, $n = 1$, has an energy of

$$-\left(\frac{m}{m^*\varkappa^2}\right)\mathrm{Ry} = -13.5\left(\frac{m}{m^*\varkappa^2}\right)\mathrm{ev}$$

For germanium, $m^* \simeq 0.2m$ and $\varkappa = 12$. Consequently, the binding energy of the electron in the ground state will be only $13.5/720 = 0.02$ ev. As for the hydrogen atom, Eq. (6.54) allows not only a ground state but the entire hydrogenic spectrum of discrete excited states, whose energies are also suitably scaled by the factor $(m/m^*\varkappa^2)$. This spectrum of energy levels has been observed through infrared spectroscopy on Ge and Si, and the results are shown in Figs. 6.20 and 6.21. Moreover, the

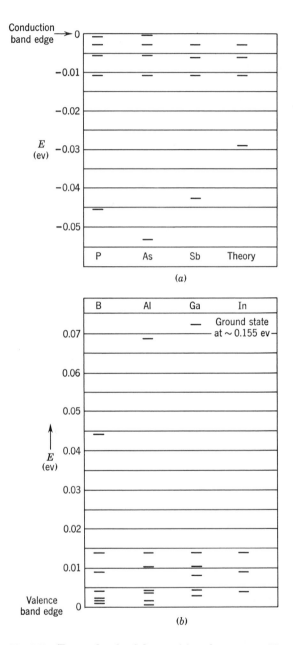

Fig. 6.21 Energy levels of donors (*a*) and acceptors (*b*) in silicon. [*After W. Kohn, Solid State Phys.*, **5**: 264 (1954).]

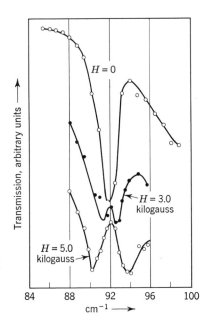

Fig. 6.22 Zeeman splitting of phosphorus donor levels in germanium. [*From B. Lax and S. Zwerdling, in A. F. Gibson (ed.), "Progress in Semiconductors," vol. 5, p. 246, John Wiley & Sons, Inc., New York, 1961.*]

Zeeman splitting of hydrogenic levels in a magnetic field is also evident in the spectra of donor and acceptor states (see Fig. 6.22). This Zeeman pattern is, however, somewhat complicated as a result of the complexity of the valence and conduction bands, which are not of the standard quasi-free-electron form.

A scaling factor also applies to the orbits of the bound states. The "Bohr radius" of the ground state is

$$a^* = \frac{\hbar^2 \varkappa}{m^* \mathrm{e}^2} = a_0 \left(\frac{\varkappa m}{m^*} \right) \tag{6.55}$$

For n-type Ge, $a^* \simeq 60 a_0$. Thus, the orbit of even the ground state is huge, encircling thousands of unit cells, and orbits of excited states are even larger. Consequently, the approximation of the impurity potential by Eq. (6.52) is well justified, especially for the excited states. The approximation will be poorest for the ground state, a $1s$-like state in which the probability for finding the electron in the unit cell occupied by the impurity is, though still quite small, larger than for any other state. It is, therefore, not surprising that experiment and theory are in least accord in this instance. The polarization of the crystal will have no effect in the immediate neighborhood of the impurity ion, and here the potential probably approaches the much larger value $V(r) = \mathrm{e}/r$. We should expect, then, that the ground-state energy is depressed below the theoretical estimate, Eq. (6.54), and this is what is observed experimentally.

B.   Scattering of Electrons (or Holes) by Ionized Impurities

Were it not for the presence of some free (conduction) electrons, the potential presented to a wandering electron by an ionized donor impurity would be that of Eq. (6.52). As in metals, the mobile electrons tend to screen the scattering center, and the potential assumes the form

$$V'(r) = \frac{\mathfrak{e}}{\varkappa r} \, e^{-r/r_0} \tag{6.56}$$

The screening radius for a nondegenerate electron gas is the Debye-Hueckel radius, given by

$$r_0{}^2 = \frac{\varkappa k T}{4\pi e^2 n'} \qquad n' = n + (n + N_m)\left(1 - \frac{n + N_m}{N_M}\right) \tag{6.57}$$

Here, N_m and N_M are the number of minority and majority impurities, that is, N_D and N_A for p-type and N_A and N_D for n-type specimens, respectively; n is the number of carriers, either electrons or holes. The Debye-Hueckel screening radius in semiconductors is considerably larger than the screening radius in metals. This enhanced range of the potential and the rather lower energy of the conduction electrons compared to the metallic case suggest that the Born approximation, which is invalid for scattering of electrons by ionized impurities in metals, must surely fail dismally here. In fact, this is not necessarily true, because the effective scattering potential is greatly reduced in the same way as the binding energy of the quasi-hydrogenic impurity. That is, the carriers are scattered by a long range, but extremely weak, potential.

Of course, the Born approximation will inevitably fail to give the correct answer for sufficiently slow electrons. As the temperature is lowered, these slow electrons will comprise an ever-increasing fraction of the Boltzmann distribution. Simultaneously, however, the screening radius decreases as $T^{\frac{1}{2}}$, so that the situation does not become serious until fairly low temperatures are attained. Phase-shift calculations show that for typical cases, Ge and Si, with roughly 10^{16} carriers, mobilities deduced by the Born approximation are correct down to temperatures of about 50°K. At lower temperatures the Born approximation leads to excessively large cross sections and, therefore, to unrealistically small mobilities.

In the Born approximation, the differential scattering cross section is given by Eq. (6.27). Substitution of Eq. (6.56) then leads to

$$\begin{aligned}
\sigma(\theta) &= 2\pi \left(\frac{2m^* \mathfrak{e}^2}{\varkappa \hbar^2}\right)^2 \left[(|\mathbf{k} - \mathbf{k'}|)^2 + \left(\frac{1}{r_0}\right)^2\right]^{-2} \\
&= 2\pi \left(\frac{2m^* \mathfrak{e}^2}{\varkappa \hbar^2}\right)^2 \left[\left(2k \sin \frac{\theta}{2}\right)^2 + \left(\frac{1}{r_0}\right)^2\right]^{-2}
\end{aligned} \tag{6.58}$$

where we have used the fact that the scattering is elastic and have also integrated over the azimuthal angle ϕ.

The relaxation time is given by Eq. (6.25).   The integral over θ presents no problem and one obtains

$$\frac{1}{\tau(\epsilon)} = \frac{\pi e^4 N_I}{2^{\frac{1}{2}}\varkappa^2 m^{*\frac{1}{2}}\epsilon^{\frac{3}{2}}} F(b) \tag{6.59}$$

where

$$F(b) = \ln(1 + b) - \frac{b}{1 + b} \qquad b = \frac{2m^*\epsilon\varkappa kT}{\pi e^2 n'\hbar^2} \tag{6.60}$$

and N_I in Eq. (6.59) denotes the total number of ionized impurities, both donors and acceptors.

C. Scattering by Neutral Impurities

With decreasing temperature, the probability for ionization of uncompensated impurities is diminished.   At sufficiently low temperatures there will generally exist a significant number of neutral impurity atoms.   The scattering of a conduction electron (or hole) by a neutral impurity is quite analogous to scattering of a slow electron by a hydrogen atom. The scattering cross section may be deduced by suitably scaling the results of Massey and Moisewitch, as was done by Erginsoy [14].   At electron energies roughly less than one-quarter of the ionization energy, the relaxation time is given to good approximation by

$$\frac{1}{\tau} = \frac{20N_n\hbar a^*}{m^*} \tag{6.61}$$

where a^* is the effective Bohr radius, Eq. (6.55).   Equation (6.61) is nearly always adequate.   At temperatures such that a fair fraction of the electrons have energies exceeding one-quarter of the ionization energy, the number of ionized impurities, even in nearly uncompensated samples, is so large that ionized-impurity scattering completely dominates over neutral-impurity scattering.

D. Scattering by Dislocations

It is evident from Fig. 6.1 that, in a covalent crystal near the core of an edge dislocation, the normal disposition of interatomic bonds cannot be preserved.   In the diamond- and zincblende-type crystals, of which Ge, Si, InSb, and numerous other semiconductors are members, an edge dislocation creates a broken, or "dangling," bond per unit cell.   No dangling bonds appear at screw dislocations, and the number of broken bonds is, in fact, proportional to the sine of the angle between the dislocation line and its Burgers vector.

Each dangling bond provides an attractive site for trapping of an extra electron, thereby completing the bond, but creating, however, a localized negative charge at the same time. Consequently, edge- or partly edge-type dislocations introduce acceptor levels in a crystal. The energy levels of these acceptor states fall near the middle of the energy gap; i.e., they are, in semiconductor parlance, deep acceptor levels.

The experimental evidence which supports this model is unequivocal. Plastic deformation of a well-annealed n-type specimen decreases the electron concentration and, in extreme cases, may even convert it to p-type as though by the addition of acceptor impurities. Simultaneously, plastic deformation of n-type specimens also decreases the mobility of the majority carriers.

In contrast, p-type material is nearly unaffected by plastic deformation, the hole concentration and mobility remaining relatively unaltered.

In an n-type sample, a dislocation line will become negatively charged as its deep acceptor levels are filled. This negative line charge will then be surrounded by an extensive cylindrical region of positive space charge. Conduction electrons are excluded from this cylindrical region, and such carriers as do approach are deflected from it. Thus, dislocation lines in n-type materials scatter electrons very effectively. This mechanism is not operative in plastically deformed p-type specimens.

Provided the cylindrical space-charge regions are well separated, their differential scattering cross section per unit length is given by the classical expression

$$\sigma(\theta) = R \sin \frac{\theta}{2} \tag{6.62}$$

where R is the radius of the space-charge cylinder. If R is large, and the distance between the cylinders is smaller than the mean free path of electrons in the annealed sample, one cannot calculate the relaxation time and mobility from the above expression. In that case, the presence of the cylinders distorts the flow of electrons so severely that the most reliable estimate of the mobility is obtained experimentally by an analog method, wherein one measures the conductivity of a two-dimensional medium suitably riddled by nonconducting holes.

Dislocations in semiconductors can also scatter carriers by virtue of their surrounding strain fields. This effect can be calculated by deriving a deformation potential from the known strain field. Scattering due to dislocation strain fields is totally unimportant in n-type materials but is, presumably, the dominant mechanism in p-type samples.

REFERENCES

1. Taylor, G. I.: *Proc. Roy. Soc. London*, **A145**: 362 (1934).
2. Orowan, E.: *Z. Physik*, **89**: 614, 635 (1934).
3. Maxwell, E.: *Phys. Rev.*, **78**: 477 (1950); C. A. Reynolds, B. Serin, W. H. Wright, and L. B. Nesbitt: *Phys. Rev.*, **78**: 487 (1950).
4. Houston, W. V.: *Phys. Rev.*, **34**: 279 (1929). L. Nordheim, *Ann. Physik*, **9**: 607 (1931).
5. Bardeen, J.: *Phys. Rev.*, **52**: 688 (1937).
6. Friedel, J.: *Phil. Mag.*, [7] **43**: 153 (1952); *Advan. Phys.*, **3**: 446 (1954).
7. Hunter, S. C., and F. R. N. Nabarro: *Proc. Roy. Soc. London*, **A220**: 542 (1953).
8. Harrison, W. A.: *J. Phys. Chem. Solids*, **5**: 44 (1958).
9. Bardeen, J., and W. Shockley: *Phys. Rev.*, **80**: 72 (1950).
10. Seeger, A.: *Can. J. Phys.*, **34**: 1219 (1956).
11. Howie, A.: *Phil. Mag.*, **5**: 251 (1960). See also A. Seeger and H. Statz; *Phys. Status Solids*, **2**: 857 (1962).
12. Allcock, G. R.: *Advan. Phys.*, **5**: 412 (1956); H. Froehlich; *Advan. Phys.*, **3**: 325 (1954).
13. Low, F., and D. Pines: *Phys. Rev.*, **91**: 193 (1953); T. Lee, F. Low, and D. Pines: *Phys. Rev.*, **90**: 297 (1953).
14. Erginsoy, C.: *Phys. Rev.*, **79**: 1013 (1950).

BIBLIOGRAPHY

Blatt, F. J.: Theory of Mobility of Electrons in Solids, *Solid State Phys.*, **4**: 199 (1957).

Friedel, J.: "Dislocations," Pergamon Press, New York, 1964.

Muto, T., and Y. Takagi: The Theory of Order-Disorder Transitions in Alloys, *Solid State Phys.*, **1**: 193 (1955).

Sham, L. J., and J. M. Ziman: The Electron-Phonon Interaction, *Solid State Phys.*, **15** (1964).

Van Bueren, H. G.: "Imperfections in Crystals," North Holland Publishing Company, Amsterdam, 1960.

Ziman, J. M.: "Electrons and Phonons," Oxford University Press, London, 1960.

7
Conductivity and Related Phenomena: Metals

7.1 INTRODUCTION

The words "metal" and "conductor" are almost synonymous, and justly so. Though the conductivity of metals varies over a wide range, it still far exceeds that of other substances. At the same time, one must beware of automatically associating a high mobility of the charge carriers with this large conductivity. The mobility in semiconductors often surpasses that in metals. It is the tremendous abundance of charge carriers rather than their inherent mobility that sets metals apart from other conductors.

In this chapter we collect the results of nearly all the previous ones, especially those of Chaps. 5 and 6. We shall now also make frequent reference to experiment to illustrate and substantiate theoretical deductions. However, to attempt a complete account of existing data on transport properties, while this might be useful from a practical, handbook point of view, would enlarge this book to several volumes and make for excruciatingly dull reading (and writing). Some tabulations have been inserted to allow an appreciation of the orders of magnitude and range of the physical quantities with which we shall now be concerned.   The experimental results have been selected to illustrate the general rather than to focus attention on peculiar eccentricities of the deviant.   At the same time, an effort has been made to avoid creating the wrong impression that all is now completely understood in this particular corner of the physical sciences.   We have also steered clear of detailed discussions of experimental techniques.   It is the author's firm conviction that these cannot be studied from books, however carefully written, but must be learned in the laboratory.

7.2   ELECTRICAL CONDUCTIVITY

A.   Resistivity Due to Lattice Scattering

At all but the lowest temperatures the resistivity of most pure metals is due predominantly to electron-phonon scattering.   In Chap. 5 we considered this relaxation process qualitatively and concluded that only at high temperatures could it be considered quasi-elastic; thus, in general, a correct calculation rests on the use of the variational, or equivalent, methods.   Therefore, the expression for ρ which must be the point of departure is Eq. (5.62).   In this equation we must substitute for $\mathfrak{S}(\mathbf{k},\mathbf{k}')$ the appropriate result derived in the preceding chapter, namely, Eq. (6.22).

Before embarking on the somewhat lengthy variational calculation of the resistivity of metals, we consider first the expression for the conductivity based on the relaxation-time approximation; moreover, we shall here assume spherical energy surfaces.

When $\mathbf{H} = 0$ and $\boldsymbol{\nabla} T = 0$ we have from Eq. (5.18)

$$\phi = \tau \mathbf{E} \cdot \mathbf{v} \tag{7.1}$$

The current density is given by

$$\mathbf{J} = \frac{e}{4\pi^3} \int f\mathbf{v} \, d\mathbf{k} = -\frac{e^2\mathbf{E}}{4\pi^3} \int \tau(\mathbf{v}\mathbf{v}) \frac{\partial f_0}{\partial \epsilon} \, d\mathbf{k}$$

$$= -\frac{e^2\mathbf{E}}{12\pi^3} \iint (\tau v^2) \frac{dS}{|\boldsymbol{\nabla}_\mathbf{k}\epsilon|} \frac{\partial f_0}{\partial \epsilon} \, d\epsilon = e^2\mathbf{E}\mathfrak{K}_1 \tag{7.2}$$

Here

$$\mathfrak{K}_n = -\frac{1}{4\pi^3} \int \tau(\mathbf{v}\mathbf{v})\epsilon^{n-1} \frac{\partial f_0}{\partial \epsilon} \, d\mathbf{k} \tag{7.3}$$

For spherical energy surfaces the integral reduces to

$$\mathfrak{K}_n = -\frac{4}{3m^*} \int \mathcal{N}(\epsilon)\tau(\epsilon)\epsilon^n \frac{\partial f_0}{\partial \epsilon} \, d\epsilon \tag{7.4}$$

and is clearly an integral of the form of Eq. (3.17). In the degenerate limit it may be evaluated as a power series in kT/η.

When the lowest nonvanishing term of the series is retained, one obtains the well-known result

$$\sigma = \frac{J}{E} = \frac{n_0 e^2 \tau(\eta)}{m^*} \tag{7.5}$$

In some cases $\mathcal{N}(\epsilon)$, $\tau(\epsilon)$, $\partial\epsilon/\partial k$, or several of these parameters, may be very sensitive functions of the energy in the immediate vicinity of the Fermi energy. Then the next-higher term of the Taylor expansion of Eq. (7.4) could contribute significantly to the final result. It is convenient to define

$$\sigma(\epsilon) = \frac{e^2}{4\pi^3} \int \frac{\tau(\mathbf{vv})}{|\nabla_{\mathbf{k}}\epsilon|} d\mathbf{S} \tag{7.6}$$

the conductivity associated with electrons on the energy surface ϵ. Applying the expansion (3.18) we have

$$\sigma = \sigma(\eta) + \frac{\pi^2}{6}(kT)^2 \left[\frac{\partial^2\sigma(\epsilon)}{\partial\epsilon^2}\right]_\eta \tag{7.7}$$

One might expect the second term in Eq. (7.7) to be prominent primarily at high temperatures; in some situations that is what seems to occur. For example, the temperature dependence of the resistivity of transition metals at high temperatures may be explained within this framework. However, in some few conductors, generally alloys, the second term in Eq. (7.7) provides the dominant temperature dependence even at low temperatures.

Suppose the band structure is such that two bands overlap at the Fermi energy. Assume that one of these, the conduction band (s band), is of normal width, with effective mass roughly equal to the free-electron mass, while the other band (d band, we shall call it) is rather narrow and has a large effective mass $m_d^* \gg m_s^* \approx m$. The corresponding density-of-states curves are shown in Fig. 7.1. From these curves we see that $\mathcal{N}_s(\epsilon)$ is relatively small and is a fairly slowly varying function of the energy; $\mathcal{N}_d(\epsilon)$ on the other hand is large and depends critically on ϵ near $\epsilon = \eta$. Though $\mathcal{N}_d(\eta) \gg \mathcal{N}_s(\eta)$, it does not follow that the electrons in the narrow d band are the important charge carriers. On the contrary, their large effective mass so severely limits their mobility that $\sigma_d < \sigma_s$. Even so, the presence of the narrow d band plays a major role in determining σ_s.

An electron in the s band near the Fermi surface can be scattered into either another state in the s band or into an unoccupied state in the

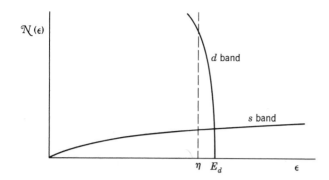

Fig. 7.1   The density-of-states curves for two overlapping bands.

d band.   Since the density of states in the d band greatly exceeds that in the s band, s-d scattering would be expected to, and indeed does, dominate over s-s scattering.   Since the transition probability is proportional to the density of final states, one is led to $\tau(\epsilon) \propto [\mathcal{N}_d(\epsilon)]^{-1}$.   If, then, $\mathcal{N}_d$ is a rapidly varying function of the energy, the second term in Eq. (7.7) will play an important role.

In an alloy at low temperatures the resistivity is largely due to scattering by stationary imperfections, a mechanism which contains no explicit temperature dependence.   Nevertheless, under the conditions just discussed, imperfection scattering can lead to a temperature dependence of the conductivity.   If, for example, we assume that s-d scattering only need be considered, then, with a d band of standard form, the resistivity is given by

$$\rho = \rho(\eta)\left[1 - \frac{\pi^2}{6}\left(\frac{kT}{E_d - \eta_0} \right)^2 \right] \tag{7.8}$$

where E_d is the energy at the edge of the d band.   The presence of the narrow, overlapping d band thus leads to a quadratic decrease of the resistivity with temperature.   Figure 7.2 shows the resistivity of several uranium alloys as a function of temperature; the behavior suggests that the above mechanism may be important here.

In most cases, however, terms in $(kT/\eta)^2$ are negligible; and in what follows we shall neglect all but the first nonvanishing term in the usual expansion of Fermi integrals.

The first step in a proper variational calculation of the resistivity is the selection of a trial function.   Here we allow ourselves a swindle, as outlined in the last paragraph of Chap. 5.   We know that at high tem-

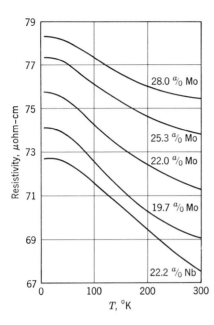

Fig. 7.2 The resistivities of several γ-phase uranium-molybdenum alloys as functions of temperature. Note the decrease of resistivity with temperature, particularly in the low-temperature range. [*From F. J. Blatt, J. Phys. Chem. Solids,* **17**: 180 (1961).]

peratures, and also at sufficiently low temperatures where impurity scattering dominates, $\phi(\mathbf{k})$ is given by Eq. (5.18), and we shall use a function of that form in our variational expression. We also need to know the shape of the Fermi surface so as to evaluate $\mathbf{v_k}$. Even when this is known, the evaluation of the variational integrals can usually be performed only with the aid of high-speed computers. The obvious escape from that unpleasant task is to assume a spherical surface at the start and replace $\mathbf{v_k}$ by $\hbar\mathbf{k}/m^*$. Thus, our trial function takes the form

$$\phi(\mathbf{k}) = \mathbf{k} \cdot \mathbf{E} = Ek_x$$

where we have taken the electric field along the x direction. Since a constant factor in the trial function must cancel in the numerator and denominator of Eq. (5.62), we further simplify the trial function to

$$\phi(\mathbf{k}) = k_x \tag{7.9}$$

The justification for Eq. (7.9) is rather pragmatic. It allows us to proceed with the calculation analytically and leads to results in surprisingly good agreement with experiment, both as regards the temperature dependence of the resistivity and its magnitude.

We now proceed to evaluate Eq. (5.62).   The denominator is

$$\frac{e^2}{16\pi^6}\left(\int \frac{\hbar k_x^2}{m^*}\frac{\partial f_0}{\partial \epsilon}\,d\mathbf{k}\right)^2 = \frac{e^2\hbar^2}{16\pi^6 m^{*2}}\left(\iint k_x^2 \frac{d\mathbf{S}}{|\nabla_{\mathbf{k}}\epsilon|}\frac{\partial f_0}{\partial \epsilon}\,d\epsilon\right)^2$$

$$= \frac{e^2}{16\pi^6\hbar^2}\left(\iint k\frac{\partial f_0}{\partial \epsilon}\frac{d\mathbf{S}\,d\epsilon}{3}\right)^2$$

$$= \left(\frac{ek_0\mathcal{Q}_0}{12\pi^3\hbar}\right)^2 \qquad (7.10)$$

where $\mathcal{Q}_0$ is the area of the Fermi surface.

To evaluate the numerator, we replace $\mathfrak{S}(\mathbf{k},\mathbf{k}')$ by Eq. (6.22). The two terms, corresponding to absorption and emission of a phonon, will lead to nearly identical expressions in Eq. (5.62); the only difference appears in the energy delta function and in the factors n_q and $n_q + 1$, respectively.   We use an abbreviated form for $\mathfrak{S}(\mathbf{k},\mathbf{k}')$, namely,

$$\mathfrak{S}(\mathbf{k},\mathbf{k}') = G(\mathbf{s})(\mathbf{s}\cdot\boldsymbol{\xi})^2\frac{n_q}{\omega_q}\delta(\epsilon_{\mathbf{k}'} - \epsilon_{\mathbf{k}} - \hbar\omega_q)$$

$$+ G(\mathbf{s})(\mathbf{s}\cdot\boldsymbol{\xi})^2\frac{n_{q'}+1}{\omega_{q'}}\delta(\epsilon_{\mathbf{k}'} - \epsilon_{\mathbf{k}} + \hbar\omega_{q'}) \quad (7.11)$$

where $\mathbf{s} = \mathbf{k} - \mathbf{k}'$.   Concentrating our attention on phonon absorption we have, in the numerator of Eq. (5.62),

$$(\phi,\mathbf{C}_a\phi)$$

$$= \frac{1}{2kT}\iint (s_x)^2(\mathbf{s}\cdot\boldsymbol{\xi})^2 G(\mathbf{s})f_0(\epsilon)[1 - f_0(\epsilon')]\frac{n_q}{\omega_q}\delta(\epsilon_{\mathbf{k}'} - \epsilon_{\mathbf{k}} - \hbar\omega_q)\,d\mathbf{k}\,d\mathbf{k}'$$

$$(7.12)$$

where, of course, $\mathbf{s}$ must satisfy the selection rule

$$\mathbf{s} = \mathbf{q} + \mathbf{K} \qquad (6.13)$$

We next apply the usual technique for integration over $\mathbf{k}$ space, replacing $\int d\mathbf{k}$ by $\iint d\mathbf{S}\,d\epsilon/|\nabla_{\mathbf{k}}\epsilon|$.   One integration, say that over $d\epsilon'$, removes the energy delta function.   In the evaluation of the second energy integral we recall that $f_0(\epsilon)[1 - f_0(\epsilon)]$ is nonvanishing over only a very small energy interval near the Fermi energy.   Since ϵ' differs from ϵ by a small increment $\hbar\omega$, the product which appears in Eq. (7.12) will behave similarly.   The remaining factors in that integrand are, by comparison, slowly varying functions of the energy and may be considered constants for the purpose of integration.   Thus, the second energy integration reduces to a constant times the following expression,

$$\int f_0(\epsilon)[1 - f_0(\epsilon')]\, d\mathbf{k} = \iint \frac{kT}{(e^y + 1)(1 + e^{-(y+z)})} \frac{d\mathbf{S}\, dy}{\hbar\mathbf{v}} \tag{7.13}$$

where $z = \hbar\omega/kT$ and $y = (\epsilon - \eta)/kT$. Although the integral over y should extend only over the range $-\eta/kT$ to $+\infty$, the error introduced by extending the range to $-\infty$ is negligible (see Sec. 3.11). The integral is elementary and we have

$$\int f_0(\epsilon)[1 - f_0(\epsilon')]\, d\mathbf{k} = \frac{kTz}{1 - e^{-z}} \int \frac{d\mathbf{S}}{\hbar\mathbf{v}} \tag{7.14}$$

Equation (7.12) now reduces to

$$(\phi, \mathbf{C}_a\phi) = \frac{1}{2kT} \iint (s_x)^2 (\mathbf{s} \cdot \boldsymbol{\xi})^2 \frac{G(\mathbf{s})}{\hbar(e^z - 1)(1 - e^{-z})} \frac{d\mathbf{S}}{\mathbf{v}} \frac{d\mathbf{S}'}{\mathbf{v}'} \tag{7.15}$$

where we have assumed that $\mathfrak{n}_q$ is given by the equilibrium Bose-Einstein distribution

$$\mathfrak{n}_q^0 = [e^{\hbar\omega_q/kT} - 1]^{-1}$$

This Bloch hypothesis neglects the possibility that the phonon distribution may be perturbed by interaction with a nonequilibrium electron distribution. We shall return later to consider the validity of this assumption.

Before we carry the integration to its bitter end, we pause here to examine the variational integral corresponding to electron scattering by phonon emission. The difference between $(\phi, \mathbf{C}_a\phi)$ and $(\phi, \mathbf{C}_e\phi)$ is restricted to two factors. First, the sign in front of $\hbar\omega$ in the delta function is reversed. Therefore, in place of Eqs. (7.13) and (7.14) we shall have instead

$$\int f_0(\epsilon)[1 - f_0(\epsilon')]\, d\mathbf{k} = \iint \frac{kT}{(e^y + 1)(1 + e^{-(y-z)})} \frac{d\mathbf{S}\, dy}{\hbar\mathbf{v}} = \frac{kTz}{(e^z - 1)} \int \frac{d\mathbf{S}}{\hbar\mathbf{v}}$$

$$\tag{7.14a}$$

Second, we must replace $\mathfrak{n}_q^0 = [\exp(z) - 1]^{-1}$ by

$$\mathfrak{n}_q^0 + 1 = \frac{e^z}{e^z - 1} = \frac{1}{1 - e^{-z}}$$

Evidently the product of exponential factors which appears is again $\{[\exp(z) - 1][1 - \exp(-z)]\}^{-1}$. Thus, $(\phi, \mathbf{C}_e\phi) = (\phi, \mathbf{C}_a\phi) = \frac{1}{2}(\phi, \mathbf{C}\phi)$.

At this point, we must specify the function $G(\mathbf{s})$ before we can proceed further; the Fermi surface has already been assumed spherical, this being the only shape consistent with our trial function (7.9).

We now divide the remaining integration into two portions, one for N and the other for U processes. For N processes, only longitudinal phonons participate; that is, $(\mathbf{s} \cdot \boldsymbol{\xi})^2 = (\mathbf{q} \cdot \boldsymbol{\xi})^2 = q^2$. We also replace, as in the evaluation of the denominator of Eq. (5.62), s_x^2 by $s^2/3 = q^2/3$, the average over a sphere. The result of the integration is

$$(\phi, \mathbf{C}\phi)_N = \frac{k_0^2}{6\pi^4 v_F^2 \hbar} \int_0^{q_0} \frac{q^5 G(q)\, dq}{(1 - e^{-z})(e^z - 1)} \tag{7.16}$$

Here the integration terminates at the maximum phonon wave vector

$$q_0 = \left(\frac{6\pi^2}{\Omega}\right)^{\frac{1}{3}}$$

the radius of the Debye sphere.

The evaluation of the double integral for U processes is rather more involved. Ziman [1] has shown that it can also be reduced to the same form as Eq. (7.16), provided a function $G_U(q)$ is suitably defined.

If we now insist on employing the "correct" function $G(q)$, characterized principally by the factor $\mathfrak{F}(|\mathbf{s}|r_s)$ in Eq. (6.21), the final integration must be performed numerically. This labor has been undertaken by Ziman [1], and we shall presently return to discuss his results. A simpler result can be extracted from Eq. (7.16) by resorting to Bloch's second assumption. Umklapp processes are neglected altogether, and for N processes it is assumed that

$$G(s) = G(O) = \frac{4\pi}{9} \frac{\eta^2}{NM} \tag{7.17}$$

Now $G(O)$ can be taken outside the integral in Eq. (7.16). This procedure clearly overestimates scattering by N processes, since $G(s)$ decreases quite rapidly as s increases. This error will be offset in part, at least, by the total neglect of U processes. In any event, though the numerical results must now be suspect, the temperature dependence of the resistivity should be essentially correct.

We collect the various fragments of the calculation, and obtain

$$\rho_i(T) = 4\Re \left(\frac{T}{\Theta}\right)^5 \mathscr{J}_5\left(\frac{\Theta}{T}\right) \tag{7.18}$$

Here

$$\Re = \frac{3\hbar q_0^6 G(0)}{16 e^2 k_0^4 v_F^2 k \Theta_D} \tag{7.19}$$

and

$$\mathscr{J}_5(x) = \int_0^x \frac{z^5 \, dz}{(e^z - 1)(1 - e^{-z})} \tag{7.20}$$

Equations (7.18) to (7.20) comprise the Bloch-Grüneisen formula, which reproduces the temperature dependence of the ideal resistivity of many metals with surprising faithfulness.

A convenient scheme for displaying $\rho_i(T)$ is through the reduced resistivity defined by the ratio

$$\mathfrak{r}(\mathfrak{t}) = \frac{\rho_i(T)}{\rho_i(\Theta)}$$

which, according to Eq. (7.18), should be a universal function of the reduced temperature $\mathfrak{t} = T/\Theta$. Representative results are shown in Fig. 7.3.

In general, the integral $\mathscr{J}_5(x)$ must be evaluated numerically. Its values are given in Table 7.1. There are, however, two limiting cases for which simple analytic expressions are readily obtained by suitable expansions.

At high temperatures, $\Theta/T = x \ll 1$, the variable in the integrand of Eq. (7.20) is also restricted to small values. Expansion of the exponentials gives, to lowest order,

$$\mathscr{J}_5(x) = \int_0^x z^3 \, dz = \tfrac{1}{4}x^4 \qquad x \ll 1 \tag{7.21}$$

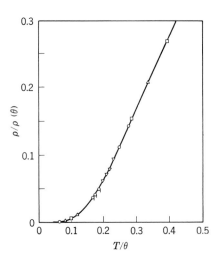

Fig. 7.3 The reduced resistivity $\mathfrak{r}$—$[\rho_i(T)/\rho_i(\Theta)]$—as a function of the reduced temperature $\mathfrak{t}$—$[T/\Theta]$—according to the Bloch-Grüneisen relation, Eq. (7.18). Experimental points for a number of metallic conductors demonstrate the generally excellent agreement between theory and experiment. $\triangle$ Au, $\Theta = 175$; $\square$ Na, $\Theta = 202$; $\bigcirc$ Cu, $\Theta = 333$; $\triangledown$ Al, $\Theta = 395$; $\lhd$ Ni, $\Theta = 472$. (*After E. U. Condon and H. Odishaw, "Handbook of Physics," p. 475, McGraw-Hill Book Company, New York, 1958.*)

Table 7-1   The Function $_n(x)$ **for** n = **3, 4, 5, and 7**

x^n ╲ n	3	4	5	7
1.0	0.4798	0.3172	0.23662	0.15665
1.2	0.6788	0.5365	0.47907	0.45534
1.5	1.0269	1.0079	1.1199	1.6538
2	1.706	2.2016	3.2293	8.3763
3	3.211	5.9632	12.771	72.010
4	4.579	10.7293	29.488	281.75
5	5.614	15.3671	50.263	705.56
6	6.3033	19.1210	70.873	1,328.9
8	6.9581	23.5874	101.48	2,798.8
10	7.1505	25.2812	116.38	3,972.1
13	7.2061	25.9273	123.14	4,809.8
20	7.2123	25.9639	124.42	5,078.2
∞	7.2124	25.9757	124.43	5,082.1

When $x \gg 1$ we may extend the upper limit to infinity, since the contribution to $\mathscr{J}_5(x)$ from large values of z will be quite small.   Partial integration gives

$$\mathscr{J}_5(x) = -\left.\frac{x^5}{e^x - 1}\right|_0^\infty + 5\int_0^\infty \frac{z^4}{e^z - 1}\,dz$$

The first term vanishes at the two limits, 0 and ∞.   The remaining integral is

$$\int_0^\infty \frac{z^4}{e^z - 1}\,dz = 4!\sum_{n=1}^\infty \frac{1}{n^5} = 4!\zeta(5)$$

where $\zeta(y)$ is the Riemann zeta function of y.   Thus,

$$\mathscr{J}_5(x) = 5!\zeta(5) = 124.4 \qquad x \gg 1 \tag{7.22}$$

From Eqs. (7.18) and (7.21)

$$\rho_i(T) = \frac{\mathfrak{R}T}{\Theta} \qquad T \gg \Theta \tag{7.23}$$

Equation (7.23) predicts the well-known linear increase of ρ_i with temperature at high temperatures.   Actually, Eq. (7.23) is a reasonably good approximation down to temperatures as low as $T = 2\Theta/3$ ($x = \frac{3}{2}$), where the error is only 10 percent.   Since the characteristic temperatures of most metals are below 400°K, Eq. (7.23) is usually valid at room temperature and above.

At low temperatures, Eqs. (7.18) and (7.22) combine to yield

$$\rho_i(T) = 497.6 \Re \left(\frac{T}{\Theta}\right)^5 \qquad T \ll \Theta \tag{7.24}$$

Here the Bloch theory predicts a T^5 law for the ideal resistivity. This, as well as the linear dependence of $\rho_i(T)$ at high temperatures, was deduced from simple physical arguments in Chap. 5.

The Debye temperature Θ appears naturally as an important parameter in the expression for the ideal resistivity. Its value character-izes the degree of excitation of the vibrational modes of the lattice at any temperature, and, consequently, the probability of electron-phonon scattering. It follows that measurements of ρ_i versus T could serve as a means for determining the Debye temperature. One finds that the characteristic temperature Θ_D, deduced from specific heats, does not, in general, agree with Θ_R, the value obtained by fitting $\rho_i(T)$ to the Bloch-Grüneisen relation, although the discrepancies between Θ_D and Θ_R are frequently fairly small [2]. Table 7.2 shows typical values for a number of metals.

It is not difficult to find the cause for these discrepancies. First, and foremost, is the simplification represented by Eq. (7.17). As we remarked then, the true behavior of $G(s)$ is markedly different from the assumed. Ziman, in his numerical evaluation of $\rho_i(T)$, used a func-tion $G(s)$ which, though not identical to the Bardeen formula, bears close resemblance to it. In the case of the electrical resistivity, the result of his computation is essentially the same as Eq. (7.18), except that the effective Θ is now slightly less than the Debye (specific-heat) temperature.

Another simplifying approximation introduced at the very outset relates to the form of the "variational trial function." True variational calculations by Kohler [3] and Sondheimer [4] have demonstrated that, though near $T = \Theta/10$ the Bloch-Grüneisen formula overestimates $\rho_i(T)$ by about 10 percent, Eq. (7.18) is correct at both high and low temper-

Table 7.2 The Debye Temperatures of Several Metals Determined from Calorimetric (Θ_D) and Resistivity (Θ_R) Measurements

	Substance							
	Li	Na	Cu	Ag	Au	Pb	Al	W
Θ_R	363	202	333	203	175	86	395	333
Θ_D	340–430	159	330–310	212	168–186	82–88	385	357–305

atures. Sondheimer also considered the validity of Matthiessen's rule and concluded that deviations therefrom should not exceed about 1 percent of the residual resistivity ρ_r. The deviation from Matthiessen's rule is most pronounced in that temperature range where $\rho_i(T) \approx \rho_r$. It must be remembered, however, that Sondheimer concerned himself only with the idealized case in which phonon and electron spectra are assumed unaffected by the introduction of impurities into the crystal.

Finally, the reduction of the variational integral for U processes to a form similar to Eq. (7.16) is not possible at low temperatures. The difficulty is that if the Fermi surface does not touch the zone boundaries, the phonon wave vector in U processes must exceed a minimum value $\mathbf{q}'$, as shown schematically in Fig. 6.11. For N processes, of course, there is no lower limit to the phonon wave vector in phonon-electron interactions. At very low temperatures, then, the number of phonons which contribute to U processes will decrease roughly exponentially; that is,

$$n_{\mathbf{q}'}^0 \approx e^{-\hbar\omega_{\mathbf{q}'}/kT} = e^{-\Theta^*/T}$$

where $\Theta^*/\Theta = q'/q_0$. The dominant temperature dependence of ρ_U at low temperatures should, therefore, be given by the same exponential factor. The parameter Θ^* may be estimated from the number of conduction electrons and the crystal structure. For a body-centered monovalent metal $\Theta^* \approx \Theta/7$. Thus, at temperatures below about $\Theta/10$, $\rho_U(T)$ should decrease far more rapidly than the Bloch theory predicts. Since various estimates indicate that at high temperatures ρ_U is rather in excess of ρ_N, this exponential deviation from Eq. (7.18) should be readily observable.

In fact, no such deviation has been detected. In alkali metals, where one would expect to observe this behavior, the velocity of sound for transverse modes in the directions of $\mathbf{q}'$ is exceptionally small. Thus, the characteristic temperature for these particular modes is especially low and U processes persist to temperatures much lower than one would at first suspect. Accurate data on ρ_i at very low temperatures are difficult to obtain, because here the residual resistivity so exceeds the ideal that small deviations from the theoretical behavior of $\rho_i(T)$ could well remain hidden. The exponential decay of U processes at low temperatures has, however, been observed in studies of the thermoelectric effect [5].

The characteristic temperature Θ_R may be defined in several ways, for example, by taking the ratio of the ideal resistivity at high and low temperatures. According to Eqs. (7.23) and (7.24),

$$\Theta_R = T_L \left[497.6 \frac{T_L}{T_H} \frac{\rho_L}{\rho_H} \right]^{\frac{1}{4}} \tag{7.25}$$

Alternatively, one may relate Θ_R to the temperature coefficient of resistivity at high and low temperatures. Whichever method is employed (and they do not lead to identical results by any means), one finds that, as with Θ_D, the characteristic temperature is itself a function of the temperature. Although Θ_R and Θ_D follow much the same pattern, Θ_R generally varies over a wider range, as shown in Fig. 7.4.

Next, we consider the quantitative predictions of the Bloch theory. Here we first restrict our attention to the monovalent metals, since we assumed spherical Fermi surfaces throughout the calculation. Comparison with experiment should be most favorable for the alkali metals, somewhat poorer for the close-packed noble metals, and none too good for the polyvalent metals. The resistivities at 273°K of a number of metals are given in Table 7.3; the mean values are shown for anisotropic conductors.

We have previously remarked that the high-temperature approximation (7.23) is fairly accurate to temperatures as low as $2\Theta/3$. We now rewrite Eq. (7.23) in slightly different form, namely,

$$\rho_i(T) = \frac{(3\pi^2)^{\frac{1}{3}}\pi^3\hbar^3}{4e^2k} \frac{1}{n_a^{\frac{2}{3}}\Theta^2 M(\Omega)^{\frac{1}{3}}} T \qquad (7.26)$$

In the above expression nearly all electronic parameters, for example, the effective mass and Fermi energy, are conspicuous by their absence. They appear in such a way in the relaxation time τ (which is a well-defined parameter at high temperatures) as to cancel each other

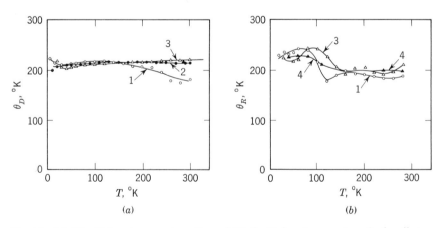

(a)   *(b)*

Fig. 7.4 *(a)* The Debye temperature Θ_D and *(b)* the Debye temperature Θ_R for silver. The numerals refer to results of several methods for extracting Θ_D and Θ_R from the experimental data. [*From F. M. Kelly, Can. J. Phys.*, **32** : 86, 87 (1954).]

Table 7-3   Ideal Resistivities at 273°K of a Number of Monovalent, Divalent, Trivalent, and Transition Metals
The last column gives a comparison of the experimental and theoretical—Eq. (7.26)—results

Element	Valence	Resistivity at 273°K, μohm-cm	ρ_{exp}/ρ_{theor}
Li	1	8.5	1.40
Na	1	4.27	0.77
K	1	6.3	0.80
Rb	1	11.6	1.31
Cs	1	19.0	1.50
Cu	1	1.55	1.87
Ag	1	1.50	1.16
Au	1	2.04	3.26
Be	2	2.78	7.33
Cd	2	6.73	8.05
Mg	2	3.94	3.23
Zn	2	5.45	5.75
Al	3	2.50	3.62
In	3	8.2	8.2
Co	Trans	5.2	14.7
Cr	Trans	15.0	34.2
Fe	Trans	8.71	26.0
Mo	Trans	5.03	25.2
Ni	Trans	6.58	9.9
Pd	Trans	9.77	13.0
Pt	Trans	9.81	17.2
Ta	Trans	12.4	36.9
Ti	Trans	42	81.0
V	Trans	18.2	48.6
W	Trans	4.89	35.2

and the effective mass m^* in the expression

$$\rho = \frac{m^*}{n_0 e^2 \tau} \tag{7.27}$$

This cancellation occurs, however, only by virtue of the special assumptions relating to the electron-phonon interaction that lead to Eq. (7.23).

Theory and experiment are compared in the fourth column of Table 7.3, where we have listed the ratio ρ_{exp}/ρ_{theor}.   For the monovalent metals the agreement is quite satisfactory, especially in view of the many approximations which paved the road to Eq. (7.26). Still, the theory nearly always predicts rather smaller values than those observed. This discrepancy can be traced largely to one assumption, namely, Eq. (7.17). The numerical work of Ziman, to which we have previously referred, leads to high-temperature resistivities roughly 1.6 times as large as Eq. (7.26). The source of remaining discrepancies is presumably hidden in the details of the band structure and the uncertainty in Θ_R.

As expected, the Bloch theory is less reliable when applied to the polyvalent metals. Still, in order of magnitude—which is about all one has a right to look to—there is adequate agreement for the most part. The one outstanding exception is the group of transition metals. These we shall examine in Secs. 7.5 and 7.6.

B. Residual Resistivity

As the temperature is lowered toward absolute zero, the resistivity of normal metals approaches a constant value, the residual resistivity. The notorious exceptions to this rule are the superconducting metals and alloys, whose resistivity vanishes altogether below a certain critical temperature T_c. In a superconducting torus a persistent current can be, and has been, maintained for days and months. This phenomenon has nothing to do with the decrease in the ideal resistivity as electron-phonon scattering is reduced. On the contrary, it was known even some years before an adequate theory of superconductivity had been proposed that the electron-phonon interaction played a crucial role in the super-conducting transition. Indeed, as a general rule it is poorly conducting metals, such as lead, mercury, tin, zinc, and niobium, that generally become superconductive, for it is in these materials that the electron-phonon interaction is strong, limiting the conductivity above the transition temperature.

The residual resistivity of normal metals arises from scattering of conduction electrons by stationary imperfections. It is such a sensitive measure of the perfection of a specimen that in current practice the over-all purity and perfection of a metal crystal are often specified by quoting its resistance ratio, $p = R_{273°}/R_{4.2°}$. Copper, 99.999 percent pure, available commercially, has a resistance ratio of about 1,000. Higher values of p may be achieved by further purification through additional zone-refining processes and preparation of the specimen in single-crystal form. It was only when such ultrapure metals became available that much of the recent fundamental progress in our understanding of metals could occur.

Residual resistivity due to point imperfections A discussion of the relaxation times associated with various kinds of stationary imperfections is contained in the previous chapter. We shall concern ourselves here primarily with the experimental results. Extensive measurements, encompassing the work of many years and many countries, have provided data on the change in resistivity due to impurities in metals.

Alloying affects the resistivity in several ways. First, the impurities represent local disturbances in an otherwise perfect lattice (except, of course, for the phonon imperfections). Second, alloying will, in general, modify the band structure, change the Fermi energy, and change the density of states and the effective mass, parameters which determine, in part, the ideal resistivity of a metal. Third, alloying often affects the elastic constants; consequently, the lattice-vibration spectrum is modified and this, in turn, must reflect upon the ideal resistivity.

Resistivity studies of dilute alloys normally are aimed at the determination of the residual resistivity due to a particular impurity and the determination of deviations from Matthiessen's rule. The latter states (see page 114) that the total resistivity is the sum of the resistivities due to scattering by the impurities and the ideal resistivity of the pure metal. Significant deviations from Matthiessen's rule are often observed. Some of these deviations may well reflect on the validity of the basic assumptions involved in the calculation of ρ_i; it is, however, certain that the second and third factors mentioned in the preceding paragraph also contribute substantially.

By far the most important effect on the resistivity of dilute alloys is that mentioned first. Experimentally, it is found that the resistivity of monovalent metals increases with alloying in proportion to the solute concentration c, provided $c \ll 1$, and that the increase per atomic percent of solute depends in a systematic way on the location of the solute atom in the periodic table. Linde's rule

$$\Delta\rho_r = a + bZ'^2 \tag{7.28}$$

where $\Delta\rho_r$ is the residual resistivity per atomic percent solute, reflects the observations reasonably well. Here a and b are constants which depend on the solvent metal and on the row of the periodic table to which the impurity atom belongs; Z' is the difference in valence between the solute and solvent atoms. We pointed out already [see Eq. (6.27)] that a Z'^2 dependence is expected. The more refined phase-shift calculations, though no longer predicting an exact Z'^2 behavior, lead to roughly the same dependence on Z'. The numerical results of such calculations, especially when the effect of lattice distortion in the immediate vicinity of the impurity is taken into account, are in good agreement with observation (see Fig. 7.5). Table 7.4 summarizes the experimental results.

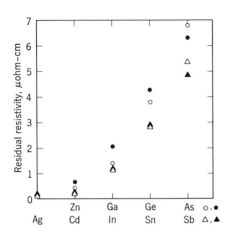

Fig. 7.5 Experimental and calculated residual resistivities of copper due to a one-atomic-percent impurity concentration. $\bigcirc$, $\triangle$ experimental points; ●, ▲ calculated results.

The resistivities of vacancies and interstitials have been estimated theoretically by treating these defects as substitutional impurities in a free-electron gas on a background of a fixed homogeneous positive charge distribution (the metal ions). The calculated results are of considerable practical interest because vacancies and interstitials are produced prolifically when a metallic sample is subjected to radiation by energetic particles—for example, neutrons from a reactor, or ions from an accelerator. The extent of radiation damage is most conveniently determined by resistivity measurements, and recovery (annealing) of irradiated material may also be followed by similar means. Although the results of different workers are not in complete agreement, the best current estimate for these imperfections in copper is

$$\Delta\rho_{\text{vac}} = 1.0 - 1.5 \ \mu\text{ohm-cm/atomic percent}$$

$$\Delta\rho_{\text{int}} = 0.5 - 1.0 \ \mu\text{ohm-cm/atomic percent}$$

Resistivity due to plastic deformation; dislocations It has been common knowledge since the turn of the century that plastic deformation generally increases the resistivity of pure metals. Further, a sample which has been drawn through dies or suffered cold-rolling will show a marked reduction in resistivity if it is annealed at a sufficiently high temperature.

Only part of the resistivity increase due to plastic deformation is attributable to scattering of electrons by dislocations, the extended defects responsible for and generated by plastic flow. This conclusion is based on the results of annealing studies.

Following cold-work at low temperatures, the conductivity recovers in several fairly well-defined temperature ranges. From a knowledge of the temperature at which recovery occurs and of the annealing kinetics,

Table 7-4   Residual Resistivities per Atomic Percent Solute for Various Solutes in Eleven Solvent Metals, μohm-cm

Impurity \ Host element	Cu	Ag	Au	Al	Mg	Pb	Ti	Fe	Ni	Pd	Pt
Ag	0.2		0.36	1.1	0.75	0.11				1.5	
Al	0.95	1.95	1.87		2.0		12	5.8			
As	6.7	8.5	8.0								
Au	0.55	0.4						4.9		1.0	
B	1.4										
Be	0.65										
Bi		7.3	6.5		8.8	0.96					
Ca	0.3			0.3							
Ce					9.1						
Cd	0.3	0.4	0.63	0.5	0.68	3.02					
Co	6.9		6.1		0.13			0.6			
Cr	4.0		4.3	8.5				5.0	6.4		
Cu		0.1	0.45	0.75			15	6.8	1.5		
Fe	9.3		7.9						6.8		
Ga	1.4	2.35	2.2	0.3							
Ge	3.7	5.5	5.2	0.8							
Hg	1.0	0.8	0.44			2.3					
In	1.1	1.8	1.4		2.0	1.13					
Ir	6.1										1.5
Li				0.94	0.75						
Mg	0.8	0.5	1.3	0.45		4.0					
Mn	2.9	1.6	2.4	6.5	3.8			5.9	2.5		
Mo								5.8			
Nb							1.8				
Ni	1.1	1.1	0.8	0.1				3.2			
P	7.0							6.0			
Pb	3.3	4.6	3.9	1.3	6.3						
Pd	0.95	0.45	0.4								0.6
Pt	2.0	1.5	1.0							0.7	
Rh	4.4		4.15								0.7
Sb	5.5	7.25	6.8			1.24					
Si	3.1			0.7				6.9			
Sn	3.1	4.3	3.36		4.8	0.29	17				
Te	8.0				3.2						
Ti	16		13	5.5							
Tl		2.2	1.9			0.635					
V				8.0				4.6			
W								4.8			
Zn	0.3	0.6	0.95	0.22							
Zr				4.5			1.8				

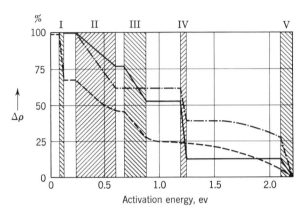

Fig. 7.6 Recovery stages of the residual resistivity in plastically deformed, quenched, and irradiated pure copper. Index: — recovery after deformation; — · — recovery after quenching; — — — recovery after irradiation. (*After A. N. Gerritsen, Metallic Conductivity, in "Encyclopedia of Physics," vol. XIX, p. 203, Springer-Verlag OHG, Berlin, 1956.*)

it is possible to assign activation energies to these thermally activated processes.   Comparison of the activation energies with those determined from annealing studies of irradiated samples shows several interesting similarities (see Fig. 7.6).   Although there still remains some uncertainty with respect to the finer details of the recovery steps, the following scheme appears to be widely accepted.

Stage 1.   This recovery stage is observed in samples irradiated near liquid-helium temperature.   Reduction in resistivity is believed due to recombination of vacancies and interstitials which are in close proximity to each other.

Stage 2.   This stage is probably the result of recombination of vacancies and interstitials distributed at random within the sample and of annealing of interstitials by diffusion to dislocation lines and internal boundaries that can act as interstitial sinks.

Stage 3.   Here the activation energy agrees closely with the migration energy of vacancies as deduced from quenching and self-diffusion experiments.   The resistivity recovery is presumably related to annealing of remaining vacancies.   It is possible that these do not all disappear at sinks, but coagulate internally to form small clusters.

Stages 4 and 5.   These recovery steps are most pronounced in plastically deformed samples and are presumably related to the annealing of dislocations, most probably through the mechanism of dislocation climb.

The presence of interstitials and vacancies in cold-worked samples has been explained by Seitz [6], who showed that generation of these defects will occur whenever dislocation lines cross as they move during plastic flow.   Conversely, generation of dislocations during irradiation is expected also: The amount of energy released per unit length as an ionizing particle traverses the crystal is sufficient to cause local internal melting.   The molten region, which quickly recrystallizes, known as a *thermal spike*, generally contains a fairly large number of dislocations.

Calculated and experimentally observed resistivities due to vacancies and interstitials are in reasonably good agreement.   The resistivities due to dislocations, however, are often significantly larger than predicted by the most reliable calculations.   The discrepancy reflects two inadequacies of the theory.   First, the resistivity arising from the "core" of the dislocation line, difficult to calculate precisely, is apparently quite substantial, and second, stacking faults may make sizeable contributions to the resistivity of plastically deformed specimens, and must be included in the complete calculation (see page 159).

Resistivity of concentrated alloys   The residual resistivity of alloys is a linear function of the solute concentration only if $c \ll 1$.   For binary alloys containing c mole fraction of metal A and $1 - c$ mole fraction of metal B, Nordheim [7] proposed the relation

$$\rho_r(c) \propto c(1 - c) \tag{7.29}$$

Nordheim's rule closely approximates the behavior of most binary systems, provided they suffer no phase transformation and provided neither component belongs to the transition group.   The first proviso reflects the fact that, generally, significant changes in the band structure accompany phase transitions.   The reason for exclusion of transition metals from Nordheim's rule will become clear after Sec. 7.5, wherein we consider the electrical properties of ferromagnetic and transition metals and their alloys.

There are numerous binary systems which satisfy the conditions for the validity of Eq. (7.29), among them Ag-Au and Au-Cu alloys. The latter system, however, transforms into ordered lattices at the compositions $AuCu_3$ and $AuCu$.   Ordering can be inhibited by rapid quenching of the disordered phase from high temperature.   Figure 7.7, showing the resistivity of the Au-Cu system in the ordered and disordered phases, demonstrates Nordheim's rule.

Equation (7.29) can be made plausible as follows.   Let us define an average cellular potential $\bar{V}$ for the $A_c B_{1-c}$ alloy by

$$\bar{V} = cV_A + (1 - c)V_B \tag{7.30}$$

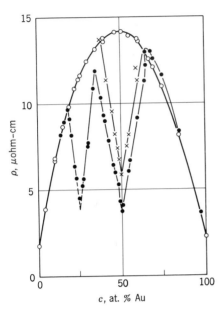

Fig. 7.7 Resistivity of Cu-Au alloys at 20°C. —○—○—○— quenched from 600°C; —×—×— cooled slowly; —●—●—●— tempered for 120 hr at 200°C. (*From J. Olsen, "Electron Transport in Metals," p. 46, Interscience Publishers, Inc., New York, 1962.*)

Assume that in a cell occupied by an A atom an electron sees a perturbation potential $V_A - \bar{V}$, and similarly for a B atom. The scattering potentials are

$$V_A - \bar{V} = (1 - c)(V_A - V_B) \qquad V_B - \bar{V} = c(V_B - V_A)$$

In the Born approximation the scattering probability per scattering center is proportional to the square of the matrix element of the perturbation potential connecting the initial and final states. Thus, the total scattering probability, and hence the residual resistivity, will be proportional to

$$c(1 - c)^2 |\langle |V_A - V_B|\rangle|^2 + (1 - c)c^2 |\langle |V_B - V_A|\rangle|^2 = c(1 - c)|\langle V_{AB}\rangle|^2$$

in agreement with Nordheim's rule.

7.3 THERMAL CONDUCTIVITY

In the region in which the relaxation-time approximation has validity, the distribution function is characterized by the solution

$$\phi = \tau \mathbf{P} \cdot \mathbf{v}$$

Formal expressions for the charge and energy current densities are

$$\mathbf{J} = \mathfrak{K}_1 \left[e^2 \mathbf{E} - eT\mathbf{\nabla}\left(\frac{\eta}{T}\right) \right] - \mathfrak{K}_2 \left(\frac{e}{T}\right) \mathbf{\nabla} T \tag{7.31}$$

$$\mathbf{Q} = \mathfrak{K}_2 \left[e\mathbf{E} - T\mathbf{\nabla}\left(\frac{\eta}{T}\right) \right] - \mathfrak{K}_3 \left(\frac{1}{T}\right) \mathbf{\nabla} T \tag{7.32}$$

where $\mathfrak{K}_n$ is given by Eq. (7.3) or Eq. (7.4).

The usual experimental arrangement for measurement of thermal conductivity allows no flow of charge. We therefore set $\mathbf{J} = 0$ and solve for $\mathbf{E}$:

$$\mathbf{E} = \frac{1}{e}\left[\mathbf{\nabla}\eta + \left(\frac{\mathfrak{K}_2}{\mathfrak{K}_1 T} - \frac{\eta}{T}\right) \mathbf{\nabla} T \right] \tag{7.33}$$

Substitution of Eq. (7.33) into Eq. (7.32) gives

$$\mathbf{Q} = \frac{\mathfrak{K}_2{}^2 - \mathfrak{K}_1\mathfrak{K}_3}{\mathfrak{K}_1 T} \mathbf{\nabla} T \tag{7.34}$$

The thermal conductivity κ is defined by

$$\mathbf{Q} = -\kappa \mathbf{\nabla} T$$

Comparison with Eq. (7.34) shows that

$$\kappa = \frac{\mathfrak{K}_1\mathfrak{K}_3 - \mathfrak{K}_2{}^2}{\mathfrak{K}_1 T} \tag{7.35}$$

If only the lowest-order terms of the expansions for $\mathfrak{K}_n$ are used in Eq. (7.35), the result vanishes identically. Keeping terms to order $(kT/\eta)^2$, one obtains the result

$$\kappa = \frac{\pi^2 k^2 T}{3e^2} \sigma \tag{7.36}$$

We have here the Wiedemann-Franz law which states that the ratio

$$\frac{\kappa}{\sigma T} = \frac{\pi^2}{3}\left(\frac{k}{e}\right)^2 = 2.45 \times 10^{-8} \text{ watt-ohm/(deg)}^2 = L_0 \tag{7.37}$$

is a constant for all metals. This result is valid whenever a meaningful relaxation time can be defined. The Wiedemann-Franz law holds even if the constant-energy surfaces are not spheres. From our discussion of Sec. 5.4 it follows that the Wiedemann-Franz law should be obeyed by all metals at high temperatures ($T > \Theta$), and also at temperatures so low that scattering by stationary imperfections is dominant. In comparing experimental and theoretical values of $\kappa/\sigma T$, one must bear in mind, however, that the thermal conductivity which we have calculated here is that due to energy transport by the quasi-free-electrons only. There is, in addition, heat flow via lattice vibrations; this is the mechanism which provides for heat conduction in an insulator. Thus, the total measured thermal conductivity should, and generally does, exceed $L_0 \sigma T$. In good metallic conductors of high purity the fraction of the heat carried by lattice vibrations is normally very small. In semimetals, however, κ_g, the lattice thermal conductivity, may be comparable to that due to the conduction electrons.

From Eqs. (7.23) and (7.37) it follows that at high temperatures the electronic thermal conductivity will be independent of temperature, whereas at very low temperatures, when $\rho_r \gg \rho_i$, κ should be proportional to T. This is, indeed, the behavior generally observed, as illustrated by Fig. 7.8, which shows the thermal conductivity of gold over a wide temperature range.

In the intermediate temperature region, extending roughly from $T = \Theta$ down to the temperature at which $\rho_r \gg \rho_i$ (the lower limit clearly depends on the purity of the specimen), a solution of the transport equation in terms of a single relaxation time cannot be found. The correct expression for the ideal electronic thermal resistivity (i.e., that associated with scattering by lattice waves) is best found by application of the variational scheme. The formal procedure commences with Eq. (5.63) and follows the pattern for the calculation of the electrical resistivity in the intermediate temperature range (see pages 183 to 189). We shall not display this calculation here, but simply state the final result:

$$\frac{1}{\kappa_i} = W_i = \frac{4\Re}{L_0 T}\left(\frac{T}{\Theta}\right)^5 \left\{\left[1 + \frac{3}{\pi^2}\left(\frac{k_0\Theta}{q_0 T}\right)^2\right] \mathscr{J}_5\left(\frac{\Theta}{T}\right) - \frac{1}{2\pi^2}\mathscr{J}_7\left(\frac{\Theta}{T}\right)\right\} \quad (7.38)$$

This result is based on the Bloch approximation, Eq. (7.17), for the scattering function, and on the total neglect of Umklapp scattering. Moreover, only the first-order variational trial function was employed in the derivation of Eq. (7.38). However, before embarking on a detailed criticism of Eq. (7.38), let us first examine its predictions.

At high temperature, Eq. (7.38) approaches Eq. (7.36), as it should. It is at low temperatures that the behavior of Eq. (7.38) is particularly interesting. Here the dominant term is the last one in the square brackets; the thermal resistivity then reduces to

$$W_i = \frac{12\Re}{L_0\pi^2} \times 124.4\left(\frac{k_0}{q_0}\right)^2\frac{T^2}{\Theta^3} = Bn_a^{\frac{2}{3}}W_\infty\left(\frac{T}{\Theta}\right)^2 \qquad T \ll \Theta \qquad (7.39)$$

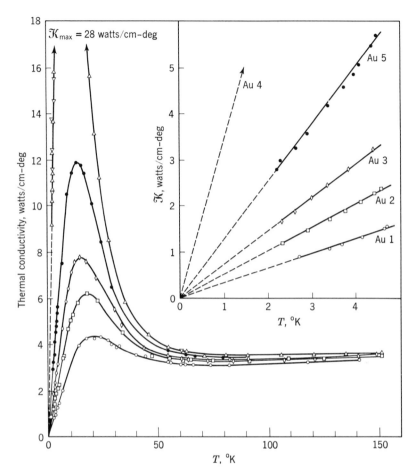

Fig. 7.8 The thermal conductivity of gold in varying states of physical and chemical purity. ○ Au 1, 99.9% pure, unannealed; □ Au 2, 99.9% pure, annealed; ◇ Au 3, JM 3226, freshly drawn; △ Au 4, JM 3226, annealed; ▽ Au 4, JM 3226, annealed—2d run; ● Au 5, JM 3226, redrawn. (*From J. Olsen.* "*Electron Transport in Metals,*" *p. 50, Interscience Publishers, Inc., New York, 1962.*)

where n_a is the number of conduction electrons per atom, and W_∞ the thermal resistivity at high temperature.

The ideal thermal resistivity at low temperatures is proportional to T^2, and not to T^4 as direct application of the Wiedemann-Franz law would predict. The failure of the Wiedemann-Franz law in this situation can be traced directly to the absence of a universal relaxation time; the problem was discussed in Chap. 5, where we derived the T^2 dependence of W_i using only qualitative arguments. These are now supported by the more rigorous treatment on which the derivation of Eq. (7.39) is based.

The constant B appearing in Eq. (7.38) equals 95.3 if the first-order variational trial function is used. Variational calculations carried to higher order suggests that this value is on the high side. Numerical solutions of the integral equation [8] lead to $B = 64.0$, the value currently accepted.

Although theory and experiment are in substantial agreement as regards the gross features, there remain several details in which the theory is evidently deficient. These difficulties are best exhibited by considering the following parameters:

$$D_1 = 64.0 \, \frac{W_\infty}{W_i(T)} \left(\frac{T}{\Theta}\right)^2 \qquad T \ll \Theta \tag{7.40}$$

$$D_2 = \frac{64.0}{497.6} \, \frac{\rho_i(T)}{L_0 W_i(T)} \, \frac{\Theta^2}{T^3} \qquad T \ll \Theta \tag{7.41}$$

Both parameters should equal $(1/n_a)^{\frac{1}{3}}$; for monovalent metals we would expect $D_1 = D_2 = 1$.

In fact, the thermal resistivity at low temperatures is considerably smaller than predicted by theory and by the limiting thermal resistivity at high temperature, W_∞, as indicated by the relatively large values of D_1 (see Table 7.5). Moreover, D_2 also exceeds the predictions by roughly an order of magnitude. Finally, a plot of κ_i according to Eq. (7.38) exhibits a distinct minimum near $T/\Theta = 0.2$. This minimum, which persists even when impurity scattering is included, has never been observed.

Table 7-5 Thermal-conductivity
Parameters D_1 and D_2 of the
Monovalent Metals
See Eqs. (7.40) and (7.41)

Element	D_1	D_2
Li	0.7	
Na	5.3	1.8
K	3.7	16
Rb	3.3	9
Cs	8	10
Cu	6.2	5.4
Ag	5.2	4.2
Au	4.8	4.5

These three discrepancies (the large values of D_1 and D_2 and the absence of a minimum in κ_i) can be traced to the assumption of spherical energy surfaces and the neglect of Umklapp scattering. Umklapp scatterings are large-angle events and, thus, quite effective in relaxing the distribution. As the temperature is lowered, U processes, which require phonons of relatively large wave vector, are gradually quenched (see Fig. 6.11). It can be shown that generally the proportion of the total thermal resistivity attributable to U processes decreases with decreasing temperature. Consequently, when U processes are included in the theory, the ratio $W_\infty/W_i(T)$ for $T \ll \theta$ will be larger than if U processes are neglected altogether.

The large values of D_2 can be explained if we discard the assumption of spherical energy surfaces. We recall that at low temperatures, N processes are small-angle scattering events. Roughly, then, τ_σ^N is, at low temperatures, the time required for an electron to "diffuse" over the Fermi surface from one side to the opposite in a sequence of a large number of small random steps. Suppose the distortion of the Fermi surface is so great that it touches the zone boundary near certain symmetry points. In that case, an electron can reach the "opposite" portion of the Fermi surface by diffusing to a point of contact with the zone boundary, where it can now partake of a U process. Thus, the distance of travel via small steps over the Fermi surface is greatly reduced, roughly halved in the case of fcc metals touching at (111) faces, and the ideal resistivity at low temperature will now be about four times as large as it would be in the absence of zone contact. The same mechanism, although it plays some role, contributes much less to the thermal resistance, since at low temperatures this is limited primarily by small-angle *inelastic* scattering events. Thus, as a result of contact of the Fermi surface with a zone boundary, the low-temperature electrical resistivity is significantly increased without a commensurate increase of the thermal resistivity. Consequently, the true value of D_2 will be larger than the one based on a model which assumes spherical Fermi surfaces.

More detailed arguments suggest that, in the monovalent metals, D_2 should be roughly equal to 5 if there is contact at the (111) faces of the BZ. From Table 7.5 it would seem that contact occurs in all three noble metals. This qualitative conclusion has now been quite firmly established by experimental methods, which we shall describe toward the end of the text.

7.4 THERMOELECTRIC EFFECTS; PHONON DRAG

There are three thermoelectric effects: the Seebeck, Peltier, and Thomson effects.

Whenever a current flows through a normal metallic conductor Joule heat is generated; this is the I^2R loss. If a temperature gradient is maintained along the conductor, an additional heat generation takes place. This extra heat is created reversibly; i.e., a reversal of the current or of the thermal gradient (not both simultaneously) causes this heat to be absorbed from the surroundings. The reversible heat generated per unit volume per second is called the *Thomson heat*. The Thomson coefficient μ is defined by

$$\mu = \frac{Q_T}{\mathbf{J} \cdot \nabla T} \tag{7.42}$$

and is taken positive if heat is liberated reversibly when $\mathbf{J}$ and ∇T are antiparallel, i.e., when the direction of current flow is from the high- to the low-temperature end of the sample.

The *Peltier effect* relates to the reversible heat generated at the junction of two different conductors when a current passes across the junction. The Peltier coefficient Π_{AB} is the heat generated per second per unit current flow from conductor A to B.

The *Seebeck effect* is the best known of the three thermoelectric effects, since it underlies the operation of commercial thermocouples. It concerns the emf developed in a circuit composed of two different conductors whose junctions are maintained at different temperatures (see Fig. 7.9).

The voltage $V_{AB}(T_0, T)$, which appears across the terminals of the circuit of Fig. 7.9, is a function of the temperatures T_0, T, and depends on the conductors A and B which are joined to form the couple. The thermoelectric power S_{AB} of the circuit is defined by

$$S_{AB}(T_0) = \left[\frac{\partial V_{AB}(T, T_0)}{\partial T} \right]_{T_0} \tag{7.43}$$

and S_{AB} is taken positive if the emf that is developed is such that as T increases, the potential of the terminal connected to the junction at the temperature T also increases.

We shall shortly derive an expression for the *absolute* thermoelectric power (TEP) of a conductor, a parameter which refers, as does the

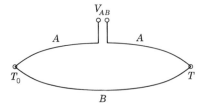

Fig. 7.9 The thermoelectric circuit.

Thomson coefficient, to an intrinsic property of a particular substance. We shall then find that $S_{AB} = S_A - S_B$, where S_A and S_B are the absolute TEP's of metals A and B, respectively.

The three thermoelectric effects are intimately related. The relationships between them, first derived by Lord Kelvin and named in his honor, have been placed on firm foundation with the development of the thermodynamics of irreversible processes. The Kelvin relations are

$$\mu_A = T \frac{\partial S_A}{\partial T} \qquad S_A = \int_0^T \frac{\mu_A}{T'} dT' \qquad \Pi_{AB} = T(S_B - S_A) \qquad (7.44)$$

The electric field developed in a conductor on which we impose the boundary condition $\mathbf{J} = 0$ is given by Eq. (7.31). Since, in steady state, $\nabla \eta = 0$, one defines the absolute TEP by

$$\mathbf{E} = S \nabla T$$

with

$$S = \frac{\mathcal{K}_2 - \eta \mathcal{K}_1}{e \mathcal{K}_1 T} \qquad (7.45)$$

Consider now the circuit of Fig. 7.9. The thermoelectric potential is given by

$$V_{AB}(T_0, T) = -\int \mathbf{E} \cdot d\mathbf{s} = \int_{T_0}^{T} (S_A - S_B) \, dT \qquad (7.46)$$

from which Eq. (7.43) follows directly.

Although the absolute TEP is an interesting and informative property of a material, it cannot generally be measured directly. Measurements of the Seebeck and Peltier effects refer to differences between the properties of two conductors, rather than to the properties themselves. The Thomson effect, however, can be observed in a homogeneous substance, and from it S and Π may be derived by application of the Kelvin relations, Eq. (7.44).

The determination of S by the aforementioned technique is beset with experimental difficulties. Moreover, from the integral relation Eq. (7.44) it follows that, in principle, one need measure μ to absolute zero of temperature. Here, one of the many unusual properties of superconductors may be used advantageously. It is expected on theoretical grounds and confirmed by experiment that the absolute TEP of a superconductor is identically zero. Thus, the absolute TEP of any normal metal at low temperature may be determined by simply forming a thermocouple consisting of the metal and a superconductor. The thermoelectric emf generated in the couple within the temperature region in which the superconductor is below its critical temperature is then characteristic of the normal metal of the couple. A convenient superconducting zero reference is Nb_3Sn, whose transition temperature is near 18°K. Above that temperature the integration of μ/T cannot be avoided.

Using these techniques the absolute TEP of pure lead has been established, and this material is now commonly used as a secondary standard in thermoelectric measurements (see Table 7.6).

Returning to the formal expressions for the thermopower, substitution of Eq. (7.4) into Eq. (7.45) gives

$$S = \frac{\pi^2 k^2 T}{3e}\left[\frac{\partial \ln \sigma(\epsilon)}{\partial \epsilon}\right]_\eta = \frac{2C_e}{3n_0 e}\left[\frac{\partial \ln \sigma(\epsilon)}{\partial \ln \epsilon}\right]_\eta \qquad (7.47)$$

where $\sigma(\epsilon)$ is given by Eq. (7.6) and C_e is the electronic specific heat. The order of magnitude assumed by S can be estimated as follows. At high temperatures, $\tau(\epsilon)$ is proportional to $\epsilon^{\frac{3}{2}}$ and $\int[v^2(\epsilon)/|\nabla_\kappa\epsilon|]\,dS$ is also proportional to $\epsilon^{\frac{3}{2}}$, provided we assume spherical energy surfaces. Consequently, under these idealized conditions, $\sigma(\epsilon)$ is proportional to ϵ^3 and its logarithmic derivative evaluated at $\epsilon = \eta$ is $3/\eta$. At very low temperatures, where $1/\tau$ is determined by scattering from impurities, $\tau(\epsilon) \propto \epsilon^{-\frac{1}{2}}$, corresponding to a constant electronic mean free path. The logarithmic derivative of $\sigma(\epsilon)$ thus leads to the factor $1/\eta$ in this temperature range.

Table 7-6   The Absolute Thermoelectric Power (TEP) of Pure Lead between 0 and 300°K

T, °K	S, $\mu v/deg$	T, °K	S, $\mu v/deg$
0	0	60	-0.77_9
5	0	70	-0.78_4
7.5	-0.22_1	80	-0.79_4
8	-0.25_7	90	-0.82_4
8.5	-0.29_7	100	-0.86_5
9	-0.34_3	113.2	-0.91
10	-0.43_4	133.2	-0.96
11	-0.51_6	153.2	-1.02
12	-0.59_3	173.2	-1.06
14	-0.70_6	193.2	-1.10_5
16	-0.77_1	213.2	-1.15
18	-0.78_{45}	233.2	-1.18
20	-0.78_4	253.2	-1.21
30	-0.77_4	273.2	-1.25
40	-0.76_4	293.2	-1.27_5
50	-0.77_4		

It follows that for the ideal metal

$$S = \frac{\pi^2 k^2 T}{e\eta} \qquad T > \Theta \tag{7.48}$$

$$S = \frac{\pi^2 k^2 T}{3e\eta} \qquad T \ll \Theta \tag{7.49}$$

Upon substitution of reasonable values for the Fermi energy, one finds that S at room temperature will be of the order of 1 $\mu v/°K$.

Equation (7.47) suggests that the small absolute thermoelectric power of metals may be related to the degeneracy of the electron gas. That is indeed true in the sense that, as with the electronic specific heat, only a small fraction (roughly kT/η) of the conduction electrons are influenced by the presence of a temperature gradient in the sample. We shall find that, in a semiconductor to which classical statistics may be applied, the thermoelectric power is in fact larger by several orders of magnitude; i.e.,

$$S_{sc} \approx S_{met} \frac{\eta}{kT} \approx \frac{\pi^2 k}{e}$$

Comparison of the above theory with experiment allows only one conclusion: The theory is woefully inadequate in explaining the observed thermopowers of even the monovalent metals. These frequently prove to be positive, rather than negative as Eq. (7.48) would predict. Moreover, the temperature dependence usually differs drastically from that expected, especially at low temperatures. In many instances S, though negative and roughly proportional to T at high temperatures, reverses sign at low temperatures. Also, the approach of S to zero as T approaches $0°K$ is usually linear only at very low temperatures, $T \ll 4°K$.

A glance at Fig. 7.10 reveals that more often than not S increases approximately linearly with temperature at high temperatures. It is in the region near and below liquid air ($80°K$) that the major discrepancy often appears. The inadequacy of the theory may be traced, in part at least, to the Bloch approximation, the assumption that the lattice vibration spectrum is at equilibrium even though a temperature gradient is imposed on the sample.

We know, of course, since insulators do conduct heat, that a temperature gradient will induce heat transport via lattice vibrations. Thus, there exists a net current of phonons traveling from the hot to the cold end of a specimen, which contributes to the thermal conductivity of the sample. The phonon mean free path l_g is limited by a variety of mechanisms, such as phonon-phonon, phonon-electron, and phonon-imperfection

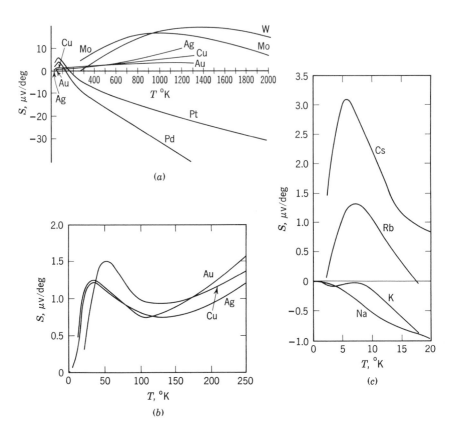

Fig. 7.10 The thermoelectric power of metals. (a) Refractory and noble metals over a wide temperature range [*From N. Cusack and P. Kendall, Proc. Phys. Soc.,* **72**: 899 (1958).]; (b) copper, silver, and gold between 0° and 250°K (*From D. K. C. MacDonald, "Principles of Thermoelectricity," p.* 71, *John Wiley & Sons, Inc., New York,* 1962.); (c) alkali metals at low temperatures. (*From D. K. C. MacDonald, "Principles of Thermoelectricity," p.* 97, *John Wiley & Sons, Inc., New York,* 1962.)

scattering. Its average value may be deduced from the kinetic-theory relation for the lattice thermal conductivity κ_g,

$$\kappa_g = \tfrac{1}{3}C_g u l_g \tag{7.50}$$

where u is the phonon velocity (velocity of sound) and C_g is the lattice specific heat.

To simplify our discussion and clarify the role of the phonon current in thermoelectricity of solids, let us assume for the moment that among the scattering mechanisms mentioned above, only phonon-electron scattering is important. In each such scattering event a phonon is absorbed (or emitted) and the electron gains (or loses) the corresponding energy and crystal momentum. In the metal bar of Fig. 7.11 a phonon current flows from right to left as a result of the temperature gradient. At any point within the bar an electron will be more likely to absorb a phonon which travels to the left than one traveling to the right, since more of the former are at hand. Consequently, the electrons absorb the phonon momentum and are "dragged" along by the phonons, as in viscous flow; hence, the term *phonon drag.*

Electrons, therefore, tend to pile up at the low-temperature end of our sample. This charge unbalance gives rise to an internal electric field which exerts a retarding force on the streaming electrons; ultimately a steady state is attained. Clearly, phonon drag provides a contribution to the thermoelectric emf which is supplementary to that derived for the noninteracting free-electron gas. We shall denote the phonon-drag thermopower by the symbol S_g and the "diffusion" thermopower by S_d.

The magnitude of S_g may be deduced from the following argument. Consider an acoustic wave propagating along the x direction through a medium of charged particles that absorb sound. The radiation pressure corresponding to the spatial decay of the energy density U is

$$P_x = - \frac{dU}{dx}$$

In steady state this force per unit area must be compensated by an opposing force which we assume of electrostatic origin,

$$F_x = -n_0 \mathfrak{e} E_x$$

If we now take for U the energy density of thermal phonons, we have

$$\frac{dU}{dx} = C_g \frac{dT}{dx}$$

where C_g is the lattice specific heat.

Hence

$$S_g = \frac{E_x}{\nabla_x T} = \frac{C_g}{n_0 \mathfrak{e}} \tag{7.51}$$

Except for a numerical factor of $\frac{1}{3}$, Eq. (7.51) is correct. We can now see

T_1 $T_2 > T_1$

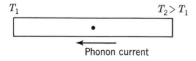

Phonon current

Fig. 7.11 A metallic bar in which a temperature gradient is maintained.

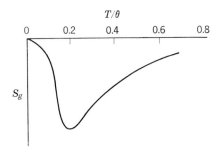

Fig. 7.12 The expected phonon-drag thermoelectric power due to Normal (N) electron-phonon scattering as a function of temperature.

why at low temperature the total TEP, the sum of S_d and S_g, displays a nonlinear temperature dependence. Whereas S_d is proportional to the electronic specific heat [see Eq. (7.47)], S_g is proportional to the lattice specific heat. The latter varies as T^3 at low temperature. Moreover, C_g is not reduced by degeneracy; thus, as T approaches Θ, S_g could approach values of about k/e, that is, (η/kT) times as large as S_d.

In practice S_g never attains such magnitudes. In the foregoing we neglected all but phonon-electron scattering. In a pure metal at reasonably low temperatures (roughly $T < \Theta/5$), phonon-electron scattering is indeed dominant. However, as T increases, phonon-phonon scattering, arising from anharmonicity of the interionic potential, asserts itself. The actual magnitude of S_g is proportional to the relative importance of phonon-electron scattering as compared to the sum total of all phonon scattering mechanisms. Hence, the true phonon-drag thermopower is given by

$$S_g = S_g^{\max}(T) \left(\frac{\tau_p'}{\tau_p' + \tau_{pe}} \right) \tag{7.52}$$

where τ_{pe} is the relaxation time associated with phonon-electron scattering, τ_p' is the relaxation time due to all other scattering events, and $S_g^{\max}(T)$ is the phonon-drag thermopower that would exist if phonons were scattered by electrons only—i.e., if $\tau_p' = \infty$.

Equation (7.52) immediately tells us the temperature dependence of S_g at high temperatures. Here $S_g^{\max} \approx k/e$, τ_{pe} is independent of temperature,† and τ_p' is inversely proportional to T, since the dominant relaxation

---

† We must not confuse here τ_{ep}, the relaxation time associated with the scattering *of* electrons *by* phonons, with τ_{pe}, the relaxation time associated with scattering *of* phonons *by* electrons. The first characteristic time appears in the expression of the electrical conductivity, and it is inversely proportional to the temperature because the number of phonons (scattering centers) increases with increasing temperature, thus reducing the electronic mean free path. The second characteristic time, τ_{pe}, is independent of T; an increase in temperature does not significantly modify the electron distribution nor does it affect the coupling of the phonon and electron fields.

mechanism is phonon-phonon scattering.   It follows that, at high temperatures, S_g is inversely proportional to T.

We arrive then at the qualitative curve for $S_g(T)$ shown in Fig. 7.12, characterized by a T^3 dependence at low temperature and a $1/T$ dependence at high temperature.

Again, we have sidestepped the ticklish question of Umklapp processes.   These electron-phonon events can also contribute to a phonon-drag effect, but it will generally be of opposite sign to that associated with

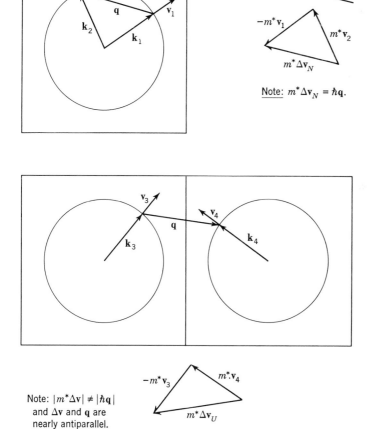

Note: $m^* \Delta \mathbf{v}_N = \hbar \mathbf{q}$.

Note: $|m^* \Delta \mathbf{v}| \neq |\hbar \mathbf{q}|$ and $\Delta \mathbf{v}$ and $\mathbf{q}$ are nearly antiparallel.

Fig. 7.13 The role of Normal (N) and Umklapp (U) scattering in phonon drag.

Normal scattering. This is best demonstrated by reference to the extended-zone scheme (Fig. 7.13), wherein Umklapp processes correspond to the transfer of an electron from a given zone to a neighboring one. Figure 7.13 shows surfaces of constant energy, assumed spherical for convenience, in adjoining zones.

We recall first that the velocity of an electron, $\mathbf{v}(\mathbf{k}) = (1/\hbar)\boldsymbol{\nabla}_{\mathbf{k}}\epsilon$, is everywhere normal to the Fermi surface. In an N process an electron with initial velocity, say, $\mathbf{v}_1$, absorbs a phonon of wave vector $\mathbf{q}$. The final velocity is now $\mathbf{v}_2$, and the change in momentum

$$m^*\Delta\mathbf{v}_N = m^*(\mathbf{v}_2 - \mathbf{v}_1)$$

is equal to $\hbar\mathbf{q}$, the crystal momentum of the phonon that has been absorbed.

An Umklapp process in which the very same phonon again participates is also shown in Fig. 7.13. Now the change in velocity is from the initial velocity $\mathbf{v}_3$ to the final velocity $\mathbf{v}_4$. The momentum of the electron has changed by $m^*(\mathbf{v}_4 - \mathbf{v}_3) = m^*\Delta\mathbf{v}_U$, and it is evident that the direction of $\Delta\mathbf{v}_U$ is nearly opposite to $\hbar\mathbf{q}$ and to $\Delta\mathbf{v}_N$. Hence, phonon drag via Umklapp scattering will tend to pile up electrons at the *hot*, and not the cold, end of an electronic conductor.

In a real metal both N and U processes occur. The net phonon-drag TEP is then the result of a partial cancellation of two contributions which may be quite large individually. Both S_g^N and S_g^U depend most sensitively on the details of the electronic band structure and the phonon spectrum. For this reason precise numerical calculations have not been attempted. However, many unusual thermoelectric properties, for example, the pronounced anisotropy of S in single-crystal cadmium samples at low temperatures, can be explained, at least semiquantitatively, in terms of Normal and Umklapp phonon drag.

7.5 CONDUCTION IN A MAGNETIC FIELD

In this section we shall consider only a few of the numerous galvano- and thermomagnetic effects; the better known are summarized in Table 7.7. A discussion of all would clearly take too much space; moreover, it has become all too obvious in recent years that galvanomagnetic effects are extremely sensitive to peculiarities of the Fermi surface, and that a theoretical model based on a quasi-free-electron approach will be grievously deficient. Indeed, magnetic phenomena provide powerful methods for probing the band structure of metals, and we shall return to that aspect of galvanomagnetic effects later.

The classical theory of galvanomagnetic effects also is suspect for reasons that have nothing to do with the spherical approximation. It is a simple matter to solve the Schroedinger equation for free electrons in a uniform magnetic field (see Appendix A). The solution bears little resemblance to the plane-wave function $\exp{(i\mathbf{k}\cdot\mathbf{r})}$, the correct eigenfunction when $\mathbf{H} = 0$. The energy spectrum, too, is modified in a profound manner. Whereas the components k_x, k_y, k_z are good quantum numbers for $\mathbf{H} = 0$, this is no longer true when the magnetic field is turned on. It follows that a correct treatment of transport, even one based on the Boltzmann equation, should be reformulated in terms of quantum numbers appropriate to the new situation.

In practice, one distinguishes between two limiting cases, known as the *weak-* and *strong-field limits*. By "strong field" one refers to a magnetic field such that $\omega_c = eH/m^*c$, the cyclotron frequency of the electron, is greater than $1/\tau$, the collision rate. Another way of expressing the same condition is to demand that in a strong field the electron's mean free path be longer than the circumference of its cyclotron orbit. Evidently, when this situation prevails, the magnetic field cannot be treated as a "small perturbation"; the sensible approach is to start with the correct quantum-mechanical description, taking full account of the magnetic field.

In the weak-field limit $\omega_c\tau \ll 1$. Although the electron still traverses a circular path in a plane normal to $\mathbf{H}$, it completes only a small arc before it suffers a collision and is scattered into another orbital state. In this instance, it does make sense to treat the magnetic field as a small perturbation giving rise to the Lorentz force. In the following, we limit our attention to the weak-field case; the strong-field limit is reserved for a later chapter.

For spherical energy surfaces the perturbed distribution function is given by Eq. (5.24). In discussing that result we already pointed out that the symmetry of the solution precluded the appearance of any longitudinal effects in the theory.

It is convenient in treating the transverse effects to select a cartesian coordinate system whose z axis is directed along the magnetic field. The electric field then lies in the xy plane. Equation (5.24) now becomes

$$\psi_x = \tau\,\frac{P_x + \omega_c\tau P_y}{1 + (\omega_c\tau)^2} \qquad \psi_y = \tau\,\frac{P_y - \omega_c\tau P_x}{1 + (\omega_c\tau)^2} \tag{7.53}$$

A. Hall Effect

From Eqs. (7.53) and (7.2) the current components are given by

$$J_x = e^2\mathcal{K}_1' E_x + e^2\mathcal{K}_1'' E_y \tag{7.54}$$

$$J_y = e^2\mathcal{K}_1' E_y - e^2\mathcal{K}_1'' E_x \tag{7.55}$$

Table 7-7   A Partial Listing of Transport Effects in a Magnetic Field

1a. Isothermal transverse effects: $H = H_z,\ J_z = E_z = \dfrac{\partial T}{\partial z} = \dfrac{\partial T}{\partial y} = 0$

1b. Adiabatic transverse effects: $H = H_z,\ J_z = E_z = \dfrac{\partial T}{\partial z} = Q_y = 0$

2. Longitudinal effects: $H = H_z,\ J_x = J_y = Q_x = Q_y = 0$

Name	Primary current	Quantity measured	Coefficient defining Eq.	Auxiliary condition
1a Magneto-resistance electrical	J_x	$\Delta\rho = \rho - \rho_0$	$B_i = \dfrac{\Delta\rho}{\rho_0 H^2}$	$J_y = \dfrac{\partial T}{\partial x} = 0$
Magneto-resistance thermal	Q_x	$\Delta\kappa = \kappa_0 - \kappa$	$B_{\kappa i} = \dfrac{\Delta\kappa}{\kappa H^2}$	$J_x = J_y = 0$
Hall effect	J_x	E_y	$R_i = \dfrac{E_y}{J_x H}$	$J_y = \dfrac{\partial T}{\partial x} = 0$
Nernst effect	Q_x	E_y	$A_{Ni} = \dfrac{E_y}{H\,\partial T/\partial x}$	$J_x = J_y = 0$
Magneto-thermo-electric effect	Q_x	$E_x;\ \Delta S = S - S_0$	$\Sigma_i = \dfrac{\Delta S}{S_0 H^2}$ $S = \dfrac{E_x}{\partial T/\partial x}$	$J_x = J_y = 0$
Corbino effect	J_x	J_y	$A_c = \dfrac{J_y}{J_x H}$	$E_y = \dfrac{\partial T}{\partial x} = 0$
1b Magneto-resistance electrical	J_x	$\Delta\rho = \rho - \rho_0$	$B_a = \dfrac{\Delta\rho}{\rho_0 H^2}$	$J_y = \dfrac{\partial T}{\partial x} = 0$
Magneto-resistance thermal	Q_x	$\Delta\kappa = \kappa_0 - \kappa$	$B_{\kappa a} = \dfrac{\Delta\kappa}{\kappa H^2}$	$J_x = J_y = 0$
Ettinghausen effect	J_x	$\dfrac{\partial T}{\partial y}$	$A_E = \dfrac{\partial T/\partial y}{J_x H}$	$J_y = \dfrac{\partial T}{\partial x} = 0$
Hall effect	J_x	E_y	$R_a = \dfrac{E_y}{J_x H}$	$J_y = \dfrac{\partial T}{\partial x} = 0$
Leduc-Righi effect	Q_x	$\dfrac{\partial T}{\partial y}$	$A_L = \dfrac{\partial T/\partial y}{H\,\partial T/\partial x}$	$J_x = J_y = 0$
Nernst effect	Q_x	E_y	$A_{Na} = \dfrac{E_y}{H\,\partial T/\partial x}$	$J_x = J_y = 0$
Magneto-thermo-electric effect	Q_x	$E_x;\ \Delta S = S - S_0$	$\Sigma_a = \dfrac{\Delta S}{S_0 H^2}$ $S = \dfrac{E_x}{\partial T/\partial x}$	$J_x = J_y = 0$
2 Magneto-resistance electrical	J_z	$\Delta\rho = \rho - \rho_0$	$B_L = \dfrac{\Delta\rho}{\rho_0 H^2}$	$\dfrac{\partial T}{\partial z} = 0$
Magneto-resistance thermal	Q_z	$\Delta\kappa = \kappa_0 - \kappa$	$B_{\kappa L} = \dfrac{\Delta\kappa}{\kappa H^2}$	$J_z = 0$
Magneto-thermo-electric effect	Q_z	$E_x;\ \Delta S = S - S_0$	$\Sigma_L = \dfrac{\Delta S}{S_0 H^2}$ $S = \dfrac{E_z}{\partial T/\partial z}$	$J_z = 0$

provided $\nabla T = 0$.   In the above expressions

$$\mathcal{K}_n' = -\frac{1}{12\pi^3} \iint \frac{\tau v^2 \epsilon^{n-1}}{[1 + (\omega_c \tau)^2]|\nabla_k \epsilon|} \, dS \frac{\partial f_0}{\partial \epsilon} \, d\epsilon \tag{7.56}$$

$$\mathcal{K}_n'' = -\frac{1}{12\pi^3} \iint \frac{\tau(\omega_c \tau)v^2 \epsilon^{n-1}}{[1 + (\omega_c \tau)^2]|\nabla_k \epsilon|} \, dS \frac{\partial f_0}{\partial \epsilon} \, d\epsilon \tag{7.57}$$

To lowest order in the expansion of $\mathcal{K}_1'$ and $\mathcal{K}_1''$, the components of the current density in the x and y directions are

$$J_x = \frac{e^2 n_0}{m^*} \left[\frac{\tau}{1 + (\omega_c \tau)^2} E_x + \frac{\omega_c \tau^2}{1 + (\omega_c \tau)^2} E_y \right] \tag{7.58}$$

$$J_y = \frac{e^2 n_0}{m^*} \left[\frac{\tau}{1 + (\omega_c \tau)^2} E_y - \frac{\omega_c \tau^2}{1 + (\omega_c \tau)^2} E_x \right] \tag{7.59}$$

i.e., all terms of order $(kT/\eta)^2$ in Eqs. (7.56) and (7.57) have been neglected.   Thus, the conductivity tensor $\boldsymbol{\sigma}$, defined by $\mathbf{J} = \boldsymbol{\sigma}\mathbf{E}$, is

$$\boldsymbol{\sigma} = \frac{e^2 n_0}{m^*} \frac{\tau}{1 + (\omega_c \tau)^2} \begin{pmatrix} 1 & \omega_c \tau & 0 \\ -\omega_c \tau & 1 & 0 \\ 0 & 0 & 1 + (\omega_c \tau)^2 \end{pmatrix} \tag{7.60}$$

The components of the resistivity tensor $\boldsymbol{\rho} = 1/\boldsymbol{\sigma}$ are given by

$$\rho_{ij} = \frac{\mathcal{D}_{ij}}{\mathcal{D}}$$

where $\mathcal{D}_{ij}$ is the ijth minor of $\mathcal{D}$, the determinant of $\boldsymbol{\sigma}$.   Accordingly,

$$\boldsymbol{\rho} = \frac{m^*}{n_0 e^2 \tau} \begin{pmatrix} 1 & -\omega_c \tau & 0 \\ \omega_c \tau & 1 & 0 \\ 0 & 0 & 1 \end{pmatrix} \tag{7.61}$$

Since the diagonal components of the resistivity tensor are not influenced by the magnetic field, the magnetoresistance in this case vanishes exactly.

The boundary condition imposed in the measurement of the Hall effect is $J_y = 0$, $E_y \neq 0$.   The angle between $\mathbf{E}$ and $\mathbf{J}$, the Hall angle, is given by

$$\tan \phi = \left(\frac{E_y}{E_x} \right)_{J_y = 0} = \frac{\mathcal{K}_1''}{\mathcal{K}_1'} = \omega_c \tau \tag{7.62}$$

The Hall coefficient, defined by the relation

$$E_y = R J_x H_z \tag{7.63}$$

is then

$$R = \frac{\rho_{yx}}{H_z} \tag{7.64}$$

In the weak-field limit $\sigma \approx \sigma_0$, regardless of the shape of the con-stant-energy surfaces. Combining Eqs. (7.64) and (7.6) we obtain

$$R = \frac{12\pi^3\hbar^2}{ec(m^*|\nabla_k\epsilon|\alpha)_\eta} \tag{7.65}$$

which reduces to the well-known result

$$R = \frac{1}{n_0 ec} \tag{7.66}$$

for a spherical band of standard form.

From Eq. (7.65) we see that the sign of the Hall coefficient is given by the product em^*. When the effective mass is positive (conduction by electrons), R is negative; when m^* is negative, R is positive, and it is then common practice to speak of "hole" conduction. That is to say, the charge carriers, instead of being assigned a negative effective mass are thought of as positively charged particles obeying the usual newtonian equation of motion.

Although the reciprocal of R is frequently used as a measure of the number of charge carriers n_0, it is well to bear in mind that this is at best a rough approximation (see Table 7.8).

In polyvalent metals, where the Fermi surface generally penetrates beyond the first Brillouin zone, the sections of the Fermi surface in the different zones may, when mapped into the central zone, form several closed surfaces. As a first approximation one may then think of the total current as the sum of charge transport associated with the several portions of the Fermi surface. One then frequently speaks of simul-taneous conduction by carriers of different masses, or electron and hole conduction, whichever is appropriate. Multiband models must be con-sidered only as very crude guides, especially when applied to metals rather than semiconductors. Detailed expressions for a two-band model may be found in Wilson's book. If one arbitrarily assumes that there exist two partially filled bands of standard form, the conductivity and Hall coefficient are given by

$$\sigma = \sigma_1 + \sigma_2 \tag{7.67}$$

$$R = \frac{R_1\sigma_1^2 + R_2\sigma_2^2}{(\sigma_1 + \sigma_2)^2} \tag{7.68}$$

Table 7-8   Comparison of Number of Valence Electrons and $n_0 = 1/R\epsilon c$ for a Number of Metallic Conductors
N denotes the number of atoms per cubic centimeter; NZ, the number of valence electrons per cubic centimeter

	Monovalent Metals						
Metal	*Li*	*Na*	*K*	*Cs*	*Cu*	*Ag*	*Au*
$N \times 10^{-22}$	4.6	2.5	1.3	0.85	8.5	5.8	5.9
$NZ \times 10^{-22}$	4.6	2.5	1.3	0.85	8.5	5.8	5.9
$(1/R\epsilon c) \times 10^{-22}$	3.7	2.5	1.5	0.8	11.4	7.5	8.7

	Polyvalent Metals							
Metal	*Be*	*Mg*	*Zn*	*Cd*	*Al*	*In*	*Tl*	*Sn*
$N \times 10^{-22}$	12.3	4.3	6.6	4.6	6.0	3.8	3.5	3.7
$NZ \times 10^{-22}$	24.6	8.6	13.2	9.2	18.0	11.4	10.5	14.8
$(1/R\epsilon c) \times 10^{-22}$	−2.5	6.7	−18	−10.5	21	89	−26	156

Here, $\sigma_j = n_j e^2 \tau_j / m_j^*$ and $R_j = 1/n_j e c$. Since the magnitude and the sign of the Hall coefficient for each band are determined by the characteristics of that band, it is clear from Eq. (7.68) that the measured Hall coefficient may be quite small by virtue of near cancellation of the two terms in the numerator. The two-band model, though it must be taken with quite a few ounces of salt when applied to metals, does provide the simplest physical explanation for the observed magnetoresistance effect.

B.   Magnetoresistance

The transverse magnetoresistance is also measured subject to the boundary condition $J_y = 0$. From Eq. (7.54) we have

$$J_x = e^2 \mathcal{K}_1' E_x + \frac{e^2 \mathcal{K}_1''^2 E_x}{\mathcal{K}_1'} = e^2 E_x \left[\frac{\mathcal{K}_1'^2 + \mathcal{K}_1''^2}{\mathcal{K}_1'} \right] \qquad \sigma = e^2 \left[\frac{\mathcal{K}_1'^2 + \mathcal{K}_1''^2}{\mathcal{K}_1'} \right]$$
$$(7.69)$$

To lowest order in kT/η, Eq. (7.69) leads to the result $\sigma = e^2 \mathcal{K}_1$. In the approximation of a single spherical band the magnetoresistance thus vanishes in the extreme degenerate limit.†

† A finite result is obtained if terms in $(kT/\eta)^2$ are retained in the expansions of the integrals $\mathcal{K}_1'$ and $\mathcal{K}_1''$. However, observed values of magnetoresistance are orders of magnitude larger than this theoretical prediction; moreover, the experiments do not show any evidence of the anticipated temperature dependence.

A nonvanishing result obtains in the two-band model, namely,

$$\frac{\Delta\rho}{\rho_0} = \frac{\sigma_1\sigma_2(\beta_1 - \beta_2)^2}{(\sigma_1 + \sigma_2)^2 + (\sigma_1\beta_2 + \sigma_2\beta_1)^2} \approx \frac{\sigma_1\sigma_2}{(\sigma_1 + \sigma_2)^2}(\beta_1 - \beta_2)^2 \qquad (7.70)$$

where

$$\beta_j = \tan\phi_j = \frac{e\tau_j}{m_j^*c}H \qquad (7.71)$$

It is instructive to inquire into the reason why the presence of a second group of degenerate charge carriers should lead to a pronounced qualitative change. In the case of a single spherical band, all carriers have the same drift velocity. The Hall field that must be established to satisfy the imposed boundary condition on the current now cancels exactly the Lorentz force on these carriers, with the result that even in a transverse magnetic field the net force acting on the carriers is that due to the primary field E_x.

If, however, we have two bands with, for example, carriers of different effective masses, the situation is drastically modified, as indicated schematically in Fig. 7.14. When $\mathbf{H} = 0$, the net current is $n_1e_1v_1 + n_2e_2v_2$. When $\mathbf{H} \neq 0$ and $J_y = 0$, the Hall field must be a compromise between the Hall fields that would act if the two bands carried current separately. Since the Lorentz forces on the carriers of the two types differ, the resultant drift-velocity vectors are no longer directed along the x direction, but make angles θ_1 and θ_2 with it, such that

$$n_1v_1 \sin\theta_1 + n_2v_2 \sin\theta_2 = 0$$

The x component of the current is now

$$J_x(H) = e(n_1v_1 \cos\theta_1 + n_2v_2 \cos\theta_2) < e(n_1v_1 + n_2v_2)$$

Evidently, it is the "spread" in velocity which gives rise to the observed magnetoresistance. In the single, standard-band approximation this is restricted to the thermal spread, which explains why in this model the magnetoresistance is of order $(kT/\eta)^2$.

In a real metal whose Fermi surface is not spherical, the spread in velocity at the Fermi surface comes from the fact that now $\mathbf{v} = (1/\hbar)\boldsymbol{\nabla}_k\epsilon$ depends on the point on the Fermi surface at which the energy gradient

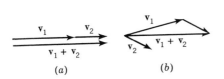

(a) (b)

Fig. 7.14 Influence of a transverse magnetic field on the current in the two-band model. We have assumed $n_1 = n_2$ and $m_1 < m_2$. (a) $\mathbf{H} = 0$ and J is proportional to $|\mathbf{v}_1 + \mathbf{v}_2| = v_1 + v_2$; (b) $\mathbf{H} \neq 0$ and directed perpendicular to the plane of the paper. $J_y = 0$ and J_x is proportional to $|\mathbf{v}_1 + \mathbf{v}_2| < v_1 + v_2$.

is calculated.   In a manner of speaking, neighboring portions of the Fermi surface may contribute to the Hall field in varying degree, the net result being qualitatively the same as in the multiband model, except for one very important difference.   A multiband model with *spherical* energy surfaces must always lead to vanishing longitudinal magnetoresistance. In practice the longitudinal magnetoresistance is often of the same magnitude as the transverse.

Observation of a finite longitudinal magnetoresistance demonstrated most forcefully the need to extend the discussion of charge transport to encompass nonspherical energy surfaces.   Now a simple, analytic solution for ψ, such as Eq. (7.53), cannot be found.   Instead, one must resort to an expansion, Eq. (5.26).   Clearly, each application of the operator $\mathbf{H} \cdot \boldsymbol{\Omega}$ will introduce one higher power of $\mathbf{H}$ in the solution of ϕ. We limit the expansion to terms in H^2.   The components of the current are then given by the general expression

$$J_i = \sigma_{ij}E_j + \sigma_{ijk}E_jH_k + \sigma_{ijkl}E_jH_kH_l \tag{7.72}$$

where the subscripts denote the cartesian components.   For the sake of brevity, we have invoked the summation convention: whenever an index is repeated in any term, that index is to be summed over all coordinates.

σ_{ij} is the ordinary zero-field conductivity tensor.   The other two tensors are given by

$$\sigma_{ijk} = \delta_{klm} \int \frac{e^3\tau^2}{c} \frac{\partial f_0}{\partial \epsilon} v_i v_m m_{jl}^{-1} \, d\mathbf{k} \tag{7.73}$$

$$\sigma_{ijkl} = \delta_{mkn}\delta_{plq} \int \frac{e^4\tau^3}{c^2} \frac{\partial f_0}{\partial \epsilon} v_i v_m \left[m_{qj}^{-1} m_{pn}^{-1} + v_p \frac{\partial}{\partial k_j} (m_{qn}^{-1}) \right] d\mathbf{k} \tag{7.74}$$

Here

$\delta_{ijk} = 0$ unless $i \neq j \neq k \neq i$

$\delta_{ijk} = +1$ if the suffixes are even permutations of 1,2,3

$\delta_{ijk} = -1$ if the suffixes are odd permutations of 1,2,3

and m_{ij}^{-1} denotes the ijth component of the reciprocal-mass tensor.

Although Eqs. (7.73) and (7.74) appear fairly compact, they prove quite unwieldy expressions when one undertakes to calculate the conductivity tensors with them.   Under cubic symmetry many components vanish, but even then the computations remain very tedious still.   For detailed discussions, the reader is referred to the original research papers [9].

This theory does predict both a transverse magnetoresistance to zero order in kT/η and a longitudinal magnetoresistance.   Their magnitudes depend critically on the assumed shape of the Fermi surface and anisotropies of the relaxation time.   If the distortion from sphericity is not too severe, one can expand the Fermi surface in spherical harmonics and treat the expansion coefficients as parameters whose magnitudes are adjusted by fitting the resulting theoretical expressions to experiment. Again, for cubic symmetry many spherical harmonics must vanish leaving only the "Kubic Harmonics." Measurements of the magnetoresistance of copper, interpreted as outlined above, suggested that the Fermi surface is so severely distorted that it touches the zone boundaries in the $\langle 111 \rangle$ directions. This conclusion is in complete agreement with detailed studies of the Fermi surface, using more sophisticated and powerful techniques based on magnetic effects in the high-field limit.

It is evident that the theory of magnetoresistance is of considerable complexity. There exists, however, one rule which appears to be obeyed in nearly every instance. From Eq. (5.17) we may write

$$\phi = \tau \mathbf{P} \cdot \mathbf{v} \left[1 - \frac{e\tau}{c\hbar^2} \mathbf{H} \cdot \mathbf{\Omega} \right]^{-1} = \phi_0 \left[1 - \frac{e\tau}{c\hbar^2} \mathbf{H} \cdot \mathbf{\Omega} \right]^{-1} \tag{7.75}$$

The current density, and hence also the conductivity, is effectively proportional to the deviation of the distribution from equilibrium—that is, to ϕ. Consequently, $\Delta\rho/\rho_0$ will be given by $(\phi_0 - \phi)/\phi$. Since the magnetic field appears in Eq. (7.75) only in the product τH, and since $\tau \propto 1/\rho_0$, it follows that

$$\frac{\Delta\rho}{\rho_0} = \Re \left(\frac{H}{\rho_0} \right) \tag{7.76}$$

where $\Re$ is a different function for each metal, but is independent of temperature and impurity content for small impurity concentrations.

Equation (7.76) is Kohler's rule. A typical example, demonstrating its applicability, is shown in Fig. 7.15. From Eq. (7.76) it is clear that magnetoresistance measurements are best performed at low temperatures, where ρ_0 is small, so that significant changes in resistivity occur already in moderate magnetic fields. Often the function $\Re(H/\rho_0)$ is displayed by means of a reduced Kohler diagram, as in Figs. 7.15 and 7.16. Here $\Delta\rho/\rho_0$ is plotted as a function of $H/\mathfrak{r}(t)$, where $\mathfrak{r}$ is the reduced resistivity $\mathfrak{r} = \rho(T)/\rho(\Theta)$.

C. Thermomagnetic Effects

Whenever a thermal current is carried by charged particles, application of a magnetic field will give rise to effects analogous to the galvanomagnetic effects. Moreover, as, in the absence of a magnetic field, coupling between charge and energy current leads to thermoelectric effects, thermomagnetic phenomena appear in the presence of a magnetic field. For example, if the sides of a Hall sample are thermally as well as electrically

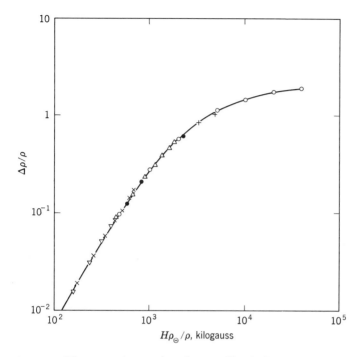

Fig. 7.15   Magnetoresistance in polycrystalline indium in a transverse magnetic field showing agreement with Kohler's rule.   Some points affected by boundary scattering have been suppressed. *Justi*, ∇, In 1: 14°K, $\rho/\rho_{273} = 0.024$;
$\times$, In 6: 14°K, $\rho/\rho_{273} = 0.0086$;
$+$, In 6: 4.2°K, $\rho/\rho_{273} = 0.0012$;
Olsen, $\bigcirc$, In 2: 4.2°K, $\rho/\rho_{273} = 6.00007$;
$\bullet$, In 2: 2°K, $\rho/\rho_{273} = 0.00003$.
(From J. Olsen, "Electron Transport in Metals," p. 67, Interscience Publishers, Inc., New York, 1962.)

insulated, one finds that concurrently with the Hall field a transverse temperature gradient is established (Ettinghausen effect).   One can readily derive suitable expressions for the various coefficients defined in Table 7.7 by solving the Boltzmann equation, subject to the correct boundary conditions.   For a single band of standard form

$$A_{N_i} = -\frac{\pi^2 k^2 T^2}{3m^*c}\left(\frac{\partial \tau}{\partial \epsilon}\right)_{\eta} \tag{7.77}$$

$$A_E = -\frac{T}{m^*c}\left(\frac{\partial \ln \tau}{\partial \epsilon}\right)_{\eta} \tag{7.78}$$

$$A_L = \frac{e\tau}{m^*c} \tag{7.79}$$

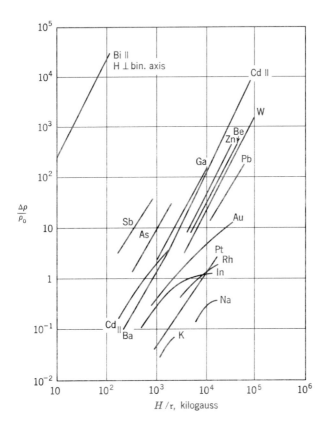

Fig. 7.16 $(\Delta\rho_H/\rho_0)$ against H/τ (double logarithmic scales) for several metals. (*From A. N. Gerritsen, Metallic Conductivity, in "Encyclopedia of Physics," vol. XIX, p. 185, Springer-Verlag OHG, Berlin, 1956.*)

The corresponding expressions for a two-band model are given in Wilson's book. Such formulas are, however, of limited value. First, anisotropy of the Fermi surface will again greatly modify the results. Second, as in the case of the thermoelectric effects, phonon drag plays an important role over a fairly wide temperature range.

7.6 ELECTRICAL PROPERTIES OF FERROMAGNETIC METALS

The electrical behavior of transition metals reveals a variety of peculiarities that appear to be intimately related to their unusual magnetic properties. First, the temperature dependence of the resistivity differs markedly from that of normal metals. In the ferromagnetic metals ρ increases rapidly below the Curie temperature T_c. Well above T_c, $d\rho/dT$ is approximately constant, but the extrapolation of the straight line to $T = 0°\text{K}$ does not intersect the ordinate at $\rho \approx 0$ as in the case of normal metals (see Fig. 6.7). These observations point to an additional resistance associated with the decrease in spontaneous magnetization as T approaches T_c.

In the nonferromagnetic transition metals, such as Pd and Pt, there is, of course, no sharp discontinuity in $d\rho/dT$ such as exists in nickel. However, the resistivity is significantly larger than in other metals with a comparable number of conduction electrons (see Table 7.3). Moreover, the ideal, that is to say, temperature-dependent, part of the resistivity of ferromagnetic as well as nonferromagnetic transition metals deviates from the Bloch-Grüneisen T^5 law at low temperatures, where, instead, a T^2 behavior is approached.

Second, the magnetoresistance of ferromagnets is anomalous. At low fields, $\Delta\rho_l/\rho$, the longitudinal magnetoresistance, is positive, whereas $\Delta\rho_t/\rho$, the transverse magnetoresistance, is negative. However, once saturation has been attained, i.e., all magnetic domains are aligned parallel to the external field, both transverse and longitudinal magnetoresistances are negative. If the magnetoresistance is extrapolated to zero field, one finds that $|\Delta\rho_l/\Delta\rho_t| \approx 2$.

Third, the thermoelectric power of ferromagnetic metals exhibits a pronounced anomaly near the Curie temperature, as shown in Fig. 6.8.

Fourth, the Hall effect of ferromagnetics shows quite remarkable features. Typical curves of the Hall field E_H versus B are shown in Fig. 7.17. Since the Lorentz force on an electron is $(e/c)(\mathbf{v} \times \mathbf{B})$, a linear relationship between E_H and B is to be expected. The knees of the curves appear at values of B corresponding to magnetic saturation. If one then writes the Hall field per unit current density, $E_H = R_0 H + R_1 M$, where M is the magnetization, one finds that while R_0 is of reasonable magnitude and is only weakly temperature-dependent, R_1 is several orders of magnitude larger and is a sensitive function of temperature, increasing sharply as T approaches T_c.

These, then, are some of the peculiar electrical properties of transition metals that need be explained. The earliest attempt in this direction was by Mott [10], who based his theory on the itinerant, or band, model for the d electrons, as contrasted with the Heisenberg theory of ferromagnetism, where d electrons are presumed localized on the individual magnetic ions. Accordingly, Mott considered a metal in which a fairly broad $4s$ conduction band overlaps a much narrower $3d$ band, as indicated schematically in Fig. 7.1. Since the d band is nearly full, it is more convenient to talk in terms of d holes rather than d electrons.

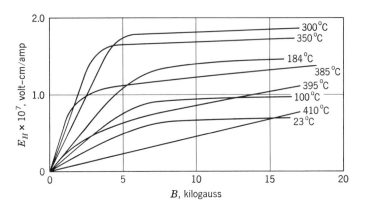

Fig. 7.17 The Hall field E_H per unit current density in nickel as a function of magnetic induction B between room temperature and 410°C. [*From F. J. Blatt, Solid State Phys.*, **4**: 266 (1953).]

Above the Curie temperature the d holes of both spin orientations are present in equal concentration. However, for $T < T_c$, the number of spin-up ($\uparrow$) holes, say, increases, while the spin-down ($\downarrow$) d band is gradually filled until, at $T = 0°$K, only $\uparrow$ holes exist. If the polarization of the s band is negligible—a fair approximation—the number of d holes can then be determined from the saturation magnetization at $T = 0°$K; that is,

$$M(0) = \mu n_d^\uparrow = \mu n_d$$

At finite temperatures, $M(T) = \mu(n_d^\uparrow - n_d^\downarrow)$, $n_d^\uparrow + n_d^\downarrow = n_d$. Since the Fermi energy must be the same for $\uparrow$ and $\downarrow$ holes, the increase in magnetization with decreasing temperature, in the band model, is viewed as a gradual relative displacement in energy of the $\uparrow$ and $\downarrow$ d bands due to the exchange interaction. Since $m_d^* > m_s^*$ and the relaxation times τ_d and τ_s are presumably about equal, the contribution of the d holes to the current may be neglected in first approximation. The argument of Mott proceeds, then, as follows.

Under the influence of lattice vibrations—or other imperfections—an s electron may be scattered into an empty state in the s or d band. Thus, $1/\tau_s = 1/\tau_{ss} + 1/\tau_{sd}$. Assuming equal coupling constants, the relaxation rates τ_{ss}^{-1} and τ_{sd}^{-1} will be proportional to the density of final states. Since $\mathcal{N}_d > \mathcal{N}_s$, it follows that $\tau_{sd} < \tau_{ss}$. Below T_c, $\mathcal{N}_d(\eta)$ depends on the spin orientation and, for a given spin orientation, on the temperature through the temperature dependence of $M(T)$.

To lowest order in perturbation theory, lattice scattering cannot induce spin flips. Spin flips can take place if we include spin-orbit interaction, which for the moment, however, we shall neglect. Thus, an $s\uparrow$ electron scatters into either an empty $s\uparrow$ or $d\uparrow$ state, and similarly for an $s\downarrow$ electron.

We, therefore, view the spin $\uparrow$ and spin $\downarrow$ bands separately and consider $s\uparrow \rightarrow d\uparrow$ and $s\downarrow \rightarrow d\downarrow$ scattering independently. We now have the following:

$$\frac{1}{\tau_{sd}^\uparrow} \propto \mathcal{N}_d^\uparrow \qquad \frac{1}{\tau_{sd}^\downarrow} \propto \mathcal{N}_d^\downarrow$$

Since the density of states is proportional to $\epsilon^{\frac{1}{2}}$, where ϵ is measured relative to the band edge, and the Fermi energy is proportional to the $\frac{2}{3}$ power of the density of electrons (or holes), we have

$$\frac{1}{\tau_{sd}^\uparrow} \propto (n_d^\uparrow)^{\frac{1}{3}} = \left[\frac{(1+z)n_d}{2}\right]^{\frac{1}{3}}$$
$$\frac{1}{\tau_{sd}^\downarrow} \propto (n_d^\downarrow)^{\frac{1}{3}} = \left[\frac{(1-z)n_d}{2}\right]^{\frac{1}{3}}$$

(7.80)

where $z = M(T)/M(0)$. The conductivities of the $\uparrow$ and $\downarrow$ s bands are thus

$$\sigma^\uparrow = c\left[\frac{1}{\alpha + (1+z)^{\frac{1}{3}}}\right] \qquad \sigma^\downarrow = c\left[\frac{1}{\alpha + (1-z)^{\frac{1}{3}}}\right]$$

(7.81)

where α is the relative probability of s-s to s-d scattering at $T > T_c$. The total conductivity is the sum $\sigma^\uparrow + \sigma^\downarrow$.† Hence,

$$\rho = \text{const}\left[\frac{1}{(1+z)^{\frac{1}{3}} + \alpha} + \frac{1}{(1-z)^{\frac{1}{3}} + \alpha}\right]^{-1}$$

(7.82)

If $\alpha = \frac{1}{4}$, $\rho(z=0)/\rho(z=1) = 3$, which demonstrates the important influence of the magnetization on the resistivity. As T_c is approached, the magnetization decreases very sharply (see Fig. 7.18) and, hence, the temperature dependence of ρ is very strong here.

The presence of a narrow overlapping d band implies not only a large, but also a strongly energy-dependent, density of states at the Fermi energy. Consequently, $[\partial \ln \sigma(\epsilon)/\partial \ln \epsilon]_\eta$ will also be large below T_c, and Eq. (7.81) leads to rough agreement with experimental results on the thermoelectric power.

Mott's theory, despite its apparent success, is deficient in several respects. In the simple two-band model employed by Mott, the Fermi

---

† If we allow spin flip during scattering, we should average the resistivities rather than add the conductivities.

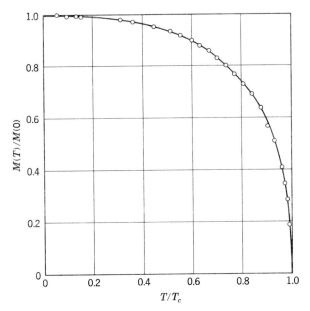

Fig. 7.18 The saturation magnetization of nickel as a function of temperature. (*After C. Kittel, "Introduction to Solid State Physics," John Wiley & Sons, Inc., New York, 1956.*)

surfaces of s and d bands neither touch nor intersect. Thus, a certain minimum crystal momentum is required for an s-d transition so that, below some temperature T^*, phonon-induced s-d scattering should decay exponentially, which leads to a resistivity contribution of the form

$$\rho \propto \exp\,(-T^*/T)$$

Of course, the true Fermi surfaces are surely nonspherical and contact is then quite possible. In that case, however, ρ_i should again go roughly as T^5, as contrasted with the observed T^2 variation at low temperatures. Finally, Mott and Stevens [11] have argued that in some transition metals a model of localized spins is to be preferred over the band model.

An alternative explanation for the resistivity of ferromagnetic transition metals is based on the Heisenberg model. The additional resistivity is now a consequence of scattering of s electrons by localized spins through the mechanism of exchange interaction. At high temperatures, i.e., near the Curie temperature, the theories rely on a molecular-field approximation, whereas at low temperatures the process can be discussed in terms of scattering of conduction electrons by spin waves.

This spin-disorder scattering also leads to a substantial resistivity contribution and, moreover, the theory predicts the observed T^2 dependence at very low temperatures. Finally, the phenomenon of the resistance minimum and the associated thermoelectric and magnetoresistance anomalies observed in various metals contaminated with transition-metal impurities also can be understood within the framework of spin-disorder scattering.

The s-d and spin-disorder scattering mechanisms differ in a quite fundamental way, by which they may be distinguished experimentally. In s-d scattering, the new feature is the presence of a narrow band whose effective density of states varies with magnetization. Its principal influence on the resistivity is through a magnetization-dependent relaxation rate. However, the basic electron-imperfection coupling itself—be it electron-phonon or electron-impurity interaction—is in no way altered. By contrast, spin-disorder scattering is a *new* interaction, and in this theory the resistivity is increased not by the enhancement of an existing relaxation rate, but by the addition of an altogether new one. Suppose we now introduce a small number of impurities in a pure ferromagnet. They will give rise to yet another relaxation mechanism, electron-impurity scattering. In the spin-disorder theory these impurities should simply contribute a *temperature-independent* residual resistance. In the Mott model, on the other hand, the perturbation which induces s-d transitions is immaterial. Consequently, in this case, impurities should further enhance the magnetization-dependent, i.e., *temperature-dependent* resistivity. The different behavior is exemplified in Fig. 7.19. Experimental results of Coles indicate that the Mott model is a good approximation for nickel, whereas spin-disorder scattering is probably dominant in iron.

Neither model, however, can account for the T^2 dependence of the resistivity of nonferromagnetic transition metals. A satisfactory explanation involves electron-electron scattering and will be discussed in the following section.

The low-field magnetoresistance of ferromagnetic metals can be understood if the resistance in a domain depends on the direction of its magnetization relative to that of the current. If the resistance is greatest when **M** and **J** are parallel, the initial change of resistivity with sample magnetization can be attributed to domain rotation. If this interpretation is correct, domain alignment through magnetostriction should result in a corresponding resistance change. In agreement with these expectations, it is found that under tension the resistance decreases in a material with negative magnetostriction, but increases if the magnetostriction is positive. The model also leads directly to the ratio $|(\Delta\rho_l/\Delta\rho_t)|_{H\to 0} = 2$, if one assumes that originally the domains are ori-

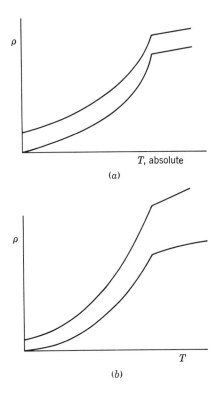

ρ

T, absolute

(a)

ρ

T

(b)

Fig. 7.19 Predicted behavior of the electrical resistivity of iron and nickel alloys. (a) Iron and iron-ruthenium; (b) nickel and nickel-palladium. [*From B. R. Coles, Advan. Phys.,* **7**: 63 (1958).]

ented at random.   Once saturation has been achieved, further enhancement of the applied field causes an increase of the spontaneous magnetization, regardless of orientation.   On either the s-d or spin-disorder scattering models, an increase of M should reduce the resistivity, in agreement with observation.

An explanation of the large extraordinary Hall coefficients of ferromagnets was given by Karplus and Luttinger [12].   The crucial interaction is spin-orbit coupling of the slightly polarized conduction electrons. An alternative theory, also involving spin-orbit coupling, was advanced by Smit [13].   Both theories predict that R_1 be proportional to ρ^n with $n \approx 2$, in reasonably good accord with experimental results.

7.7 ELECTRON-ELECTRON SCATTERING: METALS

In the preceding, we have not considered electron-electron interactions, more specifically, the mutual scattering of charge carriers.   As shown by Bohm and Pines, the collective motion of the electron gas in a metal provides for fairly effective screening of the long-range mutual coulomb interaction, leaving only a residual short-range interaction of the form

$$V(r) = \frac{e^2}{r} e^{-r/r_0} \tag{7.83}$$

where r_0 is of the order of the Wigner-Seitz radius r_s. This potential should lead to electron-electron scattering with a differential scattering cross section of the same order of magnitude as that for polyvalent impurities in monovalent metals (see page 156). The latter, we know, have a pronounced effect on the conductivity; and since electrons, now viewed as scattering centers, exist in great profusion in a metal, we might expect that electron-electron scattering will also be an important resistance mechanism.

Normal electron-electron scattering, however, cannot contribute to the electrical resistivity, because in such collisions charge and momentum must be conserved. Thus, normal electron-electron scattering is unable to relax a distribution with a net momentum such as the one shown in Fig. 5.1.

If Umklapp processes are included, momentum can be imparted to the lattice as a whole through electron-electron collisions, and they can then contribute to the electrical resistivity. The magnitude of this contribution is, however, greatly reduced by the operation of the exclusion principle. An electron-electron scattering event, N or U, can occur only if *both* initial states are occupied and *both* final states unoccupied. Thus, both electrons must originate and terminate in states within kT of the Fermi energy. This double application of the exclusion principle reduces the transition rate by the factor $(kT/\eta)^2$ and accounts for the characteristic T^2 temperature dependence of the calculated resistivity. Although the calculations indicate that electron-electron collisions should give an observable resistivity in the alkali metals below about 2°K, no evidence for it has as yet been found.

In transition metals, however, curves of $\ln \rho$ versus $\ln T$ generally show a change from an approximate T^5 behavior toward a T^2 law below about 10°K. Here the situation is rather different, in that the low-mass, mobile s-band electrons, which are the effective charge carriers, can be scattered by the relatively heavy, nearly stationary d-band electrons, and normal scattering now does lead to a nonvanishing resistivity. According to Appel [14], the resistivity should be given by

$$\rho = \frac{1 + (\gamma\sigma_0^d + \gamma^{-1}\sigma_0^s)[C(kT)^2/(A - \eta)\eta]}{\sigma_0^s + \sigma_0^s + \sigma_0^s\sigma_0^d(\gamma + \gamma^{-1} - 2)[C(kT)^2/(A - \eta)\eta]}$$

$$\gamma = \frac{n_s}{n_d}\left(\frac{m_s}{m_d}\right)^{\frac{1}{2}} \qquad C = \frac{Q_{sd}(m_s m_d)^{\frac{1}{2}} v_{sd}}{e^2} \tag{7.84}$$

where σ_0^s and σ_0^d are the conductivities of the s- and d-band carriers in the absence of s-d scattering. Here a model of two overlapping bands of standard form has been assumed, with A the energy difference between the s- and d-band edges and Q_{sd} the s-d-scattering cross section (integrated with the $1 - \cos \theta$ weighting factor). At very low temperatures, σ_0^s and σ_0^d are temperature-independent, being limited by impurity scattering, and the initial increase of ρ with T should be dominated by the $(kT)^2/(A - \eta)\eta$ term in Eq. (7.84).

The electron distribution in thermal conduction (Fig. 5.2) is already one which carries no charge current. Hence, normal processes should be capable of reducing the thermal conductivity even in ordinary metals. In other words, we are concerned here with the relaxation of an energy current as contrasted with a particle current, and the conditions

$$\mathbf{k}_1^i + \mathbf{k}_2^i = \mathbf{k}_1^f + \mathbf{k}_2^f$$

$$\epsilon_1^i + \epsilon_2^i = \epsilon_1^f + \epsilon_2^f$$

do not imply conservation of energy flow in each collision; that is,

$$\mathbf{k}_1^i\epsilon_1^i + \mathbf{k}_2^i\epsilon_2^i \neq \mathbf{k}_1^f\epsilon_1^f + \mathbf{k}_2^f\epsilon_2^f$$

The calculated thermal resistivity due to electron-electron scattering is proportional to T, consistent on one hand with the direct application of the Wiedemann-Franz law to Eq. (7.84), and, on the other, with the simple kinetic-theory expression for the thermal conductivity

$$\kappa_{ee} = \tfrac{1}{3}C_e v_e l_{ee} \tag{7.85}$$

where C_e is the electronic specific heat, proportional to T, and l_{ee} is the mean free path for electron-electron scattering, proportional to $(\eta/kT)^2$.

Even in transition metals, however, in the temperature range where $\rho \propto T^2$, the ideal thermal resistivity remains proportional to T^2 as in normal metals, showing no tendency toward a linear temperature behavior. This is not altogether surprising if we recall that the ideal thermal resistivity decreases only as T^2 at low temperatures, whereas the electrical resistivity falls as T^5. As we pointed out in Chap. 5, the rapid decrease of ρ with T at low temperatures is in part due to the limitation of electron-phonon scattering to small-angle events so that

$$\frac{1}{\tau_\sigma} = \left\langle \frac{1}{\tau} (1 - \cos \theta) \right\rangle \approx \frac{1}{\tau}\left(\frac{T}{\Theta}\right)^2$$

whereas $1/\tau_\kappa = 1/\tau$ (see page 126). Thus, in comparison with its effect on electrical resistivity, electron-phonon scattering is $(\Theta/T)^2$ times as influential in limiting the thermal resistivity. Consequently, the contribution of electron-electron scattering, though evident in measurements of ρ, will be masked by electron-phonon scattering if one attempts to observe its effect in measurements of the thermal resistivity.†

7.8 SIZE EFFECTS; THIN FILMS AND WIRES

In the preceding sections we have tacitly assumed that the electrical properties of a given specimen are independent of its shape and size. Indeed, only under these conditions does the concept of resistivity as an intrinsic material property make sense.   Of course, one may still define a resistivity by

$$\rho = \frac{A}{L}\, R \tag{7.86}$$

where A and L are the cross section and length of the sample and R is its resistance, even though ρ proves to be a function of A and/or L.   In this section, the "resistivity" is to be interpreted in this context.

The experimental conditions under which the resistivity, as defined by Eq. (7.86), will depend on sample dimensions are fairly obvious.   As long as l, the electronic mean free path (mfp) in the bulk material, is a small fraction of the distance between sample boundaries, the presence of these boundaries cannot significantly influence the intrinsic transport properties.   When, however, by drawing or etching, the diameter d of a wire is reduced to the point where d approaches l, a significant fraction of conduction electrons will strike and be scattered at the surface rather than in the bulk.   Since it is very rarely specular, surface scattering will augment the bulk relaxation mechanisms substantially and diminish the effective relaxation time.

Specular reflection of waves requires that surface irregularities be smaller than the wavelength.   In metals, the de Broglie wavelength of electrons on the Fermi surface, $\lambda_0 = 2\pi/k_0$, is of the order of one interatomic distance.   Hence, even the most carefully prepared macroscopically "flat" surface fails to meet such a stringent requirement.   It is interesting, however, to note that specular reflection has been observed in thin bismuth films.   This is consistent with the extremely small number of conduction electrons (approximately 10^{-5} per atom) in this semimetal.   Thus, in bismuth, k_0 is correspondingly small and λ_0 is several hundred interatomic spacings.

The theory of transport in thin films and wires rests on the solution of the Boltzmann equation subject to appropriate boundary conditions. In the case of diffuse surface scattering, the solution must be such that the distribution function for electrons immediately adjacent to and traveling away from the surface is the equilibrium distribution.   Using this boundary condition, Fuchs [15] and Dingle [16] solved the transport

† See, however, G. K. White and R. J. Tainsh, *Phys. Rev. Letters,* **19,** 165 (1967).

equation (for $H = 0$) for thin films and wires, respectively, and obtained expressions for the resistivities which, in the limits $d \gg l$ and $d \ll l$, reduce to

$$\begin{array}{ccc} & d \gg l & d \ll l \\ \text{Film:} & \rho = \rho_b \left(1 + \dfrac{3}{8}\dfrac{l}{d}\right) & \rho = \rho_b \left[\dfrac{4}{3}\dfrac{l}{d}\left(\ln\dfrac{l}{d}\right)^{-1}\right] \\ \text{Wire:} & \rho = \rho_b \left(1 + \dfrac{3}{4}\dfrac{l}{d}\right) & \rho = \rho_b \dfrac{l}{d} \end{array} \tag{7.87}$$

where ρ_b is the bulk resistivity.

The above expressions can be interpreted simply in terms of a reduction of the mfp due to surface scattering. If surface-scattering and bulk-relaxation mechanisms are assumed statistically independent, we can write

$$\frac{1}{l_{\text{eff}}} = \frac{1}{l} + \frac{1}{l_s} \tag{7.88}$$

where l and l_s are the bulk mfp and the mfp associated with surface scattering. If we further assume that $l_s \approx d$ and recall that

$$\rho = \frac{m^*}{n_0 e^2 \tau_{\text{eff}}} = \frac{m^* v_F}{n_0 e^2 l_{\text{eff}}} \tag{7.89}$$

where v_F is the Fermi velocity, we obtain directly

$$\rho = \rho_b \left(1 + \frac{l}{l_s}\right) = \rho_b \left(1 + \frac{l}{d}\right) \tag{7.90}$$

For cylindrical wires the resistivity calculated from Eq. (7.90) is within 5 percent of Dingle's exact numerical results over the entire range $0 < l/d < \infty$.

It follows from Eq. (7.90) that the bulk mfp l can be deduced from measurements of the resistivity as a function of wire diameter.

Figure 7.20 shows a plot of ρ versus $1/d$ from which ρ_b and l can be determined. Moreover, since the product $\rho_b l$ depends only on the concentration of conduction electrons and their Fermi momentum [see Eq. (7.89)], plots of ρ versus $1/d$ derived from measurements at different temperatures should appear as parallel straight lines. In many instances, however, significant deviations from the anticipated behavior have been observed [17]. These suggest that, in a thin specimen, electron-phonon scattering is a more effective resistive mechanism than in the bulk. A theory which explains the behavior was developed by Blatt and Satz [18] following a suggestion of Olsen.

The magnetoresistance of thin films and wires also displays several unusual and interesting features. If one applies a longitudinal magnetic

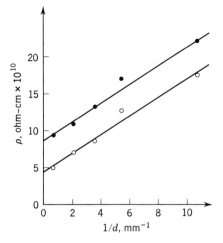

Fig. 7.20   The resistivity of thin indium wires as a function of $1/d$.
● $- T = 4.2°$K; ○ $- T = 0°$K (extrapolated from measurements to $1°$K). [*After P. Wyder, Phys. Kondens. Materie,* **3**: 263 (1965).]

field to a thin sodium wire, the resistance, following a brief initial rise, diminishes with increasing magnetic field to the value of the bulk material in the magnetic field (see Fig. 7.21).

Under the influence of the longitudinal field, the conduction electrons follow helical trajectories whose axes coincide with that of the wire. Thus, electrons, which in the absence of the magnetic field might have terminated their mfp at the surface, are deflected away from the surface by the Lorentz force and traverse mfp equal to that in the bulk metal. The radius of the helix is given by

$$r_H = \frac{m^* v_{FC}}{eH} \sin \theta$$

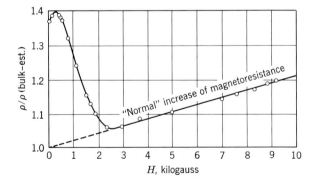

Fig. 7.21   Longitudinal magnetoresistance of a thin sodium wire at $4.2°$K. (*From D. K. C. MacDonald, Electrical Conductivity of Metals and Alloys at Low Temperature, in* "*Encyclopedia of Physics,*" *vol.* XIV, *Springer-Verlag OHG, Berlin,* 1956.)

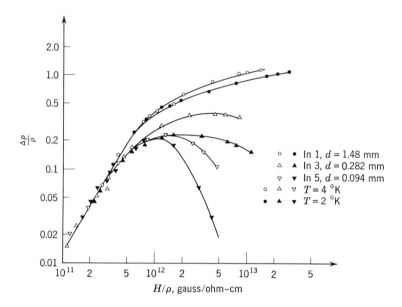

Fig. 7.22 Longitudinal magnetoresistance of thin indium wires. [*After P. Wyder, Phys. Kondens. Materie,* **3**: 263 (1965).]

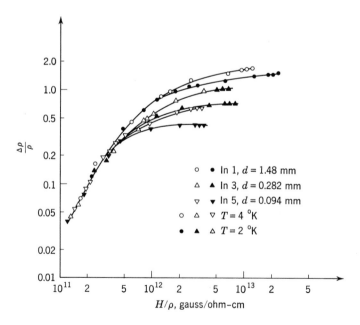

Fig. 7.23 Transverse magnetoresistance of thin indium wires. [*After P. Wyder, Phys. Kondens. Materie,* **3**: 263 (1965).]

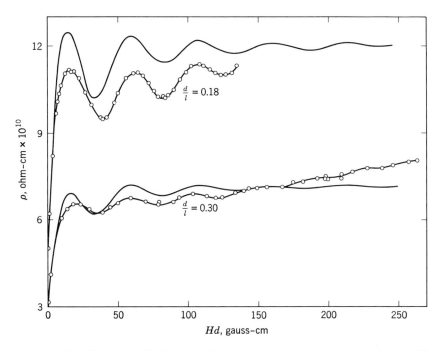

Fig. 7.24 Sondheimer oscillations in the resistivity of thin aluminum films. The abscissa is normalized—the values are Hd in gauss-cm, where d is the film thickness. The ratio d/l for the two film samples is shown in the figure. The solid curves are calculated using Sondheimer's theory and assuming an average electron Fermi momentum of 1.33×10^{-19} g-cm/sec. [*After K. Forsvoll and I. Holwech, Phil. Mag.,* **9**: 435 (1964).]

where θ is the angle between the velocity vector and **H**. Thus, as **H** increases, an ever larger fraction of the conduction electrons is prevented from striking the surface by the focusing effect of the magnetic field, and the behavior of the sample approaches that of a bulk specimen. One can show that the magnetoresistance of the wire should reach its low-field maximum (approximately 400 gauss in Fig. 7.21) when

$$r_{H_c}(\theta = 90°) = \frac{m^* v_F c}{e H_c} \approx \frac{d}{2}$$

Thus, if this critical field H_c is measured as a function of d, the Fermi momentum $m^* v_F$ can be estimated. The effect shown in Fig. 7.21 will be observable either in metals whose bulk magnetoresistance is quite low, e.g., sodium, or in metals whose magnetoresistance saturates, provided d is sufficiently small that at the saturation field r_H is still in excess of d. An example of the latter instance is shown in Fig. 7.22.

Although the theory of transverse galvanomagnetic effects in thin wires is as yet incomplete, qualitative arguments suggest, and experimental results show, a similar negative transverse magnetoresistance under suitable conditions (see Fig. 7.23). As Wyder [19] has demonstrated, the electronic thermal conductivity of thin wires follows the pattern established by the electrical conductivity.

Another interesting transverse magnetoresistance effect in thin films was predicted by Sondheimer [20] and has been verified experimentally in a number of metals. Sondheimer showed that, if the magnetic field is oriented perpendicular to the plane of the film, the galvanomagnetic effects should display an oscillatory pattern. Since the period of the oscillations is a function of the Fermi momentum, one can use the phenomenon to measure this parameter. Experimental results on aluminum films and calculated curves are shown in Fig. 7.24.

PROBLEMS

7.1. The resistivity of copper at 273°K is 1.55×10^{-6} ohm-cm. Using an effective mass $m^* = 1.5m$, calculate:

(a) The relaxation time τ
(b) The mean free path of conduction electrons
(c) The cyclotron angular frequency ω_c in a field of 50 kilogauss
(d) The resistivity for which $\omega_c\tau = 1$ in a field of 50 kilogauss
(e) The magnetic field for which $\omega_c\tau = 1$ at 4.2°K if, by cooling to 4.2°K, the resistivity of copper is reduced from its value at 273°K by a factor of 4,000

7.2. The table below gives the ideal resistivity of a metal between 4°K and room temperature.

Resistivity of a Metal as a Function of Temperature

T, °K	ρ_i, $\mu ohm\text{-}cm$	T, °K	ρ_i, $\mu ohm\text{-}cm$
4	3.6×10^{-6}	80	0.85
6	4.3×10^{-5}	90	1.03
8	2.5×10^{-4}	100	1.21
10	8.5×10^{-4}	120	1.57
15	0.0056	140	1.92
20	0.017	160	2.27
25	0.039	180	2.63
30	0.077	200	2.99
40	0.19	220	3.36
50	0.34	250	3.93
60	0.51	273	4.40
70	0.675	295	4.84

(a) Determine, using at least two different methods, the Debye temperature Θ_R of this metal.

(b) Using the result of (a), calculate $\rho_i(T)$ from the tabulated values of $\mathscr{J}_5(\Theta/T)$ at the temperatures corresponding to the tabulated values of Θ/T. Estimate the observed values of $\rho_i(T)$ at the same values of Θ/T by interpolation. Plot $\rho_i^{\text{calc}}(T) - \rho_i^{\text{exp}}(T)$. Discuss the significance of this curve.

7.3. The addition of impurities generally influences the Debye temperature of a metal. For example, Θ_R of pure copper is about $335°K$, but Θ_R of an alloy of copper with 0.78 atomic percent As is about $313°K$. The residual resistivity of this alloy, measured at $4.2°K$, is 4.83 μohm-cm. Calculate the resistivity of the alloy at $78°$ and $273°K$ and compare these results with those obtained by direct application of Matthiessen's rule.

7.4. Derive the expressions for the Hall coefficient and magnetoresistance in the two-band model, Eqs. (7.68) and (7.70).

7.5. The resistance of pure indium at $4.2°K$ is 8.7×10^{-10} ohm-cm and its transverse magnetoresistance ratio $\Delta\rho/\rho_0$ in a field of 1,000 gauss is 0.7 and proportional to H^2. Assuming that resistance can be measured to an accuracy of one part in 10^4, at what magnetic field can $\Delta\rho/\rho_0$ be determined to an accuracy of 10 percent at $273°K$. ρ_0 of indium at $273°K$ is 8.4×10^{-6} ohm-cm.

7.6. The accompanying figure shows the resistivity of sodium at elevated temperatures. Assuming that the deviation from the linear Bloch-Grüneisen relation

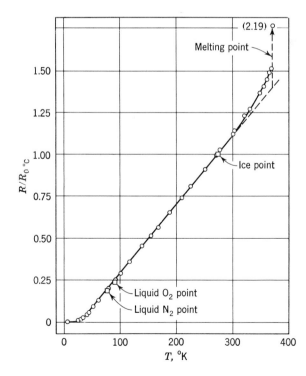

at high temperature is due to vacancies in thermodynamic equilibrium at these temperatures, calculate:

(a)   The activation energy for formation of vacancies in sodium

(b)   The resistivity in sodium due to a vacancy concentration of one atomic percent.

7.7.   From Fig. 7.20 determine the mean free path and average Fermi momentum of electrons in indium at 4.2°K.   Compare this value of the Fermi momentum with that obtained from the results of Fig. 7.22 using the criterion discussed on page 239.   (The curves for the thinnest wire at 4° and 2°K should be used.)

REFERENCES

1.   Ziman, J. M.: *Proc. Roy. Soc. London*, **A226**: 436 (1954).
2.   Meaden, G. T.: "Electrical Resistance of Metals," p. 100, Plenum Press, New York, 1965.   (Presents a comprehensive list of Θ_D and Θ_R.)
3.   Kohler, M.: Z. *Physik*, **124**: 772 (1948); **125**: 679 (1949).
4.   Sondheimer, E. H.: *Proc. Roy. Soc. London*, **A203**: 75 (1950).
5.   Guénault, A. M., and D. K. C. MacDonald: *Proc. Roy. Soc. London*, **A274**: 154 (1963).
6.   Seitz, F.: *Advan. Phys.*, **1**: 43 (1952).
7.   Nordheim, L.: *Ann. Physik*, **9**: 607 (1931).
8.   Klemens, P. G.: *Proc. Phys. Soc. London*, **A67**: 194 (1954).
9.   Olson, R., and S. Rodriguez: *Phys. Rev.*, **108**: 1212 (1957).
10.   Mott, N. F.: *Proc. Phys. Soc. London*, **47**: 571 (1935); *Proc. Roy. Soc. London*, **A153**: 699 (1936); **A156**: 368 (1936).
11.   Mott, N. F., and K. W. H. Stevens: *Phil. Mag.*, **2**: 1364 (1957).
12.   Karplus, R., and J. M. Luttinger: *Phys. Rev.*, **95**: 1154 (1954).
13.   Smit, J.: *Physica*, **21**: 877 (1955).
14.   Appel, J.: *Phil. Mag.*, **8**: 1071 (1963).
15.   Fuchs, K.: *Proc. Cambridge Phil. Soc.*, **34**: 100 (1938).
16.   Dingle, R. B.: *Proc. Roy. Soc. London*, **A201**: 545 (1950).
17.   Yaqub, M., and J. F. Cochran: *Phys. Rev.*, **137**: A1182 (1965); B. N. Aleksandrov; *Soviet Phys. JETP*, **16**: 286 (1963).
18.   Blatt, F. J., and H. G. Satz: *Helv. Phys. Acta*, **33**: 1007 (1960).
19.   Wyder, P.: *Phys. Kondens. Materie*, **3**: 263 (1965).
20.   Sondheimer, E. H.: *Phys. Rev.*, **80**: 401 (1950).

BIBLIOGRAPHY

General

Blatt, F. J.: Theory of Mobility of Electrons in Solids, *Solid State Phys.*, **4**: 199 (1957).

Jones, H.: Theory of Electrical and Thermal Conductivity in Metals, "Encyclopedia of Physics," vol. XIX, p. 227, Springer-Verlag OHG Berlin, 1956.

Olsen, J. L.: "Electron Transport in Metals," Interscience Publishers, New York, 1962.

Pippard, A. B.: The Dynamics of Conduction Electrons, "Low Temperature Physics," p. 3, Gordon and Breach Science Publishers, Inc., New York, 1962.

Wilson, A. H.: "The Theory of Metals," Cambridge University Press, London, 1953.

Ziman, J. M.: "Electrons and Phonons," Oxford University Press, London, 1960.

Electrical Conductivity

Broom, T.: Lattice Defects and the Electrical Resistivity of Metals, *Advan. Phys.*, **3**: 26 (1954).

Gerritsen, A. N.: Metallic Conductivity, Experimental Part, "Encyclopedia of Physics," vol. XIX, p. 137, Springer-Verlag OHG, Berlin, 1956.

MacDonald, D. K. C.: Electrical Conductivity of Metals and Alloys at Low Temperatures, "Encyclopedia of Physics," vol. XIV, p. 137, Springer-Verlag OHG, Berlin, 1956.

Meaden, G. T.: "Electrical Resistance of Metals," Plenum Press, New York, 1965.

Thermal Conductivity

Klemens, P. G.: Thermal Conductivity of Solids at Low Temperatures, "Encyclopedia of Physics," vol. XIV, p. 198, Springer-Verlag OHG, Berlin, 1956.

Mendelssohn, K., and H. M. Rosenberg: Thermal Conductivity of Metals at Low Temperatures, *Solid State Phys.*, **12**: 223 (1961).

Rosenberg, H. M.: Properties of Metals at Low Temperatures, *Progr. Metal Phys.*, **7**: 339 (1958).

Thermoelectric and Galvanomagnetic Effects

Jan, J. P.: Galvanomagnetic and Thermomagnetic Effects in Metals, *Solid State Phys.*, **5**: 1 (1957).

MacDonald, D. K. C.: "Thermoelectricity," John Wiley & Sons, Inc., New York, 1962.

Transition Metals

Bozorth, R. M.: "Ferromagnetism," D. Van Nostrand, Company, Inc., Princeton, N.J., 1951.

Coles, B. R.: Spin Disorder Effects in the Electrical Resistivities of Metals and Alloys, *Advan. Phys.*, **7**: 40 (1958).

Mott, N. F.: Electrons in Transition Metals, *Advan. Phys.*, **13**: 325 (1964).

Van den Berg, G. J.: Anomalies in Dilute Metallic Solutions of Transition Elements, "Progress in Low Temperature Physics," vol. IV, p. 194, North Holland Publishing Company, Amsterdam, 1964.

Size Effects

Sondheimer, E. H.: Electron Transport Phenomena in Metals, "Progress in Low Temperature Physics," vol. II, p. 151, North Holland Publishing Company, Amsterdam, 1957.

———: Mean Free Path of Electron in Metals, *Advan. Phys.*, **1**: 1 (1952).

8
Homogeneous Semiconductors

8.1 INTRODUCTION

In the next three chapters we shall treat the important fundamental conduction processes in semiconductors. Technological advances of recent decades have been phenomenal in all facets of physics, but perhaps most remarkable in the area of semiconductor physics and technology. Here, the amount of work and the financial support which it has received have been truly prodigious, with results that have amply justified these efforts. Basic and applied research have advanced along parallel lines and have constantly revealed device potentials of unexpected and unusual kind. Clearly, all we can attempt to do here is provide the reader with the basic knowledge essential to an understanding of the operation of the numerous devices and present a brief description of the more important ones.

A semiconductor is, strictly speaking, an insulator. At very low temperatures the valence band of the ideally pure substance is completely occupied by electrons, and there is no overlap with the next higher group of allowed energy levels. Since neither a completely full nor, of course, an empty band allows for charge transport, the conductivity of the substance is zero. Distinction between the metal and the semiconductor is truly qualitative; between the semiconductor and the insulator we have only a quantitative difference in the magnitude of the energy gap that separates the valence- and conduction-band edges. In the semiconductor, this gap is sufficiently small that a significant number of electrons are promoted into the conduction band by thermal excitation at temperatures well below the melting point of the material; in the insulator, thermal excitation of carriers across the gap is negligible.

It is not necessary, however, that carriers be excited across the entire gap separating the valence and conduction bands. Certain impurities when dissolved in the solvent matrix introduce energy levels that lie within the forbidden gap (see Sec. 6.9A). One distinguishes between *donor* and *acceptor* impurities according as the impurity level, in the zero-temperature limit, contains or is devoid of an electron. If, for example, this level contains an electron, excitation of that electron into the conduction band will be achieved more readily than the promotion of an electron from the valence band, since the donor level lies closer to the conduction-band edge. To some extent, then, whether a substance is a semiconductor or not may depend on its ability to dissolve suitable impurities; e.g., the energy gap in diamond is quite large, and one normally thinks of diamond as an insulator. Nevertheless, it is possible to endow diamond with semiconducting properties by suitable treatment.

This chapter concerns itself with the electronic properties of homogeneous semiconductors; inhomogeneous semiconductors, important in device applications, are discussed in the following chapter. We first consider the equilibrium statistics of carriers in the intrinsic and extrinsic regimes (Sec. 8.2), and then discuss, in some detail, the mobility of carriers and the conductivity of semiconductors (Sec. 8.3). The following section (8.4) is devoted to a brief outline of piezoresistance, with emphasis on the fundamental information that can be gleaned from piezoresistance measurements. Galvanomagnetic effects are the subject of the next section (8.5); and here again the focus is on the fundamental aspects rather than applications. The penultimate section (8.6) treats thermal conductivity and thermoelectricity, and the last section (8.7) describes some, but by no means all, of the common devices which employ homogeneous semiconductors.

In each section except the last we initially treat the "ideal" semiconductor, endowed with the simplest, and most improbable, band structure, and then focus our attention on two real substances, germanium and silicon, whose band structures deviate drastically from the ideal (see Sec. 6.7). There are, however, many other semiconducting materials, especially among the III-V compounds, whose band structures approximate the ideal. A typical example is gallium arsenide (others are InSb, InAs, and GaSb), whose conduction-band minimum occurs at $\mathbf{k} = 0$. The valence band is more complicated than the ideal as a consequence of degeneracy of the p-like valence-band states. This band consists of heavy- and light-hole bands, degenerate at $\mathbf{k} = 0$, and a third band which is split from the other two by spin-orbit coupling, as in the case of germanium and silicon. However, as a result of lack of inversion symmetry in GaAs, the heavy-hole band degeneracy at $\mathbf{k} = 0$ is lifted and the maxima do not lie at the center of the Brillouin zone. Thus, although for many purposes GaAs, InSb, etc., especially n-type material, approximate the ideal semiconductor, there remain some essential differences that take on special significance in optical and magnetooptical experiments (see Chaps. 10 and 11). For purposes of the present chapter, however, GaAs may be considered the prototype "ideal" semiconductor. The important band parameters and some electrical properties of a selected group of common semiconducting materials are listed in Table 8.1.

8.2 SEMICONDUCTOR STATISTICS

A. Intrinsic Regime

The band structure of the ideal, pure semiconductor is shown in Fig. 8.1. An energy gap $\epsilon_G = \epsilon_c - \epsilon_v$ separates the uppermost allowed energy level

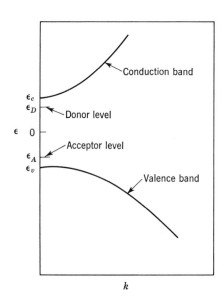

Fig. 8.1 The energy band structure of an ideal semiconductor. [*From F. J. Blatt, Solid State Phys.*, **4**: 209 (1953).]

Table 8.1 Electrical Properties and Band Parameters of Some Common Semiconductors. [After J. L. Moll, "Physics of Semiconductors," McGraw-Hill Book Company, New York, 1964, p. 70.]

Semi-conductor	Energy gap, ev		Mobility,[a] cm²/volt-sec (T = 300°K)		Mobility variation $\mu \propto T^{-n}$		Band structure[b]	Effective mass m/m_0		Dielectric constant $\varkappa$
	300°K	0°K	Electrons	Holes	Electrons	Holes		Electrons	Holes	
Ge[c]	0.67	0.75	3,950 (3,900)[d]	3,400 (1,900)[d]	1.66	2.33	A	$m_\parallel = 1.6$ $m_\perp = 0.082$	0.3, 0.04[e]	16
Si[c]	1.106	1.153	1,900 (1,350)[d]	425 (480)[d]	2.5	2.7	B	$m_\parallel = 0.97$ $m_\perp = 0.19$	0.5, 0.16[e]	12
InSb[f]	0.16	0.26	78,000	750	1.6	2.1	C	0.013	0.6	17
InAs[f]	0.33	0.46	33,000	460	1.2	2.3	C	0.02	0.41	14.5
InP[f]	1.29	1.34	4,600	150	2.0	2.4	C	0.07	0.4	14
GaSb[f]	0.67	0.80	4,000	1,400	2.0	0.9	C	0.047	0.5	15
GaAs[f]	1.39	1.58	8,500	400	1.0	2.1	C	0.072	0.5	12.5
GaP[f]	2.24	2.40	110	75	1.5	1.5	B	....	....	10

[a] The values of mobility are those obtained in the purest and most perfect material available to date. In most circumstances the actual mobilities are less than the value listed.

[b] A: germanium-like; conduction-band minimum in ⟨111⟩ direction; valence-band maximum at (000).

B: silicon-like: conduction-band minimum in ⟨100⟩ direction; valence-band maximum at ⟨000⟩.

C: GaAs-like: conduction-band minimum at ⟨000⟩; valence band consists of light-hole band with maximum at **k** = 0 and heavy-hole bands with maxima near **k** = 0 (see figure).

There are significant variations among the various semiconductors in details of the band structure beyond this A, B, C classification.

[c] E. M. Conwell, Properties of Silicon and Germanium, *Proc. IRE,* **46** : 6 (June, 1958), has a fairly comprehensive discussion of the properties of silicon and germanium.

[d] The numbers in parentheses are drift mobilities.

[e] The heavy- and light-hole masses are both given.

[f] C. Hilsum and A. C. Rose-Innes, "Semiconducting III-V Compounds," Pergamon Press, New York, 1961, list the properties of the III-V compounds and discuss the details of the band structure, etc., that must be neglected in a listing such as this.

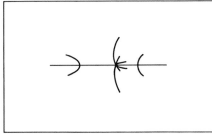

Type-C band structure.

in the valence band and the lowest energy state in the conduction band. At $T = 0°K$ the valence band is completely filled, the conduction band empty. As the temperature is raised, however, there is a finite probability that an electron in the valence band may gain sufficient energy from the lattice to make a transition into an allowed state in the conduction band. In that case the valence band will no longer be filled, and the most convenient description of this band is then in terms of holes, or unoccupied states. In the effective-mass approximation, these holes behave exactly as would electrons of positive mass and positive charge. The use of the hole concept is clearly more advantageous than the description of the valence band in terms of all the remaining electrons.

The number of electrons in the conduction band is given by

$$n = 2 \int_0^\infty \mathcal{N}_n(\epsilon) f_0(\epsilon) \, d\epsilon \tag{8.1}$$

where we have taken as our zero of energy the edge of the valence band, ϵ_v. Consistent with common semiconductor terminology, we have used the subscript n to denote the density of states in the conduction band, the band with *negative* charge carriers. The letter p is used for the valence-band properties. The number of *positively* charged holes is

$$p = 2 \int_{-\infty}^0 \mathcal{N}_p(\epsilon)[1 - f_0(\epsilon)] \, d\epsilon \tag{8.2}$$

The Fermi energy is determined by the condition of electrical neutrality

$$n = p \tag{8.3}$$

In the most general case, Eqs. (8.1) to (8.3) do not lead to an analytic solution for η, and one must resort to a table of the Fermi functions. In many instances, however, the "classical" approximation (see Sec. 3.4) is valid and Eqs. (8.1) and (8.2) can be integrated to give

$$n = A_n(kT)^{\frac{3}{2}} e^{(\eta - \epsilon_c)/kT} \tag{8.4}$$

$$p = A_p(kT)^{\frac{3}{2}} e^{-\eta/kT} \tag{8.5}$$

with

$$A_n = 2 \left(\frac{m_n}{2\pi\hbar^2} \right)^{\frac{3}{2}} \quad \text{and} \quad A_p = 2 \left(\frac{m_p}{2\pi\hbar^2} \right)^{\frac{3}{2}} \tag{8.6}$$

Here, m_n and m_p denote the density-of-states effective masses of electrons and holes, respectively. On equating Eqs. (8.4) and (8.5), we find

$$\eta = \tfrac{1}{2}\epsilon_G + \tfrac{3}{4}kT \ln \frac{m_p}{m_n} \tag{8.7}$$

From Eq. (8.7) one sees that at $T = 0°K$, the Fermi level is exactly midway between the valence- and conduction-band edges. It remains at this position at elevated temperatures also, provided $m_n = m_p$. If, however, the effective masses in the two bands are not equal, the Fermi energy will change with temperature and shift in the direction of the band which has the lower effective mass. The physical reason for this shift is as follows.

According to Eq. (3.8), the density of states $\mathcal{N}(\epsilon)$ is proportional to $m^{*\frac{3}{2}}$, so that a small effective mass corresponds to a small density of states. To maintain electrical neutrality, the relative loss in the number of available states must be compensated by an appropriate increase in the probability that an electron (or hole) occupy a particular allowed energy state.

A useful relation is obtained by multiplying Eqs. (8.4) and (8.5)

$$np = \frac{1}{2}\left(\frac{kT}{\pi h^2}\right)^3 (m_n m_p)^{\frac{3}{2}} e^{-\epsilon_G/kT} \tag{8.8}$$

Equation (8.8) exhibits the important fact that the product of n and p is, for a given material, a function of the temperature only. Provided the presence of impurities does not modify the band parameters, the introduction of, say, donors, to increase the number of conduction electrons, will result in a concomitant reduction in the number of holes, leaving the product np unaltered. This is true, however, only as long as the classical approximation is valid for both types of carriers.

B. Extrinsic Regime

It is well known that the addition of certain impurities to such semiconductors as germanium, silicon, indium antimonide, indium arsenide, lead telluride, etc., has a profound effect on their electrical properties. Germanium, silicon, and many of the intermetallic semiconducting compounds crystallize in the zincblende structure, consistent with the homopolar character of the dominant binding forces. Of the four valence electrons of, for example, germanium, each contributes to one of the four bonds between nearest neighbors. If, now, a pentavalent impurity, such as arsenic, replaces a germanium atom in the lattice, four of the five valence electrons of the impurity again participate in the binding. The remaining valence electron, however, will be bound to the impurity only through the coulomb attraction between it and the positively charged impurity ion. In Sec. 6.9A we showed that the electronic polarization of the medium and the generally small effective mass of the electron in the crystal lattice conspire to reduce this coulomb interaction, so that the ionization energy of the impurity is considerably smaller than one

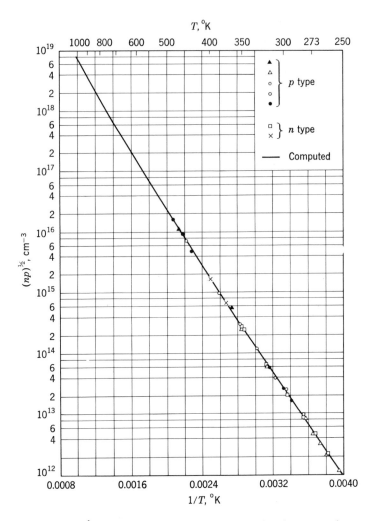

Fig. 8.2 $(np)^{\frac{1}{2}}$—the intrinsic carrier concentration in germanium—versus reciprocal temperature, plotted on a semilogarithmic scale; see Eq. (8.8). [*From F. T. Morin and J. P. Maita, Phys. Rev.,* **94**: 1527 (1954).]

Rydberg, the ionization energy of a hydrogen atom. The ionization energies of various donors and acceptors in silicon and germanium are listed in Table 8.2.

From the binding energies of Table 8.2, it is now evident why certain impurities in germanium and silicon can provide free carriers at temperatures far lower than those required for intrinsic excitation. In

Table 8-2   Ionization Energies of Donors
and Acceptors in Si and Ge, ev

Impurity	Germanium	Silicon
Donors		
Li		0.033
P	0.0120	0.044
As	0.0127	0.049
Sb	0.096	0.039
Bi		0.069
Acceptors		
B	0.0104	0.045
Al	0.0102	0.057
Ga	0.0108	0.065
In	0.0112	0.16

the following, we shall calculate the carrier density for an extrinsic semiconductor.

We consider a semiconductor containing N_D donors and N_A acceptors with localized levels at ϵ_D and ϵ_A in the forbidden gap (see Fig. 8.1). At any finite temperature, some of these impurities will be neutral, others ionized. We denote their number by N_D^0, N_A^0 and N_D^+, N_A^-, respectively. We then have

$$N_D^+ = N_D - N_D^0 \qquad N_A^- = N_A - N_A^0 \tag{8.9}$$

Further, electrical neutrality demands that

$$n + N_A^- = p + N_D^+ \tag{8.10}$$

As in the intrinsic case, the Fermi function gives the probability that a particular electronic energy state is occupied. However, the statistical considerations for localized impurity states are somewhat more complicated than for the continuum. Although an ionized donor can accommodate an electron of either spin orientation, once occupied, this state cannot then accommodate a second electron of opposite spin because of the sizeable electrostatic interaction between the two localized charge distributions. One finds [1] that, under normal conditions, N_D^0 and N_A^- are given by

$$N_D^0 = N_D \frac{1}{1 + \frac{1}{2}e^{(\epsilon_D - \eta)/kT}}$$

$$N_A^- = N_A \frac{1}{1 + \frac{1}{2}e^{(\epsilon_A - \eta)/kT}} \tag{8.11}$$

where the factor $\frac{1}{2}$ in front of the exponents would be absent if we were dealing with band states.   From Eqs. (8.4), (8.5), and (8.10) we have

$$A_n(kT)^{\frac{3}{2}}e^{(\eta-\epsilon_c)/kT} + N_A \frac{2}{2 + e^{(\epsilon_A-\eta)/kT}}$$

$$= A_p(kT)^{\frac{3}{2}}e^{-\eta/kT} + N_D \frac{2}{2 + e^{(\eta-\epsilon_D)/kT}} \quad (8.12)$$

In general, Eq. (8.12) cannot be solved analytically for the Fermi energy, and graphical and numerical methods have frequently been employed. To illuminate the pertinent physical features, it suffices, however, to consider certain special situations that, fortunately, are also of considerable practical interest.

We focus attention first on the uncompensated n-type semiconductor.   *Compensation* is a term that refers to the doping of a semiconductor containing predominantly impurities of one kind, say, donors, with impurities of the opposite type, i.e., acceptors.   In the totally uncompensated n-type semiconductor, $N_A = 0$.   We further assume that in the temperature range of interest here, N_D greatly exceeds the number of intrinsic carriers that would be present in the pure sample. From this last assumption and Eq. (8.8) it follows that $p \ll n$ and, hence, from Eqs. (8.4) and (8.5),

$$e^{-\eta/kT} \ll e^{(\eta-\epsilon_c)/kT} \quad (8.13)$$

since presumably m_n and m_p do not differ by more than an order of magnitude.   Consequently, Eq. (8.12) simplifies to

$$N_D \frac{2}{2 + e^{(\eta-\epsilon_D)kT}} = A_n(kT)^{\frac{3}{2}}e^{(\eta-\epsilon_c)/kT} \quad (8.14)$$

The left-hand side of Eq. (8.14) is the number of ionized donor impurities; the right-hand side, the number of conduction electrons.   In the limit $T \to 0°K$, we would expect to find only neutral donor atoms, since ionization does require an expenditure of energy $\epsilon_c - \epsilon_D$.   Since, as $T \to 0°K$, all donor states are occupied and all conduction-band states empty, the Fermi energy must lie somewhere between ϵ_D and ϵ_c.   Moreover, since $N_D^+ \ll N_D$, $\exp[(\eta - \epsilon_D)/kT] \gg 1$.   Consequently,

$$e^{(\epsilon_c-\epsilon_D)/kT} \gg 1 \quad (8.15)$$

Making use of Eqs. (8.15) and (8.13), Eq. (8.14) can be solved for the Fermi energy η, and one obtains

$$e^{\eta/kT} \approx \left(\frac{N_D}{A_n}\right)^{\frac{1}{2}} (kT)^{-\frac{3}{4}} e^{(\epsilon_c-\epsilon_D)/2kT} \quad (8.16)$$

and for the carrier density,

$$n = \left(\frac{N_D A_n}{2}\right)^{\frac{1}{2}} (kT)^{\frac{3}{4}} e^{-\epsilon_d/2kT} \tag{8.17}$$

where $\epsilon_d = \epsilon_c - \epsilon_D$ is the donor ionization energy.

As one might have anticipated, the number of carriers in this low-temperature region increases approximately exponentially with temperature. In principle, then, it should be possible to determine the impurity ionization energy from experimental results on the temperature dependence of the conduction-electron concentration as measured by the Hall effect. However, in practice, as one approaches the low-temperature region, one very often reaches the situation where the number of acceptor impurities that exist in even the most perfect n-type material exceeds the number of conduction electrons. These minority impurities have energy levels well below those of the donor states and are, therefore, ionized by the donor impurities at all temperatures. Consequently, even as $T \to 0°K$, the probability that a donor state be ionized must remain finite, and this requirement necessarily fixes the Fermi energy at ϵ_D. In this case, then, the exponential term will be of the form $\exp(-\epsilon_d/kT)$ rather than as in Eq. (8.17). One can show that if $N_D > N_A$ and $n < N_A$, the carrier concentration is given by [1]

$$n = \frac{N_D - N_A}{2N_A} A_n (kT)^{\frac{3}{2}} e^{-\epsilon_d/kT} \tag{8.18}$$

Let us now turn to the high-temperature region, but remember that we must remain well below the intrinsic regime. As T increases, so will, according to Eq. (8.17), the carrier concentration n. Clearly, this cannot continue indefinitely, for all the donor atoms will ultimately be ionized, at which point no further source of conduction electrons will exist, except the valence band which we have excluded by the condition (8.13). We might expect that this "exhaustion region" will be attained at temperatures such that $kT > \epsilon_d$. Since the left-hand side of Eq. (8.14) is just N_D^+, we may then set it equal to N_D and obtain for the Fermi energy

$$\eta = \epsilon_c + kT \ln\left[\frac{N_D}{A_n(kT)^{\frac{3}{2}}}\right] \tag{8.19}$$

Typically, $A_n(kT)^{\frac{3}{2}}$ is considerably greater than N_D. For example, in germanium at $300°K$, $A_n(kT)^{\frac{3}{2}} \cong 2 \times 10^{18}$ cm^{-3}, corresponding to a doping concentration rather higher than usually employed. Thus, we see that as the temperature increases and one enters the exhaustion region, the Fermi energy falls further and further toward the center of the

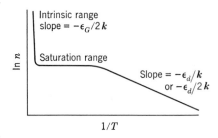

Fig. 8.3 Carrier concentration in an n-type semiconductor as a function of temperature. (*After R. A. Smith, "Semiconductors," Cambridge University Press, London*, 1959.)

forbidden region. Of course, ultimately, if the temperature is raised even more, the sample will become intrinsic in the sense that

$$n = N_D^+ + p \simeq p$$

In this limit, the Fermi energy is given by Eq. (8.7), and the carrier concentration once again increases approximately exponentially with temperature. The carrier concentration as a function of temperature for a typical case is shown schematically in Fig. 8.3. Of course, all that has been said above for the n-type semiconductor applies, *mutatis mutandis*, to p-type materials as well.

8.3 MOBILITY AND CONDUCTIVITY

Evidently the number of charge carriers in a semiconductor is generally a sensitive function of temperature and purity, in sharp contrast to the prevailing situation in a metal. It is largely for this reason that it is preferable to focus attention on the mobility μ, instead of the conductivity σ. The former is in many respects of more fundamental significance than the conductivity which can change by many orders of magnitude in going from one sample to another simply because the carrier concentration has altered. Of course, once μ is known, σ is directly at hand through the relation

$$\sigma = ne\mu_n + pe\mu_p \tag{8.20}$$

where μ_n and μ_p are the electron and hole mobilities. The mobility is just the proportionality constant relating the average drift velocity of the charge distribution to the applied electric field:

$$v_d = \mu E \tag{8.21}$$

Mobility values are normally given in units of cm²/volt-sec. If the carrier concentration is n cm^{-3}, the conductivity in units of ohm^{-1}-cm^{-1} is

$$\sigma = 1.6 \times 10^{-19} n\mu \tag{8.22}$$

When charge transport is due to the combined motion of several distinct groups of charge carriers (e.g., electrons and holes) the multiband model may be employed with good justification.

As in the preceding chapter, we shall base our discussion on the "standard-band" model, unrealistic though it may be, for the very good reason that the attempt to carry through the corresponding calculations for a band structure appropriate to germanium would so complicate matters as to obscure the physics altogether. However, having derived results for spherical energy contours, we shall then retrace our steps and show where modifications must be made if one wishes to apply the same general treatment to the more realistic situation. We shall also give at least a qualitative discussion of the changes that these modifications may bring forth in the ultimate result.

A.   Lattice-scattering Regime

Ideal semiconductor   We first treat the scattering of charge carriers through their interaction with acoustic vibrations and return subsequently to optical-mode scattering. In Chap. 6 we showed that in the present instance a meaningful relaxation time can be defined, since the scattering event is substantially elastic. Consequently, the results of Sec. 7.2 are directly applicable, and we can proceed immediately to the calculation of the appropriate relaxation time τ. We then evaluate the transport coefficients using now the classical limit of the Fermi distribution, rather than the degenerate limit suitable to metallic conductors.

The calculation of the relaxation time poses no difficulties, for we need only substitute the transition probability $\mathfrak{S}(\mathbf{k},\mathbf{k}')$ as given by Eq. (6.42) into Eq. (5.28). For elastic collisions $|\mathbf{k}| = |\mathbf{k}'|$; hence, the factor $1 - [\phi(\mathbf{k}')/\phi(\mathbf{k})]$ may be replaced by $1 - \cos\theta$, where θ, the angle between $\mathbf{k}$ and $\mathbf{k}'$, is related to q by

$$q = 2k \sin \frac{\theta}{2}$$

We obtain

$$\tau_L = \frac{\hbar \rho u_l^2}{2\pi k T \mathcal{N}(\epsilon) \mathcal{E}_1^2} = \frac{2\pi \hbar^4 \rho u_l^2}{(2m^*)^{\frac{3}{2}} \mathcal{E}_1^2} \frac{\epsilon^{-\frac{1}{2}}}{kT} = \tau_0 \frac{\epsilon^{-\frac{1}{2}}}{kT} \tag{8.23}$$

where ρ denotes the mass density. We note here that since $l = \tau v$ and $v \propto \epsilon^{\frac{1}{2}}$, the mean free path of electrons limited by lattice scattering is independent of their energy.

To calculate the mobility, Hall coefficient, Seebeck coefficient, and so on, we need only carry through the integration and determine the coefficients $\mathfrak{K}_n$, Eq. (7.4). In the classical limit, which is generally applicable in most semiconductor problems, one obtains from Eqs. (7.4), (3.22), and (3.24),

$$\mathfrak{K}_n = \frac{4n}{3m^*\pi^{\frac{1}{2}}} \int_0^\infty \tau(\epsilon)\epsilon^{n-1}x^{\frac{3}{2}}e^{-x}\,dx \tag{8.24}$$

where

$$x = \frac{\epsilon}{kT}$$

According to Eqs. (7.5) and (8.20) we now have for the mobility

$$\mu = \frac{e}{n}\,\mathfrak{K}_1 = \frac{4e}{3m^*\pi^{\frac{1}{2}}} \int_0^\infty \tau(\epsilon)x^{\frac{3}{2}}e^{-x}\,dx = \frac{e}{m^*}\langle\tau\rangle$$

$$\langle\tau\rangle \equiv \frac{4}{3\pi^{\frac{1}{2}}} \int_0^\infty \tau(\epsilon)x^{\frac{3}{2}}e^{-x}\,dx \tag{8.25}$$

In the case of acoustic-mode scattering we obtain, on substituting Eq. (8.23) into the above expression,

$$\mu = \frac{4e\tau_0}{3m^*\pi^{\frac{1}{2}}}\,(kT)^{-\frac{1}{2}} = \frac{2^{\frac{3}{2}}\pi^{\frac{1}{2}}h^4\rho u_l^2}{3\mathcal{E}_1{}^2}\,m^{*-\frac{5}{2}}(kT)^{-\frac{3}{2}} \tag{8.26}$$

The important qualitative features of Eq. (8.26) are contained in the last two factors. Accordingly, in that region of temperature in which lattice scattering by acoustic phonons plays the dominant role, the mobility should decrease with increasing temperature as $T^{-\frac{3}{2}}$. In fact, this predicted temperature dependence is observed only infrequently, but there are good reasons for the deviations from this power law which we shall discuss presently. What matters at the moment is that a $T^{-\frac{3}{2}}$ variation of the mobility is, except at elevated temperatures, a reasonably good indication of acoustic-mode scattering of carriers. We also note that the mobility should be large if the effective mass of the carriers is small. It is this dependence that endows electrons in certain semiconductors, such as InSb, with unusually high mobilities.

We can understand the temperature and also effective mass dependence of Eq. (8.26) from the following simple physical arguments. The $T^{-\frac{3}{2}}$ variation results from a combination of two factors. First, as the temperature increases so does the average energy of the carriers (they are presumed to obey classical statistics). Consequently, the average density of states, which determines the scattering probability, also increases. Since $\mathcal{N}(\epsilon)$ is proportional to $\epsilon^{\frac{1}{2}}$ we have accounted for a $T^{-\frac{1}{2}}$ factor in the relaxation time. The remaining factor T^{-1} arises simply because the num-

ber of phonons is proportional to the absolute temperature.   As regards
the variation of μ with m^*, the density of states once again plays an
important role, contributing here a factor $m^{*-\frac{3}{2}}$ to the relaxation time.
The remaining factor m^{*-1} has its origin in the classical relation between
the electric field and the acceleration of a charged particle.

   In very pure samples, scattering of charge carriers through the
absorption or emission of acoustic phonons may be important to fairly
low temperatures.   Interaction of electrons or holes with optical vibrations, on the other hand, is usually significant only at room temperature
and above, for the simple reason that as T falls well below Θ_0, the characteristic Einstein temperature for optical modes, the number of such
phonons in the vibration spectrum decreases exponentially.   Simultaneously, the number of charge carriers with sufficient energy to emit
such a quantum also decreases at the same rate.   If, in this temperature
range, the mobility were limited primarily by optical mode scattering,
we would expect to find $\mu \propto e^{\Theta_0/T}$.

   The actual calculation of the mobility due to optical-mode scattering
is complicated by the essentially inelastic nature of the collision process,
wherein a charge carrier must change its energy by an amount $k\Theta_0$.
Consequently, the solution of the transport equation must now follow
along the lines of the variational principle.   This in itself is not a serious
hurdle; however, in this particular instance a simple trial function,
comprising a single term, proves inadequate.   If a trial function is
chosen of the form

$$\phi(\mathbf{k}) = \sum_n \beta_n(\epsilon_k)^n \mathbf{k} \cdot \mathbf{P}$$

where $\mathbf{P}$ is a unit vector in the direction of the applied electric field, it
turns out that no single term of the series provides a satisfactory solution
at all temperatures of interest.   At high temperatures the situation is
simplest, for here it suffices to take $\beta_0 \neq 0$ and $\beta_n = 0$ for $n \geq 1$.   In a
polar crystal this procedure leads to the result

$$\mu_0 = \frac{3\pi^{\frac{1}{2}}\hbar^2 \varkappa'}{2^{\frac{5}{2}}em^{*\frac{3}{2}}} \, (kT)^{-\frac{1}{2}} \qquad T > \Theta_0 \tag{8.27}$$

where $\varkappa'$ is the effective dielectric constant defined by Eq. (6.46).

   At low temperatures the variational calculation yields

$$\mu_0 = \frac{\hbar^2}{(2e^2m^{*3}k\Theta_0)^{\frac{1}{2}}} \, (e^{\Theta_0/T} - 1) \qquad T < \Theta_0 \tag{8.28}$$

which displays the expected $e^{\Theta_0/T}$ temperature dependence for $T < \Theta_0/4$.

   Equations (8.27) and (8.28) are the results of a perturbation treatment of scattering of charged particles by optical phonons.   In Sec. 6.8,

we already commented on the inadequacy of perturbation theory in describing these processes because of the strength of the interaction. More satisfactory treatments of the problem using field-theoretic techniques borrowed from elementary-particle theory have been given by Low and Pines [2] and Schultz [3]. Application of these more sophisticated methods results in a multiplicative factor $F(m^*, \alpha)$, where α is the coupling constant defined in Sec. 6.8. Qualitatively, the effect is to give μ_0 an effective-mass dependence rather nearer to $m^{*-\frac{3}{2}}$ than to the $m^{*-\frac{1}{2}}$ of Eqs. (8.27) and (8.28).

Optical modes can scatter carriers also in covalent crystals. Here, the calculation of the mobility is encumbered by the uncertainty in the proper choice of the coupling constant. One approach that has been used is tantamount to extending the deformation-potential approximation into a region of doubtful validity. This procedure yields an expression for the mobility, the analog of Eq. (8.26), which is proportional to $m^{*-\frac{3}{2}}$ and $(kT)^{-\frac{3}{2}}$ at high temperatures, $T > \Theta_0$; at low temperatures the mobility should once again follow an exponential relation.

To summarize: Charge carriers in a semiconductor with the ideal band structure may suffer collisions through interaction with phonons belonging to either the acoustical or optical branches of the vibration spectrum. If limited by interaction with acoustical phonons, the mobility should decrease with increasing temperature as $T^{-\frac{3}{2}}$. The same temperature dependence also applies to high temperatures, even though the mobility is restricted primarily through scattering by optical phonons. In general, there will be an intermediate region where the rather more rapid, exponential temperature dependence of the mobility due to optical-mode scattering for $T < \Theta_0$ comes in evidence. For all types of electron-phonon scattering, the resulting mobility should be greater the smaller the effective mass of the carriers: in covalent crystals, theory predicts $\mu \propto m^{*-\frac{5}{2}}$.

Gallium arsenide, germanium, and silicon   Let us now turn our attention from the realm of fiction to the complexities of the real world. Regretfully, no known semiconductor has yet obliged us by displaying the ideal band structure. However, as we mentioned earlier, a number of intermetallic compounds do approximate this band structure. The mobilities of n- and p-type GaAs samples are shown in Fig. 8.4. The temperature dependence of μ_n of the purer samples above 100°K follows approximately a T^{-1} law; the hole mobility above 100°K shows a $T^{-2.1}$ dependence. Evidently, neither electron nor hole mobilities can be interpreted simply in terms of acoustic-mode scattering. In the case of n-type GaAs, Ehrenreich [4] has shown that this temperature dependence can be explained by a combination of polar-mode scattering and ionized-impurity

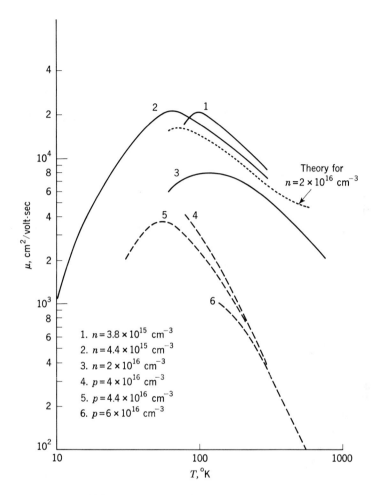

Fig. 8.4   Mobilities of electrons and holes in GaAs.   *(After C. Hilsum and A. C. Rose-Innes, "Semiconducting III-V Compounds," Pergamon Press, New York, 1961.)*

scattering (see Sec. 8.3*B*).   His theoretical result is shown by the dotted curve in Fig. 8.4.   The analysis of hole mobility is complicated by the complexity of the valence-band structure.

The conduction bands of germanium and silicon are of the many-valley type already described in Sec. 6.7.   Their valence bands are two-fold degenerate at $\mathbf{k} = 0$ (fourfold degenerate if we include spin degeneracy), but this degeneracy is lifted as one leaves the center of the Brillouin zone.   The constant-energy contours for the two valence bands are not spheres, however, but are distorted (warped) in such a manner as to maintain cubic symmetry. We shall now consider the suitable modifications in the expressions for μ arising from this more complicated band structure.

In the conduction band, where there are several spheroidal minima in $\mathbf{k}$ space, positioned symmetrically about $\mathbf{k} = 0$, the energy near the ith minimum is given by

$$\epsilon_i(k) = \frac{\hbar^2}{2}\left(\frac{k_\parallel^2}{m_\parallel} + \frac{k_\perp^2}{m_\perp}\right) \tag{8.29}$$

Here $k_\parallel$ and $k_\perp$ are the components of the wave vector parallel and perpendicular to the major axis of the spheroid and $m_\parallel$ and $m_\perp$ are the corresponding effective masses. The origin in $\mathbf{k}$ space has been translated to the center of the ith spheroid so that in Eq. (8.29) the vector $\mathbf{k}$ is to be measured from this new origin.

With the aid of the equations of motion, Eqs. (5.1) and (5.2), it is now a simple matter to generalize the transport equation and find its solution in this case. The not unexpected result is

$$J_\parallel = n_i e \mu_\parallel E_\parallel \qquad J_\perp = n_i e \mu_\perp E_\perp \tag{8.30}$$

where $\mu_\parallel = e\tau_\parallel/m_\parallel$ and $\mu = e\tau_\perp/m_\perp$.

Although the mobility associated with any one spheroid is clearly anisotropic, in the cubic crystals Ge and Si the symmetric disposition of the spheroids in $\mathbf{k}$ space guarantees an isotropic total mobility. If there are r such spheroids, each containing n/r electrons, one then has

$$J = ne\left(\frac{\mu_\parallel}{3} + \frac{2\mu_\perp}{3}\right)E$$

and total mobility

$$\mu = \frac{\mu_\parallel}{3} + \frac{2\mu_\perp}{3} \tag{8.31}$$

If the relaxation time τ is approximately isotropic, as may well be the case, one may define a "conductivity effective mass" m_c through

$$\frac{1}{m_c} = \frac{1}{3}\left(\frac{1}{m_\parallel} + \frac{2}{m_\perp}\right) \tag{8.32}$$

and write

$$\mu = \frac{e\tau}{m_c} \tag{8.33}$$

The expression for the mobility, Eq. (8.26), contains $m^{*-\frac{3}{2}}$, of which the factor $m^{*-\frac{3}{2}}$ has its origin in the density of states that always appears in transition probabilities, i.e., in $1/\tau$. To see how we should modify Eq. (8.26) so as to apply to spheroidal energy surfaces, we must find the appropriate form for the density of states. This is most conveniently achieved by introducing new coordinates through the transformation defined by

$$k'_{\parallel} = \left(\frac{m'}{m_{\parallel}}\right)^{\frac{1}{2}} k_{\parallel} \qquad k'_{\perp} = \left(\frac{m'}{m_{\perp}}\right)^{\frac{1}{2}} k_{\perp}$$

Constant-energy contours in $\mathbf{k}'$ space are once again spherical, and formally the derivation for the density of states proceeds exactly as in Sec. 3.1. However, the volume element $\Delta k'_{\parallel} \Delta k'^2_{\perp}$ now contains quantum states that belong to the element $(m'^{\frac{3}{2}}/m_{\perp}m_{\parallel}^{\frac{1}{2}})\Delta k_{\parallel}\Delta k_{\perp}^2$ in the original $\mathbf{k}$ space. Clearly, then, the appropriate combination of effective masses which should be used whenever the factor $\mathcal{N}(\epsilon)$ makes its appearance is

$$m_N^* = (m_{\parallel}m_{\perp}^2)^{\frac{1}{3}} \tag{8.34}$$

known as the *density-of-states effective mass*.

Thus, the factor $m^{*-\frac{3}{2}}$ in Eq. (8.26) should be replaced by the product $\frac{1}{3}(1/m_{\parallel} + 2/m_{\perp})(m_{\parallel}m_{\perp}^2)^{-\frac{1}{2}}$, that is, $m_c^{-1}m_N^{*-\frac{1}{2}}$. According to Eq. (8.32), the conductivity effective mass is determined primarily by the smaller of the two masses, $m_{\parallel}$ and $m_{\perp}$. The density-of-states effective mass is clearly determined largely by $m_{\perp}$. If $m_{\perp} \ll m_{\parallel}$, the "mobility effective mass," defined by

$$m_{\mu} = (m_c^{-1}m_N^{*-\frac{3}{2}})^{-\frac{2}{5}} \tag{8.35}$$

is then of the same magnitude as $m_{\perp}$. This is the situation encountered in germanium and silicon. In the former, for example, cyclotron resonance measurements yield the following effective masses: $m_{\parallel} = 1.58m$, $m_{\perp} = 0.082m$, where m is the free-electron mass. From Eqs. (8.33), (8.34), and (8.35) we obtain

$$m_c = 0.12m$$

$$m_N^* = 0.22m$$

$$m_{\mu} = 0.17m$$

all of the same order of magnitude as $m_{\perp}$, but an order of magnitude smaller than $m_{\parallel}$.

The replacement of m^* by m_{μ} is not, however, the only, nor the most important or interesting, consequence of the many-valley-band structure as regards electron-phonon scattering. Through absorption or emission of a phonon an electron may make a transition from its initial state $\mathbf{k}_i^{(i)}$ in the ith valley to a final state $\mathbf{k}_f^{(i)}$ in the same valley or to a state $\mathbf{k}_f^{(j)}$ in another spheroidal energy valley. The former process, known as *intravalley* scattering, is the exact analog of acoustic-mode scattering in the ideal case, and here the use of m_μ in place of m^* should suffice. The second possibility, known as *intervalley* scattering, is stimulated by phonons whose wave vector is roughly equal to $\mathbf{k}_0^{(j)} - \mathbf{k}_0^{(i)}$ and, thus, involves quanta of vibrational energy $\hbar(\mathbf{k}_0^{(j)} - \mathbf{k}_0^{(i)})u$. The energy of the phonon that is emitted or absorbed will depend on the disposition of the energy minima in the Brillouin zone, and there may be several phonon energies characteristic of intervalley scattering. For example, in silicon, where the minima appear along the $\langle 100 \rangle$ directions about two-thirds of the way to the zone boundary, intervalley scattering draws upon two distinct groups of phonons. Scattering from, say, the $\langle 100 \rangle$ to the $\langle 010 \rangle$, $\langle 001 \rangle$, $\langle 0\bar{1}0 \rangle$, and $\langle 00\bar{1} \rangle$ minima proceeds via phonons whose energy is roughly equal to $k\Theta_D$; scattering to the $\langle \bar{1}00 \rangle$ minimum, however, is an Umklapp process requiring a phonon whose wave vector is about $\frac{2}{3}q_0$ and whose energy is, therefore, approximately $\frac{2}{3}k\Theta_D$.

In many respects intervalley scattering is, thus, quite similar to optical-mode scattering, for once again we are dealing with a decidedly inelastic process. We expect that the mobility, if restricted largely by intervalley scattering, should obey a $T^{-\frac{3}{2}}$ law only at high temperatures and display a rather more rapid exponential variation at temperatures well below Θ_D; the onset of the exponential behavior may not be very well defined, however, since two or more groups of phonons with different characteristic energies could stimulate intervalley scattering.

Before leaving this topic, it may be well to mention yet another complication, namely, the participation of transverse as well as longitudinal modes in electron-phonon scattering. Deformation-potential theory in its most elementary version predicts that only longitudinal phonons can interact with electrons. This same conclusion was reached in the analogous case for metals with spherical energy surfaces. We recall here that transverse phonons could interact with conduction electrons in metals if either Umklapp processes were considered or if the effective mass showed some anisotropy, i.e., if the energy contours were not spherical. In semiconductors the same generalization applies. Indeed, in some cases it is thought that scattering by transverse modes is rather more effective than scattering by longitudinal modes. Frequently, group theory can be employed to advantage here; using arguments which rest solely on symmetry considerations, one often can deduce selection rules that prohibit certain transitions. Of course, such methods cannot be used to ascertain the relative strengths of the various allowed scattering events.

Scattering by transverse as well as longitudinal modes introduces yet another set of characteristic temperatures in intervalley and optical-mode scattering, since the energies of the two differently polarized vibrations are generally quite different.

To summarize the arguments in this section, we may say first that as concerns intravalley scattering the results of the ideal model should be fairly reliable, provided one replaces m^* by m_μ; although the relaxation time may be somewhat anisotropic for a particular valley, it is generally thought that in the case of lattice scattering, at any rate, τ is nearly isotropic. A many-valley structure does, however, allow for an entirely new process, intervalley scattering, which has many of the attributes of optical-mode scattering, particularly as regards the temperature dependence of the mobility. To illustrate how intervalley scattering may modify the overall temperature dependence of the mobility in a certain temperature range, we reproduce here a set of theoretical curves calculated by Herring [5] (Fig. 8.5). The curves are based on the assumption that only two processes are operative, ordinary lattice scattering (intravalley scattering) and intervalley scattering characterized by a single "Debye" temperature. The different curves correspond to different assumptions regarding the relative strengths of the two interactions, and the slopes at various points along the curves show that over a limited temperature range a power law may seem reasonable indeed. Clearly, if one were to include optical-mode scattering and the possibility of several characteristic temperatures for intervalley scattering, one could easily obtain curves for which the apparent power-law dependence is considerably extended.

We next turn our attention to lattice scattering of holes in germanium and silicon. A calculation of the relaxation time which takes full account of the warping of the energy contours has not been performed. Presumably, the model which features two valence bands, degenerate at $\mathbf{k} = 0$ and characterized by two isotropic effective masses m_l and m_h (light and heavy holes, respectively), should give fairly good results. In some cases it has been necessary to introduce the warping explicitly, but even then an isotropic relaxation time was assumed.

The unique feature introduced by the valence-band degeneracy is the possibility of interband scattering, i.e., scattering of a light hole into a state in the heavy-hole band, and vice versa. These scattering events differ from intervalley scattering in that now only long-wavelength, low-energy phonons are involved, and the relaxation process can be described in terms of a suitable relaxation time. Since the ratio of the transition probabilities for scattering into the two bands is proportional to the ratio of the density of states, that is to $(m_h/m_l)^{\frac{3}{2}}$, most scattering events should leave the hole in the heavy-mass band. Provided the coupling constant between the holes and the phonon spectrum does not change drastically as one goes from the light- to the heavy-mass

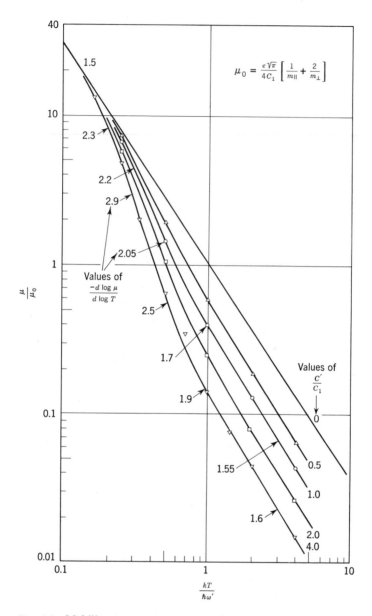

Fig. 8.5 Mobility-temperature curves for pure lattice scattering, neglecting scattering by optical modes. The quantities C_1 and C' measure the strength of the coupling of the carriers to intra- and intervalley modes, respectively; ω' is the frequency of the intervalley mode. [*From C. Herring, Bell System Tech. J.*, **34**: 237 (1955).]

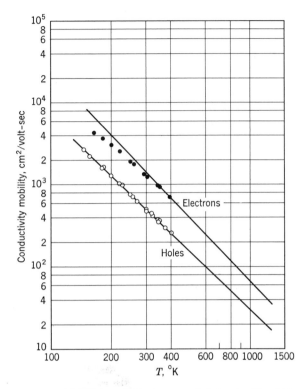

Fig. 8.6   Mobilities of electrons and holes in Si.   [*After F. T. Morin and J. P. Maita, Phys. Rev.*, **96**: 28 (1954).]

band, the relaxation times for the two types of holes should be almost identical and characteristic of the heavy-hole density-of-states mass. The mobilities, of course, will differ, with the light holes displaying the higher mobility.

Mobilities of electrons and holes in germanium and silicon in the temperature range where only lattice scattering should be important have been measured by several workers, and some of the results are shown in Figs. 8.6 and 8.7.   With the exception of electrons in germanium, the curves reveal significant deviations from the $T^{-\frac{3}{2}}$ law predicted by the elementary theory.   In each case the departure from this power law is in the direction of a more rapid temperature dependence, which is just what we might expect if intervalley and/or optical-mode scattering were to come into prominence in the temperature range covered by these experiments.   It was demonstrated by Brown and Bray [6] that reasonable choices of coupling constants and characteristic temperatures will

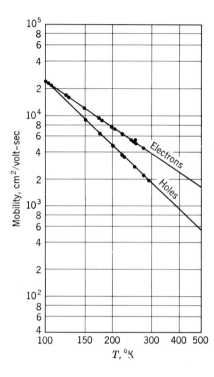

Fig. 8.7 Mobilities of electrons and holes in Ge. [*After F. T. Morin and J. P. Maita, Phys. Rev.*, **94**: 1526 (1954).]

yield curves in excellent agreement with experimental hole mobilities (see Fig. 8.8).   In the case of n-type silicon, combination of optical-mode and intervalley scattering provides such a variety of choices among coupling constants and characteristic temperatures that there is no problem in fitting the data with a reasonable theoretical expression.

Finally, there is some evidence that the conduction-band minima in germanium are nonparabolic; that is, $\epsilon_i(k_\perp) \neq \alpha |\mathbf{k}_\perp - \mathbf{k}_0^{(i)}|^2$. Hence, the effective mass $m_\perp$ defined in terms of the second derivative of $\epsilon(k)$—Eq. (4.58)—depends on the energy.   Consequently, as the temperature is increased and higher-energy states in the conduction band are occupied, the average mobility mass changes, and this effect introduces yet another temperature-dependent factor in the mobility expression.

B.   Impurity-scattering Regime

Ionized impurity scattering   The relaxation time for scattering of charge carriers by ionized impurities is given by Eq. (6.59), and the mobility in the region where this scattering mechanism is of paramount importance may be obtained by substituting Eq. (6.59) into Eq. (8.25). The integration over energy is complicated, however, by the presence of the logarithmic function $F(b)$ defined by Eq. (6.60), and one generally resorts to the following simplification.

Upon examination of the relevant quantities one finds that in the temperature range in which the Born approximation, upon which Eq. (6.59) is based, is justified, the parameter b is generally significantly larger than unity for all but a relatively small number of rather slow electrons. The function $F(b)$ may then be approximated by $F(b) \cong \ln b - 1$, and proves to be a rather slowly varying function of the electron energy. Consequently, one can obtain a fairly reliable analytic expression for μ by taking the factor $\ln b - 1$ outside the integral and setting ϵ in Eq. (6.60) equal to $\epsilon_m = 3kT$, the energy at which the remaining integrand attains its maximum. The result of this procedure is

$$\mu = \frac{2^{\frac{5}{2}}(kT)^{\frac{3}{2}}\varkappa^2}{\pi^{\frac{3}{2}}e^3 m^{*\frac{1}{2}} N_I} \left\{ \ln\left[\frac{24m^*\varkappa(kT)^2\pi}{n'e^2h^2}\right] - 1 \right\}^{-1} \tag{8.36}$$

In Eq. (8.36), the dominant temperature dependence derives from the factor $(kT)^{\frac{3}{2}}$—provided, of course, that the number of scattering

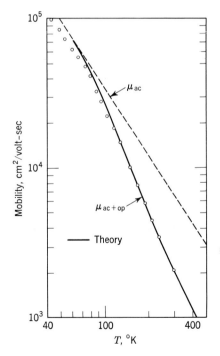

Fig. 8.8 Comparison of theory and experiment for a sample of p-type Ge, $T >$ 100°K. Theoretical curve includes acoustical and optical mode lattice scattering. Dashed line shows extrapolated mobility for pure acoustical scattering. [*From D. M. Brown and R. Bray, Phys. Rev.,* **127:** 1598 (1962).]

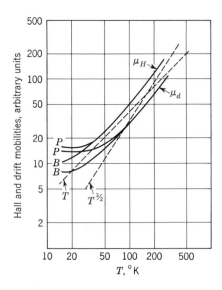

Fig. 8.9 Hall and drift mobilities as functions of the temperature for the case $m^* = 0.33$, $\kappa = 11.8$, $n = 2 \times 10^{16}$, and no compensation. The curves labeled P were obtained using the results of the partial wave method. The curves labeled B were obtained using the results of the Born approximation. Also shown are the straight lines corresponding to a $T^{\frac{3}{2}}$ and a linear temperature dependence. [*From F. J. Blatt, Solid State Phys.*, **4**: 350 (1953).]

centers does not change with temperature—and it is often stated that in the ionized impurity range μ is proportional to $T^{\frac{3}{2}}$. In the exhaustion region, N_I is independent of temperature, but as the temperature is lowered, carriers begin to "freeze out" on donors (or acceptors) and the number of *ionized* impurities decreases very rapidly. When that happens, the mobility increases rather than decreases with decreasing temperature. Even in the exhaustion region, a simple $T^{\frac{3}{2}}$ law would seem to be oversimplifying matters a bit. At temperatures sufficiently low that lattice scattering is insignificant, the temperature dependence of the logarithmic term, though slow, is not altogether negligible. The theoretical mobility does not follow a $T^{\frac{3}{2}}$ law except at fairly high temperatures. A typical curve of μ versus T is shown in Fig. 8.9. To verify that the approximation leading to Eq. (8.36) is not in serious error, the mobility was also calculated by integrating the relaxation time over the Boltzmann distribution using numerical methods. The good agreement between the two curves is gratifying. The deviation from the $T^{\frac{3}{2}}$ law is, however, quite pronounced at lower temperatures, where a linear T dependence may be a better approximation. Such behavior seems to be observed in practice.

At rather low temperatures the Born approximation, i.e., Eq. (6.59), loses validity and Eq. (8.36) cannot be trusted. Here one should really resort to tedious phase-shift calculations of scattering cross sections. Such calculations have been performed for some cases. There is some evidence that phase-shift calculations do give more reliable results than the Born approximation, since experimentally one observes that majority impurities present larger scattering cross sections than do minority impurities; this is in accord with the predictions of phase-shift calculations, whereas the Born approximation does not distinguish between minority and majority ionized impurities.

If the energy surfaces are spheroidal, as in n-type Ge and Si, the relaxation time within one spheroid may well be highly anisotropic. Calculations by Ham [7] suggest that $\tau_\perp/\tau_\parallel = 12$ in Ge, where $m_\parallel/m_\perp = 19$.

As regards scattering of holes in these substances, interband scattering appears to be unimportant, except possibly for rather high impurity concentrations; this is because such transitions involve relatively large changes in the wave vector; the Fourier transform of the shallow, long range screened coulomb potential of ionized impurities contains predominantly long-wavelength terms. Only as N_I increases and the screening length is reduced do components with shorter wavelengths take on increasing importance. Except at high impurity concentrations, the two hole bands can be treated independently in the ionized impurity region.

Neutral-impurity scattering   At very low temperatures, the number of neutral impurities in a semiconductor containing only a minimum number of minority impurities will become quite large compared to the number of ionized impurities. At the same time the number of free carriers decreases sharply. The relaxation time for scattering by neutral impurities is given by Eq. (6.61). Since τ_N is independent of energy, the corresponding mobility is simply

$$\mu_N = \frac{e}{m^*}\tau_N \qquad\qquad (8.37)$$

Although τ_N does not depend on energy or temperature explicitly, there is, in fact, a very pronounced temperature dependence that has its origin in the number of neutral scattering centers N_N, which increases very rapidly as the temperature is lowered. Although neutral-impurity scattering should be of some importance in many samples at low temperatures, there does not appear to be any precise experimental determination of this effect.

In all of the above we have neglected the effects of electron-electron, electron-hole, and hole-hole scattering. This matter has been subjected to careful scrutiny in recent years and the results are summarized below.

C. Carrier-carrier Scattering

Although the total momentum, and consequently the current, is conserved in electron-electron scattering, these events can still exert a profound influence on the total mobility. To see how this can come about one need only consider an extreme case. Suppose the relaxation process which restores equilibrium is characterized by a strongly energy-dependent relaxation time which increases with increasing electron energy. In that case, electrons in the high-energy tail of the Boltzmann distribution will have a long mean free path and will, therefore, carry a disproportionately large amount of the current. At the same time, the steady-state distribution function will show a significant departure from a Boltzmann distribution whose center in velocity space has suffered a displacement equal to the drift velocity. Clearly, the low-energy part of the distribution, relaxing more rapidly toward equilibrium, will be displaced less than the high-energy portion.

Now electron-electron scattering, though conserving total momentum, can redistribute momentum and energy among the electrons. Indeed, if no other relaxation mechanism is active and the accelerating field is turned off, the ultimate distribution achieved through these collisions will be a Boltzmann distribution whose momentum has been shifted in $\mathbf{k}$ space. Thus, electron-electron scattering tends to maintain a normal distribution, feeding electrons into states whose relaxation time is relatively short. Clearly, electron-electron scattering will be more important the stronger the energy dependence of the dominant momentum-relaxation process. It is of no consequence whatever in neutral-impurity scattering, is relatively unimportant for lattice scattering, and cannot be ignored in treating the effect of ionized-impurity scattering.

The influence of electron-electron scattering on the thermal conductivity is generally greater than on the electrical conductivity. The reason is simply that while momentum conservation demands that

$$\mathbf{v}_1^i + \mathbf{v}_2^i = \mathbf{v}_1^f + \mathbf{v}_2^f$$

where i and f refer to initial and final states, in general,

$$\epsilon_1^i \mathbf{v}_1^i + \epsilon_2^i \mathbf{v}_2^i \neq \epsilon_1^f \mathbf{v}_1^f + \epsilon_2^f \mathbf{v}_2^f$$

That is, though charge current is conserved in any one collision, energy flow is not.

Carrier-carrier collision is most effective, however, when interband scattering can occur. In this case, conservation of crystal momentum

$$\mathbf{k}_1^i + \mathbf{k}_2^i = \mathbf{k}_1^f + \mathbf{k}_2^f$$

does not imply conservation of velocity or current. Interband scattering is possible in a variety of extrinsic semiconductors, for example p-type Si and Ge (light-hole–heavy-hole scattering) and all intrinsic semiconductors (electron-hole scattering).

Carrier-carrier scattering is discussed by Paige and McLean [8]

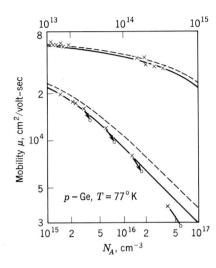

Fig. 8.10 Calculated and measured majority carrier (hole) mobilities in p-type Ge. The dashed curve represents the calculated mobility without hole-hole scattering; the solid curve includes hole-hole scattering. The experimental data are shown by $\times$ (Hall mobilities) and $\bigcirc$ (drift mobilities). [*From J. Appel and R. Bray, Phys. Rev.*, **127**: 1603 (1962).]

and by Appel [9], who bases his theoretical treatment on an extension of the variational method. The profound influence of interband collisions on the electrical conductivity is apparent from the result

$$\sigma = \frac{\sigma_n + \sigma_p - \sigma_n\sigma_p[(1 - n/p) + (1 - p/n)]Q}{1 + [(n/p)\sigma_p + (p/n)\sigma_n]Q} \tag{8.38}$$

where Q is a constant that depends on the electron-hole relaxation time and σ_n, σ_p are electron and hole conductivities neglecting n-p scattering.

Theory predicts a most startling effect, namely, a negative mobility (or conductivity) for minority carriers under suitable conditions. If holes and electrons are present, an external field accelerates these in opposite directions, both groups normally contributing to charge flow. Let us assume, for example, that $n \gg p$ and that the mean free path for n-p scattering is short compared to other electron-scattering events. Electrons will then share the momentum which they have gained from the field with the holes, and may drag them along in a direction opposite to that of the accelerating field. The situation is analogous to the phonon-drag mechanism described in the preceding chapter. In n-type InSb, the conditions for observing this negative mobility of holes should be experimentally realizable.

The influence of carrier-carrier scattering on the mobility of minority and majority carriers has been studied experimentally by Paige [10] and by Appel and Bray [11]. The effect is, as expected, more prominent in the case of minority carriers, as can be seen by a comparison of Figs. 8.10 and 8.11.

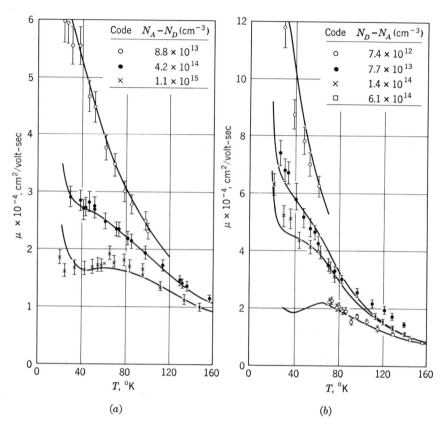

Fig. 8.11 (a) The drift mobility of minority carriers (electrons) in p-type Ge as a function of temperature. The solid curves are calculated, including effects of carrier-carrier scattering. Note the decrease in *minority* mobility with increasing *majority* carrier concentration. (b) The drift mobility of minority carriers (holes) in n-type Ge as a function of temperature. The solid curves are calculated, including effects of carrier-carrier scattering. Note the decrease in minority mobility with increasing majority carrier concentration. [*From A. F. Gibson (ed.), "Progress in Semiconductors," vol. 8, p. 138, John Wiley & Sons, Inc., New York, 1964.*]

D. Temperature Dependence of Mobility and Conductivity

Now that we have discussed in some detail each of the important scattering processes in semiconductors, we should be able to predict the typical behavior of the mobility.

At very low temperatures one may expect that neutral-impurity scattering should dominate the behavior in most cases, leading to a mobility which increases exponentially with increasing temperature as the number of neutral scattering centers diminishes. Although neutral-impurity scattering is not always negligible, it is rarely decisive. The reason is that the scattering cross section presented to carriers by ionized impurities is far greater than that due to neutral impurities; since most samples contain some, say, N_m, minority impurities, the number of ionized scattering centers, even at the lowest temperature, is $2N_m$, and ionized impurity scattering is important to the lowest temperatures.   An increase in mobility due to a diminution of neutral impurities with increasing temperature will never materialize, because the concomitant increase in the concentration of ionized impurities leads to the opposite effect, namely, a reduction in the mobility.   A further rise in temperature establishes the region of ionized impurities in restricting the mobility. Until the exhaustion region is attained, the mobility will decrease with increasing temperature because of the increase in the number of scattering centers.   In the exhaustion region, the true character of ionized-impurity scattering manifests itself.   Here, one expects, and one generally does find, the $T^{\frac{3}{2}}$ behavior.   Soon, however, the mobility reaches a maximum and scattering of carriers by phonons takes over.   Depending on which portion of the phonon spectrum is chiefly responsible for scattering of charge carriers, the mobility may fall with increasing temperature as $T^{-\frac{3}{2}}$ or more rapidly.   A few typical experimental curves are shown in Figs. 8.12 and 8.13.

In the preceding discussion we focused attention on one or another relaxation mechanism.   All too often this is not realistic.   When two or more scattering mechanisms are operative, the resulting mobility is *not* given by the equivalent of Matthiessen's rule, i.e.,

$$\frac{1}{\mu} \neq \sum_i \frac{1}{\mu_i}$$

Instead, the mobility must be computed by inserting the effective relaxation time

$$\tau_{\text{eff}} = \left(\sum_i \frac{1}{\tau_i} \right)^{-1} \tag{8.39}$$

into Eq. (8.25).   Since the energy dependence of the effective relaxation time is now no longer a simple power law, the actual computation is often rather tedious, demanding numerical methods.   A number of reasonable approximate expressions have been given for certain specific cases, and for others, integrals of the type generally encountered have been evaluated numerically.   The reader who wishes to probe further into this subject should consult the references [12].

The temperature variation of the conductivity mirrors the mobility in only a very restricted temperature range, the exhaustion region.   At

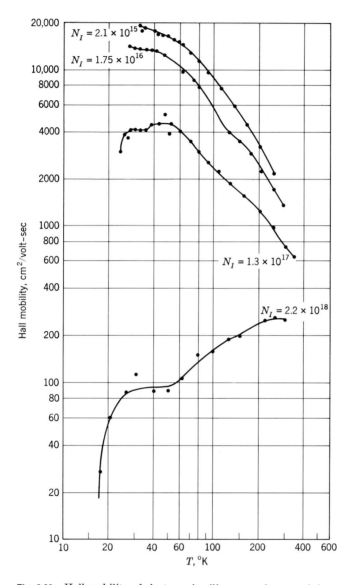

Fig. 8.12 Hall mobility of electrons in silicon samples containing arsenic as a function of absolute temperature. [*After F. T. Morin and J. P. Maita, Phys. Rev.*, **96**: 28 (1954).]

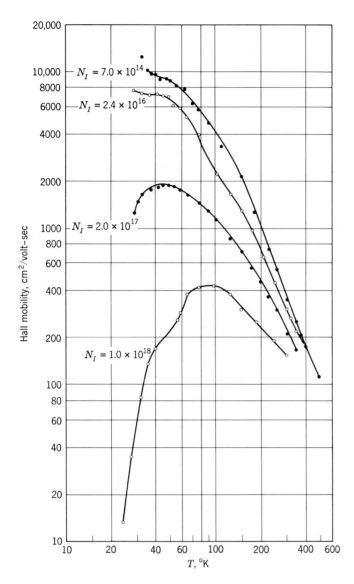

Fig. 8.13 Hall mobility of holes in silicon samples containing boron as a function of absolute temperature. [*After F. T. Morin and J. P. Maita, Phys. Rev.*, **96**: 28 (1954).]

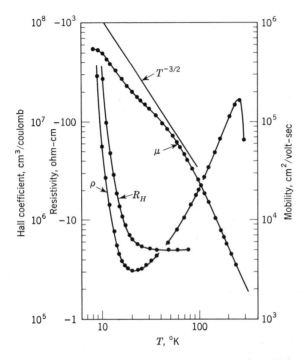

Fig. 8.14 Experimental Hall, resistivity, and mobility data for a sample of p-type germanium. [*From D. M. Brown and R. Bray, Phys. Rev.*, **127**: 1597 (1962).]

higher as well as lower temperatures, the variation of σ is determined primarily by the number of charge carriers.

As the high-temperature portion of the exhaustion region is approached, one frequently finds that the resistivity increases with increasing temperature, reminiscent of metallic behavior (see Fig. 8.16). Here n (or p) is temperature-independent and μ is limited principally by lattice scattering; hence, the decrease of μ and σ with increasing T.

If, now, the temperature is raised further, thermal excitation of carriers begins to make itself felt. Since the number of thermally excited (intrinsic) carriers increases roughly exponentially, the transition region between extrinsic and intrinsic conduction is quite narrow. The number of intrinsic carriers rapidly dominates the scene, and as the temperature is raised the conductivity falls exponentially. Indeed, the temperature variation of the conductivity in the intrinsic region is one good measure of the energy gap.

We have seen earlier that theory predicts a $T^{-\frac{3}{2}}$ dependence for the mobility at quite high temperatures, even if optical-mode and/or inter-

valley scattering accompany acoustical-mode scattering.   It then follows
from Eqs. (8.4), (8.5), (8.25), and (8.20) that $\sigma \propto \exp\left(-\epsilon_G/2kT\right)$ in the
intrinsic region.   Accordingly, a plot of σ versus $1/T$ should be a
straight line with a slope equal to $-\epsilon_G/2k$.   While such semilogarithmic
plots obey the expected straight-line behavior, the energy gap determined
by this method is generally not in good agreement with that deduced
from optical absorption or photoconductivity experiments.   The reason
for the discrepancy is that the energy gap itself is temperature dependent.
If one assumes that all terms but the linear term in a Taylor series expansion of $\epsilon_G(T)$ are negligibly small, and writes

$$\epsilon_G(T) = \epsilon_G(T=0) + \beta T \tag{8.40}$$

it is clear that Eq. (8.8) would be multiplied by a constant factor
$\exp\left(-\beta/k\right)$.   Thus, the energy gap corresponding to the slope of a σ vs.
$1/T$ plot is, to first approximation, the energy gap at $T = 0°K$.   When

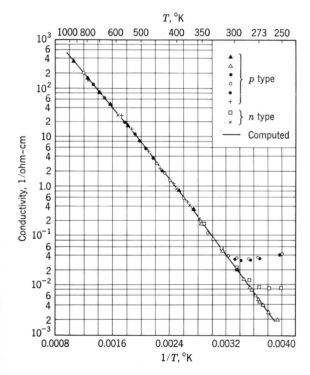

Fig. 8.15   Conductivity versus $1/T$ for n- and p-type germanium samples.   [*From F. T. Morin and J. P. Maita,
Phys. Rev.*, **94**: 1526 (1954).]

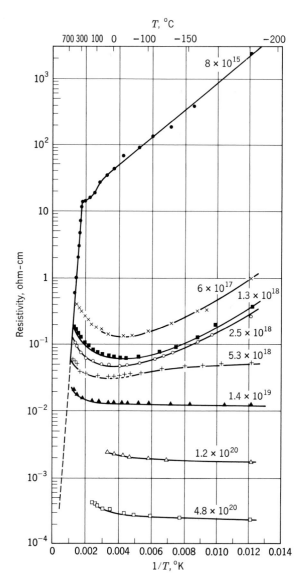

Fig. 8.16   The resistivity as a function of temperature for
p-type specimens.   Number of acceptor impurities is
shown on curves.   [*After G. L. Pearson and J. Bardeen,
Phys. Rev.*, **75**: 865 (1949).]

comparison is made with optically measured gaps at low temperatures the agreement is now quite good.   Figures 8.15 and 8.16 show typical curves of conductivity as a function of temperature.

If the temperature is reduced below the lower limit of the exhaustion region, the conductivity again displays an exponential pattern, this time because thermal ionization of the doping impurities diminishes. According to Eq. (8.17) a logarithmic plot of σ versus $1/T$ should approximate a straight line with a slope of $-\epsilon_d/2\mathbf{k}$.   Thus, donor- and acceptor-ionization energies can be determined by measuring the conductivity as a function of temperature in uncompensated n- and p-type samples. Since impurity ionization energies are very much smaller than the energy gap, the slopes of lines of σ versus $1/T$ in the two regions are vastly different, as can be seen from Fig. 8.16.

Impurity-band conduction   As one can observe from Fig. 8.16, the resistivity of the more heavily doped samples does not increase exponentially with decreasing temperature down to the lowest temperatures. Instead, below some temperature which depends on the degree of doping, the resistivity remains substantially constant.   This quasi-metallic behavior is known as *impurity-band conduction*, a term which was originally thought to be descriptive of the basic mechanism of conduction. Actually, there are two kinds of "impurity-band conduction" that are encountered.

If the concentration of impurities is fairly high, e.g., in Ge some 5×10^{16} cm^{-3} or more, the wave functions of the electrons bound to the neutral donor impurities will overlap to a significant extent.   Such overlap can occur in semiconductors at such dilutions because, as we remarked in Sec. 6.9, the high dielectric constant and small effective mass result in a vastly expanded Bohr orbit.   As we pointed out in Sec. 4.6, the N-fold degenerate level of an assembly of N well-separated atoms is broadened into a band of closely spaced nondegenerate levels when the atoms are brought into such close proximity that their wave functions overlap.   Although in the case of impurities placed at random in a semiconductor one cannot expect a Brillouin-zone structure—this being a property of a *periodic* lattice—overlap of wave functions will lead once again to an energy band.   The width of the band will depend on the degree of overlap.   Thus, as the impurity concentration is increased, we expect a reduction of the quasi-metallic resistivity for two reasons: (1) With increasing concentration the number of carriers is increased; provided the relaxation time does not decrease in proportion, the resistivity should fall.   (2) As the concentration increases, so should the bandwidth; this implies a reduction in the carrier effective mass, and hence an increase in mobility and a concomitant reduction in resistivity.   Measurements of resistivity and Hall effect at low temperatures in moderately to heavily doped samples support these qualitative conclusions.

As the impurity concentration is reduced further, impurity conduction persists, even though the impurities are now sufficiently far apart to allow only a negligible degree of direct overlap. Here a hopping process, suggested by Mott [13], seems to be the principal mechanism of charge transport. Since an n-type semiconductor will be contaminated to some extent by acceptor impurities, some of the donor impurities will be ionized even at the lowest temperatures. Thus, an electron localized on one donor could "hop" to a nearby ionized donor, leaving the first ionized and neutralizing the other. Normally, this process will occur in a purely random manner. In the presence of an applied electric field, however, there is an enhanced probability for a jump toward the lower potential. The result is a net charge flow. The process is in this sense completely analogous to ionic conductivity, which is basically directed diffusion. In the present instance, the theoretical description of the problem is complicated by the random distribution of donors and acceptors in the host lattice. Acceptable theories were provided by Miller and Abrahams [14] and Mott and Twose [15], and the experimental results compare very well with these theories. In particular, there are two crucial experiments that show that hopping rather than the band-conduction mechanism is important at low impurity concentrations. According to theory, the hopping process cannot take place in a sample which contains N_D donors and no acceptors whatever. If, now, one gradually adds compensating acceptor impurities, keeping the donor concentration fixed, the conductivity should show a rapid rise as more and more unoccupied hopping sites become available to electrons bound to the neutral donor impurities. This dependence of conductivity on the degree of compensation is consistent with hopping but not with quasi-metallic conduction. Measurements by Fritzsche [16] have confirmed the hopping model. According to the second theory, the frequency dependence of the conductivity should be quite different for hopping and band conduction. One can show that in the former, σ should increase with increasing frequency, at least at reasonably low frequencies, whereas σ should decrease with increasing frequency if the band model applies. Once again, measurements on only moderately doped samples have demonstrated the existence of the hopping process.

8.4 PIEZORESISTANCE

The term *piezoresistance* refers to the change of the resistivity due to an applied stress. Although from the experimental, operational point of view this is by far the best description, the interpretation of the effect in terms of band parameters is more conveniently formulated for the *elastoresistance*, the change of resistance due to an elastic strain. Since stress and strain are connected through the elastic-constant tensor, one effect uniquely determines the other.

We must remember that when we write Ohm's law

$$\mathbf{J} = \sigma\mathbf{E}$$

the conductivity σ, relating two vectors to each other, is a second-rank tensor. The elastoconductivity relates to the change $\delta\sigma_{ij}$ in σ_{ij} due to a strain ϵ_{kl}. Thus, the general linear set of equations between the two tensors $\delta\sigma$ and ϵ is

$$\delta\sigma = \mathfrak{M} : \epsilon \tag{8.41}$$

where $\mathfrak{M}$ is a fourth-rank tensor with 36 components. In analogy with elasticity theory, $\delta\sigma$ and ϵ are expressed as six-component vectors and $\mathfrak{M}$ as a six-by-six matrix, whose independent components are generally severely limited by requirements of crystal symmetry. In the cases which we shall discuss, Ge and Si, cubic symmetry reduces Eq. (8.41) to Eq. (8.42):

$$
\begin{pmatrix}
\delta\sigma_{11} \\
\delta\sigma_{22} \\
\delta\sigma_{33} \\
\delta\sigma_{23} \\
\delta\sigma_{31} \\
\delta\sigma_{12}
\end{pmatrix}
=
\begin{pmatrix}
M_{11} & M_{12} & M_{12} & 0 & 0 & 0 \\
M_{12} & M_{22} & M_{12} & 0 & 0 & 0 \\
M_{12} & M_{12} & M_{11} & 0 & 0 & 0 \\
0 & 0 & 0 & M_{44} & 0 & 0 \\
0 & 0 & 0 & 0 & M_{44} & 0 \\
0 & 0 & 0 & 0 & 0 & M_{44}
\end{pmatrix}
\begin{pmatrix}
\epsilon_{11} \\
\epsilon_{22} \\
\epsilon_{33} \\
\epsilon_{23} \\
\epsilon_{31} \\
\epsilon_{12}
\end{pmatrix}
\tag{8.42}
$$

Interest in elastoresistance effects in semiconductors stems not only from the magnitude of the effect, often some hundreds of times that encountered in metals, but the fact that the anisotropy casts much light on the band structure. Moreover, some of the deformation-potential constants that are needed in mobility calculations can be determined experimentally from elastoresistance data.

There are only two practical experimental configurations that are suitable. In the first, the sample is subjected to uniform hydrostatic pressure. Since the elastic constants of Ge and Si are isotropic, as is demanded by cubic symmetry, the resulting strain is a pure dilatation. The second practical arrangement is that of uniaxial tension, from which the shear coefficients can be deduced. Clearly, to form a complete picture of the elastoconductivity tensor, it is necessary to use several crystals, in cylindrical shapes, with the cylinder axis along different crystallographic directions.

Pressure can modify the band structure, and thereby the conductivity of a semiconductor in two ways. First, the energy gap depends on strain, and, second, the effective mass also changes with a change in lattice parameter. These two effects are, in fact, quite intimately related, because the effective mass in a particular band, which we denote by β, is given by

$$\frac{1}{m_{ij}^{*\beta}} = \frac{1}{m} + \frac{2}{m^2} \sum_{\delta} \frac{\langle \beta | \mathbf{p}_i | \delta \rangle \langle \delta | \mathbf{p}_j | \beta \rangle}{\epsilon_\beta - \epsilon_\delta} \qquad (8.43)$$

where $\mathbf{p}_i$ is the ith component of the momentum operator and δ is a band index (see Sec. 4.7). Clearly, the energy bands which exert the greatest influence in deciding the effective-mass tensor in the β band will be those bands which are energetically close to the β band, for then the energy denominators will be small. Consequently, any change in the energy gap between the valence and conduction bands will reflect itself in variations of the effective masses of these two bands.

In the intrinsic region the change in energy gap with pressure is much more important than the change in effective mass, because the number of charge carriers depends exponentially on the energy gap, whereas the mobility only goes as some power—roughly the $\frac{5}{2}$ power of m^*. If, for the moment, we neglect changes in the mobilities altogether, we obtain from Eq. (8.20)

$$\frac{d \ln \sigma}{dP} = \frac{d \ln n}{dP} = \frac{1}{2kT} \frac{d\epsilon_G}{dP} = \frac{\kappa}{2kT} \frac{d\epsilon_G}{d \ln V} = \frac{\kappa}{2kT} E_1 \qquad (8.44)$$

where κ is the compressibility. Here E_1 has the dimensions and appearance of a deformation potential constant; it represents the *combined* shift of the valence- and conduction-band edges under a uniform dilatation. The magnitude of E_1 is usually several electron volts and may be positive or negative, depending on the substance.

As the temperature is reduced and one enters the extrinsic region, the elastoconductivity is greatly diminished, though by no means negligible. The effect which one observes now reflects the change in mobility with pressure, since the total number of electrons (holes) remains constant.

The very large and highly anisotropic elastoresistance effect in n-type germanium and silicon under shear strain is a direct consequence of the multivalley band structure shown schematically in Fig. 8.17. Figure 8.17b, which shows the valleys along the $\langle 100 \rangle$ directions, corresponds to the silicon band structure. As we mentioned previously, overall isotropy of σ is assured by the symmetry conditions which allow valleys to be transformed into each other by a rotation about the $\langle 111 \rangle$ axis and/or reflection in a plane perpendicular to the $\langle 111 \rangle$ axis.

Tension along the z direction destroys this symmetry and will shift

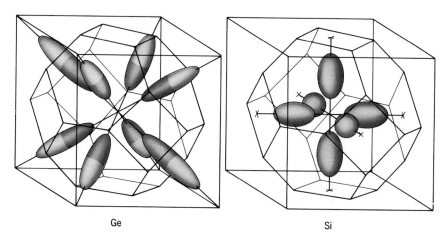

Ge   Si

Fig. 8.17 Constant-energy surfaces for electrons in Ge and Si. (*After J. M. Ziman,* "*Electrons and Phonons," Oxford University Press, London, 1960.*)

the energies of the x and y minima relative to the z spheroids. If, for example, the z minima are lowered, electrons from the other four will "spill over" into the z spheroids. Since, for the z spheroids alone, the mobility is higher in the x, y directions than in the z direction ($m_\perp \ll m_\parallel$) and these minima now contribute heavily to the total current, the conductivity becomes anisotropic.

If, however, tension is applied along the $\langle 111 \rangle$ axis, the important symmetry elements, namely, those which transform the valleys into each other, are not destroyed. Consequently, the carrier concentration in the valleys remains unchanged, and, to first order, the elastoresistance should vanish. The situation is exactly reversed in germanium where the minima are oriented along the $\langle 111 \rangle$ axes in the crystal. In this case tension along the $\langle 111 \rangle$ axis will result in a large, anisotropic elastoresistance, whereas one should find no effect for a strain along the $\langle 100 \rangle$ axis.

The experimental results for n-type germanium and silicon are shown in polar plots in Fig. 8.18. The disposition of the energy minima in these materials is evident from these curves.

The shift in the band edges of the valleys can be described in the deformation-potential formalism by

$$\delta\epsilon^i = \mathcal{E}^i : \epsilon \tag{8.45}$$

where $\mathcal{E}^i$ is the deformation-potential tensor for the ith minimum. According to Eq. (8.4), a shift of the band edge of the ith valley must

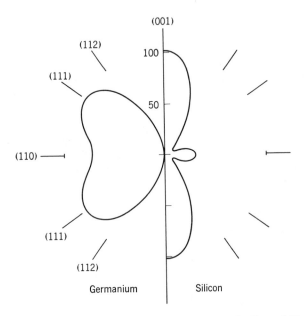

Fig. 8.18   Room temperature piezoresistance in Ge and Si.
[*From R. W. Keyes, Solid State Phys.*, **11**: 197 (1960).]

result in a concentration change δn^i given by

$$\delta n^i = -n^i \frac{\delta(\epsilon^i - \eta)}{kT} \tag{8.46}$$

Since the total number of electrons must remain unchanged,

$$\sum_i \delta n^i = 0 = -\frac{n}{kT}\left(\sum \delta\epsilon^i - \gamma\eta\right) \tag{8.47}$$

where γ is the number of valleys.   With the aid of Eqs. (8.45) and (8.47), Eq. (8.46) can be written

$$\delta n^i = -\frac{n}{kT}\left(\boldsymbol{\varepsilon}^i - \frac{1}{\gamma}\sum \boldsymbol{\varepsilon}^i\right)\!:\!\boldsymbol{\epsilon} \tag{8.48}$$

and the conductivity of the ith valley is changed by an amount

$$\delta\boldsymbol{\sigma}^i = \delta n^i e \boldsymbol{\mu}^i \tag{8.49}$$

where we have assumed that, at least to first order, $\boldsymbol{\mu}^i$ is independent of strain.

We have carried the formal theory to this point to demonstrate that the elastoconductivity in the extrinsic region can be used to measure the deformation-potential constants, and to show that $\delta\sigma/\sigma$ should increase with decreasing temperature. Experiments by Fritzsche [17] have verified this temperature dependence to quite low temperatures. At 7°K the dimensionless parameter $m_{44} = M_{44}/\sigma$ attains a value of 4,000, so that a relatively small strain of 2.5×10^{-4} along the $\langle 111 \rangle$ direction produces in Ge a change in resistance equal to the resistance of the unstrained material.

When intervalley scattering is important, a strain may also induce very large changes in the mobility. We recall that the transition probability for scattering from the ith to the jth valley depends on the density of final states, that is, the density of states in the jth valley. If the energy of the electron in the ith valley, relative to the band edge, is ϵ, then the density of final states in the jth valley is proportional to $[\epsilon \pm \hbar\omega_q + (\epsilon^i - \epsilon^j)]^{\frac{1}{2}}$; here, the energy of the phonon, $\hbar\omega_q$, cannot be neglected, since we are considering an intervalley process (see p. 169). If the strain lowers ϵ^i relative to ϵ^j, the last term in the bracket is negative, and the transition probability is correspondingly reduced. Thus, the mobility in the ith valley is increased; at the same time, this same shift in the valleys increases the number of electrons in the ith valley and diminishes those in the jth valley. These two effects augment each other and may be of roughly the same order of magnitude. Deviations of the predicted $1/T$ dependence of the elastoresistance may, therefore, be expected in that temperature range where intervalley scattering begins to play a significant role in limiting the mobility (i.e., near the Debye temperature).

Sizeable piezoresistance effects also occur in p-type germanium and silicon (and other semiconductors) where the many-valley model clearly

Table 8-3   Elastoresistance Coefficients of Some Semiconductors

| | *Temperature, °K* | *No. of carriers, cm^{-3}* | *Shear coefficients* | | *Volume dilation coefficient $(m_{11} + 2m_{12})/3$* |
			$(m_{11} - m_{12})/2$	m_{44}	
n-InSb	77		-1.1	-1.3	-16.0
n-GaSb	300	4.6×10^{18}		-38.6	
n-GaAs	300		$+0.5$	-1.4	-7.5
n-Si	300		-79.5	-10.8	$+5.0$
n-Ge	300	$\sim 5 \times 10^{18}$	$+0.1$	-93.4	-13.6
p-InSb	77		$+21.0$	$+101.0$	-4.4
p-Si	300		$+3.9$	$+110.0$	$+6.0$
p-Ge	300		$+66.0$	-6.0	$+1.0$

is inappropriate. Presumably, a shear strain severely distorts the "warped" surfaces of constant energy and, thereby, produces a large anisotropy. Of course, the dependence of the phonon spectrum on strain also contributes to elastoresistance, as do various other lesser sources. Their importance quickly diminishes as the temperature is lowered.

Piezoresistance measurements on n-type GaAs agree with expectations for a spherical band centered at $\mathbf{k} = 0$. In particular, both shear coefficients are small and the elastoresistance is nearly isotropic. Experimental results on a number of semiconductors are listed in Table 8.3.

8.5 MAGNETORESISTANCE AND THE HALL EFFECT

A. Ideal Semiconductor

We begin the discussion of the galvanomagnetic effects in semiconductors within the framework of the idealized band structure. As in the preceding section, we shall subsequently consider the modifications called forth by a many-valley configuration. The reasoning which led to a vanishing longitudinal magnetoresistance in metals with spherical energy surfaces remains valid also for the nondegenerate distribution, and we, therefore, limit our discussion at first to the transverse effects.

Extrinsic region (single band) The current components J_x and J_y in the presence of a magnetic field $\mathbf{H} = (0,0,H_z)$ are given by Eqs. (7.54) and (7.55). In the nondegenerate limit the coefficients $\mathcal{K}_n'$ and $\mathcal{K}_n''$ are given by Eq. (8.24) with $\tau(\epsilon)$ replaced by

$$\frac{\tau}{1 + (\omega_c\tau)^2} \quad \text{for the } \mathcal{K}_n' \tag{8.50}$$

and by

$$\frac{\tau(\omega_c\tau)^2}{1 + (\omega_c\tau)^2} \quad \text{for the } \mathcal{K}_n'' \tag{8.51}$$

where ω_c is the cyclotron frequency

$$\omega_c = \frac{eH}{m^*c} \tag{8.52}$$

The experimental boundary condition $J_y = 0$ gives

$$E_y = E_x\omega_c \frac{\langle \tau^2/(1 + \gamma^2)\rangle}{\langle \tau/(1 + \gamma^2)\rangle} \qquad \gamma \equiv \omega_c\tau \tag{8.53}$$

For the derivation of the transverse magnetoresistance it is convenient to expand Eq. (8.50) and write

$$\frac{\tau}{1 + \gamma^2} = \tau - \frac{\tau\gamma^2}{1 + \gamma^2} \tag{8.54}$$

Using Eqs. (8.24), (8.53), and (8.54), one finds

$$J_x = \frac{ne^2}{m^*} E_x \left\{ \langle\tau\rangle + \omega_c^2 \left[\frac{\langle\tau^2/(1 + \gamma^2)\rangle^2}{\langle\tau/(1 + \gamma^2)\rangle} - \left\langle \frac{\tau^3}{1 + \gamma^2} \right\rangle \right] \right\} \tag{8.55}$$

The transverse magnetoresistance coefficient

$$B \equiv \frac{\Delta\rho}{\rho_0 H^2} \tag{8.56}$$

is given by

$$B = \left(\frac{e}{m^*c}\right)^2 \frac{1}{\langle\tau\rangle} \left[\left\langle \frac{\tau^3}{1 + \gamma^2} \right\rangle - \frac{\langle\tau^2/(1 + \gamma^2)\rangle^2}{\langle\tau/(1 + \gamma^2)\rangle} \right] \tag{8.57}$$

and from Eqs. (8.53) and (8.55) and the defining Equation (7.63), the Hall coefficient is

$$R = \frac{1}{nec} \frac{\langle\tau^2/(1 + \gamma^2)\rangle}{\langle\tau/(1 + \gamma^2)\rangle} \left\{ \langle\tau\rangle + \omega_c^2 \left[\frac{\langle\tau^2/(1 + \gamma^2)\rangle^2}{\langle\tau/(1 + \gamma^2)\rangle} - \left\langle \frac{\tau^3}{1 + \gamma^2} \right\rangle \right] \right\}^{-1} \tag{8.58}$$

There are four limiting cases of physical interest, namely: (1) the low-field, (2) the classical high-field, (3) the quantum, and (4) the extreme-quantum limits.

Case 1.   The low-field limit is defined by the condition $\gamma \ll 1$ and, physically, describes the situation wherein the charge carriers traverse only a small fraction of a cyclotron orbit before they are scattered.

Case 2.   In the classical high-field limit $\gamma > 1$. Now an electron completes several orbits before it is scattered. The absence of quantum effects is assured by the second requirement, $kT \gg \hbar\omega_c$; thus, levels with very large quantum numbers as well as low-lying levels are now occupied and, by the correspondence principle, the behavior is that of a classical system. Alternatively, one may say that the thermal spread is so great as to smear out any evidence of orbital quantization. Although for free electrons and with reasonable room-temperature relaxation times ($\tau \simeq 10^{-14}$ sec) a fairly strong field is required to reach the high-field limit, in semiconductors the small effective mass of some carriers brings the onset of the high-field region into the range of 1 to 10 kilogauss. To determine the critical magnetic field from mobility data it is convenient to write $\gamma = \mu H/c$. Electrons in indium antimonide have, at room temperature, a mobility in the neighborhood of 7×10^4 cm^2/volt-sec, or about 2×10^7 esu. Thus, region 2 commences for $H = 1,500$ gauss at

$T = 300°K$, and at much lower fields at liquid-air temperature. As we shall see presently, the onset of the high-field region for one group of carriers in a multicarrier system can lead to quite pronounced field variations of the galvanomagnetic properties.

Cases 3 and 4. To observe the effects of orbital quantization we must meet the conditions $\gamma > 1$ *and* $kT < \hbar\omega_c$. In case 3 the charge carriers occupy a number of quantized levels, whereas in case 4 all carriers have condensed into the lowest-lying, highly degenerate orbital level. Even under most favorable circumstances, magnetic fields in the range of 100 kilogauss are required for case 4. Case 3, on the other hand, can generally be attained from case 2 merely by performing the experiment at sufficiently low temperatures. We shall defer discussion of all quantum effects until Chap. 11, and restrict our attention to cases 1 and 2.

Case 1. ($\gamma \ll 1$). The expressions for the magnetoresistance and the Hall coefficient, Eqs. (8.57) and (8.58), now reduce to

$$B = \left(\frac{e}{m^*c}\right)^2 \frac{\langle\tau^3\rangle\langle\tau\rangle - \langle\tau^2\rangle^2}{\langle\tau\rangle^2} \tag{8.59}$$

$$R = \frac{1}{nec} \frac{\langle\tau^2\rangle}{\langle\tau\rangle^2} \tag{8.60}$$

According to Eq. (8.59) the magnetoresistance is a consequence of the energy dispersion of the relaxation time τ, consonant with our remarks of the preceding chapter in connection with the vanishing magnetoresistance of a totally degenerate free-electron gas. Clearly, if τ were independent of energy the numerator in Eq. (8.59) would vanish. The magnitude of B is, thus, indicative of the energy dependence of the relaxation time, and, especially if used in conjunction with the temperature dependence of the mobility, can provide some information concerning the relaxation mechanism.

Similarly, the Hall coefficient, Eq. (8.60), is not equal to, but only proportional to, $1/nec$, since $\langle\tau^2\rangle/\langle\tau\rangle^2 \geq 1$, and the value of the ratio is a function of the energy dependence of τ. In particular,

$$\frac{\langle\tau^2\rangle}{\langle\tau\rangle^2} = \frac{3\pi}{8} = 1.18 \qquad \text{if } \tau(\epsilon) \propto \epsilon^{-\frac{1}{2}} \text{ (lattice scattering)}$$

$$\frac{\langle\tau^2\rangle}{\langle\tau\rangle^2} = \frac{315\pi}{512} = 1.93 \qquad \text{if } \tau(\epsilon) \propto \epsilon^{\frac{3}{2}} \text{ (ionized-impurity scattering)} \tag{8.61}$$

If we take the product $R\sigma c$ we obtain from Eqs. (8.25) and (8.60)

$$R\sigma c = \frac{e}{m^*} \frac{\langle\tau^2\rangle}{\langle\tau\rangle} \equiv \mu_H \tag{8.62}$$

μ_H is known as the *Hall mobility* and is proportional to, but not equal to, the drift mobility, Eq. (8.25).   The ratio of Hall to drift mobility depends on the energy dispersion of the relaxation time, and for the two cases of lattice- and ionized-impurity scattering it is given by Eq. (8.61).   As mentioned in the preceding section, several relaxation mechanisms often operate simultaneously, and the effective relaxation time is then

$$\tau_{\text{eff}} = \left(\sum_i \frac{1}{\tau_i} \right)^{-1}$$

where the individual τ_i are different functions of ϵ.   In that case, which is frequently encountered in practice, the integrals $\langle \tau \rangle$ and $\langle \tau^2 \rangle$ must be evaluated by numerical methods.

The most direct determination of the mobility is by the Haynes-Shockley drift method, wherein the drift velocity of charge carriers in a known electric field is measured.   The experimental arrangement is shown schematically in Fig. 8.19.   A pulse of minority carriers is injected at the emitter and, under the influence of the applied field, drifts toward C.   Here, the carriers are "collected" and appear as a blip on the scope. From the distance EC and the measured transit time, one obtains the

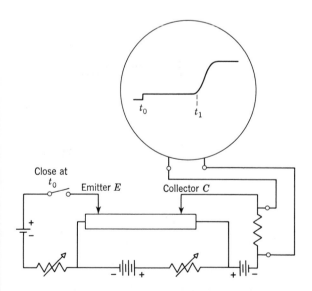

Fig. 8.19   Arrangement for measuring the drift mobility of electrons in a p-type sample.   *(From W. C. Dunlap, "An Introduction to Semiconductors," p. 200, John Wiley & Sons, Inc., New York, 1957.)*

drift velocity. The experiment can succeed only if the lifetime of the minority carriers is longer than the transit time. Moreover, the assumption, made when these experiments were initiated, that the drift mobility of, say, electrons as minority carriers in a p-type sample is the same as when they constitute the majority carriers, is surely invalid in view of carrier-carrier scattering. For these reasons, usually Hall mobilities are measured and reported in the literature.

Case 2. ($\gamma > 1$; $kT \gg \hbar\omega_c$). When $\omega_c\tau \gg 1$, Eq. (8.55) reduces to

$$J_x = \frac{ne^2}{m^*} E_x \left\langle \frac{1}{\tau} \right\rangle^{-1} \tag{8.63}$$

and one obtains

$$B = \frac{1}{H^2} \frac{(\langle 1/\tau \rangle)^{-1} - \langle \tau \rangle}{\langle \tau \rangle} \tag{8.64}$$

$$R = \frac{1}{nec} \tag{8.65}$$

The magnetoresistance coefficient B again depends on the dispersion of τ, though in a different manner than in the low-field limit. Of greater moment is the fact that B goes as H^{-2}, i.e., the magnetoresistance saturates at high fields and attains a value characteristic of $\tau(\epsilon)$. Clearly, high-field magnetoresistance measurements also provide a method for determining the relaxation mechanism and may be used as an independent check on deductions based on unrelated data.

The Hall coefficient, in contrast to B, is, at high fields, independent of $\tau(\epsilon)$. It, therefore, provides the most reliable measure of carrier density. The ratio $R_0/R_\infty = \langle \tau^2 \rangle/\langle \tau \rangle^2$ generally falls between 1.0 and 2.0 [see Eq. (8.61)].

Multicarrier system   We must now extend our discussion to the multicarrier system so that we may treat the phenomena in intrinsic materials (electrons and holes) and in p-type germanium and silicon (light and heavy holes). In the case of intrinsic Ge and Si, and possibly other semiconductors as well, one must allow for three groups of carriers.

We shall now disregard the energy dependence of τ for the two carriers. As will be apparent presently, the changes of R and $\Delta\rho$ with magnetic field are so great for a two-carrier system, even assuming a constant relaxation time, that the effects due to dispersion can be neglected. (We recall that in the degenerate case the transverse magnetoresistance vanishes for a single band but is finite for two or more bands.)

One can then derive the following expressions:

$$\rho = \frac{\Sigma(n_i e_i \mu_i)/(1 + \gamma_i^2)}{[\Sigma(n_i e_i \mu_i)/(1 + \gamma_i^2)]^2 + [\Sigma(n_i e_i \mu_i \gamma_i)/(1 + \gamma_i^2)]^2} \tag{8.66}$$

$$R = \frac{\dfrac{1}{c}[\Sigma(n_i e_i \mu_i^2)/(1 + \gamma_i^2)]}{[\Sigma(n_i e_i \mu_i)/(1 + \gamma_i^2)]^2 + [\Sigma(n_i e_i \mu_i \gamma_i)/(1 + \gamma_i^2)]^2} \tag{8.67}$$

where n_i is the number of carriers of type i, e_i is the charge of carriers of type i, μ_i is the mobility of carriers of type i, $\gamma_i = e_i \tau_i H / m_i c = \mu_i(H/c)$, and the following sign convention must be adhered to: the charge e_i is negative for electrons and positive for holes; the masses m_i, relaxation times τ_i, and concentrations n_i are always positive; and consequently, the mobilities μ_i and cyclotron frequencies ω_i must be taken positive for holes and *negative for electrons*. Although this is not the only sign convention that can be employed, it seems the most sensible in view of the usual assignment of positive masses and negative and positive charges for electrons and holes, respectively.

In the case of two groups of carriers we have

$$\rho = \frac{\dfrac{n_1 e_1 \mu_1}{1 + \gamma_1^2} + \dfrac{n_2 e_2 \mu_2}{1 + \gamma_2^2}}{\left(\dfrac{n_1 e_1 \mu_1}{1 + \gamma_1^2} + \dfrac{n_2 e_2 \mu_2}{1 + \gamma_2^2}\right)^2 + \left(\dfrac{n_1 e_1 \mu_1 \gamma_1}{1 + \gamma_1^2} + \dfrac{n_2 e_2 \mu_2 \gamma_2}{1 + \gamma_2^2}\right)^2} \tag{8.68}$$

$$R = \frac{\dfrac{1}{c}\left(\dfrac{n_1 e_1 \mu_1^2}{1 + \gamma_1^2} + \dfrac{n_2 e_2 \mu_2^2}{1 + \gamma_2^2}\right)}{\left(\dfrac{n_1 e_1 \mu_1}{1 + \gamma_1^2} + \dfrac{n_2 e_2 \mu_2}{1 + \gamma_2^2}\right)^2 + \left(\dfrac{n_1 e_1 \mu_1 \gamma_1}{1 + \gamma_1^2} + \dfrac{n_2 e_2 \mu_2 \gamma_2}{1 + \gamma_2^2}\right)^2} \tag{8.69}$$

Already for a two-carrier system, the formulas display sufficient complexity to allow for fairly extensive field variations of ρ and R, such as are shown in Figs. 8.20 and 8.21.

In the high-field limit, the Hall coefficient of a two-carrier system approaches the value

$$R_\infty = \frac{1}{c(n_1 e_1 + n_2 e_2)} \tag{8.70}$$

If $e_2 = -e_1$, i.e., if the carriers are electrons and holes, R_∞ can be very large, provided $n_1 - n_2$ is small, in other words if the number of electrons and holes are nearly equal. The result, it is worth noting, is independent

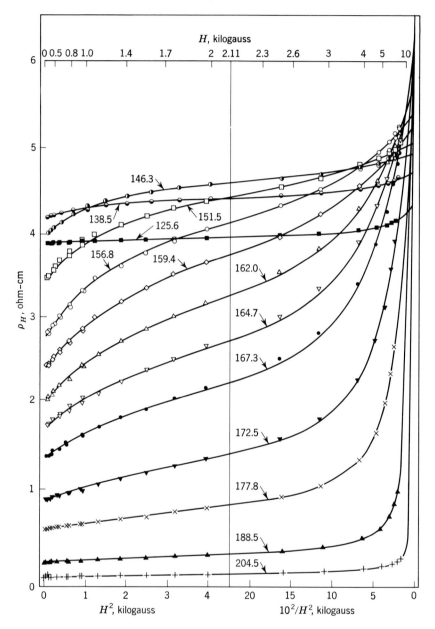

Fig. 8.20 Resistivity of p-type InSb as a function of magnetic field at various temperatures. Note the change in scale on the abscissa to bring out the important features near $H = 0$ and $H \rightarrow \infty$. The points are experimental and the curves calculated using a three-band model. [*From G. Fischer, Helv. Phys. Acta.*, **33**: 474 (1960).]

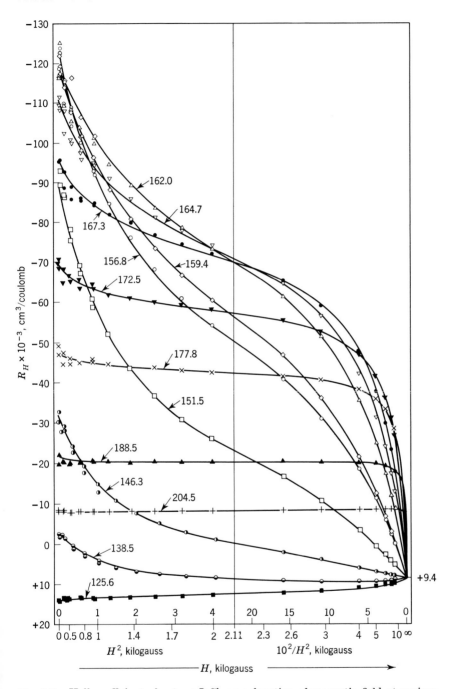

Fig. 8.21   Hall coefficient of p-type InSb as a function of magnetic field at various temperatures.   The points are experimental and the curves calculated using a three-band model.   [*From G. Fischer, Helv. Phys. Acta.,* **33**: 472 (1960).]

of the mobility ratio, $b \equiv \mu_2/\mu_1$. If, however, $n_1 = n_2$ exactly,

$$R_\infty = \frac{1}{n_1 e_1 c} \frac{1 - b}{1 + b} \tag{8.71}$$

If, now, $b = 1$ we have $R_\infty = 0$, according to Eq. (8.71) for $n_1 = n_2$, whereas according to Eq. (8.70), $R_\infty \to \infty$ as $n_1 \to n_2$. To probe the source of this paradox one need only expand Eq. (8.69) for $\gamma \gg 1$ in powers of γ^{-1}. One then finds that Eq. (8.70) and Eq. (8.71) are, in fact, both correct in the proper circumstances. If n_1 is *very nearly* equal to n_2, it turns out that for fields such that $1 \ll \gamma^2 \ll n_1/(n_1 - n_2)$, Eq. (8.71) is correct. Only when $\gamma^2 \gg n_1/(n_1 - n_2)$, i.e., at *very* high fields, does Eq. (8.70) hold.

The various features of $R(H)$ are displayed very clearly in the curves of Fig. 8.21. At the lowest temperature, $T = 125.6°K$, the sample is extrinsic p type, and one might expect that a one-carrier model should suffice. The Hall coefficient is positive throughout but decreases by a factor of roughly 1.5 from the low- to the high-field limit. This can be understood in terms of a two-band model, i.e., two sets of holes of different masses and mobilities. As the temperature is increased, electrons are thermally excited into the conduction band and, because of their very high mobility, quickly dominate the low-field Hall effect. This same high mobility is responsible for the onset of the "high-field" region already at very small magnetic fields. At temperatures in excess of about 170°K the two "high-field" limits show up very beautifully: following an initial increase of R (decrease of its magnitude) as H is increased to about 1,000 gauss, the Hall coefficient remains almost constant to a much higher field, where R once again increases to the ultimate, temperature-independent high-field value of $+9.4$. As T is increased from 172.5 to 204.5°K, the number of intrinsic carriers increases and so does the ratio $n_1/(n_1 - n_2)$. Accordingly, the intermediate region of nearly constant R should and does extend to higher fields as T increases.

It is apparent that such measurements can provide a wealth of information, such as mobility ratios and carrier concentrations at various temperatures. Of course, the mobility ratio b may also be deduced from the Hall effect in the low-field limit. Here Eq. (8.69) reduces to

$$R = \frac{n_1 e_1 \mu_1^2 + n_2 e_2 \mu_2^2}{c(n_1 e_1 \mu_1 + n_2 e_2 \mu_2)^2} \tag{8.72}$$

and, provided $e_2 = -e_1$, R vanishes when

$$b^2 = \frac{n_1}{n_2} \tag{8.73}$$

Let the subscripts 1 and 2 stand for electrons and holes, respectively, and assume, as is most frequently the case, that

$$\mu_2 = \mu_p < |\mu_1| = |\mu_n|$$

If we start with a p-type sample in the extrinsic region ($n_1 = n = 0$), the Hall coefficient is positive and a measure of $n_2 = p$. Now as the temperature is increased and the sample passes into the intrinsic range, R decreases, goes to zero, and changes sign (see Fig. 8.22). The electron and hole concentrations at the temperature T', where R = 0 can be calculated from Eq. (8.8), provided the band parameters and energy gap are known, and from the known difference $p - n = p(\text{extr})$, as determined from the Hall effect in the extrinsic region. The mobility ratio is then given by Eq. (8.73). The critical temperature T' can be adjusted over some range by varying the doping.

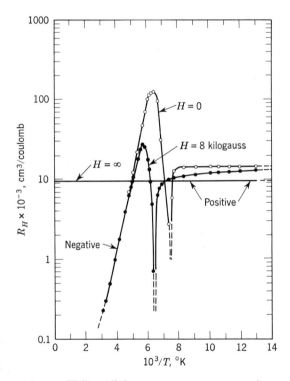

Fig. 8.22 Hall coefficient versus temperature of a single crystal of InSb at magnetic fields of 0 and 8.0 kilooersteds and $H \to \infty$. Note the field dependence as well as the temperature dependence of R. [*From G. Fischer, Helv. Phys. Acta.*, **33**: 467 (1960).]

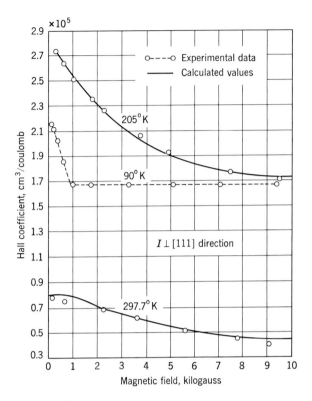

Fig. 8.23 Hall coefficient of a p-type Ge crystal as a function of magnetic field at three temperatures. [*From A. C. Beer, Solid State Phys. Suppl., No. 4, 168 (1962).*]

In p-type Ge, Si, and InSb, where two types of holes occur, Eqs. (8.73) and (8.8) must be corrected to account for the three-carrier intrinsic situation encountered here, while in the extrinsic region in these substances a two-carrier model must be employed. In the latter case the heavy holes, despite their greater mass, make the dominant contribution to the current. We recall that in this case the relaxation times for both groups of holes are nearly equal (see page 263). Since the carrier concentration is proportional to $(m^*)^{\frac{3}{2}}$ [see Eqs. (8.5) and (8.6)], the conductivity ratio $\sigma_h/\sigma_l = (m_h/m_l)^{\frac{3}{2}} > 1$, although $\mu_h/\mu_l = m_l/m_h < 1$.

The relative contribution of the two types of carriers to the Hall coefficient is, according to Eq. (8.72), given by $n_h\mu_h^2/n_l\mu_l^2$; here, then, the role is reversed, and the light holes largely determine the magnitude of the Hall coefficient at low fields. However, as a result of their high mobility, these low-mass carriers also enter the high-field region for relatively small values of H, and the Hall effect in p-type germanium exhibits pronounced field dependence at moderate fields (see Fig. 8.23).

Before considering the temperature dependence of R, we call attention to a complication that sets in with strong electric and magnetic fields in the intrinsic region. Since electrons and holes experience a Lorentz force in the same direction, the concentration of electron-hole pairs is enhanced on one side of the specimen, thereby generating a transverse concentration gradient in the sample. The unbalance is, of course, counteracted by thermal excitation on the depleted side and recombination on the opposite one. At strong fields ($H > 10,000$ gauss) and in pure samples these concentration gradients may become significant and a theory based on a homogeneous distribution loses validity.

The temperature dependence of the low-field Hall effect is completely described by Eq. (8.72)—or its extension to the three-carrier model—together with Eqs. (8.8) and (8.25). Let us, for the moment, disregard changes in mobility in comparison with changes in concentration. The former will be altogether negligible except in the exhaustion range, and even here only variations in the energy dispersion of τ, but not its actual value, can influence the Hall coefficient. We also assume in the following that $\mu_p < |\mu_n|$.

A typical set of curves for an n-type sample is shown in Fig. 8.24. R is negative at all temperatures. In the extrinsic region it is independent of temperature, consistent with a fixed carrier concentration. In the purer samples, and with decreasing temperature, R increases exponentially as the carriers "freeze out" on donor impurities. At high temperatures, as one enters the intrinsic region, both n and p increase with $n - p$ constant. Since $|\mu_n| > \mu_p$, electrons remain decisive in the Hall effect and $|R|$ decreases precipitously.

In p-type materials the situation is not altered (except for sign) at low temperatures. However, in the transition to the intrinsic region, R changes sign (see Fig. 8.22). As was pointed out earlier, the temperature at which $R = 0$ depends on the extrinsic carrier concentration and on the mobility ratio for any given semiconductor.

At very low temperatures and in moderate to heavily doped semiconductors, $|R|$ attains a maximum as T is reduced, and upon further reduction in temperature diminishes and then approaches a constant value. This behavior is characteristic of impurity-band conduction: $|R|$ decreasing from its maximum as more and more carriers contribute to impurity-band conduction, until, at very low temperatures, all carriers are "frozen out" and the concentration in the "impurity band" remains fixed. The greater the doping, the higher the temperature at which the transition to impurity-band conduction occurs, as can be seen from Fig. 8.25.

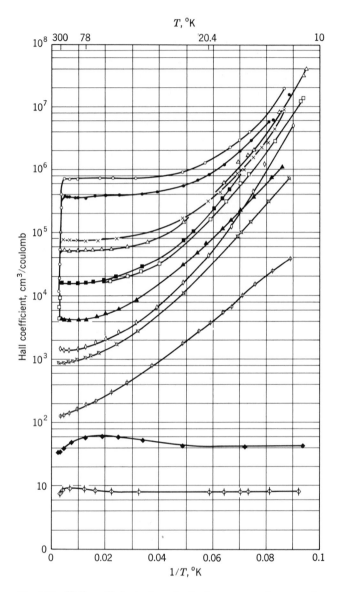

Fig. 8.24 Hall coefficient of a set of n-type germanium samples (arsenic-doped) as a function of inverse absolute temperature. [*After P. P. Debye and E. M. Conwell, Phys. Rev.,* **93**: 694 (1956).]

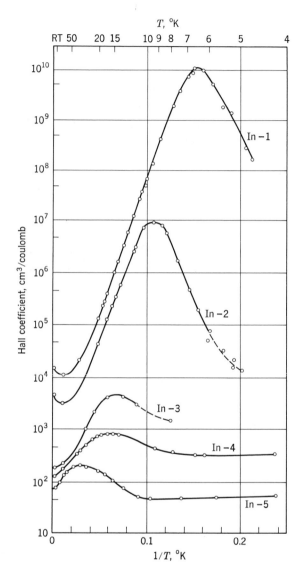

Fig. 8.25 The Hall coefficient of p-type Ge samples at low temperatures. The impurity concentration increases in going from sample IN-1 to IN-5. [*After H. Fritzsche, Phys. Rev.*, **99**: 406 (1955).]

As indicated in the discussion of Figs. 8.20 to 8.22, the multiband model in which the individual energy bands are assumed of standard form leads to reasonably good agreement with experimental results on magnetoresistance and Hall effect in indium antimonide. Similarly, in n-type gallium arsenide the longitudinal magnetoresistance is, as expected, very small. The transverse magnetoresistance at room temperature is proportional to H^2 up to fields of 10,000 gauss and is relatively small even at this field. The value of $\Delta\rho/\rho$ depends sensitively on the purity of the specimen; for relatively impure samples, for which ionized impurity scattering is of some importance even at room temperature (see page 259), $\Delta\rho/\rho$ at 10 kilogauss is about 0.004, whereas in high-purity samples ($n = 4 \times 10^{15}$ cm^{-3}) $\Delta\rho/\rho$ at 10 kilogauss is about 0.02.

B. Multivalley Semiconductors

To evaluate the Hall and magnetoresistance coefficients in n-type germanium and silicon it is necessary to take into account explicitly the nonspherical shape of the constant-energy contours of the individual spheroids. This can be accomplished in various ways, one of which was outlined in Chap. 5. There we saw that the distribution function could be written as an expansion in H, provided the approach to equilibrium could be represented in terms of a relaxation time τ. The method will, therefore, be strictly valid in a semiconductor at all temperatures, unless optical-mode or intervalley scattering are important. Even when this condition is not satisfied, experience has shown that the relaxation-time approximation leads to results almost identical with those of the variational method. Thus, the method outlined in Chap. 5 should be a good approximation procedure under all conditions.

The calculation, which we shall here only sketch, proceeds along the following lines. In the expression for the current, Eq. (7.2), we replace the function f by $-\phi(\mathbf{k},\mathbf{r})(\partial f_0/\partial\epsilon)$, where $\phi(\mathbf{k},\mathbf{r})$ is now given by Eq. (5.26). A bit of algebra then leads to the result, correct to H^2,

$$J_i^\beta = \Sigma\sigma_{ik}^\beta E_k + \Sigma\sigma_{ikl}^\beta E_k H_l + \Sigma\sigma_{iklm}^\beta E_k H_l H_m \qquad (8.74)$$

where the subscripts refer to cartesian coordinates 1, 2, 3, and the superscript to the particular spheroid. σ_{ik}^β is the usual conductivity tensor for $H = 0$; the remaining coefficients are given by Eqs. (7.73) and (7.74).

Clearly, the calculation of $\mathbf{J}^\beta$ using these general formulas is exceedingly complex and tedious, even when, as in the cubic case, crystal symmetry reduces the number of independent tensor components. Here, we confine ourselves to presentation of the final results and refer the interested reader to the original literature [18]. The low-field Hall coefficient reduces to

$$R = \frac{1}{nec} \frac{\langle \tau^2 \rangle}{\langle \tau \rangle^2} \left[3 \frac{1 + 2m_\perp/m_\parallel}{(2 + m_\perp/m_\parallel)^2} \right] \tag{8.75}$$

which is identical to Eq. (8.60), except for the correction factor in the brackets. Since $m_\perp$ is generally small compared to $m_\parallel$, this correction factor is not very important, ranging between 0.75 and 1.0.

The magnetoresistance coefficient in the many-valley case depends on the disposition of the valleys in **k** space and on the relative orientation of **J** and **H**. There are, however, certain simple relations between the

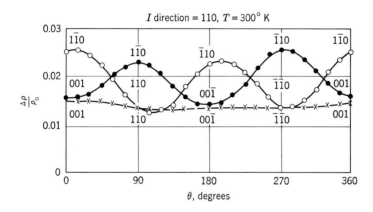

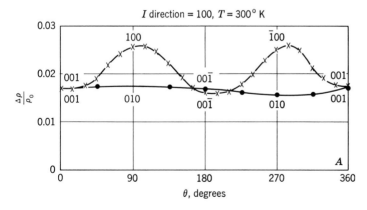

Fig. 8.26 Variations of $\Delta\rho/\rho_0$ in n-type germanium as H is rotated through an angle θ from 0 to 360°. The magnitude of H is 4,000 gauss, and certain cardinal directions of H are as indicated. The fixed directions of I are shown. [*From A. F. Gibson (ed.), "Progress in Semiconductors," vol. 3, p. 10, John Wiley & Sons, Inc., New York, 1958.*]

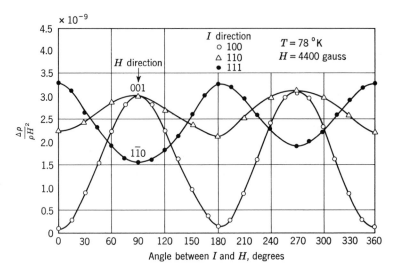

Fig. 8.27 Variations in $\Delta\rho/\rho H^2$ as H is rotated with respect to I in n-type silicon. Certain cardinal directions of H are as indicated. The fixed directions of I are as given. [*From A. F. Gibson (ed.), "Progress in Semiconductors," vol. 3, p. 20, John Wiley & Sons, Inc., New York, 1958.*]

various magnetoresistance coefficients which prove quite useful in deciding on the arrangement of the valleys in the Brillouin zone. These are given below.

For valleys oriented along $\langle 100 \rangle$ directions:

$$B_{100}^{100} = 0$$
$$B_{110}^{1\bar{1}0} = B_{100}^{010} - B_{110}^{110} \tag{8.76}$$
$$B_{110}^{001} = B_{100}^{001}$$

For valleys oriented along $\langle 111 \rangle$ directions:

$$B_{110}^{110} = \tfrac{1}{2}B_{100}^{100}$$
$$B_{110}^{1\bar{1}0} = \tfrac{1}{2}B_{100}^{100} + B_{100}^{010} \tag{8.77}$$
$$B_{110}^{001} = B_{100}^{001}$$

In the above relations the superscripts give the direction of the magnetic field and the subscripts, the direction of current flow. The magnetoresistivity of n-Si and n-Ge single crystals as functions of magnetic-field orientation are shown in Figs. 8.26 and 8.27. The excellent agreement with the predictions of Eqs. (8.76) and (8.77) at the various symmetry points testifies to the utility of magnetoresistance measurements in establishing important features of the band structure.

8.6 THERMAL CONDUCTIVITY AND THERMOELECTRIC POWER

A. Thermal Conductivity

The electronic thermal conductivity and thermoelectric power of an extrinsic, single-band semiconductor are given by Eqs. (7.35) and (7.45). In the nondegenerate limit the coefficients $\mathcal{K}_n$ are to be evaluated according to Eq. (8.24) and one obtains directly

$$\kappa = \frac{n}{Tm^*} \frac{\langle \tau \rangle \langle \tau \epsilon^2 \rangle - \langle \tau \epsilon \rangle^2}{\langle \tau \rangle} \tag{8.78}$$

and, for the Lorentz number,

$$L = \frac{\kappa}{\sigma T} = \frac{\langle \tau \rangle \langle \tau \epsilon^2 \rangle - \langle \tau \epsilon \rangle^2}{e^2 T^2 \langle \tau \rangle^2} \tag{8.79}$$

We have seen that the energy dependence of the relaxation time can often be expressed in the form

$$\tau = \tau_0 \epsilon^q \tag{8.80}$$

For example, $q = -\frac{1}{2}$ for acoustic-mode scattering, while for scattering by ionized impurities, $q = \frac{3}{2}$. When Eq. (8.80) holds, the averages $\langle \tau \rangle$, $\langle \tau \epsilon \rangle$, and $\langle \tau \epsilon^2 \rangle$ over the Boltzmann distribution are

$$\langle \tau \rangle = \frac{\tau_0 \Gamma(\frac{5}{2} + q)}{\Gamma(\frac{5}{2})}$$

$$\langle \tau \epsilon \rangle = \frac{\tau_0 kT \Gamma(\frac{7}{2} + q)}{\Gamma(\frac{5}{2})} \tag{8.81}$$

$$\langle \tau \epsilon^2 \rangle = \frac{\tau_0 (kT)^2 \Gamma(\frac{9}{2} + q)}{\Gamma(\frac{5}{2})}$$

Substitution of Eq. (8.81) into Eqs. (8.78) and (8.79) gives

$$\kappa = \frac{k^2 T}{e^2} \left(\frac{5}{2} + q \right) \sigma \qquad L = \frac{k^2}{e^2} \left(\frac{5}{2} + q \right) \tag{8.82}$$

Evidently, the thermal conductivity depends to some extent on the dispersion of the relaxation time. In particular, the thermal conductivity will be large if $q > 0$, small if $q < 0$. It is not difficult to understand this behavior. If $q > 0$, high-energy electrons in the distribution have a longer-than-average relaxation time. Since these electrons carry more than average energy while carrying, of course, the average charge, an enhanced Lorentz number is to be expected in this instance.

In the intrinsic region a two-band model must be used. It is then essential, since the Fermi energy for the two groups of carriers is the same, that the transport coefficients $\mathcal{K}_n$ be referred to the same zero of energy. After a bit of algebra one then finds

$$\kappa = \frac{k^2 T}{e^2} \left\{ \left[\left(\frac{5}{2} + q_n \right) \sigma_n + \left(\frac{5}{2} + q_p \right) \sigma_p \right] \right.$$
$$\left. + \left[(5 + q_n + q_p) + \frac{\epsilon_G}{kT} \right]^2 \frac{\sigma_n \sigma_p}{\sigma_n + \sigma_p} \right\} \quad (8.83)$$

The first term in Eq. (8.83) is the anticipated result for two independent groups of carriers. The second term is new and of considerable interest, since it may be orders of magnitude larger than the first under certain circumstances. If we divide Eq. (8.83) by the total electrical conductivity times T, and also assume for convenience $q_n = q_p = q$ (i.e., the same dispersion for τ_p and τ_n), we obtain

$$L = \frac{k^2}{e^2} \left(\frac{5}{2} + q \right) + \frac{k^2}{e^2} \left(5 + 2q + \frac{\epsilon_G}{kT} \right)^2 \frac{\sigma_n \sigma_p}{(\sigma_n + \sigma_p)^2} \quad (8.84)$$

The first term is of order $(k/e)^2$. If, now, σ_n and σ_p are of roughly the same magnitude, the second term is of order $(k/e)^2(\epsilon_G/kT)^2$, i.e., about $(\epsilon_G/kT)^2$ times as great as the first. Since $\epsilon_G \gg kT$, this last term can be extremely important in an intrinsic material.

The physical mechanism responsible for this additional energy flux is not hard to find. We recall that, according to Eq. (8.8), the product np is a sensitive function of temperature. In the presence of a temperature gradient this relation will remain valid at every point in the sample. Consequently, a temperature gradient will generate a concentration gradient of electron-hole pairs in the sample. Under the action of this concentration gradient the carriers diffuse toward the region of low concentration, that is, toward the cold end. This tendency, as a result of diffusion, to reduce np at the hot end and increase it at the cold end in relation to the equilibrium value (Eq. 8.8) is constantly balanced by generation and recombination, respectively. However, in the process of diffusion down the temperature gradient each electron-hole pair transports the energy ϵ_G that was expended in its creation. Ultimately, as recombination takes place, this same energy is liberated in a region of lower temperature. It is this transport of ionization energy through *ambipolar diffusion* that is responsible for the second term in Eqs. (8.83) and (8.84).

Since the carrier concentration in a semiconductor is, almost by definition, many orders of magnitude smaller than in a metal, it follows that the electronic portion of the thermal conductivity will generally be much smaller than the lattice thermal conductivity. This is, of course, the exact inverse of the situation normally encountered in metals. It is only when $\sigma_n \simeq \sigma_p$ and the ambipolar diffusion term is large that the electronic thermal conductivity becomes sizeable.

B.   Thermoelectric Power

Diffusion thermopower   Stimulated by the possibility of a wide range of applications, the thermoelectric properties of semiconductors have been studied quite intensively in recent years.   We shall return to the practical aspects shortly, but shall first present the formal results and consider their significance.

From Eqs. (8.24) and (7.45) one obtains

$$S = \frac{1}{eT}\left(\frac{\langle \tau \epsilon \rangle}{\langle \tau \rangle} - \eta\right) = \frac{k}{e}\left[\left(\frac{5}{2} + q\right) - \frac{\eta}{kT}\right] \tag{8.85}$$

Here the Fermi energy η is measured relative to the appropriate band edge; it is, therefore, negative for electrons and positive for holes, assuming nondegenerate samples where the Fermi level falls into the forbidden gap.

In the saturation region of an extrinsic semiconductor there is a simple relation between the temperature, doping concentration, effective mass, and Fermi energy, namely, Eq. (8.19).   If we make use of Eq. (8.19) and set $\epsilon_c = 0$ (since we are measuring energies relative to the band edge), we obtain the so-called Pisarenko formula

$$S = \frac{k}{e}\left[\frac{5}{2} + q + \ln\frac{2(2\pi m^* kT/h^2)^{\frac{3}{2}}}{N_D}\right] \tag{8.86}$$

for an n-type semiconductor, and a corresponding expression for a p-type material.   It must be emphasized that Eq. (8.86) is valid only in the exhaustion region, whereas Eq. (8.85) is correct whenever transport is limited to a single band.

In an intrinsic or otherwise multiband sample one can calculate the thermoelectric power from the simple relation

$$S = \frac{\Sigma(S_i \sigma_i)}{\Sigma(\sigma_i)} \tag{8.87}$$

Since S_n and S_p, the thermopowers for electrons and holes, are of opposite sign and often of roughly equal magnitude, the thermopower in an intrinsic sample is decided primarily by the carriers of the higher mobility.   Normally, this means that S at higher temperatures is negative and decreases in magnitude with increasing temperature, since, in Eq. (8.85), the contribution due to η/kT diminishes as T increases.   In the exhaustion region the sign of S is given by the charge of the carriers, positive for holes and negative for electrons. Moreover, according to Eq. (8.86), we expect that S will increase slowly in magnitude with increasing temperature. Finally, it also follows from Eq. (8.86) that the thermoelectric power not only allows for a quick determination of the sign of the charge carriers, but of the density-of-states effective mass as well. It is only necessary to know the number of uncompensated donor (or acceptor) impurities, and this one can determine from the Hall effect. It is not even essential that q be known precisely, since the last term is generally much larger than unity.

A typical curve of S as a function of T is shown in Fig. 8.28. The curve agrees with expectation quite well at high temperatures but shows a large anomaly at low temperatures.

Measurements of thermopower of semiconductors display the anticipated temperature and concentration dependence, except at low temperatures, where the thermoelectric power in pure samples often attains values larger than the theoretical by factors of about 20. Effective

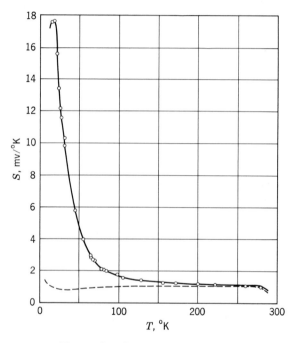

Fig. 8.28 Thermoelectric power of p-type Ge (1.5×10^{14} acceptors per cubic centimeter). Dashed curve represents the calculated value using Eq. (8.85). The difference between the curves is the result of phonon drag. (*After J. Tauc, "Photo and Thermoelectric Effects in Semiconductors," p. 156, Pergamon Press, New York, 1962.*)

masses deduced from high-temperature thermopower data are generally in fair agreement with values obtained from cyclotron resonance experiments. However, a survey of existing data leads to the conclusion that while thermopower gives a good estimate of effective mass, this method cannot be relied upon for a precise determination of that parameter.

Phonon-drag thermopower   The anomalously large values of S at low temperatures arise from the same mechanism responsible for a similar behavior in metals—the phonon-drag effect. In the semiconductor the situation is somewhat different in detail. Whereas in the metal *all* phonons participate in electron-phonon scattering, and the phonons of maximum wave vector impart with each collision the greatest momentum to the electron, in a semiconductor we know that *only long-wavelength* (small wave vector) phonons can interact with the charge carriers (neglecting for the moment intervalley scattering). The treatment of phonon-drag thermoelectricity must, therefore, be modified so as to account for the fact that only a small portion of the phonon spectrum contributes to the effect. We present here an alternative discussion which is particularly suitable to the phenomenon in semiconductors, following arguments initially phrased by Herring [19].

We start by ascribing to the phonon distribution a drift velocity v_d' which we define in terms of the thermal conductivity through the kinetic equation

$$v_d' = \frac{\kappa'}{U'} \nabla T = \frac{C'l'u'}{3U'} \nabla T \tag{8.88}$$

where we have used the primes to indicate that we are restricting the symbols to that group of long-wavelength phonons which can interact with the charge carriers. In Eq. (8.88) U' is the energy density, C' the specific heat, u' the sound velocity, and l' the mean free path for that group of phonons. Since we are concerned only with the low-frequency part of the spectrum, we can apply classical results and write

$$U' = C'T \tag{8.89}$$

and obtain

$$v_d' = \frac{l'u'}{3T} \nabla T \tag{8.90}$$

If we now neglect all electron-relaxation processes except electron-phonon scattering, then the electron distribution will gradually acquire this drift velocity from the phonon distribution. From the definition of the mobility it then follows that such a drift velocity is equivalent to some electric field, or, alternatively, that to prevent such a drift, and prevent a flow of charge current, an electric field

$$E = \frac{v_d'}{\mu} \tag{8.91}$$

must be generated in the sample to offset phonon drag. The corresponding phonon-drag thermopower is, therefore,

$$S_g = \frac{l'u'}{3\mu T} = \frac{m^* u'^2}{3eT} \frac{\tau_p'}{\tau_e} \tag{8.92}$$

where we have made the substitutions $l' = u'\tau_p'$ and $\mu = e\tau_e/m^*$ so as to display the dependence of S_g on the ratio of phonon to electron relaxation times. To predict the temperature dependence of S_g we must then inquire into the temperature dependence of these relaxation times.

According to Herring, $\tau_p' \propto \lambda^2/T^3$, where λ is the phonon wavelength. Since the average electron energy and wave vector depend on the temperature according to $T \propto \epsilon_{avg} \propto k_{avg}^2$, the wave vector of the phonons that can scatter electrons also increases with increasing T. Consequently, $\tau_p' \propto T^{-4}$. Consistent with our initial assumption that τ_e is limited by electron-phonon scattering, we take $\tau_e \propto T^{-1.5}$. Combining these results we conclude that Eq. (8.92) predicts a $T^{-3.5}$ dependence for the phonon-drag thermopower. Indeed, if the theoretical diffusion thermopower is subtracted from the data of Hull and Geballe, the remainder does go as $T^{-3.2}$ for the purest samples which these investigators studied. In p-type silicon, S_g is proportional to $T^{-2.3}$; this somewhat slower temperature dependence is what we should expect, since for this material the mobility in the lattice-scattering regime goes as $T^{-2.3}$, and not as the theoretical $T^{-1.5}$.

The preceding results suggest that S_g will increase indefinitely as the temperature is lowered. Clearly, this cannot be true, and experimentally one finds a maximum whose value and temperature depend sensitively on the purity of the sample and also upon its dimensions. The dependence of S_g on sample size is interesting because it makes its appearance long before other physical properties exhibit a size dependence. The reason is, of course, that in this instance only long-wavelength phonons are important, and these have much longer mean free paths than the average for the entire phonon spectrum. The dependence of S_g on sample size at low temperatures arises because, with decreasing temperature, scattering of long-wavelength phonons at boundaries becomes an important dissipative mechanism. Since under these conditions τ_p' should be independent of temperature and wavelength, S_g should now go as $(\mu T)^{-1}$.

Simultaneously, as T is reduced, scattering of carriers by ionized impurities becomes increasingly important. The carriers can now dissipate the momentum acquired from the phonon current against these scattering centers.

8.7   DEVICES USING HOMOGENEOUS SEMICONDUCTORS

We conclude this chapter with a few remarks on practical applications of semiconductors, leaving, however, to the next chapter a more detailed, though by no means exhaustive, treatment of rectifiers and transistors. Many volumes have been written on the subject and all but a cursory outline is clearly beyond the scope of this book.   At the end of the chapter we list some of the more recent reviews and books which may be consulted for further study.

A.   Thermistor

In device terminology a *thermistor* is a circuit element whose resistance is a sensitive function of the temperature.   Clearly any intrinsic semiconductor comes under this heading, and most common units are constructed of such materials, generally metal oxides.   The basic constituents are selected so that over the operating range the temperature coefficient of resistance is high, while the resistance is reasonably low. Typical applications are in industrial temperature measurement and control.   In the laboratory, microwave and infrared power levels are frequently measured with thermistor bolometers which have a small bead of semiconducting material as the active element.

In recent years, germanium has found its way into many low-temperature laboratories, where it serves as a stable, reliable, and extremely sensitive resistance thermometer in the temperature range between 1° and 20°K.   Germanium resistance thermometers whose active range extends to 78°K and higher are also available, though a single unit cannot cover the entire temperature range effectively.   These thermometers are now displacing the carbon-composition resistor as resistance thermometers.   The latter is quite unstable and requires recalibration each time it is used.

B.   Varistor

Removed from thermal contact with a heat bath, a semiconductor which carries a current I will experience a temperature increase as a result of Joule heating.   If the semiconductor is intrinsic, this increase in temperature will lower its resistance.   Clearly, we have here the makings of a decidedly nonohmic device whose resistance decreases with increasing current flow.   One common application of such a nonohmic resistor, called a *varistor*, is as a lightning arrestor or other surge-protection device. The unit, generally fashioned from silicon carbide, is connected in shunt across the equipment, for example, a transformer at a substation, and under normal conditions draws very little current. However, when a high voltage is applied, the resistance of the unit drops rapidly and the surge passes through the protecting device. Compact units capable of withstanding surge currents in excess of 100,000 amp for several microseconds are in common use. On a smaller scale, varistors find frequent application as control elements for current and voltage stabilization.

C. Hall-effect Devices

The Hall effect in semiconductors has also been put to practical use in a variety of ways. If the magnetic field for the device is produced by passing the current in a power line (or a known fraction thereof) through a set of coils, while the primary current in the device is made proportional to the line voltage, the Hall voltage will be proportional to the product IV. In short, the unit illustrated schematically in Fig. 8.29 will serve as a compact and sturdy wattmeter.

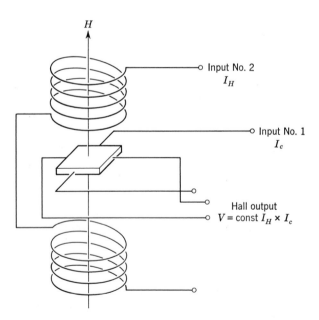

Fig. 8.29 Schematic of a Hall-effect wattmeter; I_H is proportional to line current; I_c is proportional to line voltage. (*From W. C. Dunlap, "An Introduction to Semiconductors," p. 400, John Wiley & Sons, Inc., New York, 1957.*)

Gaussmeters utilizing the Hall effect have been available commercially for many years.   Here, the primary current is derived from a well-regulated dc supply and the Hall voltage is proportional to the unknown magnetic field.   These units have many advantages over the conventional rotating-coil magnetometer—they contain no moving parts, are of rugged construction, and, especially advantageous in many situations, can be made quite small.   The last feature is particularly important when the unknown field is highly nonuniform and has steep field gradients.   The disadvantage of Hall-effect gaussmeters is that the active element, a semiconductor, is somewhat sensitive to the temperature.   In some cases where a probe of high sensitivity is demanded, calling for an active element with a high mobility, it has been necessary to incorporate temperature stabilization.   This temperature stabilization is generally achieved by means of yet another semiconducting device (see below).

D.   Thermoelectric Devices

The best known application of thermoelectricity is the *thermocouple*, consisting of two dissimilar conductors, usually a pure metal and an alloy or two alloys (for example, Pt-PtRh, Cu-constantan, AuCo-AgAu).   One junction is immersed in a fixed temperature bath at the temperature T_0 (for example, ice water, 0°C), and the other is placed in contact with the substance whose temperature T_1 is to be measured.   The voltage developed across the thermocouple is a monotonic function of $T_1 - T_0$, and there are standard conversion tables from which the temperature T_1 may be read for a given voltage and reference temperature.

The most important and interesting application of thermoelectricity in semiconductors is the direct conversion of heat to electrical energy and the reverse process, Peltier cooling.   One need hardly dwell on the numerous advantages of such conversion devices over conventional units, provided they are of comparable efficiency: absence of moving parts, negligible maintenance, a very long lifetime, completely noiseless operation, and compact construction.   The general principle of the device is illustrated in Fig. 8.30.   The elements 1 and 2 are two semiconductors with a large difference in their thermopowers S_1 and S_2.   Thus, 1 might be an n-type and 2 a p-type material.   These are connected in series through metallic conductors which are maintained at temperatures T_1 and T_0.   To operate the cell as a current generator a load R is connected to the terminals and a temperature difference $T_1 - T_0$ must be maintained by means of a heater and a heat sink.   If, on the other hand, a current is sent through the unit, one end will be heated and the other cooled as a result of the Peltier effect at the junctions.   The unit can then serve as a refrigeration element.   We now calculate the optimum

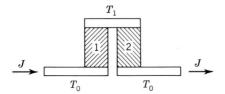

Fig. 8.30 Schematic of a thermoelectric generation (Peltier cooling) unit. (*After J. Tauc, "Photo and Thermo-electric Effects in Semiconductors," p. 164, Pergamon Press, New York, 1962.*)

efficiency when used as a generator, leaving as a problem the analogous calculation of refrigeration efficiency.

If the thermopowers of 1 and 2 are S_1 and S_2, and $S_1 > 0$, $S_2 < 0$, the total thermopower of the couple is $S = S_1 + |S_2|$. We denote by ρ_1, ρ_2, κ_1, κ_2, and A_1, A_2 the resistivities, thermal conductivities, and cross sections of elements 1 and 2, which we assume of equal length l.

The internal resistance of the generator is then

$$r = \left(\frac{\rho_1}{A_1} + \frac{\rho_2}{A_2}\right) l \tag{8.93}$$

and the thermal conductance is

$$K = \frac{\kappa_1 A_1 + \kappa_2 A_2}{l} \tag{8.94}$$

The Peltier heat received by the two junctions is

$$Q_1 = S T_1 I \qquad Q_0 = -S T_0 I \tag{8.95}$$

$$I = \frac{S(T_1 - T_0)}{R + r} \tag{8.96}$$

and we have assumed that $S(T_1) = S(T_0) = S$.

The heat flow from the hot to the cold junction is

$$Q_h = K(T_1 - T_0) \tag{8.97}$$

and the Joule heat generated in the unit is

$$Q_J = I^2 r \tag{8.98}$$

of which half goes to the hot and half to the cold junction.

If we set $R/r = m$, the Peltier heat loss at the hot junction is, from Eqs. (8.95) and (8.96),

$$Q_1 = \frac{S^2 T_1 (T_1 - T_0)}{r(1 + m)} \tag{8.99}$$

and using Eq. (8.96), the useful power consumed by the load is

$$P_L = I^2 R = \frac{S^2 m (T_1 - T_0)^2}{r(1 + m)^2} \tag{8.100}$$

The efficiency of the generator is defined as the ratio of useful power to the power taken from the heat source.   For the latter we have from Eqs. (8.97), (8.98), and (8.99),

$$Q = Q_1 + Q_h - \tfrac{1}{2}I^2r$$
$$= \frac{S^2 T_1 (T_1 - T_0)}{r(1 + m)} + K(T_1 - T_0) - \frac{S^2(T_1 - T_0)^2}{2r(1 + m)^2} \tag{8.101}$$

The ratio of Eq. (8.100) to Eq. (8.101) gives the efficiency

$$\eta = \frac{T_1 - T_0}{T_1} \left\{ \frac{m/(1 + m)}{[1 + Kr(m + 1)/S^2 T_1] - [(T_1 - T_0)/2(m + 1)]} \right\} \tag{8.102}$$

The first factor in Eq. (8.102) is just the Carnot term, the efficiency of an ideal heat engine operating between the temperatures T_1 and T_0. The second term is a function of the intrinsic properties of the materials and of the geometry.   In fact, just two parameters appear, S^2/Kr and m.   The first of these should be as large as possible, and takes its maximum value for a given pair of semiconductor elements when $(A_1/A_2)^2 = (\rho_1 \kappa_2 / \rho_2 \kappa_1)$.   Under these conditions

$$Z \equiv \left(\frac{S^2}{Kr} \right)_{\text{opt}} = \frac{S^2}{(\sqrt{\kappa_1 \rho_1} + \sqrt{\kappa_2 \rho_2})^2} \tag{8.103}$$

Optimum energy transfer occurs when $m = 1$; η is then

$$\eta_{\text{opt}} = \frac{1}{2} \left[\frac{T_1 - T_0}{T_1 + 2/Z - (T_1 - T_0)/4} \right] \tag{8.104}$$

For maximum efficiency, on the other hand, we must set

$$m = M = \left[1 + \frac{Z}{2}(T_1 - T_0) \right]^{\frac{1}{2}}$$

and obtain

$$\eta_{\text{max}} = \frac{T_1 - T_0}{T_1} \frac{M - 1}{M + T_0/T_1} \tag{8.105}$$

The central problem in the application of thermoelectric devices has been that of finding suitable materials with the highest Z, or to be more exact, the highest ZT values in the operating range.   In this connection the main obstacle is the relatively high thermal conductivity due to phonons in semiconductors.   In an effort to reduce κ, research has concentrated on compounds of heavy elements, such as PbS, $PbSe$, $PbTe$, Bi_2Te_3, Bi_2Se_3, and ternary mixtures, for example, $Bi_4Te_3Se_3$. Despite fairly intensive effort, efficiencies of the order of 10 to 15 percent are the best that have been attained, and it is becoming increasingly apparent that thermoelectric power generation using semiconducting elements will probably never be of great commercial interest.

The situation is rather different with regard to refrigeration. Again, the efficiency of such devices is relatively low, but so is that of a small standard compressor unit. It has been possible to reach temperature differences of 70 to 80°C with the hot junction held at room temperature, and, since for normal household applications the maximum temperature difference is unlikely to exceed 50°C, Peltier-cooling units should be quite useful. Indeed, small refrigerators using Peltier junctions are now manufactured commercially and are in use in modern hotels and camping trailers. Peltier junctions also find wide application where the temperature of a small region must be maintained constant near room temperature, as, for example, the probe in a sensitive Hall-effect gaussmeter. The reversible feature of the device is here particularly welcome, since it permits one to raise or lower the temperature of the junction merely by reversing the primary current.

PROBLEMS

8.1. Gallium antimonide (GaSb) has an energy gap $\epsilon_G = 0.8$ ev and a dielectric constant $\mathbf{x} = 15.2$. The effective masses of electrons and holes in GaSb are $m_n = 0.047m$ and $m_p = 0.4m$.

(a) Calculate the donor and acceptor ionization energies in this semiconductor and the radii of Bohr orbits of the lowest bound state for these impurities.

(b) What should be the donor concentration in an uncompensated sample so that $n = 10^{15}$ cm^{-3} at 14°K?

(c) For the sample (b) find the temperature at which $p = n/2$.

8.2. A sample of semiconductor 3 cm long, 6 mm wide, and 1 mm thick has a resistance of 500 ohms. Placed in a magnetic field of 5 kilogauss normal to the plane of the slab, it develops a Hall voltage of 5 mv when the current through the sample is 10 ma. Assuming that the sample is extrinsic:

(a) Determine the Hall mobility of the carriers.

(b) Find the carrier density.

Using a sketch indicate how you would determine the sign of the charge carriers.

8.3. Design a Hall-effect gaussmeter using an n-type Ge slab with a thickness of 1 mm. The unit should have a nearly temperature-independent response between $+60°$ and $-100°C$ and provide maximum sensitivity.

8.4. A semiconductor has the following properties: The energy gap, determined from measurements of resistivity versus temperature at elevated temperatures ($T > 350°K$), is 0.16 ev. At 78°K and also at 120°K the Hall coefficient has the value of $+160$ cm^3/coul. The resistivity at 78°K is 0.04 ohm-cm, and at 120°K it is 0.076 ohm-cm. The thermoelectric power of this sample at 120°K is 520 μv/°K. The low-field Hall coefficient of the sample vanishes at 254°K. The effective mass of electrons is known to be $0.07m$.

Determine the effective mass of holes, the density of acceptor impurities (assuming no compensation), and the mobility of electrons and holes, the resistivity, thermoelectric power, and the high-field Hall coefficient of the sample at 254°K.

8.5. A p-type sample of silicon contains 10^{18} acceptor and 10^{17} donor impurities per cubic centimeter. Estimate the relative importance of lattice scattering, ionized-impurity scattering, and neutral-impurity scattering at $T = 10°$, $20°$, $100°$, and $200°$K.

8.6. Derive an expression for the efficiency of a Peltier refrigerator.

REFERENCES

1. Brooks, H.: *Advan. Electron. Electron Phys.*, **7**: 87 (1955).
2. Low, F. E., and D. Pines: *Phys. Rev.*, **98**: 414 (1955).
3. Schultz, T. D.: Solid State and Molecular Theory Group, *Tech. Rept No. 9*, M.I.T., 1956.
4. Ehrenreich, H.: *Phys. Rev.*, **120**: 1951 (1960).
5. Herring, C.: *Bell System Tech. J.*, **34**: 237 (1955).
6. Brown, D. M., and R. Bray: *Phys. Rev.*, **127**: 1593 (1962).
7. Ham, F. S.: *Phys. Rev.*, **100**: 1251 (1955). (See also Ref. 1, p. 158.)
8. McLean, T. P., and E. G. S. Paige: *J. Phys. Chem. Solids*, **16**: 220 (1960).
9. Appel, J.: *Phys. Rev.*, **125**: 1815 (1962).
10. McLean, T. P., and E. G. S. Paige: *J. Phys. Chem. Solids*, **18**: 139 (1961).
11. Appel, J., and R. Bray: *Phys. Rev.*, **127**: 1603 (1962).
12. Jones, H.: *Phys. Rev.*, **81**: 149 (1951).
    Johnson, V. A., and W. J. Whitesell: *Phys. Rev.*, **89**: 961 (1953).
    Beer, A. C., J. A. Armstrong, and I. N. Greenberg: *Phys. Rev.*, **107**: 1506 (1957).
    Gibson, A. F., J. W. Granville, and E. G. S. Paige: *J. Phys. Chem. Solids*, **19**: 198 (1961).
13. Mott, N. F.: *Phil. Mag.*, **6**: 287 (1961).
14. Miller, A., and E. Abrahams: *Phys. Rev.*, **120**: 745 (1960).
15. Mott, N. F., and W. D. Twose: *Advan. Phys.*, **10**: 107 (1961).
16. Fritzsche, H.: *J. Phys. Chem. Solids*, **6**: 69 (1958).
17. Fritzsche, H.: *Phys. Rev.*, **115**: 336 (1959).
18. Herring, C.: *Bell System Tech. J.*, **34**: 237 (1955).
    Abeles, M., and S. Meiboom: *Phys. Rev.*, **95**: 31 (1954).
    Shibuya, M.: *Phys. Rev.*, **95**: 1385 (1954).
    Herring, C., and E. Vogt: *Phys. Rev.*, **101**: 944 (1956).
19. Herring, C.: "Semiconductors and Phosphors," p. 184, Interscience Publishers, New York, 1958.

BIBLIOGRAPHY

General

Beam, W. R.: "Electronics of Solids," McGraw-Hill Book Company, New York, 1965.
Burstein, E., and P. H. Egli: The Physics of Semiconductor Materials, *Advan. Electron. Electron Phys.*, **7**: 1 (1955).

Hilsum, C., and A. C. Rose-Innes: "Semiconducting III-V Compounds," Pergamon Press, New York, 1961.
Moll, J. L.: "Physics of Semiconductors," McGraw-Hill Book Company, New York, 1964.
Smith, R. A.: "Semiconductors," Cambridge University Press, London, 1959.
Spenke, E.: "Electronic Semiconductors," McGraw-Hill Book Company, New York, 1958.
Welker, H., and H. Weiss: Group III—Group V Compounds, *Solid State Phys.*, **3**: 1 (1956).

Statistics

Blakemore, J. S.: "Semiconductor Statistics," Pergamon Press, New York, 1962.

Mobility; Germanium and Silicon

Blatt, F. J.: Theory of Mobility of Electrons in Solids, *Solid State Phys.*, **4** (1957).
Brooks, H.: Theory of the Electrical Properties of Germanium and Silicon, *Advan. Electron. Electron Phys.*, **7**: 87 (1955).
Fan, H. Y.: Valence Semiconductors, Germanium and Silicon, *Solid State Phys.*, **1** (1955).
Paige, E. G. S.: The Electrical Conductivity of Germanium, *Progr. Semiconductors*, **8** (1964).
Scanlon, W. W.: Polar Semiconductors, *Solid State Phys.*, **9** (1959).

Piezoresistance

Keyes, R. W.: The Effects of Elastic Deformation on the Electrical Conductivity of Semiconductors, *Solid State Phys.*, **11** (1960).
Paul, W., and H. Brooks: Effect of Pressure on the Properties of Germanium and Silicon, *Progr. Semiconductors*, **7**:135 (1963).

Galvanomagnetic Effects

Beer, A. C.: "Galvanomagnetic Effects in Semiconductors," Academic Press, Inc., New York, 1963.
Glicksman, M.: Magnetoresistivity of Germanium and Silicon, *Progr. Semiconductors*, **3**: 1 (1958).

Thermal Conductivity, Thermopower

Appel, J.: Thermal Conductivity of Semiconductors, *Progr. Semiconductors*, **5**: 141 (1960).
Cadoff, I. B., and E. Miller: "Thermoelectric Materials and Devices," Reinhold Publishing Corporation, New York, 1960.
Drabble, J. R., and H. J. Goldsmid: "Thermal Conduction in Semiconductors," Pergamon Press, New York, 1961.
Ioffe, A. F.: "Semiconductor Thermoelements and Thermoelectric Cooling," Info-search, Ltd., London, 1957.
Tauc, J.: "Photo and Thermoelectric Effects in Semiconductors," Pergamon Press, New York, 1962.

Devices

Dunlap, W. C.: "An Introduction to Semiconductors," John Wiley & Sons, Inc., New York, 1957.
Greiner, R. A.: "Semiconductor Devices and Applications," McGraw-Hill Book Company, Inc., New York, 1961.

9
Rectifying Junctions
and Transistors

9.1 INTRODUCTION

In the preceding chapters we discussed equilibrium and steady-state conditions in a homogeneous material only. Solid-state rectifiers and amplifiers (transistors) depend for their action on the presence of inhomogeneities, and we must, therefore, extend our treatment now in this direction.

In this chapter we present a cursory survey of junction diodes and transistors without even attempting to explore the many interesting and complex problems relating to performance characteristics and design considerations. The primary aim is to acquaint the reader with sufficient background so that he may understand the principles of operation of these devices and appreciate more careful and detailed discussions in books and periodicals that often emphasize technological aspects at the expense of the fundamental physics.

We first consider the equilibrium properties of an inhomogeneous semiconductor and discuss, qualitatively, the principal mechanisms responsible for electron-hole recombination. We then discuss barrier rectification, first at a metal-semiconductor interface, and then at a semiconductor p-n junction; the section concludes with a brief account of tunnel diodes. Section 9.4 is devoted to a qualitative treatment of n-p-n transistors and concludes with a few paragraphs on one of many transistor refinements, the n-p-i-n transistor.

The discussion of the performance of semiconductor devices presented here is, admittedly, greatly oversimplified. To carry the topic beyond the elementary, descriptive stage would take us quickly into the realm of semiconductor-device technology and out of the mainstream of semiconductor physics. The reader interested in further details and discussion of other types of transistors—field-effect, unipolar, graded-base transistors—should consult one of the relevant texts listed in the bibliography.

9.2 EQUILIBRIUM CONDITIONS IN INHOMOGENEOUS SEMICONDUCTORS

A. Diffusion Currents

Whenever the carrier concentrations vary with position, currents due to carrier diffusion may flow. These we could, of course, neglect in the preceding chapters. This particle flux is related to the concentration gradient through the diffusion equation

$$\mathcal{J}_n = -D\nabla n \tag{9.1}$$

where D is the diffusion coefficient and $\mathcal{J}_n$ the number of particles which, per unit time, cross a unit area normal to the direction of the concentration gradient. The electric current resulting therefrom is†

$$J_n^d = |e|D_n \frac{\partial n}{\partial x} \tag{9.2a}$$

$$J_p^d = -|e|D_p \frac{\partial p}{\partial x} \tag{9.2b}$$

for electrons and holes, respectively.

The total current is now

$$J = J_n + J_p = |e|(n\mu_n + p\mu_p)E_x + |e|\left(D_n \frac{\partial n}{\partial x} - D_p \frac{\partial p}{\partial x}\right) \tag{9.3}$$

Clearly, if the concentration gradients do not vanish and we impose the boundary condition $J = 0$, an electric field E_x will be established in the region of the concentration gradients which is of just such magnitude and direction that the conduction and diffusion currents cancel. Not only

---

† We restrict ourselves hereafter to essentially one-dimensional geometries.

must this condition prevail, but the electron and hole currents must vanish individually; otherwise we should not be able to maintain local thermal equilibrium. Application of this last requirement leads to a very useful relation between the mobilities and diffusion constants.

From the condition

$$J_n^c + J_n^d = 0 \tag{9.4}$$

it follows that

$$n\mu_n E_x = -D_n \frac{\partial n}{\partial x} \tag{9.5}$$

The electric field E_x will, therefore, establish within the sample a potential

$$\phi = -E_x x \tag{9.6}$$

In the classical limit, the carrier concentration, in thermal equilibrium, must be proportional to the Boltzmann factor; that is,

$$n = c e^{-|e|\phi/kT} \tag{9.7}$$

Substitution of Eqs. (9.6) and (9.7) into Eqs. (9.5) leads directly to the Einstein relation

$$D_n = \frac{kT}{|e|} \mu_n \tag{9.8}$$

An analogous expression holds, of course, for the hole diffusion constant and mobility.

The Einstein relation is quite generally valid whenever the diffusion process is characterized by a pure random walk. However, if successive steps are not random but correlated, deviations from Eq. (9.8) do occur.

B. Recombination Mechanisms

Let us consider next the processes which tend to restore the equilibrium concentration of holes and electrons in a semiconductor wherein n and p deviate from equilibrium by amounts Δn and Δp. Such departures from equilibrium may be obtained by injecting carriers at properly biased metal contacts or by the creation of electron-hole pairs optically or through irradiation with high-energy electrons.

As regards the recombination process, there are three important basic mechanisms, namely, direct recombination, recombination at imperfections (recombination centers), and surface recombination. In direct recombination an electron in the conduction band drops directly into an unoccupied state in the valence band; energy is conserved by the emission of a phonon, $\hbar\omega = \epsilon_G$, while crystal momentum must also be conserved.

As we shall see in the next chapter, the latter condition often requires the simultaneous emission or absorption of a phonon; one then speaks of an "indirect" optical transition. In principle, direct recombination could take place without the emission of a light quantum, all the energy appearing as lattice vibration. However, since $k\Theta \ll \epsilon_G$ even in narrow-gap semiconductors, this process would necessitate the simultaneous emission of a large number of phonons, an extremely unlikely event.

The mean lifetime of excess carriers subject to direct optical recombination can be computed relatively easily from the known absorption coefficient. One then finds that the calculated minority-carrier lifetimes are often considerably longer than the experimental values, showing that direct recombination is not the limiting mechanism. For example, the observed lifetimes in germanium at room temperature are less than 10^{-3} sec, as compared to the calculated value of 0.75 sec.

However, in some compound semiconductors, (e.g., InSb, GaAs, and InAs), direct recombination is the major mechanism, often over a wide temperature range. The principal reason for the low probability of direct recombination in Si and Ge is that, in these crystals, the transition is "indirect" and can occur only with the simultaneous absorption or emission of a phonon or in the vicinity of a crystal imperfection. Since the direct recombination lifetimes decrease as ϵ_G diminishes, it is reasonable that this mechanism should be important in narrow-band-gap materials with type-C band structures (see Table 8.1).

The fact that there exist competing processes which may mask direct recombination does not mean that it is too weak to be observed experimentally. However, a high nonequilibrium carrier concentration is then necessary, and this can be achieved at a p-n junction biased in the forward direction (see below). Recombination radiation has been studied in a variety of substances, and at p-n junctions it can be exceedingly intense. Indeed, the junction lasers which have been developed in recent years employ this very process.

Recombination at recombination centers—that is, at impurities whose acceptor or donor levels lie relatively far from the respective band edges—seems to be the process that limits the lifetime of carriers in the interior of many substances. Recombination now proceeds in two or more stages. An electron is first captured at a trapping site and may remain in this state for a considerable time. Ultimately, a hole attracted to the region by its electrostatic interaction with the trapped electron recombines with it, leaving the center free to trap another electron. The initial capture may well be a multistage process itself. It is quite probable that the initial capture of the electron is into a highly excited state of the trapping center, since this would be a state with a large Bohr orbit and, hence, large capture cross section. The electron subsequently drops into the ground state of the trap through the emission of one or more phonons.   Once it has decayed into the ground state, reexcitation into the conduction band through thermal agitation would be quite improbable.

Carriers can recombine not only in the interior of a semiconductor but also, and quite effectively, at the surfaces where surface states serve as recombination centers.   Since the electrons and holes must diffuse to the surface before this recombination mechanism can come into play, the surface-recombination lifetime will be a function of the dimensions of the sample as well as of the surface properties themselves.   It is then convenient to employ the concept of a surface-recombination velocity, defined by

$$s = \frac{S_a}{\Delta p} \tag{9.9}$$

where S_a is the recombination rate per unit surface area and Δp (or Δn) is the excess carrier concentration immediately below the surface.   The surface-recombination velocity so defined is, of course, independent of the sample dimension.   It is, however, a sensitive function of the state of preparation of the surface, highest for rough, sandblasted surfaces and smallest for carefully electropolished and etched surfaces.   In germanium, surface-recombination velocities may range between 15 and 100,000 cm/sec at room temperature.

For small deviations from equilibrium we can write

$$\frac{d\Delta p}{dt} = -\frac{\Delta p}{\tau_h} + \Re \tag{9.10}$$

where $\Re$ is the rate at which excess holes are created.   The approach to steady state is, thus, exponential and proceeds with a characteristic time τ_h.   We denote the characteristic lifetimes by τ_e and τ_h, respectively, using these subscripts to avoid confusion with the mobility relaxation times τ_n and τ_p, which are normally many orders of magnitude smaller.

Consider, then, a one-dimensional semi-infinite bar of n-type semiconductor in which, at $x = 0$, holes are continually injected so as to maintain an excess minority-carrier concentration Δp_0.   Under steady-state conditions and vanishingly small electric fields the equation of continuity

$$\frac{\partial \rho}{\partial t} = -\boldsymbol{\nabla} \cdot \mathbf{J} \tag{9.11}$$

reduces to

$$0 = \frac{\Delta p}{\tau_h} - D_p \frac{d^2 \Delta p}{dx^2} \tag{9.12}$$

whose solution is

$$\Delta p = \Delta p_0 e^{-x/L_p} \qquad L_p = (D_p \tau_h)^{\frac{1}{2}} \qquad\qquad (9.13)$$

The length L_p is called the *minority-carrier diffusion length* for holes and, together with its counterpart L_n, plays an important role in the performance of junction transistors. In germanium at room temperature, when $\tau_h = 10^{-3}$ sec, the diffusion length $L_p = 0.2$ cm.

9.3 BARRIER RECTIFICATION

Rectification occurs quite generally whenever a current is made to flow across a high-resistance interface separating two dissimilar conductors. The most common rectifiers employ either a semiconductor and a metal or two semiconductors (*p-n* junction).

A. Metal-semiconductor Junctions

In Fig. 9.1*a* we show, schematically, a metal and an n-type semiconductor just prior to contact. The energies are referred to a standard zero which corresponds to an electron at rest far removed from either conductor. The energies W_m and W_s are the work functions of the metal and semi-conductor; generally, $W_m > W_s$, as in Fig. 9.1.

As soon as contact is established between these two materials, electrons will flow from the semiconductor into the metal, since in so doing they can reduce their energies. This transient flow of carriers depletes the semiconductor surface region of electrons, leaving it posi-

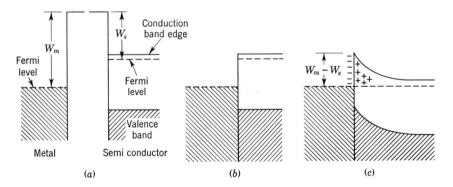

Fig. 9.1 Formation of a barrier layer in an n-type semiconductor at a metal-semi-conductor junction. (*a*) Metal and semiconductor before contact; (*b*) metal and semiconductor after contact has been established; (*c*) junction after equilibrium has been established. Fermi level is shown by the dashed line.

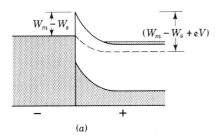

$W_m - W_s$

$(W_m - W_s + eV)$

(a)

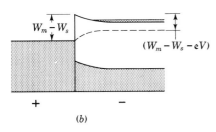

$W_m - W_s$

$(W_m - W_s - eV)$

+   −

(b)

Fig. 9.2 Metal-semiconductor junction with (a) reverse and (b) forward bias. (*After L. V. Azaroff and J. J. Brophy, "Electronic Processes in Materials," p. 231, McGraw-Hill Book Company, New York, 1963.*)

tively charged. The positive charge, of course, attracts the mobile electrons in the metal, and the double layer which forms is of just the correct strength to maintain a constant Fermi level, as shown in Fig. 9.1c.

Thus, within the semiconductor there will be a region immediately adjacent to the surface which is depleted of carriers and forms an insulating layer between the metal and the bulk of the semiconductor. Typically, the barrier height and width may be of order 1 volt and 10^{-6} cm. Since the resistivity of the layer is exceedingly high compared to that of the metal and bulk semiconductor, any voltage applied across the junction will appear almost entirely across the thin barrier.

The effect of imposing a voltage in the "reverse" and "forward" directions across the junction is shown in Fig. 9.2a and b. The important feature to note here is that, whereas the barrier height as viewed from the semiconductor depends on the applied voltage, the height seen by electrons approaching the interface from the metal is always the same. It is, fundamentally, this asymmetry that leads to rectification.

To calculate the current flowing across the junction, consider separately the currents flowing from right to left and left to right. The number of electrons striking the interface from the left is $N\bar{v}/4$, where $\bar{v}$ is an average electron velocity. The probability that the electron will surmount the barrier is given by the Boltzmann factor $\exp(-e\phi_0/kT)$, where ϕ_0 is the height of the barrier. Hence the current to the right is given by $(Ne\bar{v}/4)\exp(-e\phi_0/kT)$. Using identical arguments the current flowing in the opposite direction is $(Ne\bar{v}/4)\exp[-e(\phi_0 - V)/kT]$.

Thus the net current flow is

$$J = \frac{N e \bar{v}}{4} e^{-\epsilon\phi_0/kT} \left(e^{\epsilon V/kT} - 1 \right)$$

$$= J_R(e^{\epsilon V/kT} - 1)$$

(9.14)

Evidently $J = 0$ in the absence of an applied potential. When a voltage is applied in the forward direction, the current increases exponentially with V and may become quite large if $V \gg kT/\epsilon$. Since at room temperature $kT/\epsilon = 0.025$ volt, the voltages involved here are relatively small. Conversely, with reverse voltage the current very quickly approaches the reverse-current saturation value J_R.

B.   Semiconductor p-n Junctions

p-n junction rectifiers are single crystals of germanium or other semiconductors containing an n- and a p-type region separated by a thin interface. Such devices cannot be constructed by simply attaching a p-type to an n-type crystal, because an essential requirement for the operation of the rectifier is that minority carriers can diffuse across the transition layer. At the surfaces of the two crystals, surface recombination would prevent the diffusion process. It is also important that the material be a single crystal containing relatively few imperfections, since the device functions most effectively if the minority-carrier diffusion length is long. Over the years a variety of techniques have been developed for growing single crystals incorporating p-n junctions. The description of these methods would take us rather far afield and we refer the reader to various books on semiconductor technology for such details.

As always, the Fermi energy at equilibrium must be a constant throughout the domain. Thus, as we pass from the n to the p region, the energy bands must bend as shown in Fig. 9.3. Clearly, an electric field exists in the transition region such that an electron in the n region must overcome a substantial potential hill to pass into a conduction-band state in the p region.

The electric field which brings forth the displacement of the energy bands shown in Fig. 9.3 may be thought of as arising in the following way. If, initially, no field exists across the junction, then, under the influence of the electron and hole concentration gradients near the junction, electrons will diffuse toward the p-type region and holes, toward the n-type region. Consequently, we shall be left with an excess number of positively charged donor ions in the n-type region, and an excess number of negatively charged acceptor ions in the p-type region near the interface. The dipole layer which is established in this manner will grow until the resulting electric field is sufficient to prevent further flow of diffusion

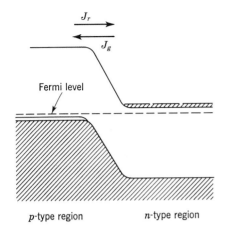

Fig. 9.3 Energy bands and Fermi level in a *p-n* junction at equilibrium. Note that the directions of the recombination and generation currents are opposite to the directions of electron motion for these currents because of the negative charge on the electron.

currents, or—more precisely—until the diffusion and conduction currents just cancel.

Even under the equilibrium conditions shown in Fig. 9.3, some electrons will diffuse into the *p* region and recombine there with holes. In equilibrium this current is exactly balanced by the flow of electrons thermally excited into the conduction band in the *p* region which then diffuse into the *n* region, compensating for the loss of electrons that have moved in the opposite direction and recombined with holes. We shall use the symbols J_r^n and J_g^n to denote electron-recombination and electron-generation currents, respectively. Similarly, corresponding hole currents will, of course, also flow across the junction.

Suppose we now apply a potential across the junction. As in the metal-semiconductor diode, here, also, almost the entire voltage appears across the thin layer that separates the *p* and *n* regions and which is denuded of carriers. If the potential is in the "forward" direction, i.e., as shown in Fig. 9.4*b*, electrons can diffuse much more readily into the *p* region, there to recombine with holes, since the potential barrier which they must surmount has been diminished by the applied potential. Thus J_r^n increases. The generation current, on the other hand, remains effectively unaltered; it depends only on the rate of generation of minority carriers in the *p*-type region and their diffusion length. If they are generated within a distance of roughly L_n from the interface, they stand a fair chance of diffusing to the *n*-type region; once they are in the layer separating *n* and *p* regions, the dipole field only pushes them along. For the device to operate effectively it is only necessary that the minority-carrier diffusion lengths be large compared to the thickness of the interface, so that there may be a substantial recombination current arising from carriers that have "made it" successfully across the interface.

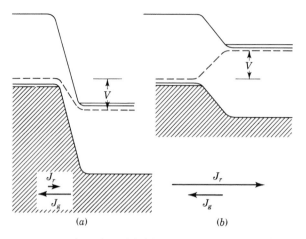

Fig. 9.4 p-n junction with (a) reverse and (b) forward bias.

Conversely, if V is reversed J_r^n diminishes, since the electrons must now overcome a larger potential barrier, and J_g^n once again remains almost unaffected.

At equilibrium, and for $V = 0$, $J_r^n = J_g^n$. As in the metal-semiconductor case, the recombination current will be determined by the Boltzmann factor $\exp(-\epsilon\phi/kT)$, where ϕ is the height of the potential barrier between the p and n regions. This barrier is, of course, subject to modulation by the applied voltage. Thus we have

$$J_r^n / J_{r_0}^n e^{\epsilon V/kT} = J_g^n e^{\epsilon V/kT} \tag{9.15}$$

where we have made use of the fact that the generation and recombination currents must be of equal magnitude when $V = 0$. Hence, the net electron current is

$$J_n = J_r^n - J_g^n = J_g^n(e^{\epsilon V/kT} - 1) \tag{9.16}$$

A few moments reflection will show that a forward voltage for electrons also serves as a forward voltage for holes which move in the opposite direction across the junction. The total current flowing in the device is then given by

$$J = J_g(e^{\epsilon V/kT} - 1) \tag{9.17}$$

How very closely the performance of a germanium p-n junction conforms to theory is illustrated in Fig. 9.5. Once the reverse bias exceeds a few $kT/\epsilon \simeq 0.025$ volts, the reverse current saturates. In the forward direction, on the other hand, the current increases exponentially, and with comparable applied voltages attains already large values.

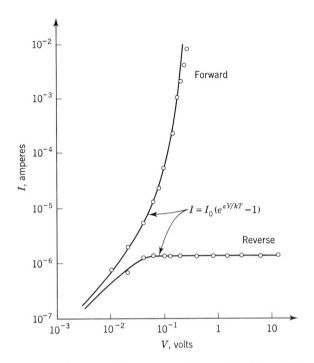

Fig. 9.5 Current-voltage curve of a p-n junction. The solid line represents the rectifier equation, whereas the circles represent experimental values. (*From L. V. Azaroff and J. J. Brophy, "Electronic Processes in Materials," p. 275, McGraw-Hill Book Company, New York, 1963.*)

From Eq. (9.17) it is apparent that the performance characteristics of a p-n junction depend sensitively on the operating temperature. First, the relative change in the diode current in the forward direction is an exponential function of eV/kT; thus the lower the temperature, the lower the voltage increment that is needed to produce a given fractional current change. Second, the generation current J_g, which is, of course the same as the reverse-bias saturation current, depends on the rate of thermal generation of electron-hole pairs and on the diffusion lengths of these carriers. Generally, the temperature dependence of thermal generation, given by the Boltzmann factor $\exp(\epsilon_G/kT)$, largely determines the temperature variation of J_g. As the temperature is increased the reverse current increases and the rectifying characteristics become poor for this reason also.

Complete failure of the device sets in at even higher temperatures when the intrinsic region is attained. In that case the Fermi level on *both* sides of the junction is almost at the same position relative to the band edges—somewhere near the center of the energy gap—and the potential barrier, essential for rectification, vanishes altogether.   Since the intrinsic range commences at a higher temperature the larger the band gap, silicon is better suited to high-temperature applications than germanium, even though the mobilities are more favorable in the latter substance.

Departures from the ideal p-n junction characteristic are, however, fairly common in some substances, for example, GaAs and GaP.   The major cause for such deviations apparently stems from a variation of electron and hole current densities within the depletion layer due to carrier recombination.   In the preceding discussion it was assumed that these currents are constant.   The theory may be extended to include this contingency, and the diode characteristic then depends on the electron and hole recombination times.

C. Tunnel Diodes

A rather interesting current voltage characteristic obtains when the doping level in the p and n regions is so great that degeneracy is reached on both sides of the junction.   Since, under these conditions, the Fermi level lies above the conduction-band edge on the one side and below the valence-band edge on the other, the energy-level scheme is as shown in Fig. 9.6.   Here we have shown the occupied electronic energy levels as shaded.

If we now apply a small forward bias, an electron current will flow which is only partly the result of diffusion and recombination, as described in the preceding section.   In addition to the recombination current via diffusion there will also arise a current which has its origin in a quantum-mechanical tunnel effect.   According to quantum theory a particle has a finite probability of penetrating (tunneling) through a potential barrier, even though classically it may not have sufficient energy to actually surmount the barrier.   Thus, with a small forward bias, electrons can tunnel into unoccupied valence-band states in the degenerate p region. If, however, the forward bias is increased so much that the energy band scheme is as shown in Fig. 9.6c, all tunnel current must cease, for there are now no energy levels available to the electrons on the p side.   (In the tunnel process, energy must be conserved and an acceptable unoccupied final state must exist on the other side of the barrier.)   If the forward bias is increased still further, the current will again increase, the diode current now being entirely due to the usual minority-carrier recombination process described earlier.   Thus, in the forward direction the I-V characteristic is of the form shown in Fig. 9.7.   In the reverse direction the current is at first nearly the same as in the forward.   As one can see from Fig. 9.6d, application of reverse bias permits tunneling of electrons from the valence band on the p side to empty conduction-band states.

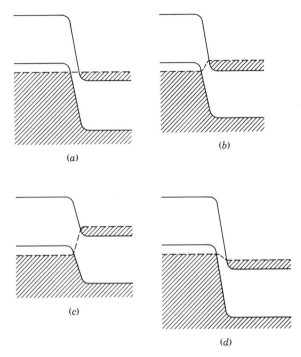

Fig. 9.6   Energy bands and Fermi level in a tunnel diode.
(a) Equilibrium; (b) small forward voltage; (c) larger
forward voltage, preventing tunneling; (d) reverse bias,
allowing tunneling in opposite direction.

The probability for tunneling in the reverse direction is about the same
as in the forward direction, and consequently the reverse current and
forward current do not differ significantly for small applied voltages.
Clearly, this device is not a very satisfactory "diode" in the usual sense
of the word.

It is the unusual current-voltage characteristic in the forward
direction that makes the tunnel diode such an important new development in semiconductor applications.   Over a well-defined region the
device has a *negative* resistance.   If operation is maintained between
V_1 and V_2, the diode can serve as an active, rather than a passive, circuit
element.   Moreover, it can be made very small, and requires no auxiliary
electrical energy, such as the power to heat a vacuum tube filament.   It
is, thus, ideally suited for fast switching circuits, particle counters in
high-energy physics, and microwave oscillators.   In the latter capacity
it has the advantage over the conventional klystron of ease of tuning, not
to mention all the other advantages of solid-state devices over vacuum

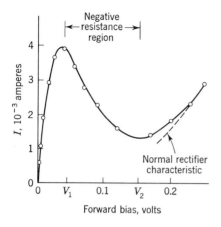

Normal rectifier characteristic

Fig. 9.7 Current-voltage characteristic of a tunnel diode. (*From L. V. Azaroff and J. J. Brophy, "Electronic Processes in Materials," p.* 285, *McGraw-Hill Book Company, New York,* 1963.)

tubes. Tunnel-diode oscillators have been used in the 10-, 3-, and 1-cm wavelength bands, and recently operation at nearly 50,000 Mc has been achieved.

9.4 TRANSISTORS

It is hardly an exaggeration to say that the development of the transistor, which earned its inventors the Nobel Prize, has completely revolutionized electronic instruments and the electronics industry. Improvements of the basic device aimed at extending its frequency range on the one hand and enhancing its current-carrying capacity on the other have continued over the years and are still in progress. The reliability of the units is exceptionally good, and their lifetimes, provided they are not maltreated, almost unlimited. There are no filaments which gradually evaporate and burn out with time, no vacuum jacket which slowly admits gas from the surroundings. Mechanically, transistors are also superior to vacuum tubes. The essential portion is a small single crystal of germanium or silicon. Transistors are, thus, capable of withstanding many g's of acceleration and are free of microphonics. And last, but by no means least, they are cheap. Many books have been written about transistors and transistor circuits, and the reader should consult these for more detailed information. Here, we limit ourselves to a qualitative description of the operation of the simplest unit, the *n-p-n* transistor, and a few remarks concerning one of the many refinements.

A. *n-p-n* Transistor

An *n-p-n* transistor consists of a single crystal of germanium or other semiconductor, containing a central narrow *p*-type region bounded by

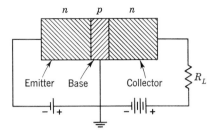

Fig. 9.8   The *n-p-n* transistor, biased for grounded base operation, with load resistor R_L.

the two *n*-type portions.† These three parts of the transistor are called the *base* (the central *p* region) and the *emitter* and *collector* (the two *n*-type regions). When operated as an amplifier, the emitter is biased in the forward direction, and reverse bias is applied across the base-collector junction. In the case of the *n-p-n* transistor this means that, with the base grounded, a negative potential is applied to the emitter, a positive potential to the collector (see Fig. 9.8). The energy bands in the transistor are then displaced relative to each other, as shown in Fig. 9.9.

With the emitter-base *n-p* junction biased in the forward direction a substantial electron current flows from the emitter into the base region; electrons are *emitted* into the base, hence the name. In the *n-p* junction diode we called this current the *electron recombination current,* since these charge carriers would ultimately recombine with the holes in the *p* region. In the transistor, however, the *p* region is made so very narrow that the electrons stand a good chance of diffusing across the base toward the collector before recombining. Once they reach the base-collector junction they are pulled into the collector region by the applied reverse bias and constitute the collector current. From the *n-p* junction characteristic it is clear that a rather small change in forward bias can induce a very substantial change in the current flowing across the junction. On flowing through the load resistor R_L, which, as we shall see, can be made quite large, this current change appears as an amplified signal voltage.

† We purposely refrain from any mention of the means of preparation of transistors. This is as much art as it is technology; new methods are constantly being developed, and old ones improved. Here again, the reader should consult other books and the periodical literature.

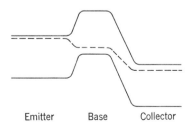

Fig. 9.9   Energy bands and Fermi level in an *n-p-n* transistor biased as shown in Fig. 9.8.

The performance of the transistor is thus in many ways quite analogous to that of a three-element vacuum tube, with the emitter playing the role of cathode, the base that of the grid, and the collector acting as the plate. However, the transistor, though it has only three basic parts, performs more like a pentode than a triode, in that the collector (plate) impedance is very high, permitting a large voltage gain. The current across the emitter junction is determined by the Boltzmann factor $\exp(eV_e/kT)$, and increases by a factor $e = 2.72$ whenever V_e increases by $kT/e \simeq 0.025$ volt at room temperature. As can be seen from Fig. 9.10, a potential of a few volts at most, and indeed just a few tenths of a volt, at the collector will suffice to draw off the entire emitter current that traverses the base region. In other words, the transistor operates in the saturation region, as does the pentode. Quite substantial changes in collector voltage hardly influence the collector current; i.e., the collector impedance is very high, as we said above, and, as with a pentode, the load resistance can be correspondingly large.

There are two essential requirements for proper transistor operation, apart from the obvious biasing conditions. First, the base layer must be reasonably thin. Second, the impurity concentration in the emitter must be considerably greater than in the base.

A thin base is desirable for several reasons. First, efficient operation demands that almost all the carriers leaving the emitter be received by the collector. Some of the carriers will inevitably diffuse to the base connector instead of traversing the base toward the collector. The fraction that finds its way to the base connector depends on the geometry of the base and will be small if the base is thin. In vacuum-tube parlance what we are saying is that the grid current, which should be as small as possible compared to the plate current, is decreased by reducing the base thickness.

Second, the probability that an emitted electron will recombine in the base before diffusing to the collector is diminished if the base is thin. Since the current carriers of the transistor constitute minority carriers in the base, it is here that recombination is most probable and must be kept at a minimum.

Third, the performance of a transistor falls off at high frequency and the limiting frequency is determined largely by the thickness of the base layer. The device can function properly only as long as the transit time of carriers across the base is short compared to the period of the ac signal. Clearly, if the signal voltage reverses before most of the emitted electrons have traversed the base, the collector current will contain only a small alternating component. We must also bear in mind that the electrons do not move across the base as a "bunch" but diffuse, and thus a narrow pulse of emitted electrons spreads out as it crosses to the emitter. The

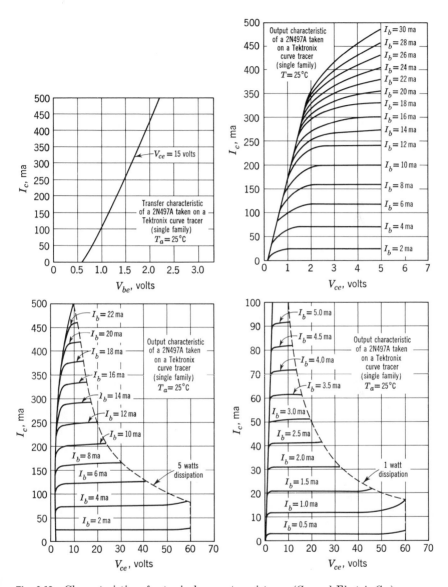

Fig. 9.10   Characteristics of a typical *n-p-n* transistor.   (*General Electric Co.*)

spread will be more severe the wider the base. In transistors intended for low-power applications (portable radios, hearing aids, etc.) the thickness of the base may range between 0.0002 and 0.001 in.

The reasons for keeping the doping level in the base substantially lower than in the emitter are also easy to understand. First, the higher the doping level, the larger the number of holes in the base of the n-p-n transistor. Consequently, the greater also is the probability that an emitted electron will recombine with a hole in the base region before reaching the collector.

Second, with the emitter biased in the forward direction relative to the base, not only will electrons flow from the emitter to the base with considerable ease, but a hole current will flow from the base to emitter. To keep the base current small compared to the collector current, the doping level in the base should be small.

B. n-p-i-n Transistor

Although a very thin base is desirable for the reasons given above, there is a lower limit to the base thickness that is not imposed by technical limitations. While voltages applied across a transistor are small compared to those used in vacuum-tube circuits, breakdown ("punchthrough" in transistor jargon) across the base region occurs if the base is too thin. The n-p-i-n (and p-n-i-p) transistor was developed to overcome this limitation to high-frequency response.

In this device an intrinsic, and hence high-resistivity, layer is placed between the collector and a very narrow base region. The base itself is made as thin as possible, 0.0001 in. or less. After the emitted electrons have diffused across the base they are accelerated across the intrinsic region by the large electric field that exists there as a result of the high resistivity of the intrinsic material. The transit time is therefore determined by the thin p-type base, while the high-resistance intrinsic layer prevents punch-through between collector and emitter.

The n-p-i-n transistor is only one of the many modifications of the standard n-p-n unit. Other variants are in common use today and are discussed in modern texts on the subject.

BIBLIOGRAPHY

Beam, W. R.: "Electronics of Solids," McGraw-Hill Book Company, New York, 1965.
Biondi, F. J. (ed.): "Transistor Technology," D. Van Nostrand Company, Inc., Princeton, N.J., 1958.
Moll, J. S.: "Physics of Semiconductors," McGraw-Hill Book Company, New York, 1964.
Valdes, L. B.: "The Physical Theory of Transistors," McGraw-Hill Book Company, New York, 1961.

10
Optical Properties of Semiconductors

10.1 INTRODUCTION

In this chapter we present a survey of the optical properties of semi-conductors, laying particular stress on the fundamental aspects and on the relation between optical and electrical phenomena in these materials. Clearly, one could easily devote an entire book to the topic, and for additional material the reader is directed to just such volumes.

Broadly, two mechanisms are responsible for absorption of electro-magnetic radiation in semiconductors. The first, arising from the accel-eration of free carriers by the oscillating electric field, can be discussed adequately within the framework of classical electrodynamics. The sec-ond, the excitation of electrons from the valence band into the conduction band or into bound electron-hole states (excitons), must be treated quantum mechanically. The two processes are known as *free-carrier absorption* and *interband*, or *fundamental, absorption*, respectively, and we shall now consider these in turn. Following a fairly careful discussion of the physics of the absorption process, we then turn our attention to photoelectric effects. These we shall treat in somewhat less detail, elucidating only the essential features without attempting to go into the technology of device application. Nevertheless, this material should help the reader in understanding the operation and limitations of photo-electric devices.

10.2 FREE CARRIER ABSORPTION

If a time-varying electric field

$$E_x(t) = Ee^{i\omega t} \tag{10.1}$$

acts on a free electron, the equation of motion of the charge carrier is

$$m\ddot{x} + \frac{m}{\tau}\dot{x} = \mathfrak{e}Ee^{i\omega t} \tag{10.2}$$

where the second term on the left-hand side of (10.2) is the damping term arising from a relaxation mechanism having a characteristic relaxation time τ. The solution of (10.2) is

$$x(t) = xe^{i\omega t} \qquad x = \frac{\mathfrak{e}E/m}{i\omega/\tau - \omega^2} \tag{10.3}$$

If we have a concentration of n electrons per unit volume, the polarization is $n\mathfrak{e}x$ and the polarizability $\mathfrak{p}^*$ is $n\mathfrak{e}x/E$. We recall here that the polarizability $\mathfrak{p}^*$, dielectric constant $\mathbf{x}^*$, and refractive index $\mathfrak{n}^*$ are related through

$$\mathbf{x}^* = \frac{1 + \mathfrak{p}^*}{\varepsilon_0} \tag{10.4}$$

where ε_0 is the permittivity of free space, and

$$(\mathfrak{n}^*)^2 \equiv (\mathfrak{n} - i\mathfrak{f})^2 = \mathbf{x}^* \tag{10.5}$$

Here we have used the asterisks to indicate that the various quantities generally are complex. The significance of the real, $\mathfrak{n}$, and imaginary, $\mathfrak{f}$, parts of the complex index of refraction is immediately apparent if we write the usual expression for a wave propagating through a refractive medium,

$$E(z,t) = Ee^{i(\omega t - \omega \mathfrak{n}^* z/c)} = Ee^{i(\omega t - \omega \mathfrak{n} z/c)}e^{-\omega \mathfrak{f} z/c} \tag{10.6}$$

which shows that in the medium the wave progresses with a phase velocity $c/\mathfrak{n}$ and is attenuated in the z direction at a rate proportional to $\mathfrak{f}$.

From Eqs. (10.3) to (10.5) we now obtain

$$\mathbf{x}^* = (\mathfrak{n} - i\mathfrak{f})^2 = \frac{n\mathfrak{e}^2/m\varepsilon_0}{i\omega/\tau - \omega^2} + \mathbf{x}' \tag{10.7}$$

We have written $\varkappa'$ rather than unity on the right-hand side of (10.6) as a reminder that even in the absence of free carriers the material may exhibit a dielectric constant different from that of free space.   For the real and imaginary parts of the dielectric constant we obtain

$$\varkappa_r = \mathfrak{n}^2 - \mathfrak{k}^2 = -\frac{\tau^2 n e^2 / m \varepsilon_0}{1 + \omega^2 \tau^2} + \varkappa' = -\frac{\tau \sigma_0}{\varepsilon_0(1 + \omega^2 \tau^2)} + \varkappa' \tag{10.8}$$

and

$$\varkappa_i = 2\mathfrak{n}\mathfrak{k} = \frac{\tau n e^2 / \omega m \varepsilon_0}{1 + \omega^2 \tau^2} = \frac{\sigma_0}{\omega \varepsilon_0(1 + \omega^2 \tau^2)} \tag{10.9}$$

where we have used the elementary expression for the dc conductivity, $\sigma_0 = n e^2 \tau / m$.   In so doing we have neglected to account for the energy dependence of the relaxation time.   More properly we should express (10.7) and (10.8) in terms of the now familiar averages over a Boltzmann distribution.   Accordingly, if $\tau = \tau_0 \epsilon^p$, we should multiply Eq. (10.8) by the factor

$$Q(p) = \frac{\Gamma(\tfrac{5}{2} - p)\Gamma(\tfrac{5}{2} + p)}{\Gamma^2(\tfrac{5}{2})}$$

Hereafter we shall neglect these refinements and proceed on the simplifying assumption that τ is energy-independent.

The quantity commonly measured is, of course, not $\mathfrak{k}$ but rather the absorption coefficient α, defined by

$$\mathbf{P}(z) = \mathbf{P}_0 \epsilon^{-\alpha z}$$

where $\mathbf{P}$ is the Poynting vector.   Since $\mathbf{P}$ is proportional to E^2, we conclude from (10.6) that

$$\alpha = \frac{2\omega \mathfrak{k}}{c} = \frac{4\pi \mathfrak{k}}{\lambda_0} \tag{10.10}$$

where λ_0 is the wavelength of the radiation in free space.   According to (10.9)

$$\alpha = \frac{\sigma_0}{\mathfrak{n} c \varepsilon_0 (1 + \omega^2 \tau^2)} \tag{10.11}$$

It is convenient, at this point, to consider separately two limiting cases: long wavelength ($\omega \tau \ll 1$), and short wavelength ($\omega \tau \gg 1$). Since τ is a sensitive function of temperature and purity in any substance, it is impossible to draw a sharp boundary between these two situations.   In germanium, at room temperature, $\tau_n \simeq 1.3 \times 10^{-12}$ and

$\tau_p \simeq 7 \times 10^{-13}$ sec, and $\omega\tau \sim 1$ for $\omega \sim 10^{12}$, corresponding to a wavelength of about 2 mm. Thus the long-wavelength case obtains in the usual microwave region ($\lambda > 1$ cm), whereas measurements in the near and far infrared belong to the short-wavelength case.

A. Long-wavelength Limit ($\omega\tau \ll 1$)

Equations (10.8) and (10.11) now reduce to

$$\varkappa_r = \varkappa' - \frac{\tau\sigma_0}{\varepsilon_0} \tag{10.12}$$

and

$$\alpha = \frac{\sigma_0}{\mathfrak{n}c\varepsilon_0} \tag{10.13}$$

Two extreme situations are instructive. In the first instance, σ_0 is relatively small and the electronic contribution to the dielectric constant is small compared to $\varkappa'$. Then $\mathfrak{n} \sim (\varkappa_r)^{\frac{1}{2}}$ and

$$\alpha = \sigma_0 \frac{(\varkappa_r)^{-\frac{1}{2}}}{\varepsilon_0 c}$$

$$= 3.75 \frac{\sigma_0}{\mathfrak{n}} \text{ cm}^{-1} \tag{10.14}$$

if σ_0 is in (ohm-cm)$^{-1}$. The appropriate condition prevails, for example, in reasonably pure germanium which, at room temperature, may have a resistivity of about 10 ohm-cm and a relaxation time of about 10^{-12} sec, so that $\tau\sigma_0/\varepsilon_0 \sim 1$, whereas $\varkappa'$ is about 16. Under these conditions α is independent of frequency but does depend on temperature through σ_0.

If, on the other hand, σ_0 is large, as will happen frequently in a more highly doped sample, $\tau\sigma_0/\varepsilon_0$ may exceed $\varkappa'$, and $\varkappa_r$ will become negative; i.e., the material behaves essentially like a metal. If we neglect $\varkappa'$ altogether (that is, assume $\varkappa' \ll \tau\sigma_0/\varepsilon_0$)

$$\mathfrak{n}^2 - \mathfrak{f}^2 = -\frac{\tau\sigma_0}{\varepsilon_0} \tag{10.15}$$

$$2\mathfrak{n}\mathfrak{f} = \frac{\sigma_0}{\omega\varepsilon_0} \tag{10.16}$$

from which we obtain

$$\omega\tau = \frac{(\mathfrak{f}/\mathfrak{n})^2 - 1}{2(\mathfrak{f}/\mathfrak{n})}$$

Since $\omega\tau \ll 1$ we must have $(\mathfrak{f}/\mathfrak{n}) \sim 1$, and, from (10.16),

$$\mathfrak{n} = \left(\frac{\sigma_0}{2\omega\varepsilon_0}\right)^{\frac{1}{2}} \tag{10.17}$$

Substitution of (10.17) into (10.13) gives the absorption coefficient

$$\alpha = \left(\frac{2\sigma_0\omega}{\varepsilon_0 c^2}\right)^{\frac{1}{2}} \tag{10.18}$$

We see that, as in a metal, there exists a skin depth $\delta = 1/\alpha$ into which the radiation penetrates, and that this skin depth diminishes as the square root of the dc conductivity and the frequency.

B.   Short-wavelength Limit $(\omega\tau \gg 1)$

This situation, as we have already mentioned, normally falls into the frequency region extending upward of the far infrared. Although in principle all short-wavelength radiation is of interest in free-carrier absorption, experimentally this mechanism takes on a very minor role once $\hbar\omega$ exceeds ϵ_G and interband transitions can be induced by the applied electromagnetic field. Moreover, as we shall see presently, the absorption coefficient due to free-carrier absorption diminishes with increasing frequency in this domain, so that free-carrier absorption is of little consequence in the intrinsic, or fundamental, absorption region.

From Eqs. (10.8), (10.9), and (10.11) we now obtain

$$\mathbf{x}_r = \mathbf{x}' - \frac{\sigma_0}{\varepsilon_0\omega^2\tau} \tag{10.19}$$

$$2\mathfrak{n}\mathfrak{f}\omega = \frac{\sigma_0}{\varepsilon_0\omega^2\tau^2} \tag{10.20}$$

$$\alpha = \frac{\sigma_0}{\mathfrak{n}c\varepsilon_0\omega^2\tau^2} = \frac{n\lambda_0^2 e^3}{4\pi^2\varepsilon_0 m^{*2}c^3\mathfrak{n}\mu} \tag{10.21}$$

where μ is the mobility, m^* is the conductivity effective mass of the free carriers, and λ_0 is the wavelength in free space. According to Eq. (10.21) the absorption coefficient in this frequency range should be nearly proportional to the square of the wavelength ($\mathfrak{n}$ does depend slightly on wavelength also), to the number of free carriers, and to the reciprocal of their mobility. These variations contrast sharply with those in the long-wavelength domain; there, according to (10.14), α is independent of wavelength and increases with increasing mobility, and in the quasi-metallic case the absorption still increases with increasing mobility.

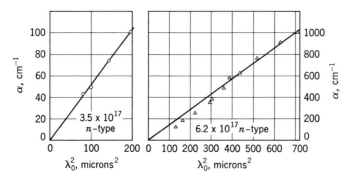

Fig. 10.1 Absorption coefficient of n-type InSb versus (wavelength)^2. (*From T. S. Moss, "Optical Properties of Semiconductors," Academic Press Inc., New York, p. 32, 1959.*)

These functional relationships have been verified in a variety of materials (see Fig. 10.1). Of course, as λ_0 is increased, the absorption coefficient does not grow without limit, but, in the long-wavelength limit, approaches the value given by (10.14).

According to (10.19), $\varkappa_r$ changes sign as ω decreases. The condition $\varkappa_r = 0$, corresponding to total reflection—that is, to an infinite absorption coefficient—is of particular interest, since the singularity in α suggests the appearance of a resonance behavior. The resonance frequency is given by

$$\omega_p{}^2 = \frac{ne^2}{m^*\varkappa'\varepsilon_0} \tag{10.22}$$

and is known as the *plasma frequency*. This is the frequency at which a classical dissipationless plasma of free charge carriers exhibits its normal mode of undamped oscillations. In germanium, doped to an electron concentration of 10^{16} carriers and with $m^* = m/8$ and $\varkappa' = 16$, one finds that the plasma frequency should be roughly 2×10^5 Mc, falling into the rather difficult millimeter-wave region. The plasma frequency can, of course, be reduced by diminishing n to, say, 10^{14} cm^{-3} or less; but a sharp resonance absorption can be observed only if $\omega_p\tau \gg 1$, and this requirement can be met in the microwave region only by working with quite pure samples and at low temperatures. Alternatively, one may go to even higher concentrations and look for plasma effects in the far-infrared spectrum. Both techniques have been employed with success in recent years.

Plasma oscillations appear also in metals, but there, because of the very high electron concentration, the resonance frequency falls into the far ultraviolet, corresponding to a photon energy of the order of 10 to 20 ev.   Resonance absorption has been studied in metals not by optical methods but by observing the characteristic energy losses suffered by electrons which penetrate through a thin metal foil.

Free-carrier absorption in semiconductors has been used extensively to study the relaxation time and to determine the conductivity effective mass of electrons and holes.   For example, in the range $\omega\tau \ll 1$, the relaxation time may be deduced by comparing $\varkappa_r$ in two samples with different, but known, carrier concentrations, provided their dc conductivities have also been measured.   This technique was used successfully at an early stage in the history of semiconductor research by Benedict and Shockley [1], who obtained, in this manner, the temperature dependence of the electron and hole relaxation times.   Of course, once τ, n, and σ_0 are known, one can calculate the conductivity effective mass of the majority carriers; and, this too was done by these workers who obtained values in good agreement with later cyclotron resonance experiments.

Similarly, the absorption coefficient for $\omega\tau \gg 1$ also yields values of m^* once n and μ have been found by other means—e.g., from measurements of conductivity and Hall effect.   These optical methods are particularly valuable when the more precise and elegant resonance methods fail, as they do at normal temperatures and in fairly heavily doped samples where τ is so short that only in the optical range can one expect to achieve the condition $\omega\tau > 1$.

10.3 FUNDAMENTAL ABSORPTION

When the energy of the incident photon exceeds ϵ_G, an electron can be excited from the valence into the conduction band.   Clearly, the study of optical properties in this frequency region will prove to be an invaluable tool for band-structure investigations.   Moreover, nearly all the fundamentally interesting and technologically important photoelectric phenomena arise from such interband excitations of charge carriers.

The absorption coefficient associated with this process depends on the probability per unit time that an electron will make a transition from the valence to the conduction band under the influence of radiation of intensity $I(\nu)$ at the frequency ν.   The problem of calculating this transition probability is strictly quantum-mechanical, since the energy-level structure of electrons in crystals falls quite outside the realm of classical physics.   We shall here touch on all the important and interesting features without carrying the calculation through in full detail.

The important expression, derived from first-order time-dependent perturbation theory, which we have already used in the calculation of the electron-phonon relaxation time (see Sec. 6.5), is [see Eq. (A.63)]

$$W_i = \frac{2\pi}{h} |\mathfrak{K}'_{if}|^2 \rho(\epsilon_f) \tag{10.23}$$

Here W_i is the probability for a transition from an initial state i to a group of final states f in a continuum, $\mathfrak{K}'_{if}$ is the matrix element of the perturbation which connects the states i and f of the system, and $\rho(\epsilon_f)$ is the density of final states.

In the present instance the perturbation is due to the incident electromagnetic field, and the only important matrix element is that corresponding to electric dipole transitions, for which $\mathfrak{K}'_{if}$ has the form

$$\mathfrak{K}'_{if} \propto \int \psi_i^* \nabla \psi_f \, d\tau = \int u_v^*(\mathbf{k}_i, \mathbf{r}) e^{-i\mathbf{k}_i \cdot \mathbf{r}} \, \nabla [u_c(\mathbf{k}_f, \mathbf{r}) e^{i\mathbf{k}_f \cdot \mathbf{r}}] \, d\tau \tag{10.24}$$

from which we obtain two terms:

$$\int u_v^*(\mathbf{k}_i, \mathbf{r}) \nabla u_c(\mathbf{k}_f, \mathbf{r}) e^{i(\mathbf{k}_f - \mathbf{k}_i) \cdot \mathbf{r}} \, d\tau \tag{10.25a}$$

and

$$i\mathbf{k}_f \int u_v^*(\mathbf{k}_i, \mathbf{r}) u_c(\mathbf{k}_f, \mathbf{r}) e^{i(\mathbf{k}_f - \mathbf{k}_i) \cdot \mathbf{r}} \, d\tau \tag{10.25b}$$

Both integrands contain the factor $\exp[i(\mathbf{k}_f - \mathbf{k}_i) \cdot \mathbf{r}]$ which oscillates rapidly unless

$$\mathbf{k}_f = \mathbf{k}_i \tag{10.26}$$

so that, unless (10.26) is satisfied, $\mathfrak{K}'_{if}$ will be vanishingly small. This requirement is, of course, that of crystal momentum conservation. Strictly, we should have

$$\mathbf{k}_f = \mathbf{k}_i + \mathbf{q} \tag{10.27}$$

where $\mathbf{q}$ is the wave vector of the photon that is absorbed in the process [compare (10.27) with (6.13)]. In the limit of the dipole approximation, however, $\mathbf{q}$ is negligibly small compared to $\mathbf{k}_i$ or $\mathbf{k}_f$ (except for $\mathbf{k}_i = 0$, which is unimportant, as we shall see presently). The physical reason for neglecting $\mathbf{q}$ is as follows.

The wave vector $\mathbf{k}$ ranges from $\mathbf{k} = 0$ to $\mathbf{k} = \mathbf{k}_{BZ}$, where k_{BZ} is the value of the wave vector at the Brillouin zone. Since lattice parameters are of the order of a few angstroms, $k_{BZ} \sim (2-5) \times 10^7$ cm^{-1}. Therefore all but a negligibly small number of the electrons in the valence band are in states with $\mathbf{k}$ vectors greater than 5×10^5 cm^{-1}. The energy of a photon which induces transitions across the forbidden gap will be somewhat larger than ϵ_G. Thus we may take $h\nu$ to be of the order of 1 ev for a typical semiconductor. The photon frequency will, therefore, be in the neighborhood of 2×10^{14} sec^{-1} corresponding to a wavelength $\lambda \sim 1.5 \times 10^{-4}$ cm $= 1.5\mu$, which places the spectral range of interest in the infrared. The wave vector of the photon is

$$q = \frac{2\pi}{\lambda} \sim 4 \times 10^4 \text{ cm}^{-1}$$

Clearly, $q \ll k$ for all but an insignificant number of states.

Since ∇ is an odd operator, the expression (10.25a) will vanish unless u_v and u_c are of opposite symmetry, that is, unless one is an odd and the other an even function of **r**. The situation here is completely analogous to that encountered in atomic physics, and surely well known to the reader, where one of the selection rules for optical transitions declares that the two states must have opposite parity. It is therefore common practice to employ here the terminology of spectroscopy and denote transitions as *allowed* if (10.25a) is nonvanishing and as *forbidden* if (10.25a) is zero. Though forbidden, such a transition is not "strictly forbidden," since (10.25b) can and does contribute to $\mathfrak{K}'_{if}$. However, whereas for allowed transitions $\mathfrak{K}'_{if}$ is, to first approximation, independent of k_i and, hence, of the initial energy, the matrix element for forbidden transitions is proportional to k_i, so that in this case $|\mathfrak{K}'_{if}|^2 \propto k^2 \propto \epsilon$. Hence the energy, i.e., frequency dependence of the absorption coefficient, will tell us whether u_v and u_c are of the same or of opposite parity, though we cannot say which is even or odd if the transition is allowed, nor whether they are both even or both odd if the transition is forbidden.

We must now look somewhat closer at the band structure of the valence and conduction bands. Two possible configurations, shown in Figs. 10.2 and 10.3, must be distinguished. Figure 10.2 shows the ideal semiconductor band structure, of which InSb is a reasonable approximation. Figure 10.3 is characteristic of Ge, Si, and a number of other materials.

A.   Direct (Vertical) Transitions

In the case of Fig. 10.2 the valence-band maximum and the conduction-band minimum appear at the same point in the Brillouin zone, namely, at $\mathbf{k} = 0$. Evidently, the energy gap ϵ_G is also the minimum energy for direct, "vertical" optical transitions. To deduce the energy dependence of the absorption coefficient near the edge of the fundamental absorption band, we need only calculate the density of states, $\rho(\epsilon_f)$ in Eq. (10.23). We recall here that

$$\epsilon_n = \epsilon_c + \frac{\hbar^2 k^2}{2m_n} \tag{10.28a}$$

and

$$\epsilon_p = \epsilon_v - \frac{\hbar^2 k^2}{2m_p} \qquad (10.28b)$$

Hence,

$$h\nu = \epsilon_n - \epsilon_p = \epsilon_G + \frac{\hbar^2 k^2}{2m_r} \qquad (10.29)$$

where m_r is the "reduced mass"

$$m_r \equiv \frac{m_n m_p}{m_n + m_p} \qquad (10.30)$$

Now, following the same arguments as in Chap. 3, Eqs. (3.6) to (3.8), we have

$$\rho(\epsilon_f) = \frac{(2m_r)^{\frac{3}{2}}}{2\pi^2 \hbar^3} (h\nu - \epsilon_G)^{\frac{1}{2}} \qquad (10.31)$$

From (10.31) and (10.23) we conclude that

$$\alpha_d^a = C_d^a (h\nu - \epsilon_G)^{\frac{1}{2}} \qquad \text{for allowed direct transitions} \qquad (10.32)$$

for which $\mathcal{3C}'_{if}$ is independent of k, whereas

$$\alpha_d^f = C_d^f (h\nu - \epsilon_G)^{\frac{3}{2}} \qquad \text{for forbidden direct transitions} \qquad (10.33)$$

for which $\mathcal{3C}'_{if} \propto k$.

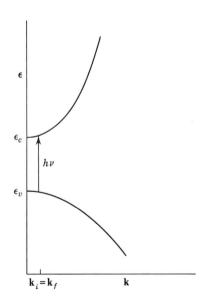

Fig. 10.2 A direct, "vertical," optical transition near the fundamental absorption edge in a semiconductor with the ideal band structure.

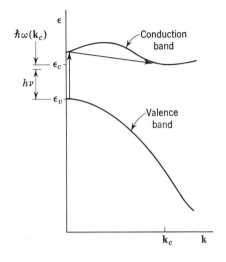

Fig. 10.3   An indirect, "nonvertical," optical transition near the fundamental absorption edge in a semiconductor with a many-valley conduction band. Here $h\nu$ is the energy of the photon that is absorbed and $\hbar\omega(\mathbf{k}_c)$ the energy of the phonon that is absorbed in the indirect transition.

B. Indirect (Nonvertical) Transitions

When the band structure is as in Fig. 10.3—for example, in germanium—the minimum energy required for a direct optical transition exceeds the thermal energy gap ϵ_G.   Nevertheless, the optical absorption edge and the thermal energy gap agree quite well experimentally.   Clearly, some new process must enter which permits indirect, "nonvertical" transitions to take place.

The mechanism for indirect optical transitions generally involves the simultaneous emission (or absorption) of a phonon with the absorption of the photon, although in highly doped samples scattering of the electron by an impurity can serve the same purpose as phonon-electron scattering. We shall here consider only the phonon interaction.   Indirect transition is fundamentally a process which can arise only in second order in a perturbation expansion.   The steps are indicated schematically in Fig. 10.3.   The electron, initially in the valence band at $\mathbf{k} = 0$, is raised in a vertical transition to the intermediate state, also at $\mathbf{k} = 0$, in the conduction band; it then absorbs, or emits, a phonon of wave vector $\mathbf{q} = \mathbf{k}_c$ or $\mathbf{q} = -\mathbf{k}_c$ and makes the transition to the conduction-band minimum.

We also show, in Fig. 10.3, for the case of phonon absorption the photon and phonon energies involved in the indirect transition.   It is immediately apparent that energy is not conserved in the transition to the intermediate state, since the photon energy is less than the direct energy gap at $\mathbf{k} = 0$.   This apparent violation of a fundamental conservation law, characteristic of second-order processes, is, however, consistent if viewed within the limitations imposed by the uncertainty principle.   The energy of the intermediate state is known only within an uncertainty $\Delta\epsilon \sim \hbar/\tau_i$, where τ_i is the lifetime of the intermediate

state. Provided the second transition follows within a time short compared to $[\epsilon_G(k = 0) - h\nu]/\hbar$, no fundamental physical laws are violated.
We can also see that the transition probability for the second-order
process will depend not only on the usual density-of-states factor and on
the matrix elements for electron-photon and electron-phonon interactions, but also on the difference between the energy in the intermediate
state and the energy provided through the absorption of the photon.
Clearly, the greater this energy difference, the shorter must be the lifetime
of the intermediate state, i.e., the shorter must be the time interval which
elapses, so to speak, between the first and second step in this two-step
process. Since the probability for electron-phonon scattering is proportional to the time interval allowed (that is, the transition probability
per unit time is a constant), the transition probability for the second-order
process should be proportional to τ_i. Thus here, as in all such instances,
the complete matrix element for the indirect transition contains an
"energy denominator" equal to $\epsilon' - \epsilon_i$, where ϵ' is the energy provided
by the absorbed quantum and ϵ_i is the energy of the intermediate state,
relative to the ground-state energy.

   It is the appearance of this energy denominator which makes the
alternative process, shown in Fig. 10.4, rather unlikely. Here an electron
in the valence band at $\mathbf{k} = \mathbf{k}_c$ is excited by the incident photon into the
conduction-band minimum; the hole which is left at $\mathbf{k} = \mathbf{k}_c$ in the valence
band is then scattered to $\mathbf{k} = 0$ in the valence band. Under the circumstances shown in Fig. 10.4 the energy denominator will be significantly
larger than in the case considered first (Fig. 10.3), and the transition
probability will be correspondingly diminished.

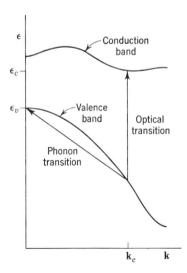

Fig. 10.4   An alternative indirect transition
process.

Let us now consider these indirect processes in somewhat more detail. As before, we are principally concerned with the frequency dependence of α. We shall have to distinguish carefully between processes involving emission and absorption of phonons, since, for a particular transition between a given initial and final state, the frequency of the photon depends on which phonon process takes place. In the case of phonon absorption we have

$$h\nu = \epsilon_n - \epsilon_p - \hbar\omega_q \qquad \text{(phonon absorption)} \qquad (10.34a)$$

while for phonon emission

$$h\nu = \epsilon_n - \epsilon_p + \hbar\omega_q \qquad \text{(phonon emission)} \qquad (10.34b)$$

That is, a photon of a given energy $h\nu$ connects different groups of initial and final states, depending upon the phonon process.

We shall assume that the transition probability via phonon absorption (or emission) from a state $\mathbf{k}_p$ near $\mathbf{k} = 0$ in the conduction band to a state $\mathbf{k}_n$ near $\mathbf{k} = \mathbf{k}_c$ is independent of $\mathbf{k}_n$ and $\mathbf{k}_p$. This is a reasonable presumption, provided we restrict our attention to situations in which $\mathbf{k}_p$ and also $\mathbf{k}_n - \mathbf{k}_c$ are small compared to $\mathbf{k}_c$.

The transition probability for an indirect process depends, as for direct transition, on the total matrix element (including the energy denominator) and the effective density of states. Overall energy conservation now gives, for a phonon-absorption process,

$$h\nu = \epsilon_G - \hbar\omega_q + \frac{\hbar^2(\mathbf{k}_n - \mathbf{k}_c)^2}{2m_n} + \frac{\hbar^2 k_p{}^2}{2m_p} \qquad (10.35)$$

Here $\mathbf{k}_n$ and $\mathbf{k}_p$ are the wave vectors in the initial and final states, which now differ by $\mathbf{q}$, the wave vector of the absorbed phonon. Although (10.35) is written as though the energy surfaces about the minimum in the conduction band were spherical, the generalization to spheroidal surfaces requires only that m_n be replaced by the density-of-states effective mass [see Eq. (8.34)].

Let us now consider transitions from a specific state of energy ϵ_p in the valence band induced by photons of energy $h\nu$. The density of final conduction-band states is

$$\rho_c(\epsilon_n) = a_c(\epsilon_n - \epsilon_c)^{\frac{1}{2}} = a_c(h\nu - \epsilon_G - \epsilon_p + \hbar\omega_q)^{\frac{1}{2}} \qquad (10.36)$$

where a_c is a constant. To find the total absorption we must now integrate over all initial states for which (10.35) can be satisfied. That there is a band of states over which we must sum is apparent from the following consideration. We assume that $h\nu = \epsilon_G - \hbar\omega_q + \delta$, where δ is small compared to ϵ_G. From Fig. 10.3 it is then apparent that transitions can take place for all initial states in the interval between $\epsilon_p = \epsilon_v$ and $\epsilon_p = \epsilon_v - \delta$. If we write for the density of states in the valence band

$$\rho(\epsilon_p) = a_v(\epsilon_v - \epsilon_p)^{\frac{1}{2}}$$

the effective density of states for the transition is

$$\rho(h\nu) \propto \int_0^\delta \rho_c(\epsilon)\rho_v(\epsilon)\, d\epsilon_p = a_c a_v \int_0^\delta (\delta - \epsilon_p)^{\frac{1}{2}}\epsilon_p^{\frac{1}{2}}\, d\epsilon_p$$

$$= C_i^a \delta^2 = C_i^a(h\nu - \epsilon_G + \hbar\omega_q)^2 \tag{10.37}$$

The probability for absorption of a phonon of frequency ω_q is, of course, proportional to the density of such phonons, as given by Planck's law, namely,

$$\mathfrak{n}(\hbar\omega_q) = (e^{\hbar\omega_q/kT} - 1)^{-1} \tag{10.38}$$

As before, we must ask whether the direct optical portion of the indirect transition is allowed or forbidden. In the latter case the k dependence of the optical matrix element will once again introduce an additional energy factor in the final expression. Combining the above results we finally obtain for the absorption coefficient due to indirect transitions involving phonon absorption

$$\alpha_a^a = C_{ia}^a \frac{(h\nu - \epsilon_G + \hbar\omega_q)^2}{e^{\hbar\omega_q/kT} - 1} \tag{10.39a}$$

$$\alpha_a^f = C_{ia}^f \frac{(h\nu - \epsilon_G + \hbar\omega_q)^3}{e^{\hbar\omega_q/kT} - 1} \tag{10.39b}$$

for allowed and forbidden transitions, respectively.

The calculation of indirect optical absorption involving the emission instead of the absorption of phonons follows along identical lines. We need only bear in mind that the probability for phonon emission is proportional to $\mathfrak{n}(\hbar\omega_q) + 1$ and that the conservation condition is now (10.34b). The final result, for optically allowed indirect transitions, the only situation that has been encountered in practice, is then

$$\alpha_i = C_i \left[\frac{(h\nu - \epsilon_G + \hbar\omega_q)^2}{e^{\hbar\omega_q/kT} - 1} + \frac{(h\nu - \epsilon_G - \hbar\omega_q)^2}{1 - e^{-\hbar\omega_q/kT}} \right] = \alpha_{ia} + \alpha_{ie} \tag{10.40}$$

In (10.40) the argument within each set of parentheses must be positive. Clearly, indirect transitions with phonon absorption extend to somewhat lower frequencies than those involving phonon emission.

We have devoted considerable space to these matters, because in the hands of a careful experimenter the study of optical absorption can yield a wealth of information. Some we shall now discuss, and others will be presented shortly.

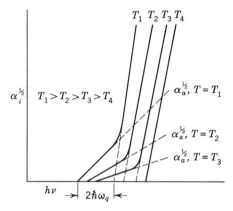

Fig. 10.5 $\alpha_i{}^{\frac{1}{2}}$ as a function of photon energy at four temperatures (theoretical). Dashed lines show $\alpha_a{}^{\frac{1}{2}}$ and $\alpha_e{}^{\frac{1}{2}}$. (*After R. A. Smith, "Semiconductors," p. 205, Cambridge University Press, London, 1959.*)

According to (10.40) a plot of $\alpha_i{}^{\frac{1}{2}}$ vs. photon energy should yield a curve consisting largely of two straight-line segments, as shown in Fig. 10.5. At the lowest photon energies, only α_{ia} contributes, and the plot of $\alpha_{ia}{}^{\frac{1}{2}}$ vs. $h\nu$ intersects the axis at $h\nu = \epsilon_G - \hbar\omega_q$. When $h\nu > \epsilon_G + \hbar\omega_q$, α_{ie} also comes into play, and, especially at lower temperatures, soon becomes the dominant term. Since the intercept of $\alpha_{ie}{}^{\frac{1}{2}}$ versus $h\nu$ occurs at $h\nu = \epsilon_G + \hbar\omega_q$, it is possible to determine not only the energy gap ϵ_G, but also the energy of the phonons which participate in indirect transitions. If, moreover, measurements are carried out at several temperatures, the slopes of the straight-line segments, corresponding to α_{ia} and α_{ie}, should be proportional to $(e^{\hbar\omega_q/kT} - 1)^{-\frac{1}{2}}$ and $(1 - e^{-\hbar\omega_q/kT})^{-\frac{1}{2}}$, respectively. As the temperature is lowered toward $T = 0°$K, the slope of the $\alpha_{ia}{}^{\frac{1}{2}}$ line approaches zero and α_{ia} becomes vanishingly small, while the slope for $\alpha_{ie}{}^{\frac{1}{2}}$ tends to the value $C_i{}^{\frac{1}{2}}$.

Thus, from a series of careful measurements, all the critical physical parameters in Eq. (10.40) can be determined. Indeed, the measurements afford an opportunity to check the theory for internal consistency, since the dependence of the slopes on temperature also yields a value for the phonon energy $\hbar\omega_q$ which can be compared with the difference in energy between the intercepts of the two straight-line segments.

However, this is by no means all. In the preceding we have assumed that only one type of phonon mode participates in indirect transitions. This is, generally, not the case, and transverse and longitudinal acoustic, as well as optical, phonons can contribute to the indirect process. The treatment can, of course, be generalized without difficulty to take account of this contingency, and one obtains

$$\alpha_i = \Sigma_s(\alpha_{ia}^s + \alpha_{ie}^s)$$

where s is an index which characterizes the phonon mode. The analysis of the data proceeds along the lines outlined above.   Using high spectral resolution, Macfarlane and coworkers [2] were able to show that, in germanium, transverse and longitudinal acoustic modes participate and that the relevant energies of these phonons are 0.008 ev and 0.027 ev, corresponding to Debye temperatures of 90 and 320°K, respectively. Since the energy minima in the conduction band of germanium are known to occur at the (111) zone boundaries, these phonon energies are characteristic of the shortest wavelength for these two modes for propagation along the [111] directions.   It is a tribute to the excellence of the infrared work, as well as a testimonial to the value of such studies in providing fundamental data, that subsequent measurements of the vibration spectrum of germanium using neutron-diffraction techniques have fully confirmed the infrared results.

If the photon energy is raised sufficiently one observes a rather sharp increase in the absorption coefficient, which marks the onset of direct transitions at $\mathbf{k} = 0$.   Thus, one can also deduce the direct optical as well as the thermal energy gap.   For this purpose magnetooptical experiments, which will be discussed in the next chapter, are even better suited, and these have yielded extremely accurate values for the direct gap.   Actually, even before the onset of direct transitions one can see,

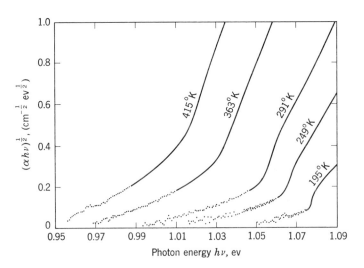

Fig. 10.6 Low-level absorption spectrum of high-purity silicon at various temperatures. At the higher levels the experimental points define the curves unambiguously; at the lower levels the experimental points are shown individually. [*From G. G. Macfarlane, T. P. McLean, J. E. Quarrington, and V. Roberts, Phys. Rev.*, **111**: 1249 (1958).]

under high resolution, the appearance of a fairly sharp absorption line at an energy slightly below that of the direct absorption edge. This absorption peak has been attributed to exciton production, and it therefore behooves us to consider excitons briefly.

10.4 EXCITON ABSORPTION

Exciton is the name given to the system of electron and hole bound to one another by their mutual coulomb attraction. Excitation of an electron into the conduction band, corresponding in a sense to complete ionization, leads to a free electron and hole, capable of moving independently under the influence of an applied field. Other, lower-energy, excited configurations also exist in which the electron and hole move as a bound, neutral unit. This system is entirely analogous to positronium, the bound positron-electron pair, and the exciton energy levels are given, as for positronium, by the Bohr model of hydrogen with the replacement of the free-electron mass by the reduced mass

$$m_r = \frac{m_n m_p}{m_n + m_p}$$

Further, since the exciton exists in the crystal and not in free space, the coulomb interaction is reduced by the dielectric constant. Thus one obtains for the exciton energy spectrum

$$E_n^x = -\frac{m_r}{mn^2\varkappa^2} E_H \tag{10.41}$$

where E_H is the ionization energy of hydrogen, 13.5 ev, and $\varkappa$ denotes the dielectric constant. Substituting reasonable values for m_n and m_p and setting $\varkappa = 16$, one obtains a ground-state energy of -0.005 ev for the exciton in germanium. In other words, there should be a set of energy levels, corresponding to different values of n in (10.41), lying just below the conduction band, with the lowest level about 0.005 ev below ϵ_c^0, where ϵ_c^0 is the conduction-band edge at $\mathbf{k} = 0$. These energies are to be associated with the bound electron-hole state.

We have so far neglected the possibility that the exciton might move as a unit through the crystal. Such center-of-mass motion is, in principle, perfectly possible and, indeed, is believed to contribute to energy transport in certain situations. To the energy of the stationary exciton one would then need to add its kinetic energy, and this, one might think, would lead to a broadening of the exciton line spectrum into bands. However, for excitons formed in direct transitions the center-of-mass motion must vanish for the following reason.

In a direct transition, $\mathbf{k}_n$ and $\mathbf{k}_p$, the wave vectors of the electron and hole that are created, must be equal and *opposite* so as to conserve crystal momentum. But if the electron and hole are excited into a *bound* state they must *move together*, not in opposite directions. These two conditions can be satisfied only if $\mathbf{k}_n = \mathbf{k}_p = 0$. Hence the spectrum for direct exciton absorption should consist of a series of sharp lines.

It is the ground-state ($n = 1$) level which has been observed as an absorption peak on the long-wavelength side of the direct absorption edge. As in the determination of the direct gap itself, the most accurate measurement of the exciton level has come from magnetooptical studies, which are described in the following chapter.

If the exciton is formed with the simultaneous emission or absorption of a phonon, the exciton may acquire a center-of-mass momentum $\hbar\mathbf{K}$, corresponding to the momentum of the phonon which participates in the transition. Now the exciton levels *will* be spread into bands. The absorption coefficient due to exciton formation is then given by an expression of the form

$$\alpha_{ex}^i = C_{ex}^i (h\nu - \epsilon_{ex} \pm \hbar\omega_q)^{\frac{1}{2}} \qquad (10.42)$$

if the optical transition is allowed. Although no absorption peak can be

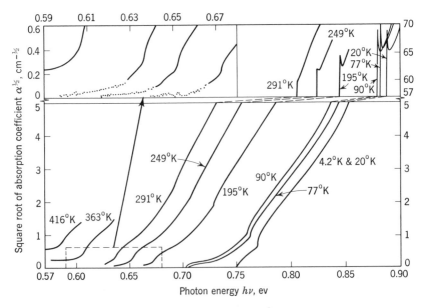

Fig. 10.7 The absorption spectrum of high purity Ge at various temperatures showing the characteristic exciton features in both the indirect and direct transition regions. [*After G. G. Macfarlane, T. P. McLean, J. E. Quarrington, and V. Roberts, J. Phys. Chem. Solids,* **8**: 390 (1959).]

expected now, the presence of indirect exciton absorption should still be noticeable as a sharp rise in the absorption coefficient. These "bumps" in the indirect absorption region are evident in the results of Macfarlane et al., shown in Fig. 10.7.

To summarize, optical absorption studies can provide a wealth of information on the band structure of semiconductors. From the frequency and the temperature dependence of the absorption coefficient one can determine not only the energy gap, but one can also see if the minimum energy gap corresponds to direct or indirect transitions, i.e., whether the valence and conduction band extrema occur at the same or at different points in the Brillouin zone. In the latter instance the direct as well as the thermal energy gaps can be determined. Moreover, it is possible to ascertain the energy of the phonons that contribute to indirect transitions. From this, one can either deduce the Debye temperature if the positions of the band extrema are known, or, if the Debye temperature has been established from other measurements, determine the approximate relative location of the valence band maximum and conduction band minimum. Finally, the existence and ground-state energies of direct and indirect exciton levels can be determined.

10.5 PHOTOELECTRIC EFFECTS

In the following we shall describe some of the most important photoelectric effects in semiconductors and indicate their major technological applications. We first treat the case of a homogeneous semiconductor and, at the end of the chapter, make a few remarks concerning devices which depend on the photoelectric properties of p-n junctions. Our primary aim here is the elucidation of the physical phenomena, and no serious attempt is made to give a detailed discussion of the design and operation of various devices. Nevertheless, the material in these sections should help the reader understand the function and limitation of such devices.

A. Photoconduction

All photoelectric effects in semiconductors rest on the fact that excess carriers are generated whenever a sample is illuminated with light of wavelength shorter than the fundamental absorption edge. Of these, the most obvious phenomenon is that of photoconductivity, that is, the change in conductivity induced by illumination.

The basic arrangement for the measurement of photoconductivity is shown in Fig. 10.8. A slab of length l, width W, and thickness d is fitted with electrodes at its ends and is uniformly illuminated over its

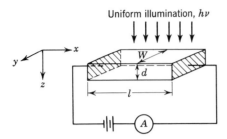

Fig. 10.8 Basic arrangement for observation of photoconduction.

surface. The current-voltage characteristic is then measured as a function of wavelength and light intensity.

Since fundamental absorption (as distinguished from free-carrier absorption) is a process which generates electron-hole pairs, the photoconductive threshold should coincide with the fundamental absorption edge. This is true even if the absorption edge is due to exciton formation, because at all but very low temperatures an exciton, due to its very small binding energy, will quickly dissociate thermally into a free electron and hole. Thus a study of photoconductivity serves as yet another method for measuring the energy gap, and, as we shall see presently, several other important physical parameters as well.

The energy gap of most semiconductors falls into the range between 0.2 and 2.5 ev, corresponding to threshold wavelengths of 6.2 and 0.5 microns. These materials therefore can be, and are used extensively as detectors of infrared and visible light. The lead salts, PbS, PbTe, and PbSe, appear to be especially suitable for such applications.

If, then, as a result of illumination the electron and hole concentrations are enhanced by Δn and Δp, with $\Delta n = \Delta p$, the concomitant relative change in conductivity will be

$$\frac{\Delta\sigma}{\sigma_0} = \frac{\Delta n\mu_n + \Delta p\mu_p}{n_0\mu_n + p_0\mu_p} = \frac{(1 + b)\,\Delta n}{n_0 b + p_0} \tag{10.43}$$

where n_0 and p_0 are the equilibrium electron and hole concentrations in the dark, and b is the mobility ratio, $b = \mu_n/\mu_p$. Equation (10.43) is correct, provided the mobilities do not depend on the carrier concentrations. This is a valid assumption as long as Δn is small compared to n_0 in an n-type sample. However, when Δn and Δp are large, electron-hole scattering may become important and reduce the mobility (see Sec. 8.3C). We shall limit ourselves to small changes in carrier concentration.

The steady-state excess-carrier concentrations depend on the intensity and wavelength of the incident radiation and on the rate of recombination. Moreover, the distribution of the charge carriers also depends on the boundary conditions and the absorption coefficient, and we shall consider here two limiting cases, defined by the inequalities $\alpha d \ll 1$ and $\alpha d \gg 1$.

If $\alpha d \ll 1$, the intensity of the radiation will be practically uniform throughout the interior of the sample. Furthermore, one can show that if I is the incident intensity, multiple internal reflection results in a uniform rate of absorption given by αI per unit volume. The rate of electron-hole generation is then

$$\mathfrak{R} = \frac{\alpha I}{h\nu}\,\eta \tag{10.44}$$

where η, the *quantum efficiency*, is the probability that an electron-hole pair is created when a photon of energy $h\nu$ is absorbed. Generally there will be competing absorption processes, so that η is less than unity. Clearly, a high quantum efficiency will be one of the requirements for good photoconductive devices.

If $\alpha d \gg 1$, multiple internal reflection is ruled out, since the intensity of the beam upon reaching the back surface is already negligible. The intensity within the sample is now given by

$$I'(z) = I(1 - R)e^{-\alpha z} \tag{10.45}$$

where R is the reflection coefficient at the front surface. The rate of generation is therefore

$$\mathfrak{R} = \frac{\alpha \eta I (1 - R)e^{-\alpha z}}{h\nu} = \mathfrak{R}_0 e^{-\alpha z} \tag{10.46}$$

Let us now return to the case $\alpha d \ll 1$. We neglect, for the moment, surface recombination. Under steady-state conditions we have, according to Eqs. (9.10) and (10.44),

$$\Delta p = \mathfrak{R}\tau_h = \frac{\alpha I \tau_h \eta}{h\nu} \tag{10.47}$$

In germanium, α at a wavelength of 1.0 μ is about 10^4 cm^{-1}. If $\tau_h = 10^{-4}$ sec and $\eta = 1$, we obtain, for an intensity of 10^{-4} watt/cm^2,

$$\Delta p = 5 \times 10^{14} \text{ cm}^{-3}$$

i.e., a fairly substantial enhancement in carrier concentration. It is clear that even with a reasonably weak light intensity the carrier concentration can be greatly enhanced, especially if the recombination time is long. Also we see that, since $\alpha \sim 10^3$ to 10^5 cm^{-1} for most materials in the intrinsic absorption region, the condition $\alpha d \ll 1$ can be fulfilled only through the use of thin films. In that case, however, we are no longer justified in neglecting surface recombination.

In very thin films the diffusion length L_p will normally be much longer than d. In that case the effect of surface recombination is simply to diminish the lifetime to τ'_h, given by

$$\frac{1}{\tau'_h} = \frac{1}{\tau_h} + \frac{2s}{d} \tag{10.48}$$

If we take $s = 100$ cm/sec and $d = 10^{-4}$ cm, then

$$\frac{2s}{d} = 2 \times 10^6 \text{ sec}^{-1}$$

which is much larger than $1/\tau_h$. Thus in thin films, surface recombination rather than the bulk lifetime limits the excess-carrier concentration, which will then be considerably smaller than we have just estimated. From the above it also follows that a large absorption coefficient is by no means essential nor even desirable very often, but that long lifetimes are of primary concern in the manufacture of photoconductive cells.

The photocurrent (that is, the change in current due to the photo-electrically induced change in conductivity) is, according to Eqs. (10.43) and (10.47),

$$i_p = Wd\Delta\sigma E = \frac{Wde\eta\alpha I\tau'_h(1 + b)\mu_p E}{h\nu} \tag{10.49}$$

For weak intensities, τ'_h is constant and the photocurrent is then proportional to the light intensity. On the other hand, at strong intensities, when $\Delta p \gtrsim p_0$, τ'_h is a function of the excess-carrier concentration and a nonlinear relationship between i_p and I results. It is left as a problem to show that, if $\Delta p \gg n_0$ or p_0 and if, moreover, radiative recombination is the process which limits the lifetime, then i_p is proportional to $I^{\frac{1}{2}}$.

If the sample is thick so that $\alpha d \gg 1$, the intensity within the sample is given by (10.45). Since, now, the rate of generation varies with depth according to (10.46), diffusion will play an important role. The continuity equation which must be satisfied is

$$\frac{\Delta p}{\tau_h} - D\frac{d^2\Delta p}{dz^2} = \mathcal{R}_0 e^{-\alpha z} \tag{10.50}$$

If the diffusion length $L = (D\tau_h)^{\frac{1}{2}}$ is much longer than d, the solution of (10.50) is

$$\Delta p = \frac{\mathcal{R}_0\tau_h}{\alpha^2 L^2 - 1}\left(\frac{\alpha L^2 + s\tau_h}{L + s\tau_h}e^{-z/L} - e^{-\alpha z}\right) \tag{10.51}$$

Equation (10.51) is obtained when the constant of integration is evaluated for the boundary condition at the surface:

$$D \frac{\partial \Delta p}{\partial z} = s\,\Delta p \qquad z = 0$$

To calculate the photocurrent we now integrate over z, and we shall replace the upper limit $z = d$ by $z = \infty$. We then have

$$i_p = W e E (1 + b)\mu_p \int_0^\infty \Delta p \, dz$$

$$= \frac{e\eta W L I \tau_h \mu_p (1 + b)(1 - R)E}{h\nu(L + s\tau_h)}\left[1 + \frac{s\tau_h}{L(1 + \alpha L)}\right] \qquad (10.52)$$

For constant intensity the dependence of i_p on wavelength is now no longer simply determined by $\alpha(\lambda)$, as was the case for $\alpha d \ll 1$ [see Eq. (10.49)]. If $s\tau_h \ll L$, the photocurrent increases monotonically with decreasing wavelength, as shown in Fig. 10.9. However, if the surface recombination velocity is large and $s\tau_h \gg L$, i_p will exhibit a maximum when $\alpha(\lambda) \sim 1/L$. The reason for the subsequent decrease of i_p with increasing absorption coefficient is that, when $\alpha L \gg 1$, all carriers are generated close to the surface, where their lifetimes are severely curtailed, whereas for smaller values of α a fair number of carriers are produced in the bulk, where their lifetimes are limited by the longer volume recombination time τ_h.

In the foregoing discussion of photoconductivity we have completely neglected the influence of *traps*, as contrasted with recombination centers. These traps accept only carriers of one kind and ultimately release the trapped electron or hole through thermal excitation. The presence of such traps will tend to enhance rather than reduce the photocurrent, since the effective lifetime of excess carriers is thereby increased. Although traps therefore appear to be desirable imperfections on first glance, they are actually deleterious, since they increase the response time of a device. For example, if the illumination is suddenly

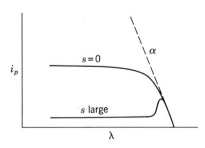

Fig. 10.9 Variation of photocurrent with wavelength for large and small values of the surface recombination velocity s. (*From R. A. Smith, "Semiconductors,"* p. 311, *Cambridge University Press, London,* 1959.)

switched off at time $t = 0$, the photocurrent in a sample containing no traps would decay with the characteristic time τ_h'. If traps are present the current decays until the traps have been emptied, which generally takes much longer than recombination.

Trapping centers, i.e., impurities with negligible cross section for capture of one type of carrier, are used in practically every photoconductive device to enhance the gain at the expense of response time. Generally, hole traps are employed, and the kind and concentration used will depend on the required frequency response.

B. Photovoltaic Effect

We consider an n-type semiconductor illuminated in the fundamental absorption band. We also presume that $\alpha d \gg 1$. Excess carriers, electrons and holes, are then generated in the material at a rate which diminishes exponentially with distance from the illuminated surface, according to Eq. (10.46). The resulting concentration gradients now cause a flow of electron and hole diffusion currents which cancel only if the mobilities of the two carriers are identical. To see this we need only rewrite Eq. (9.3), making use of the Einstein relation (9.8) and the condition $\Delta n = \Delta p$, and obtain

$$J_z = J_{nz} + J_{pz} = e(bn + p)\mu_p E_z + (b - 1)kT\mu_p \frac{\partial \Delta p}{\partial z} \qquad (10.53)$$

If we now impose the boundary condition $J_z = 0$ we see that, unless $b = 1$, an electric field

$$E_z = - \frac{kT}{e} \left(\frac{b - 1}{nb + p} \right) \frac{\partial \Delta p}{\partial z} \qquad (10.54)$$

will be established. The resulting photovoltage between the dark and illuminated faces is

$$V = \frac{kT}{e} \frac{\eta I \alpha L \tau_h (1 - R)(b - 1)}{(n_0 b + p_0)(L + \tau_h s)(1 + \alpha L)} \qquad (10.55)$$

Equation (10.55) shows the expected functional dependences: (1) The photovoltage is proportional to the light intensity I. (2) For fixed intensity, V increases with increasing lifetime τ_h, greater quantum efficiency η, diffusion length L, and mobility ratio b. (3) V vanishes identically if $b = 1$.

Since, in contrast to the photoconductivity effect, the photovoltaic effect requires no external voltage source, photocells based on this phenomenon are commonly employed as active elements in light detectors and flux meters. For light-sensitive switching devices ("electric-eye" door activators and similar applications) photodiodes which rely on the photovoltage developed across a *p-n* junction are generally employed.

C.   Photomagnetic (PEM) Effect

If, in addition to the incident light flux, we also apply a magnetic field parallel to the illuminated surface, say, in the y direction in Fig. 10.8, electrons and holes, diffusing in the z direction away from the illuminated surface will experience opposite Lorentz forces and will, therefore, tend to separate.   Consequently, if the boundary conditions preclude the flow of net current in the x direction, an electric field is generated in the x as well as the z directions.

With the aid of Eqs. (8.20) and (8.62) and the assumption that τ is independent of energy so that we need not distinguish between Hall and drift mobilities, Eq. (7.58) can be brought into the more convenient form

$$J_{nx} = \mu_n(enE_x - H_y J_{nz}/c) \tag{10.56a}$$

$$J_{px} = \mu_p(epE_x + H_y J_{pz}/c) \tag{10.56b}$$

where we have interchanged coordinates to conform with the present choice of axes.   The electron and hole currents in the z direction are

$$J_{nx} = en\mu_n E_z + eD_n \frac{\partial \Delta n}{\partial z} \tag{10.57a}$$

$$J_{pz} = ep\mu_p E_z - eD_p \frac{\partial \Delta p}{\partial z} \tag{10.57b}$$

As in the derivation of the photovoltaic effect, we impose the boundary condition $J_z = J_{nz} + J_{pz} = 0$, so that the electric field has a z component given by (10.54).   Accordingly, setting $\Delta n = \Delta p$, the z components of the electron and hole currents are

$$J_{nz} = eD \frac{\partial \Delta n}{\partial z} \qquad J_{pz} = -J_{nz} \tag{10.58}$$

where D is the *ambipolar diffusion coefficient*

$$D \equiv \frac{D_n D_p}{D_n + D_p} \tag{10.59}$$

In the calculation of the x component of the electric field we cannot demand that $J_x = J_{nx} + J_{px} = 0$.   The solution would then be a function of z and cannot be correct, since, for constant magnetic field, **E** must be irrotational.   Since $\partial E_z/\partial x = 0$ it then follows that $\partial E_x/\partial z$ must also vanish.   The correct boundary condition

$$\int_0^d (J_{nx} + J_{px})\, dz = 0 \tag{10.60}$$

allows for the flow of internal circulating electron and hole currents.

We now obtain

$$\begin{aligned}
E_x &= \frac{H(b+1)}{ced(n_0 b + p_0)} \int_0^d J_{pz}\, dz \\
&= \frac{DH(b+1)}{cd(n_0 b + p_0)} [\Delta p(z = 0) - \Delta p(z = d)] \\
&= \frac{DH(b+1)}{cd(n_0 b + p_0)} \frac{\eta I(1 - R)\tau_h}{h\nu(L + \tau_h s)} \frac{\alpha L}{(1 + \alpha L)}
\end{aligned} \tag{10.61}$$

where we have assumed $\alpha d \gg 1$, and $d \gg L$, have accordingly set $\Delta p(z = d) = 0$ and have also made use of Eq. (10.51).

If, instead of fixing our attention on the open-circuit voltage, we calculate the short-circuit current flowing in the x direction (maintaining the condition $J_z = 0$), we find

$$i_{\mathrm{pem}} = \frac{e\mu_p(b+1)H\eta I(1 - R)L^2}{ch\nu(L + s\tau_h)} \frac{\alpha L}{(1 + \alpha L)} \tag{10.62}$$

Equations (10.52) and (10.62) are very similar in appearance, and taking the ratio of the two currents, one obtains

$$\frac{i_{\mathrm{pem}}}{i_p} = \frac{H}{cE} \frac{\alpha L^2}{\tau_h(1 + \alpha L + s\tau_h/L)} \tag{10.63}$$

and in the limit $\alpha L \gg 1$,

$$\frac{i_{\mathrm{pem}}}{i_p} = \frac{H}{cE} \frac{L}{\tau_h} = \frac{H}{cE} \left(\frac{D}{\tau_h}\right)^{\frac{1}{2}} \tag{10.64}$$

Since D can be determined from mobility data and Eq. (9.8), the measurement of photocurrent and photomagnetic current under conditions for which $\alpha L \gg 1$ and $\alpha d \gg 1$ provides a means for establishing the recombination time τ_h.   This procedure is rather more convenient than direct injection methods, especially if the recombination times are small, 1 μsec or less.   Moreover, from the spectral variation of this current ratio, that is, by changing α, the surface recombination velocity can also be deduced by fitting the experimental results to Eq. (10.63).   This procedure is to be preferred over that of selecting s so as to match (10.52) or (10.62) separately to the spectral dependence of the photocurrent or photomagnetic current, because the quantum efficiency generally depends on the wavelength of the radiation.   By taking the ratio of the two currents this factor is eliminated.

D. ⸱ Photoelectric Effects at p-n Junctions

We shall, finally, consider the behavior of a junction diode under illumination in the fundamental absorption range.   The effects, which we shall describe very briefly, are of great technologic interest and are basic to various devices, of which the solar battery is of particular moment today in view of its use as a power source in space vehicles.

Photodiodes   Consider, then, a p-n junction diode illuminated uniformly, as shown in Fig. 10.10.   In the region far from the junction the effect of the light is merely one of reducing the resistivity of the material through the photoconductive effect.   However, within distances L_p and L_n to the right and left, respectively, of the barrier layer, carriers generated photoelectrically can diffuse across the barrier and thereby alter the property of the junction in a pronounced way.

The electron of an electron-hole pair created in the p-type region immediately adjacent to the barrier will, upon diffusing to the barrier, "fall" down the potential hill into the n-type region.   Similarly, the excess holes created photoelectrically on the n side of the barrier flow into the p region upon reaching the barrier.   In short, the effect of illumination is simply to increase the generation current in the same way as would a local increase in temperature.   This additional current is just

$$J_p = -e\Re(L_p + L_n) \tag{10.65}$$

where we have used the negative sign to indicate that the current, a generation current, flows in the reverse direction with respect to the standard polarity of a diode circuit.   We must now add to this the current which flows in the junction under normal operation and obtain

$$J = J_g(e^{eV/kT} - 1) - e\Re(L_n + L_p) \tag{10.66}$$

If we bias the junction in the reverse direction, so that, in the dark, the current is the reverse saturation current $-J_g$, the change in reverse saturation current under illumination is proportional to the light intensity.

Uniform illumination, $h\nu$

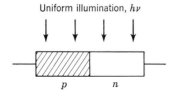

p n

Fig. 10.10   The p-n junction photodiode, schematic.

Alternatively, we may operate the diode under open-circuit conditions. In that case $J = 0$, and from (10.66) we conclude that a voltage

$$V_p = \frac{kT}{e} \ln \left[\frac{1 + e\mathfrak{R}(L_p + L_n)}{J_g} \right] \tag{10.67}$$

is developed across the terminals of the diode. Equation (10.67) is correct only for small light intensities; in that case V_p is at first proportional to $\mathfrak{R}$, i.e., to the intensity. However, as $\mathfrak{R}$ is increased, the voltage across the diode does not increase without limit. Ultimately the photovoltage will attain the value of the barrier voltage and no further increase is possible. In other words, under strong illumination the junction behaves as though the temperature were increased to the point where the material becomes intrinsic, and an essentially flat-band condition is attained where the existence of the junction can play no further role.

In edge-on illumination the effective area is small, only $L_p + L_n$ wide. A larger effective area can be achieved by constructing a diode with only a very thin n (or p) layer over a thicker p (or n) crystal. Generally, this is accomplished by allowing suitable doping impurities to diffuse, at elevated temperatures, a short distance into the p-type bulk crystal. Electrical contact is made to the illuminated n-type face of the diode by deposition of a semitransparent metallic layer. Illumination is now over the entire front surface, and such diodes, presenting large effective areas, are generally employed in solar batteries.

Since the open-circuit voltage of a photodiode is only of the order of 1 volt, large numbers are normally connected in series. Though this does provide a substantial working voltage it has the disadvantage that, if one of the series elements fails accidentally, or if it is not illuminated, the internal resistance of the battery is then quite high and the performance suffers accordingly.

For purposes of power generation, what matters, of course, is neither the open-circuit voltage nor the short-circuit current but the power that can be delivered to a load under optimum load conditions. In the case of solar batteries the illumination is not monochromatic but covers the entire electromagnetic spectrum and corresponds fairly closely to radiation from a "blackbody" at about 6000°K. To utilize as much of this radiation as possible, a narrow band-gap material might appear desirable. However, as we have seen, the theoretical maximum voltage that can be developed by each cell is limited to ϵ_G/e. In practice, the maximum open-circuit voltage is closer to $\frac{2}{3}(\epsilon_G/e)$. Thus a compromise must be effected between maximum utilization of the available radiant energy and high output voltage. Calculations show that for a solar battery the optimum band gap is about 1.4 ev, and that under idealized conditions (e.g., no reflection losses) efficiencies of about 30 percent could be realized. Working efficiencies of about 15 percent are commonly attained.

p-n junction lasers (injection lasers)   We conclude this chapter with a brief, qualitative description of one of the more recent developments in semiconductor technology, which promises to be one of the more important and far-reaching developments as well.   The effect, the emission of a coherent, intense beam of light from a p-n junction diode biased in the forward direction and carrying a fairly high current, is the inverse of the photodiode phenomenon which we discussed in the preceding section.

The word *laser* derives from *maser*, which stands for *m*icrowave *a*mplification by *s*timulated *e*mission of *r*adiation.   A laser is a device, also operating on the principle of stimulated emission, where the radiation is *l*ight; that is, the wavelength falls into the visible or infrared rather than the microwave region of the spectrum.   The fundamental principle of operation of these devices is simple enough, though detailed analysis has its ramifications, which, however, need not concern us here.

Consider a system of N particles of which each may exist in one of three quantum states, as shown in Fig. 10.11.   We denote these states by the numbers 1, 2, 3, and the corresponding energies by E_1, E_2, E_3. The state of energy E_1 is clearly the ground state.   Let us, for convenience, consider only the case for $T = 0°K$.   At equilibrium all N particles are in the ground state.

If we now irradiate the system with radiation such that

$$h\nu = h\nu_{13} = E_3 - E_1$$

we will induce transitions between states 1 and 3, provided the optical transition is allowed.   If the intensity of the radiation is sufficient, and neglecting for the moment the existence of state 2, we will quickly achieve a steady state in which $N_1 = N_3 = N/2$.   The system is then said to be *saturated;* that is, there are as many particles in the excited state 3 as there are in the ground state 1.   No further net absorption of radiation takes place, since the number of quanta absorbed will equal the number emitted as particles decay from state 3 to the ground state.

Let us further assume that the transition from state 3 to state 2

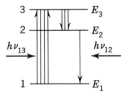

Fig. 10.11   Energy levels for a three-level maser.

has a high probability, that from state 2 to state 1, a low probability; that is, the lifetime τ_{32} is very short but τ_{21} is extremely long. In that case, some of the particles in state 3 will decay to state 2, rather than to the ground state, during the course of irradiation. The deficiency in N_3 relative to N_1 is, however, quickly made up through absorption of incident photons of energy $h\nu_{13}$. Clearly, as time goes on, we shall attain a distribution such that $N_2 \gg N_1 = N_3$, a distribution in which most particles find themselves in the metastable state 2. One has then arrived at the condition known as *population inversion* as regards states 1 and 2. Since, at equilibrium at finite temperatures $N_2/N_1 = e^{-(E_2-E_1/kT)}$, the inverted distribution can be characterized by allowing T to take on negative values. The concept of a *negative temperature* has been employed widely and, though it is not essential to an understanding of the physical phenomena, the student will often find it used in the literature.

Having attained this population inversion we now illuminate with radiation of frequency $\nu_{12} = (E_2 - E_1)/h$. We thereby *stimulate* transitions from state 2 to state 1 with the emission of radiation of frequency ν_{12}, and, for a brief period immediately after application of the stimulating radiation, the number of quanta emitted at this frequency will greatly exceed those absorbed. Thus amplification of a weak stimulating signal of frequency ν_{12} is achieved.

Masers have certain important advantages over conventional microwave amplifiers, as well as some disadvantages. As regards the former, we might mention first the extreme sensitivity—a few photons per second may suffice to trigger the device—and second, the practically noiseless operation. The principal disadvantages are: (1) Masers must be operated at very low temperatures (liquid helium or hydrogen) to maintain long τ_{12}. (2) The bandwidth is extremely narrow—though this can also be advantageous in certain circumstances. (3) Some additional microwave or optical source is required to supply the pump energy, i.e., quanta of frequency ν_{13}.

It is, of course, possible to incorporate a feedback loop and operate the maser as an oscillator rather than as an amplifier. This can be done, for example, by painting a semitransparent metallic coating over the end surfaces of the maser crystal,† whose length is a multiple of $\lambda_{12}/2$. Under these conditions the few photons that are liberated within the crystal due to spontaneous emission are reflected internally and may themselves stimulate further transitions before they emerge from the crystal. The

---

† Many masers are molecular crystals containing certain impurity atoms which constitute the active maser particles. The most common is ruby, aluminum oxide with some chromium impurities. However, gas masers and lasers are also frequently employed. Many books have appeared recently which discuss these devices in considerable detail.

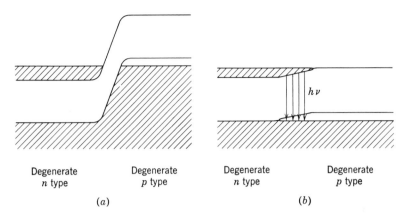

Degenerate   Degenerate   Degenerate   Degenerate
n type   p type   n type   p type

(a)   (b)

Fig. 10.12   The junction laser.   (a) No applied bias; (b) large forward bias.

crystal now acts as a cavity resonator enforcing constructive interference, and the radiation which emerges from the end surfaces is coherent.   This coherence is one of the most essential and important aspects of maser and laser radiation.

The p-n junction injection laser also depends on a population inversion.   Here, however, this condition is achieved not by optical or microwave pumping but by biasing the junction in the forward direction, thus forcing electrons to flow from the n to the p side and holes from the p to the n side.   The resulting carrier distribution is shown schematically in Fig. 10.12.   In the junction region, recombination of electrons and holes will take place.   For low currents, nonradiative recombination may be dominant; but when the electron and hole concentration is sufficiently high, radiative recombination takes on increasing importance.

In contrast to the three-level maser the emitted radiation, as shown in Fig. 10.13, encompasses a fairly wide frequency range.   At first this recombination radiation appears in all directions and with random polarization.   At higher injection levels a so-called superradiant state is attained.   Here the photons which propagate in the plane of the junction trigger further recombination elsewhere in the junction.   Consequently, the radiation is now sharply peaked in the plane of the junction.   Moreover, since the probability for self-stimulated emission is quite frequency sensitive, the spectral distribution becomes decidedly peaked.

The emerging radiation is, however, not coherent.   Coherence can be enforced by preparing the crystal so that the front and back faces are exactly parallel.   The radiation is then reflected internally a number of times.   In the superradiant state the intensity is insufficient to overcome the reflection losses.   If the junction current is further increased, standing waves are set up in this Fabry-Perot interferometer, and only waves which interfere constructively survive. The emerging radiation is now coherent and polarized perpendicular to the plane of the junction. The intensity of the radiation increases with increased junction current, since electrons and holes must be supplied to the junction by the current in sufficient quantity to offset the loss due to recombination. Requisite current densities are quite high, in excess of 10^3 amp/cm². In the junction the power dissipation is therefore exceedingly high, ranging from 10^7 watt/cm³ upward. Though much of this energy is converted into light rather than into heat in the junction, and good thermal contact with the rest of the crystal carries away this heat fairly rapidly, at present junction lasers can only be operated under pulse conditions at room temperature. At liquid-air and lower temperatures continuous operation is possible.

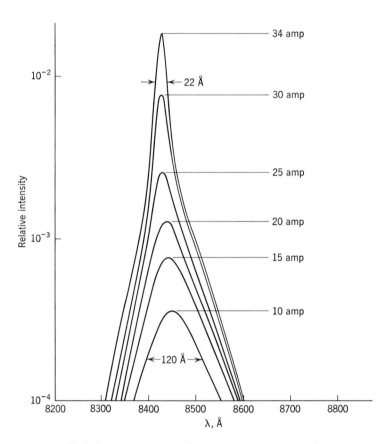

Fig. 10.13   Emission spectra from a GaAs junction in super radiant region.

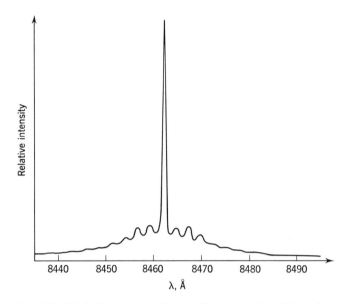

Fig. 10.14 Emission spectrum from a GaAs laser biased just above the laser threshold.

The radiation from the junction laser comes only from the junction region, that is, from a very narrow slit whose width is perhaps about 5×10^{-4} cm. Consequently, the angular spread of the coherent beam is fairly wide. In this respect a ruby crystal is a superior laser. The coherent light emerging from a ruby rod of 1 cm diameter is confined into a narrow pencil whose apex angle is roughly 10^{-4} rad. The energy density in this beam is therefore almost unbelievably high and the electric field intensity is correspondingly large. Since the motion of ions in a crystal is governed by Hooke's law only if the displacement from equilibrium is small, such intense electric fields can be used to study nonlinear effects in solids. The availability of intense electromagnetic radiation has thus opened up a wide range of new fundamental investigations.

Intense and narrow light beams are also of considerable practical value. Several years ago illumination of a small surface of the moon by a laser stationed on earth was observed. More recently, laser rather than radar beams have been used for tracking and communicating with satellites.

To return to the junction laser, this device does have decided advantages over other crystal and gas lasers. First, the latter require a fair amount of auxiliary equipment for optical pumping, whereas very little is needed to operate a junction laser. Second, the light intensity from the laser can be modulated with great ease by simply varying the bias.

Third, the junction laser is probably the most efficient device known today for the conversion of electrical energy into light. At high injection level the quantum efficiency in the junction approaches 100 percent. Fourth, the response time of the junction laser is apparently faster than that of any other device yet discovered. Pulses of 10^{-9} sec duration are reproduced faithfully, and only at a frequency of 10^{11} sec^{-1} does the laser fail to respond perfectly.

PROBLEMS

10.1. Consider the following fictitious semiconductor. The crystal structure is hexagonal with $c = 2.8$ Å. The energy of the conduction band at $\mathbf{k} = 0$ is 1.0 ev, and at $\mathbf{k}_{0001} = \pm \dfrac{\pi}{c}$ the energy is 0.9 ev above the valence-band maximum, which occurs at $\mathbf{k} = 0$. Assume optical transitions from the valence to the conduction band are allowed. The velocity of sound for propagation along the c direction is 4×10^5 cm/sec. Sketch curves showing the absorption coefficient as a function of photon energy, for photon energies in excess of 0.85 ev, at $T = 0°$ and $300°$K, showing all relevant features, i.e., energies at which absorption commences and changes significantly, and the energy dependence of the absorption coefficient.

10.2. The accompanying figure shows the absorption coefficient of germanium as a function of photon energy at $T = 300°$K. A slab of n-type germanium, 0.2 cm thick, 1 cm wide, and 3 cm long, with carrier concentration of 10^{17} electrons per cubic centimeter, is illuminated at normal incidence from a monochromatic light source with light of wavelength 15,340 Å. The incident intensity is 2×10^{-4} watt/cm^2.

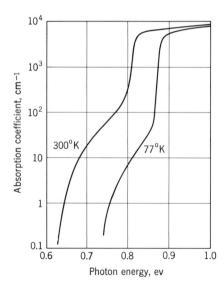

Fig. P10.2 Absorption in germanium. (*Dash and Newman*, 1955; *Courtesy American Physical Society.*)

(a) Find the number of photons per second incident on the slab.

(b) Find the depth within the germanium slab at which the light intensity is 1 percent of its value at the surface.

(c) Find the number of electron-hole pairs created per second in this slab, assuming a quantum efficiency of 0.85.

(d) Find the photoconductance i_p/E if the diffusion length is 1 mm and surface recombination is neglected.

(e) Find the voltage developed between the front and back surfaces of the specimen under open-circuit conditions.

10.3. Repeat Prob. 10.2, parts *a, c, d, e,* using as the wavelength of the incident radiation 19,110 Å.

10.4. Show that if the light intensity incident on an *n*-type semiconductor is such that $\Delta p \gg n_0$, and if radiative recombination limits the lifetime of excess carriers, the photocurrent is proportional to the square root of the light intensity.

REFERENCES

1. Benedict, T. S., and W. Shockley: *Phys. Rev.*, **89**: 1152 (1953).
2. Macfarlane, G. G., T. P. McLean, J. E. Quarrington, and V. Roberts: *J. Phys. Solids*, **8**: 388 (1959).

BIBLIOGRAPHY

Birnbaum, G.: Optical Masers, *Advan. Electron. Electron Phys., Suppl.* **2** (1964).

Greiner, R. A.: "Semiconductor Devices and Applications," McGraw-Hill Book Company, New York, 1961.

Heavens, O.: "Optical Masers," John Wiley & Sons, Inc., New York, 1964.

Lengyel, B. A.: "Introduction to Laser Physics," John Wiley & Sons, Inc., New York, 1966.

McLean, T. P.: The Absorption Edge Spectrum of Semiconductors, *Progr. Semiconductors*, **5**: 53 (1960).

Moll, J. L.: "Physics of Semiconductors," McGraw-Hill Book Company, New York, 1964.

Moss, T. S.: "Optical Properties of Semiconductors," Academic Press Inc., New York, 1959.

Ryvkin, S. M.: "Photoelectric Effects in Semiconductors," Consultants Bureau, New York, 1964.

Smith, R. A.: "Semiconductors," Cambridge University Press, London, 1959.

Tauc, J.: "Photo and Thermoelectric Effects in Semiconductors," Pergamon Press, New York, 1962.

11

Properties of Semiconductors and Metals in Strong Magnetic Fields

11.1 INTRODUCTION

This chapter is devoted to some of the most interesting and exciting developments that have unfolded in solid-state physics during the last decade. The phenomena which we shall discuss—cyclotron resonance, magnetoacoustic resonance, magnetoresistance, and the de Haas-van Alphen effect—have all contributed enormously to our present understanding of metals, particularly the detailed features of the Fermi surface. Cyclotron resonance and magnetooptical studies have similarly revealed the band structure of semiconductors in considerable detail.

In every instance the most startling and precise results are obtained when the relaxation time of the charge carriers is long compared to the cyclotron period. We shall, therefore, be principally concerned with this high-field region, defined by the condition

$$\omega_c \tau = \frac{eH}{m^*c}\tau > 1 \tag{11.1}$$

The full theory of most of the effects, taking account of departures of energy bands from standard form, of spin-orbit coupling, and of band-edge degeneracies, is far too complex to be presented here. We shall, instead, rely heavily on the free-electron approximation and shall content ourselves with qualitative discussions of those occasionally profound changes that arise when this approximation fails.

In this chapter we reverse the usual order of presentation, focusing our attention first on semiconductors, leaving the rather more tricky metals to the last.

11.2 HIGH–FIELD EFFECTS IN SEMICONDUCTORS

We consider a semiconductor whose valence and conduction bands are nondegenerate, parabolic, and spherically symmetric in **k** space. In the absence of a magnetic field the energies in the two bands are

$$\epsilon_n(\mathbf{k}) = \epsilon_c + \frac{\hbar^2}{2m_n} (k_x^2 + k_y^2 + k_z^2) \tag{11.2a}$$

$$\epsilon_p(\mathbf{k}) = \epsilon_v - \frac{\hbar^2}{2m_p} (k_x^2 + k_y^2 + k_z^2) \tag{11.2b}$$

This energy spectrum is fundamentally altered by application of a magnetic field **H**, which we take directed along the z axis. As shown in Sec. A.4 of Appendix A, the motion in the plane perpendicular to **H** is quantized in "Landau levels," but remains continuous along **H**. The energies are now

$$\epsilon_n(k_z, l_c) = \epsilon_c + \hbar\omega_c(l_c + \tfrac{1}{2}) + \frac{\hbar^2 k_z^2}{2m_n} \tag{11.3a}$$

$$\epsilon_p(k_z, l_v) = \epsilon_v - \hbar\omega_v(l_v + \tfrac{1}{2}) - \frac{\hbar^2 k_z^2}{2m_p} \tag{11.3b}$$

where ω_c and ω_v are the cyclotron frequencies of the electrons and holes, respectively.

We see that in the presence of a uniform magnetic field the valence and conduction bands are split into a series of one-dimensional sub-bands, each subband identified by the "orbital" quantum number l, which can take on only integral values. The minimum energy of the lowest, $l_c = 0$, subband in the conduction band is $\hbar\omega_c/2$ above the zero-field conduction band edge; the maximum energy of the highest, $l_v = 0$, subband of the valence band is $\hbar\omega_v/2$ below the zero-field valence band edge. The subbands are separated by constant energy differences $\hbar\omega_c$ and $\hbar\omega_v$, respectively, and this separation is independent of the other

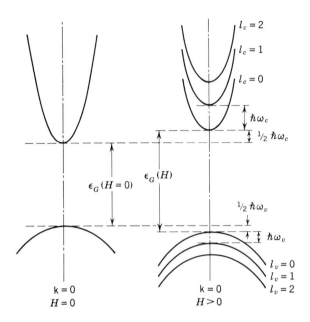

Fig. 11.1 Energy bands for a simple semiconductor for $H = 0$ and for $H > 0$. [*After E. Burstein, G. S. Picus, R. F. Wallis, and F. J. Blatt, Phys. Rev.*, **113**: 16 (1959).]

quantum number k_z (see Fig. 11.1). To take account of spin we should add to both (11.3a) and (11.3b) a term $g\beta H m_s$, where g is the effective g factor of the carriers and m_s is the magnetic quantum number, $\pm\frac{1}{2}$.

A. Cyclotron Resonance

In cyclotron resonance the incident microwave radiation is so polarized that the electric field vector is perpendicular to the constant applied magnetic field, and the sample, placed in the microwave cavity, is located at an electric field antinode. With this arrangement, transitions will be induced between Landau levels when the frequency ν of the microwave radiation satisfies the condition of energy conservation

$$h\nu = \hbar\omega_c \quad \text{or} \quad h\nu = \hbar\omega_v \tag{11.4}$$

To calculate the transition rate between Landau levels one can again make use of time-dependent perturbation theory, following the same procedure as in Chap. 10. However, whereas previously our unperturbed states were Bloch states, $u_n(\mathbf{r}) \exp(i\mathbf{k} \cdot \mathbf{r})$, we must now use wave functions appropriate to electrons in a magnetic field, i.e., functions of the form

$$\psi_n(\mathbf{r},l,k_z) = u_n(\mathbf{r})F_{l,k_z}(\mathbf{r}) \tag{11.5}$$

where

$$F_{l,k_z}(\mathbf{r}) = G_l(t)e^{i(k_x x + k_z z)} \tag{11.5a}$$

and $G_l(t)$ is the harmonic oscillator function (Hermite polynomial) of the variable

$$t = s^{\frac{1}{2}}\left(y - \frac{k_x}{s}\right) \qquad s = \frac{eH}{\hbar c} \tag{11.5b}$$

In cyclotron resonance the transitions occur between subbands of the same band. Hence the modulating function $u_n(\mathbf{r})$ remains unchanged. For dipole transitions the harmonic-oscillator selection rules $\Delta l = \pm 1$ apply, which shows that, in this case, only transitions between neighboring subbands are allowed to first order in the perturbation.

The transition probability depends, however, not only on the matrix elements connecting the initial and final states but also on the density of states, which we now calculate. First, we recognize that although three quantum numbers, namely, l, k_x, and k_z, are required to specify a particular state, only two of these, l and k_z, appear in the expression for the energy. Thus each energy level is degenerate in k_x, the degree of degeneracy being given by the possible values this quantum number can take. It is left as a problem to show that in fact the degeneracy per unit area normal to $\mathbf{H}$ is $s/2\pi$. For given k_x and l, the number of states per unit length in the z direction in the energy interval $d\epsilon$ is $[(dN/dk_z)(d\epsilon/dk_z)]\,d\epsilon$; multiplying by the degeneracy $s/2\pi$ we have the desired result

$$\mathcal{N}_l(\epsilon) = \frac{2s}{h}(2m^*)^{\frac{1}{2}}(\epsilon - \epsilon_l)^{-\frac{1}{2}} \tag{11.6}$$

where ϵ_l is the energy at the edge of the lth subband.

It is instructive to compare (11.6) with the corresponding expression for an ordinary, three-dimensional band, Eq. (3.8). We note that whereas $\mathcal{N}(\epsilon)$ vanishes as $\epsilon \to \epsilon_0$, $\mathcal{N}_l(\epsilon)$ approaches infinity in the corresponding limit $\epsilon \to \epsilon_l$. The density-of-states curves for the valence and conduction bands of the ideal semiconductor with and without a magnetic field are shown in Fig. 11.2.

The singularities in the density-of-states curve play an essential role in the interband magnetooptic (IMO) effects, which we shall discuss shortly. In cyclotron resonance this $\mathcal{N}_l(\epsilon)$ function simply tells us that principally states near $k_z = 0$ will contribute to the absorption line.

Although we could have treated the problem classically, we have approached the phenomenon of cyclotron resonance from the quantum-mechanical viewpoint, so that we need not start afresh with our discussion of the closely related IMO effects. Moreover, elementary meth-

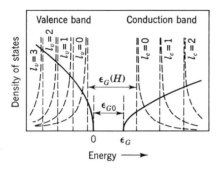

Fig. 11.2 Densities of states for a simple semiconductor for $H = 0$ (solid lines) and for $H > 0$ (heavy dashed lines). [*After E. Burstein, G. S. Picus, R. F. Wallis, and F. J. Blatt, Phys. Rev.,* **113**: 17 (1959).]

ods cannot be used to extend the treatment of cyclotron resonance so as to include degeneracy effects and spin-orbit coupling. On the other hand, the classical approach has the merit that it provides a vivid pictorial description and thereby allows good insight into the physics of the phenomenon.

The classical motion of a charged particle in a uniform magnetic field is a helix whose axis points along the field direction. The sense of rotation about the field direction is determined by the charge of the particle, and the circular frequency is the cyclotron frequency $\omega_c = eH/m^*c$. If we now apply an alternating electric field in the plane of the cyclotron orbit and set the frequency ω equal to ω_c, the charged particle will remain in phase with the alternating field and be accelerated by it. Thus, classically, its energy and also its orbit continually increase. If one represent the alternating field as the sum of two circularly polarized fields, one can show that only the left circularly polarized part accelerates electrons, whereas the right circularly polarized part interacts with holes orbiting in the magnetic field. It is, therefore, possible to determine the type of carrier responsible for resonant absorption at a given frequency through the use of circularly polarized instead of plane polarized radiation.

To obtain a reasonably sharp absorption peak it is, of course, necessary that the relaxation time τ of the carriers be at least as long as the cyclotron period, so that the orbiting carriers remain in phase with the applied rf field for at least one complete cycle. From the point of view of quantum theory, a finite lifetime τ implies an uncertainty $\Delta\epsilon$ in the energy of each orbital level, where $\Delta\epsilon \approx \hbar/\tau$. The energy levels will then overlap significantly if $\Delta\epsilon > \hbar\omega_c$, and the condition $\Delta\epsilon < \hbar\omega_c$ again leads to the requirement $\omega_c\tau > 1$. For this reason cyclotron resonance is normally performed at helium temperatures and in very pure single crystals.

Germanium and silicon In germanium and silicon the constant-energy surfaces of electrons are spheroids located at equivalent positions in the

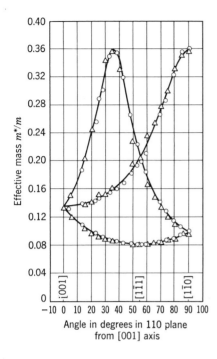

Angle in degrees in 110 plane
from [001] axis

Fig. 11.3 Effective mass of electrons in germanium at 4°K for magnetic-field direction in the (110) plane. [*From G. Dresselhaus, A. F. Kip, and C. Kittel, Phys. Rev.*, **98**: 376 (1955).]

Brillouin zone, and the effective mass for each spheroid is a tensor with two independent components $m_\parallel$ and $m_\perp$.   In this case the cyclotron frequency will be a function of orientation of the magnetic field relative to the major axis of the spheroid.   If **H** makes an angle θ with this axis one can show that

$$\omega_c^2 = \omega_\perp^2 \cos^2\theta + \omega_\perp\omega_\parallel \sin^2\theta \tag{11.7}$$

where

$$\omega_\perp = \frac{eH}{m_\perp c} \quad \text{and} \quad \omega_\parallel = \frac{eH}{m_\parallel c}$$

The *cyclotron resonance effective mass* is therefore given by

$$\left(\frac{1}{m^*}\right)^2 = \frac{\cos^2\theta}{m_\perp^2} + \frac{\sin^2\theta}{m_\perp m_\parallel} \tag{11.8}$$

For an arbitrary direction of **H** the cyclotron resonance effective masses are now different for different spheroids of the energy surface, and more than one resonance line is observed.   For example, in silicon, where the spheroidal axes are along the [100] directions, one finds two electron resonances if the magnetic field is also oriented along [100].   One of these corresponds to $m^* = m_\perp$, while for the other, $m^* = (m_\perp m_\parallel)^{\frac{1}{2}}$. Only in certain special field directions do the resonance lines overlap. It is, then, a relatively simple matter to determine the disposition of the spheroidal surfaces in the Brillouin zone by cyclotron resonance methods and to measure the masses. Figures 11.3 and 11.4 show the effective-mass anisotropies in n-type silicon and germanium. The currently accepted values for the effective masses of electrons are

	Ge	Si
$m_\perp/m_0$	0.0819 ± 0.0003	0.192 ± 0.001
$m_\parallel/m_0$	1.64 ± 0.03	0.90 ± 0.02

For holes in germanium and silicon the theory of cyclotron resonance is quite complicated. In these substances the p-like valence band is split by spin-orbit interaction into a fourfold degenerate (including spin) $p_{\frac{3}{2}}$ and a twofold degenerate $p_{\frac{1}{2}}$ state at $\mathbf{k} = 0$, with the $p_{\frac{3}{2}}$ state lying about 0.3 ev above the $p_{\frac{1}{2}}$ level. As we move away from the center of the zone the twofold orbital degeneracy of the $p_{\frac{3}{2}}$ state is lifted and one obtains two bands, the light- and heavy-hole bands.

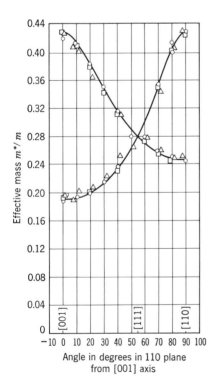

Fig. 11.4 Effective mass of electrons in silicon at 4°K for magnetic-field direction in the (110) plane. [*From G. Dresselhaus, A. F. Kip, and C. Kittel, Phys. Rev.,* **98**: 377 (1955).]

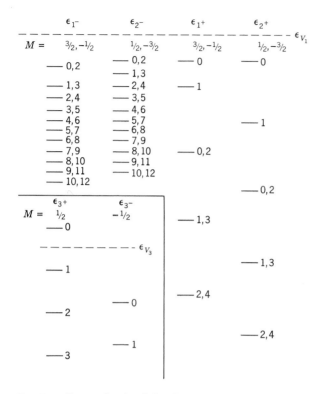

Fig. 11.5 Energy levels of the three valence bands in Ge in the presence of a magnetic field. The numbers next to each level are the l values that characterize that level. [*From E. Burstein, G. S. Picus, R. F. Wallis, and F. J. Blatt, Phys. Rev.*, **113**: 25 (1959).]

The degeneracy at $\mathbf{k} = 0$ greatly increases the complexity of the energy-level spectrum in a magnetic field. Provided one confines one's attention to Landau levels that are far from the band edges, i.e., to large l values, the energy levels form two sets of "ladders" whose rungs are uniformly spaced. The closely spaced rungs correspond to the heavy, the widely spaced rungs to the light holes. For small l, however, mixing of degenerate states results in large deviations from this uniform spacing (Fig. 11.5).

If, for the moment, we disregard the low l states, holes in germanium and silicon will show two cyclotron resonance lines. The normal experimental arrangement is one in which ν is held fixed and H, hence, ω_v, is varied, so that the light-hole line appears at the low-field value. Since transitions between the irregularly spaced low l levels occur at still different fields we may expect some fine structure. To observe the fine structure, however, only the lowest quantum levels should be populated in thermal equilibrium, and excitation to the higher quantum states must be kept at a minimum. The predicted fine structure has been observed by Fletcher [1] and collaborators and more recently by Stickler, Zeiger, and Heller [2], who used extremely sensitive microwave spectrometers and maintained their samples at very low temperature.

A second complication of the degeneracy of the valence bands is that the constant-energy contours near $\mathbf{k} = 0$ are "warped" spheres, that is,

$$\epsilon_p(\mathbf{k}) = \frac{\hbar^2}{2m} \{Ak^2 \pm [B^2k^4 + C^2(k_x^2k_y^2 + k_y^2k_z^2 + k_z^2k_x^2)]^{\frac{1}{2}}\} \tag{11.9}$$

There are two consequences of this ϵ versus k relation. First, the cyclotron resonance effective masses for light and heavy holes are anisotropic, as shown in Fig. 11.6. Second, cyclotron resonance absorption can also take place at harmonics of the fundamental frequency, the amplitudes of the harmonic absorption depending upon the degree of warping. In the case of the light holes the warping is quite small, as can be seen from the nearly isotropic effective mass (Fig. 11.6), and the harmonics are therefore too weak to be seen. Second- and third-harmonic resonances in germanium have been observed for the heavy holes by Dexter, Zeiger, and Lax [3].

In the preceding pages we have only touched on the most essential aspects of cyclotron resonance in semiconductors. Additional details, experimental and theoretical, are contained in the excellent review article by Lax and Mavroides.

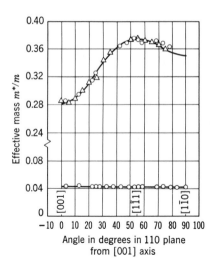

Fig. 11.6 Effective mass of holes in germanium at 4°K for magnetic-field directions in the (110) plane. [From G. Dresselhaus, A. F. Kip, and C. Kittel, Phys. Rev., **98**: 382 (1955).]

B. Interband Magnetooptic (IMO) Effects

Whereas cyclotron resonance involves transitions of carriers between Landau levels of one band, IMO effects arise as a result of interband transitions in a magnetic field.   Three interband absorption processes have been studied; to wit, direct, indirect, and exciton transitions.

Direct IMO absorption   Direct, i.e., vertical, interband transitions are indicated schematically in Fig. 11.7.   We assume here that these are allowed transitions.   In that case, to lowest order in perturbation theory, the selection rule is $\Delta l = 0$.   By contrast, the selection rule for cyclotron resonance is $\Delta l = \pm 1$.   Moreover, whereas in cyclotron resonance the energy difference between initial and final states was independent of k_z, the energy difference now depends markedly on k_z.   Thus, even in the absence of line broadening due to finite lifetime of the quantum states, no sharp absorption peaks should be expected.   Nevertheless, theory predicts a well-defined oscillatory pattern which is a consequence of the regular appearance of singularities in the density-of-states curve in a magnetic field (see Fig. 11.2).   According to Fig. 11.2, as we increase the frequency of the incident radiation we should observe an initial sharp absorption peak when $h\nu = \epsilon_G + \frac{1}{2}\hbar(\omega_c + \omega_v)$, followed by additional peaks at regular intervals of $\hbar(\omega_c + \omega_v)$.   Each peak should be characterized by a sharp rise on the low-frequency side, followed by a tail on the high-frequency side, corresponding to the gradual decay of the density of states with increasing energy.   Lifetime effects will, of course, further broaden the absorption pattern, and a theoretical curve of the form of Fig. 11.8 may be anticipated.

The experimental results reveal their oscillatory features most dramatically if the ratio of the intensity of the transmitted radiation with and without a magnetic field is plotted, as in Fig. 11.9.   This curve

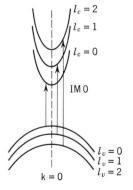

Fig. 11.7   Interband transitions for a simple semiconductor in the presence of a magnetic field.   [*After E. Burstein, G. S. Picus, R. F. Wallis, and F. J. Blatt, Phys. Rev.*, **113**: 19 (1959).]

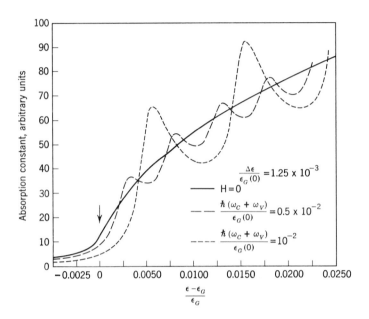

Fig. 11.8 Interband absorption spectrum for a simple semiconductor for $H = 0$ and $H > 0$. [*After E. Burstein, G. S. Picus, R. F. Wallis, and F. J. Blatt, Phys. Rev.*, **113**: 20 (1959).]

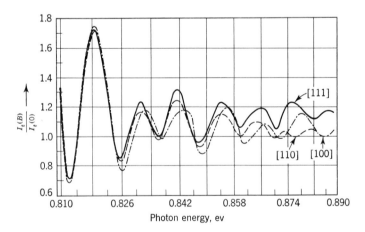

Fig. 11.9 Oscillatory magnetoabsorption of the direct transition in germanium at room temperature. $\mathbf{H} = 35.7$ kilogauss along the directions indicated. [*From B. Lax and S. Zwerdling, in A. F. Gibson (ed.), "Progress in Semiconductors," vol. 5, p. 226, John Wiley & Sons, Inc., New York*, 1961.]

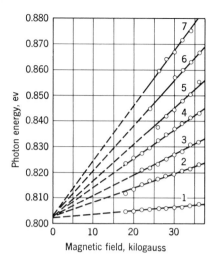

Fig. 11.10 Energy values of transmission minima versus magnetic field for successive transitions of electrons between Landau levels of valence and conduction bands in germanium. The convergence of lines yields an energy-gap value $\epsilon_G = 0.803 \pm 0.001$ ev at room temperature. [*From B. Lax and S. Zwerdling, in A. F. Gibson (ed.), "Progress in Semiconductors," vol. 5, p. 227, John Wiley & Sons, Inc., New York, 1961.*]

also exhibits an anisotropy which reflects the anisotropic character of the valence band in germanium, to which we have already referred.

Since absorption maxima appear at photon energies

$$h\nu = \epsilon_G + (n + \tfrac{1}{2}) \frac{eH}{c} \frac{m_n + m_p}{m_n m_p} \tag{11.10}$$

a plot of the position of a given peak (n fixed) as a function of H should be a straight line which extrapolates to ϵ_G as H goes to zero. A set of these lines is shown in Fig. 11.10. From such measurements the direct energy gap can be determined to great accuracy. In germanium it has the value $\epsilon_G = 0.803 \pm 0.001$ ev. Moreover, from the spacing between adjacent absorption peaks,

$$\frac{eH}{c} \frac{m_n + m_p}{m_n m_p}$$

the effective mass of electrons at $\mathbf{k} = 0$ can be determined, since the heavy-hole mass m_p is known from cyclotron resonance results. (The light holes, in consequence of the reduced density of states, do not play an important role in this absorption process.) The experimental value $m_n(\mathbf{k} = 0) = (0.037 \pm 0.0001)m$ is in excellent agreement with theoretical estimates.

In the foregoing we completely disregarded the spin of the electron and the splitting of the twofold spin degeneracy by the magnetic field. In the discussion of cyclotron resonance this was permissible, because the selection rule for this process is $\Delta m_s = 0$. Thus, though the $m_s = +\tfrac{1}{2}$

and $m_s = -\frac{1}{2}$ states are shifted by $g\beta H/2$, the resonance frequency is not affected by this shift.

In the IMO effect, on the other hand, first-order transitions occur for $\Delta m_s = 0, \pm 1$; which of these transitions is excited is determined by the polarization of the incident radiation. The situation is completely analogous to the usual Zeeman effect: If the Poynting vector is parallel to **H**, $\Delta m_s = +1$ transitions are induced by left circularly polarized light, and $\Delta m_s = -1$ transitions are induced by right circularly polarized light. In this configuration $\Delta m_s = 0$ transitions cannot be excited. If the Poynting vector is perpendicular to **H**, light polarized parallel to **H** causes $\Delta m_s = 0$ transitions, and, if $\mathbf{E} \perp \mathbf{H}$, $\Delta m_s = \pm 1$ transitions are excited. Figure 11.11 shows the difference between the IMO absorption pattern in germanium for right and left circularly polarized light. The somewhat complicated structure of the absorption curve is the result of nonuniform spacing of the first few Landau levels in the valence band of germanium, which has been mentioned previously. These quantum effects can be studied far more readily using interband transitions than by using cyclotron resonance. Further, from comparison of the spectra for two different polarizations, the g value of electrons in the conduction band could be determined and gave the anomalous value of -2.5. The g-factor anomaly is even more pronounced in InSb, where, in consequence of the small energy gap, small electron effective mass, and large spin-orbit

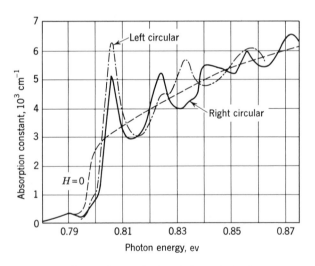

Fig. 11.11 Comparison of circularly polarized magneto-absorption spectra of the direct transition in germanium. [*From B. Lax and S. Zwerdling, in A. F. Gibson (ed.), "Progress in Semiconductors," vol. 5, p. 228, John Wiley & Sons, Inc., New York, 1961.*]

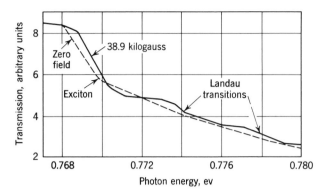

Fig. 11.12   The magnetoabsorption spectrum of the indirect transition in germanium at 1.5°K showing the exciton absorption edge at zero field and the development of the "staircase" absorption edges for the Landau transitions at higher energies at 38.9 kilogauss. [*From B. Lax and S. Zwerdling, in A. F. Gibson (ed.), "Progress in Semiconductors," vol. 5, p. 233, John Wiley & Sons, Inc., New York, 1961.*]

coupling, it is -54.   This is in very good agreement with theoretical estimates, which yield $g = -56$.

Indirect IMO absorption   The shape of the indirect absorption edge is also sensitive to a magnetic field, although the changes are not as spectacular as for direct transitions.   The principal reason is that, as a result of the additional phonon interaction, there are no selection rules limiting Δl, and all values of Δl consistent with the available photon energy are permitted.   Consequently, the spectrum is now no longer a series of fairly sharp lines followed by tails on the high-frequency side, but is a succession of steps, each new step indicating the onset of a transition to or from a new Landau level.   Finite relaxation times again broaden the pattern so that the steps appear with finite slope, as shown in Fig. 11.12. By plotting the derivative of the transmission curve against photon energy, the position of the "steps" can be fixed fairly accurately.   As before, a plot of the energy of the nth step against the magnetic field is a straight line which extrapolates to the indirect gap at zero field, plus (or minus) the energy of the phonon which participates in the indirect transition (see Fig. 11.13).   Measurements at 1.5°K have shown that the indirect gap in germanium is 0.744 ± 0.001 ev.

Exciton IMO absorption   The first step in Fig. 11.12 is actually the result of exciton formation rather than of interband transitions.   That it is not an interband transition is apparent from the fact that (1) the energy

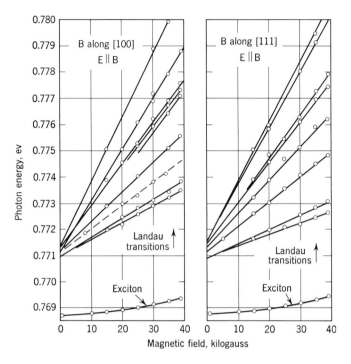

Fig. 11.13   Position of indirect transitions in germanium at 1.5°K as a function of magnetic field showing the quadratic Zeeman effect of the exciton and linear convergence of the Landau levels. [*From B. Lax and S. Zwerdling, in A. F. Gibson (ed.), "Progress in Semiconductors," vol. 5, p. 233, John Wiley & Sons, Inc., New York, 1961.*]

shift is quadratic rather than linear in H, and (2) the curve in Fig. 11.13 marked "exciton" extrapolates to an energy well below that of all the other lines.   Careful measurements using high-resolution techniques have revealed the presence of two exciton lines corresponding to binding energies of 2.1×10^{-3} and 3.2×10^{-3} ev.

The direct exciton has also been studied by the IMO method, and experimental and theoretical results are again in good accord.

Evidently, the study of optical absorption in a magnetic field is a very versatile and powerful method for determining a variety of fundamental and interesting properties of semiconductors.   These studies do not duplicate, but rather extend and supplement, cyclotron resonance work.

Further discussion may be found in the review article by Lax and Zeiger, who also consider other magnetooptic phenomena, such as Faraday rotation and the Zeeman splitting of impurity levels by a magnetic field.

11.3 HIGH–FIELD EFFECTS IN METALS

We begin our discussion by treating orbital quantization of electrons anew, this time using what may be called a geometric approach. This line of argument will prove extremely valuable in the latter portions of the chapter.

Consider, then, an electron in the state $\mathbf{k}$ with energy $\epsilon(\mathbf{k})$. The velocity of this electron, $\mathbf{v}(\mathbf{k}) = (1/\hbar)\nabla_{\mathbf{k}}\epsilon$, need not be directed along $\mathbf{k}$. Under the influence of a magnetic field $\mathbf{H}$ the electron will move according to

$$\dot{\mathbf{k}} = \frac{e}{\hbar c}\, \mathbf{v} \times \mathbf{H} = \frac{e}{\hbar^2 c}\, (\nabla_{\mathbf{k}}\epsilon) \times \mathbf{H} \tag{11.11}$$

over the surface of constant energy $\epsilon(\mathbf{k})$. It is now evident from (11.11) that the path of the $\mathbf{k}$ vector traces out the curve formed by the intersection of the surface of constant energy and the plane which passes through the initial value of $\mathbf{k}$ and is perpendicular to $\mathbf{H}$. The rate at which the representative point moves along this curve is proportional to $\mathbf{H}$ and to the component of velocity normal to $\mathbf{H}$. If we write $\dot{\mathbf{r}}$ for $\mathbf{v}(\mathbf{k})$ and integrate (11.11) the result

$$\mathbf{k}(t) = \frac{e}{\hbar c}\, \mathbf{r}(t) \times \mathbf{H} \tag{11.12}$$

shows that the orbits in $\mathbf{k}$ space and in real space are identical, except for the scale factor $H(e/\hbar c)$ and a rotation by $\pi/2$ about an axis parallel to $\mathbf{H}$.

Two qualitatively different situations can now arise. Either the orbit in $\mathbf{k}$ space traces out a closed curve, or, in the periodically extended zone scheme, the trajectory is an open orbit, passing from one zone into the adjacent one, never returning to its starting point. The intermediate case, an extended, though closed, orbit in the extended zone scheme, is also possible, but for present purposes this situation is fundamentally a closed orbit.

To show how closed and open electron and hole orbits can arise we take a simple cubic lattice in which the Fermi surface touches the zone boundaries in the [100] directions. In the extended zone scheme the Fermi surface is then a relatively simple, though multiply connected surface, as shown in Fig. 11.14a.

If now the magnetic field is oriented along one of the cube axes, say, the z axis, there arise two extremal areas from the intersections of the (001) plane with the Fermi surface, one corresponding to closed electron orbits and the other to closed hole orbits. These are shown in

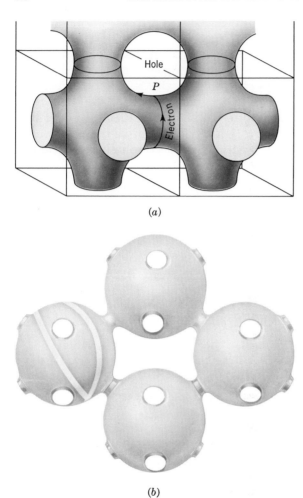

(a)

(b)

Fig. 11.14 (a) A multiply connected Fermi surface showing "electron" orbits and "hole" orbits. At a point such as P the carriers may belong to both types. (*From J. M. Ziman, "Principles of the Theory of Solids," p. 264, Cambridge University Press, London, 1964.*) (b) Model of the Fermi surface of gold in the periodically extended-zone scheme showing the belly orbits (white rings), neck orbits (black rings), and the central "dog's-bone" hole orbit. (*From H. M. Rosenberg, "Low Temperature Solid State Physics," Oxford University Press, London, 1963.*)

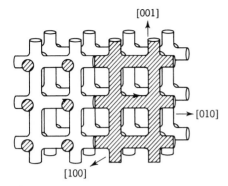

[001]

[010]

[100]

Fig. 11.15 One possible type of open Fermi surface for a cubic metal, showing two sections of constant k_H for **H** along [100]. Left: electron orbits; right: hole orbits. (*After C. Kittel, "Quantum Theory of Solids," p. 232, John Wiley & Sons, Inc., New York, 1963.*)

Fig. 11.15.   A closed electron orbit may be defined as one in which the path of the **k** vector over the constant-energy surface encloses an occupied region in **k** space; a closed hole orbit encloses a region of unoccupied states in the extended zone.

To produce an open orbit we need only tilt the magnetic field in the (100) plane.   As shown in Fig. 11.16, regions of closed orbits are now separated by open orbits in **k** space.   This particular open orbit is "periodic" in the sense that the motion in **k** space repeats as the orbit passes from one zone into the adjacent zone.   A slight, arbitrary tilt of **H** away from the (010) plane results in electron and hole orbits that are then separated by an aperiodic open orbit, as demonstrated in Fig. 11.17.

As we shall see presently, open orbits have a profound effect on the magnetoresistance at high magnetic fields.   For the moment we merely note the following features concerning open orbits.   First, the plane of the orbit in **k** space is always perpendicular to the magnetic field, as is, of course, also true for closed orbits.   Second, since the velocity of an electron is perpendicular to the constant-energy surface, the average velocity of an electron in an open orbit is perpendicular to both **H** and the average direction of the orbit in **k** space.   Thus, if with **H** in the

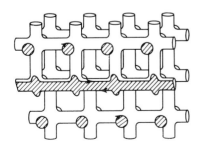

Fig. 11.16 Section of Fermi surface for **H** in (010) plane, showing the periodic open orbits bounding the central shaded strip.   Electron orbits above and below.   (*From C. Kittel, "Quantum Theory of Solids," p. 232, John Wiley & Sons, Inc, New York, 1963.*)

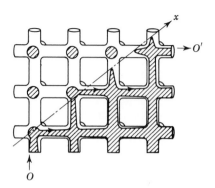

Fig. 11.17 As in Fig. 11.16 but with **H** tilted slightly away from [100] in an arbitrary direction. Regions of electron orbits (top left) and hole orbits (bottom right), separated by an aperiodic open orbit OO'. Direction of open orbit taken as x axis. (*From C. Kittel, "Quantum Theory of Solids,"* p. 233, *John Wiley & Sons, Inc., New York,* 1963.)

z direction there exists an open orbit directed along k_x, the electron in this orbit will carry a current in the y direction. This situation is in sharp contrast to that which prevails for closed orbits, for which the average velocity vanishes.

If the Fermi surface is a simply connected closed surface, all orbits are closed. In that case one can rederive the orbital quantization condition directly from the Bohr theory. The Bohr quantization condition is

$$\oint \mathbf{p} \cdot d\mathbf{s} = (n + \beta)h \tag{11.13}$$

where $\mathbf{p}$ and $\mathbf{s}$ are canonically conjugate momenta and coordinates, n is an integer, and β is a phase factor. In the presence of a magnetic field the linear momentum $\mathbf{p}$ must be replaced by $\mathbf{p} - (e/c)\mathbf{A}$, and writing $\hbar\mathbf{k}$ for $\mathbf{p}$ we have

$$\oint \left(\hbar\mathbf{k} - \frac{e}{c}\mathbf{A} \right) \cdot d\mathbf{s} = (n + \beta)h \tag{11.14}$$

Now

$$\oint \mathbf{A} \cdot d\mathbf{s} = \mathcal{S}H \tag{11.15}$$

where $\mathcal{S}$ is the area enclosed by the orbit. From (11.12)

$$\oint \hbar\mathbf{k} \cdot d\mathbf{s} = \frac{e}{c} H \oint \mathbf{r} \times d\mathbf{s} = 2 \frac{e}{c} \mathcal{S}H \tag{11.16}$$

Thus (11.14) becomes

$$\frac{e}{c} \mathcal{S}H = (n + \beta)h \tag{11.17}$$

Finally, according to (11.12), the area of the orbit in **k** space is just

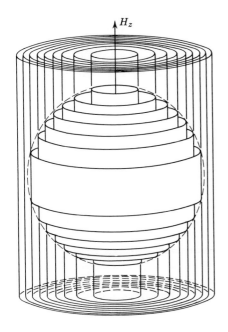

Fig. 11.18   The quantization of the energy spectrum in the xy-plane into discrete cylindrical surfaces in k space under the influence of an applied magnetic field H_z. (*From H. M. Rosenberg, "Low Temperature Solid State Physics,"* p. 352, *Oxford University Press, London,* 1963.)

$(eH/c\hbar)^2$ times the area in real space, so that (11.17) is equivalent to

$$\mathscr{A}(\epsilon) = \frac{2\pi eH}{\hbar c}(n + \beta) \tag{11.18}$$

where $\mathscr{A}(\epsilon)$ is the area of the orbit in $\mathbf{k}$ space.

For a free-electron gas, $\mathscr{A}(\epsilon) = \pi k_\perp{}^2 = 2\pi m\epsilon_\perp/\hbar^2$, where $\epsilon_\perp$ is the energy associated with motion normal to $\mathbf{H}$. Thus (11.18) corresponds to the quantization condition (11.3a), provided β is chosen $\frac{1}{2}$. Motion along $\mathbf{H}$ is, of course, not quantized. Thus in the magnetic field the allowed-energy states are not distributed uniformly in $\mathbf{k}$ space but instead lie on right cylinders whose cross sections satisfy (11.18). This is shown in Fig. 11.18, together with the Fermi surface (dashed circle), in the absence of a magnetic field.

As H is increased the cylinders of constant n move outward and the furthest will pass through the Fermi surface when

$$\frac{2\pi eH}{\hbar c}(n + \tfrac{1}{2}) = \mathscr{A}_0$$

where $\mathscr{A}_0$ is the *extremal cross-sectional area* of the Fermi surface in a plane normal to $\mathbf{H}$. Thus, when

$$\frac{1}{H} = (n + \tfrac{1}{2})\frac{2\pi e}{\hbar c \mathscr{A}_0} \tag{11.19}$$

the nth cylinder just touches the Fermi surface and will pass beyond it if H is increased ever so slightly.

We have already noted that, in one-dimensional subbands, $\mathcal{N}_l(\epsilon)$ has a singularity at $k_z = 0$. Consequently, we expect that whenever (11.19) is satisfied, $\mathcal{N}(\eta)$ will attain a maximum and then fall sharply to a smaller value, rising to another maximum as H is further increased and (11.19) is once again satisfied with n diminished by one. Moreover, since the orbital degeneracy $s = eH/\hbar c$ increases with H, these oscillations in $\mathcal{N}(\eta)$ should also increase in amplitude. To summarize, then, $\mathcal{N}(\eta)$ should exhibit periodic variations in $1/H$, whose period $2\pi e/\hbar c \mathcal{A}_0$ is a measure of the extremal cross section of the Fermi surface in a plane perpendicular to $\mathbf{H}$, and whose amplitude increases with increasing magnetic field.

Now we have seen in the preceding chapters, particularly Chaps. 3 and 7, that practically all electronic properties of metals depend on the density of states at the Fermi energy. This is true of the electronic specific heat, paramagnetic susceptibility, conductivity, Hall effect, thermoelectric power, and others which have not yet been mentioned, such as the diamagnetic susceptibility. Indirectly, $\mathcal{N}(\eta)$ also plays a role in such apparently nonelectronic properties as velocity of sound and bulk modulus. It now follows from what has just been said that, under appropriate experimental conditions, periodic variations should manifest themselves in every one of these phenomena. All experiments to date have substantiated this prediction.

There are basically two "appropriate experimental conditions" for the observation of oscillatory effects. First, the thermal spread of the distribution function must be small compared to the spacing between orbitally quantized levels, so that the effect of quantization is not "washed out." Thus we require that $kT < 2\beta^*H$, where β^* is the effective Bohr magneton

$$\beta^* = \frac{e\hbar}{2m^*c} \tag{11.20}$$

and m^* is an effective mass defined by

$$m^* = \frac{1}{2\pi}\left(\frac{d\mathcal{A}_0}{d\epsilon}\right) \tag{11.21}$$

Second, the sample must be sufficiently pure and the temperature sufficiently low so that the relaxation time is long. Otherwise uncertainty broadening of the levels will prevent the appearance of well-defined oscillations. The condition here is the same as in cyclotron resonance, namely, $2\beta^*H > \tau/\hbar$, or $\omega_c\tau > 1$.

Finally, we must work with a material in which the electron density is high enough so that $\eta > 2\beta^*H$ when H has attained the necessary magnitude to meet the first two conditions. If this last requirement on the Fermi energy is not fulfilled all electrons will have condensed into the lowest orbital state before any oscillations can be observed.

To appreciate the orders of magnitude involved here, let us calculate the pertinent parameters for a free-electron gas having a density corresponding to that in metallic sodium. We take $m^*/m = 1$, in agreement with calculation and recent experimental results. In this case, then $2\beta^*/k = 0.15°K/kilogauss$. Our first condition now tells us that we should need fields in excess of 20 kilogauss, even if we maintain the sample near 1°K. For spherical energy surfaces, $\mathscr{A}_0 = \pi k_F{}^2$; for Na, $\mathscr{A}_0 \simeq 3 \times 10^{16}$ cm^{-2}. According to (11.19) the period in $1/H$ is then $\Delta(1/H) \simeq 5 \times 10^{-10} \simeq \Delta H/H^2$. Consequently, at a field of 20 kilogauss the intervals between successive maxima would be about 0.2 gauss.

Evidently the conditions for observing oscillatory effects are not particularly favorable in sodium. For ease of observation we should like a small effective mass so that β^* will be large, and a sufficiently small effective number of carriers so that $\mathscr{A}_0$ will be small, making $\Delta(1/H)$ fairly large. In this last phrase the words "effective number" are crucial. What concerns us here is the area $\mathscr{A}_0$ of closed portions of the Fermi surface in any Brillouin zone. In general then, polyvalent metals are more likely candidates for oscillatory behavior than are monovalent metals. In the latter the first Brillouin zone can easily accommodate within a closed Fermi surface all the valence electrons. In the former, however, band overlap is bound to occur, and the Fermi surface in the various Brillouin zones then forms several surfaces for which $\mathscr{A}_0$ may be quite small. In a divalent metal, for example, we may find a small group of holes in the first zone and an equally small group of electrons in the second zone. Both will in general contribute to oscillatory effects. Moreover, in these cases the effective masses are frequently small fractions of the free-electron mass. The first observations of the de Haas-van Alphen effect in bismuth, followed by measurements in Sb and As (pentavalent), graphite and Sn (tetravalent), Al, Ga, In, and Tl (trivalent), and Zn, Cd, and Hg (bivalent), predate the first successful experiments on Cu, Ag, Au, and the alkali metals by decades not despite, but rather in consequence of, the complexity of the Fermi surface of polyvalent metals as compared to that of the monovalent metals.

A.   De Haas-van Alphen (HA) Effect

Of the several oscillatory effects, the de Haas-van Alphen (HA) effect is the best known and most extensively studied. It concerns the periodic variations of the magnetic susceptibility with magnetic field at low temperatures. Although often described as oscillations in the diamagnetic susceptibility, the spin susceptibility also participates, though it normally plays only a minor role. The reason for this is that, in most metals, HA oscillations originate primarily from those regions of the Fermi surface where m^* is very small. Since the nonperiodic part of the diamagnetic susceptibility of an electron gas is

$$\chi_d = -\frac{\hbar\beta^*}{2\eta} \tag{11.22}$$

HA observations, pronounced when β^* is large, are most dramatic in highly diamagnetic materials. The dominant term of the oscillatory part of the magnetic susceptibility is of the form

$$\chi_{\text{osc}} = -C\frac{(\beta^*)^{\frac{1}{2}}kT}{(H)^{\frac{3}{2}}}\, e^{-\pi^2 kT_e/\beta^* H}\, \sin\left[\frac{\hbar c\mathscr{A}_0}{2\pi e H} - 2\pi \mp \frac{\pi}{4}\right]\cos\left(\frac{\pi m^*}{m}\right) \tag{11.23}$$

Here the last factor, $\cos(\pi m^*/m)$, has its origin in the paramagnetic contribution and is often omitted, since m^*/m is usually so small that the factor itself is very nearly one. In some cases, for example, in copper, it plays an essential role and can cause the disappearance of the oscillatory term for certain orientations of the magnetic field. T_e in the exponential factor is an effective temperature which includes the effect of uncertainty broadening of the oscillations. Under reasonable simplifying assumptions one obtains

$$T_e = T + \frac{\hbar}{\pi k\tau} \tag{11.24}$$

Finally, the sign of the phase in the argument of the sine depends on whether the surface in question is electron- or hole-like, i.e., whether the extremal area $\mathscr{A}_0$ is a maximum ($-$ sign) or a minimum ($+$ sign). The full expression for the oscillatory portion of χ contains higher harmonics not included in (11.23) which are, however, usually damped out very quickly at even fairly low temperatures.

It would be difficult to overstate the role of the HA effect in the elucidation of the Fermi surface of metals. The extremal cross section of the Fermi surface as a function of crystal orientation can be determined directly from measurement of the period of the HA oscillations. With this information plus a knowledge of the crystal symmetry and the total number of valence electrons, a nearly complete three-dimensional picture of the Fermi surface can often be constructed. In almost all cases certain complications do arise. For one, with the exception of the alkali metals, the HA pattern is normally a superposition of several

oscillatory terms of different frequencies, because with arbitrary orientation of $\mathbf{H}$, and a fairly complicated Fermi surface, there exist several
extremal areas. Thus the curve of χ versus $1/H$ may have a complicated appearance and must be Fourier analyzed to extract the desired
information.

     To demonstrate the origin of such complicated patterns let us
consider a simple square lattice of polyvalent atoms and assume that
the magnetic field is directed normal to the plane of this two-dimensional
lattice.   The orbital plane is then the plane of Fig. 11.19.   The first
zone in the figure is completely filled.   The Fermi circle intersects the
second, third, and fourth Brillouin zones and, by the usual translation
through reciprocal-lattice vectors, these surfaces can be reformed, as they
appear in Fig. 11.20.   Now we know that at the Brillouin-zone boundaries of such a square lattice the Fermi surface must always be normal to
the zone face, so that the true energy surface is more nearly as shown in
Fig. 11.19b.   Hence the various sections of the Fermi surface will have
their corners rounded somewhat.   However, the general features of these
surfaces are still preserved.   As Harrison has demonstrated [4], this
simple geometrical construction, extended to three dimensions, frequently
yields energy surfaces in quite good agreement with HA results and

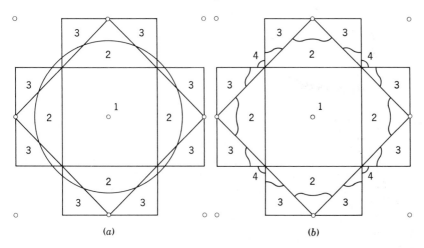

(a)   (b)

Fig. 11.19 (a) First three Brillouin zones of a simple square lattice. Reciprocal-
lattice points are shown as dots.   Zone boundaries are the bisectors of lines joining
reciprocal-lattice points.   The numbers denote the zone in order of increasing energy
(as measured by k^2) to which the segment belongs.   The circle drawn represents a
Fermi surface with area in zones 2, 3, and 4 (not shown).   (b) Same as (a), but showing distortion of Fermi surface by a weak crystal potential.   The Fermi surface is
made to intersect the zone boundaries at right angles.   *(From C. Kittel, "Quantum
Theory of Solids," p. 257, John Wiley & Sons, Inc., New York, 1963.)*

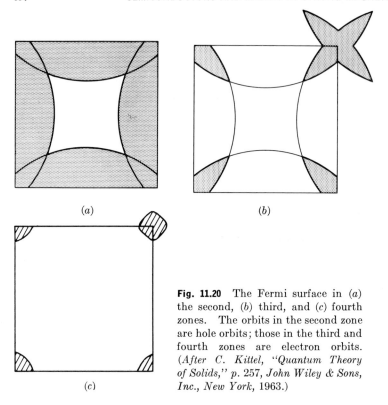

(a)   (b)

Fig. 11.20 The Fermi surface in (a) the second, (b) third, and (c) fourth zones. The orbits in the second zone are hole orbits; those in the third and fourth zones are electron orbits. (*After C. Kittel, "Quantum Theory of Solids," p. 257, John Wiley & Sons, Inc., New York, 1963.*)

(c)

invariably serves as an excellent guide in the interpretation of HA measurements.

Harrison has also given a simple recipe for constructing the Fermi surface in the free-electron, or single orthogonalized-plane-wave (OPW) approximation. We draw a circle (in three dimensions, a sphere) of the correct size to accommodate all valence electrons about each point of the reciprocal lattice, as shown in Fig. 11.21. Then a point in **k** space contained within at least one sphere lies within the first zone. Points contained within two spheres correspond to occupied states in the second zone, and so on. The second-, third-, and fourth-zone surfaces, using the Harrison construction, are shown in Fig. 11.21.

In this particular, two-dimensional example, there are three closed orbits, a hole orbit (second zone) and two electron orbits (third and fourth zones), and the corresponding HA pattern would be a superposition of three oscillatory terms.

In addition to size and shape of the Fermi surface, further information may be extracted if the amplitudes of HA oscillations are studied as functions of the field and temperature. Provided $kT/\beta^*H \ll 1$, then the amplitude A divided by the temperature should increase exponentially with decreasing temperature.   Hence a plot of $\ln (A/T)$ versus kT should be a straight line of slope $-\pi^2/\beta^*H$.   This behavior is generally observed, except at very high fields and low temperatures, where deviations occur that are attributable to the appearance of harmonics that have been neglected in (11.23).[†]   Relative amplitude measurements over a range of temperatures are therefore of interest because they provide a measure of β^*, that is, of $d\mathcal{A}_0/d\epsilon$ at the Fermi energy.

One may also measure the amplitude of HA oscillations as a function of H at constant temperature.   Equation (11.23) predicts that a plot of $\ln (AH^{\frac{3}{2}}T^{-1})$ versus $1/H$ should be a straight line of slope $-\pi^2 kT_e/\beta^*$.   If β^* has been obtained from the temperature dependence of A, the effective relaxation time can be determined [see Eq. (11.24)].

[†] Actually, the magnetic induction $\mathbf{B} = \mathbf{H} + 4\pi\mathbf{M}$ rather than $\mathbf{H}$ should appear on the right-hand side of Eq. (11.23).   This correction greatly complicates the theoretical pattern, since the relationship between $\mathbf{M}$ and $\mathbf{H}$ (or χ and $\mathbf{H}$) is now an implicit transcendental equation which has the approximate form

$$M = D \sin \left(\frac{\hbar c \mathcal{A}_0}{H + 4\pi M} \right)$$

where D is a constant.   Nonlinear effects attributable to this correction are quite pronounced in beryllium and have also been observed in other metals.

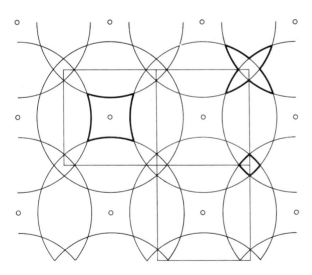

Fig. 11.21   Harrison construction for the square lattice of Fig. 11.19(a) showing Fermi surfaces in the second, third, and fourth zones.   (*From C. Kittel, "Quantum Theory of Solids," p. 259, John Wiley & Sons, Inc., New York, 1963.*)

The results of amplitude measurements generally confirm the validity of (11.23). The values of τ, however, are often much shorter than the relaxation time deduced from the residual resistivity. This discrepancy is still not entirely resolved. Of course, there is little justification for assuming that the relaxation time which characterizes the randomizing of linear momentum (conductivity) should be the same as that which describes the lifetime in an angular-momentum quantum state (HA lifetime). Moreover, the portions of the Fermi surface which contribute to χ_{osc} do not normally make the dominant contribution to the conductivity, and the relaxation times may well differ substantially over different portions of a complicated Fermi surface.

Turning now to the experimental side, two methods have been used extensively in the study of the HA effect, and a third, which holds great promise for certain special situations, has been developed in recent years. The first, and oldest, method is the direct measurement of χ, using a torque balance, in a steady magnetic field. Excellent, reliable results have been obtained over the years by this technique on a variety of metals. The principal disadvantage of the method is that only long-period oscillations can be studied with relative ease.

The pulse method was devised especially to allow observation of short-period oscillations. Here the sample is located inside one of a pair of identical coils connected in series opposition. Both coils, the dummy and the sample, are placed inside a solenoid carefully wound to produce a field of high homogeneity over the region occupied by the two coils. Normally the solenoid is placed in the liquid air jacket of a helium dewar, and only the sample and the pickup coils are kept at helium temperatures. Fields of several hundred kilogauss are produced by discharging a condenser bank through the solenoid. As the field increases, the emf generated in each coil is proportional to dM/dt, hence to dM/dH. In the coil containing the sample the induced emf has an oscillatory component due to the oscillatory part of the sample magnetization. The output signals are usually displayed on a double-beam oscilloscope, one trace of which shows the magnetic field and the other the oscillatory signal from the pickup coils.

Besides extending the range of available magnetic fields by at least an order of magnitude, the pulse method has further advantages. Since the signal is proportional to dM/dH, not M/H as in the steady-state method, the signal amplitude is enhanced by a factor $2\pi/H\Delta(1/H)$. Moreover, if the field pulse is carefully shaped, oscillations in $(1/H)$ can be made to appear as periodic oscillations in time. If then the pickup coils are made part of a tuned LC circuit, the Fourier decomposition of the HA oscillations can be accomplished electrically by simply adjusting the resonant frequency of the pickup circuit.

There are, of course, some disadvantages to the pulse method as well.   First, it is not well suited to measurements of the absolute or relative amplitudes of oscillations.   Second, from the necessary geometry of the experimental apparatus it is clear that the relative orientation of the field and crystal axes cannot be altered readily.   Third, eddy currents in high-conductivity samples result in a nonuniform field in the sample, even though the applied field is homogeneous.   Fortunately, in most materials the magnetoresistance reduces eddy currents sufficiently to permit the observation of the HA effect with the pulse method.

In the third method, developed by Shoenberg and Stiles [5], the magnetic field is maintained absolutely constant and the sample, surrounded by a pickup coil, is rotated slowly in the field.   The susceptibility now oscillates, because $\mathscr{A}_0$ changes with orientation.   Since the argument of the sinusoidal function in (11.23) is very large in most cases (for Na in a field of 20 kilogauss, $\hbar c \mathscr{A}_0 / 2\pi eH \sim 10^5$), an extremely small fractional change of $\mathscr{A}_0$ results in rapid oscillations of χ and induces thereby a high-frequency signal in the pickup coil.   The method is ideally suited for investigations of the anisotropy of nearly spherical Fermi surfaces, such as those of the alkali metals.   The technique can only succeed if the magnetic field is absolutely steady, a condition that can now be met with a superconducting magnet operating in the persistent-current mode.

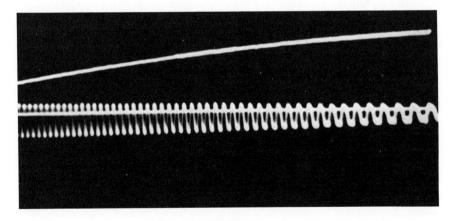

(a)

Fig. 11.22   Examples of de Haas-van Alphen oscillations.   (a) De Haas-van Alphen oscillations in a copper crystal at about 10^5 gauss, obtained using the pulsed field technique.   The curved trace across the picture shows the manner in which the field varies during the impulsive discharge through the coil.   (*From H. M. Rosenberg,* "*Low Temperature Solid State Physics,*" *Oxford University Press, London,* 1963.)

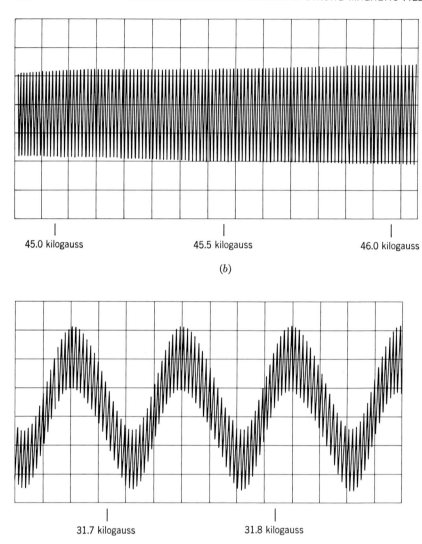

45.0 kilogauss   45.5 kilogauss   46.0 kilogauss

(b)

31.7 kilogauss   31.8 kilogauss

(c)

Fig. 11-22 (*Continued*)   (*b*) De Haas-van Alphen effect in gold with $H \parallel$ [110].   The oscillation is from the dog's-bone orbit of Fig. 11.14*b*.   The signal is related to the second derivative of the magnetic moment with respect to field.   The results were obtained by a field modulation technique in a high-homogeneity superconducting solenoid at about 1.2°K.   (*c*) De Haas-van Alphen effect in gold with $H \parallel$ [111], showing the belly (fine spacing) and neck (coarse spacing) oscillations.   [(*b*) *and* (*c*) *from C. Kittel, "Introduction to Solid State Physics," p. 295, John Wiley & Sons, Inc., New York, 1956.*]

B.   Cyclotron (Az'bel-Kaner) Resonance

The usual cyclotron resonance experiments, which work so well in semi-conductors, cannot be carried out in metals, because at frequencies such that $\omega_c\tau > 1$ the skin depth is so small that the electromagnetic radiation penetrates only a fraction of a mean free path into the metal.   In pure copper, for example, the relaxation time at 4°K is roughly 10^{-10} sec and the velocity at the Fermi surface is about 1.6×10^8 cm/sec.   Hence the mean free path is about 10^{-2} cm.   If $\omega_c\tau$ is to be larger than 1, the applied magnetic field must be of such strength that $\omega_c > 10^{10}$ sec^{-1}. At 24,000 Mc, a frequency at which many measurements have been performed, the skin depth δ is only about 10^{-5} cm; i.e., we are well into the anomalous skin-depth region where $\delta \ll l$.

Not only is $\delta \ll l$, but $\delta \ll r_c$, where r_c is the radius of a cyclotron orbit, $r_c = v_F/\omega_c \sim 10^{-3}$ cm.   Az'bel and Kaner [6] first suggested that one could take advantage of this large ratio of r_c/δ in the following ingenious manner.   If the applied magnetic field is oriented parallel to the surface of a highly polished specimen, electrons near the surface

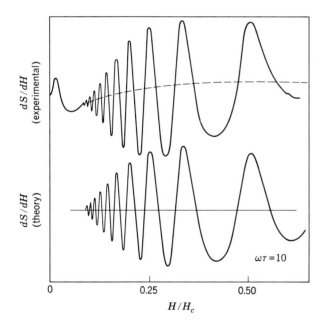

Fig. 11.23 Cyclotron resonance absorption in copper; comparison of calculations of the magnetic-field dependence of the derivative of the surface resistivity with experimental results at 24,000 Mc. (*From C. Kittel, "Quantum Theory of Solids," p. 318, John Wiley & Sons, Inc., New York, 1963.*)

of the sample will describe helical orbits which penetrate the skin depth once every cyclotron period. If now the angular frequency of the rf field equals ω_c, then each time the electron surfaces into the skin depth it will be in phase with the oscillating electric field and can be accelerated by it. During the portion of the rf cycle when the electric field is in such a direction as to decelerate the electron, the particle is deeply submerged below the skin depth and is unaware of the existence of the rf field. Resonant absorption will occur not only when $\omega_c = \omega$, but for all subharmonics; i.e., whenever $\omega_c = \omega/p$, where p is an integer. In that case the rf field completes p cycles between successive penetrations of the electron into the skin-depth region. The observed and theoretically predicted pattern for a single crystal of pure copper is shown in Fig. 11.23, in which the subharmonic pattern is beautifully displayed.

In contrast to the HA effect, the resonant frequency in the AK resonance experiment is a measure of the average effective mass

$$m_c = \frac{1}{2\pi} \frac{d\mathscr{A}_0}{d\epsilon}$$

over an extremal orbit. Wherever effective masses from AK and HA experiments are available they are in good agreement. The determination of effective masses by the AK technique is, of course, much more precise and also an easier matter experimentally.

C. Ultrasonic Resonances

Before turning to the galvanomagnetic effects, we mention yet another quasi-resonance technique that has been employed with considerable success in the study of Fermi surfaces of metals.

If a longitudinal sound wave with wave vector q_x is propagated through a metal, the alternating regions of compression and dilatation will establish a sinusoidally varying electric field within the crystal. If we also impose a steady magnetic field perpendicular to the direction of propagation of the sound wave, a resonance condition can arise when the spatial extension of the cyclotron orbit is an integral multiple of the sonic wavelength. In the theoretical analysis of the phenomenon it is permissible to neglect the velocity of the sound wave, since it is orders of magnitude smaller than that of an electron at the Fermi surface. Thus, one considers the electric field as permanently frozen in the lattice, with electrons moving under the influence of this temporally steady, spatially sinusoidally varying electric and uniform magnetic field. The condition for maxima in the absorption of the ultrasonic wave is then found to be

$$\Delta x \simeq (n + \gamma)\lambda_q \tag{11.25}$$

where Δx is the extension of the cyclotron orbit in the x direction, λ_q is the wavelength of the ultrasonics, and γ is a phase factor of about $\pi/4$. Since the orbits in real space and reciprocal space are identical except for the scale factor $eH/\hbar c$ and a rotation by $\pi/2$, the condition for "geometrical" resonance is

$$\frac{1}{H} = (n + \gamma) \frac{e\lambda_q}{2\hbar c \, \Delta k_y} \tag{11.26}$$

Thus we find once again an oscillatory behavior in $1/H$. However, in contrast to the HA oscillations, the period is now determined by the "caliper" dimension Δk_y and not by the area of an extremal orbit. The techniques thus complement rather than duplicate each other.

If the Fermi surface is such as to support open orbits, another very interesting resonance phenomenon can occur. Let us assume that with **H** transverse to q_x as before, there is an open orbit which, in **k** space, extends along k_y. In real space the electron will therefore move along the x direction with an average velocity $\bar{v}_x$ on which there is superimposed a periodic variation corresponding to the periodic pattern of its motion along the trajectory in **k** space. The periodicity in **k** space is just equal to a reciprocal lattice vector **K**, and thus in real space is equal to $\dfrac{\hbar c}{eH} K$. Consequently, a resonant condition obtains when

$$\lambda = \frac{\hbar c}{eH} K \tag{11.27}$$

There is an essential and fundamental difference between this open orbit resonance and all other resonance phenomena that have been discussed previously. According to Eq. (11.27) the resonance condition involves no features of the Fermi surface whatever, neither the size of an extremal orbit, nor the effective mass, nor a caliper dimension. The only quantity that appears is the length of a reciprocal lattice vector, a parameter uniquely determined by the *crystal* structure, *not* the electronic *band* structure.

Let us further consider the open orbit case, but in an experimental situation where the velocity v_s of the sound wave enters in an important way in the phenomenon. Previously we assumed that the direction of the applied magnetic field was exactly perpendicular to the propagation vector **q** of the sound wave, so that the average motion of the electrons was also normal to **q**. If, however, we tilt **H** through a small angle θ toward **q**, the electrons now describe a helical path whose average velocity in the direction of **q** is $v_H \sin \theta$, where v_H is the drift velocity of electrons in the direction of the magnetic field. Of course, v_H depends on

k_H and will thus vary over the Fermi surface. However, there will be a maximum value v_H^m which is characteristic of the Fermi velocity for the particular direction of the magnetic field. Now when the angle θ is such that $v_H^m \sin \theta = v_s$, the electrons on that portion of the Fermi surface will remain in phase with the propagating sound wave and can continuously absorb energy from it. Hence we expect that a plot of ultrasonic absorption versus θ will show a sharp increase at the critical angle $\theta_c = \arcsin [v_s/v_F(H)]$. The tilt effect thus provides a direct measure of the Fermi velocity in the direction of $\mathbf{H}$. By suitable orientation of the crystal it is possible to obtain a complete mapping of this quantity over the Fermi surface; i.e., one can determine $\nabla_{\mathbf{k}}\epsilon(\mathbf{k})$ over the entire Fermi surface.

D. Transport Properties

We have already seen that in the special case of spherical energy surfaces a single-band model predicts a vanishing magnetoresistance. We discussed the physical reason for this result, namely, the exact cancellation of Lorentz and Hall forces on electrons at the Fermi surface, and showed that a simple extension to a two-band model does lead to results in qualitative and fair quantitative agreement with experiments at low magnetic fields. Let us now consider this model in the high-field limit, and, furthermore, let us assume that the two bands correspond to electrons and holes, respectively.

We now have

$$\mathbf{J}_1 = \frac{n_1 e^2 \tau_1}{m_1} \mathbf{E} + \frac{e\tau_1}{m_1 c} \mathbf{J}_1 \times \mathbf{H} \tag{11.28a}$$

$$\mathbf{J}_2 = \frac{n_2 e^2 \tau_2}{m_2} \mathbf{E} - \frac{e\tau_2}{m_2 c} \mathbf{J}_2 \times \mathbf{H} \tag{11.28b}$$

where subscripts 1 and 2 denote electrons and holes, respectively. Since we are now interested in the high-field limit where $\omega_c \tau \gg 1$, we may neglect, in Eqs. (11.28), $\mathbf{J}_1$ and $\mathbf{J}_2$ on the left-hand side of the equations in comparison with the last term on the right-hand sides. We then obtain, in cartesian coordinates with the usual choice $\mathbf{H} = (0,0,H_z)$,

$$n_1 e E_x + \frac{J_{1y}}{c} H_z = n_2 e E_x - \frac{J_{2y}}{c} H_z = 0$$

and for the total current in the y direction

$$J_y = J_{1y} + J_{2y} = \frac{(n_2 - n_1)ec}{H_z} E_x \tag{11.29}$$

An interesting and important consequence of (11.29) is that J_y vanishes even in the absence of a Hall field E_y, provided $n_2 = n_1 = n$. In this very special case, then, $E_y = 0$ at high fields, and the conductivity tensor has vanishing off-diagonal components. The resistivity component ρ_{xx} is then simply σ_{xx}^{-1}, that is,

$$\rho_{xx} = \frac{H^2}{nc^2} \frac{\tau_1 \tau_2 / m_1 m_2}{\tau_1 / m_1 + \tau_2 / m_2} \tag{11.30}$$

This result, which also follows from Eq. (7.70) if arbitrarily extended into the high-field region, is of considerable importance, for it shows that if the number of electrons and holes are exactly equal the transverse magnetoresistance does not saturate but instead increases indefinitely in proportion to H^2.

Experimental results on many even-valent metals at high fields and low temperatures show this absence of saturation. However, in some odd-valent metals as well, where the condition $n_1 = n_2$ cannot hold, the

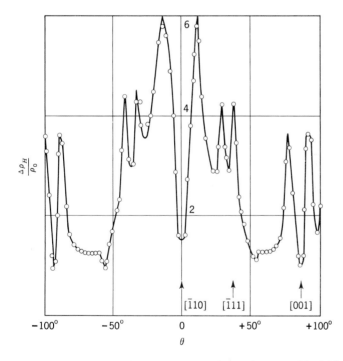

Fig. 11.24 Variation of transverse magnetoresistance with field direction in a field of 23.5 kilogauss, for a single crystal Au specimen with current || [110]. (*From C. Kittel, "Quantum Theory of Solids," p. 239, John Wiley & Sons, Inc., New York, 1963.*)

magnetoresistance often fails to saturate for certain crystallographic directions. A polar plot of the high-field magnetoresistance as a function of crystal orientation frequently displays a strikingly anisotropic pattern with sharp peaks (nonsaturation) separated by regions of low magnetoresistance (saturation), as shown in Fig. 11.24. For a long time these patterns remained an unexplained mystery, and only in the last decade has this phenomenon been clarified theoretically. Quite naturally this understanding has sparked a renaissance of magnetoresistance studies.

Let us assume that the Fermi surface of the metal is multiply connected, so that, in a properly oriented magnetic field, open orbit trajectories can exist. Let us further assume that there is such an open orbit in the k_x direction with **H** along the z direction. Then the electrons in these open orbits carry a current in the y direction whose magnitude is not influenced by the magnetic field. Hence, in the high-field limit the conductivity tensor (7.60) takes the form

$$
\sigma = \frac{n_0 e^2 \tau}{m} \begin{pmatrix} (\omega_c \tau)^{-2} & (\omega_c \tau)^{-1} & 0 \\ -(\omega_c \tau)^{-1} & (\omega_c \tau)^{-2} + \beta & 0 \\ 0 & 0 & 1 \end{pmatrix} \simeq \frac{n_0 e^2 \tau}{m} \begin{pmatrix} (\omega_c \tau)^{-2} & (\omega_c \tau)^{-1} & 0 \\ -(\omega_c \tau)^{-1} & \beta & 0 \\ 0 & 0 & 1 \end{pmatrix}
$$

$$(11.31)$$

where β denotes the contribution of the open orbit electrons to the current in the y direction, which will be large compared to $(\omega_c \tau)^{-2}$ when $\omega_c \tau \gg 1$.

We can then write the expressions for the x and y components of the current, namely,

$$
J_x = \frac{n_0 e^2 \tau}{m} \left(\frac{E_x}{(\omega_c \tau)^2} + \frac{E_y}{(\omega_c \tau)} \right)
$$

$$(11.32a)$$

$$
J_y = \frac{n_0 e^2 \tau}{m} \left(-\frac{E_x}{\omega_c \tau} + \beta E_y \right)
$$

$$(11.32b)$$

The usual boundary condition $J_y = 0$ now leads to

$$
E_y = \frac{E_x}{\beta \omega_c \tau}
$$

$$
J_x = \frac{n_0 e^2 \tau (\beta + 1)}{m \beta (\omega_c \tau)^2} E_x
$$

and a resistivity

$$
\rho = \frac{E_x}{J_x} = \frac{(\omega_c \tau)^2 m \beta}{n_0 e^2 \tau (1 + \beta)}
$$

$$(11.33)$$

which evidently fails to saturate at high fields.   The existence of open orbits, though necessary, is not a sufficient condition for absence of saturation, for not only must these orbits exist but they must carry current almost exactly perpendicular to the applied magnetic and electric fields.

With multiply connected Fermi surfaces the Hall coefficient also shows pronounced anisotropy which can be traced to the existence of open orbits.

Thus conventional low-temperature transport measurements as a function of field orientation can provide useful topological information on the Fermi surface.   The results by themselves are generally too ambiguous to permit the construction of a unique Fermi surface, but with the aid of reasonable models based on the Harrison construction it is often possible to go a long way with such elementary experimental methods.   Despite their obvious limitations these measurements have the decided advantage of experimental simplicity over the more exotic techniques for Fermi surface studies.   Moreover, if τ is relatively short, resonance methods may prove impractical, because the cyclotron frequency at fields such that $\omega_c \tau > 1$ may fall outside the range for which microwave techniques have been developed.   No such limitation restricts the use of transport measurements.

It is rather remarkable that the various methods for the study of the Fermi surface in metals not only complement each other to perfection but give just enough redundant information to allow a cross check.   Each method measures primarily one essential property of the Fermi surface: extremal areas (HA effect), effective masses (cyclotron resonance), caliper dimensions (magnetoacoustic resonance), Fermi velocity (magnetoacoustic tilt effect), and general topology—existence and orientation of open orbits (magnetoresistance).   The totality of the data is thus capable of painting for us a picture of the Fermi surface with far greater clarity and definition than would have seemed possible a decade ago.   As a result, in this last decade Fermi surface investigations have replaced Fermi surface speculations.   A compilation of experimental Fermi surface studies to the year 1964 has been prepared by Shoenberg [7].

As in nearly every significant advance in physics, here, too, the ingenuity of those who devised a variety of precise and beautiful experiments was further stimulated by theoretical advances that not only enhanced the value of their results but often suggested further fruitful research.

PROBLEMS

11.1. Prove that the degeneracy per unit area of each orbital quantum state of a free-electron gas in a uniform magnetic field is equal to $s/2\pi$.

11.2. Show that plane polarized light can be decomposed into two circularly polarized components. Also show that only one of these will lead to resonant absorption by electrons orbiting in a constant magnetic field.

11.3. Prove that the cyclotron resonance frequency for spheroidal energy surfaces is given by Eq. (11.7).

11.4. It is of interest to determine the effective mass of electrons in germanium as a function of temperature. In a typical experiment, the electrons are generated optically and their mean free path is limited by lattice scattering. If $m^*(T)$ is to be found between 4.2° and 70°K, what is the lowest possible resonant frequency at which a reasonably sharp resonance can be observed? What magnetic fields would be required for the experiment?

11.5. Consider a fictitious metal which crystallizes in a simple cubic lattice and in which the conduction-electron density corresponds to 1.5 electrons per atom.

(a) Calculate the radius of the Fermi sphere in **k** space for this metal.
(b) Use the Harrison construction to exhibit the orbits if the magnetic field is directed along one of the cube axes.
(c) Determine the periods of the HA oscillations, and state which correspond to electron and which to hole resonances.

REFERENCES

1. Fletcher, R. C., W. A. Yager, and F. R. Merritt: *Phys. Rev.*, **100**: 747 (1955).
2. Stickler, J. J., H. J. Zeiger, and G. S. Heller: *Phys. Rev.*, **127**: 1077 (1962).
3. Dexter, R. N., H. J. Zeiger, and B. Lax: *Phys. Rev.*, **104**: 637 (1956).
4. Harrison, W. A.: *Phys. Rev.*, **116**: 555 (1959); **118**: 1190 (1960).
5. Shoenberg, D., and P. J. Stiles: *Proc. Roy. Soc. London*, **A281**: 62 (1964).
6. Az'bel, M. I., and E. A. Kaner: *Soviet Phys. JETP*, **3**: 772 (1956).
7. Shoenberg, D.: "Low Temperature Physics," LT 9, part B, p. 680, Plenum Press, New York, 1965.

BIBLIOGRAPHY

Daunt, J. G., D. O. Edwards, F. J. Milford, M. Yaqub (eds.): "Low Temperature Physics," LT9, part B, Plenum Press, New York, 1965.
Fawcett, E.: High-field Galvanomagnetic Properties of Metals, *Advan. Phys.*, **13**: 139 (1964).
Harrison, W. A., and M. B. Webb (eds.): "The Fermi Surface," John Wiley & Sons, Inc., New York, 1960.
Lax, B., and J. G. Mavroides: Cyclotron Resonance, *Solid State Phys.*, **11**: 261 (1960).
——— and S. Zwerdling: Magneto-optical Phenomena in Semiconductors, *Progr. Semiconductors*, **5**: 221 (1960).

Appendix A
Summary of Elementary
Quantum Mechanics

The purpose of this appendix is the presentation of the basic postulates of quantum mechanics and their application to those situations that are encountered in the body of the text. The material in this appendix is not intended as a short course in quantum mechanics; the aim is primarily to present the reader, who is either unfamiliar with quantum mechanics or has, perhaps, had only a phenomenological introduction to the topic, with sufficient background so that he can follow the arguments in various sections of the text. The appendix is subdivided into the following sections: 1. Basic Postulates and the Schroedinger Equation; 2. The Free Particle in a Box and the One-dimensional Potential Well; 3. The Harmonic Oscillator; 4. Charged Particles in a Uniform Magnetic Field; 5. Stationary Perturbation Theory; and 6. Time-dependent Perturbation Theory and Transition Probabilities.

A.1 BASIC POSTULATES AND THE SCHROEDINGER EQUATION

Classical mechanics concerns itself with the dynamics of a physical system consisting of particles that may interact with one another and respond to external forces.   Such a system is characterized by N coordinates q_i which uniquely specify the configuration of the particles.   Such a system possesses a lagrangian $\mathcal{L}(q_i,\dot{q}_i,t)$, from which the canonically conjugate momenta are defined by

$$p_i = \frac{\partial \mathcal{L}}{\partial \dot{q}_i}$$

These are used to construct the hamiltonian function

$$\mathcal{H}(q_i,p_i,t) = \sum_{i=1}^{N} p_i \dot{q}_i - \mathcal{L}(q_i,\dot{q}_i,t)$$

and the dynamics of the system is then obtained from the solution of Hamilton's equations

$$\dot{p}_i = -\frac{\partial \mathcal{H}}{\partial q_i} \qquad \dot{q}_i = \frac{\partial \mathcal{H}}{\partial p_i}$$

These equations define a set of trajectories in phase space.   The particular trajectory along which the system moves, determined by the initial conditions, provides an exact specification of the coordinates and momenta at all subsequent times.   Thus, in classical mechanics, the state of the system is specified by a statement of the exact values of the coordinates and momenta at some initial time.   The state of the system subsequently is determined uniquely by the solution of the equations of motion.   Moreover, all dynamical variables, such as kinetic and potential energies and angular momenta, can also be calculated exactly from the known coordinates and momenta.

The basic postulates of quantum mechanics negate this concept of predestination and absolute precision.   According to the Heisenberg uncertainty principle, a coordinate and its canonically conjugate momentum cannot simultaneously be specified precisely; the product of the uncertainties of the two conjugate variables must be greater than $\hbar = h/2\pi = 1.05443 \times 10^{-27}$ erg-sec.   Thus, for example,

$$\Delta x \Delta p_x \geq \hbar \qquad \Delta \phi \Delta J_\phi \geq \hbar \qquad \Delta E \Delta t \geq \hbar \qquad \text{(A.1)}$$

where x and ϕ are position and angle coordinates, p_x and J_ϕ are the conjugate linear and angular momenta, t is the time variable, and E is the energy of the system.

Since the initial state of a quantum-mechanical system cannot be prepared with the same absolute precision as in classical mechanics, it follows that its time development also can no longer be predicted precisely.   In contrast to classical mechanics, quantum mechanics, therefore, concerns itself with probabilities rather than certainties.

Postulate 1.   There exists a complex function $\psi(q_i,t)$, called the *state function* of the quantum-mechanical system, such that the probability that the system at time t will be found within the ranges between q_i and $q_i + dq_i$ is

$$P(q_i,t)\, dq_1\, dq_2\, \cdots\, dq_N = \psi^*(q_i,t)\psi(q_i,t)\, dq_1\, dq_2\, \cdots\, dq_N$$

where the asterisk denotes complex conjugation.

The state function is generally normalized to meet the requirement

$$\int\psi^*\psi\, dq_1\, \cdots\, dq_N = \int\psi^*\psi\, d\tau = 1 \tag{A.2}$$

Postulate 2.   To every dynamical observable there corresponds a *linear hermitian operator* **R**.   The result of a physical measurement of the observable R on the quantum-mechanical system characterized by the state function ψ is given by the expectation value $\langle\mathbf{R}\rangle$ of the corresponding operator defined by

$$\langle\mathbf{R}\rangle \equiv \int\psi^*\mathbf{R}\psi\, d\tau \tag{A.3}$$

The requirement of linearity assures that the superposition principle will retain validity in quantum mechanics.   The hermitian property, that is,

$$\int\psi^*\mathbf{R}\varphi\, d\tau = \int\varphi(\mathbf{R}\psi)^*\, d\tau \tag{A.4}$$

guarantees that the expectation value is a real quantity.   The quantum-mechanical operator for the linear momentum is $\mathbf{p} = -i\hbar\nabla$.

Postulate 3.   The state function $\psi(q_i,t)$ is a solution of the *time-dependent Schroedinger equation*

$$\mathfrak{IC}\psi = i\hbar\, \frac{\partial\psi}{\partial t} \tag{A.5}$$

where $\mathfrak{IC}$ is the hamiltonian operator constructed by replacing the classical variables by their quantum-mechanical operator equivalents.   In the simple case where the single-particle classical hamiltonian is just a sum of the kinetic and potential energies, that is,

$$\mathfrak{IC} = \frac{p^2}{2m} + V(r)$$

Eq. (A.5) becomes

$$-\frac{\hbar^2}{2m}\,\nabla^2\psi + V\psi = i\hbar\,\frac{\partial\psi}{\partial t} \tag{A.6}$$

Provided $\mathcal{3C}$ does not involve the time explicitly, the left-hand side of (A.6) is independent of the time. Consequently, we can separate ψ into a product

$$\varphi(r)\chi(t)$$

and obtain

$$\chi(t) = Ce^{i\epsilon t/\hbar} \tag{A.7}$$

The equation which $\varphi(r)$ must satisfy,

$$\mathcal{3C}\varphi = \epsilon\varphi \tag{A.8}$$

is called the *time-independent Schroedinger equation*. The quantity ϵ in Eq. (A.8) is the energy of the quantum-mechanical system. Its value(s) depends on $\mathcal{3C}$ and on the boundary conditions imposed on φ. An equation of the form (A.8) is called an *eigenvalue equation*, its solution is the *eigenfunction*, and ϵ itself is the *eigenvalue*. The eigenfunction $\varphi(\mathbf{r})$ and its first derivative must be continuous. Moreover, if $\varphi(\mathbf{r})$ is to be normalized then $\varphi(\mathbf{r})$ must vanish as $\mathbf{r} \rightarrow \infty$.

The expectation value of the energy is, according to (A.3),

$$\langle\epsilon\rangle = \int\varphi^*\mathcal{3C}\varphi \, d\tau = \epsilon \tag{A.9}$$

Hence the system whose state function φ is a solution of Eq. (A.8) has an energy which is precisely equal to the eigenvalue ϵ. The system is therefore in a "stationary energy state," i.e., the state does not change its energy with time.

It may happen that the eigenfunction of the energy operator $\mathcal{3C}$ is also an eigenfunction of another eigenvalue equation involving the quantum-mechanical operator $\mathbf{R} \neq \mathcal{3C}$. In that case, not only the energy, but also the dynamical variable R of the system, can be determined precisely and both will maintain their eigenvalues indefinitely. It is easily shown that the necessary and sufficient condition for this is that the operators commute, that is,

$$[\mathcal{3C},\mathbf{R}] \equiv (\mathcal{3C}\mathbf{R} - \mathbf{R}\mathcal{3C}) = 0 \tag{A.10}$$

An important property of the set of eigenfunctions corresponding to the totality of eigenvalues of a particular dynamical operator $\mathbf{R}$ is that they constitute a complete orthogonal set. To demonstrate their orthogonality, we consider two eigenfunctions φ_m and φ_n which are solutions of

$$\mathbf{R}\varphi_m = R_m\varphi_m \quad \text{and} \quad \mathbf{R}\varphi_n = R_n\varphi_n \tag{A.11}$$

We multiply the first of the equations by φ_n^*, the second by φ_m^*, subtract the complex conjugate of the second equation from the first, and integrate over coordinate space. Thus,

$$\int[\varphi_n^* \mathbf{R}\varphi_m - \varphi_m(\mathbf{R}\varphi_n)^*]\, d\tau = (R_m - R_n^*)\int\varphi_n^*\varphi_m\, d\tau = (R_m - R_n)\int\varphi_n^*\varphi_m\, d\tau \tag{A.12}$$

the last following from the fact that the eigenvalues of a hermitian operator are real. But, from Eq. (A.4),

$$\int[\varphi_n^* \mathbf{R}\varphi_m - \varphi_m(\mathbf{R}\varphi_n)^*]\, d\tau = 0 = (R_m - R_n)\int\varphi_n^*\varphi_m\, d\tau$$

Consequently, either

$$R_m - R_n = 0 \tag{A.13a}$$

or

$$\int\varphi_n^*\varphi_m\, d\tau = 0 \tag{A.13b}$$

If $R_n = R_m$ the eigenvalues are said to be *degenerate*. In the nondegenerate case the wave functions must evidently be orthogonal. If the eigenvalues R_n and R_m are degenerate and φ_n and φ_m are nonorthogonal, it is always possible to construct linear combinations of these functions that will be mutually orthogonal. Since the eigenfunctions of $\mathbf{R}$ constitute a complete orthogonal set, another wave function, which need not correspond to a particular eigenvalue of $\mathbf{R}$, is expressible as a linear combination of functions from this set.

Suppose, then, that

$$\psi = \sum_{j=0}^{\infty} a_j\varphi_j \tag{A.14}$$

and

$$\mathbf{R}\varphi_j = R_j\varphi_j \tag{A.15}$$

where the φ_j are assumed normalized and we also assume, for convenience, that the eigenvalues R_j are nondegenerate. Now

$$\int \psi^*\psi\, d\tau = \sum_{j=0}^{\infty}\sum_{k=0}^{\infty} a_j^* a_k \int \varphi_j^*\varphi_k\, d\tau$$

$$= \sum_{j=0}^{\infty}\sum_{k=0}^{\infty} a_j^* a_k \delta_{jk} = \sum_{j=0}^{\infty} a_j^* a_j = 1 \tag{A.16}$$

Thus, if the function ψ is normalized in the usual way, the sum of the squares of the absolute values of the expansion coefficients must be unity.

Next, consider the expectation value of **R** in the state characterized by the eigenfunction ψ.   We have

$$\int \psi^* \mathbf{R} \psi \, d\tau = \sum_{j=0}^{\infty} \sum_{k=0}^{\infty} a_j^* a_k \int \varphi_j^* \mathbf{R} \varphi_k \, d\tau$$

$$= \sum_{j=0}^{\infty} \sum_{k=0}^{\infty} a_j^* a_k R_k \delta_{jk} = \sum_{k=0}^{\infty} a_k^* a_k R_k \qquad (A.17)$$

The physical meaning of this result is as follows.   If, in the state ψ, we perform a measurement of the dynamical variable R the result will be one of the eigenvalues R_j, and the probability that the measurement will yield a particular value R_k is given by $a_k^* a_k = |a_k|^2$.

The quantity

$$\int \psi_\alpha^* \mathbf{R} \psi_\beta \, d\tau \equiv \langle \alpha | \mathbf{R} | \beta \rangle \equiv R_{\alpha\beta} \qquad (A.18)$$

is commonly known as the *matrix element* of **R** between (or connecting) states α and β.

A.2 FREE PARTICLES AND THE ONE–DIMENSIONAL POTENTIAL WELL

The simplest system we can consider is a single particle confined to a volume **V** wherein the potential energy is a constant, which we take to be zero.   Thus Eq. (A.8) reduces to

$$\mathcal{H}\varphi = -\frac{\hbar^2}{2m} \nabla^2 \varphi = \epsilon \varphi \qquad (A.19)$$

whose solution is

$$\varphi = \frac{1}{\mathbf{V}^{\frac{1}{2}}} e^{i\mathbf{k}\cdot\mathbf{r}} \qquad (A.20)$$

The factor $1/\mathbf{V}^{\frac{1}{2}}$ is the normalization factor imposed by the requirement (A.2).   The energy is given by

$$\epsilon = \frac{\hbar^2 k^2}{2m} \qquad (A.21)$$

The eigenfunction (A.20) is also an eigenfunction of the linear momentum operator, that is,

$$\mathbf{p}\varphi = -i\hbar\nabla\varphi = p\varphi \qquad (A.22)$$

has the solution

$$\varphi = \frac{1}{V^{\frac{1}{2}}} e^{i\mathbf{k}\cdot\mathbf{r}} \tag{A.23}$$

with eigenvalue $\mathbf{p} = \hbar\mathbf{k}$.

The one-dimensional well   We consider the one-dimensional problem of a particle moving under the influence of the potential shown in Fig. (A.1). For $|x| < a$,

$$\mathcal{H}\varphi = -\frac{\hbar^2}{2m}\nabla^2\varphi = -\frac{\hbar^2}{2m}\frac{\partial^2\varphi}{\partial x^2} = \epsilon\varphi \tag{A.24}$$

while for $|x| > a$,

$$\mathcal{H}\varphi = -\frac{\hbar^2}{2m}\frac{\partial^2\varphi}{\partial x^2} + V_0\varphi = \epsilon\varphi \tag{A.25}$$

whose solutions are

For $|x| < a$: $\varphi(x) = A \sin \beta x + B \cos \beta x$ $\beta = +\sqrt{\dfrac{2m\epsilon}{\hbar^2}}$ (A.26)

For $|x| > a$: $\varphi(x) = Ce^{-\gamma x} + De^{\gamma x}$ $\gamma = +\sqrt{\dfrac{2m(V_0 - \epsilon)}{\hbar^2}}$ (A.27)

If $\varphi(x)$ is to vanish at $x = \pm\infty$, we must have $C = 0$ if $\varphi(x)$ is to represent the solution for $x > a$ and $D = 0$ if $\varphi(x)$ is to represent the solution for $x < a$. If we now impose the condition that $\varphi(x)$ and $d\varphi/dx$ are continuous at $x = a$ and $x = -a$, we find that

If $A = 0$: $\beta \tan \beta a = \gamma$ (A.28a)

If $B = 0$: $\beta \cot \beta a = -\gamma$ (A.28b)

These two solutions show that the corresponding eigenvalues can be associated with even ($A = 0$) or odd ($B = 0$) eigenfunctions $\varphi(x)$. This division of the eigenfunctions into even and odd types is a direct consequence of the symmetry of the potential $V(x)$. Let $\mathbf{P}$ be an operator

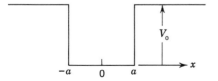

Fig. A.1   One-dimensional square potential well.

which changes x into $-x$.   Thus

$$\mathbf{P}\varphi(x) = P\varphi(x) = \varphi(-x) \tag{A.29}$$

and

$$\mathbf{P}(\mathbf{P}\varphi) = P^2\varphi(x) = \varphi(x) \tag{A.30}$$

Hence

$$P = +1 \quad \text{or} \quad -1 \tag{A.31}$$

i.e., the *parity operator* $\mathbf{P}$ can have eigenvalues $+1$ or -1.   If

$$V(x) = V(-x)$$

$\mathbf{P}\mathfrak{K} = \mathfrak{K}$, since $\mathfrak{K}$ is then an even function of x.   Consequently, $[\mathbf{P},\mathfrak{K}] = 0$ and eigenfunctions of $\mathfrak{K}$ will also be eigenfunctions of the parity operator. It follows that the eigenfunctions of $\mathfrak{K}$ can be classified according as they have even or odd parity.   This is but the most elementary example showing the relation between symmetry and the form of the eigenfunctions.   In crystal physics, symmetry considerations are extremely important, because they dictate the form of the eigenfunctions in much more complicated situations.

A.3   ONE-DIMENSIONAL HARMONIC OSCILLATOR

The classical hamiltonian of the one-dimensional harmonic oscillator is

$$\mathfrak{K} = \frac{p^2}{2m} + \frac{1}{2} Kx^2 \tag{A.32}$$

Hence, the Schroedinger equation is

$$-\frac{\hbar^2}{2m} \frac{\partial^2 \varphi_n}{\partial x^2} + \frac{1}{2} Kx^2 \varphi_n = \epsilon_n \varphi_n \tag{A.33}$$

We make the substitution $\zeta = \alpha x$, where $\alpha = (Km/\hbar^2)^{\frac{1}{4}}$, and obtain

$$\varphi_n'' + (\beta_n - \zeta^2)\varphi_n = 0 \qquad \beta_n = \frac{2\epsilon_n}{\hbar} \left(\frac{m}{K}\right)^{\frac{1}{2}} \tag{A.34}$$

where each prime denotes differentiation with respect to ζ.
    The solutions of (A.34) are

$$\varphi_n(\zeta) = N_n e^{-\frac{1}{2}\zeta^2} H_n(\zeta) \tag{A.35}$$

where $N_n = (\alpha/\pi n!2^n)^{\frac{1}{2}}$ is the normalization factor demanded by the requirement $\int_{-\infty}^{\infty} \varphi_n^* \varphi_n \, dx = 1$, and $H_n(\zeta)$ is the nth hermite polynomial defined by

$$H_n(\zeta) = (-1)^n e^{\zeta^2} \frac{d^n(e^{-\zeta^2})}{d\zeta^n} \tag{A.36}$$

The corresponding eigenvalues for β_n are

$$\beta_n = 2n + 1$$

from which we obtain the energy eigenvalues

$$\epsilon_n = (n + \tfrac{1}{2})\hbar\omega \tag{A.37}$$

where $\omega = \sqrt{K/m}$ is the classical angular resonant frequency of the oscillator.

The matrix element of $\mathbf{x}$ between two harmonic-oscillator eigenstates appears in several important calculations. The result

$$\langle n|\mathbf{x}|m\rangle = \langle m|\mathbf{x}|n\rangle = \left(\frac{n+1}{2\alpha^2}\right)^{\frac{1}{2}} \qquad \text{for } m = n + 1 \tag{A.38}$$

$\langle n|\mathbf{x}|m\rangle = 0$ if $|n - m| \neq 1$ is derived in standard quantum-mechanics texts.

A.4 CHARGED PARTICLES IN A UNIFORM MAGNETIC FIELD

The classical lagrangian of a charged particle in an electromagnetic field is

$$\mathfrak{L} = \tfrac{1}{2}m\dot{x}_i\dot{x}_j + \frac{\mathfrak{e}}{c}\dot{x}_j A_j - \mathfrak{e}\phi \tag{A.39}$$

where ϕ and $\mathbf{A}$ are the scalar and vector potentials. Following the procedure outlined in Sec. A.1 we obtain

$$\mathfrak{IC} = \left(-i\hbar\nabla - \frac{\mathfrak{e}}{c}\mathbf{A}\right)^2 - \mathfrak{e}\phi \tag{A.40}$$

We now choose our coordinate system such that the z axis points along the direction of the uniform magnetic field $\mathbf{H}$. We can then take $\mathbf{A} = \tfrac{1}{2}\mathbf{H} \times \mathbf{r}$, set $\phi = 0$, and obtain the following Schroedinger equation:

$$-\frac{\hbar^2}{2m}\nabla^2\psi - i\frac{\mathfrak{e}H}{2mc}\hbar\left(x\frac{\partial}{\partial y} - y\frac{\partial}{\partial x}\right)\psi + \frac{H^2\mathfrak{e}^2}{8mc^2}(x^2 + y^2)\psi = \epsilon\psi \tag{A.41}$$

If we make the substitution

$$\psi = u(x)e^{i(k_y y + k_z z)}e^{H\mathfrak{e}xy/2\hbar c} \tag{A.42}$$

Eq. (A.41) reduces to

$$-\frac{\hbar^2}{2m}\frac{\partial^2 u}{\partial x^2} + \frac{1}{2m}\left(\hbar k_y + \frac{eH}{c}x\right)^2 u = \left(\epsilon - \frac{\hbar^2 k_z^2}{2m}\right)u \qquad (A.43)$$

Comparison with Eq. (A.33) shows that Eq. (A.43) is the Schroedinger equation of a harmonic oscillator centered at $x_0 = -(\hbar c/eH)k_y$ with a resonant (cyclotron) frequency $\omega_c = eH/mc$. Hence, the energy eigenvalues are

$$\epsilon_n = \hbar\omega_c(n + \tfrac{1}{2}) + \frac{\hbar^2 k_z^2}{2m} \qquad (A.44)$$

From (A.42) and (A.44) we see that the z component of the eigenfunction and the z component of the energy are the same as for a free particle. In the plane perpendicular to the magnetic field, however, the energy is now quantized.

A.5 STATIONARY PERTURBATION THEORY

In quantum mechanics, as in classical mechanics, there are very few physically interesting problems to which an exact analytic solution can be found. Generally, then, one must resort to suitable approximation methods. The discussion of two of these occupies the final sections of this appendix.

Stationary perturbation theory concerns itself with the approximate solution of the time-independent Schroedinger equation (A.8). It rests upon the assumption that the complete hamiltonian $\mathcal{3C}$ can be separated into two parts: $\mathcal{3C}_0$, the unperturbed, or zero-order, hamiltonian, and $\mathcal{3C}'$, the perturbation term. $\mathcal{3C}_0$ is selected so that the eigenvalue equation

$$\mathcal{3C}_0\varphi_{n0} = \epsilon_{n0}\varphi_{n0} \qquad (A.45)$$

is one whose eigenvalues and eigenfunctions are known. Moreover, the desirable separation of $\mathcal{3C}$ into $\mathcal{3C}_0$ and $\mathcal{3C}'$ is one in which $\mathcal{3C}'$ is a small perturbation. The approximate solution of the complete Schroedinger equation is now obtained in the form of a power series expansion. We let

$$\mathcal{3C} = \mathcal{3C}_0 + \alpha\mathcal{3C}' \qquad (A.46)$$

where α is a coefficient which may vary continuously between zero and one, and write

$$\varphi_n = \varphi_{n0} + \alpha\varphi_{n1} + \alpha^2\varphi_{n2} + \cdots$$
$$\epsilon_n = \epsilon_{n0} + \alpha\epsilon_{n1} + \alpha^2\epsilon_{n2} + \cdots \qquad (A.47)$$

where

$$\mathcal{H}\varphi_n = \epsilon_n\varphi_n \tag{A.8}$$

Evidently the approximate solutions to Eq. (A.8) will be useful only if the power series (A.47) converge fairly rapidly for $\alpha = 1$. One now substitutes (A.46) and (A.47) into (A.8) and equates coefficients of equal powers of α. Thus

$$\mathcal{H}_0\varphi_{n0} = \epsilon_{n0}\varphi_{n0}$$
$$\mathcal{H}_0\varphi_{n1} + \mathcal{H}'\varphi_{n0} = \epsilon_{n0}\varphi_{n1} + \epsilon_{n1}\varphi_{n0} \tag{A.48}$$
$$\mathcal{H}_0\varphi_{n2} + \mathcal{H}'\varphi_{n1} = \epsilon_{n0}\varphi_{n2} + \epsilon_{n1}\varphi_{n1} + \epsilon_{n2}\varphi_{n0} \quad \text{etc.}$$

If we multiply the second of Eqs. (A.48) by φ_{m0}^*, integrate, sum over m, and utilize the orthonormality of the functions φ_{n0} and the hermitian property of $\mathcal{H}_0$ we obtain

$$\epsilon_{n1} = \int \varphi_{n0}^* \mathcal{H}' \varphi_{n0} \, d\tau = \langle n0|\mathcal{H}'|n0\rangle \equiv \mathcal{H}'_{nn} \tag{A.49}$$

Thus, the first-order correction to the unperturbed energy is just equal to the expectation value of $\mathcal{H}'$ in the unperturbed eigenstate φ_{n0}.

To calculate the first-order correction to the wave functions, we expand φ_{n1} in terms of the orthonormal set φ_{n0}, that is,

$$\varphi_{n1} = \sum_{j=0}^{\infty} a_{j1}\varphi_{j0} \tag{A.50}$$

If we replace φ_{n1} in the second line of (A.48) by (A.50), multiply by φ_{m0}^*, and integrate, we obtain

$$a_{m1} = \frac{\langle m0|\mathcal{H}'|n0\rangle}{\epsilon_{n0} - \epsilon_{m0}} = \frac{\mathcal{H}'_{mn}}{\epsilon_{n0} - \epsilon_{m0}} \quad n \neq m \tag{A.51}$$

Finally, $a_{n1} = 0$ follows from the normalization condition on the perturbed state function, $\varphi_n = \varphi_{n0} + \varphi_{n1}$.

It frequently happens that $\mathcal{H}'$ has vanishing diagonal matrix elements, so that $\epsilon_{n1} \equiv 0$. For example, if the perturbation hamiltonian $\mathcal{H}'$ is an *odd* function of the coordinates, $\mathcal{H}'_{nn} \equiv 0$. [See, for example, (A.38).] To calculate the lowest-order correction in the energy resulting from the perturbation, it is then necessary to carry the expansion to the next higher order. Starting with the third line of (A.48), following the same procedure as before, and making use of (A.49) and (A.51) one obtains

$$\epsilon_{n2} = \sum_{m=0}^{\infty}{}' \frac{|\mathcal{H}'_{nm}|^2}{\epsilon_{n0} - \epsilon_{m0}} \tag{A.52}$$

where the prime on the summation denotes that the term $n = m$ is to be omitted from the sum.

A.6 TIME-DEPENDENT PERTURBATION THEORY

Frequently the perturbation which is imposed on a quantum-mechanical system fluctuates with time. For example, we may subject the system to electromagnetic radiation and investigate its behavior under this stimulus. To calculate the response of the quantum-mechanical system to a time-dependent perturbation, we now start with the time-dependent Schroedinger equation (A.5).

As in the preceding section, we write

$$\mathcal{H}_0 \varphi_{n0} = \epsilon_{n0} \varphi_{n0} \tag{A.45}$$

$$\mathcal{H} = \mathcal{H}_0 + \alpha \mathcal{H}'(t) \tag{A.46}$$

shall ultimately let α approach unity, and expand the solution of

$$\mathcal{H}\psi = i\hbar \frac{\partial \psi}{\partial t} \tag{A.5}$$

in power series in α. We first express the wave function ψ in terms of the eigenfunctions of the *time-dependent* unperturbed wave equation $\psi_{n0} = \varphi_{n0} \exp(-i\epsilon_{n0}t/\hbar)$. Since the perturbation $\mathcal{H}'(t)$ is a function of time, the expansion coefficients must also be time dependent. We write

$$\psi = \sum_{n=0}^{\infty} a_n(t) \varphi_{n0} e^{-i\epsilon_{n0}t/\hbar} \tag{A.53}$$

which we now substitute into (A.5). Thus

$$\sum_n i\hbar \dot{a}_n \varphi_{n0} e^{-i\epsilon_{n0}t/\hbar} + \sum_n a_n \epsilon_{n0} \varphi_{n0} e^{-i\epsilon_{n0}t/\hbar} = \sum_n a_n (\mathcal{H}_0 + \mathcal{H}') \varphi_{n0} e^{-i\epsilon_{n0}t/\hbar}$$

We multiply by ψ_{m0}^*, integrate, make use of the orthogonality of the unperturbed wave functions, and obtain

$$\dot{a}_m = \frac{1}{i\hbar} \sum_n \mathcal{H}'_{mn} a_n e^{i\omega_{mn}t} \tag{A.54}$$

where

$$\hbar\omega_{mn} \equiv \epsilon_{m0} - \epsilon_{n0} \tag{A.55}$$

If we now expand in powers of α, i.e., write

$$a_n = a_{n0} + \alpha a_{n1} + \alpha^2 a_{n2} + \cdots$$

substitute in (A.54), and equate coefficients of equal power of α, we obtain the set of differential equations

$$\dot{a}_{m0} = 0 \qquad \dot{a}_{m,k+1} = \frac{1}{i\hbar} \sum_n \mathfrak{K}'_{mn} a_{n,k} e^{i\omega_{mn}t} \tag{A.56}$$

Equations (A.56) can be integrated successively to any order.

Let us now assume that before the perturbation $\mathfrak{K}'$ is applied at $t = 0$ the quantum-mechanical system is in a particular eigenstate of $\mathfrak{K}_0$, say, the state φ_{n0}. Thus all expansion coefficients except a_{n0} vanish and $a_{n0} = 1$. We now obtain the first-order coefficients a_{m1} by integrating (A.56). Thus

$$a_{m1}(t) = \frac{1}{i\hbar} \int_0^t \mathfrak{K}'_{mn}(t') e^{i\omega_{mn}t'} \, dt' \tag{A.57}$$

If $\mathfrak{K}'$ is independent of time except for being turned on at $t' = 0$ and off at $t' = t$, Eq. (A.57) gives

$$a_{m1}(t) = \mathfrak{K}'_{mn} \frac{1 - e^{i\omega_{mn}t}}{\hbar\omega_{mn}}$$

Hence, the probability that the system will be found in the quantum state m as a result of the perturbation is, to first order,

$$|a_{m1}(t)|^2 = \frac{4|\mathfrak{K}'_{mn}|^2 \sin^2\left(\dfrac{\omega_{mn}t}{2}\right)}{\hbar^2 \omega_{mn}^2} \tag{A.58}$$

It is generally not $|a_{m1}(t)|^2$ but the transition probability per unit time between an initial state i and a final state f that is of physical interest. This is given by

$$\frac{\partial}{\partial t} |a_{fi}(t)|^2 = \frac{2\pi}{\hbar} |\mathfrak{K}'_{fi}|^2 \mathcal{O}(E_f - E_i) \tag{A.59}$$

where

$$\mathcal{O}(x) = \frac{\sin(xt/\hbar)}{\pi x} \tag{A.60}$$

The function $\mathcal{O}(x)$ peaks at $x = 0$ and has significant magnitude only for $|x|t < \hbar$. Since

$$\int_{-\infty}^{\infty} \mathcal{O}(x) \, dx = 1$$

$\mathcal{O}(x)$, in the limit of large t, is a representation of the Dirac delta function $\delta(x)$. In Eq. (A.59), $\mathcal{O}(E_f - E_i)$—or $\delta(E_f - E_i)$—is then just a formal statement of energy conservation.

Frequently, one is also interested in the transition probability per unit time from the initial state to all states accessible through the perturbation interaction. In that case, one seeks the rate W_n, defined by

$$W_n = \frac{1}{t} \sum_m |a_{mn}(t)|^2 \tag{A.61}$$

We assume that the states of the quantum-mechanical system are closely spaced in energy and, thus, constitute a quasi continuum about ϵ_n, and define the density of final states $\rho(\epsilon_m)$ such that $\rho(\epsilon_m) \, d\epsilon_m$ equals the number of energy states of the quantum-mechanical system in the energy interval between ϵ_m and $\epsilon_m + d\epsilon_m$. Equation (A.61) now becomes

$$W_n = \frac{1}{t} \int |a_{m1}(t)|^2 \rho(\epsilon_m) \, d\epsilon_m$$

$$= \frac{1}{t} \int_{-\infty}^{\infty} \frac{4|\mathcal{3C}'_{mn}|^2 \rho(\epsilon_m) \sin^2 \left(\dfrac{\omega_{mn} t}{2} \right)}{\hbar \omega_{mn}^2} \, d\omega_{mn} \tag{A.62}$$

The quantity $\sin^2(\omega_{mn} t/2)/\omega_{mn}^2$ as a function of ω_{mn} is shown in Fig. (A.2).

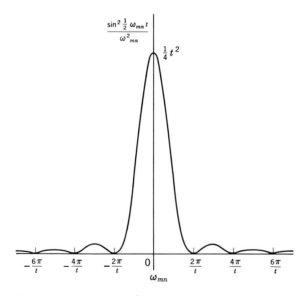

Fig. A.2 $\sin^2(\omega_{mn} t/2)/\omega_{mn}^2$ as a function of ω_{mn}. The scales for abscissa and ordinate depend on t, as shown. The central peak will thus be the sharper and higher the longer the duration of the perturbation. (*From L. I. Schiff, "Quantum Mechanics," 2d ed., p. 198, McGraw-Hill Book Company, New York, 1955.*)

Evidently the dominant contribution to (A.62) will come from the region near $\omega_{mn} = 0$.   If we assume that $\mathcal{3C}'_{mn}$ and $\rho(\epsilon_m)$ are slowly varying functions of energy near $\epsilon = \epsilon_n$, we can replace (A.62) by

$$W_n = \frac{1}{t} \frac{4|\mathcal{3C}'_{mn}|^2}{\hbar} \rho(\epsilon_m) \int_{-\infty}^{\infty} \frac{\sin^2\left(\frac{\omega_{mn}t}{2}\right)}{\omega_{mn}^2} d\omega_{mn}$$

and obtain the "golden rule"

$$W_n = \frac{2\pi}{\hbar} |\mathcal{3C}'_{mn}|^2 \rho(\epsilon_m) \tag{A.63}$$

Appendix B
Units and Conversion Factors

In this text we have employed both practical mks units and rationalized gaussian units in conformity with current practice in physics. The following table gives the defining relationships, mks and gaussian units, and the conversion factors.

Quantity	Defining equation Mks	Defining equation Gaussian	Mks unit	Gaussian unit	Equivalence
Mass, length, time			Kilogram, meter, second	Gram, centimeter, second	1 kg $= 10^3$ gm 1 m $= 10^2$ cm
Force	$F = ma$		newton = kilogram-meter/second^2	dyne = gram-centimeter/second^2	1 newton $= 10^5$ dyne
Work, energy	$W = \int \mathbf{F} \cdot \mathbf{ds}$		joule = newton-meter	erg = dyne-centimeter	1 joule $= 10^7$ erg
Power	$P = dW/dt$		watt = joule/second	erg/second	1 watt $= 10^7$ erg/sec
Charge	$q = \int I\, dt$	$F = qq'/r^2$	coulomb = ampere-second	statcoulomb; [stat-coulomb] $= $ [dyne]$^{1/2}$ [centimeter]	1 coul $\simeq (c/10)$ stat-coul $\simeq 3 \times 10^9$ statcoul
Current	$I = dq/dt$		ampere; [ampere] $=$ [newton]$^{1/2}/\mu_0^{1/2}$	statampere = stat-coulomb/second $=$ $(1/c)$ abampere	1 amp $= (1/10)$abamp $= (c/10)$ statamp $\simeq$ 3×10^9 statamp
Current density	$J = \lim \Delta I/\Delta S$		ampere/meter^2	statampere/centimeter^2	1 amp/m$^2 = (c/10^5)$ statamp/cm$^2 \simeq$ 3×10^5 statamp/cm^2
Electric field intensity	$\mathbf{E} = \lim \Delta\mathbf{F}/\Delta q$		newton/coulomb $=$ volt/meter	dyne/statcoulomb $=$ statvolt/centimeter	1 newton/coul $=$ $(10^6/c)$ dynes/statcoul $\simeq (10^{-4}/3)$ dynes/statcoul

Quantity	mks	gaussian	mks unit	gaussian unit	conversion
Electric potential Capacitance	$V = \int \mathbf{E} \cdot d\mathbf{s}$ $C = Q/V$; farad = coulomb/volt; [farad] = ϵ_0[meter]		volt farad = coulomb/volt; [farad] = ϵ_0[meter]	statvolt statfarad = statcoulomb/statvolt; [statfarad] = [centimeter]	1 volt = $\frac{1}{300}$ statvolt 1 farad = $(10^{-9}/c^2)$ statfarad $\simeq 9 \times 10^{11}$ statfarad
Electric dipole moment	$\mathbf{p}_e = q\mathbf{r}$		meter-coulomb	centimeter-statcoulomb	1 m-coul = $(10c)$ cm-statcoul $\simeq 3 \times 10^{11}$ cm-statco 1
Electric polarization	$\mathbf{P} = \dfrac{\Sigma\mathbf{p}}{V}$		coulomb/meter²	statcoulomb/centimeter²	1 coul/m² = $(10^{-5}c)$ statcoul/cm² $\simeq 3 \times 10^5$ statcoul/cm²
Relative permittivity or dielectric constant; electric susceptibility	$\epsilon_r = D/(\epsilon_0 E)$ $= \epsilon/\epsilon_0$ $\chi = \epsilon_r - 1$	$\epsilon_r = D/E$ $\chi = \dfrac{(\epsilon_r - 1)}{4\pi}$	dimensionless ratio	dimensionless ratio (statcoulomb²/dyne-cm)	χ same in both systems; 1 unit of χ(mks) = $(1/4\pi)$ unit of χ (gaussian)
Displacement	$\mathbf{D} = \epsilon_0\mathbf{E} + \mathbf{P}$	$\mathbf{D} = \mathbf{E} + 4\pi\mathbf{P}$	coulomb/meter²	dyne/statcoulomb	1 coul/m² = $(4\pi \times 10^{-5}c)$ dyne/statcoul $\simeq 12\pi \times 10^5$ dyne/statcoul of $\mathbf{D}$
Resistance	$R = V/I$		ohm = volt/ampere [ohm] = [second/meter]/ϵ_0 $= \mu_0$[meter/second]	statohm = statvolt/statampere; [statohm] = [second/centimeter]	1 ohm = $(10^9/c^2)$ statohm $\simeq (10^{-11}/9)$ statohm
Conductance	$G = I/V$		mho = ampere/volt	statmho = statampere/statvolt	1 statmho = $(c^2/10^9)$ statmho $\simeq 9 \times 10^{11}$ statmho
Resistivity	$\varrho = E/J$		ohm-meter	statohm-centimeter	1 ohm-m = 100 ohm-cm = $(10^{11}/c^2)$ statohm-cm $\simeq (10^{-9}/9)$ statohm-cm

Units and Conversion Factors (*Continued*)

Quantity	Defining equation		Mks unit	Gaussian unit	Equivalence
	Mks	*Gaussian*			
Electrical conductivity	$\sigma = J/E$		Mho/meter	Statmho/centimeter	1 mho/m = $(c^2/10^{11})$ statmhos/cm $\simeq$ 9 × 10⁹ statmhos/cm
Magnetic induction (B)	$\mathbf{F} = q(\mathbf{v} \times \mathbf{B})$	$\mathbf{F} = (q/c)(\mathbf{v} \times \mathbf{B})$	weber/meter² = tesla = newton/ampere-meter	gauss = (c) dyne/statampere-centimeter (= oersted); [gauss] = μ_0[oersted] = $\mu_0^{1/2}$[dyne$^{1/2}$/cm]	1 weber/m² 1 = 10⁴ gauss
Magnetic flux	$\Phi = \int \mathbf{B} \cdot d\mathbf{S}$		weber = tesla-meter² = volt-second = joule/ampere = ampere-henry; [weber] = $\mu_0^{1/2}$[newton$^{1/2}$-meter]	maxwell = gauss-centimeter² = (c) erg/statampere (= oersted/centimeter²)	1 weber = 10⁸ maxwells
Relative permeability μ_r; magnetic susceptibility χ	$\mu_r = \mu/\mu_0$ $\chi = \mu_r - 1$	$\mu_r = \mu$ $\chi = \dfrac{\mu - 1}{4\pi}$	dimensionless ratio	dimensionless ratio	μ_r same in both systems; 1 unit of χ(mks) = $(1/4\pi)$ unit of χ (gaussian)
Magnetic moment	$\left.\begin{array}{l}\mathbf{\mu} = I\mathbf{A} \\ \mathbf{p}_m = \mu_0 I\mathbf{A}\end{array}\right\}$	$\mathbf{\mu} = (I/c)\mathbf{A}$	$\left\{\begin{array}{l}\text{ampere-meter}^2 \\ \text{weber-meter}\end{array}\right.$	gauss-centimeter³ = erg/oersted (= erg/gauss)	1 amp-m² = 4π × 10^{-7} weber-m = 10³ gauss-cm³ of m
Magnetization	$\mathbf{M} = \dfrac{\Sigma\mathbf{\mu}}{V}$		$\left\{\begin{array}{l}\text{ampere/meter} \\ \text{weber/meter}^2\end{array}\right.$	gauss (= oersted)	1 amp/m = 4π × 10^{-7} weber/m² = 10^{-3} gauss (= 10^{-3} oersted) of **M**

Units and Conversion Factors (Concluded)

Quantity	Mks unit	Defining equation		Gaussian unit	Equivalence
		Mks	Gaussian		
Magnetic intensity ($\mathbf{H}$)	ampere/meter	$\mathbf{H} = \mathbf{B}/\mu_0 - \mathbf{M}$	$\mathbf{H} = \mathbf{B} - 4\pi\mathbf{M}$	oersted ($= $ gauss) $= (1/c)$ statampere/ centimeter; [oersted] $= $ [dyne$^{1/2}$/centi-meter]	1 amp/m $= 4\pi \times 10^{-3}$ oersted of $\mathbf{H}$
Hall coefficient	volt-meter^3/ampere-weber $= $ meter^3/coulomb	$R = \mathbf{E}_H/JB$		statvolt-centimeter/ statampere-gauss $= $ centimeter$^3/(c)$ statcoulomb	1 volt-m^3/amp-weber $= (10^7/c^2)$ statvolt-cm/statampere-gauss $\simeq (10^{-13}/9)$ stat-volt-cm/statamp-gauss
Thermopower, Thomson coefficient	volt/degree Centigrade $= $ joule/coulomb-degree Centigrade	$\dfrac{dV}{dT} = S$		statvolt/degree K	$1\,V/°\mathrm{K} = (10^8/c)$ statvolt/$°\mathbf{K} \simeq$ (1/300) statvolt/$°\mathrm{K}$

Appendix C
The Periodic Table

H¹	
(1.008)	
$1s$	

The notation used to describe the outer electronic configuration of atoms and ions is discussed in all textbooks of introductory atomic physics. The letters s, p, d, . . . signify electrons having orbital angular momentum 0, 1, 2, . . . in units $\hbar$; the number to the left of the letter denotes the principal quantum number of one orbit, and the superscript to the right denotes the number of electrons in the orbit. The number in parentheses gives the atomic weight.

Li³	Be⁴
(6.940)	(9.013)
$2s$	$2s^2$

Na¹¹	Mg¹²
(22.990)	(24.32)
$3s$	$2s^2$

K¹⁹	Ca²⁰	Sc²¹	Ti²²	V²³	Cr²⁴	Mn²⁵	Fe²⁶	Co²⁷
(39.100)	(40.08)	(44.96)	(47.90)	(50.95)	(52.01)	(54.94)	(55.85)	(58.94)
		$3d$	$3d^2$	$3d^3$	$3d^5$	$3d^5$	$3d^6$	$3d^7$
$4s$	$4s^2$	$4s^2$	$4s^2$	$4s^2$	$4s$	$4s^2$	$4s^2$	$4s^2$

Rb³⁷	Sr³⁸	Y³⁹	Zr⁴⁰	Nb⁴¹	Mo⁴²	Tc⁴³	Ru⁴⁴	Rh⁴⁵
(85.48)	(87.62)	(88.92)	(91.22)	(92.91)	(95.95)	(98)	(101.2)	(102.91)
		$4d$	$4d^2$	$4d^4$	$4d^5$	$4d^6$	$4d^7$	$4d^8$
$5s$	$5s^2$	$5s^2$	$5s^2$	$5s$	$5s$	$5s$	$5s$	$5s$

Cs⁵⁵	Ba⁵⁶	La⁵⁷	Hf⁷²	Ta⁷³	W⁷⁴	Re⁷⁵	Os⁷⁶	Ir⁷⁷
(132.91)	(137.36)	(138.92)	(178.6)	(180.95)	(183.85)	(186.22)	(190.2)	(192.2)
			$4f^{14}$					
		$5d$	$5d^2$	$5d^3$	$5d^4$	$5d^5$	$5d^6$	$5d^9$
$6s$	$6s^2$	$6s^2$	$6s^2$	$6s^2$	$6s^2$	$6s^2$	$6s^2$	—

Fr⁸⁷	Ra⁸⁸	Ac⁸⁹
(223)	(226.05)	(227)
		$6d$
$7s$	$7s^2$	$7s^2$

Ce⁵⁸	Pr⁵⁹	Nd⁶⁰	Pm⁶¹	Sm⁶²	Eu⁶³
(140.13)	(140.92)	(144.24)	(145)	(105.35)	(152.0)
$4f^2$	$4f^3$	$4f^4$	$4f^5$	$4f^6$	$4f^7$
$6s^2$	$6s^2$	$6s^2$	$6s^2$	$6s^2$	$6s^2$

Th⁹⁰	Pa⁹¹	U⁹²	Np⁹³	Pu⁹⁴	Am⁹⁵
(232.05)	(241.1)	(238.07)	(237)	(242)	(243)
—	$5f^2$	$5f^3$	$5f^4$	$5f^6$	$5f^7$
$6d^2$	$6d$	$6d$			
$7s^2$	$7s^2$	$7s^2$	$7s^2$	$7s^2$	$7s^2$

								He[2]
								(4.003)
								$1s^2$

			B[5]	**C**[6]	**N**[7]	**O**[8]	**F**[9]	**Ne**[10]
			(10.81)	(12.011)	(14.007)	(16.00)	(19.00)	(20.182)
			$2s^22p$	$2s^22p^2$	$2s^22p^3$	$2s^22p^4$	$2s^22p^5$	$2s^22p^6$

			Al[13]	**Si**[14]	**P**[15]	**S**[16]	**Cl**[17]	**Ar**[18]
			(26.98)	(28.09)	(30.97)	(32.066)	(35.453)	(39.946)
			$3s^23p$	$3s^23p^2$	$3s^23p^3$	$3s^23p^4$	$3s^23p^5$	$3s^23p^6$

Ni[28]	**Cu**[29]	**Zn**[30]	**Ga**[31]	**Ge**[32]	**As**[33]	**Se**[34]	**Br**[35]	**Kr**[36]
(58.71)	(63.54)	(65.38)	(69.72)	(72.59)	(79.91)	(78.96)	(79.91)	(83.80)
$3d^8$	$3d^{10}$	$3d^{10}$						
$4s^2$	$4s$	$4s^2$	$4s^24p$	$4s^24p^2$	$4s^24p^3$	$4s^24p^4$	$4s^24p^5$	$4s^24p^6$

Pd[46]	**Ag**[47]	**Cd**[48]	**In**[49]	**Sn**[50]	**Sb**[51]	**Te**[52]	**I**[53]	**Xe**[54]
(106.4)	(107.87)	(112.40)	(114.82)	(118.69)	(121.74)	(127.61)	(126.91)	(131.3)
$4d^{10}$	$4d^{10}$	$4d^{10}$						
—	$5s$	$5s^2$	$5s^25p$	$5s^25p^2$	$5s^25p^3$	$5s^25p^4$	$5s^25p^5$	$5s^25p^6$

Pt[78]	**Au**[79]	**Hg**[80]	**Tl**[81]	**Pb**[82]	**Bi**[83]	**Po**[84]	**At**[85]	**Rn**[86]
(195.09)	(197.0)	(200.6)	(204.39)	(207.2)	(209.0)	(210)	(211)	(222)
$5d^9$	$5d^{10}$	$5d^{10}$						
$6s$	$6s$	$6s^2$	$6s^26p$	$6s^26p^2$	$6s^26p^3$	$6s^26p^4$	$6s^26p^5$	$6s^26p^6$

Gd[64]	**Tb**[65]	**Dy**[66]	**Ho**[67]	**Er**[68]	**Tm**[69]	**Yb**[70]	**Lu**[71]
(157.25)	(158.92)	(162.50)	(164.93)	(167.3)	(169)	(173.04)	(174.98)
$4f^7$	$4f^8$	$4f^{10}$	$4f^{11}$	$4f^{12}$	$4f^{13}$	$4f^{14}$	$4f^{14}$
$5d$	$5d$						$5d$
$6s^2$	$6s^2$	$6s^2$	$6s^2$	$6s^2$	$6s^2$	$6s^2$	$6s^2$

Cm[96]	**Bk**[97]	**Cf**[98]	**Es**[99]	**Fm**[100]	**Md**[101]	**(No)**[102]	**Lw**[103]
(247)	(249)	(251)	(254)	(255)	(256)	(255)	(257)
$5f^7$							
$6d$							
$7s^2$							

Appendix D
Values of Some Important Physical Constants and Some Convenient Conversion Factors

Quantity	Value
Avogadro's number, N	$(6.025438 \pm 0.000107) \times 10^{23}$ g mol^{-1} (phys.)
Electronic charge, $\mathfrak{e}$	$-(4.802233 \pm 0.000071) \times 10^{-10}$ esu
Electron rest mass, m	$(9.107208 \pm 0.000246) \times 10^{-28}$ grams
Planck's constant, h	$(6.623773 \pm 0.000180) \times 10^{-27}$ erg sec
$\hbar = h/2\pi$	$(1.054206 \pm 0.000028) \times 10^{-27}$ erg sec
Velocity of light, c	(299790.22 ± 0.86) km sec^{-1}
Specific charge of the electron, $\mathfrak{e}/m$	$(1.758897 \pm 0.000032) \times 10^{7}$ emu g^{-1}
First Bohr radius, $a_0 = \hbar^2/m\mathfrak{e}^2$	$(5.291508 \pm 0.000035) \times 10^{-9}$ cm
Classical radius of the electron, $r_0 = \mathfrak{e}^2/mc^2$	$(2.817515 \pm 0.000056) \times 10^{-13}$ cm
Atomic weight of hydrogen	1.0081284 (phys.) ± 0.0000030
Ratio proton mass to electron mass	1836.1388 ± 0.0339
Boltzmann's constant, $\boldsymbol{k}$	$(1.3802565 \pm 0.0000615) \times 10^{-16}$ erg deg^{-1}
Bohr magneton, $\boldsymbol{\mu}_B = \mathfrak{e}\hbar/2mc$	$-(0.92712031 \pm 0.0000219) \times 10^{-20}$ erg gauss^{-1}
Wavelength associated with 1 ev	$(12396.44 \pm 0.174) \times 10^{-8}$ cm
Frequency associated with 1 ev	$(2.418357 \pm 0.000032) \times 10^{14}$ sec^{-1}
Wave number associated with 1 ev	(8066.832 ± 0.113) cm^{-1}
Energy associated with 1 ev	$(1.601864 \pm 0.000024) \times 10^{-12}$ erg
Energy associated with unit wave number	$(1.985742 \pm 0.000054) \times 10^{-16}$ erg
Energy associated with 1 rydberg	13.60353 ± 0.00210 ev
Speed of 1-ev electron	$(5.931099 \pm 0.000055) \times 10^{7}$ cm sec^{-1}
Energy associated with 1° Kelvin	$(8.616562 \pm 0.000357) \times 10^{-5}$ ev
"Temperature" associated with 1 ev	$(11{,}605.556 \pm 0.480)°$K

Appendix E
List of Symbols

This list includes every symbol which appears in the text with the exception of a very few used only rarely and then in a single section only (e.g., **s**, long-range order parameter, see p. 143).   On rare occasion the same symbol is used to denote two different quantities; these few duplications should not cause confusion.

Vectors are represented by boldface symbols and their magnitudes by the corresponding italic symbols (e.g., electronic wave vector **k**, of magnitude k).   Tensors and operators are usually shown in boldface sans serif type.

Symbol	Meaning	First Appearance in Text	
		Equation	*Page*
A	vector potential	11.14	388
$\mathcal{A}_0$	area of Fermi surface	7.10	187
$\mathscr{A}_0$	extremal cross sectional area of Fermi surface	11.19	389
$\mathbf{a}_n$	lattice coordinate vector	2.28	33

Symbol	Meaning	First Appearance in Text	
		Equation	*Page*
a_0	Bohr radius	6.55	177
a^*	effective Bohr radius	6.55	177
B	magnetic induction		227
B	magnetoresistance coefficient	8.56	287
b	mobility ratio		294
C_v	specific heat at constant volume	2.40	39
C	collision operator	5.53	133
c	velocity of light in vacuum	5.12	112
D	diffusion coefficient	1.1	7
D_n, D_p	diffusion coefficient of electrons, holes	9.2	318
d	diameter of wire	7.87	236
d	thickness of semiconducting film		355
E	total energy	2.46	42
E	electric field	5.12	112
$\mathcal{E}_i$	deformation potential constant	6.41	170
e	electronic charge	1.1	7
F	force	2.1	25
$\mathfrak{F}_n$	Fermi-Dirac integral of order n	3.14	59
$\mathfrak{F}(x)$	interference function	6.21	152
$f_0(\epsilon)$	Fermi-Dirac distribution function	3.11	58
$f(\mathbf{k,r})$	distribution function of electrons		109
$f_1(\mathbf{k,r}) = f(\mathbf{k,r}) - f_0(\epsilon)$		5.8	112
$g(\omega)$	spectral density, phonons	2.51	43
g	Lande g-factor	3.34	68
H	magnetic field	3.30	67
$\mathcal{3C}$	Hamiltonian	4.1	76
$h = 2\pi\hbar$	Planck's constant	2.37	38
I	intensity of incident radiation	10.44	355
J	current density	5.3	110
J_r	recombination current density		325
J_g	generation current density		325
$\mathscr{J}_n(x)$	transport integral of order n	7.20	190
K	reciprocal lattice vector	2.33	35
$\mathcal{K}_n$	transport coefficient	7.3	183
$\mathcal{K}'_n, \mathcal{K}''_n$	transport coefficients in a magnetic field	7.56	219
$\mathbf{k}$	wave vector, electrons	3.2	55
k_0	Fermi wave vector		158
k	Boltzmann's constant	1.1	7
$\mathfrak{k}$	refractive index, imaginary part	10.5	336

Symbol	Meaning	First Appearance in Text Equation	Page
L	Wiedemann-Franz ratio	5.38	127
L_0	Lorenz number		127
L_n, L_p	diffusion length—electrons, holes	9.13	322
l	mean free path		236
l_c, l_v	Landau level quantum number	11.3	371
M	mass of crystal ion	2.28	33
$\mathbf{M}$	magnetization	3.31	68
m	mass of free electron	3.1	55
m^*	effective mass, scalar	4.46	96
m	effective mass, tensor	4.58	102
m_n, m_p	effective masses in semiconductor—electrons, holes	8.6	248
N_0	Avogadro's number		39
N_D, N_A	density of donor, acceptor impurities	6.57	178
$\mathcal{N}(\epsilon)$	density of states	3.6	56
n	density of electrons, semiconductor	8.1	248
n_0	density of conduction electrons, metal	3.9	57
n_a	number of conduction electrons per atom	7.26	194
$\mathfrak{n}_q$	phonon occupation number	2.37	38
$\mathfrak{n}^*$	complex refractive index	10.4	336
$\mathfrak{n}$	refractive index, real part	10.5	336
$\mathbf{P} = \mathfrak{e}\mathbf{E} - (\epsilon - \eta)\mathbf{\nabla} \ln T$, effective force field		5.14	114
$\mathbf{P}(\mathfrak{r})$	electric polarization	6.44	171
$\mathbf{p}$	momentum operator	4.53	100
p	density of holes, semiconductor	8.2	248
$\mathfrak{p}^*$	complex electric polarizability	10.4	336
Q_q	normal coordinate, lattice vibrations	2.28	33
Q	heat current density	7.32	203
$\mathbf{Q}, \mathbf{Q}^*$	phonon annihilation, creation operators	2.39	39
q	wave vector, phonon	2.28	33
q_0	Debye wave vector (magnitude)		123
R	universal gas constant		39
R	Hall coefficient	7.63	219
$\mathfrak{R}$	normalized ideal resistivity	7.18	189
$\mathfrak{R}$	rate of generation of excess carriers	9.10	321
$\mathfrak{r}$	position vector	1.3	14
r_s	radius of Wigner-Seitz sphere	4.49	98
$\mathfrak{r}$	reduced resistivity		190

Symbol	Meaning	First Appearance in Text	
		Equation	*Page*
S	thermoelectric power	7.43	208
S_g	phonon-drag thermoelectric power	7.51	213
S	entropy	5.42	131
$\mathfrak{S}(\mathbf{k},\mathbf{k}')$	a priori scattering rate	5.6	111
$d\mathbf{S}$	surface element on a surface of constant energy in $\mathbf{k}$-space	7.6	184
s	polarization index	2.28	33
s	surface recombination velocity	9.9	321
T	absolute temperature	1.1	7
$\mathbf{T}$	translation operator	4.10	80
t	time	2.4	25
t	reduced temperature		190
$U(\mathbf{r})$	perturbation potential	6.4	147
u	velocity of sound	5.40	129
$u_{\mathbf{k}}(\mathbf{r})$	periodic part of Bloch function	4.7	79
$\mathbf{u}$	displacement vector	2.28	33
$V(\mathbf{r})$	potential, potential energy	4.1	76
V	volume		36
$v(\mathbf{r})$	ionic potential	6.7	148
$v(\mathbf{K})$	Fourier coefficient of $V(\mathbf{r})$	4.25	87
$\mathbf{v}_{\mathbf{k}}, \mathbf{v}(\mathbf{k})$	velocity of electron in state $\mathbf{k}$	4.55	101
v_F	Fermi velocity	7.16	189
W	thermal resistivity	5.63	135
$y = (\epsilon - \eta)/kT$		7.13	188
$z = \hbar\omega/kT$		7.13	188
α	absorption coefficient	10.10	337
α_n	overlap integral, tight-binding approximation	4.42	93
β	spring constant	2.1	25
β_n	overlap integral, tight-binding approximation	4.42	93
β^*	effective Bohr magneton, $e\hbar/2m^*c$	11.20	390
γ	electronic specific heat coefficient		66
$\gamma = \omega_c\tau$		8.53	286
$\delta(x)$	Dirac delta function	6.6	148
δ_l	phase shift of lth partial wave		157
$\Delta(\mathbf{r})$	dilatation	6.31	158
ϵ	single-particle energy, phonon or electron	2.37, 3.1	38, 55
ϵ_c	conduction band edge, semiconductor		246

Symbol	Meaning	Equation	Page
		First Appearance in Text	
ϵ_v	valence band edge, semiconductor		246
ϵ_G	energy gap, semiconductor		246
$\boldsymbol{\epsilon}$	strain tensor	8.41	281
ε_0	permittivity of vacuum	10.4	336
$\zeta(x)$	Riemann zeta function of x		47
η	Fermi energy	3.11	58
η_0	Fermi energy at $T = 0°\mathrm{K}$	3.10	57
$\boldsymbol{\eta}$	quantum efficiency	10.44	355
Θ_E	Einstein temperature	2.48	42
Θ_D	Debye temperature	2.60	46
Θ_R	Debye temperature from resistivity measurements		192
Θ_0	Einstein temperature for optical modes		257
κ	thermal conductivity	5.37	126
$\varkappa$	dielectric constant	6.46	171
λ	wavelength		27
μ	mobility		164
μ_n, μ_p	mobility of electrons, holes	8.20	254
μ_H	Hall mobility	8.62	288
$\boldsymbol{\mu}$	magnetic moment		67
$\boldsymbol{\mu}_B$	Bohr magneton	1.2	12
$\boldsymbol{\mu}$	Thomson coefficient	7.42	208
ν	frequency	2.41	40
$\boldsymbol{\xi}$	polarization vector of phonons	2.28	33
Π	Peltier coefficient	7.44	209
$\boldsymbol{\rho}, \rho$	resistivity tensor, scalar	5.60	134
$\boldsymbol{\sigma}, \sigma$	conductivity tensor, scalar	7.60, 1.1	219, 7
$\sigma(\theta,\varphi)$	differential scattering cross section		154
τ	relaxation time	5.13	113
$\langle\tau\rangle$	relaxation time, Boltzmann average	8.25	256
τ_n, τ_p	mobility relaxation time of electrons, holes		321
τ_e, τ_h	minority carrier lifetime—electrons, holes	9.10	321
$d\boldsymbol{\tau}$	element of volume	4.26	88
$\phi_n(\mathbf{r})$	atomic wave function	4.35	91
$\phi(\mathbf{k},\mathbf{r}) = -f_1/(\partial f_0/\partial\epsilon)$		5.9	112
χ	magnetic susceptibility	1.2	12
$\psi_{\mathbf{k}}(\mathbf{r})$	electronic wave function in crystal, Bloch function	3.2	55

Symbol	Meaning	First Appearance in Text	
		Equation	*Page*
$\psi = \mathbf{k}\phi(\mathbf{k},\mathbf{r})/k^2$		5.22	119
Ω	volume of unit cell		36
Ω_B	volume of Brillouin zone in $\mathbf{k}$-space	2.36	36
$\Omega = \nabla_{\mathbf{k}}\epsilon \times \nabla_{\mathbf{k}}$		5.16	115
ω	angular velocity, $2\pi\nu$	2.4	25
ω_c	cyclotron angular frequency		217
$d\omega$	element of solid angle	6.23	155

Index